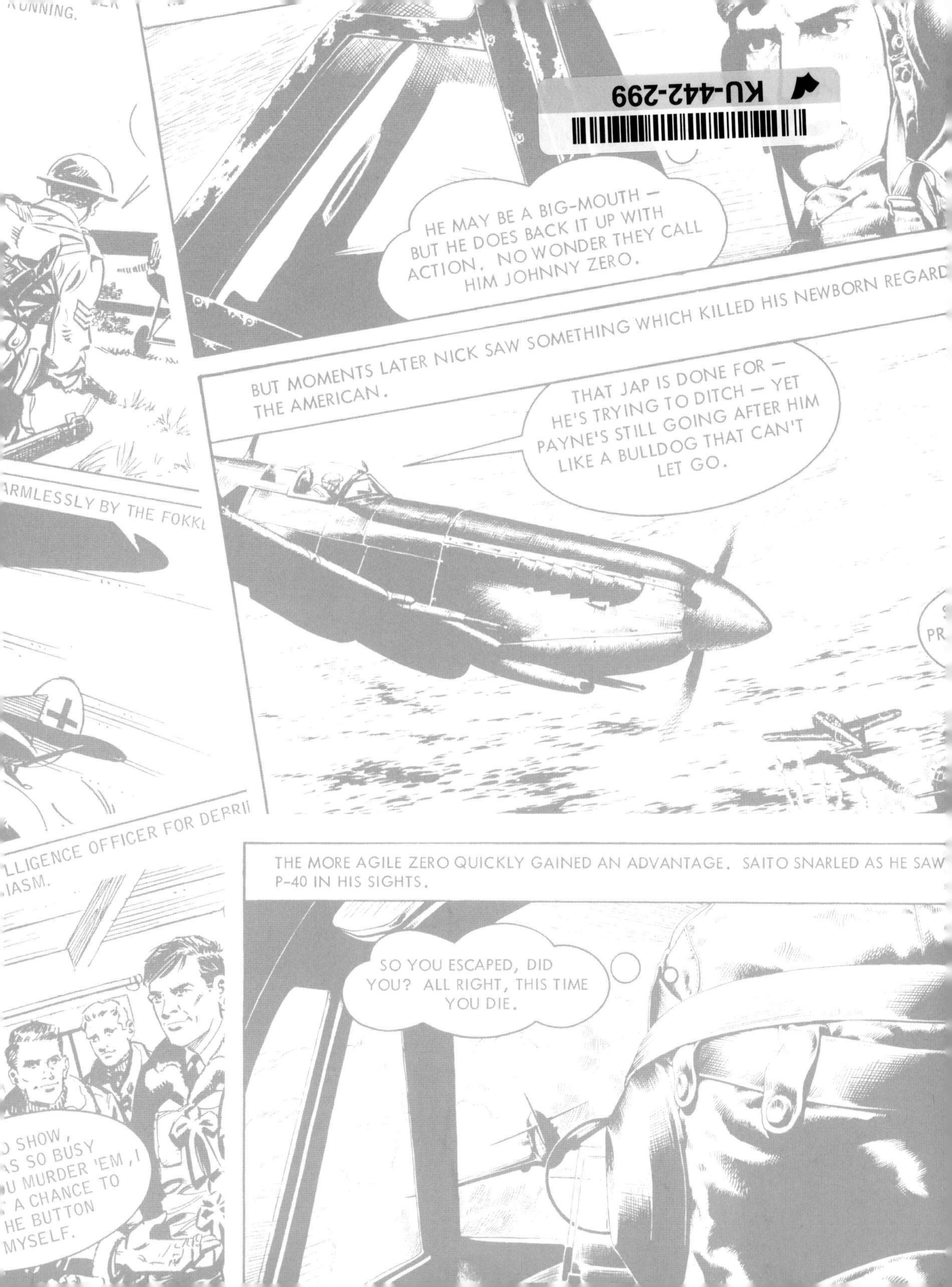
RUNNING.
HE MAY BE A BIG-MOUTH — BUT HE DOES BACK IT UP WITH ACTION. NO WONDER THEY CALL HIM JOHNNY ZERO.
BUT MOMENTS LATER NICK SAW SOMETHING WHICH KILLED HIS NEWBORN REGARD FOR THE AMERICAN.
THAT JAP IS DONE FOR — HE'S TRYING TO DITCH — YET PAYNE'S STILL GOING AFTER HIM LIKE A BULLDOG THAT CAN'T LET GO.
ARMLESSLY BY THE FOKK
LLIGENCE OFFICER FOR DEBRI
IASM.
THE MORE AGILE ZERO QUICKLY GAINED AN ADVANTAGE. SAITO SNARLED AS HE SAW P-40 IN HIS SIGHTS.
SO YOU ESCAPED, DID YOU? ALL RIGHT, THIS TIME YOU DIE.
SHOW, AS SO BUSY U MURDER 'EM, I A CHANCE TO HE BUTTON MYSELF.

Commando

FOR ACTION AND ADVENTURE

BANDITS AT 12 O'CLOCK

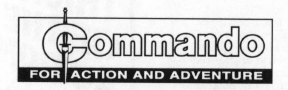

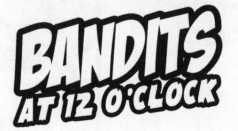

Published in 2008 by Carlton Books
Limited
An imprint of the Carlton Publishing
Group
20 Mortimer Street
London W1T 3JW

A catalogue record for this book is
available from the British Library.

ISBN 978-1-84732-128-2

Printed and bound in Thailand
10 9 8 7 6 5 4 3 2 1

Commando

FOR ACTION AND ADVENTURE

**THE 12 BEST AIR-COMBAT
COMMANDO BOOKS EVER!**

EDITED BY GEORGE LOW, EX-EDITOR OF COMMANDO

CARLTON
BOOKS

Contents

Introduction

JIM PULLED HIS SLOW PLANE INTO A STEEP CLIMB WHILE DICK DISCOURAGED ANY PURSUIT WITH HIS LEWIS GUN.

ALL AIRCRAFT JETTISON YOUR FISH AND GET BACK TO THE CARRIER, MAKE FOR THE CLOUDS.

JUST LIKE CLAY PIPES IN A SHOOTING-GALLERY IN THIS OLD TUB.

Everybody who has ever turned a page of a Commando war library has a favourite air story that stands out above the others for some reason or other. The first thing to catch the attention are the names … Spitfire, Hurricane, Typhoon, Tempest, Whirlwind, Mosquito. Who wouldn't want to read a story with aircraft like that twisting and turning through the pages, machine guns or cannon flaming, rockets ricocheting in every direction?

And then there are the men who flew the fighters, bombers, seaplanes, flying boats and transport aircraft into combat. These pilots of every nationality had one aim … to make sure that they won their duels high in the skies over the fields of Kent, the dense jungles of Burma or the cold and hungry sea waiting below for the loser.

There was also a sense of old-fashioned chivalry in some of the clashes between enemy aces, as if they were knights from centuries long past. They were no longer jousting with war horses and lances, but were strapped into tiny, uncomfortable cockpits, lethal streams of fire lancing across the sky.

It's a great combination … these men and their machines …

for a writer to bring together in an action yarn for the reader to enjoy, and then there's the added bonus of the work of an artist skilled in the technique of reproducing the looks and characteristics of all the amazing aircraft that flashed across the skies from the First World War onwards. It's not an easy job to make

BUT IN THE CELL AT LEAST ONE PARTISAN, GASTON BRENNER, THE LOCAL INNKEEPER, WASN'T HAPPY WITH THE DECISION AT ALL. HIS PALE, FAT FACE WAS BEADED WITH COLD SWEAT.

BUT THIS IS MADNESS! WE SHALL BE CRUSHED LIKE BEETLES, IS IT NOT? I SAY NON, NON MERCI!

LIKE FAT SLUGS, YOU MEAN, GASTON! BE QUIET, YOU FOOL. IT IS OUR ONLY CHANCE.

AND SO THE DESPERATE DECISION WAS PASSED ON TO OLD JACQUES.

these fighting machines look realistic, and also make them appear as if they are actually flying, but the "air artists" can do that. There's also the attention to detail needed to show how many wing guns or cannon a certain mark of fighter should carry. Or in which way an undercarriage lowers or rises back into place.

It all adds up to merge into this ace collection which you have in front of you and it features many of these very able writers and artists and a lot of the credit must go to them. The Commando staff were the lucky ones because they saw it all come together before the issues hit the streets, but now here's another chance to see the best of air action … so take your time and enjoy. Concentrate hard enough and you'll hear the roar of the engines and the chatter of the wing guns. And don't feel ashamed to duck if you think the action is coming too close!

THREE THROTTLES SLAMMED WIDE OPEN. THE SURGING POWER OF THE MIGHTY SABRE ENGINES ROCKETED THEM SKYWARDS AS THEY PULLED THEIR STICKS BACK.

UPS A DAISY!

George Low.

George Low,
EX-EDITOR, COMMANDO

Commando FLY PAST

No. 2 — MESSERSCHMITT
Bf109E-3

Shown in the markings of
Jagdgeschwader 26, Luftwaffe,
at Caffiers, France, during August, 1940.

BATTLE SQUADRON

THIS IS A STORY OF MEN AND MACHINES. THE MEN ARE THE AIRCREWS OF THE ADVANCED AIR STRIKING FORCE, THE MACHINES ARE THE FAIREY "BATTLE" AIRCRAFT THEY FLEW. THE FAIREY BATTLE WAS SLOW, POORLY ARMED, HELPLESS AGAINST THE CANNON OF THE MESSERSCHMITTS.

IT IS A STORY OF HEAVY LOSSES AGAINST OVERWHELMING ODDS, BUT ALSO A STORY OF COURAGE AND DEVOTION TO DUTY IN THE HIGHEST TRADITIONS OF THE ROYAL AIR FORCE.

IT BEGINS IN SOUTH AMERICA, AUTUMN 1938, WHERE ANOTHER OF THE MANY REVOLUTIONS WAS DRAWING TO ITS CLOSE.

FIVE MINUTES TO TARGET...

THREE LIGHT BOMBERS WERE ON THEIR WAY TO ATTACK THE FLEEING REMNANTS OF THE REBEL FORCES.

FLYING THE LEAD MACHINE WAS MIKE STALLARD, AN EX-R.A.F. PILOT WHOSE LUST FOR ADVENTURE LED HIM WHEREVER THE FIGHTING WAS FIERCEST.

THIS LITTLE SHOW SHOULD SOON BE OVER. THEN BACK TO ENGLAND FOR A WHILE.

MIKE HAD BEEN HIRING OUT HIS SERVICES AS A COMBAT PILOT FOR FIVE YEARS. IN CHINA, SPAIN, AND NOW SOUTH AMERICA, HE HAD SEEN WAR AT ITS MOST CRUEL.

SHARP EYES PICKED OUT A STRAGGLING ENEMY COLUMN TRUDGING ACROSS THE HILLY COUNTRY BELOW. ROCKING HIS WINGS, MIKE DROPPED THE NOSE OF HIS MACHINE, HIS HAND CLOSING ON THE BOMB RELEASE.

THE WEARY, RAGGED WRETCHES WERE ALREADY SCATTERING FOR THEIR LIVES AS THE BOMBS WHISTLED DOWN.

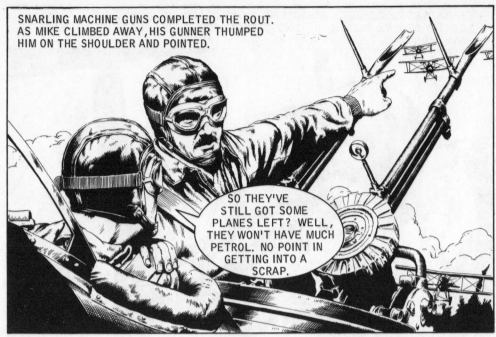

SNARLING MACHINE GUNS COMPLETED THE ROUT. AS MIKE CLIMBED AWAY, HIS GUNNER THUMPED HIM ON THE SHOULDER AND POINTED.

SO THEY'VE STILL GOT SOME PLANES LEFT? WELL, THEY WON'T HAVE MUCH PETROL. NO POINT IN GETTING INTO A SCRAP.

AT HIS SIGNAL THE THREE BOMBERS RACED AWAY AT LOW LEVEL, SKIMMING THROUGH THE VALLEYS, EASILY AVOIDING THE HALF-HEARTED ATTACKS OF THE FIGHTERS.

WELL, THAT WRAPS IT UP. THE REVOLUTION'S OVER. MIGHT AS WELL START PACKING AS SOON AS WE GET BACK.

MIKE KNEW THAT WITH THE END OF THE FIGHTING HIS SERVICES WOULD NO LONGER BE REQUIRED. HIS SENTIMENTS WERE SHARED BY A FELLOW PILOT, AN AMERICAN.

WELL, MIKE, GUESS IT'S TIME TO MOVE ON AND FIND MY-SELF ANOTHER WAR. HOW ABOUT YOU?

HAVEN'T YOU HEARD? THERE'S A KING-SIZE SCRAP BREW-ING UP BACK HOME. THAT'S WHERE I'M HEADING.

MIKE HAD LEARNED TO FLY IN THE R.A.F., AND WAS IN THE RESERVE. HE INTENDED TO REJOIN THE NOW RAPIDLY EXPANDING AIR FORCE.

SO YOU'RE GOING TO BE "OFFICIAL" NOW? RECKON THE OLD "YES SIR, NO SIR" WILL COME A BIT HARD. STILL, GOOD LUCK.

THANKS, CHET, I'LL HAVE TO START BRUSHING UP MY SALUTE.

MIKE DID FIND SOME DIFFICULTY IN ADJUSTING TO SERVICE BEHAVIOUR, BUT HE SATISFACTORILY COMPLETED THE REFRESHER COURSE AND RESUMED HIS RANK OF FLYING OFFICER.

YOUR POSTING IS TO A LIGHT BOMBER SQUADRON JUST FORMING. YOU'VE HAD SOME EXPERIENCE IN THAT LINE, I UNDERSTAND.

YES, SIR, QUITE A BIT.

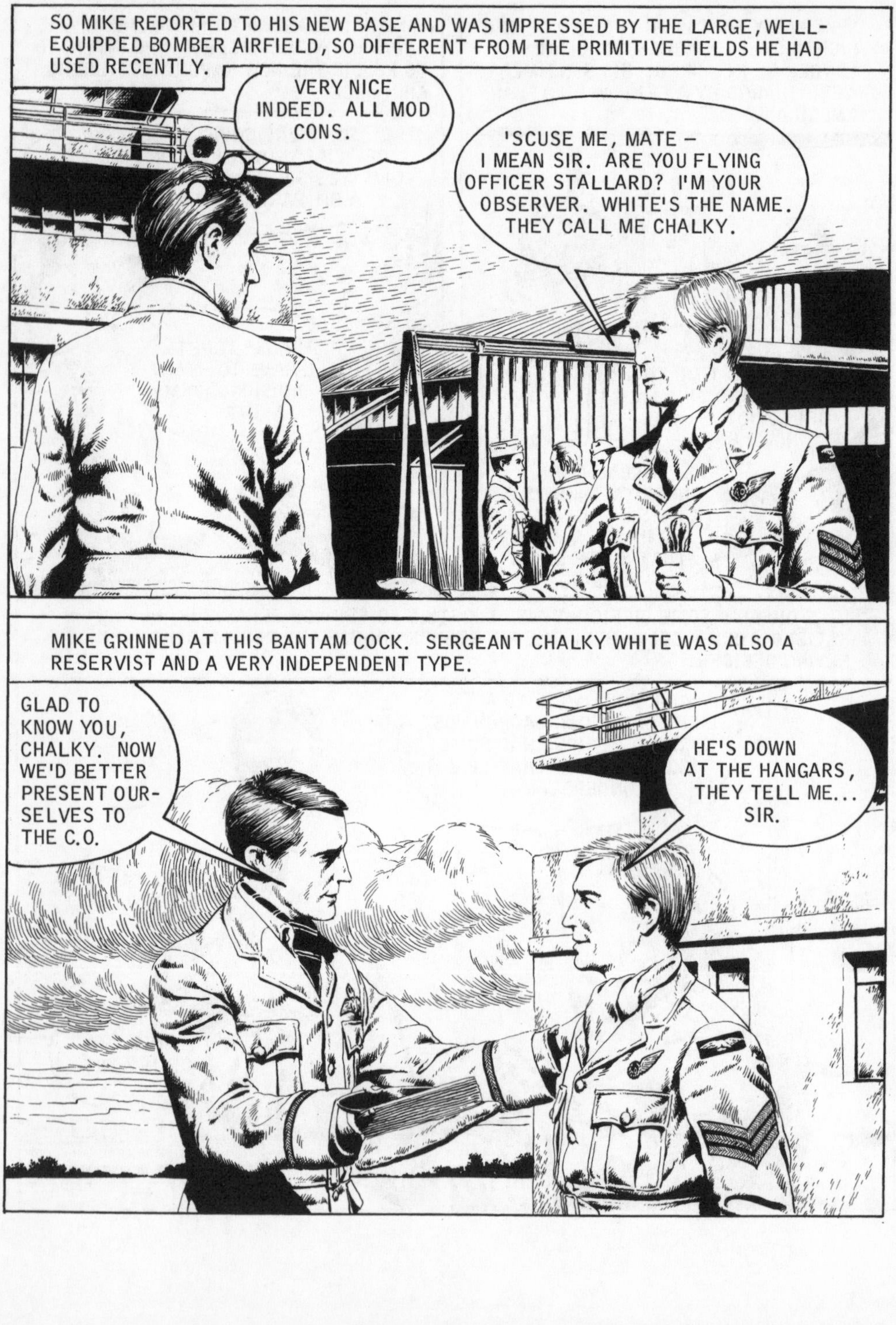
SO MIKE REPORTED TO HIS NEW BASE AND WAS IMPRESSED BY THE LARGE, WELL-EQUIPPED BOMBER AIRFIELD, SO DIFFERENT FROM THE PRIMITIVE FIELDS HE HAD USED RECENTLY.
VERY NICE INDEED. ALL MOD CONS.
'SCUSE ME, MATE – I MEAN SIR. ARE YOU FLYING OFFICER STALLARD? I'M YOUR OBSERVER. WHITE'S THE NAME. THEY CALL ME CHALKY.
MIKE GRINNED AT THIS BANTAM COCK. SERGEANT CHALKY WHITE WAS ALSO A RESERVIST AND A VERY INDEPENDENT TYPE.
GLAD TO KNOW YOU, CHALKY. NOW WE'D BETTER PRESENT OURSELVES TO THE C.O.
HE'S DOWN AT THE HANGARS, THEY TELL ME... SIR.

THE SQUADRON LEADER WAS JAMES BELL, NEWLY PROMOTED AND A GRADUATE FROM CRANWELL.   THERE HE HAD LEARNED THE RULE BOOK BY HEART, AND NOW NEVER INTENDED TO FORGET IT.

RESERVISTS, OBVIOUSLY. YOU NEED A HAIRCUT, SER-GEANT. LET'S HOPE YOUR FLYING IS AN IMPROVE-MENT ON YOUR TURNOUT.

ER — DO YOU THINK WE COULD HAVE A LOOK AT OUR AIRCRAFT, SIR?

MIKE MET BELL'S GLARE STEADILY. THE SQUADRON-LEADER WAVED HIS HAND AT ONE OF THE PARKED AIRCRAFT AND STALKED AWAY.

I DON'T THINK HE LIKES US.

THAT'S HIS PROBLEM. THIS IS SUPPOSED TO BE A BOMBER SQUADRON, NOT A FASHION PARADE. LET'S HAVE A LOOK AT OUR KITE.

WHAT MIKE SAW DID NOT IMPRESS HIM. WHEN INTRODUCED, THE FAIREY "BATTLE" HAD BEEN A BIG ADVANCE OVER THE TYPES THEN IN SERVICE, BUT HAD LONG BEEN LEFT BEHIND BY MODERN DEVELOPMENTS.

IT'S PATHETIC. ONE GUN IN THE WING, ANOTHER IN THE REAR COCKPIT. JUST TWO GUNS. THE OLD CRATES I FLEW WERE BETTER ARMED.

HEAVY ARMAMENT IS UNNECESSARY, STALLARD. THIS AIRCRAFT RELIES ON SPEED FOR ITS PROTECTION.

BOTH TURNED AT THE INTERRUPTION. IT WAS BELL AGAIN.

AT THAT PRECISE MOMENT A FLIGHT OF SPITFIRES, SLEEK AND DEADLY AS SHARKS, ROARED OVERHEAD. CHALKY NODDED TOWARDS THE FIGHTERS.

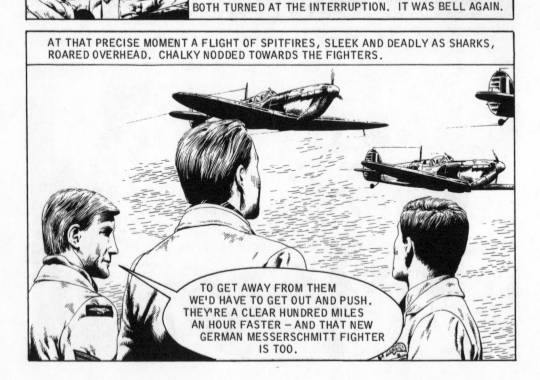

TO GET AWAY FROM THEM WE'D HAVE TO GET OUT AND PUSH. THEY'RE A CLEAR HUNDRED MILES AN HOUR FASTER — AND THAT NEW GERMAN MESSERSCHMITT FIGHTER IS TOO.

MIKE SAID NOTHING, MERELY COCKED AN ENQUIRING EYEBROW AT BELL, WHO AGAIN TURNED AND STAMPED ANGRILY AWAY.

OPERATIONAL TRAINING GOT UNDER WAY, BUT TO MIKE'S DISGUST BELL SEEMED ONLY INTERESTED IN PRECISION FORMATION FLYING.

"COMBAT" PRACTICE WOULD HAVE BEEN LAUGHABLE IF IT HADN'T BEEN PATHETIC. THE FIGHTERS MADE TEXTBOOK ATTACKS, THE BATTLES TOOK TEXTBOOK EVASIVE ACTION AS FAR AS THE IMPOSSIBLY TIGHT FORMATION ALLOWED.

MIKE'S IMPATIENCE WAS NEARING BOILING POINT AT THESE DRILL-BOOK METHODS, WHICH HE KNEW WOULD BE USELESS IN ACTUAL COMBAT.

WATCHED BY BELL, EACH CREW TOOK ITS TURN TO BE "ATTACKED" BY A VERY BORED HURRICANE PILOT.

HERE HE COMES, SIR. SAME ANGLE, SAME SPEED, SAME EVERYTHING.

RIGHT. HANG ON AND HAVE YOUR CAMERA GUN READY.

MIKE HAULED THE HEAVY BATTLE ROUND AND SCREAMED PAST THE HURRICANE, GIVING THE PILOT THE SHOCK OF HIS LIFE.

WHAT THE BLAZES?

LOVELY GRUB. GOT HIM RIGHT IN THE BELLY.

MIKE PLUNGED INTO A CLOUD, GRINNING AS HE HEARD THE HURRICANE PILOT'S VOICE IN HIS EARS, CURSING WILDLY.

DEAR ME, WHAT LANGUAGE! WANT TO POP OUT AND GIVE HIM ANOTHER SQUIRT?

NO, I THINK WE'VE MADE OUR POINT.

BUT WHEN THEY ARRIVED BACK AT BASE, THEY FOUND THAT BELL ALSO HAD A FEW POINTS TO MAKE.

YOU COMPLETELY IGNORED THE TACTICS YOU'VE BEEN TAUGHT — TACTICS DEVISED BY MEN OF VAST FLYING EXPERIENCE...

WHO HAVEN'T FIRED A SHOT IN ANGER FOR TWENTY YEARS, IF EVER. LET'S GET THE CAMERA GUN FILMS DEVELOPED.

THE PICTURES SHOWED THAT CHALKY HAD SCORED HITS ON THE HURRICANE'S ENGINE AND BELLY, WHILE THE FIGHTER HAD MISSED THEM ENTIRELY.

ALL RIGHT, BUT YOU MADE A TOTALLY UNEXPECTED MANOEUVRE, AND...

OF COURSE I DID, AND IF WHITE HAD BEEN USING LIVE AMMUNITION HE WOULD HAVE CLOBBERED THE ENGINE AND PROBABLY KILLED THE PILOT. YOU CAN'T FIGHT A WAR TO FIXED RULES.

AND WAR WAS LOOMING VERY CLOSE. ON 2ND SEPTEMBER, 1939, THE ADVANCED AIR STRIKING FORCE FLEW TO FRANCE...

THEY'RE GIVING US A BIG SEND-OFF.

WHAT BOTHERS ME IS HOW MANY OF OF US WILL COME BACK.

THEIR NEW BASE WAS A FAR CRY FROM THE LAVISHLY-EQUIPPED AIRFIELDS TO WHICH MOST OF THE CREWS WERE ACCUSTOMED.

BIT PRIMITIVE, ISN'T IT?

JUST LIKE OLD TIMES. I THINK OVER BY THE WOODS WILL BE THE BEST PLACE TO PARK.

MIKE'S OLD INSTINCT FOR PROTECTION CAUSED HIM TO CHOOSE THIS SPOT, BUT HE WAS FORESTALLED.

OVER THERE, SIR, PLEASE, IN LINE WITH THE REST.

BUT THAT'S WIDE OPEN, AND RIGHT NEXT TO THE PETROL DUMP!

MIKE TRIED TO ARGUE THE POINT — BUT TO NO AVAIL.

SQUADRON-LEADER'S ORDERS, SIR. THEY'LL BE EASIER TO GUARD AND TO REFUEL HERE.

AND THEY'LL MAKE A SITTING TARGET, TOO. OH, WHAT'S THE USE!

MIKE PUT HIS OBJECTIONS TO BELL, BUT RECEIVED THE EXPECTED REBUFF.

ONCE AND FOR ALL, STALLARD, I COMMAND THIS SQUADRON. THIS ISN'T ONE OF YOUR REVOLUTIONS, YOU KNOW.

I KNOW, AND THAT'S WHAT WORRIES ME.

ON 3RD SEPTEMBER, 1939, AT 11.15 a.m...

IT'S ON! IT'S JUST COME OVER THE RADIO — WE'RE AT WAR WITH GERMANY!

RIGHT, THAT'S IT. WE'RE THE STRIKING FORCE, SO WHEN DO WE GET STARTED?

AS SOON AS WE RECEIVE ORDERS.

THAT SAME AFTERNOON THE LOCAL ARMY COMMANDER CALLED ON A TOUR OF INSPECTION. THE BRIGADIER TOOK ONE LOOK AND EXPLODED.

GREAT HEAVENS, MAN, YOU'RE A BOMBER PILOT. DID YOU EVER SEE SUCH A READY-MADE TARGET? GET THEM UNDER COVER AND CAMOUFLAGED!

THEY'RE SPACED OUT AT THE DISTANCE LAID DOWN IN THE MANUAL, SIR.

THE R.A.F. CONSIDERED THE CAMOUFLAGE COLOUR SCHEME PAINTED ON THE AIRCRAFT SUFFICENT PROTECTION, BUT THE BRIGADIER HAD OTHER IDEAS.

CUT BAYS IN THOSE WOODS. USE THE FOLIAGE WITH YOUR CAMOUFLAGE NETTING TO MAKE COVERED PENS. AND GET THAT PETROL AS FAR FROM THE PLANES AS POSSIBLE.

YES, SIR, I'LL PUT THE WORK IN HAND AT ONCE.

MIKE REFRAINED FROM SAYING "I TOLD YOU SO", BUT HIS LOOK SPOKE VOLUMES. IF NOTHING ELSE, BELL WAS AN EXCELLENT ORGANISER, AND THE WORK PROCEEDED APACE.

BET THOSE POOR BLOKES ARE FURIOUS AT LOSING THEIR SUNDAY AFTERNOON.

AND US STANDING WATCHING DOESN'T HELP. COME ON, LET'S MUCK IN.

THE OTHER AIRCREW QUICKLY FOLLOWED MIKE'S EXAMPLE, AND WITH THE EXTRA HANDS THE BACK-BREAKING JOB QUICKLY NEARED COMPLETION.

FIRST-CLASS JOB. AND YOUR OFFICERS LENDING A HAND WAS GOOD FOR MORALE.

ER...THANK YOU, SIR.

YET THESE ELABORATE PRECAUTIONS SEEMED POINTLESS, FOR THIS WAS THE PERIOD OF THE "PHONEY WAR", WHEN NEITHER SIDE MADE ANY AGGRESSIVE MOVE.

WE ARE TO PATROL A SECTOR OF THE MAGINOT LINE. LET'S HAVE GOOD FLYING, AND KEEP YOUR EYES PEELED.

IF WE CAN AVOID BASHING INTO EACH OTHER.

AS MIKE EXPECTED, BELL'S MAIN CONCERN WAS MAINTAINING CLOSE FORMATION.

KEEP CLOSED UP. REMEMBER THE FRENCH ARE WATCHING. WE MUST CREATE A GOOD IM-PRESSION.

BUT THE GERMANS WERE WATCHING TOO.

VERY PRETTY. IT MUST TAKE CARE AND ATTENTION TO FLY LIKE THAT.

EXACTLY. SO THEY WON'T BE KEEPING A PROPER LOOKOUT. COME ON.

THE MESSERSCHMITTS WORKED THEIR WAY UP-SUN, THEN SWOOPED. CHALKY SPOTTED THE GLINT OF THEIR WINGS AT THE LAST MOMENT.

BANDITS! COMING OUT OF THE SUN!

REACTING INSTINCTIVELY, MIKE KICKED THE RUDDER, SKIDDING HIS BATTLE TO ONE SIDE. THE MURDEROUS TRACER SLASHED BY, MISSING HIM BY INCHES. HIS OPPOSITE NUMBER WAS NOT SO FORTUNATE.

WHAT THE DEVIL? WHERE DID THEY COME FROM?

THE IMPORTANT THING IS THAT THEY'RE HERE!

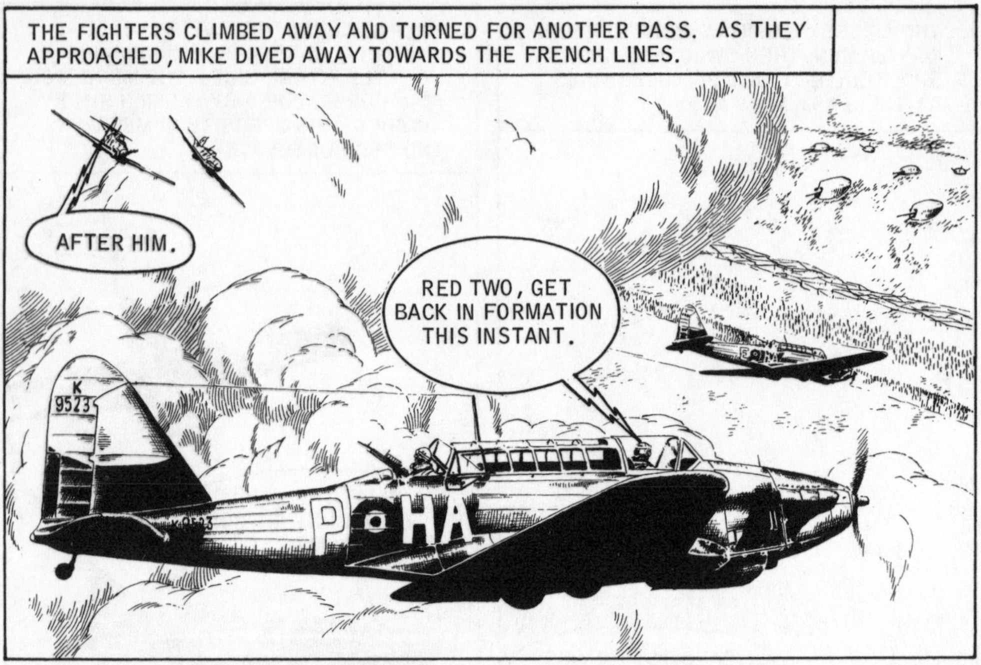
THE FIGHTERS CLIMBED AWAY AND TURNED FOR ANOTHER PASS. AS THEY APPROACHED, MIKE DIVED AWAY TOWARDS THE FRENCH LINES.
AFTER HIM.
RED TWO, GET BACK IN FORMATION THIS INSTANT.

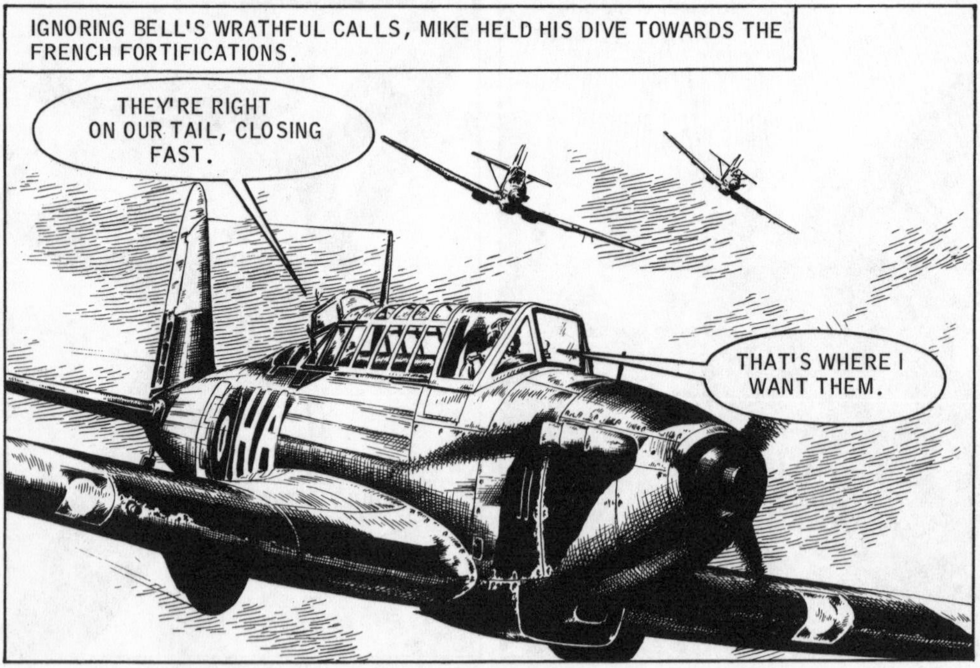
IGNORING BELL'S WRATHFUL CALLS, MIKE HELD HIS DIVE TOWARDS THE FRENCH FORTIFICATIONS.
THEY'RE RIGHT ON OUR TAIL, CLOSING FAST.
THAT'S WHERE I WANT THEM.

AND HE LED THE EAGERLY PURSUING MESSERSCHMITTS RIGHT ON TO THE WAITING ANTI-AIRCRAFT GUNS.

SMART THINKING, SKIPPER.

IF THE FRENCH HADN'T COTTONED ON, WE'D HAVE BEEN IN REAL TROUBLE.

BUT CHALKY WHITE'S ENTHUSIASM WAS NOT SHARED BY SQUADRON LEADER BELL. AT THE AIRFIELD...

GIVE ME ONE GOOD REASON FOR NOT COURT-MARTIALLING YOU FOR THAT PERFORMANCE.

COURT-MARTIAL? WE BROKE UP THE ATTACK AND GOT ONE JERRY SHOT DOWN. WHAT'S WRONG WITH THAT?

YOU TURNED TAIL AND RAN. OUR DUTY IS TO FIGHT, NOT RUN AWAY.

RUBBISH! WE ALSO HAVE A DUTY TO SURVIVE, TO FIGHT AGAIN. NOT TO BE KNOCKED OFF LIKE CLAY PIGEONS.

BUT BELL WAS NOT TO BE STOPPED.

YOUR ACTION SET A VERY BAD EXAMPLE.

TELL THAT TO TO POOR DEVILS WHO WERE SHOT DOWN! IT WAS THE FAULT OF THE RIDICU-LOUSLY TIGHT FORMA-TION YOU INSIST ON.

AGAIN CAME BELL'S ANGRY REPLY.

ARE YOU SUGGESTING THAT THE ENTIRE FLIGHT SHOULD HAVE RETREATED?

YES I AM. THOSE JERRIES WOULD HAVE CUT US TO PIECES. THANKS TO MY "COWARDICE" TWO VALUABLE AIRCRAFT AND THEIR CREWS HAVE SURVIVED. THIS IS A WAR, MAN, NOT AN AIR SHOW!

SO ENDED THE SQUADRON'S FIRST ACTION. A FEW DAYS LATER THEY WERE ELATED TO HEAR THAT A NIGHT RAID ON A GERMAN INDUSTRIAL TOWN WAS PLANNED. MIKE ATTENDED THE BRIEFING WITH HIGH HOPES.

THIS MISSION WILL PROVIDE EXCELLENT NIGHT NAVIGATION EXPER- IENCE. THE LEAFLETS YOU WILL DROP...

LEAFLETS?

MIKE'S LOUD EXCLAMATION STOPPED BELL IN MID-SENTENCE AND ALL EYES TURNED ON THE YOUNG PILOT.

I SUPPOSE, AS USUAL, YOU HAVE AN OBJECTION?

YES, I DO. WE SHOULD BE HAMMER- ING AWAY AT THE GERMANS. GETTING IN THE FIRST BLOW, NOT TRYING TO FRIGHTEN THEM WITH BITS OF PAPER.

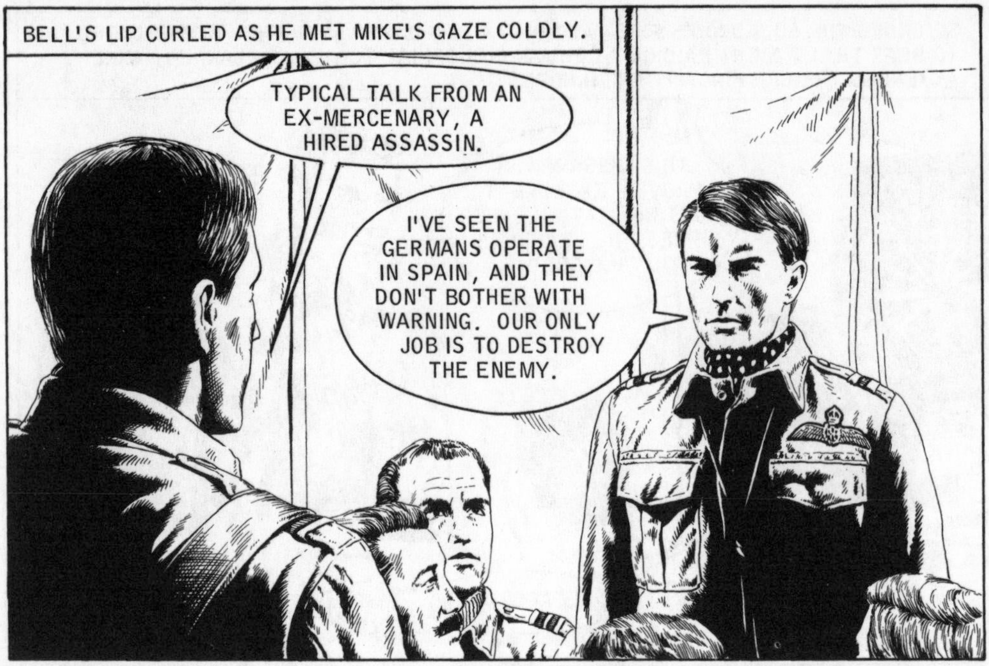
BELL'S LIP CURLED AS HE MET MIKE'S GAZE COLDLY.
TYPICAL TALK FROM AN EX-MERCENARY, A HIRED ASSASSIN.
I'VE SEEN THE GERMANS OPERATE IN SPAIN, AND THEY DON'T BOTHER WITH WARNING. OUR ONLY JOB IS TO DESTROY THE ENEMY.

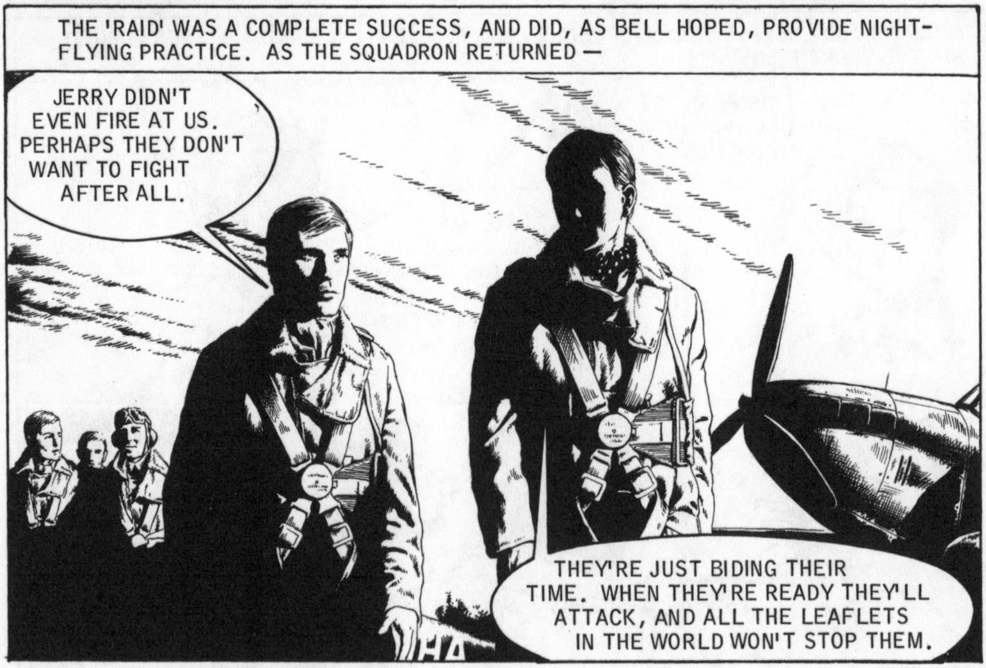
THE 'RAID' WAS A COMPLETE SUCCESS, AND DID, AS BELL HOPED, PROVIDE NIGHT-FLYING PRACTICE. AS THE SQUADRON RETURNED —
JERRY DIDN'T EVEN FIRE AT US. PERHAPS THEY DON'T WANT TO FIGHT AFTER ALL.
THEY'RE JUST BIDING THEIR TIME. WHEN THEY'RE READY THEY'LL ATTACK, AND ALL THE LEAFLETS IN THE WORLD WON'T STOP THEM.

10TH MAY, 1940. GERMAN ARMOURED COLUMNS BURST THROUGH THE ARDENNES FOREST, OUTFLANKING THE VAUNTED MAGINOT LINE. SWARMS OF AIRCRAFT ROSE FROM LUFTWAFFE AIRFIELDS. THE "PHONEY WAR" WAS OVER.

NO WORD REACHED THE ALLIED AIRFIELDS. THE DAY STARTED QUITE NORMALLY, UNTIL FROM THE EAST A SWARM OF DOTS APPEARED.

AS THE MEN FLUNG THEMSELVES INTO SLIT TRENCHES, THE FIRST OF THE UGLY, CROOKED-WINGED DIVE BOMBERS WAS HURTLING DOWN, PRECEDED BY ITS EAR-PIERCING, NERVE-SHATTERING SCREAM.

BANG GOES THE OFFICERS' MESS.

THEY'RE PLASTERINC EVERYTHING IN SIGHT, BUT THEY OBVIOUSLY HAVEN'T SPOTTED THE AIRCRAFT.

THE "NEEDLESS" PRECAUTIONS WERE PAYING OFF. THE MOMENT THE STUKAS LEFT, MIKE SPRINTED THROUGH THE DUST AND SMOKE TO HIS MACHINE. APART FROM A FEW SHRAPNEL HOLES IT WAS UNDAMAGED.

THE OTHERS ARE THE SAME, SIR. WE'LL HAVE THEM FIXED IN AN HOUR OR SO. THEY MISSED THE PETROL AND BOMB DUMPS TOO.

BUT THEY'VE MADE A MESS OF THE AIRFIELD. LOOK AT THOSE CRATERS.

SQUADRON-LEADER BELL WAS FRANTICALLY TRYING TO CONTACT HEADQUARTERS WITHOUT SUCCESS. THE REST OF THE SQUADRON STOOD DUMBLY SURVEYING THE DEVASTATION.

WHILE YOU'RE SEEING TO THE AIRCRAFT I'LL ROUND UP SOME BLOKES AND GET THESE HOLES FILLED IN.

GOOD IDEA, SIR. COME ON, YOU LAYABOUTS, DON'T STAND THERE GAWPING.

BELL RETURNED TO FIND THE AIRFIELD HUMMING WITH ACTIVITY. THE WRECKAGE HAD BEEN CLEARED AWAY, MOST OF THE BOMB CRATERS FILLED. HE LEARNED THAT MIKE HAD SET THE WORK IN MOTION.

HOW DARE YOU ISSUE ORDERS WITHOUT CONSULTING ME!

IT SEEMED THE OBVIOUS THING TO DO.

ORDER EVENTUALLY BEGAN TO APPEAR OUT OF THE CHAOS CAUSED BY THE GERMAN OFFENSIVE. BUT IT WAS NOON BEFORE THE BATTLES WERE DIRECTED AT THE ADVANCING GERMAN COLUMNS.

AT THE PRECISE HEIGHT AND SPEED LAID DOWN IN THE BOOK, THE SQUADRON ATTACKED. STRAIGHT AND LEVEL THEY FLEW, RIGHT OVER THE WAITING GERMAN GUNS.

STREAMS OF BULLETS AND SHELLS HACKED SITTING TARGETS OUT OF THE SKY. BUT EVEN THE GERMANS MARVELLED AT THE UNFLINCHING WAY THE SURVIVORS CLOSED THEIR RANKS AND CAME ON.

MAGNIFICENT DISCIPLINE, BUT WHAT A WASTE.

I DON'T SEE THE C.O., SKIPPER. HE MUST HAVE BOUGHT IT.

BADLY SHAKEN, THE SURVIVORS RETURNED TO BASE. THE REAL THING HAD BEEN HORRIBLY DIFFERENT FROM THE PRACTICE FIGHTS. BELL WAS AMONG THE MISSING.

AS SENIOR FLIGHT COMMANDER, I HAVE TO ASSUME COMMAND. WE HAVE ORDERS TO REPEAT THE ATTACK AS SOON AS THE AIRCRAFT ARE REFUELLED AND REARMED.

COULD I HAVE A WORD WITH YOU IN PRIVATE?

MIKE TOOK THE FLIGHT COMMANDER ASIDE AND SUGGESTED THEY USE A DIFFERENT METHOD OF ATTACK, COMING IN BY FLIGHTS FROM DIFFERENT DIRECTIONS TO SPLIT THE ENEMY FIRE.

YOU SAW WHAT HAPPENED WHEN WE MADE THE CLASSIC APPROACH. DO YOU WANT IT TO HAPPEN AGAIN?

WE'VE NEVER PRACTISED IT...WELL, OK, BUT THE CHAPS AREN'T USED TO ACTING INDE-PENDENTLY.

THE SECOND ATTACK WAS AS BIG A DISASTER AS THE FIRST. RELEASED FROM BELL'S STRICT DISCIPLINE, THE PILOTS RAN WILD.

KEEP IN YOUR FLIGHTS, YOU CLOWNS. OH LORD, WHAT'S THE MATTER WITH THEM?

WITH UNWIELDY AIRCRAFT CHARGING ABOUT AT LOW LEVEL THE INEVITABLE HAPPENED. WATCHING TWO OF THE PLANES COLLIDING, MIKE POUNDED HIS FIST ON THE COCKPIT.

IT'S HOPELESS! THEY'VE GOT NO IDEA!

AND HERE COME THE FAST BOYS – MESSERSCHMITTS!

THE FIGHTERS GLEEFULLY FELL ON THE SCATTERED BATTLES, COMPLETING THE HAVOC.

BLUE THREE AND RED TWO. FORMATE ON ME. DO YOU HEAR ME?

THE SHARP NOTE OF COMMAND HAD ITS EFFECT. THE TWO BATTLES JOINED MIKE AND TOGETHER THEY RACED AWAY AT LOW LEVEL.

KEEP SPACED OUT TO GIVE YOUR GUNNERS A GOOD FIELD OF FIRE.

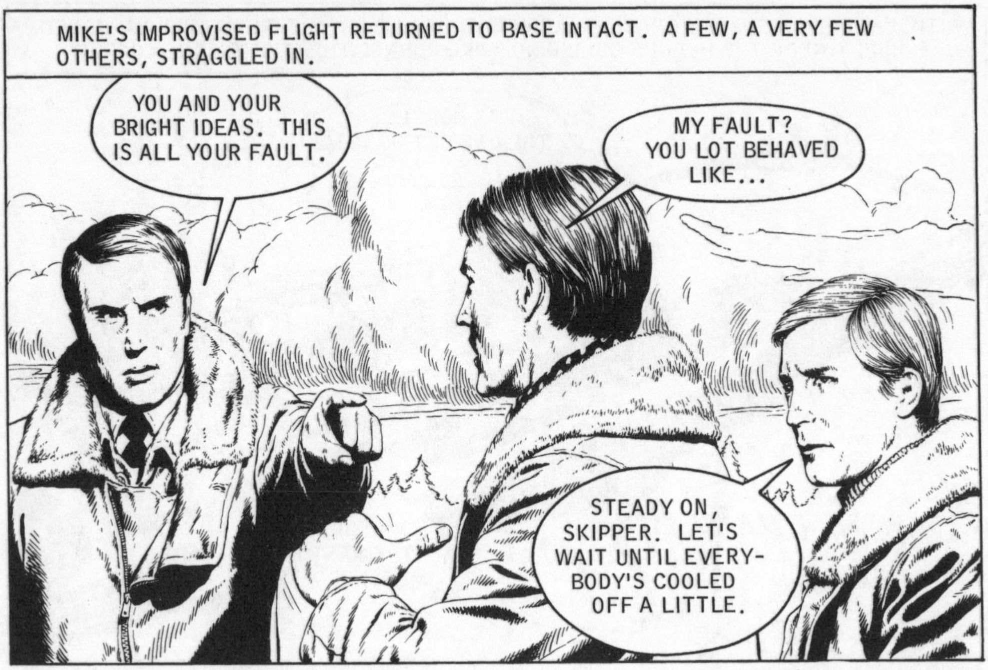
MIKE'S IMPROVISED FLIGHT RETURNED TO BASE INTACT. A FEW, A VERY FEW OTHERS, STRAGGLED IN.
YOU AND YOUR BRIGHT IDEAS. THIS IS ALL YOUR FAULT.
MY FAULT? YOU LOT BEHAVED LIKE...
STEADY ON, SKIPPER. LET'S WAIT UNTIL EVERYBODY'S COOLED OFF A LITTLE.

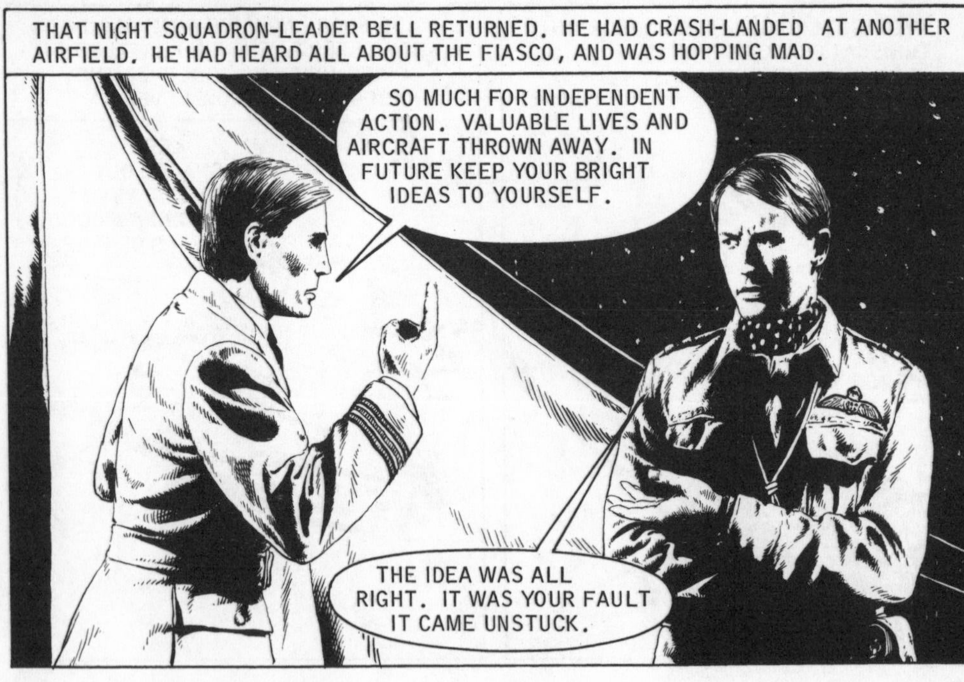
THAT NIGHT SQUADRON-LEADER BELL RETURNED. HE HAD CRASH-LANDED AT ANOTHER AIRFIELD. HE HAD HEARD ALL ABOUT THE FIASCO, AND WAS HOPPING MAD.
SO MUCH FOR INDEPENDENT ACTION. VALUABLE LIVES AND AIRCRAFT THROWN AWAY. IN FUTURE KEEP YOUR BRIGHT IDEAS TO YOURSELF.
THE IDEA WAS ALL RIGHT. IT WAS YOUR FAULT IT CAME UNSTUCK.

THE C.O. COULDN'T BELIEVE HIS EARS.

MY FAULT? BUT I TRAINED THESE MEN TO A HAIR...

EXACTLY. EVERYTHING BY THE BOOK, WITH YOU TURNING THE PAGES. THE MEN JUST DIDN'T KNOW HOW TO ACT ON THEIR OWN.

AND FOR THE FIRST TIME, DOUBT SHOWED IN BELL'S EYES.

BUT...I... I...

THINK ABOUT IT. WHY SACRIFICE BRAVE MEN FOR OUTDATED RULES AND REGULATIONS?

BUT THERE WAS LITTLE TIME FOR TACTICAL DISCUSSIONS. THE GERMAN ARMIES SWEPT ON. AT ONE POINT THEIR ADVANCE HINGED ON TWO RIVER BRIDGES, AS BELL EXPLAINED TO HIS CREWS.

THE ARMY ARE EXTREMELY CONCERNED. THEY WANT THOSE BRIDGES DESTROYED AT ANY COST. OUR PROBLEM IS LACK OF AIRCRAFT.

THE BOMBER LOSSES HAD BEEN SO HEAVY THAT IN THE ENTIRE SECTOR ONLY FIVE SERVICEABLE BATTLES COULD BE FOUND.

WE HAVE THREE, ANOTHER SQUADRON CAN RAISE TWO. I WON'T ORDER ANYBODY TO UNDER- TAKE THIS MISSION. ANY VOLUNTEERS, PLEASE STAND UP.

EVERY MAN GOT TO HIS FEET INSTANTLY.

THANK YOU, GENTLEMEN, I EXPECTED AS MUCH. WE WILL DRAW LOTS.

THREE SLIPS OF PAPER HAD CROSSES ON THEM. MIKE AND BELL WERE AMONG THOSE WHO DREW THEM.

THERE WERE TWO BRIDGES OVER A BELGIAN RIVER, ONE CONCRETE, THE OTHER STEEL, SET ABOUT A MILE APART. SQUADRON-LEADER BELL COMMANDED THE PITIFULLY SMALL FORCE WHICH SET OFF TO ATTACK THEM.

BUT THE HEAVY BATTLE COULD NOT BE DIVED STEEPLY LIKE THE STUKA. MURDEROUSLY ACCURATE FLAK CLAWED DOWN THE LEADING MACHINE BEFORE IT EVEN REACHED THE BRIDGE. THE SECOND AIRCRAFT STRUGGLED ON, ALREADY TRAILING SMOKE.

MORTALLY WOUNDED, HIS GUNNER DEAD, FLAMES LICKING AROUND HIM, THE PILOT FOUGHT TO STEADY HIS SHELL-TORN MACHINE.

BUT THE CONTROLS WERE USELESS, THE BLAZING BATTLE VEERED AWAY. GERMANS FLED FOR THEIR LIVES AS, LIKE A COMET, THE SHATTERED AIRCRAFT PLUNGED TOWARDS THE ROAD.

MIKE HAD WATCHED THIS TERRIBLE SACRIFICE, AND ALREADY THE GUNS AT THE SECOND BRIDGE WERE GETTING THE RANGE.

BELL'S FACE TIGHTENED AS TRACER BEGAN TO HISS ROUND HIS TINY FORCE. THEN HE
SAW MIKE BREAK AWAY...

WHAT THE BLAZES?
STALLARD, GET BACK!
YOU YELLOW-LIVERED,
SPINELESS....

BELL WAS NOT THE ONLY ONE WHO THOUGHT MIKE HAD CHICKENED OUT...

THE COWARDLY
ONE IS WISE,
FRANZ.

JA, THE
OTHERS WILL
NOT LIVE TO
FLY AGAIN!

BUT MIKE IGNORED THE STREAM OF CRITICISM. HE KNEW WHAT HE WAS DOING. THROTTLE WIDE, HE MADE A WIDE SWEEP AWAY FROM THE RIVER, THEN TURNED BACK BELOW THE BRIDGE.

I THOUGHT YOUR NERVE HAD GONE, SKIPPER.

I HOPE THE JERRIES THINK THE SAME, CHALKY!

EVERY GERMAN EYE WAS ON THE REMAINING TWO BATTLES, SO THEY WERE TOTALLY UNPREPARED FOR THE THIRD MACHINE THAT CAME ROARING UP BEHIND THEM.

IT'S THE ONE THAT RAN AWAY!

GET HIM!

MIKE'S BATTLE THUNDERED IN AGAIN, GUNS HAMMERING. BELL WASTED NO TIME IN QUESTIONS.

THE GERMANS QUICKLY RECOVERED FROM THEIR SHOCK AND HURLED A VERITABLE TORNADO OF SHOT AND SHELL AT THE FLEEING BATTLES.

BY LUCK AND SHEER WILL-POWER, BELL AND MIKE MANAGED TO COAX THEIR SAGGING MACHINES INTO FRIENDLY TERRITORY. BUT THE AIRCRAFT COULD ONLY STAND SO MUCH...

THE WEARY, BULLET-TORN MACHINE SLITHERED TO A HALT. BELL WAS WAITING, SMILING.

MIKE WAS RAPIDLY FINDING OUT THAT HIS INDEPENDENT ATTITUDE WAS FINE FOR REVOLUTIONS AND THE LIKE, BUT THIS WAS, AS HE SAID IN 1938, A KING-SIZE WAR.

COURAGE AND SKILL JUST AREN'T ENOUGH. THERE MUST BE ORGANISATION AND DISCIPLINE.

NEVER THOUGHT I'D HEAR YOU SAY THAT, STALLARD. COME ON, WE'VE GOT A LONG WALK AHEAD OF US.

THEY FINALLY ARRIVED BACK AT THE AIRFIELD TO FIND MANY NEW FACES IN THE MESS.

SO MANY SQUADRONS HAVE BEEN BADLY CUT UP THAT THEY'VE BEEN DISBANDED AND THE CREWS AND AIRCRAFT SENT TO MAKE UP THE NUMBERS OF OTHERS.

AS BAD AS THAT, EH? WELL, AT LEAST THEY HAVE SOME EXPERIENCE— BETTER THAN RECRUITS JUST OUT OF TRAINING.

NOTHING COULD STOP THE NAZI BLITZKREIG. OPPOSITION WAS SWEPT ASIDE, NATURAL BARRIERS SUCH AS RIVERS WERE QUICKLY BRIDGED BY THE HIGHLY EFFICIENT GERMAN ENGINEERS. AND AGAIN IT WAS UP TO THE BATTLES TO ATTACK.

THE PONTOON BRIDGES HERE MUST BE DESTROYED AT ANY COST. EVERY AVAILABLE AIRCRAFT IS TO BE USED IN A MASS RAID.

SOME THIRTY BATTLES WERE SCRAPED UP, ESCORTED BY A MOTLEY ASSORTMENT OF FRENCH AND BRITISH FIGHTERS.

QUITE AN IMPRESSIVE SIGHT, SKIPPER, AND NO SIGN OF JERRY.

TEN MINUTES MORE AND WE'LL BE OVER THE TARGET.

HARDLY HAD MIKE SPOKEN THAN MESSERSCHMITTS APPEARED ABOVE, ALL OUT FOR BLOOD.

NEVER MIND THE FIGHTERS. GET AT THE BOMBERS, SCATTER THEM.

OUTFLOWN AND OUT-GUNNED, THE FEW FIGHTERS WERE QUICKLY SWEPT ASIDE. BUT THE BATTLES REFUSED TO SCATTER, STUBBORNLY HOLDING THEIR FORMATIONS.

ONE TO US. LOOK AT OUR BOYS, SKIPPER. BORING STRAIGHT ON AS IF THIS WERE A PRACTICE FLIGHT.

THAT'S DISCIPLINE, CHALKY.

MIKE STALLARD HAD AT LAST REALISED THAT BUT FOR THE SUPERB WAY THE BATTLES KEPT TOGETHER, THE CARNAGE WOULD HAVE BEEN TEN TIMES WORSE.

THEN THEY WERE OVER THE RIVER. MIKE RELEASED HIS BOMBS.

BULL'S-EYE! AND SOME OF THE OTHERS GOT THROUGH TOO!

SOME, BUT VERY FEW. EVEN FEWER MANAGED TO ESCAPE FROM THAT CAULDRON OF SUDDEN DEATH. LATER, BACK AT BASE, BELL PASSED ON THE LATEST INFORMATION.

WE DID OUR BEST, BUT THE GERMANS HAVE REPLACED THE BRIDGES. WE ARE TO FALL BACK. AIRFIELDS HAVE BEEN PREPARED FOR US NEARER THE COAST.

THE NEW AIRFIELDS WERE MORE PRIMITIVE THAN THE ONES THEY HAD LEFT, BUT THE BATTLES HARASSED THE ONRUSHING ENEMY, ALWAYS OUTNUMBERED BUT NEVER FLINCHING.

TOMORROW'S TARGET IS A STUKA AIRFIELD. TAKE-OFF IS BEFORE DAWN, SO GET A GOOD NIGHT'S REST.

NOW WE CAN GIVE THOSE WONKY-WINGED PERISHERS A TASTE OF THEIR OWN MEDICINE.

BELL WAS LEARNING TOO. THE ATTACK WAS TIMED FOR DAWN, THE BATTLES APPROACHING UNSEEN FROM THE DARKNESS TO THE WEST, THE TARGET LIT BY THE NEWLY-RISEN SUN.

OBVIOUSLY THEY'RE NOT EXPECTING US. ATTACK FORMATION.

THE GERMANS WERE UNCONCERNEDLY PREPARING THE UGLY DIVE-BOMBERS FOR THE DAY'S OPERATIONS. WHY SHOULD THEY WORRY, THE R.A.F. WAS BEATEN...

ENGLANDERS! TAKE COVER!

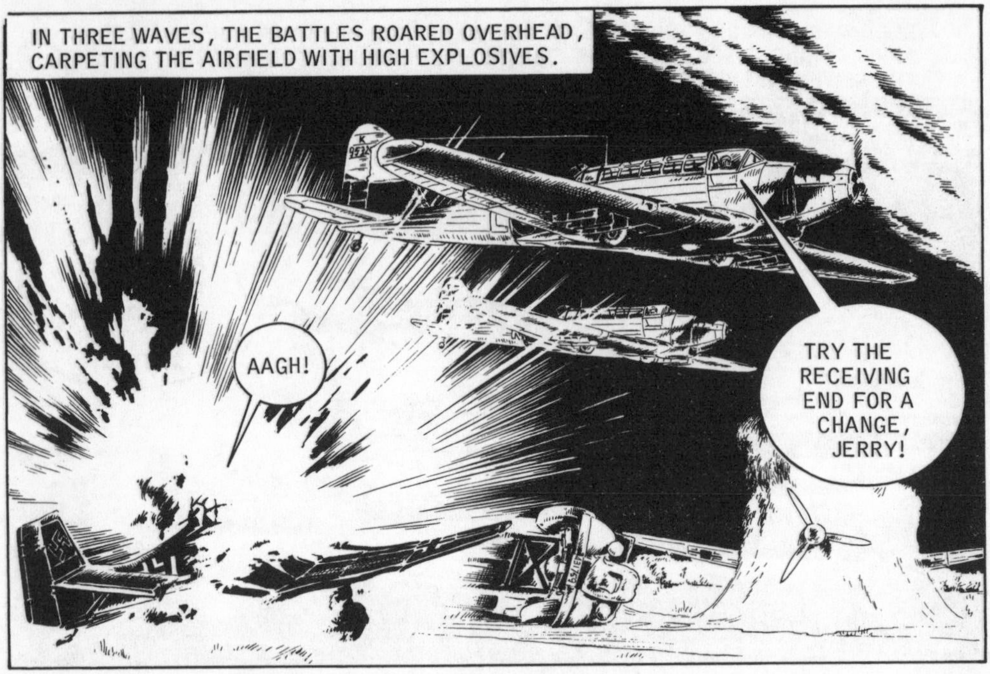
IN THREE WAVES, THE BATTLES ROARED OVERHEAD, CARPETING THE AIRFIELD WITH HIGH EXPLOSIVES.
AAGH!
TRY THE RECEIVING END FOR A CHANGE, JERRY!

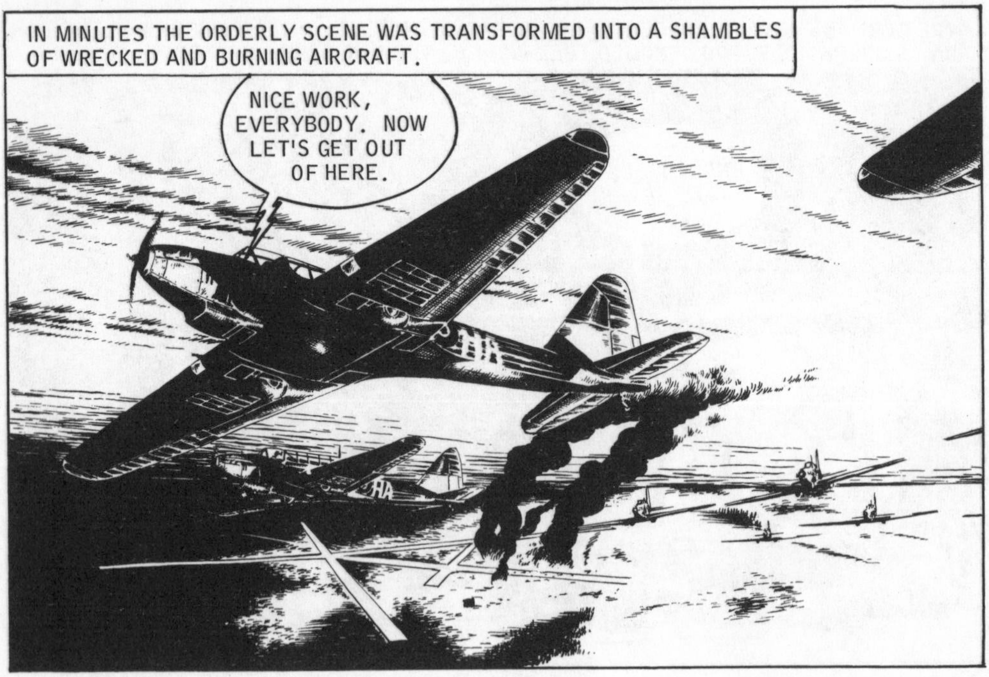
IN MINUTES THE ORDERLY SCENE WAS TRANSFORMED INTO A SHAMBLES OF WRECKED AND BURNING AIRCRAFT.
NICE WORK, EVERYBODY. NOW LET'S GET OUT OF HERE.

AT FULL THROTTLE THE BATTLES RACED FOR HOME. BUT TELEPHONE LINES HAD BEEN HUMMING TO THE FIGHTER AIRFIELDS, AND MIKE'S AIRCRAFT FELT THE FIRST BULLETS FROM ATTACKING MESSERSCHMITTS.

THERE WAS BARELY TIME FOR THEIR PARACHUTES TO OPEN BEFORE THEY THUMPED DOWN IN AN OPEN FIELD.

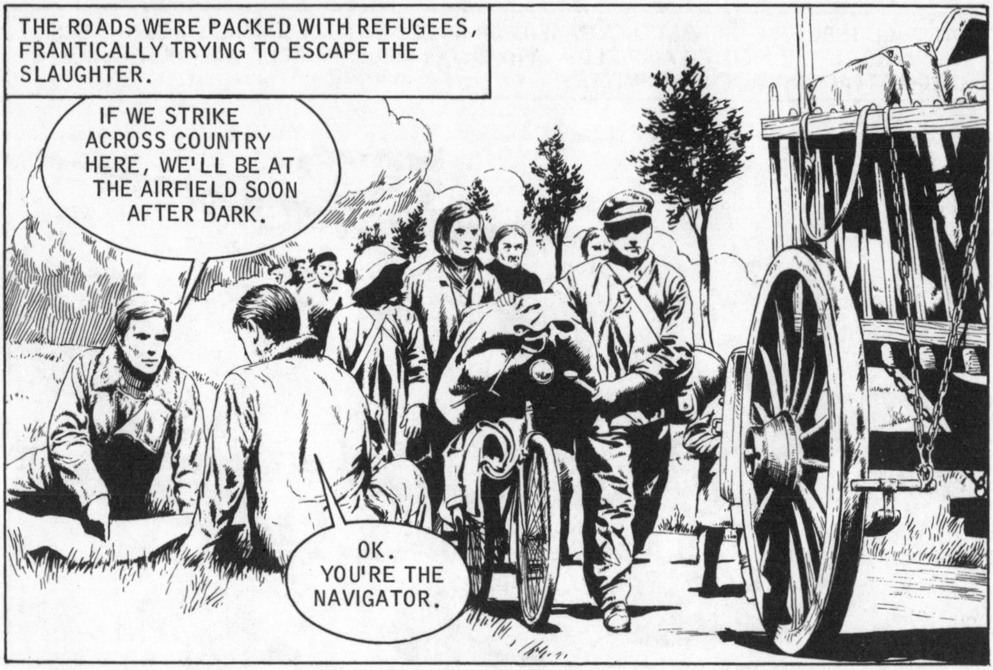
THE ROADS WERE PACKED WITH REFUGEES, FRANTICALLY TRYING TO ESCAPE THE SLAUGHTER.
IF WE STRIKE ACROSS COUNTRY HERE, WE'LL BE AT THE AIRFIELD SOON AFTER DARK.
OK. YOU'RE THE NAVIGATOR.

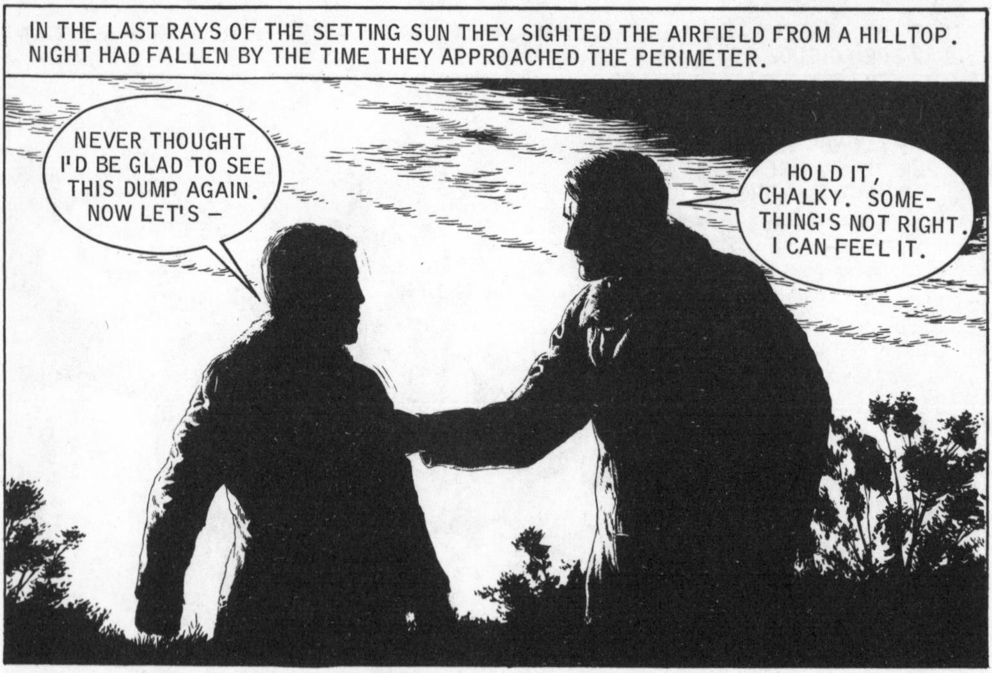
IN THE LAST RAYS OF THE SETTING SUN THEY SIGHTED THE AIRFIELD FROM A HILLTOP. NIGHT HAD FALLEN BY THE TIME THEY APPROACHED THE PERIMETER.
NEVER THOUGHT I'D BE GLAD TO SEE THIS DUMP AGAIN. NOW LET'S –
HOLD IT, CHALKY. SOME-THING'S NOT RIGHT. I CAN FEEL IT.

SOME SIXTH SENSE SET MIKE'S NERVES TINGLING. STEALTHILY HE AND CHALKY MADE THEIR WAY TO THE AIRFIELD BOUNDARY WHERE THE GUNNER GASPED IN ASTONISHMENT.

LOOK OVER THERE, SKIPPER. A JERRY ARMOURED CAR!

I THOUGHT THE PLACE WAS TOO QUIET. AND SOME OF OUR PLANES ARE STILL HERE. THE SQUADRON MUST HAVE BEEN TAKEN BY SURPRISE.

THE PICTURE WAS ALL TOO CLEAR. A FAST PANZER COLUMN HAD CAPTURED THE AIRFIELD.

WE COULD PINCH A BATTLE. BUT WHICH OF THEM IS AIRWORTHY? MOST OF THEM LOOK PRETTY KNOCKED ABOUT.

QUIET! SOMEBODY'S COMING THIS WAY.

THEY SHRANK INTO THE UNDERGROWTH AS THE SHADOWY FIGURE FLITTED FROM TREE TO TREE. WHEN IT WAS CLOSE ENOUGH, THEY SPRANG.

LET ME GO!

I'D KNOW THAT FACE ANY- WHERE. IT'S CHIEFY!

THE TOUGH OLD FLIGHT-SERGEANT EX-PLAINED THE SITUATION. ORDERS HAD BEEN RECEIVED FOR THE SQUADRON TO WITHDRAW TO ENGLAND.

CHIEFY TOLD THEM HE HAD TAKEN COVER IN THE WOODS. A STRAY SHELL HAD BURST NEARBY, STUNNING HIM. HE HAD ONLY RECOVERED A SHORT WHILE BEFORE.

...ALMOST EVERY PLANE THAT WAS IN GOOD SHAPE LEFT RIGHT AWAY. I GOT THE LADS STARTED PACKING UP WHEN SUDDENLY THERE WERE TANKS EVERYWHERE.

HOW DID YOU ESCAPE?

I WAS ON MY WAY TO SAB-OTAGE THE ONE FLYABLE BATTLE THAT WAS LEFT BEHIND.

THEN IT'S A GOOD JOB WE JUMPED YOU WHEN WE DID. SHOW US WHERE THIS MACHINE IS!

SILENTLY THEY MADE THEIR WAY TO WHERE THE BATTLE STOOD IN ITS DISPERSAL BAY.

THEY MAY HAVE PUT OBSTRUCTIONS ON THE AIRFIELD, SO WE'LL HAVE TO WAIT FOR DAYLIGHT. IS THERE A FULL LOAD OF PETROL ON BOARD, CHIEFY?

I SAID SHE WAS SERVICE-ABLE, DIDN'T I?

MIKE GRINNED AT THE OLD MECHANIC'S HURT TONE AS THEY SETTLED DOWN TO WAIT. AFTER WHAT SEEMED AN ETERNITY, THE EASTERN SKY LIGHTENED.

YOU GO FIRST, CHALKY, AND GET YOUR GUN READY.

GIVE ME A JIFFY TO PRIME THE ENGINE AND TURN THE PROP, SIR. THAT'LL SUCK IN PETROL AND SHE'LL START EASIER.

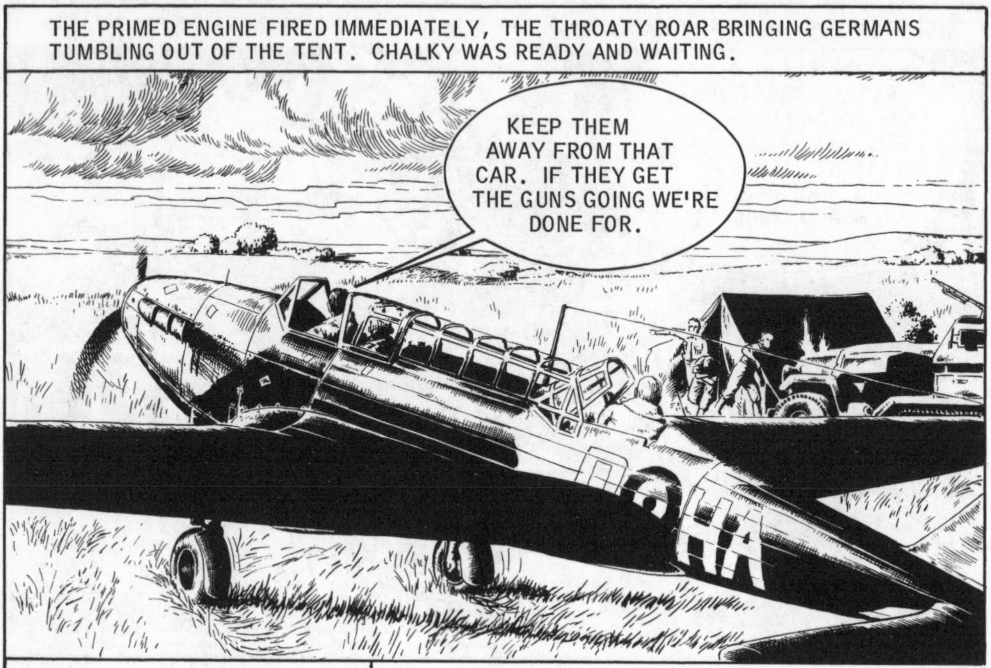
THE PRIMED ENGINE FIRED IMMEDIATELY, THE THROATY ROAR BRINGING GERMANS TUMBLING OUT OF THE TENT. CHALKY WAS READY AND WAITING.
KEEP THEM AWAY FROM THAT CAR. IF THEY GET THE GUNS GOING WE'RE DONE FOR.

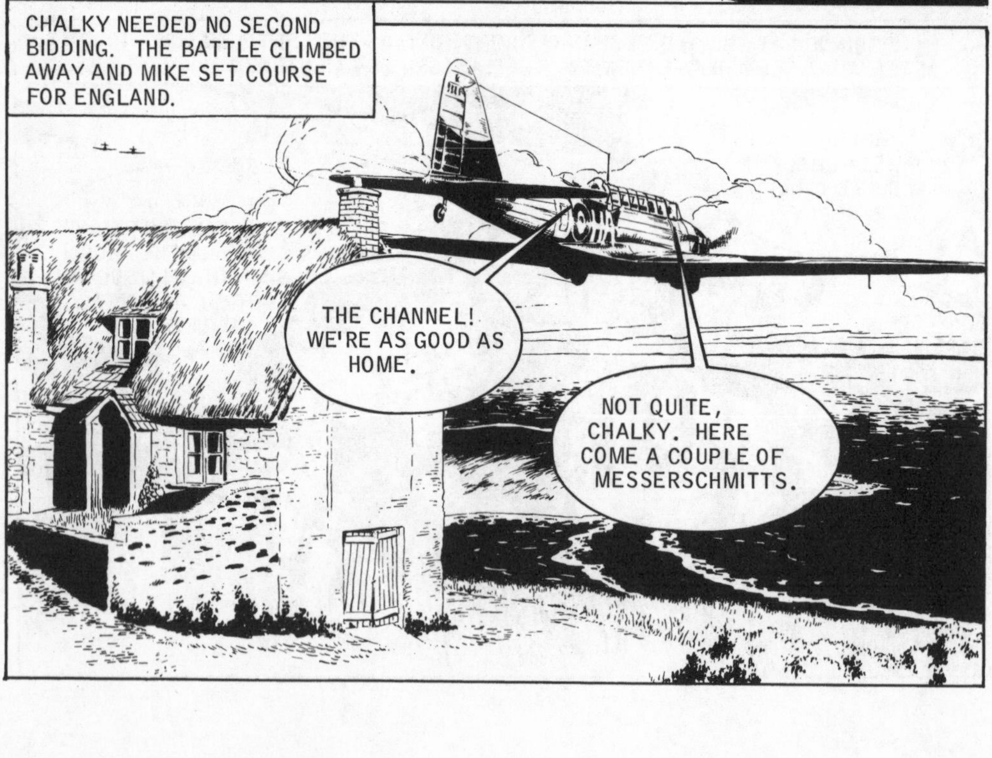
CHALKY NEEDED NO SECOND BIDDING. THE BATTLE CLIMBED AWAY AND MIKE SET COURSE FOR ENGLAND.
THE CHANNEL! WE'RE AS GOOD AS HOME.
NOT QUITE, CHALKY. HERE COME A COUPLE OF MESSERSCHMITTS.

MIKE WENT DOWN TO WAVE-TOP LEVEL, BUT THE SPEEDY MESSERSCHMITTS RACED AFTER THE BRITISH PLANE. THE COAST OF ENGLAND LOOMED TANTALISINGLY AHEAD.

BUT OTHER EYES WERE WATCHING THE CHASE.

THE LEADING GERMAN PILOT WAS CALMY LINING HIS SIGHTS ON THE HELPLESS BATTLE WHEN A SHELL EXPLODED UNDER HIM, HURLING THE MESSERSCHMITT OVER ON ITS BACK.

MEIN GOTT!

AARGH!

THE GRINNING ARTILLERYMEN WAVED AS THE BATTLE SWEPT LOW OVERHEAD, ROCKING ITS WINGS IN SALUTE.

TOO CLOSE FOR COMFORT! I'LL NEVER JOKE ABOUT THE ARMY AGAIN.

HALF AN HOUR LATER MIKE TOUCHED DOWN AT THE SAME AIRFIELD FROM WHICH HE HAD TAKEN OFF FOR FRANCE. AND THERE TO MEET HIM WAS BELL WHO HAD GOT BACK SAFELY WITH THE OTHER AIRWORTHY BATTLES.

WELL, I'M BLOWED — IT'S STALLARD. I KNEW YOU'D TURN UP SOONER OR LATER — LIKE A BAD PENNY.

BETTER LATE THAN NEVER. AND WE'VE BROUGHT OUR AIRCRAFT WITH US, FOR WHAT USE THE OLD BUS IS NOW.

BUT THERE MIKE WAS WRONG. THERE WAS STILL WORK FOR THE AGEING BATTLE. EVERY HARBOUR ON THE CHANNEL COAST OF FRANCE WAS FILLING WITH BARGES.

THOSE BARGES MEAN INVASION. ANYTHING THAT CAN FLY AND CARRY BOMBS IS TO BE USED AGAINST THEM. INCLUDING MY NEW WILD MEN.

A NEW SQUADRON? WHAT'S SO WILD ABOUT THEM?

MEN FROM THE CONQUERED COUNTRIES HAD MADE THEIR WAY TO ENGLAND, EAGER TO CONTINUE THE FIGHT AGAINST THE HATED ENEMY. AMONG THEM, AND BY FAR THE MOST FORMIDABLE, WERE THE POLES.

...THEY'RE ALL KEEN TO HIT BACK AT JERRY. I'VE GOT TO TEACH THEM THE R.A.F. WAYS. WOULD YOU BE MY SENIOR FLIGHT COMMANDER?

WHY ME?

BELL WAS REALLY AFRAID OF THESE FIERCE, PROUD POLES WHO ONLY LIVED TO KILL NAZIS.

YOU CAN DEAL WITH FOREIGNERS. I DON'T WANT TO SQUASH THEIR ENTHUSIASM AS I'VE DONE WITH OTHERS IN THE PAST.

OR LET IT RUN TO WASTE, LIKE I DID. BETWEEN US WE CAN HANDLE THEM.

EACH SQUADRON HAD BEEN ALLOTTED A PORT AS TARGET. MIKE, NOW A FLIGHT—LIEUTENANT, STUDIED THE MAP WITH BELL AND DREW UP A PLAN.

THE PLAN WAS UNORTHODOX, AND TICKLED THE FANCY OF THE POLISH FLYERS. THEY WERE KEEN TO TRY IT, A LITTLE TOO KEEN —

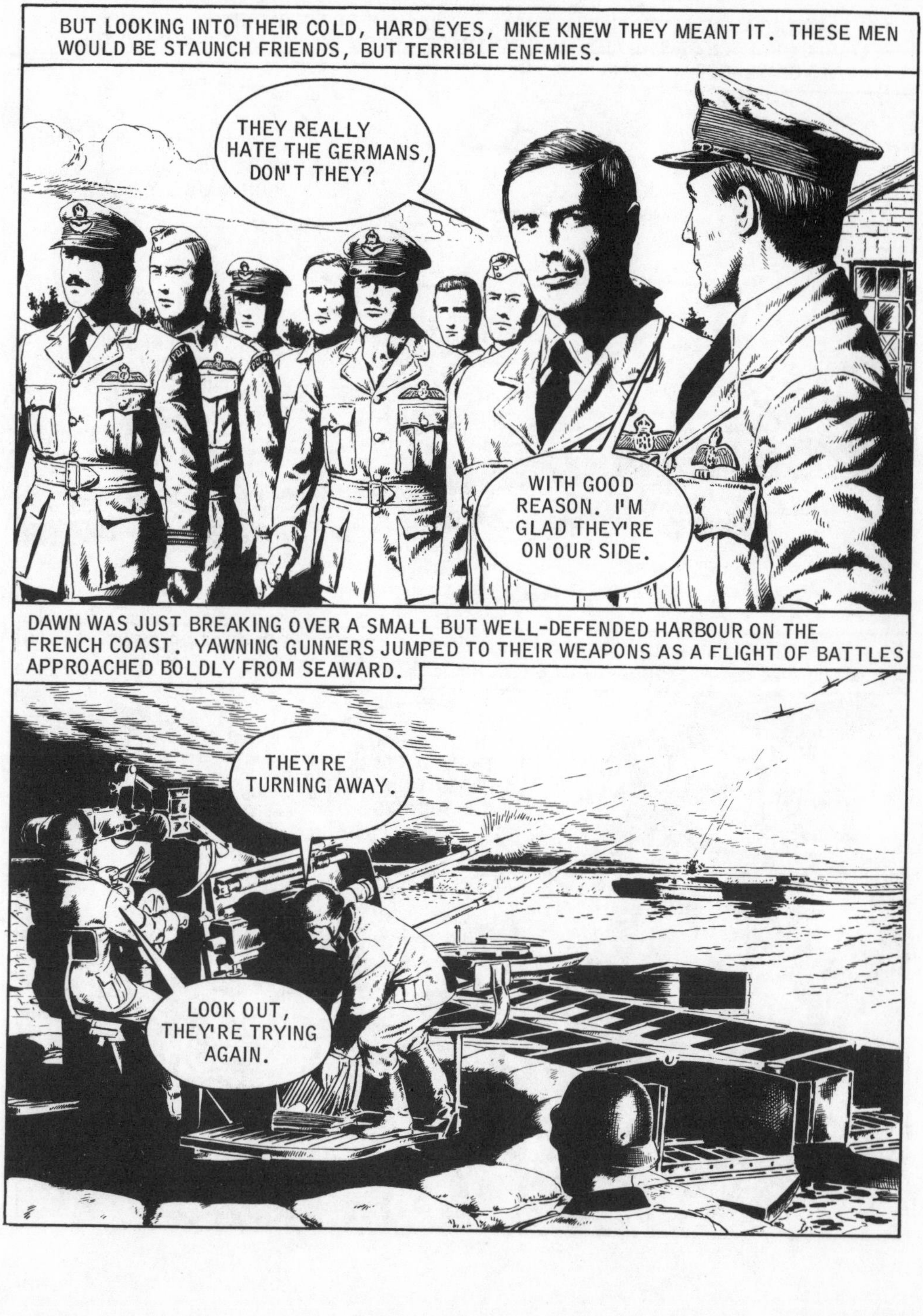
BUT LOOKING INTO THEIR COLD, HARD EYES, MIKE KNEW THEY MEANT IT. THESE MEN WOULD BE STAUNCH FRIENDS, BUT TERRIBLE ENEMIES.
THEY REALLY HATE THE GERMANS, DON'T THEY?
WITH GOOD REASON. I'M GLAD THEY'RE ON OUR SIDE.
DAWN WAS JUST BREAKING OVER A SMALL BUT WELL-DEFENDED HARBOUR ON THE FRENCH COAST. YAWNING GUNNERS JUMPED TO THEIR WEAPONS AS A FLIGHT OF BATTLES APPROACHED BOLDLY FROM SEAWARD.
THEY'RE TURNING AWAY.
LOOK OUT, THEY'RE TRYING AGAIN.

THE BOMBERS MADE SEVERAL HALF-HEARTED DASHES AT THE HARBOUR, BUT ALWAYS FELL BACK IN FACE OF THE ANTI-AIRCRAFT FIRE. FROM INLAND MIKE WATCHED THE STREAKS OF TRACER.

THE C.O.'s GOT THE FIRE-WORK DISPLAY GOING NICELY.

BETTER MOVE IN SOON, SKIPPER. I CAN HEAR OUR MATES GNASHING THEIR TEETH.

MIKE, WITH THE MAIN BODY OF THE SQUADRON, HAD CROSSED THE COAST FURTHER SOUTH AND MADE A WIDE SWEEP INLAND TO BRING HIM BEHIND THE TARGET.

HERE WE GO, THEN. ATTACK FORMATION — AND NO SHOVING!

HOLDING PERFECT FORMATION, THE BATTLES ROARED OVER THE HARBOUR, THEIR BOMBS SPLINTERING THE BARGES TO PIECES.

BY THE TIME GUNNERS HAD SWUNG THEIR WEAPONS TO MEET THIS NEW MENACE, THE BATTLES HAD GONE, AND OUT TO SEAWARD BELL IMMEDIATELY TOOK HIS CUE.

GIBBERING WITH RAGE, THE GERMANS AGAIN DRAGGED THEIR GUNS ROUND. BUT THE SKY WAS EMPTY. THE BATTLES WERE HEADING FULL THROTTLE FOR HOME, THEIR MISSION SUCCESSFULLY COMPLETED.

HERE COME BELL'S LOT. WHAT A LOVELY SPOOF WE PULLED. I'D LOVE TO SEE THOSE JERRIES' FACES.

JUST TIMING, ORGANISATION, DISCIPLINE — AND SKILL!

BACK AT BASE, THERE WAS NO NOISY CELEBRATION, BUT MIKE SAW GRIM SATISFACTION IN THE POLES' FACES, AND THAT WAS REWARD ENOUGH.

TARGET DESTROYED. NO DAMAGE OR CASUALTIES ON OUR SIDE. IT WAS A TEXT-BOOK OPERATION.

WELL DONE, SIR. OH, BY THE WAY, THE FIRST ONE ARRIVED A FEW MINUTES AGO, SIR.

MIKE WAS PUZZLED AT THE MECHANIC'S REMARK.

THE FIRST ONE OF WHAT?

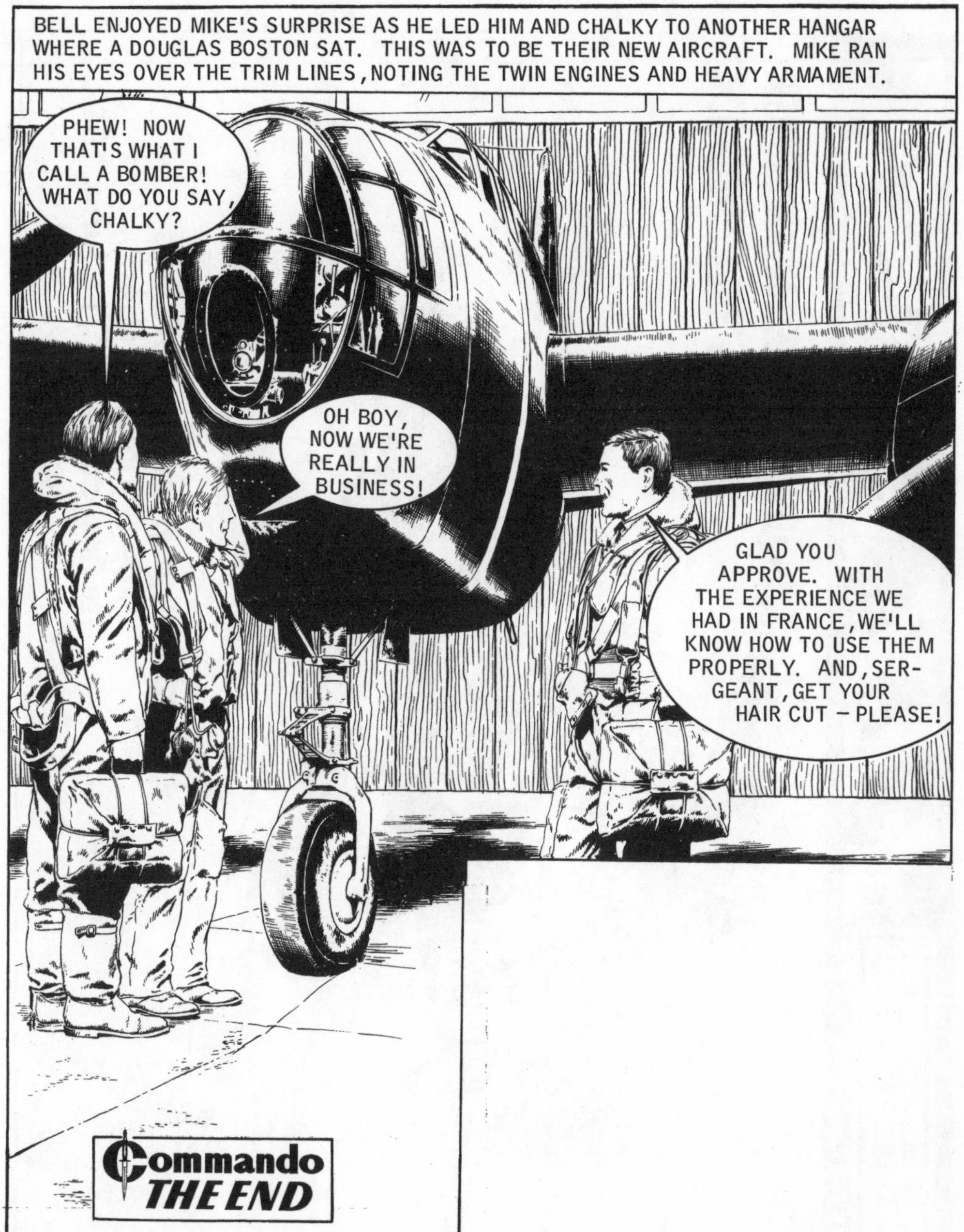
BELL ENJOYED MIKE'S SURPRISE AS HE LED HIM AND CHALKY TO ANOTHER HANGAR WHERE A DOUGLAS BOSTON SAT. THIS WAS TO BE THEIR NEW AIRCRAFT. MIKE RAN HIS EYES OVER THE TRIM LINES, NOTING THE TWIN ENGINES AND HEAVY ARMAMENT.
PHEW! NOW THAT'S WHAT I CALL A BOMBER! WHAT DO YOU SAY, CHALKY?
OH BOY, NOW WE'RE REALLY IN BUSINESS!
GLAD YOU APPROVE. WITH THE EXPERIENCE WE HAD IN FRANCE, WE'LL KNOW HOW TO USE THEM PROPERLY. AND, SERGEANT, GET YOUR HAIR CUT – PLEASE!
Commando THE END

Commando **FLY PAST**

No. 7 – SUPERMARINE SPITFIRE Mk IX

Shown in the markings of 64 Squadron, R.A.F., its first squadron, in June, 1942.

THE SIGN OF THE GRIFFIN — A SYMBOL THAT HAD HAUNTED TONY GRIEVE ALL HIS LIFE. IN THE FIRST WORLD WAR IT HAD BEEN PAINTED ON THE AIRCRAFT OF A GERMAN ACE PILOT AT A TIME WHEN TONY HADN'T EVEN BEEN BORN.
AND NOW IT WAS TO APPEAR AGAIN IN THE SECOND WORLD WAR ON ANOTHER GERMAN ACE'S AIRCRAFT...AND SERVE AS A STRANGE LINK BETWEEN THE TWO WARS!

SON OF A TRAITOR

IN 1918 CAPTAIN DICK GRIEVE CONSIDERED HIMSELF LUCKY. HE WAS FLYING ONE OF THE LATEST SOPWITH CAMEL BIPLANES, ONE OF THE BEST FIGHTERS IN THE R.F.C.

SCHWEINHUND! OUR PLANES WILL SHOOT YOU OUT OF THE SKY!

ARMED WITH TWIN MACHINE GUNS, THE CAMEL COULD ALSO CARRY FOUR BOMBS — A PRESENT FOR THE HUN ON THIS LONE SORTIE OVER THE TRENCHES.

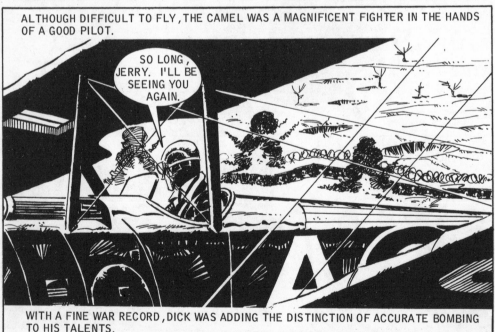

ALTHOUGH DIFFICULT TO FLY, THE CAMEL WAS A MAGNIFICENT FIGHTER IN THE HANDS OF A GOOD PILOT.

SO LONG, JERRY. I'LL BE SEEING YOU AGAIN.

WITH A FINE WAR RECORD, DICK WAS ADDING THE DISTINCTION OF ACCURATE BOMBING TO HIS TALENTS.

FOUR TIMES HE HAD MADE THE LONE RUN OVER THE GERMAN LINES TO DROP THE DEADLY EGGS.   THREE TIMES HE HAD RETURNED WITHOUT TROUBLE , BUT THIS TIME WOULD BE DIFFERENT.

A JERRY! NOW FOR SOME SPORT.

LEUTNANT FRANZ KRAUSS ALSO HAD A REPUTATION ON THE WESTERN FRONT. HE HAD MORE KILLS TO HIS CREDIT THAN THE REST OF HIS SQUADRON PUT TOGETHER.

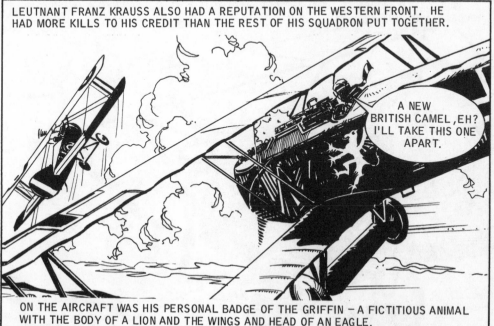

A NEW BRITISH CAMEL , EH? I'LL TAKE THIS ONE APART.

ON THE AIRCRAFT WAS HIS PERSONAL BADGE OF THE GRIFFIN – A FICTITIOUS ANIMAL WITH THE BODY OF A LION AND THE WINGS AND HEAD OF AN EAGLE.

FOR A FEW HECTIC MINUTES BOTH PILOTS MANOEUVRED FOR POSITION.   THEN DICK
REALISED WHO HE'D TAKEN ON.

EVERY R.F.C. PILOT HAD HEARD OF FRANZ KRAUSS,
THE GERMANS' GREATEST ACE IN THIS SECTOR.

THE FOKKER WAS BIGGER AND HEAVIER BUT FASTER — AND , FLOWN BY KRAUSS ,A
DEADLY OPPONENT.

WITH THE SUN IN HIS EYES, DICK FELT THE JAR OF THE GERMAN'S BULLETS SMASHING THROUGH HIS FUSELAGE AND FABRIC-COVERED WINGS.

YET HIS LUCK WAS HOLDING. HE SWUNG THE CAMEL OUT OF RANGE AND TURNED TO COME BACK. DICK GRIEVE WAS NOT THE KIND TO RUN AWAY FROM A FIGHT.

IF HE GETS THE ENGINE I'VE HAD IT.

RIGHT, MY LAD. NOW IT'S MY TURN.

THE FOKKER'S FUEL CAPACITY WAS NOT GREAT AND KRAUSS HAD BEEN AIRBORNE FOR A LONG TIME. HE HAD TO BREAK OFF THE FIGHT AS THE FUEL GAUGE NEEDLE DROPPED.

IT HAD BEEN A HARD DAY AND DICK WAS READY TO RELAX IN THE LOCAL INN THAT NIGHT AFTER HIS BATTLE WITH KRAUSS. CAPTAIN REGINALD PRICE, THE SQUADRON SECURITY OFFICER, EVIDENTLY THOUGHT LITTLE OF THE GERMAN ACE.

A WELL-TO-DO OFFICER, ALWAYS SPLASHING MONEY AROUND, PRICE HAD PLENTY OF FRIENDS EVER READY TO AGREE WITH HIM.

REGGY, YOU'RE DEAD RIGHT, AS USUAL. KRAUSS IS JUST A PHONEY.

ALTHOUGH NORMALLY A QUIET MEMBER OF THE SQUADRON, SLOW TO MAKE FRIENDS WITH HIS SNOBBISH FELLOW-OFFICERS, DICK GRIEVE HAD TO SAY SOMETHING NOW.

THAT'S A LOT OF RUBBISH, PRICE. KRAUSS IS A TOP FIGHTER-PILOT — AND I OUGHT TO KNOW. I TANGLED WITH HIM TODAY.

PRICE SNEERED –

NOW WHAT HAVE WE HERE? A GENUINE HUN-LOVER, I DO DECLARE. A PERSONAL FRIEND OF JERRY, I'LL BET.

DICK ADMIRED ANY MAN WHO KNEW HIS TRADE WELL, BE HE FRIEND OR FOE.

IF HUN-LOVER MEANS ACKNOWLEDGING A GOOD PILOT, THEN YOU CAN CALL ME THAT.

COME OFF IT. YOU'LL BEGIN TO SMELL LIKE A JERRY SOON!

TAKING HIS FRIENDS WITH HIM, PRICE MADE FOR THE DOOR.

COME ON, CHAPS, LET'S MOVE ON. THE AIR HERE IS ACQUIRING A STRONG SMELL OF GERMAN SAUSAGES.

FOR THE NEXT HOUR DICK FUMED ANGRILY AT THE EVENING'S EVENTS.

THAT FOOL PRICE JUST DOESN'T KNOW WHAT HE'S ON ABOUT...

BY THE TIME DICK LEFT, A THICK FOG HAD DESCENDED.

HECK, I'LL NEVER FIND MY WAY HOME IN THIS LOT.

ON THE WAY BACK TO THE AIRFIELD FROM THE VILLAGE ALL THE ROADS LOOKED THE SAME, AND IN THE FOG IT WAS NOT DIFFICULT TO GET LOST.

HALT, WHO GOES THERE?

CAPTAIN GRIEVE, SENTRY, AND I'M LOOKING FOR MY BED.

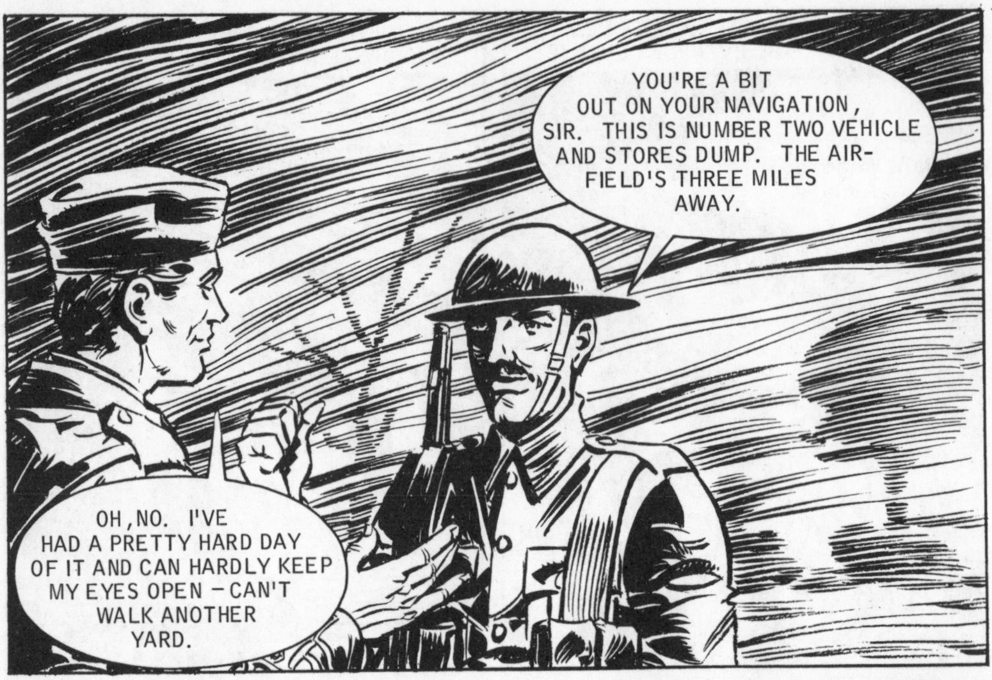
YOU'RE A BIT OUT ON YOUR NAVIGATION, SIR. THIS IS NUMBER TWO VEHICLE AND STORES DUMP. THE AIR-FIELD'S THREE MILES AWAY.
OH, NO. I'VE HAD A PRETTY HARD DAY OF IT AND CAN HARDLY KEEP MY EYES OPEN – CAN'T WALK ANOTHER YARD.

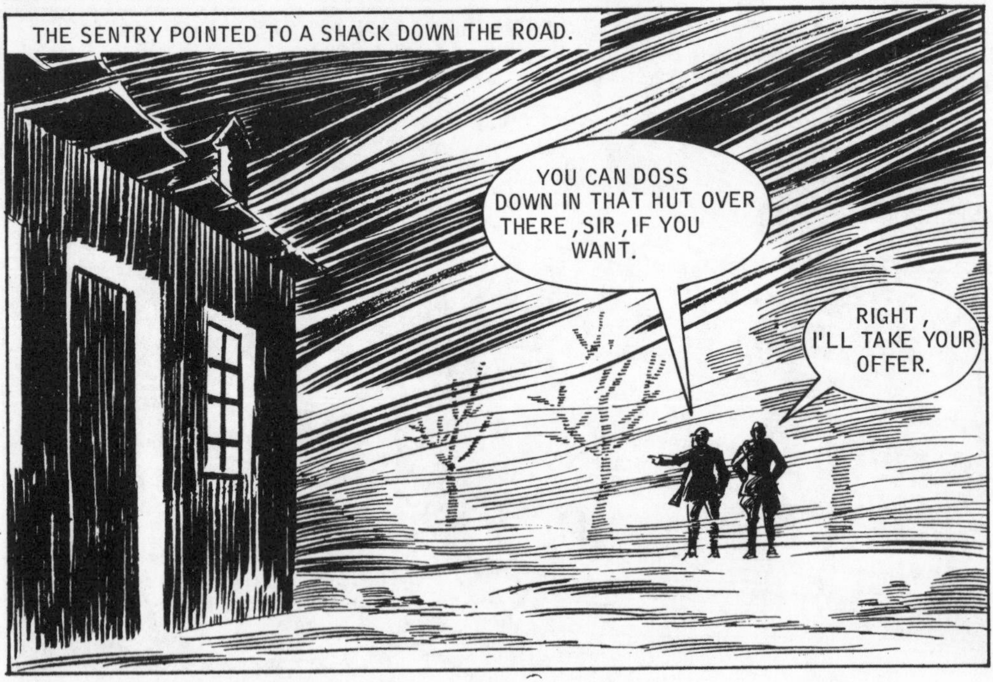
THE SENTRY POINTED TO A SHACK DOWN THE ROAD.
YOU CAN DOSS DOWN IN THAT HUT OVER THERE, SIR, IF YOU WANT.
RIGHT, I'LL TAKE YOUR OFFER.

INSIDE THE HUT HE FOUND A HEAP OF GRAIN SACKS, BUT TO DICK IT COULD HAVE BEEN A FEATHER-BED.

IT WAS THREE HOURS LATER AND DAWN WAS BREAKING WHEN THE NOISE OF AN AIRCRAFT ENGINE WOKE HIM.

HE HEADED IN THE DIRECTION OF THE NOISE AND SAW AN AIRCRAFT HE HAD LAST SEEN IN THE AIR, A FOKKER D-7 WITH A GRIFFIN SYMBOL ON IT. IT WAS FRANZ KRAUSS WHO HAD LANDED TO RENDEZVOUS WITH A MAN IN R.F.C. UNIFORM.

HEY, WHAT'S GOING ON THERE?

THE GERMAN GUNNED HIS POWERFUL ENGINE AND THE FOKKER BEGAN TO ROLL FORWARD. A SHOT FROM THE R.F.C. MAN BY THE PLANE CREASED DICK'S SKULL.

AAAGH!

DICK WAS NOT THE ONLY ONE WHO HAD HEARD THE GERMAN PLANE. TWO SOLDIERS AND A SERGEANT FROM THE DUMP CAME RUNNING.

A VOLLEY OF FIRE FROM THE SOLDIERS FLEW HARMLESSLY BY THE FOKKER.

BUT THE FOKKER TOOK OFF UNSCATHED INTO THE DAWN SKY.

HAH, KRAUSS'S LUCK HOLDS GOOD.

IT WAS THE KEEN EYES OF ONE OF THE SOLDIERS WHICH SPOTTED DICK'S UNCONSCIOUS BODY IN THE GRASS.

SARGE! IT'S A FLYING CORPS OFFICER — AND HE'S DEAD.

BUT DICK GRIEVE WAS STILL VERY MUCH ALIVE.

HE'S NOT DEAD, BULLET JUST CREASED HIM. BUT WHAT'S HE DOING HERE?

MAYBE HE HAD SOMETHING TO DO WITH THAT JERRY, SARGE.

THE NEXT THREE WEEKS WERE THE LONGEST IN DICK'S LIFE. THE SCALP WOUND WAS NOT SERIOUS, BUT HIS DISCOVERY ON THE FIELD BROUGHT HIM BEFORE A COURT-MARTIAL.

WELL, SIR, AFTER THIS GERMAN AEROPLANE GOT AWAY, WE SPOTTED THIS BODY ON THE FIELD. WE MUST HAVE HIT HIM SHOOTING AT THE PLANE.

IT HAD BEEN QUICKLY ASSUMED BY ALL THAT DICK HAD BEEN MAKING A SECRET MEETING WITH THE GERMAN TO PASS ON VALUABLE INFORMATION. NOBODY BELIEVED HIS STORY OF THE R.F.C. OFFICER HE HAD SEEN BUT FAILED TO IDENTIFY.

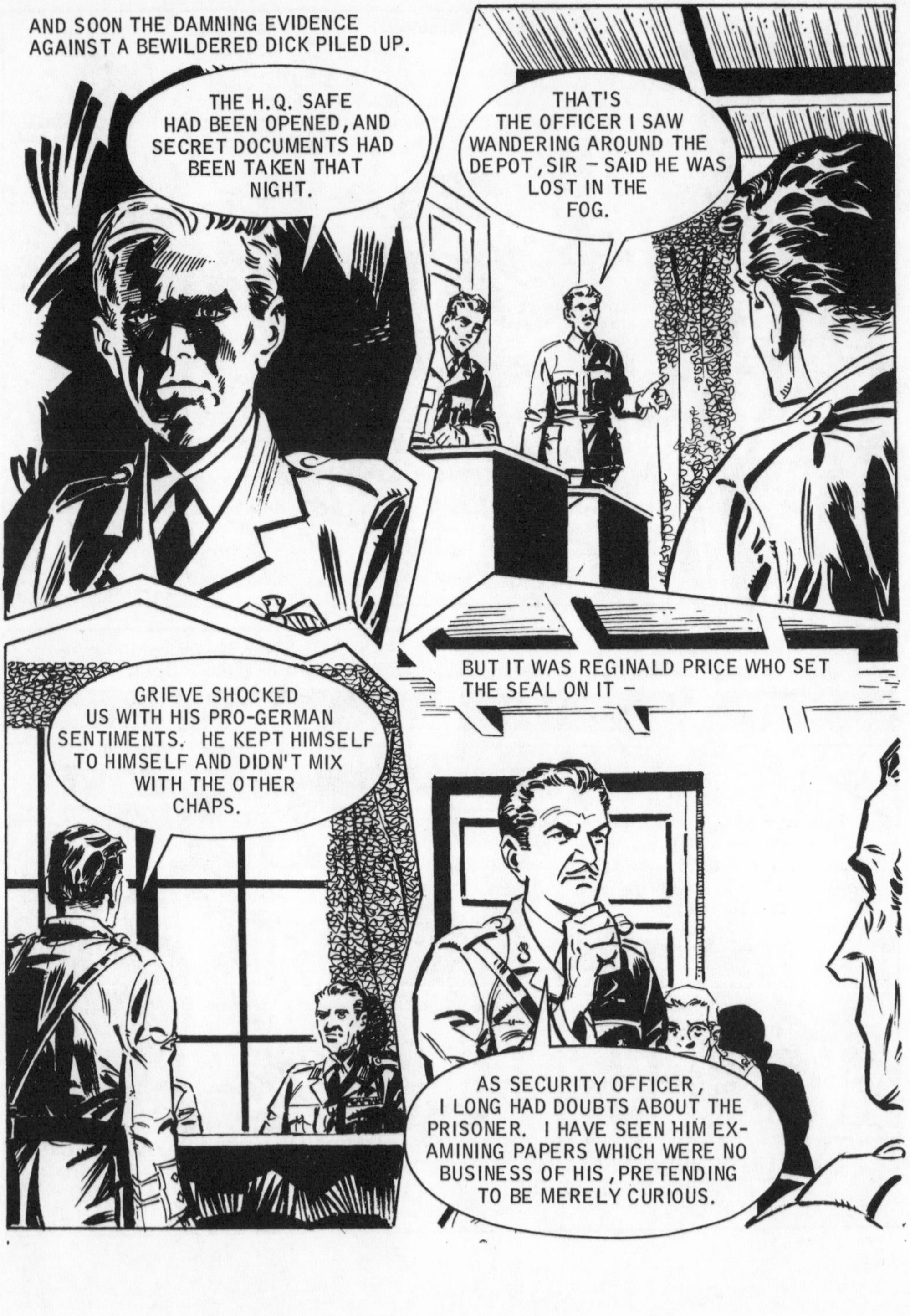
AND SOON THE DAMNING EVIDENCE AGAINST A BEWILDERED DICK PILED UP.
THE H.Q. SAFE HAD BEEN OPENED, AND SECRET DOCUMENTS HAD BEEN TAKEN THAT NIGHT.
THAT'S THE OFFICER I SAW WANDERING AROUND THE DEPOT, SIR – SAID HE WAS LOST IN THE FOG.
GRIEVE SHOCKED US WITH HIS PRO-GERMAN SENTIMENTS. HE KEPT HIMSELF TO HIMSELF AND DIDN'T MIX WITH THE OTHER CHAPS.
BUT IT WAS REGINALD PRICE WHO SET THE SEAL ON IT –
AS SECURITY OFFICER, I LONG HAD DOUBTS ABOUT THE PRISONER. I HAVE SEEN HIM EXAMINING PAPERS WHICH WERE NO BUSINESS OF HIS, PRETENDING TO BE MERELY CURIOUS.

AND SO IT WENT ON, AND DESPITE DICK'S INDIGNANT DENIALS, HE WAS FOUND GUILTY AND THE SENTENCE PRONOUNCED.

YOU HAVE BEEN FOUND GUILTY OF TREASON. BECAUSE OF THE CIRCUMSTANTIAL NATURE OF MUCH OF THE EVIDENCE YOU WILL BE DISCHARGED FROM THE SERVICE WITH DISHONOUR AND IMPRISONED FOR THE DURATION OF THE WAR.

IMPRISONMENT WAS BETTER THAN DICK COULD HAVE HOPED FOR. TREASON USUALLY MEANT THE FIRING SQUAD.

EVEN IN PRISON, DICK REMAINED A LONER. HE PREFERRED IT THAT WAY, THOUGH HE COULD HAVE FOUND FEW FRIENDS EVEN IF HE'D WANTED THEM.

WHAT'S HE IN FOR? DOESN'T LOOK A HARD NUT.

FLOGGING SECRETS TO THE FLAMING HUN – DIRTY TRAITOR.

THE CASE CAUSED A MILD SENSATION AND FOR YEARS IT WAS REGULARLY DUG UP AND SPLASHED IN THE PAGES OF CHEAP MAGAZINES. EVEN AS LATE AS 1940 –

WHY DO THEY KEEP RAKING IT UP? CAN'T THEY LEAVE WELL ENOUGH ALONE?

ON RELEASE FROM PRISON HE HAD TRIED TO MAKE A HAPPIER LIFE FOR HIMSELF. HE HAD MARRIED AND NOW HAD A SON, TONY.

WHY BUY THIS STUFF, DAD? IT ONLY MAKES YOU MISERABLE.

I KNOW. BUT IT'S THERE, TONY, REMINDING EVERYBODY THAT YOUR OLD MAN WAS A TRAITOR.

YOU A SPY? NEVER!

WHEN TONY VOLUNTEERED FOR THE FORCES, IT WAS FOR THE R.A.F. IT MAY HAVE TREATED HIS FATHER UNFAIRLY, BUT FLYING WAS IN THE BLOOD.

TAKE CARE OF YOURSELF, SON. YOU'RE LUCKY TO HAVE GOT IN, CONSIDERING THE RECORD OF THE GRIEVES.

NONSENSE. YOU WERE A FIRST-CLASS PILOT, AND THEY'RE JUST HOPING IT RUNS IN THE FAMILY.

AND YET THERE WAS SOMETHING TROUBLING TONY AS HE HEADED FOR HIS NEW LIFE. HE MADE A GRIM RESOLVE —

EVERYBODY'LL KNOW ABOUT DAD. THE CHEAP RAGS MAKE SURE IT'S NOT FORGOTTEN. BUT JUST LET ANYBODY MENTION IT TO ME IN THE WRONG WAY, AND I'LL THUMP HIM.

BUT IN THE HECTIC DAYS OF TRAINING AND LATER, WHEN THE SPITFIRE SQUADRON HE JOINED WAS LAUNCHED INTO THE BATTLE OF BRITAIN, NO ONE EVEN MENTIONED THE NAME OF DICK GRIEVE.

RED LEADER, RED LEADER. BANDITS SIGHTED AT TWO-O'CLOCK.

NOW FOR SOME FUN.

ALREADY THE SON OF THE FIRST WORLD WAR ACE HAD CHALKED UP FOUR KILLS AND THREE PROBABLES AND THIS WAS GOING TO BE ANOTHER GOOD DAY.

ONE DOWN AND TWO TO GO!

AND IT HAD NOT TAKEN HIM LONG TO REACH THE RANK OF FLYING OFFICER.

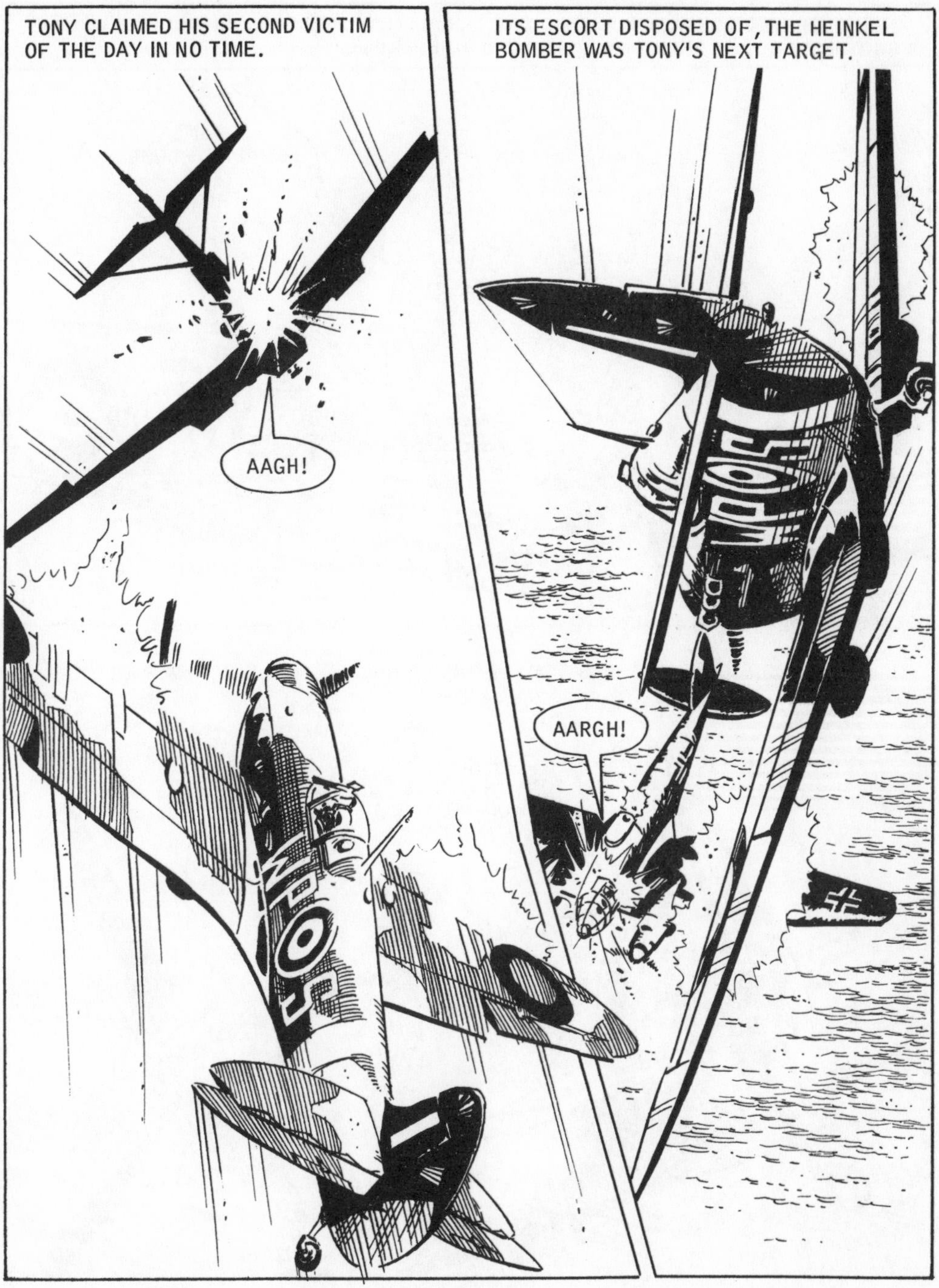
TONY CLAIMED HIS SECOND VICTIM OF THE DAY IN NO TIME.
AAGH!
ITS ESCORT DISPOSED OF, THE HEINKEL BOMBER WAS TONY'S NEXT TARGET.
AARGH!

ALTHOUGH HE'D ALREADY POLISHED OFF THREE, TONY WAS SOON ON THE LOOKOUT FOR
ANOTHER KILL.   IT DIDN'T TAKE HIM LONG TO FIND ONE.

THAT'S
JOHN IN TROUBLE.
BETTER LEND A
HAND.

PILOT OFFICER JOHN DIXON WAS GLAD OF TONY'S HELP.   DIXON WAS A FAIR PILOT, BUT
NO ACE.

THANKS,
TONY. I WAS GETTING
WORRIED FOR A
MINUTE.

THE ACTING SQUADRON LEADER, A NERVOUS, ILL-TEMPERED FLIGHT LIEUTENANT CALLED BARNES, WAS IMPATIENT. HIS AMMUNITION WAS EXPENDED AND HE WAS IN A HURRY TO GET HOME.

BARNES WAS NO GREAT PILOT. HE HAD TAKEN OVER WHEN THE LAST C.O. HAD BEEN KILLED, BUT OBVIOUSLY WOULD NEVER MAKE THE GRADE.

AS THEY FILED IN TO REPORT TO THE INTELLIGENCE OFFICER FOR DEBRIEFING, JOHNNY DIXON SHOWED HIS USUAL BOYISH ENTHUSIASM.

FLIGHT LIEUTENANT BRIAN BARNES STEPPED IN AT THAT MOMENT. HE SNAPPED AT DIXON.

YOU NEVER TRIED TO GET IN THE FIGHT, DIXON. NEXT TIME FORGET ABOUT GRIEVE HERE GRANDSTANDING IT AND HAVE A GO YOUR-SELF.

OH, SURE, SIR. BUT WASN'T HE SHARP TODAY? THREE Me's AND THAT HORRIBLE HEINKEL — ALL CERTAIN KILLS.

THERE WAS A TRACE OF JEALOUSY IN THE FLIGHT-LEADER'S VOICE AS HE SPOKE.

THAT'S AS MAYBE. THE HEINKEL WAS A CERTAIN, BUT I FANCY TWO OF THE MESSERSCHMITTS WILL BE PROBABLES.

WHAT? THEY WERE CERTS OR MY NAME'S NOT GRIEVE!

IT'S GRIEVE ALL RIGHT. NONE OF US WILL FORGET THAT. I'D ADVISE YOU NOT TO FOR-GET IT, EITHER.

THE HINT HAD NOT EVEN BEEN SUBTLE AND TONY WAS TOUCHY ABOUT ANYTHING CONCERNING HIS FATHER.

WHAT'S HE MEAN BY THAT? IF HE'S TALKING ABOUT MY OLD MAN...

HOLD IT, TONY. YOU CAN'T WIN A SCRAP AGAINST A BLOKE WITH THE RANK.

TONY HAD NEVER FORGOTTEN THE FAMILY'S BLACK MARK AND IT WAS OBVIOUS OTHERS HADN'T FORGOTTEN EITHER.

YOU KNOW ABOUT IT, DON'T YOU, JOHNNY? ABOUT MY DAD BEING A TRAITOR.

EVERYBODY KNOWS, DON'T THEY? BUT IT'S ANCIENT HISTORY, TONY. NOBODY PUTS ANY STORE BY IT.

IT WAS EASY TO SAY "FORGET IT", BUT MUCH HARDER TO DO SO. THREE DAYS LATER THE SQUADRON WAS HEADING FOR THE SOUTH COAST, AND TONY'S HEAD WAS STILL FULL OF HIS FATHER'S HISTORY.

I WONDERED WHY BARNES WAS ALWAYS SO STAND-OFFISH. NOW I KNOW.

BUT HE PUT HIS MIND TO THEIR JOB THAT DAY. THE GERMAN BOMBERS HEADING FOR THE SOUTH COAST PORT FULL OF ROYAL NAVY WARSHIPS HAD BEEN LOCATED IN TIME, BUT BARNES HAD TO PLAY IT THE HARD WAY.

CLIMB FOR THE CLOUD-BANK AT TWELVE O'CLOCK HIGH. WE'LL HANG AROUND THERE UNTIL THE BANDITS ARRIVE.

THE CLOUD WAS THICK ENOUGH TO HIDE SIX SQUADRONS.

SUNRAY TWO TO SUNRAY, CAN'T SEE A THING. WE'LL NEVER SPOT THE JERRIES IN THIS.

LISTEN, GRIEVE, WHEN I GIVE AN ORDER I DON'T WANT A DEBATE ON THE SUBJECT. I'LL DECIDE WHEN WE ATTACK.

MEANWHILE A SQUADRON OF STUKA DIVE BOMBERS, ESCORTED BY Me109s, SWEPT IN LOW BENEATH THE CLOUD-BANK, OUT OF SIGHT OR SOUND OF THE WAITING SPITFIRES.

THERE ARE THE SHIPS, LIKE FAT DUCKS ON A POND. LET'S PAY THEM A VISIT.

TO THE NAVAL OFFICERS BELOW WHO HAD BEEN PROMISED AIR PROTECTION THIS SEEMED TO BE R.A.F. INCOMPETENCE.

BLAST THE DEVILS! I'D LIKE TO GET MY HANDS ON THOSE R.A.F. PLAYBOYS.

IT'S NOT THE FIRST TIME WE'VE BEEN LET DOWN, SIR. WE SHOULD BE USED TO IT.

THE ACK-ACK GUNNERS FOUGHT VALIANTLY AND CLAIMED A VICTIM OR TWO, BUT THE DAMAGE HAD BEEN DONE.

YOU TELL THOSE POOR DEVILS DYING OUT THERE TO GET USED TO IT.

BY THE TIME BARNES REALISED HIS MISTAKE AND THE SPITFIRES ARRIVED IT WAS ALL OVER.

THEY GOT ON THE HEELS OF THE RAIDERS WITH ALL SPEED BUT THE WALL OF FLAK WHICH HIT THE SKY ON REACHING THE FRENCH COAST READ "STOP".

THE MISSION HAD BEEN A DISASTER, BUT THE BITTERNESS TONY FELT OVER THIS WAS TEMPERED BY HIS PROMOTION TO FLIGHT LIEUTENANT.

YOU DIDN'T WASTE ANY TIME PUTTING UP THAT SECOND RING, OLD BOY. YOU DESERVE IT THOUGH.

THEN BRIAN BARNES CAME IN. HE HAD SPENT A STICKY HOUR WITH THE WING-COMMANDER ON THEIR RETURN AND HAD BEEN TOLD TO HAND OVER HIS DUTIES TO TONY.

SO YOU'RE LAUGHING THIS MORNING, GRIEVE. ENJOY PUTTING UP ANOTHER RING? WELL, NOW YOU'RE TAKING OVER AS SQUADRON LEADER FROM ME.

BARNES KNEW DEEP DOWN THAT TONY WOULD DO THE JOB WELL, AND BE PROMOTED TO SQUADRON LEADER EVENTUALLY, THWARTING HIS AMBITIONS.

JOHNNY DIXON HAD LITTLE RESPECT FOR ANY NUMBER OF RANK-RINGS ON SLEEVES – ESPECIALLY WHEN THEY WERE WORN BY BARNES.

WHAT DID YOU EXPECT AFTER THAT SHAMBLES YESTERDAY? TONY DESERVES THE BOOST-UP.

YOU KEEP YOUR MOUTH SHUT. I'M TALKING TO THE PRIDE OF THE R.A.F. NOW – JUST AS HIS PA WAS THE PRIDE OF THE R.F.C., AND I DON'T THINK!

BARNES WAS AT HIS SNEERING AGAIN.

I'LL RAM THAT DOWN YOUR THROAT, BARNES. COME OUTSIDE WITH ME RIGHT NOW.

TEMPER, TEMPER!

BUT BARNES BACKED DOWN BEFORE TONY'S FURY.

FIGHT YOU? WHY, I WOULDN'T SOIL MY HANDS.

CALM DOWN, TONY. DON'T START CHUCKING DOWN THE GAUNTLETS.

TONY TOOK A GRIP ON HIMSELF. AS JOHNNY SAID, THIS WAS NO TIME FOR PRIVATE SQUABBLES.

SO TONY TOOK OVER AND RAPPED OUT HIS ORDERS IN THE AIR WITH AUTHORITY. IT HAD A GOOD EFFECT ON JOHNNY DIXON WHO WAS BECOMING A BETTER PILOT UNDER TONY'S LEADERSHIP.

ONE DAY SOME WEEKS LATER, TONY STROLLED ACROSS THE AIRFIELD LOST IN THOUGHT. HIS REVERIE WAS BROKEN BY DIXON'S EXCITED VOICE.

HEY, TONY, HEARD THE LATEST? WE'RE BEING SHIPPED TO THE DESERT, LOCK, STOCK AND BARREL.

WELL, MAYBE I'LL GET THAT SUNTAN I ALWAYS WANTED.

BUT THE NORTH AFRICAN DESERT IN 1941 WAS NO HOLIDAY RESORT. IT WAS TOUGH — VERY TOUGH. THE FIGHTING WAS SAVAGE AND COMFORTS FEW.

BIT DIFFERENT TO SWANNING OVER SUSSEX, THEN HOME FOR BACON AND EGGS, EH? THE GRUB'S LOUSY AND I HAD TO SHAVE IN THE DREGS OF MY TEA-MUG THIS MORNING.

ONE CONSOLATION IS THE JERRIES AREN'T GETTING IT ANY BETTER.

IT WAS MARCH 1941 AND WHILE THE ITALIAN AIR FORCE CRUMBLED, THE GERMAN LUFTWAFFE HAD BEGUN TO ARRIVE IN FORCE.

KEEP YOUR EYES PEELED FOR EYETIE FIGHTERS. THERE ARE STILL SOME LEFT.

THIS TIME THE PATROL DID FIND AN ENEMY, BUT THE FIGHTERS WHICH STRUCK AT THEM WERE NOT ITALIAN.

SPITFIRES BELOW. LET'S SHOW THEM OUR TEETH!

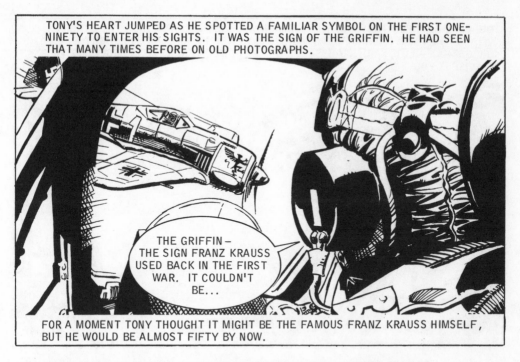

TONY'S HEART JUMPED AS HE SPOTTED A FAMILIAR SYMBOL ON THE FIRST ONE-NINETY TO ENTER HIS SIGHTS. IT WAS THE SIGN OF THE GRIFFIN. HE HAD SEEN THAT MANY TIMES BEFORE ON OLD PHOTOGRAPHS.

THE GRIFFIN — THE SIGN FRANZ KRAUSS USED BACK IN THE FIRST WAR. IT COULDN'T BE...

FOR A MOMENT TONY THOUGHT IT MIGHT BE THE FAMOUS FRANZ KRAUSS HIMSELF, BUT HE WOULD BE ALMOST FIFTY BY NOW.

WHO COULD THIS PILOT BE? SURELY NO ONE ELSE WOULD USE THE FAMOUS SYMBOL OF THE GREAT WORLD WAR ONE ACE?

WHOEVER YOU ARE, YOU'RE A TRICKY CUSTOMER, MATE.

THE DUEL BETWEEN TONY AND THE GERMAN WENT ONE WAY AND THEN THE OTHER, WITH NEITHER MAN GAINING ADVANTAGE. TONY KNEW HE WAS IN FOR A FIGHT AND THE GERMAN PILOT, KARL KRAUSS, SON OF THE FAMOUS FRANZ, WAS BEGINNING TO REALISE IT TOO.

BOTH PILOTS' AMMUNITION WAS SOON EXPENDED WITH NO RESULT. THE SONS OF TWO FORMER AIR ACES WERE PROVING A MATCH FOR EACH OTHER ALL RIGHT.

WITH BOTH AIRCRAFT ON A COLLISION COURSE, ONE MAN'S NERVE HAD TO GIVE. TONY SWERVED ASIDE JUST IN TIME.

HA, SO YOU'VE NO STOMACH FOR THIS, ENGLANDER!

BUT THEN THE DOG-FIGHT BROKE UP, AND ON THE WAY HOME TONY HAD TIME TO REFLECT.

PHEW. THAT BLOKE'S EITHER BRAVE OR NUTS — IT MUST BE THE OLD BEGGAR'S SON. IF WE MEET AGAIN I WON'T BACK DOWN...

THAT FIRST ENCOUNTER HAD ENDED IN A DRAW, BRITISH AND GERMAN BREAKING OFF THE FIGHT AS FUEL AND AMMO RAN LOW.

BUT BEFORE JOHNNY COULD ANSWER A CORPORAL CAME DASHING UP.

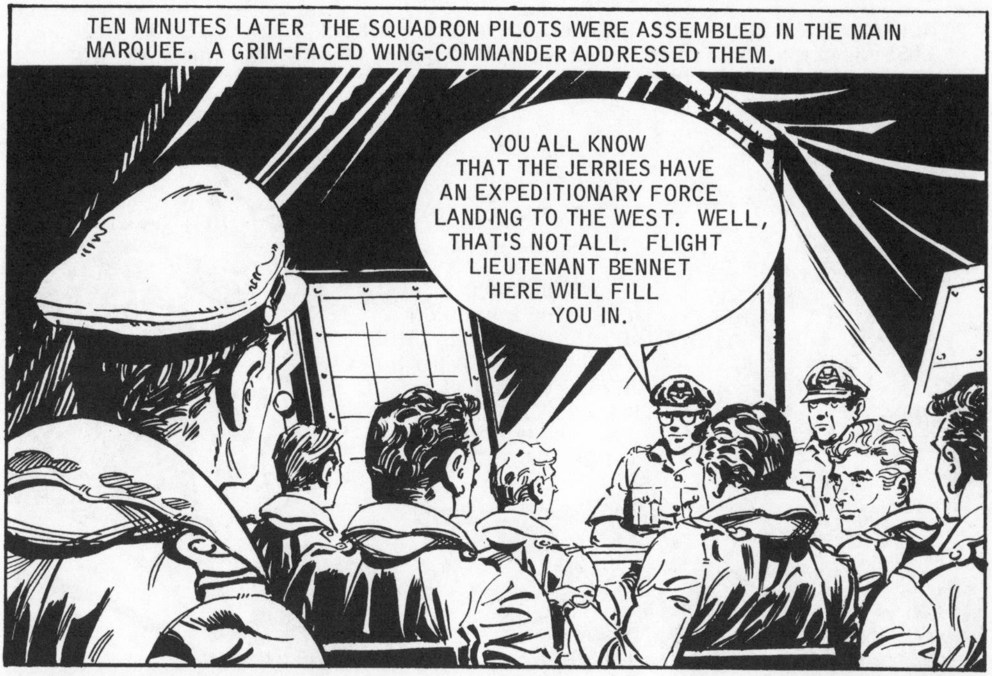
TEN MINUTES LATER THE SQUADRON PILOTS WERE ASSEMBLED IN THE MAIN MARQUEE. A GRIM-FACED WING-COMMANDER ADDRESSED THEM.
YOU ALL KNOW THAT THE JERRIES HAVE AN EXPEDITIONARY FORCE LANDING TO THE WEST. WELL, THAT'S NOT ALL. FLIGHT LIEUTENANT BENNET HERE WILL FILL YOU IN.

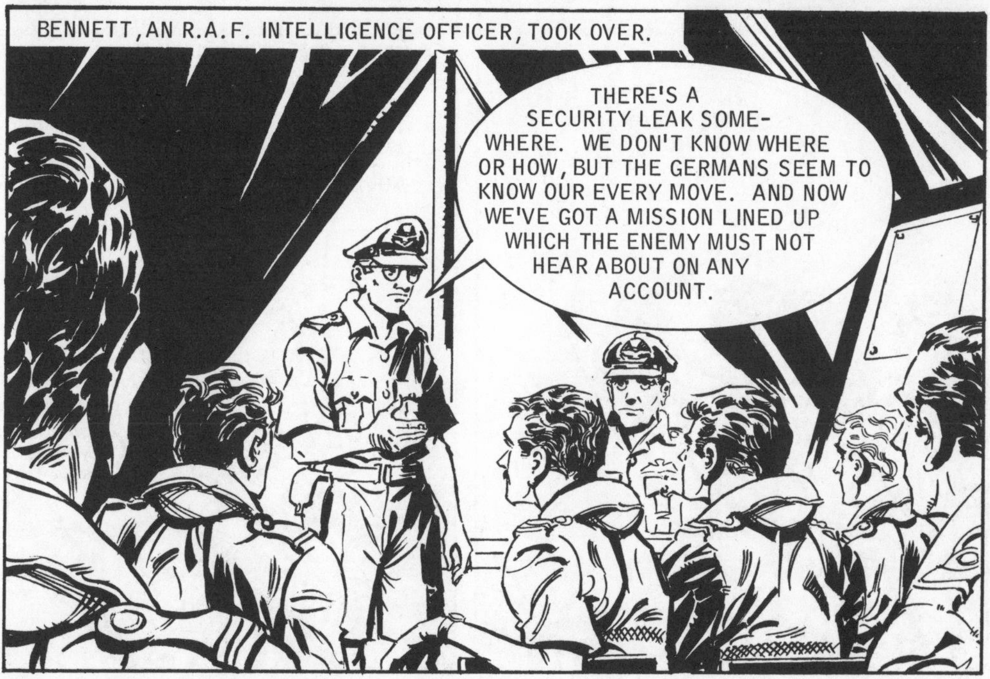
BENNETT, AN R.A.F. INTELLIGENCE OFFICER, TOOK OVER.
THERE'S A SECURITY LEAK SOME-WHERE. WE DON'T KNOW WHERE OR HOW, BUT THE GERMANS SEEM TO KNOW OUR EVERY MOVE. AND NOW WE'VE GOT A MISSION LINED UP WHICH THE ENEMY MUST NOT HEAR ABOUT ON ANY ACCOUNT.

ALREADY THE ATMOSPHERE HAD BECOME TENSE. SECURITY LEAKS LED TO THE LOSS OF MEN'S LIVES, AND TO SUSPICION AND DOUBT WHEN A MAN WAS WARY TO TRUST EVEN HIS OWN COMRADES.

WE'RE GOING TO ARM THE SQUADRON WITH BOMBS THIS TIME. THERE'S A GERMAN PANZER-CARRYING CONVOY ON ITS WAY DOWN THE COAST FROM CRETE. THAT'S THE TARGET. GATHER ROUND HERE FOR THE DETAILS.

AND WHEN THE BRIEFING ENDED BARNES WASN'T SLOW TO ACT.

ANOTHER SECURITY LEAK, EH? FUNNY HOW THEY HAPPEN WHEN THERE'S A GRIEVE IN THE SQUADRON. LIKE FATHER, LIKE SON...

BARNES HAD BEEN ASKING FOR IT FOR A LONG TIME. TONY SWUNG ROUND AND HIT OUT.

SEE IF THIS SHUTS YOUR FOUL MOUTH!

AAH!

THIS TIME NOT EVEN JOHNNY DIXON COULD STOP IT.

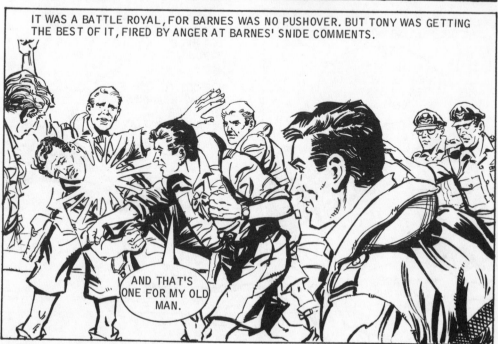

IT WAS A BATTLE ROYAL, FOR BARNES WAS NO PUSHOVER. BUT TONY WAS GETTING THE BEST OF IT, FIRED BY ANGER AT BARNES' SNIDE COMMENTS.

THE FIGHT WAS FINALLY BROKEN UP BY THE ARRIVAL OF THE WING COMMANDER.

DISGRACEFUL! TWO OF MY SENIOR OFFICERS BRAWLING IN PUBLIC. WHEN YOU COME BACK FROM THIS MISSION I'LL WANT AN EXPLANATION — AND IT HAD BETTER BE A GOOD ONE!

THE FIGHT HAD BEEN STOPPED, BUT THE ILL-FEELING WAS STILL THERE.

I HAVEN'T FINISHED WITH YOU BY A LONG CHALK.

ANY PLACE, ANY TIME — JUST AS SOON AS WE GET BACK.

NEXT DAY THEY TOOK OFF ON THE MISSION. TONY HAD COOLED DOWN, BUT HIS RESOLVE WAS JUST AS STRONG.

I'VE GOT TO SETTLE WITH BARNES ONCE AND FOR ALL. THIS BICKERING CAN'T GO ON.

BEFORE THEY EVEN SIGHTED THE PANZER-CARRYING SHIPS, YELLOW-NOSED FOCKE-WULFS DROPPED LIKE HAWKS OUT OF THE SUN AS THEY CROSSED THE COAST.

BANDITS! THEY'VE BEEN WAITING FOR US.

THE FW190s HAD BEEN WAITING, AND KARL KRAUSS WAS ONE OF THE FIRST TO TAKE ADVANTAGE OF THE SURPRISE.

ONE LESS ENGLANDER.

KRAUSS CHOSE BARNES AS HIS NEXT TARGET. DESPERATELY THE ENGLISH PILOT SWUNG BACK OVER THE DESERT, JETTISONING HIS BOMB. BUT HE HAD A KILLER ON HIS TAIL.

THERE WAS NO ESCAPE FOR BARNES NOW.

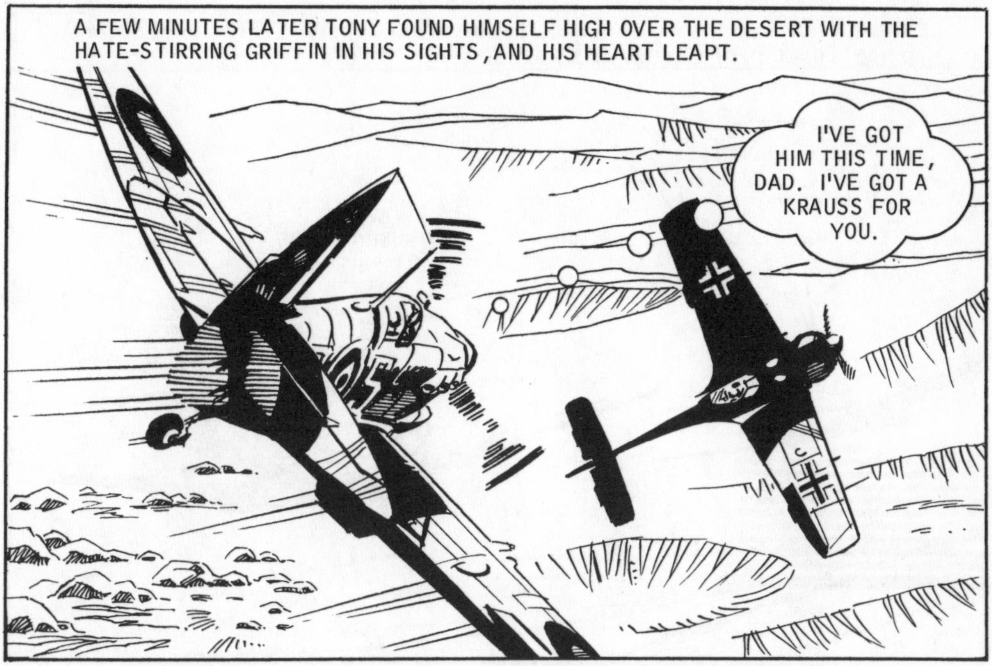
A FEW MINUTES LATER TONY FOUND HIMSELF HIGH OVER THE DESERT WITH THE HATE-STIRRING GRIFFIN IN HIS SIGHTS, AND HIS HEART LEAPT.
I'VE GOT HIM THIS TIME, DAD. I'VE GOT A KRAUSS FOR YOU.

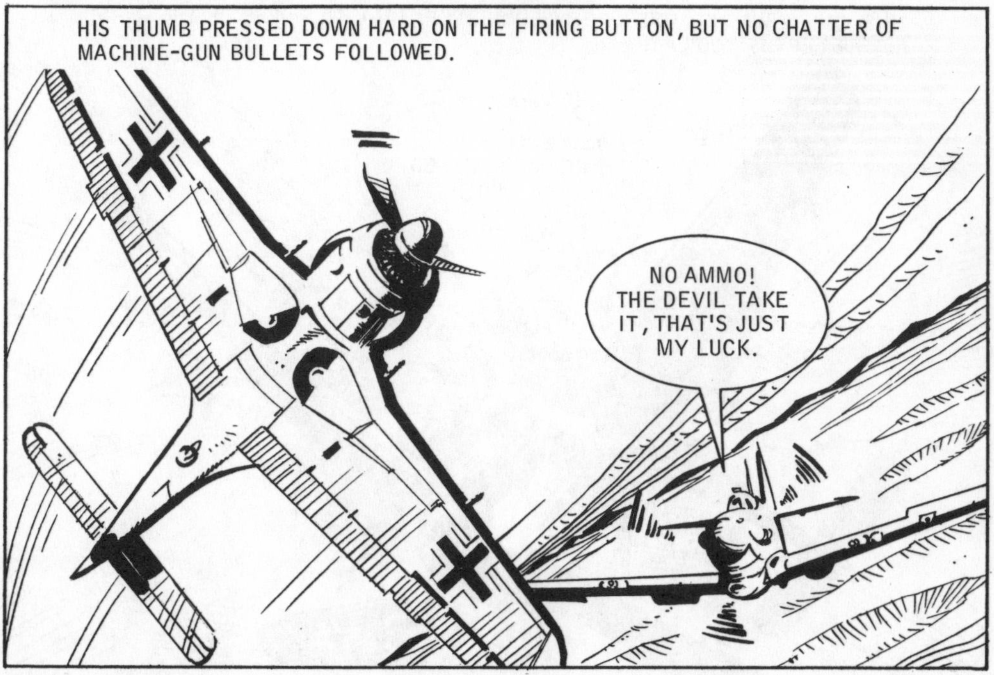
HIS THUMB PRESSED DOWN HARD ON THE FIRING BUTTON, BUT NO CHATTER OF MACHINE-GUN BULLETS FOLLOWED.
NO AMMO! THE DEVIL TAKE IT, THAT'S JUST MY LUCK.

HE MIGHT HAVE SLID TO SAFETY, BUT THIS MAN WAS THE SON OF THE GERMAN WHO HAD HAD A HAND IN DISGRACING HIS FATHER.

SO YOU WANT TO PLAY GAMES, ENGLANDER?

IT WON'T BE ME WHO DUCKS OUT THIS TIME.

THIS TIME IT WAS KRAUSS WHO TRIED DESPERATELY TO SIDE-SLIP THE CRASH. BUT HE LEFT IT TOO LATE.

ZUM TEUFEL! HE HAS FINISHED US BOTH.

BOTH MEN MANAGED TO ESCAPE AS THEIR SHATTERED AIRCRAFT PLUNGED EARTHWARDS.

SO I DIDN'T GET HIM AFTER ALL.

AND BRIAN BARNES HAD WATCHED THE DRAMATIC ENCOUNTER ABOVE HIM FROM WHERE HE HAD BROUGHT HIS KITE DOWN.

THAT WAS GRIEVE'S SPIT, OR I'M A DUTCHMAN.

TONY HIT THE DECK AFTER KRAUSS HAD GOT RID OF HIS HARNESS. THE TIME-LAG WAS TO PROVE IMPORTANT.

AND KARL KRAUSS HAD HIM COVERED BY THE TIME HE WAS FREE.

THEY HAD LANDED CLOSE TO BARNES WHO CAME RUSHING OVER –

FOR A MOMENT A THOUGHT CAME TO BARNES. HERE WAS THE OPPORTUNITY FOR HIM TO PAY OFF TWO DEBTS — ONE AGAINST THE MAN WHO HAD SHOT HIM DOWN, AND THE OTHER AGAINST THE SON OF A TRAITOR.

DROP YOUR GUN, ENGLANDER, OR I SHOOT YOUR FRIEND HERE.

BUT AS SOUR AS HE WAS, BRIAN BARNES WAS NO MURDERER. HE TOSSED THE REVOLVER TO THE GROUND.

MAYBE GRIEVE DESERVES TO DIE, BUT NOT AT THE HANDS OF A JERRY.

NOW THAT IS SHOWING GOOD SENSE, MY FRIEND.

THE DESERT HAD SEEMED EMPTY BUT THE FALLING PLANES AND PARACHUTES HAD BEEN SPOTTED BY UNFRIENDLY ARAB BANDITS WHO LIVED BY PLUNDER.

THIS WAY. THEY LANDED OVER THERE.

IGNORANT OF THE APPROACHING DANGER, THE THREE PILOTS STARTED TO WALK. SOMEWHERE TO THE NORTH WAS THE COAST. IT WOULD BE A LONG, LONG TREK, BUT THERE WAS NO OTHER WAY.

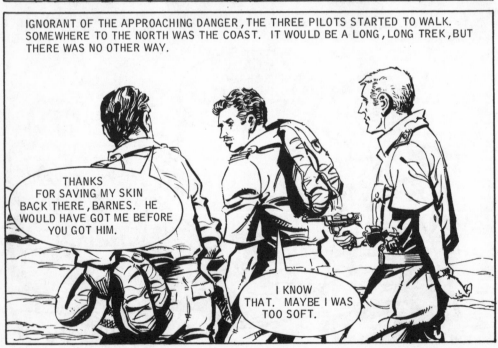

THANKS FOR SAVING MY SKIN BACK THERE, BARNES. HE WOULD HAVE GOT ME BEFORE YOU GOT HIM.

I KNOW THAT. MAYBE I WAS TOO SOFT.

AS THE THREE MEN REACHED A ROCKY GULLY, TWO SHOTS RANG OUT.

IT'S AN AMBUSH! MAKE FOR THE ROCKS.

THEY GAINED THE SHELTER OF THE ROCKS BY THE SKIN OF THEIR TEETH.

WHO IS IT?

ARAB BANDITS. THEY WOULD SLIT A MAN'S THROAT FOR HIS WRIST-WATCH.

KRAUSS THEN DECIDED THAT FELLOW AIR-
MEN WERE LESS DANGEROUS THAN NOMADIC
ARABS.

AND THE GERMAN'S MOVE PAID OFF
WHEN TONY NAILED THE FIRST
KILLER.

HERE,
TAKE THESE. THIS
WILL BE A FIGHT TO THE
DEATH.

AAARGH!

KRAUSS'S LUGER CLAIMED A SECOND ARAB BEFORE THE DESERT NIGHT FELL. YET
THEY KNEW THE FOUR ARABS LEFT WOULD NOT GO.

THEY CAN
MAKE US USE UP OUR
AMMUNITION. WILL YOUR
PEOPLE BE SENDING A
RESCUE PARTY FOR
YOU?

MAYBE, IF
ANYONE SAW US
COME DOWN.

TONY HAD TO GET ONE THING CLEAR —

THAT GRIFFIN SIGN ON YOUR PLANE. DURING THE LAST WAR A GERMAN PILOT NAMED KRAUSS USED IT. YOU COULDN'T BE...

JA, I AM KARL KRAUSS, THE SON OF FRANZ KRAUSS. IT IS STRANGE YOU KNOW ABOUT THE GRIFFIN.

I KNOW ABOUT IT ALL RIGHT. MY FATHER WAS COURT-MARTIALLED AND IMPRISONED, FALSELY ACCUSED OF PASSING SECRET INFORMATION TO YOUR FATHER.

JA, MY FATHER TOOK GREAT RISKS TO GET INFORMATION FROM A GERMAN AGENT WHO CALLED HIMSELF PRICE AND WAS PLANTED IN THE R.F.C.

THE SECURITY OFFICER IN MY FATHER'S SQUADRON!

IT ALL BECAME CLEAR. PRICE, AS SECURITY OFFICER, HAD HAD ACCESS TO ALL KINDS OF INFORMATION AND WAS ABOVE SUSPICION.

SO THAT WAS IT. WHY DIDN'T HE SPEAK UP AFTER THE WAR?

PRICE WAS JUST DOING HIS JOB. A DANGEROUS ONE, TOO, FOR LATER HE WAS KILLED IN A BOMBING RAID. STILL, I AM SORRY YOUR FATHER WAS PUNISHED FOR SOMETHING HE DID NOT DO.

AFTER ALL THESE YEARS TONY'S FATHER COULD BE CLEARED. HE TURNED TO BARNES.

DID YOU HEAR THAT, BARNES? MY FATHER WAS INNOCENT.

ALL RIGHT, ALL RIGHT. BUT WHO'S RESPONSIBLE FOR THE SECURITY LEAK IN OUR SQUADRON? TELL ME THAT, GRIEVE.

AH, YOU MEAN HOW DID WE KNOW YOU WERE OUT TO ATTACK THE CONVOY? THIS IS SIMPLE. WE BROKE YOUR RADIO CODE. I CAN TELL YOU THAT NOW, AS THE BRITISH CHANGED THEIR CODE JUST AFTERWARDS.

BARNES HAD TO AGREE. HE WAS MAN ENOUGH TO ADMIT HE HAD BEEN WRONG.

I OWE YOU AN APOLOGY, GRIEVE. AND YOU COULD CLEAR YOUR FATHER'S NAME TOO IF WE EVER GET OUT OF THIS MESS.

BUT AFTER A LONG UNCOMFORTABLE NIGHT WITHOUT WATER, THE SITUATION LOOKED VERY GRIM. BY DAWN THEIR POSITION SEEMED HOPELESS.

ARE THEY STILL THERE?

YOU BET THEY ARE. JUST WAITING FOR US TO SHOW OURSELVES.

BUT THEN THE DRONE OF A SEARCHING AIRCRAFT REACHED THEIR EARS. IT WAS GERMAN AND PILOTED BY LEUTNANT BECK, A TOUGH PILOT WHO FLEW WITH KRAUSS.

ARABS! THEY'VE GOT KRAUSS AND SOME OTHERS TRAPPED DOWN THERE.

THE LITTLE PLANE WITH ITS BLACK CROSS MARKINGS CLEARLY RECOGNISABLE CAME IN TO A BUMPY LANDING.

IT'S ONE FROM MY BASE! SOMEONE MUST HAVE SEEN ME GO DOWN.

BECK, WIELDING A SCHMEISSER EXPERTLY, DASHED FROM THE PLANE, GUNNING DOWN ONE ARAB.

AAARGH!

HE REACHED COVER SAFELY —

GOOD TO SEE YOU, BECK. PERHAPS WE'LL GET OUT OF THIS NOW.

BUT THESE TWO ARE ENGLANDERS!

BECK WAS A RUTHLESS MAN — AN OUT-AND-OUT NAZI. HE SPOKE IN CALM, CRUEL TONES.

WE GO NOW, BUT I WILL GET RID OF THESE TWO. WE HAVE NO ROOM FOR PRISONERS.

WHAT? YOU CAN'T DO THAT...

BUT BEFORE THE SCHMEISSER COULD BARK, KRAUSS SPOKE UP ANGRILY — HE HAD INHERITED HIS FATHER'S SENSE OF FAIR PLAY AS WELL.

OH, NO YOU DON'T, BECK. THESE MEN MUST BE LEFT, BUT THEY MUST HAVE A CHANCE. HAND OVER THE SCHMEISSER TO THEM.

DONNER UND BLITZEN! YOU ARE A WEAK FOOL, KRAUSS.

BEFORE THE GERMANS MADE THE DASH FOR THE HENSCHEL, KRAUSS ASSURED TONY HE WOULD SEND HELP.

HE'S A DECENT BLOKE. IF WE EVER GET OUT OF THIS, YOU CAN VOUCH FOR WHAT HE SAID ABOUT MY OLD MAN.

SURE, IF ANYBODY WILL BELIEVE US.

BUT THE GERMANS WERE NOT CLEAR YET. A VOLLEY OF FIRE FROM THE ARABS PEPPERED THE HENSCHEL'S ENGINE.

HIMMEL! THE DEVILS HAVE HIT THE ENGINE!

BECK CRASH-LANDED THE HENSCHEL BEFORE THE FLAMES TOOK A FIRM HOLD. IMMEDIATELY THE ARABS CLAMBERED DOWN FROM THE ROCKS ABOVE.

THE ARABS WILL GET THEM. COME ON, BARNES, WE OWE KRAUSS A FAVOUR.

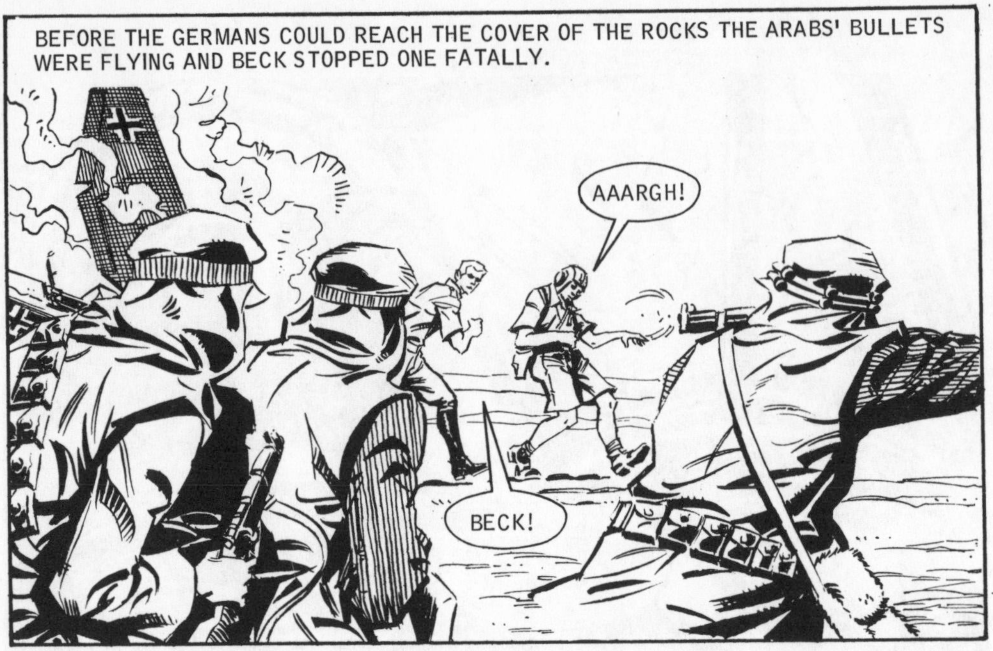
BEFORE THE GERMANS COULD REACH THE COVER OF THE ROCKS THE ARABS' BULLETS WERE FLYING AND BECK STOPPED ONE FATALLY.
AAARGH!
BECK!

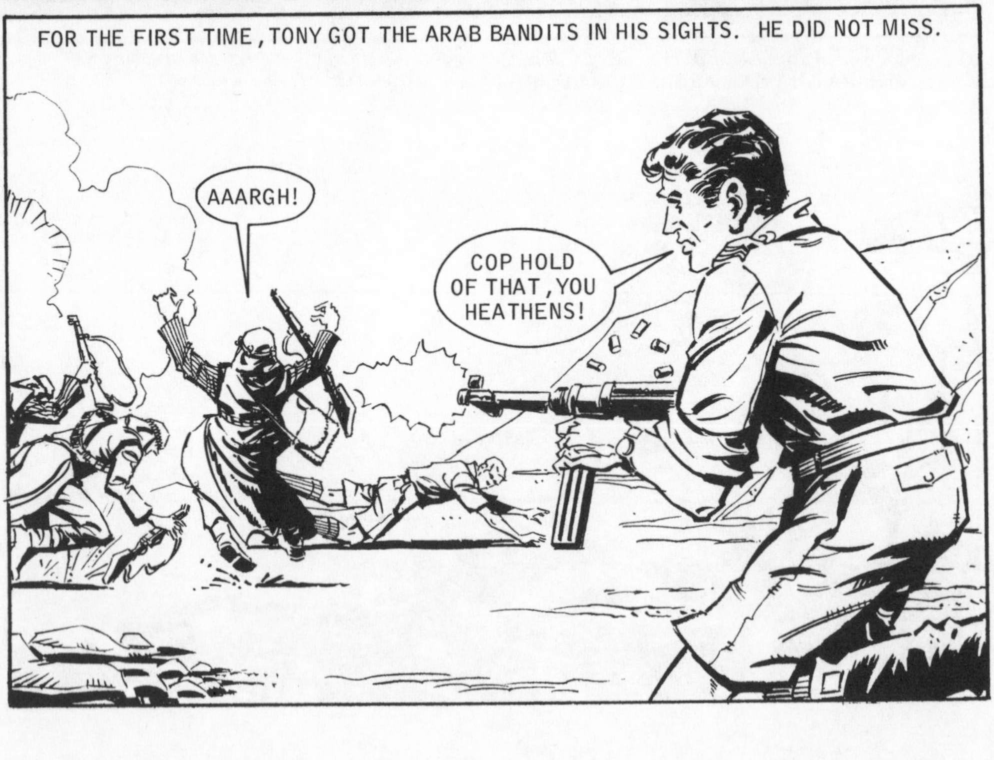
FOR THE FIRST TIME, TONY GOT THE ARAB BANDITS IN HIS SIGHTS. HE DID NOT MISS.
AAARGH!
COP HOLD OF THAT, YOU HEATHENS!

THE DANGER WAS OVER. THE THREE ARABS AND BECK LAY DEAD.

POOR BECK. HE TOOK HIS NAZI POLITICS MUCH TOO SERIOUSLY.

HEY, LOOK, IT'S A LYSANDER — ONE OF OURS!

AS KRAUSS SPOKE, BARNES SPOTTED AN R.A.F. LYSANDER SCANNING THE DESERT FOR THEM.

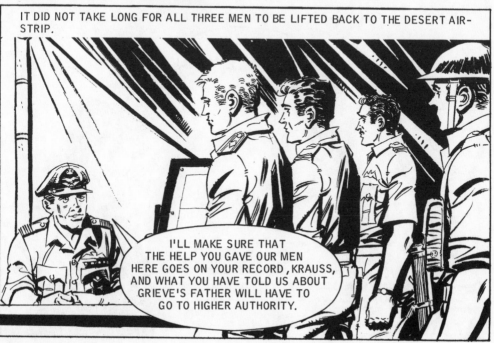

IT DID NOT TAKE LONG FOR ALL THREE MEN TO BE LIFTED BACK TO THE DESERT AIR-STRIP.

I'LL MAKE SURE THAT THE HELP YOU GAVE OUR MEN HERE GOES ON YOUR RECORD, KRAUSS, AND WHAT YOU HAVE TOLD US ABOUT GRIEVE'S FATHER WILL HAVE TO GO TO HIGHER AUTHORITY.

AND I WILL SWEAR ON OATH THAT IT IS TRUE. AN INJUSTICE HAS BEEN DONE TO AN INNOCENT MAN. IT IS STILL NOT TOO LATE TO CLEAR HIS NAME.

AFTER THE STATEMENT HAD BEEN MADE ON OATH, THE SONS OF ACES SHOOK HANDS.

THANKS, KARL. SORRY YOU HAVE TO GO BEHIND BARS.

I MAY NOT STAY LONG... GOODBYE AND GOOD LUCK, TONY.

AT LAST HIS FATHER'S NAME HAD BEEN CLEARED. TONY WAS A HAPPY MAN.

AS KRAUSS WAS DRIVEN OFF, THE WING COMMANDER EMERGED FROM THE TENT.

NOW THERE'S A LITTLE MATTER OF A BRAWL...

ENTIRELY MY FAULT, SIR. I APOLOGISE TO YOU AND TONY.

FORGET IT. WE'LL HAVE PLENTY OF SQUAREHEADS TO FIGHT WITHOUT SLUGGING EACH OTHER.

BARNES' APOLOGY WAS ACCEPTED AND THE MATTER DROPPED. IN THE MONTHS OF HARD FIGHTING AHEAD TONY AND BARNES BECAME FIRM FRIENDS — AND A DEADLY TEAM.

BANDITS BELOW. ONE-OH-NINES, I RECKON. LET'S PAY THEM A VISIT, BRIAN.

I'M RIGHT BEHIND YOU, TONY.

Commando
THE END

FLY PAST

Commando

No. 9 — VICKERS-ARMSTRONG WELLINGTON IC

Seen in the markings of 75 Squadron, Royal New Zealand Air Force, at Feltwell, Norfolk, in April, 1941.

Kennedy

DEATH OF A WIMPEY

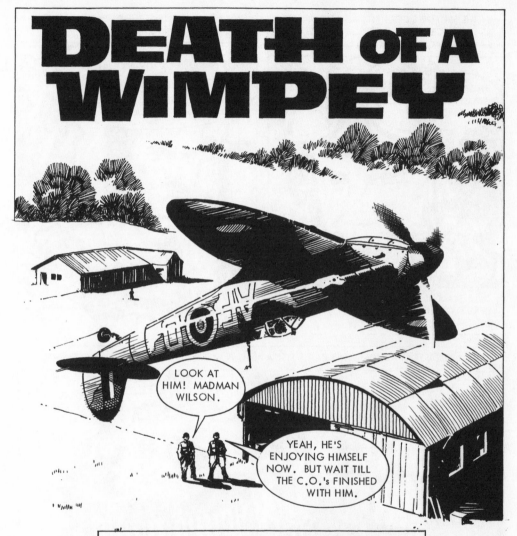

LOOK AT HIM! MADMAN WILSON.

YEAH, HE'S ENJOYING HIMSELF NOW. BUT WAIT TILL THE C.O.'s FINISHED WITH HIM.

"YOU'RE AN IRRESPONSIBLE YOUNG HALF-WIT, AND IF I HAVE MY WAY YOU'LL NEVER FLY AGAIN." IT LOOKED LIKE THE END OF PILOT OFFICER ALAN WILSON'S FLYING CAREER. JUST ONCE TOO OFTEN HE'D KICKED OVER THE TRACES AND NOW HE WAS PAYING FOR IT. BUT NOTHING COULD KEEP ALAN OUT OF THE AIR. IF THEY WOULDN'T GIVE HIM A PLANE HE'D JUST HAVE TO HELP HIMSELF TO ONE.

AND THAT'S WHAT HE DID...

IN THE SPITFIRE'S COCKPIT, ALAN GRINNED AS THE AIRCRAFT SCREAMED GROUNDWARDS IN A STOMACH-JERKING DIVE.

THIS'LL WAKE THEM UP. EVEN OLD STARCHY.

'OLD STARCHY' WAS THE C.O., SQUADRON LEADER GREENWOOD, A STERN DISCIPLINARIAN.

HE WAS WATCHING THE DISPLAY THROUGH HIS OFFICE WINDOW.

WILSON, AGAIN. THAT MAN'S GOT NO IDEA OF DISCIPLINE. TO HIM THE WHOLE WAR IS A JOKE. I WANT HIM TO REPORT TO ME THE MOMENT HE ENDS HIS IDIOTIC DISPLAY, BARNES.

YES, SIR.

THEN, DISASTER. AS ALAN PULLED HIS SCREAMING PLANE INTO A TIGHT BANKING TURN...

WHERE DID THAT CLOT SPRING FROM?

WATCH IT, YOU BLITHERING IDIOT!

SUDDENLY DEADLY SERIOUS, HIS HEART HAMMERING, ALAN HAULED HIS PLANE AWAY FROM THE CRIPPLED SPIT. BUT TOO LATE.

HIS VICTIM, ALREADY SHATTERED FROM COMBAT WITH A PACK OF Me109's, PUT ITS NOSE DOWN AND GROPED FOR THE AIRFIELD.

ALAN'S OWN PLANE, ALSO BADLY DAMAGED, BEGAN TO BUCK AND REAR. SKILFULLY HE FOUGHT IT DOWN, CRASH-LANDING WITHIN TWENTY YARDS OF THE OTHER SPITFIRE.

AS SOON AS HIS SMOKING SPIT SLITHERED TO A HALT, ALAN WAS OUT OF THE COCKPIT AND RUNNING. JUST IN TIME...

OH NO. I'LL BE FOR THE CHOP NOW.

TEN MINUTES LATER HE FACED ANOTHER EXPLOSION.

TWO PLANES PRANGED. COMPLETE WRITE-OFFS. YOU'VE DONE A GOOD DAY'S WORK FOR HITLER, WILSON!

I'M SORRY, SIR. I REALISE IT WENT SOUR...

SOUR YOU CALL IT. ONE PILOT HALF-KILLED! I CALL IT CRIMINAL RESPONSIBILITY, WILSON. YOU'RE GROUNDED. AND I MEAN GROUNDED!

AND THE C.O. MEANT IT. WITHIN TWO DAYS ALAN WAS HEADING FOR NORTH AFRICA, ON ADMINISTRATION DUTIES.

WILSON 151044

SO I'M TO SPEND THE REST OF THE WAR FIGHTING JERRY FROM BEHIND A DESK, EH? WE'LL SEE ABOUT THAT.

BUT SQUADRON LEADER GREENWOOD HAD WRITTEN ALL OVER ALAN'S SERVICE RECORDS 'GROUNDED FOR IRRESPONSIBILITY'. THAT WAS ENOUGH. THE HARD-PRESSED DESERT AIR FORCE WAS TOO SHORT OF AIRCRAFT TO RISK THEM IN THE HANDS OF A RECKLESS PILOT.

TWO MONTHS OF PUSHING A PEN AND MOVING PAPERS ABOUT. WHAT A WAY TO FIGHT. GOSH... WHAT WOULDN'T I GIVE TO BE WITH THOSE CHAPS.

HIS CHANCE CAME A FEW DAYS LATER. H.Q. TELEPHONED THE ADJUTANT, TELLING HIM THAT A V.I.P. CIVILIAN WAS FLYING FROM CAIRO AND A SPITFIRE MUST ESCORT HIM.

HE'S A TOP EXPLOSIVES EXPERT ON HIS WAY BACK TO BLIGHTY, SO HE MUST HAVE AN ESCORT. WHO'VE WE GOT?

NOBODY. ALL THE BOYS ARE OUT ON PATROL. NOT DUE BACK TILL EARLY MORNING.

THERE IS TOMMY WALKER, BUT HE'S STILL IN HOSPITAL WITH A BENT ARM.

WELL, HE'S OUR ONLY HOPE. GET HIM OVER HERE.

THE MEDICAL OFFICER WAS OPPOSED TO THE IDEA BUT YOUNG TOMMY WALKER WAS DRAGGED OVER TO THE ADJUTANT'S OFFICE AND BRIEFED ON THE MISSION.

I RECKON I CAN DO IT, SIR, IF THERE'S NOT GOING TO BE ANY ACTION.

I THINK IT'S JUST A STRAIGHTFORWARD FLIGHT, THEN HOME AGAIN. NOW HERE'S WHERE YOU RENDEZVOUS WITH THE TRANSPORT.

BUT AS TOMMY LEFT THE OFFICE...

FEEL FUNNY, LIKE THE WORLD'S SPINNING... URH!

OK, MATEY, I'VE GOT YOU.

IT WAS QUITE OBVIOUS THAT TOMMY WALKER COULD HARDLY WALK, LET ALONE FLY. ALAN WHIPPED HIM BACK TO THE HOSPITAL, THEN PUT ON HIS FLYING GEAR.

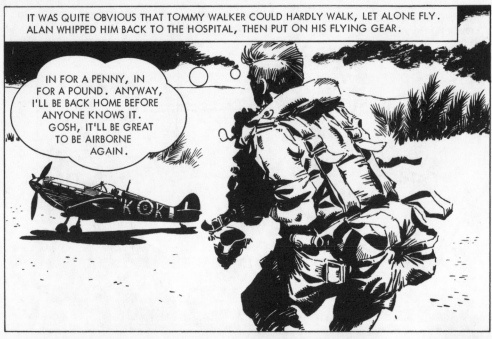

IN FOR A PENNY, IN FOR A POUND. ANYWAY, I'LL BE BACK HOME BEFORE ANYONE KNOWS IT. GOSH, IT'LL BE GREAT TO BE AIRBORNE AGAIN.

HE TOOK OFF INTO THE MOONLIT SKY.

I THOUGHT MISTER WILSON WAS SUPPOSED TO BE GROUNDED.

MUST'VE CHANGED THEIR MINDS. BLIMEY... HE DOESN'T HALF FLY A PLANE HARD, DON'T HE?

ALAN PICKED UP THE DAKOTA TRANSPORT AT THE RENDEZVOUS, AND WATCHED OVER IT AS THEY CROSSED THE MOON-BLANCHED SANDS.

SHOULD BE PEACEFUL. JERRY DOESN'T OFTEN SEND OUT PATROLS AT NIGHT.

NOT OFTEN... BUT THIS NIGHT TWO MESSERSCHMITT 109 s WERE OUT, HUNTING THE SKIES FOR ANY QUARRY THEY COULD FIND.

ONE FAT PIGEON AND ONE LEAN HAWK. WHICH WILL YOU TAKE, HANS?

TONIGHT I FEEL BOLD. THE SPITFIRE FOR ME.

AS THE TWO MARAUDERS SNARLED INTO THE ATTACK, ALAN WILSON FACED HIS FIRST AIR COMBAT.

IGNORING THE PERIL AT HIS OWN TAIL, ALAN DIVED LIKE A HAWK AT THE SECOND NAZI.

HIS BULLETS RAKED THROUGH THE NAZI PLANE, RIPPING OUT ITS HEART.

ONE DOWN!

POOR WERNER... ACH, ENGLANDER, NOW IT IS YOUR TURN.

THE SURVIVING NAZI PILOT HURLED HIS CRAFT AFTER ALAN, CANNONS BLAZING. THE BRITON HELD HIS COURSE TO THE LAST POSSIBLE SECOND, EXPECTING TO FEEL THE THUDDING SHOCK OF THE NAZI'S SHELLS HIT HIS BACK ANY MOMENT. THEN HE SIDE-SLIPPED AND THE MESSERSCHMITT'S GUNS CHATTERED INTO EMPTY SKY.

MOVE ONE!

ACH, HE'S LUCKY, THIS ENGLANDER.

ALAN SCREAMED HIS SPITFIRE UP AND ROUND IN A TIGHT, FIERCE TURN. NOW HE HAD THE HEIGHT AND THE ADVANTAGE. GRIMLY HE LEVELLED UP THE Me109 IN HIS SIGHTS AND SQUEEZED THE FIRING BUTTON.

THE NAZI MET HIS FATE ON THE MOONLIT DESERT.

HIS BLOOD SINGING, ALAN THREW HIS CRAFT ABOUT THE CLEAR SKY IN A SERIES OF WILD VICTORY ROLLS.

THEN...

HEY, I'M ON FIRE. THAT JERRY MUST HAVE CLOBBERED ME WORSE THAN I THOUGHT. ONLY ONE THING FOR IT NOW. GET A BIT OF HEIGHT...

...AND PART COMPANY.

ALAN DRIFTED DOWN THROUGH THE COLD DESERT NIGHT AIR. HE WAS IN A SPOT AND KNEW IT. NO WATER, NO IDEA OF HIS POSITION.

AND I DON'T EVEN SPEAK THE LINGO IF I'M PICKED UP BY SOME ARABS. STILL, LET'S LOOK ON THE BRIGHT SIDE. TWO KILLS TO MY NAME. IT'S BEEN A LUCKY NIGHT.

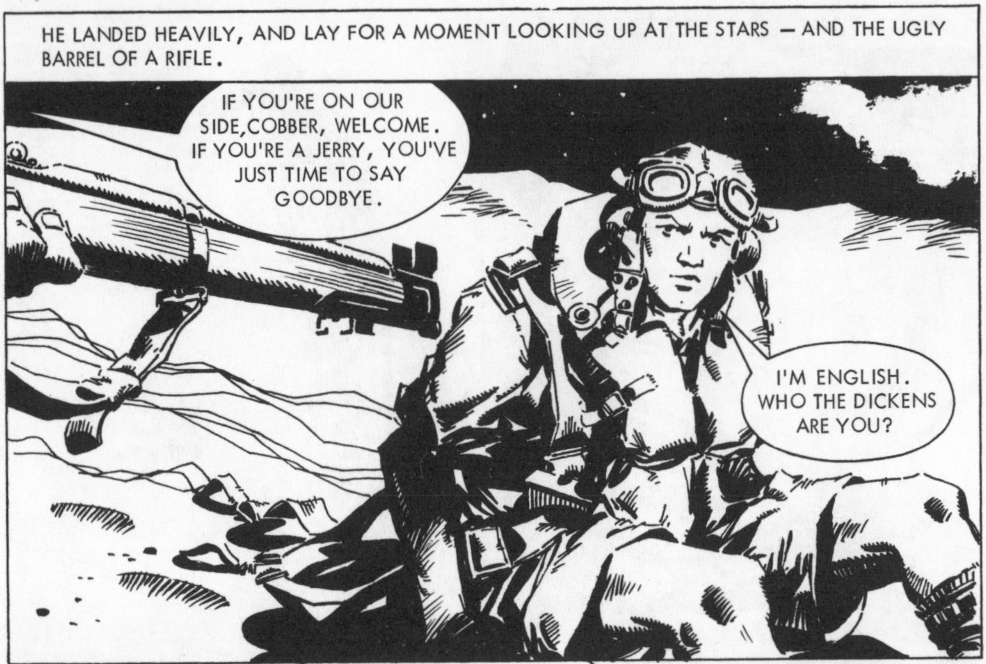
HE LANDED HEAVILY, AND LAY FOR A MOMENT LOOKING UP AT THE STARS — AND THE UGLY BARREL OF A RIFLE.
IF YOU'RE ON OUR SIDE,COBBER, WELCOME. IF YOU'RE A JERRY, YOU'VE JUST TIME TO SAY GOODBYE.
I'M ENGLISH. WHO THE DICKENS ARE YOU?

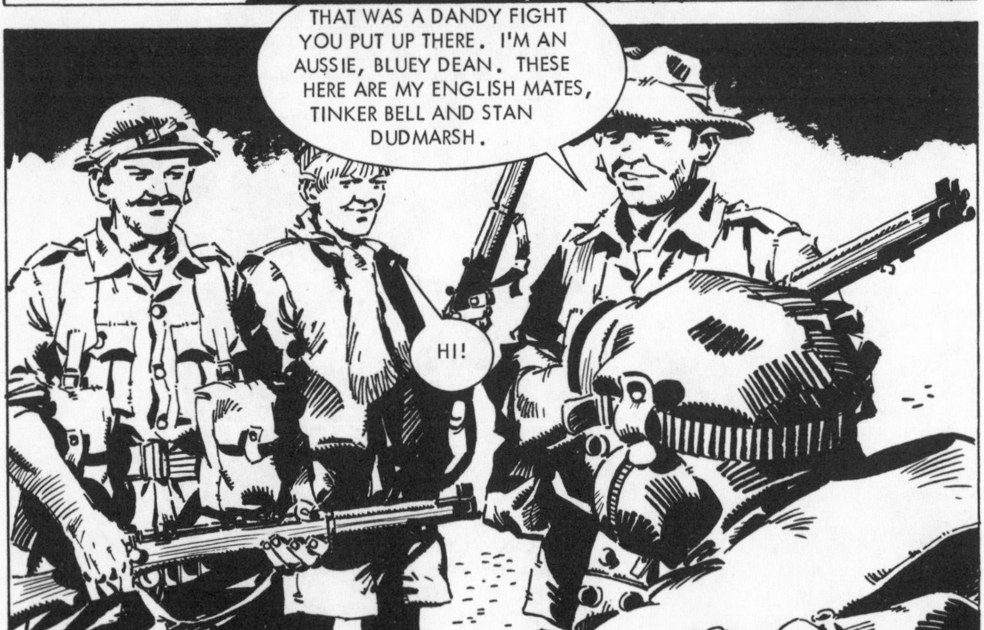
THAT WAS A DANDY FIGHT YOU PUT UP THERE. I'M AN AUSSIE, BLUEY DEAN. THESE HERE ARE MY ENGLISH MATES, TINKER BELL AND STAN DUDMARSH.
HI!

THE TOUGH TRIO LED ALAN TO THEIR TRUCK WHERE THEY ATE A TASTY SUPPER.

WE'RE ALL THAT'S LEFT OF A LONG RANGE DESERT STRIKE FORCE. WHEN OUR MATES GOT CLOBBERED WE THOUGHT WE'D CARRY ON. WE DON'T LIKE SERVING IN AN ORGANISED OUTFIT. WE'VE GOT OUR OLD TRUCK AND WE ATTACK ANY NAZIS WE SEE. BEEN DOING IT FOR THREE MONTHS NOW.

ALAN LIKED THESE RECKLESS DESERT OUTLAWS. HE TOLD THEM HIS STORY.

...SO I'VE GOT SOME MUSIC TO FACE WHEN I GO BACK.

WHY GO BACK? STEER CLEAR OF THE BIG BRASS, COBBER, AND YOU CAN HAVE A REAL WAR. STICK WITH US. WE MAKE THE RULES, DON'T BOTHER WITH KIT INSPECTIONS, HAVE A HIGH OLD TIME. RIGHT, TINKER?

RIGHT. TELL YOU WHAT, WE'VE GOT A NICE LITTLE ACTION PLANNED FOR TOMORROW. JOIN US ON THAT AND SEE HOW YOU FEEL.

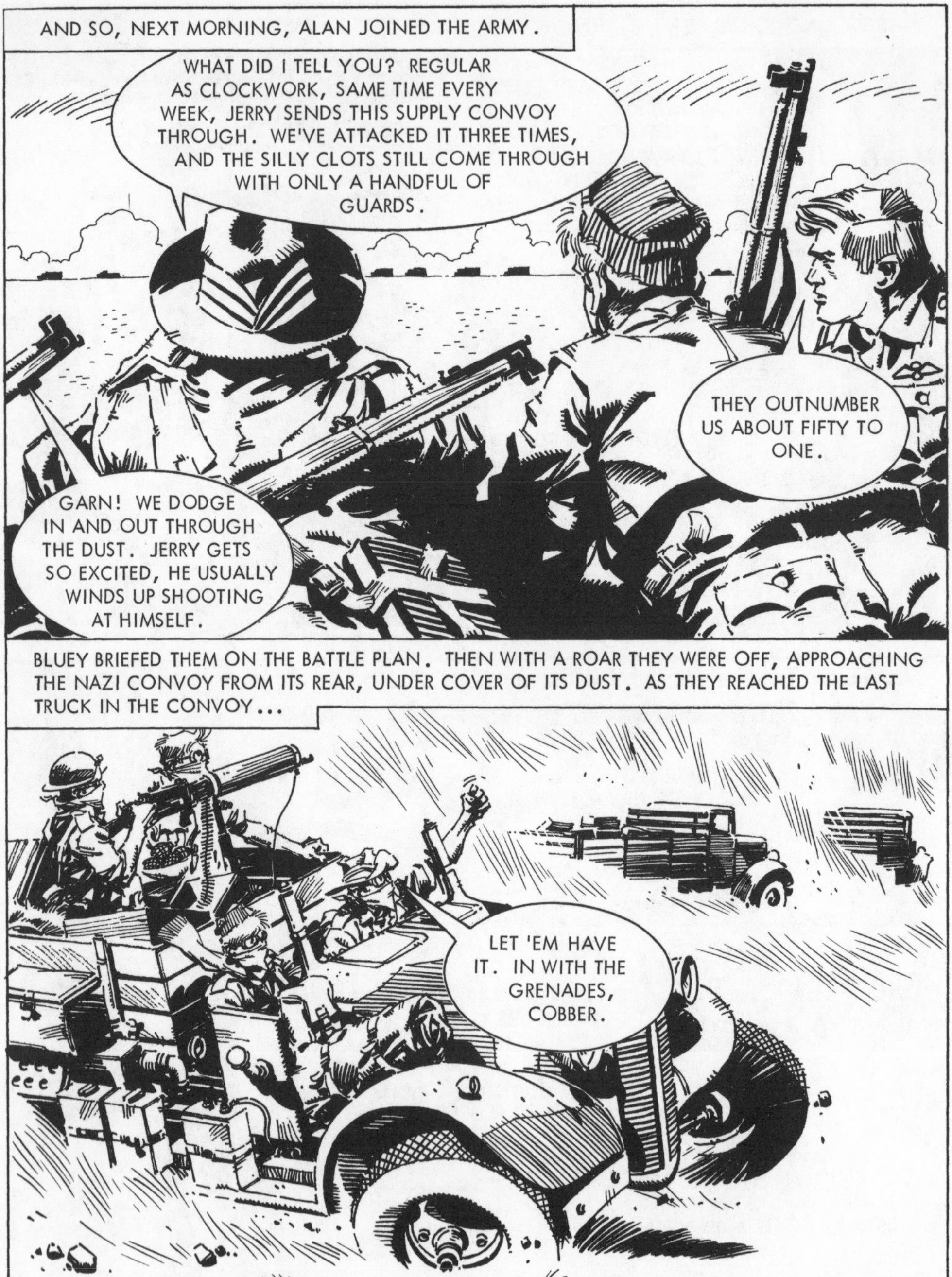
AND SO, NEXT MORNING, ALAN JOINED THE ARMY.
WHAT DID I TELL YOU? REGULAR AS CLOCKWORK, SAME TIME EVERY WEEK, JERRY SENDS THIS SUPPLY CONVOY THROUGH. WE'VE ATTACKED IT THREE TIMES, AND THE SILLY CLOTS STILL COME THROUGH WITH ONLY A HANDFUL OF GUARDS.
THEY OUTNUMBER US ABOUT FIFTY TO ONE.
GARN! WE DODGE IN AND OUT THROUGH THE DUST. JERRY GETS SO EXCITED, HE USUALLY WINDS UP SHOOTING AT HIMSELF.
BLUEY BRIEFED THEM ON THE BATTLE PLAN. THEN WITH A ROAR THEY WERE OFF, APPROACHING THE NAZI CONVOY FROM ITS REAR, UNDER COVER OF ITS DUST. AS THEY REACHED THE LAST TRUCK IN THE CONVOY...
LET 'EM HAVE IT. IN WITH THE GRENADES, COBBER.

BLUEY JUDGES THAT. HE'S GOT GREAT BUILT-IN SURVIVAL HAS OLD BLUEY. WHEN IT'S TIME FOR US TO BLOW, OFF WE GO. SO MAKE THE MOST OF YOUR TIME.

FIVE TRUCKS WERE PUT OUT OF ACTION BEFORE BLUEY CALLED A HALT. TINKER STEERED AWAY FROM THE CONVOY.

THEY STILL DON'T KNOW HOW MANY TRUCKS ARE ATTACKING THEM!

TURN NOW, TINKER, AND WE'LL HIT 'EM FROM THE FRONT.

WITH SHATTERING AUDACITY THEY CIRCLED THROUGH THE DUNES, AND WHILST THE NAZIS WERE STILL TRYING TO SORT THEMSELVES OUT, PRESSED HOME ANOTHER ATTACK FROM THE FRONT.

HIMMEL, MORE OF THEM! THEY ARE COMING FROM ALL SIDES.

ALAN CHUCKED TWO GRENADES INTO THE OPEN BACK OF THE NAZI TRUCK. STAN OPENED UP
WITH THE VICKERS AND ONE GERMAN TRUCK WENT UP WITH A ROAR. THAT WAS ONLY A START.

AS TINKER HAD PREDICTED, THE NAZI COLUMN BROKE UP IN CONFUSION. THE FEW GERMAN
ESCORT TROOPS PEERED THROUGH THE CHOKING DUST FOR THE ENEMY, SCARED TO SHOOT
IN CASE THEY HIT THEIR OWN MEN. FOR THE SINGLE ATTACKING TRUCK THIS WAS NOT A
PROBLEM. IT CRISS-CROSSED THE NAZI COLUMN, GUNS BELCHING DEATH.

ANOTHER TWO NAZI VEHICLES WERE REDUCED TO SMOKING RUIN ON THOSE CHOKING SANDS.

RIGHT, LADS, LET'S CALL IT A DAY.

PHEW, THIS BARREL'S RED-HOT.

SO AM I. HOW OFTEN DO YOU BOYS DO THIS SORT OF THING?

EVERY FEW DAYS. NOT ALWAYS LIKE THIS. SOMETIMES WE DO A FOOT OPERATION, PINCHING WEAPONS AND AMMO. BUT YOU'LL SEE.

ALAN DID SEE.

A FEW DAYS LATER THEY STOLE A GERMAN WATER WAGON AS IT CALLED ON THE FRONT-LINE TROOPS.

LET'S GO!

RIGHT BEHIND YOU, BLUEY.

SURPRISE WAS THEIR MAIN AND MOST SUCCESSFUL WEAPON. BUT THEY COULDN'T HOPE TO ESCAPE UNSCATHED EVERY TIME.

ALAN WAS ENJOYING THE LIFE. BEHIND HIM LAY ALL THOSE DEADLY DULL DAYS OF DESK WORK. THIS WAS THE ACTION HE CRAVED, THOUGH HE KNEW, DEEP DOWN, THAT HE WOULD HAVE BEEN FAR HAPPIER BEHIND THE CONTROLS OF A SPITFIRE.

TINKER'S WORDS WERE VERY NEARLY PROPHETIC. FOR NEXT MORNING AS THEY TRAMPED THE SANDS...

THEY REACHED THE WELLINGTON AND FOUND ONLY THE PILOT, SLUMPED DEAD OVER THE CONTROLS. ALAN CHECKED THE BOMBER OVER AND FOUND THAT IT WAS AIRWORTHY, DESPITE SOME FLAK DAMAGE.

HOLDING THE STICK IN HIS HANDS, ALAN EXAMINED THE CONTROLS.

I RECKON I COULD, ASSUMING IT REALLY IS AIRWORTHY. GIVE ME AN HOUR OR TWO.

YOU'RE ON. BOYS, WE'VE GOT OUR NEW TRANSPORT. ONLY NOW WE DO IT THE COMFORTABLE WAY.

AFTER THEY'D BURIED THE PILOT —

EVEN IF SHE WILL FLY, BLUEY, WHAT DO WE DO WITH HER?

WE'VE GOT ALL THE MAPS HERE. JUST FLY TO A BRITISH AIRFIELD, BOMB UP THEN TAKE OFF. WE PICK OUR OWN TARGETS AND CLOBBER 'EM.

BLUEY GRINNED AS THREE FACES STARED AT HIM IN AMAZEMENT.

YOU'RE NOT SERIOUS!

WE KNOW WEAPONS. WHAT'S SO DIFFERENT ABOUT AN AIRCRAFT'S GUNS THAT WE CAN'T LEARN? AND YOU CAN SHOW ME HOW TO DROP BOMBS.

BLUEY'S OPTIMISM WAS INFECTIOUS — BUT IT TOOK MORE THAN AUSTRALIAN OPTIMISM TO FLY A BOMBER. FOR THE NEXT WEEK THE FOUR MEN THREW THEMSELVES INTO THE TASK OF LEARNING THE NEW SKILLS THEY WOULD NEED IF THE WELLINGTON WAS EVER TO GET OFF THE GROUND.

WITH HOURS OF PRACTICE, THE FOUR MEN SOON GOT USED TO THEIR NEW JOBS, ALAN AT THE BOMBER'S UNFAMILIAR CONTROLS, BLUEY IN THE NAVIGATOR'S SEAT, STAN IN THE NOSE GUN TURRET AND TINKER IN THE LONELY TAIL POSITION.

NEXT DAY THEY WERE READY. TINKER AND STAN CROUCHED BEHIND THEIR GUNS WHILE BLUEY SAT WITH ALAN. THE POWERFUL ENGINES COUGHED, THEN ROARED INTO LIFE, AND THE WELLINGTON BEGAN RACING ACROSS THE HARD SAND.

SWEET AS A BIRD, THE BOMBER SOARED INTO THE HOT BLUE SKY.

THEY HAD TO YELL TO MAKE THEMSELVES HEARD FOR THERE WAS NO INTER-COM WORKING.

ALAN HEADED FOR AL HALFA, A FORWARD BRITISH AIRFIELD, TIMING HIS LANDING TO COINCIDE WITH THE SWIFT-FALLING AFRICAN DUSK.

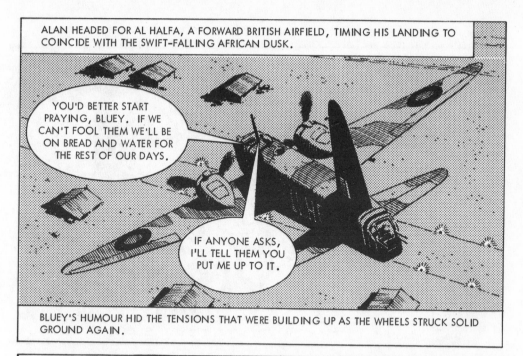

YOU'D BETTER START PRAYING, BLUEY. IF WE CAN'T FOOL THEM WE'LL BE ON BREAD AND WATER FOR THE REST OF OUR DAYS.

IF ANYONE ASKS, I'LL TELL THEM YOU PUT ME UP TO IT.

BLUEY'S HUMOUR HID THE TENSIONS THAT WERE BUILDING UP AS THE WHEELS STRUCK SOLID GROUND AGAIN.

TENSION MOUNTED AS THEY LANDED. COULD THEY BLUFF THEIR WAY PAST ANY CURIOUS OFFICERS? FAILURE WOULD MEAN THE REST OF THE WAR SPENT BEHIND BARS.

LOOK AT THAT ROPEY LANDING.

YEAH, MORE WORK FOR US BY THE LOOK OF IT.

BUT NO QUESTIONS WERE ASKED. ALAN FELT MORE CONFIDENT WHEN HE BROUGHT THE
WELLINGTON TO A HALT AND CONSULTED THE FLIGHT SERGEANT MECHANIC.

SHE FLIES BETTER THAN SHE LOOKS, FLIGHT. I WANT A FULL LOAD OF BOMBS, AMMO AND FUEL. AND AS MUCH MAINTENANCE AS YOU CAN MANAGE BEFORE DAWN. I MUST TAKE OFF AT SIX O'CLOCK.

WE'LL DO WHAT WE CAN, SIR. DOES THE C.O. KNOW YOU'RE HERE?

ALAN REPLIED THAT AT THAT VERY MOMENT HE WAS GOING TO SEE THE C.O.

AS THEIR PILOT MADE OFF IN THE GENERAL DIRECTION OF THE ADMINISTRATION BLOCK, BLUEY
AND HIS TWO PALS JUMPED FROM THE BOMBER AND, CLOAKED IN THE GATHERING DUSK,
SCOUTED AROUND FOR THE MESS HALL.

GRUB TIME! REMEMBER, IF ANYBODY ASKS, WE'RE ON A SPECIAL MISSION AN' OUR SKIPPER IS SEEING THE C.O. RIGHT NOW. OK?

YEAH. I SMELL STEW COMING FROM SOMEWHERE. HOW LONG IS IT SINCE WE HAD A STEW?

ALL THREE WERE NOW WEARING LEATHER FLYING JACKETS THEY HAD FOUND INSIDE THE
WELLINGTON.

ALAN NEVER SAW THE C.O. HE TURNED INSTEAD INTO THE OFFICERS' MESS AND GRABBED A PASSING ORDERLY.

I'VE JUST COME IN. ANY CHANCE OF AN EARLY SUPPER?

YES, SIR. THE REST OF THE GENTLE-MEN EAT ABOUT EIGHT O'CLOCK, BUT THE FOOD IS READY.

QUIETLY ALAN TOOK A SEAT IN THE EMPTY DINING ROOM AND WAITED FOR HIS SUPPER.

I THINK WE'RE GOING TO GET AWAY WITH IT. CRIKEY, WHAT A SITUATION.

LIFE ON THESE FORWARD AIRFIELDS WAS A PRETTY HECTIC AFFAIR, WITH MEN COMING AND GOING, AIRCRAFT STOPPING OVER, CONSTANTLY CHANGING PERSONNEL. IN THIS CONFUSION, BLUEY AND HIS COMPANION WERE HARDLY NOTICED.

BETTER THAN BULLY BEEF AND BISCUITS, EH?

YEAH. I'M GOING BACK FOR SECONDS.

BE CAREFUL, AND ACT LIKE SERGEANTS. ANYBODY SPEAKS TO YOU, JUST SMILE AND MOVE AWAY.

FULL OF GOOD FOOD AND MOUNTING CONFIDENCE, THE TOUGH TRIO FOUND AN EMPTY ROOM AND SETTLED FOR THE NIGHT.

DON'T SUPPOSE WE COULD SLEEP EASY ON A BED ANYWAY, US HAVING BEEN IN THE DESERT SO LONG.

NAH. BEDS MAKE YOU SOFT. KIP TIME NOW. WE'VE GOT A BOMBING RUN TO DO TOMORROW.

OVER IN THE OFFICERS' BLOCK, ALAN WASN'T HAVING IT SO EASY.

YOU JUST BRING IN THAT WELLINGTON? SAW YOU LAND. ENGINE TROUBLE?

TODAY'S MENU

YES, THEY'RE FIXING IT NOW. SHOULD BE FINE FOR AN EARLY TAKE-OFF.

THE INQUISITIVE OFFICER, A STICKLER FOR DISCIPLINE BY THE NAME OF SMYTHE-BROWN, THEN ASKED ALAN WHICH STATION HE CAME FROM.

TOOK OFF FROM SIDI MAKESH. WE'RE FLYING A SPECIAL BOMBING — RECCE FLIGHT. JERRY SEEMS TO BE BUILDING SOMETHING UP OVER THE TABORA.

BIT ODD, ISN'T IT? SENDING A HEAVY BOMBER ON A JOB LIKE THAT.

THE FLIGHT LIEUTENANT REMINDED ALAN OF THE MAN WHO HAD GROUNDED HIM, SQUADRON LEADER GREENWOOD. CURTLY HE TURNED AWAY.

THERE'S A WAR ON, YOU KNOW. GOOD NIGHT.

HE SPENT AN UNCOMFORTABLE NIGHT HUNCHED UP IN THE SHOWER ROOM, THE ONLY EMPTY SAFE PLACE HE COULD FIND.

CAN'T STAND THESE INTERFERING BLIMPS! THEY DON'T EVEN KNOW THERE'S A WAR ON. WELL, THEY CAN GO JUMP IN THE LAKE. ME AND THE BOYS, WE'LL FIGHT OUR OWN WAR.

AT FIVE THIRTY NEXT MORNING, ALAN AND HIS CREW WALKED OUT TO THEIR BOMBER.

SHE'LL BE OK, SIR. FULL LOAD OF BOMBS AND FULL AMMUNITION DRUMS. TANKS FULL. NOT TOO HAPPY ABOUT THE PORT ENGINE, BUT WE DID WHAT WE COULD IN THE TIME.

THANKS A LOT.

BY THE WAY, SIR, WE HAD FLIGHT LIEUTENANT SMYTHE-BROWN GOING OVER THE PLANE LAST NIGHT. WRITING DOWN THE NUMBER, THAT SORT OF THING. GAVE IT A REGULAR GOING OVER HE DID.

YEAH, I TALKED WITH HIM. THANKS AGAIN, FLIGHT. GREAT JOB!

IT LOOKED AS IF THE WELLINGTON WAS TAKING OFF JUST IN TIME.

AS ALAN MOVED THE HEAVY BOMBER TO THE RUNWAY, TWO PAIRS OF QUESTIONING EYES FOLLOWED IT.

RUM DO. A WELLINGTON WITH ONLY FOUR MEN ABOARD, AND HE COULDN'T GET OFF FAST ENOUGH. OH WELL, NONE OF MY BUSINESS. IT'S ME FOR BED.

SOMETHING VERY FUNNY ABOUT THAT KITE. ANYWAY I'VE GOT ITS REGISTRATION. MUST CHECK ON IT.

ALAN BREATHED A BIG SIGH OF RELIEF ONCE THEY WERE CLIMBING AWAY FROM THE AIRFIELD.

THAT'S ONE AIRFIELD WE CAN'T COME BACK TO AND IF THAT SMYTHE-BROWN CIRCULATES OUR REGISTRATION, WE'LL BE PICKED UP AT ANY FIELD WE LAND ON.

LET'S WORRY ABOUT THAT LATER. WHAT'S OUR TARGET, SKIPPER?

WHY BOTHER WITH ANYTHING SO CONVENTIONAL AS A FIXED TARGET? LET'S FLY OVER JERRY LINES, PICK OUT SOMETHING FAT, AND CLOBBER IT.

ALAN HAD REALLY SETTLED DOWN IN THIS ROUGH AND TUMBLE LIFE.

THEY ENJOYED TEN MINUTES SERENE FLYING. THEN HIGH ABOVE THEM, THEY SPOTTED A WING OF FIGHTERS — GERMAN FIGHTERS.

CRIKEY! A WHOLE GAGGLE OF MESSERSCHMITTS! TELL THE BOYS.

WELL, A FAT BRITISH BOMBER. THIS IS THE LAST SUNRISE YOU WILL SEE, MY FRIENDS.

THE SLEEK FIGHTERS CAME PLUMMETING DOWN LIKE HAWKS, EAGER TO DESTROY THE ONE UNPROTECTED WELLINGTON.

AS THE FIRST NAZI HURTLED PAST, ALAN FELT THE BOMBER SHUDDER BENEATH THE IMPACT OF CANNON SHELLS.

STAN AND TINKER POURED STREAMS OF BULLETS ACROSS THE SKY WHENEVER THEY GOT A NAZI IN THEIR SIGHTS.

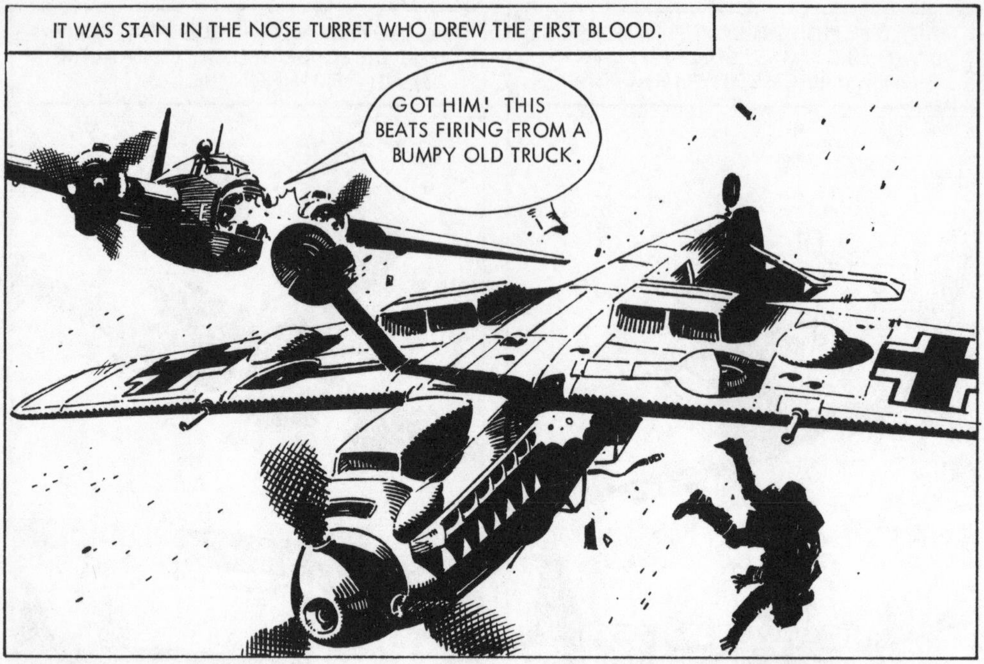
IT WAS STAN IN THE NOSE TURRET WHO DREW THE FIRST BLOOD.
GOT HIM! THIS BEATS FIRING FROM A BUMPY OLD TRUCK.

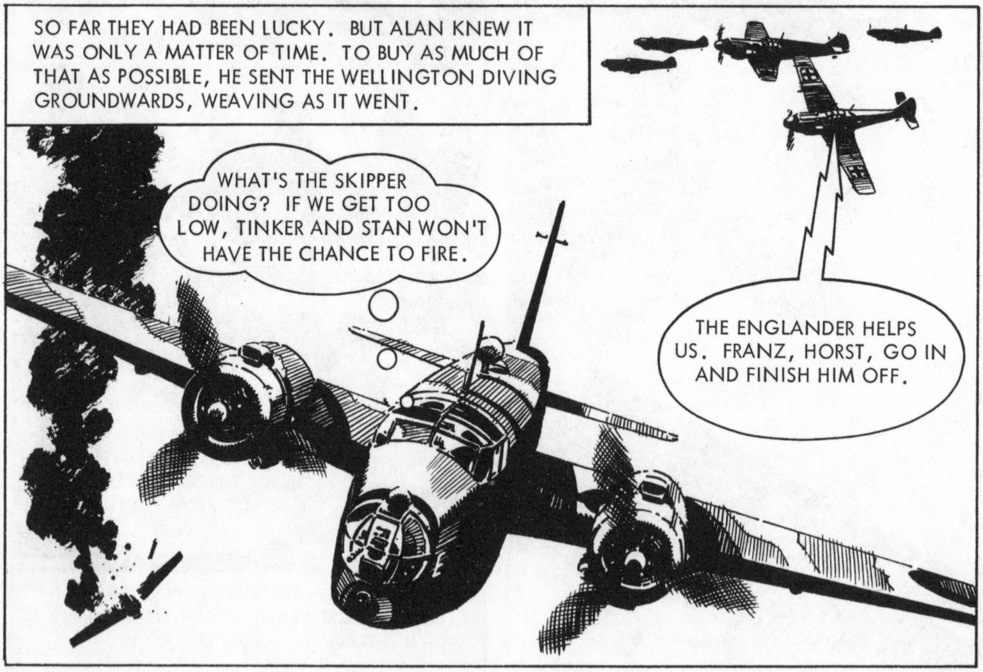
SO FAR THEY HAD BEEN LUCKY. BUT ALAN KNEW IT WAS ONLY A MATTER OF TIME. TO BUY AS MUCH OF THAT AS POSSIBLE, HE SENT THE WELLINGTON DIVING GROUNDWARDS, WEAVING AS IT WENT.
WHAT'S THE SKIPPER DOING? IF WE GET TOO LOW, TINKER AND STAN WON'T HAVE THE CHANCE TO FIRE.
THE ENGLANDER HELPS US. FRANZ, HORST, GO IN AND FINISH HIM OFF.

THE TWO MESSERSCHMITTS SHRIEKED DOWN. IN THE COCKPIT ALAN PRAYED HIS TACTICS WOULD PAY DIVIDENDS.

WHAT I WOULDN'T GIVE TO BE IN A SPIT RIGHT NOW. THIS IS LIKE FLYING A BUS IN THICK FOG.

FLYING ABOUT SIXTY FEET OFF THE DESERT AS THE TWO NAZIS FLASHED IN FOR THEIR KILL, ALAN PULLED ROUND IN A TIGHT CIRCLE.

GOOD OLD SKIPPER! YOU LINED THEM UP BEAUTIFULLY.

HE TRIES TO MAKE US DIVE INTO THE GROUND. YOU COME IN FROM THE FRONT. I'LL TAKE THE REAR.

ALAN GROANED AS HE FOUGHT TO KEEP THE BOMBER STABLE IN THE BUMPING HEAT HAZE RISING FROM THE DESERT.

NOW THEY'VE GOT US LIKE A NUT BETWEEN THE CRACKERS. WELL, LET'S BE COMPLETELY UNORTHODOX.

THROTTLES WIDE OPEN, HE THRUST THE WELLINGTON'S NOSE CLAWING BACK INTO THE SKY. THE TWO MESSERSCHMITTS WERE ON THEIR ATTACK RUN AND THE BOMBER TREMBLED BENEATH A DEADLY HURRICANE OF FIRE. THEN...

BUT THE GERMAN FLIGHT COMMANDER, IMPATIENT WITH THE EFFORTS OF HIS PILOTS, CALLED THEM BACK INTO FORMATION AND DIVED TO THE ATTACK HIMSELF.

BY NOW THEY REALISED THEY WERE REALLY UP AGAINST IT. THEIR JUBILANCE AT BEING BACK IN ACTION VANISHED AS THEY WATCHED THAT SINGLE DEADLY SHAPE STREAKING TOWARDS THEM.

THE NAZI FIGHTER SWEPT PAST, THE WELLINGTON WRITHING UNDER THE FURY OF ITS FIRE.

ONE MORE RUN AND IT WOULD ALL BE OVER. THEN...

THE SPITFIRES, OUT ON A ROUTINE PATROL, WERE RETURNING TO THEIR BASE.

WITHIN SECONDS THE SKY WAS SHUDDERING WITH ACTION. THE NAZI FLIGHT COMMANDER, BAULKED OF HIS PREY, FELL BENEATH THE FIRE-POWER OF THE BRITISH SQUADRON LEADER.

SOON ONLY ONE MESSERSCHMITT WAS STILL IN THE AIR. AND IT WAS BADLY SHOT-UP.

THE SPITFIRES STREAKED PAST THE WELLINGTON, HEADING BACK TO THEIR BASE.

THANKS, FELLERS. YOU DON'T KNOW HOW MUCH I WISH I COULD BE WITH YOU.

HECTIC, THAT WAS. I THOUGHT WE'D COPPED IT THEN FOR SURE. NICE FLYING, SKIPPER.

THANKS, BLUEY. NOW WHAT ABOUT THAT JERRY TARGET?

THE WELLINGTON WAS A TOUGH OLD BIRD. DESPITE HER RIDDLED FUSELAGE AND ONE ENGINE RUNNING ROUGH, SHE SOARED THROUGH THE HOT AIR UNTIL THEY SIGHTED A GERMAN AIRFIELD.

LOVELY. HERE'S WHERE I SHOW MY SKILL AS A BOMB-AIMER. FLY US IN NICE AND LEVEL, SKIP.

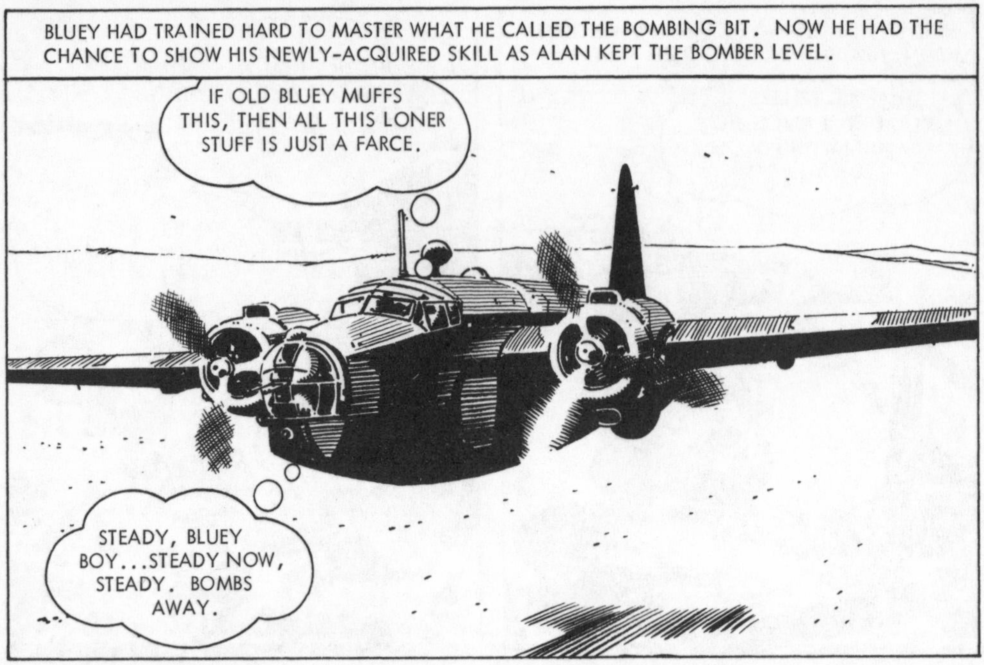
BLUEY HAD TRAINED HARD TO MASTER WHAT HE CALLED THE BOMBING BIT. NOW HE HAD THE CHANCE TO SHOW HIS NEWLY-ACQUIRED SKILL AS ALAN KEPT THE BOMBER LEVEL.
IF OLD BLUEY MUFFS THIS, THEN ALL THIS LONER STUFF IS JUST A FARCE.
STEADY, BLUEY BOY...STEADY NOW, STEADY. BOMBS AWAY.

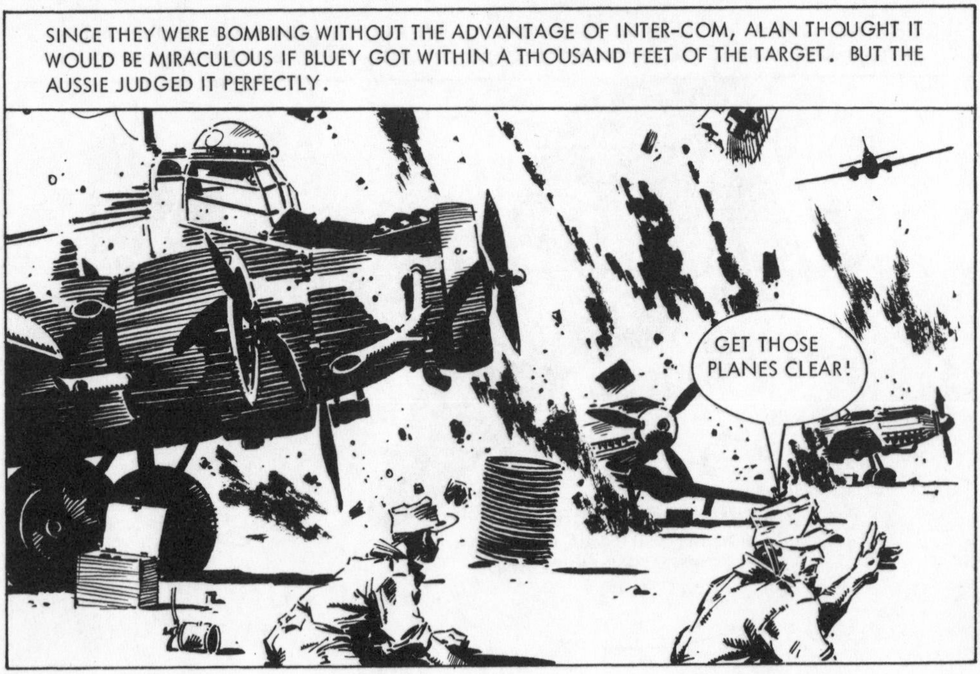
SINCE THEY WERE BOMBING WITHOUT THE ADVANTAGE OF INTER-COM, ALAN THOUGHT IT WOULD BE MIRACULOUS IF BLUEY GOT WITHIN A THOUSAND FEET OF THE TARGET. BUT THE AUSSIE JUDGED IT PERFECTLY.
GET THOSE PLANES CLEAR!

BLUEY CAME UP FROM THE BOMB-AIMER'S POSITION, AND ALAN TURNED AND HEADED AWAY FROM THEIR TARGET.

YOU'RE A BLINKING MARVEL. EVERY EGG BANG ON.

TERROR OF THE NAZIS, THAT'S ME. WHAT CHANCE HAVE I GOT OF JOINING THE R.A.F.?

WHAT CHANCE HAVE ANY OF US GOT? WE'RE ALL OUT-CASTS, FACING A SPELL IN THE CLINK IF WE'RE PICKED UP. EVERYBODY'S OUR ENEMY — GERMAN AND BRITISH.

BUT THE VERY FIRST PRIORITY WAS TO FIND A CONVENIENT AIRFIELD TO LAND ON.

THIS TIME THERE WOULD BE NO DARKNESS TO HELP THEM LAND WITHOUT DIFFICULT QUESTIONS BEING ASKED. EVERY MAN WAS TENSE AS THEY BROUGHT THE WELLINGTON DOWN ON A SMALL AIRFIELD.

THEY WOULDN'T DARE PUT ME IN THE NICK. ME, THE BEST BOMB-AIMER IN THE ARMY.

NO, THEY WOULDN'T LOCK YOU UP, BLUEY. THEY'D SHOOT YOU.

ALAN WAS PROBABLY RIGHT.

THE WELLINGTON TOUCHED DOWN SAFELY AND ALAN QUICKLY HANDED IT OVER TO THE GROUND CREWS TO SERVICE AND PROVISION. THEN THE FOUR RENEGADES WALKED TOWARDS THE ADMINISTRATION BLOCK.

THIS TIME WE TAKE NO CHANCES. TINKER, YOU LOOK AROUND FOR AN EMPTY ROOM. STAN, YOU PLUNDER SOME BLANKETS. BLUEY AND I WILL GRAB SOME FOOD AND DRINK.

AND WE STAY HOLED UP UNTIL WE TAKE OFF TOMORROW. MEET BEHIND THE ADMINISTRATION BLOCK IN FIFTEEN MINUTES.

THEY GOT FOOD AND FOUND A HUT TO SLEEP IN. BUT ALAN LAY AWAKE FOR A LONG TIME.

I DON'T WANT TO BE AN OUTCAST. I'VE GOT TO SHOW GREENWOOD AND SMYTHE-BROWNE THAT I CAN FLY RESPONSIBLY. TODAY, I DID, BUT I WANT TO DO IT WITH SPITFIRES.

AT GERMAN H.Q., A HIGH-RANKING OFFICER WAS PONDERING THE LATEST ORDERS FROM BERLIN.

ORDERS FROM HERR HITLER HIM-SELF. OUR PEOPLE'S MORALE IS SAGGING. IF WE COULD SCORE A GREAT VICTORY HERE IT WOULD CHEER THEM ALL UP. SO ONCE AGAIN WE ARE EXPECTED TO PERFORM A MIRACLE.

SO THE OFFICER CALLED HIS STAFF TOGETHER AFTER HE'D WORKED OUT A PLAN.

WE WILL MASS OUR ARMOUR AND TROOPS AT SIDI BAKA. THE BRITISH DEFENCES AT THAT POINT ARE STRETCHED VERY THIN. A BREAKTHROUGH SHOULD BE EASY. BUT THE R.A.F. COULD DESTROY US BEFORE WE ARE READY. SO MOVE BY NIGHT AND DIG IN DURING DAYLIGHT BENEATH THICK CAMOUFLAGE NETS.

WHEN DO WE ATTACK?

STAFF OFFICERS GASPED AT THE ANSWER, EVEN THE MOST BATTLE-HARDENED.

IN TWO DAYS. TOMORROW THE LUFTWAFFE WILL ATTACK HEAVILY AT SEVERAL POINTS EAST AND WEST OF SIDI BAKA. THIS WILL GIVE US SOME FREEDOM TO MOVE UNOBSERVED. THIS IS OUR LAST CHANCE FOR US IN AFRICA. WE MUST NOT FAIL.

WITHIN HOURS THE NAZI WAR MACHINE WAS ON THE MOVE. MANY TANKS WERE MOVED TOWARDS SIDI BAKA. MEN BEGAN THE MARCH THERE, TOUGH VETERANS OF THE AFRIKA KORPS.

AND AT POINTS MANY MILES EAST AND WEST, GERMAN BOMBERS POUNDED THE BRITISH LINES.

AT DAWN THAT DAY ALAN TOOK OFF WITHOUT INCIDENT AND BEGAN SEARCHING OUT A TARGET.

THAT'S FUNNY. THOUGHT I SAW SOMETHING IN THE SAND. JUST OVER THERE TO THE RIGHT.

CAN'T SEE A THING, BLUEY. PROBABLY HEAT HAZE.

NO, THERE IT IS AGAIN. IT'S TANKS, SKIPPER — DOZENS OF THEM.

YOU'RE RIGHT, THEY'RE BEING PUT UNDER HEAVY CAMOUFLAGE NETS. WHAT THE DICKENS IS JERRY UP TO?

THEY'D SPOTTED THE NAZI ATTACKING FORCE BUT ALAN KEPT FLYING STRAIGHT, PRETENDING THAT HE HAD OBSERVED NOTHING.

FOOLS! IMBECILES! IF THAT PLANE HAD SEEN THE TANKS ALL WOULD HAVE BEEN LOST. I'LL SHOOT THE MAN WHO LETS THE CAMOUFLAGE BLOW LOOSE AGAIN!

BLUEY STARED AT HIS PILOT IN DISMAY.

WHY DON'T WE CLOBBER 'EM? IT'S NOT EVERY DAY WE HAVE TANKS FOR BREAKFAST!

SOMETHING FISHY GOING ON THERE, BLUEY. MARK THE POSITION ON THE MAP. LOOKS LIKE A JERRY BUILD-UP FOR SOMETHING BIG. WE'LL HAVE TO REPORT IT.

ALAN'S MIND WAS MADE UP. HE TURNED THE WELLINGTON ROUND AND HEADED AT TOP SPEED FOR THE NEAREST AIRFIELD.

UNFORTUNATELY THE NEAREST AIRFIELD WAS AL HALFA. ALAN TOUCHED DOWN AND LEFT HIS THREE PALS IN THE BOMBER. BUT HE MET SMYTHE-BROWN —

I'VE CHECKED ON YOUR AIRCRAFT. HOW COME YOU'RE FLYING IT?

HAVEN'T GOT TIME TO TALK ABOUT IT NOW. WHERE'S THE C.O?

SOON ALAN WAS STANDING IN FRONT OF THE COMMANDING OFFICER.

BEFORE WE DO ANYTHING ELSE, SIR, CAN WE INFORM H.Q. THAT JERRY IS BUILDING UP HIS ARMOUR RIGHT THERE AT SIDI BAKA. BIG STUFF.

KEEP QUIET! FIRST TELL ME WHAT THE DICKENS YOU MEAN BY FLYING THAT AIRCRAFT AND COMING IN HERE FOR ILLEGAL SUPPLIES.

ALAN SAW RED.

JERRY IS MASSING TO ATTACK AND ALL YOU WORRY ABOUT IS A FEW BOMBS AND AVIATION FUEL.

SMYTHE-BROWN, GET TWO GUARDS AND LOCK UP THIS MADMAN.

SO ALAN WAS SEIZED.

OK, BUT JUST GET THAT GEN THROUGH TO H.Q. IF YOU DON'T, YOU COULD BE KNOWN AS THE MAN WHO LOST US THE WAR IN AFRICA.

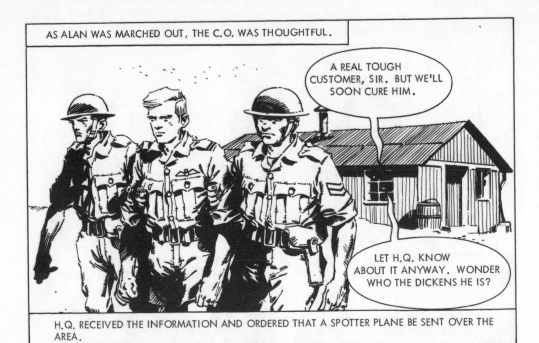

AS ALAN WAS MARCHED OUT, THE C.O. WAS THOUGHTFUL.

A REAL TOUGH CUSTOMER, SIR. BUT WE'LL SOON CURE HIM.

LET H.Q. KNOW ABOUT IT ANYWAY. WONDER WHO THE DICKENS HE IS?

H.Q. RECEIVED THE INFORMATION AND ORDERED THAT A SPOTTER PLANE BE SENT OVER THE AREA.

MEANWHILE BLUEY AND HIS PALS SAW ALAN BEING MARCHED OFF TO THE GUARD ROOM.

THEY COPPED HIM. THERE'S GRATITUDE FOR YOU.

LET'S WAIT UNTIL IT'S DARK, THEN WE'LL SPRING HIM AND TAKE OFF.

YEAH. BY THEN WE'LL BE FUELLED UP AND READY TO GO. WE STILL HAVE THOSE BOMBS ABOARD, REMEMBER. STAN, YOU STAY AROUND THE PLANE AND MAKE SURE NOBODY INTERFERES WITH IT. TINKER AND I'LL MAKE A PLAN TO GET THE SKIPPER OUT.

THE TRIO, ONCE SO SELF-CONTAINED IN THEMSELVES, FELT STRANGELY LONELY AS THEY SAW THEIR SKIPPER DISAPPEAR FROM SIGHT.

THAT NIGHT...

HEY, SKIPPER! YOU AWAKE?

BLUEY! THAT CLOT OF A C.O. DIDN'T BELIEVE ME.

ALAN WAS SEETHING.

WE'RE HERE TO SPRING YOU, SKIPPER.

NOT YET. WE CAN'T SEE THOSE TANKS IN THE DARK. WAIT TILL JUST BEFORE DAWN, THEN WE'LL CLEAR OUT OF HERE AND BOMB THE BLIGHTERS OURSELVES.

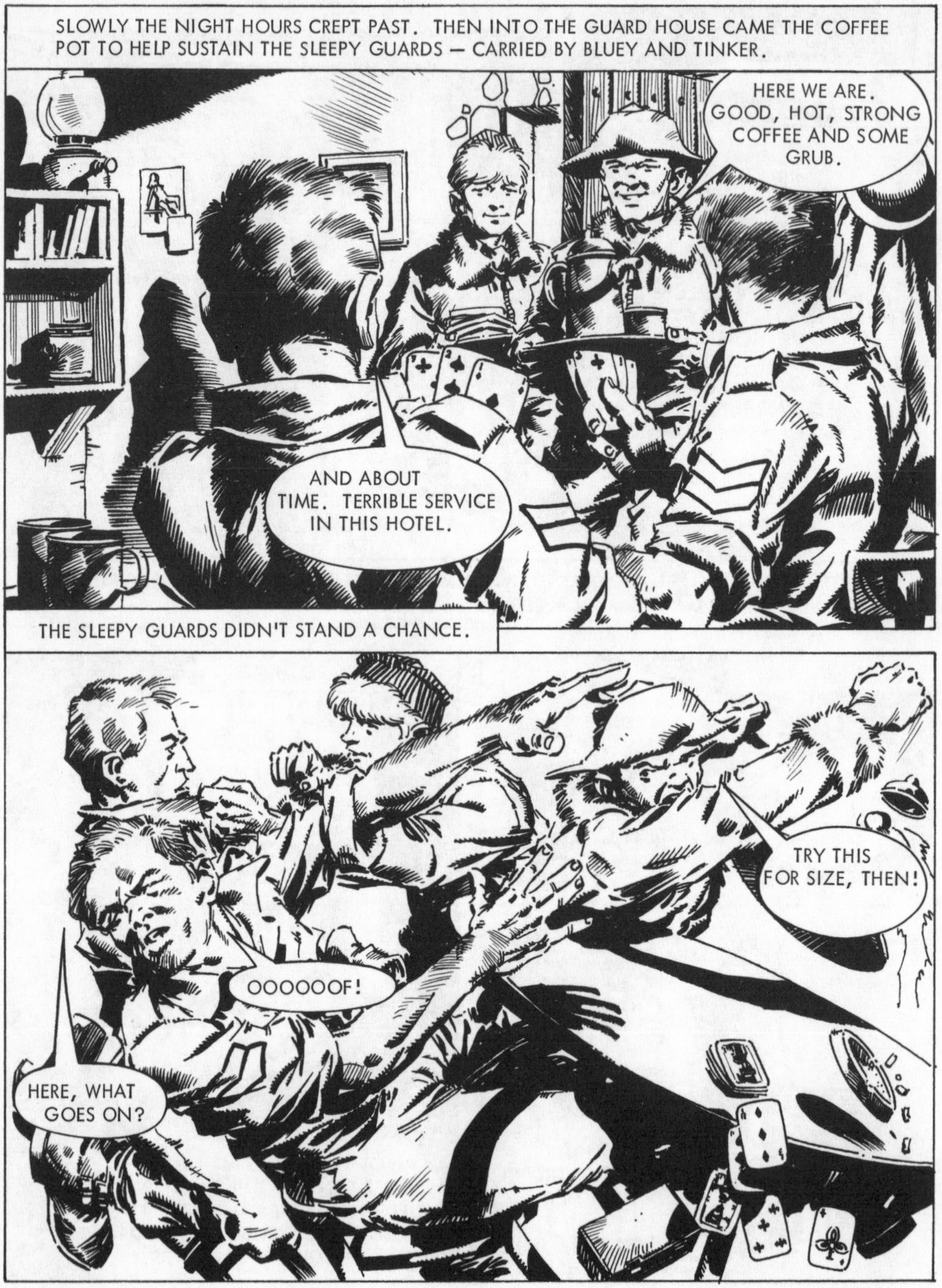
SLOWLY THE NIGHT HOURS CREPT PAST. THEN INTO THE GUARD HOUSE CAME THE COFFEE POT TO HELP SUSTAIN THE SLEEPY GUARDS — CARRIED BY BLUEY AND TINKER.
HERE WE ARE. GOOD, HOT, STRONG COFFEE AND SOME GRUB.
AND ABOUT TIME. TERRIBLE SERVICE IN THIS HOTEL.
THE SLEEPY GUARDS DIDN'T STAND A CHANCE.
TRY THIS FOR SIZE, THEN!
OOOOOOF!
HERE, WHAT GOES ON?

SECONDS LATER ALAN WAS FREED AND THEY RACED FOR THEIR PLANE.

YOU GOT HIM, THEN? IT'S ALL FUELLED AND READY, SKIPPER.

LET'S GO!

AS HIS CREW CLIMBED ABOARD, ALAN TALKED TO THE FLIGHT SERGEANT IN CHARGE OF THE GROUND CREW.

TELL THE C.O. WE'VE GONE TO BOMB THE BUILD-UP AREA. IF HE WANTS US HE CAN COME AFTER US WITH A DOZEN BOMBERS. GOT IT?

YES, SIR!

OFF THEY WENT, TURNING TOWARDS SIDI BAKA.

ROMMEL, HERE WE COME!

WHEN WE FINISH THIS WE CAN NIP ACROSS AND BOMB BERLIN.

BACK AT THE AIRFIELD, THE STARTLED FLIGHT SERGEANT ROUSED HIS IRATE C.O.

THE WELLINGTON'S GONE? YE GODS! ROUSE SMYTHE-BROWN AND TELL HIM TO GET ME H.Q. ON THE PHONE.

VERY GOOD, SIR.

SOON THE FURIOUS SQUADRON LEADER WAS TALKING TO H.Q. WHERE A COOL FLIGHT LIEUTENANT ANSWERED.

WELL, SIR, OUR SPOTTER PLANE DIDN'T FIND A BLESSED THING. BUT THE WELLINGTON HEADED STRAIGHT FOR THE AREA AND HE'S CIRCLING IT NOW. SOUNDS AS THOUGH WE'VE GOT A MANIAC ON OUR HANDS.

SLAMMING DOWN THE RECEIVER, THE C.O. SNARLED ORDERS AT THE UNFORTUNATE SMYTHE-BROWN.

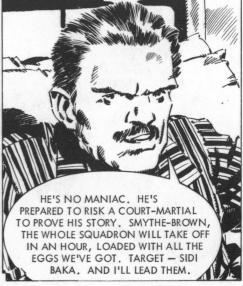

HE'S NO MANIAC. HE'S PREPARED TO RISK A COURT-MARTIAL TO PROVE HIS STORY. SMYTHE-BROWN, THE WHOLE SQUADRON WILL TAKE OFF IN AN HOUR, LOADED WITH ALL THE EGGS WE'VE GOT. TARGET — SIDI BAKA. AND I'LL LEAD THEM.

AFTER A FRENZIED HOUR THE SQUADRON OF WELLINGTONS WAS AIRBORNE.

I FLEW OVER SIDI BAKA YESTERDAY AND IT'S JUST EMPTY SAND. ANYWAY, OURS NOT TO REASON WHY.

KEEP OFF THE RADIO, YOU BLOCKHEADS, AND CONCENTRATE ON YOUR FLYING.

AS THE LAST PLANE LIFTED OFF, SMYTHE-BROWN CALLED UP H.Q.

HALLO. THE WHOLE SQUADRON HAS JUST TAKEN OFF FOR SIDI BAKA. LOOKS LIKE THIS COULD BE REALLY BIG. I THOUGHT I'D BETTER TIP YOU OFF.

SO TWO SENIOR AIR FORCE OFFICERS WERE ORDERED TO INSPECT THE AREA, KEEPING IN RADIO CONTACT WITH THE RECCE PLANE, A LYSANDER.

BIT EARLY FOR ALL THIS BOUNCING ABOUT.

HEAVEN HELP SOMEONE IF THIS IS ALL A JOKE. I'LL CALL THE LYSANDER. "HALLO SIDNEY ABLE...COME IN."

FROM THE SPOTTER PLANE THE DESERT LOOKED EMPTY.

I'VE BEEN FLYING OVER THIS DEAD WORLD FOR TWO HOURS AND NOTHING'S MOVED — NOT EVEN A SAND RAT. MIND YOU, THERE'S A LOT OF HEAT HAZE DANCING ON THE DESERT DOWN THERE.

KEEP LOOKING. EXPECT TO SEE A WELLINGTON BOMBER ANY MINUTE, FOLLOWED BY ANOTHER TWELVE. IT ALL SOUNDS MAD, BUT IT COULD BE DEADLY SERIOUS.

AT THAT MOMENT, THE ROGUE WIMPEY, BARELY SIXTY FEET OFF THE SAND, WAS APPROACHING FOR A BOMBING RUN.

WE'LL SHOOT UP THE AREA A BIT FIRST AND SEE IF THAT MAKES THEM SHOW THEMSELVES.

THAT'S BEAUTIFUL CAMOUFLAGE. JERRY MUST BE STIFLING HOT UNDER IT ALL.

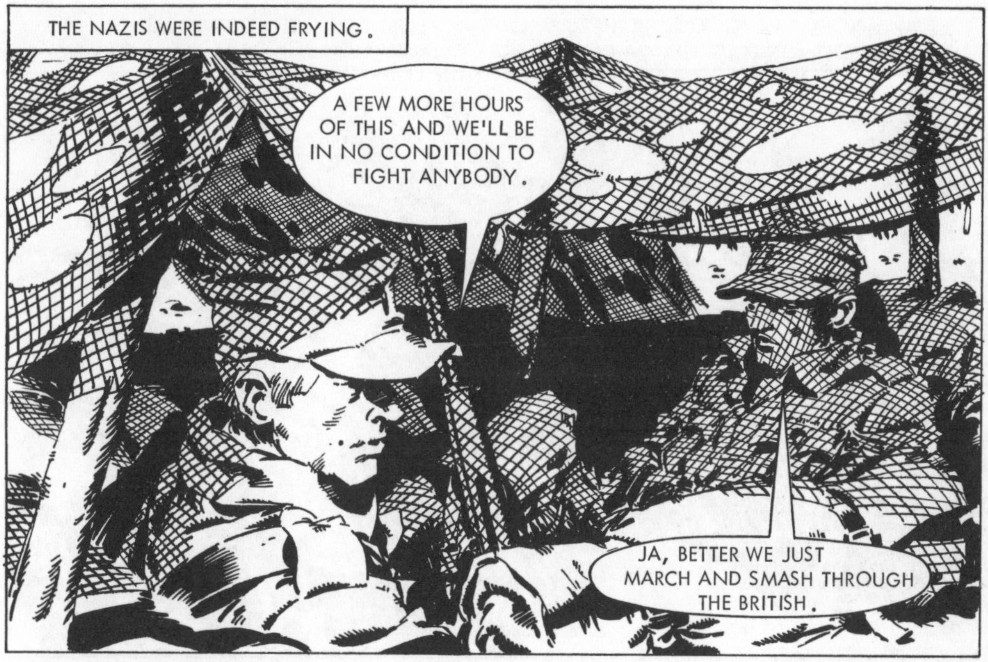
THE NAZIS WERE INDEED FRYING.
A FEW MORE HOURS OF THIS AND WE'LL BE IN NO CONDITION TO FIGHT ANYBODY.
JA, BETTER WE JUST MARCH AND SMASH THROUGH THE BRITISH.

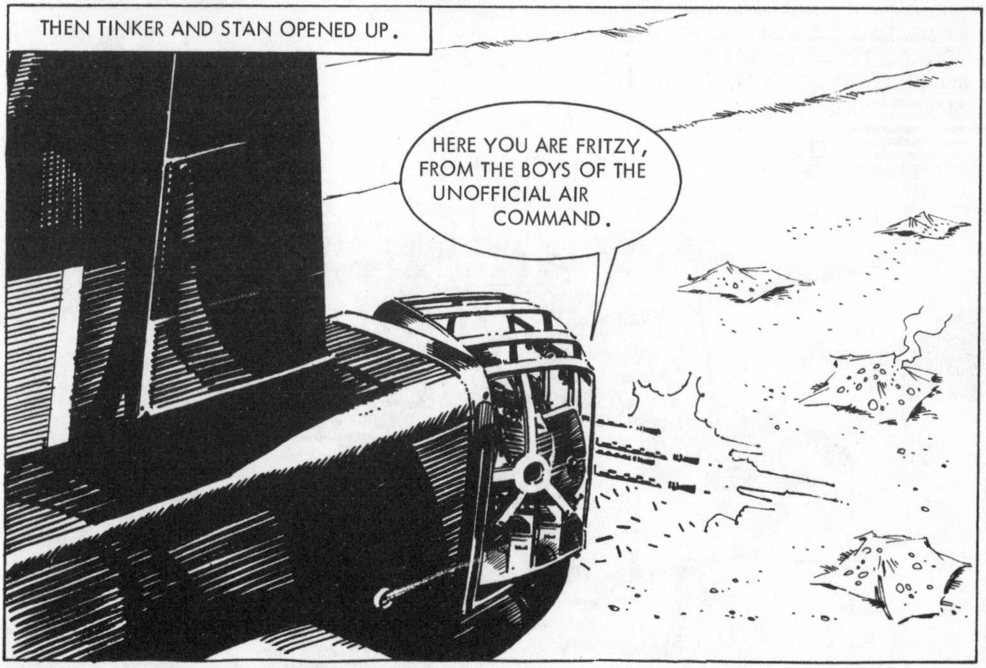
THEN TINKER AND STAN OPENED UP.
HERE YOU ARE FRITZY, FROM THE BOYS OF THE UNOFFICIAL AIR COMMAND.

AS THE HOT LEAD RAKED ACROSS THE APPARENTLY LIFELESS SAND, THE GERMANS THOUGHT THEY WERE BEING ATTACKED BY A LARGE FORCE. SECRECY NOW BEING USELESS, THEY FLUNG BACK THEIR CAMOUFLAGE AND BLASTED BACK AT THE LOW-FLYING BOMBER.

BY THE TIME ALAN HAD TURNED ROUND TO COME IN FOR HIS BOMBING RUN, THE DESERT WAS ALIVE WITH GERMANS.

THE WELLINGTON RAN INTO AN INFERNO OF EXPLODING STEEL AS EVERY ACK-ACK GUN BELOW OPENED FIRE. IT TOOK ALL OF ALAN'S IRON NERVE, EVERY OUNCE OF HIS NEW-FOUND RESPONSIBILITY, TO KEEP THE PLANE LEVEL.

BUT THIS TIME THEY PAID A HIGHER PRICE FOR THEIR AGRESSION. TINKER'S TURRET SUDDENLY DISSOLVED INTO A THRESHING RUIN.

AND SECONDS LATER, STAN MET A SIMILAR FATE.

BUT THEY DID NOT DIE IN VAIN. SOME-HOW ALAN KEPT THE BOMBER FLYING LEVEL, THOUGH JERRY THREW EVERY-THING AT THEM.

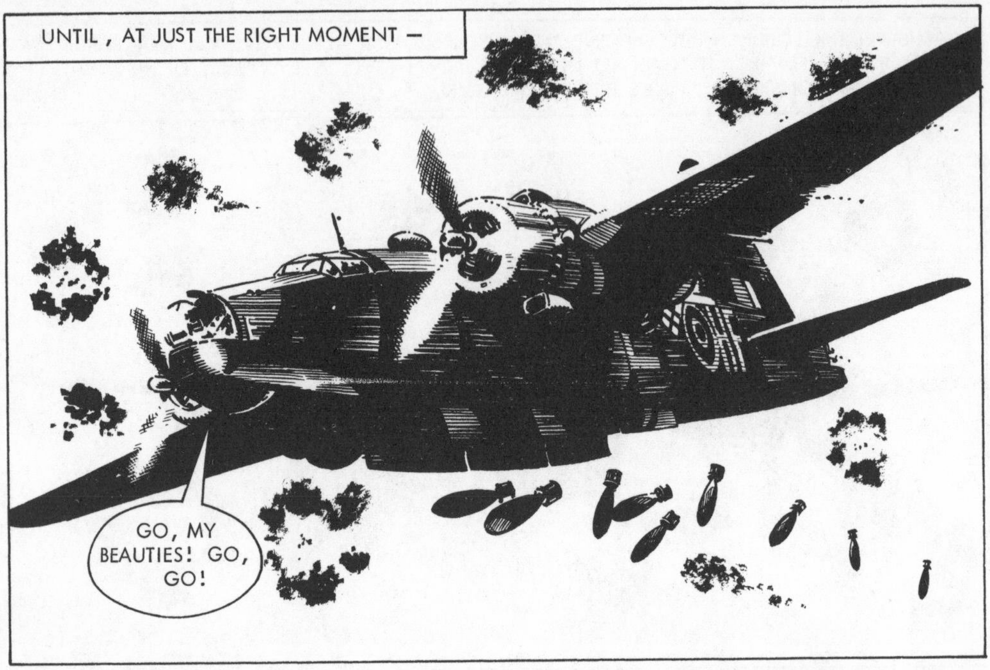
UNTIL, AT JUST THE RIGHT MOMENT –
GO, MY BEAUTIES! GO, GO!

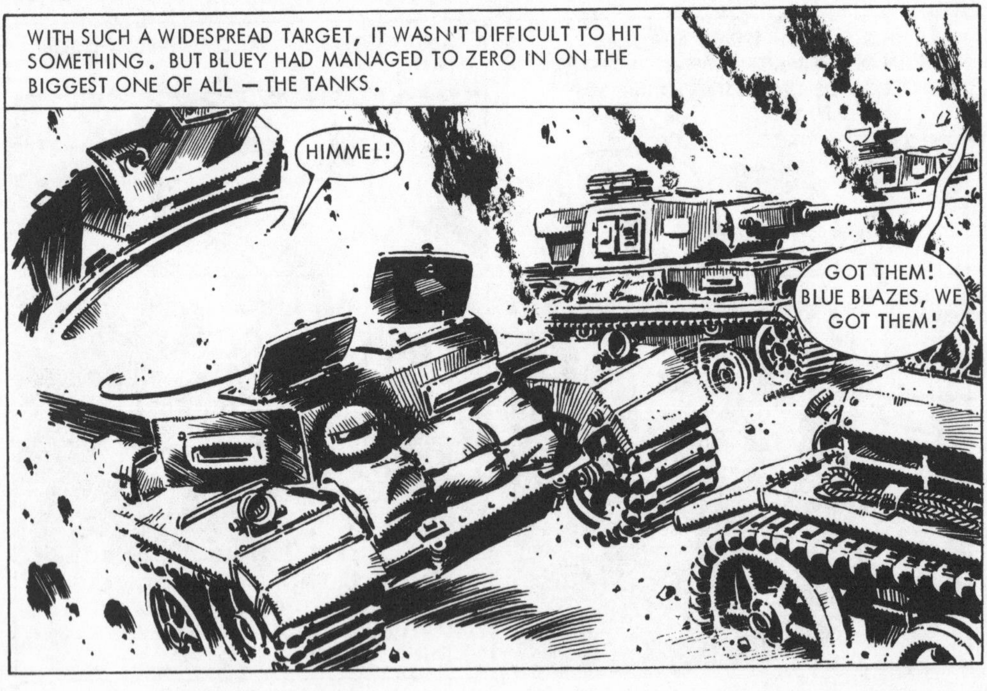
WITH SUCH A WIDESPREAD TARGET, IT WASN'T DIFFICULT TO HIT SOMETHING. BUT BLUEY HAD MANAGED TO ZERO IN ON THE BIGGEST ONE OF ALL – THE TANKS.
HIMMEL!
GOT THEM! BLUE BLAZES, WE GOT THEM!

BUT UNDER SUCH FIRE, EVEN THIS WIMPEY'S GREAT HEART BROKE. FLAMES LICKED ALONG THE BROKEN FUSELAGE AND THE GIANT WELLINGTON BEGAN TO FALL TO EARTH.

BLUEY, WE'RE GOING IN. GRAB HOLD OF SOMETHING AND HANG ON.

CONTROLS BUCKING IN HIS HANDS, ALAN PULLED BACK ON THE STICK AND FOUGHT THE BLAZING BOMBER DOWN ON TO THE SAND.

THIS IS IT!

LANDING HEAVILY, THE WIMPEY SLOWED TO A HALT. ALAN AND BLUEY FLED.

WHAT ABOUT STAN AND TINKER?

BOTH DEAD. THEY'RE FEELING NOTHING NOW.

WITH A SOUND LIKE THUNDER, THE GALLANT WELLINGTON ENDED HER DAYS.

SKIPPER — LOOK!

ABOVE HAD APPEARED THE DOZEN BOMBERS, THE CREWS ALL READY TO GO INTO ACTION.

REMIND ME TO LAY ON THE BIGGEST MESS PARTY EVER FOR THE MAD BLIGHTERS IN THAT WELLINGTON.

TWO OF THEM GOT OUT ANYWAY, SIR.

SOON ALAN AND BLUEY WERE PICKED UP BY THE TWO SENIOR OFFICERS.

GOOD SHOW ARE THIN WORDS FOR WHAT YOU'VE DONE, BUT GOOD SHOW!

THANKS, SIR. I'M PILOT OFFICER ALAN WILSON. THIS IS ARMY PRIVATE BLUEY MARSH, THE BEST BOMB-AIMER IN ALL THREE SERVICES.

ARMY?

YES, SIR. AND MY FRONT AND REAR GUNNERS WERE ARMY BODS, TOO.

SO ENDED THE EXPLOITS OF THE ROGUE BOMBER AND ITS MADCAP CREW. SO ENDED TOO, THE LAST MAJOR GERMAN THRUST IN AFRICA. ALAN AND BLUEY WERE FETED BY EVERY MESS IN THE AREA.

WHAT'S THE TOP BRASS GOING TO DO WITH YOU TWO BLOKES?

GOODNESS KNOWS. WE'VE GOT AN INTERVIEW TOMORROW MORNING. KEEP YOUR FINGERS CROSSED FOR US.

IF THEY CLOBBER YOU, EVERY PILOT IN THE COMMAND WILL GO ON STRIKE. THAT I PROMISE.

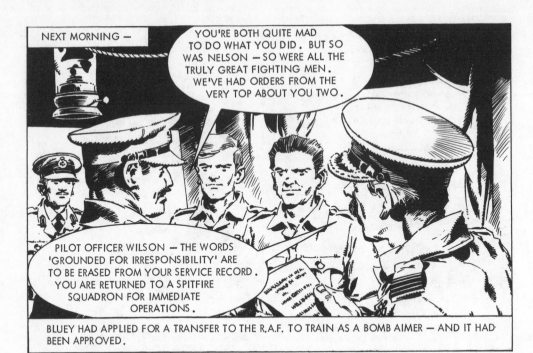

NEXT MORNING —

YOU'RE BOTH QUITE MAD TO DO WHAT YOU DID. BUT SO WAS NELSON — SO WERE ALL THE TRULY GREAT FIGHTING MEN. WE'VE HAD ORDERS FROM THE VERY TOP ABOUT YOU TWO.

PILOT OFFICER WILSON — THE WORDS 'GROUNDED FOR IRRESPONSIBILITY' ARE TO BE ERASED FROM YOUR SERVICE RECORD. YOU ARE RETURNED TO A SPITFIRE SQUADRON FOR IMMEDIATE OPERATIONS.

BLUEY HAD APPLIED FOR A TRANSFER TO THE R.A.F. TO TRAIN AS A BOMB AIMER — AND IT HAD BEEN APPROVED.

SOON ALAN WAS FIGHTING THE NAZIS AGAIN, BUT NOW FROM BEHIND THE CONTROLS OF HIS BELOVED SPITFIRE. HE WAS A MORE MATURE ALAN, MORE CALCULATED IN HIS JUDGEMENTS.

BANDIT DOWN. AM REJOINING FOR- MATION!

AS FOR BLUEY, HE FLEW IN WELLINGTONS UNTIL THE WAR'S END, FLYING NIGHTLY OVER EUROPE, BOMBING THE HEART OUT OF THE NAZI WAR DREAMS UNTIL FIRES WERE BURNING IN THE VERY CENTRE OF BERLIN ITSELF.

BUT NEITHER EVER FORGOT THEIR DAYS WITH THE ROGUE BOMBER AND ITS CREW OF FIGHTING FOOLS.

Commando
THE END

Aircraft of the Second World War — No. 4

JAPANESE "ZERO"

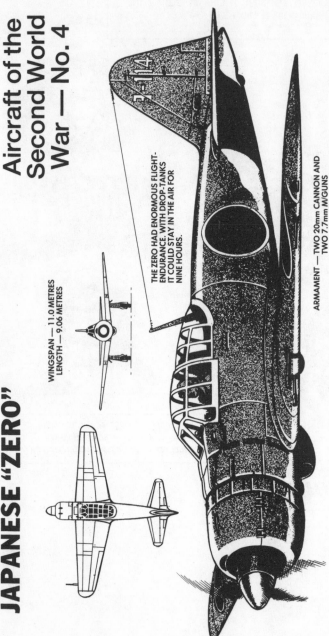

WINGSPAN — 11.0 METRES
LENGTH — 9.06 METRES

THE ZERO HAD ENORMOUS FLIGHT-ENDURANCE. WITH DROP-TANKS IT COULD STAY IN THE AIR FOR NINE HOURS.

ARMAMENT — TWO 20mm CANNON AND TWO 7.7mm M/GUNS

THE Mitsubishi Zero-sen, symbol of air supremacy to the Japanese, was first used with great success against the Chinese.

Its performance came as a great shock to the Americans when the Japs made their lightning attack on Pearl Harbour, and not until they captured one intact did they find out anything about it.

It appeared in great numbers on every front, and not only as a fighter. It was modified as a float-plane to give support to beach-storming infantry, and could also be converted into a dive bomber.

But as a dive bomber its bomb release gear was unreliable, and so Zeroes formed the first squadron of "Kamikaze" suicide planes, filled with explosives and piloted right on to targets by fanatical Jap pilots.

The Zero was master of the Pacific skies until the battle of Midway in 1942. After that, better and faster Allied planes shot it out of the skies.

THE SILVER SPITFIRE

IN THE DUSTY SQUARE OF THE SMALL TOWN OF DAKPUR IN CENTRAL BURMA, THERE STANDS ON A CONCRETE BASE A PRICELESS RELIC OF THE LAST WAR. IT IS EASILY RECOGNISED AS A SPITFIRE FIGHTER — THE GREATEST WAR PLANE OF WORLD WAR II. PAINTED ALL SILVER, UNDER THE LOVING CARE OF THE TOWNSPEOPLE IT SHINES IN THE GLARE OF THE TROPICAL SUN. AND IT HAS A NAME — THE PEOPLE CALL IT "THE SWORD OF DAKPUR".

THE STORY OF THIS SPITFIRE AND THE MAN WHO FLEW IT BEGAN BACK IN 1941, WHEN THE ARMED MIGHT OF JAPAN BURST FORTH, SWEPT OVER HALF THE EAST — AND TOUCHED ON A PEACEFUL JUNGLE VILLAGE CALLED DAKPUR...

CHEEK BY JOWL WITH THE VILLAGE OF DAKPUR AN AIRSTRIP HAD BEEN CARVED FROM THE TANGLE OF TEAK FOREST. HERE, AN R.A.F. HURRICANE SQUADRON SWEATED AND WAITED FOR THE NEXT JAP RAID.

A.C.1. TOM SHAW, FLIGHT MECHANIC, STRETCHED HIS ACHING MUSCLES. HE WAS DOG TIRED, HAVING SLAVED ALL NIGHT AND HALF THE MORNING MAKING A HURRICANE SERVICE-ABLE.

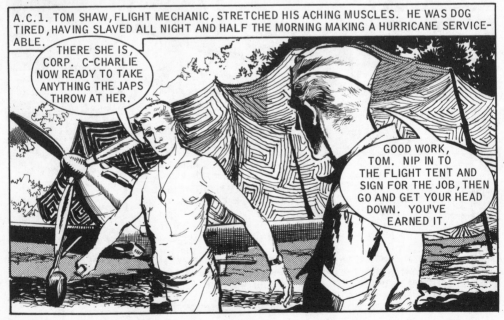

THERE SHE IS, CORP. C-CHARLIE NOW READY TO TAKE ANYTHING THE JAPS THROW AT HER.

GOOD WORK, TOM. NIP IN TO THE FLIGHT TENT AND SIGN FOR THE JOB, THEN GO AND GET YOUR HEAD DOWN. YOU'VE EARNED IT.

TOM GATHERED HIS GEAR TOGETHER AND STARTED BACK FOR HIS TENT, DREAMING OF HIS AWAITING BED...

I COULD SLEEP FOR A WEEK...

COME ON, YOU LOT. GET CRACKING! JAP RAIDERS COMING IN, DOZENS OF 'EM THIS TIME.

BUT ANY THOUGHTS TOM HAD OF SLEEP WERE HASTILY DISPELLED BY THE RAUCOUS HAMMERING ON THE MAKE-SHIFT WARNING SYSTEM.

WITHIN SECONDS THE SWARMING ZEROS STRUCK. THE FIRST SHELLS FOUND C-CHARLIE'S FUEL TANKS.

OH NO!

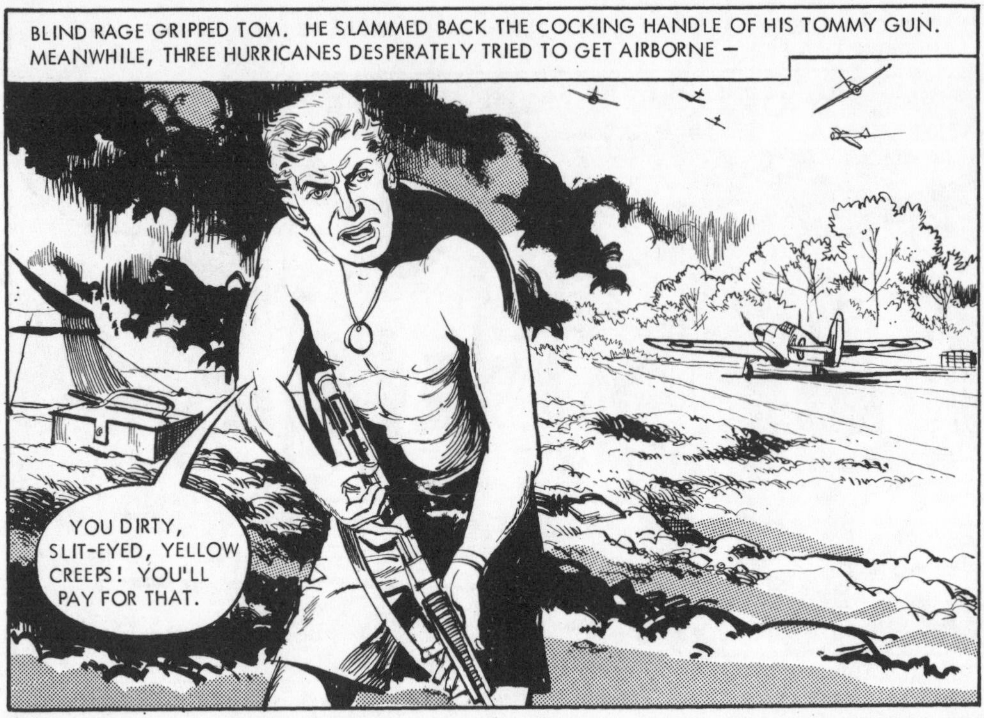
BLIND RAGE GRIPPED TOM. HE SLAMMED BACK THE COCKING HANDLE OF HIS TOMMY GUN. MEANWHILE, THREE HURRICANES DESPERATELY TRIED TO GET AIRBORNE –
YOU DIRTY, SLIT-EYED, YELLOW CREEPS! YOU'LL PAY FOR THAT.

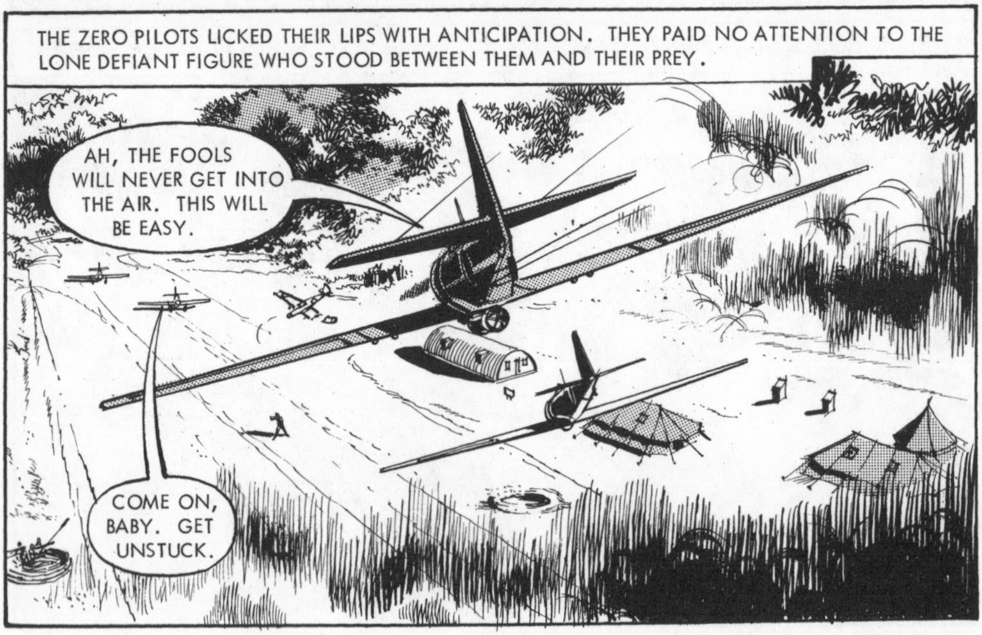
THE ZERO PILOTS LICKED THEIR LIPS WITH ANTICIPATION. THEY PAID NO ATTENTION TO THE LONE DEFIANT FIGURE WHO STOOD BETWEEN THEM AND THEIR PREY.
AH, THE FOOLS WILL NEVER GET INTO THE AIR. THIS WILL BE EASY.
COME ON, BABY. GET UNSTUCK.

AT THE PRECISE MOMENT WHEN THE JAPS' GUNS BEGAN THEIR TATTOO OF DEATH, TOM CLENCHED HIS FINGER DOWN HARD ON THE TRIGGER AND HELD IT THERE.

NOW, SEE HOW YOU LIKE SOME OF YOUR OWN MEDICINE!

EIGHT BULLETS FOUND THE JAP'S BODY. HE SLUMPED DEAD OVER HIS CONTROLS, HIS PLANE LURCHING SIDEWAYS INTO THE OTHER ZERO. FOR TWO NIPPONESE PILOTS, THE RISING SUN HAD SET — PERMANENTLY.

NEI, WE CRASH!

TOM'S LONE STAND HAD GIVEN THE HURRICANES THE CHANCE TO GET AIRBORNE. THEY NOW CIRCLED ABOVE, WATCHING ONE ZERO EXPLODE VIOLENTLY IN THE JUNGLE WHILE THE OTHER WOBBLED DRUNKENLY TOWARDS THE VILLAGE.

GLORY BE, I'VE CLOBBERED BOTH OF 'EM!

WE MADE IT, THANKS TO THAT ERK DOWN THERE. HE DESERVES A MEDAL, WHOEVER HE IS.

THE ZERO FELL INTO THE VILLAGE. TOM'S GLEE TURNED INTO STARK HORROR —

HEY! WHAT'S THE BIG IDEA?

IT'S GONE SLAP BANG INTO THE MIDDLE OF THE VILLAGE AND ITS BOMB HASN'T GONE OFF YET! I'VE GOT TO DO SOMETHING, FAST. SORRY, CHUM, I NEED YOUR JEEP MORE THAN YOU DO.

BY A MIRACLE, THE ZERO, ITS PILOT DEAD, HAD MISSED ALL THE HUTS. TO THE EXCITED VILLAGERS, THE BLAZING PYRE SHOWED THAT THE LITTLE YELLOW MEN WERE NOT SO INVINCIBLE AFTER ALL.

GET BACK! RUN FOR YOUR LIVES. HECK, THEY DON'T UNDERSTAND. IF THAT BOMB GOES UP...

AIEE! BURN YOU YELLOW DOG!

SNATCHING THE ESCAPE AXE FROM ITS STOWAGE IN THE JEEP, TOM RACED INTO THE FLAMES. THE HARDENED STEEL BLADE CHOPPED THROUGH THE LIGHT ALLOY BOMB RACKS.

PHEW, IT'S HOT. THESE VILLAGERS DON'T SEEM TO REALISE THE SPOT THEY'RE IN!

JUST AS TOM CUT THE BOMB FREE, THE VILLAGERS REALISED THE PERIL OF THE UNEXPLODED BOMBS AND SOME RUSHED TO HELP.

FOR THE LOVE OF MIKE, BE CAREFUL. THE BOMB'S FUSED READY TO EXPLODE.

TOM DROVE HIS LETHAL LOAD INTO THE JUNGLE AND DUMPED IT WHERE IT WOULD DO NO HARM.

ON HIS RETURN, OLD U WAN, THE VILLAGE HEAD MAN, WAVED TOM TO STOP.

YOU HAVE SAVED MANY LIVES, MY SON. NOW, IN RETURN, MY PEOPLE WANT TO HELP.

SURE, JUMP ABOARD ALL THAT'S COMING.

TOM KNEW THE GUNPOSTS COULD DO WITH HELP. THERE WOULD ALSO BE FIRES TO PUT OUT, A TASK MADE EASIER WITH ASSISTANCE FROM THE VILLAGERS.

THE MASSIVE JAP RAID WAS A DISASTER FOR 703 SQUADRON BUT THE VICTORY WAS DEARLY BOUGHT. THE BURNING WRECKAGE OF MANY JAP PLANES FLAMED ALL AROUND THE TINY AIRSTRIP. THROUGH IT ALL THE MEN OF DAKPUR TOILED AND SWEATED ALONGSIDE THE R.A.F. MEN, SHARING THEIR PERILS.

ONE OF THE LAST BOMBS TO FALL BLASTED THE JEEP AS TOM DROVE FURIOUSLY TOWARDS A GUN-PIT WITH THE MUCH NEEDED AMMUNITION.

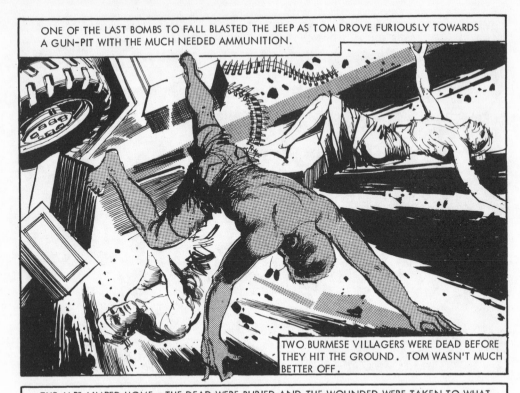

TWO BURMESE VILLAGERS WERE DEAD BEFORE THEY HIT THE GROUND. TOM WASN'T MUCH BETTER OFF.

THE JAPS LIMPED HOME. THE DEAD WERE BURIED AND THE WOUNDED WERE TAKEN TO WHAT REMAINED OF THE HOSPITAL. UNDER APPALLING CONDITIONS, THE MEDICAL OFFICER FOUGHT TO SAVE THE LIFE OF A.C.1 TOM SHAW — AND WON.

THAT LAD'S GOT THE HEART OF A LION. HE GAVE THE C.O. A CHANCE TO GET AIR-BORNE WITH A COUPLE OF OTHERS TO SHOOT UP THE NIPS. HE'S PRETTY BADLY SHOT UP NOW. MARK HIM DOWN FOR EVACUATION.

YES, SIR.

A FEW DAYS LATER, TOM AND TWENTY-FOUR OTHER SERIOUS CASES WERE AWAITING THE ARRIVAL OF A DAKOTA TO TAKE THEM TO INDIA AND THEN TO BRITAIN. THEY BROUGHT TOM A VISITOR.

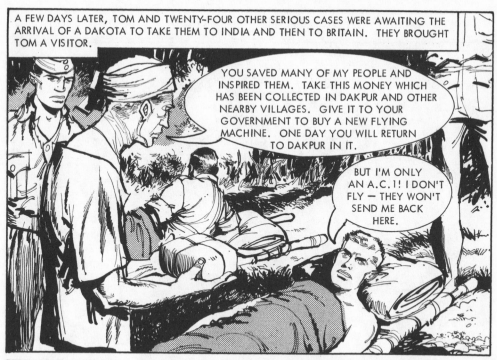

YOU SAVED MANY OF MY PEOPLE AND INSPIRED THEM. TAKE THIS MONEY WHICH HAS BEEN COLLECTED IN DAKPUR AND OTHER NEARBY VILLAGES. GIVE IT TO YOUR GOVERNMENT TO BUY A NEW FLYING MACHINE. ONE DAY YOU WILL RETURN TO DAKPUR IN IT.

BUT I'M ONLY AN A.C.1! I DON'T FLY — THEY WON'T SEND ME BACK HERE.

BUT, UNPERTURBED, THE OLD MAN PLACED A NECKLET, THE SYMBOL OF CHIEF, ROUND TOM'S NECK.

YOU CANNOT CHANGE FATE. ONE DAY YOU WILL COME BACK TO DAKPUR WITH MANY FLYING MACHINES. YOU WILL BE THEIR CHIEF AND DRIVE THE EVIL JAPANESE AWAY. THE ABILITY TO LEAD WAS BORN IN YOU, MY SON. THIS NECKLET WILL ENSURE YOUR RETURN TO US.

A WAVE OF WEAKNESS SWEPT OVER TOM. HE COULD ONLY GASP A FEEBLE PROTEST.

I'M SORRY, BUT YOU'LL HAVE TO GO NOW.

GOODBYE, MY SON. THE HOPES OF MY PEOPLE GO WITH YOU.

BUT, I CAN'T DO ANYTHING! I-I'M ONLY A FLIGHT MECHANIC.

THE DAKOTA WAS LOADED AND AIRBORNE IN A SHORT TIME.

THEY ARE GETTING READY TO LEAVE. THAT MEANS THE NIPPONESE WILL COME VERY SOON NOW. MY PEOPLE MUST BE PATIENT AND ENDURE MUCH UNTIL HE RETURNS.

ONCE AIRBORNE, TOM OPENED THE PARCEL. HE COUNTED THE MONEY SLOWLY, GOGGLING WIDELY AT THE AMOUNT.

FIVE THOUSAND QUID! THAT'S A HUGE SUM TO THESE PEOPLE. IT'S ALMOST ENOUGH TO BUY A SPITFIRE.

IT WAS A LONG, WEARY JOURNEY BY PLANE AND HOSPITAL SHIP FROM THE HUMID JUNGLE HEAT TO THE FROSTY MISTS OF WAR-TORN BRITAIN. TOM ARRANGED FOR THE MONEY TO BE HANDED OVER TO THE PROPER AUTHORITIES —

DON'T WORRY, SHAW. I'LL TAKE THE MONEY WITH ME WHEN I REPORT TO THE ADMIRALTY.

THANK YOU, SIR.

THEY SENT TOM TO A R.A.F. CONVALESCENT CENTRE WHERE HIS WOUNDS BECAME SCARS. THEN ONE DAY —

WELL, YOU'RE LUCKY. YOU'VE MADE A GOOD RECOVERY. WE CAN CLASS YOU AS A1 AGAIN.

A.1 — FIT ENOUGH TO BE A PILOT. I THINK I'LL APPLY —

WHILE TOM WAS ON THREE WEEKS' SICK LEAVE, THE STORY OF DAKPUR'S GIFT BROKE IN THE NEWSPAPERS, MUCH TO TOM'S SURPRISE AND EMBARRASSMENT.

OH MY GOSH — THEY'VE LAID IT ON A BIT THICK. I'M NO FLAMING HERO. GOOD JOB THEY DIDN'T KNOW ANYTHING ABOUT U WAN'S NECKLET. THEY'D CERTAINLY HAVE GONE TO TOWN ON THAT LOAD OF CORN — OR IS IT? I WONDER...

ECHO

DARING EXPLOITS
BY 'ERK' IN JUNGLE BLITZ. GRATEFUL NATIVES BUY SPITFIRE

RAIDS ON OIL DEPOTS

MEANWHILE, TOM'S APPLICATION FOR PILOT TRAINING WENT FORWARD FOR CONSIDERATION.

LOOK AT ALL THESE APPLICATIONS. I THINK EVERY GROUND WALLAH IN THE AIR FORCE WANTS TO BE A PILOT. WE'LL HAVE TO REJECT HALF OF THEM.

EXCUSE ME, SIR. THIS ONE IS SOMEONE SPECIAL. IT'S A.C.1 SHAW, THE MAN WHO BROUGHT BACK THAT MONEY FROM DAKPUR TO BUY A SPITFIRE.

NEVER HEARD OF HIM. AND WHERE'S DAKPUR?

IN BURMA, SIR. THE COMPLETE STORY'S IN THIS FILE.

THE WING COMMANDER WAS A SHREWD MAN. HE REALISED THE POTENTIAL APPEAL TO THE PUBLIC IF THIS MAN WAS SELECTED TO FLY DAKPUR'S FIGHTER.

REMARKABLE STORY. APPROVE HIS APPLICATION AND MAKE SURE HE FLIES DAKPUR'S SPITFIRE WHEN HE COMPLETES HIS TRAINING.

TOM REPORTED BACK FIT FOR DUTY AND WAS SENT TO A FLYING TRAINING SCHOOL. HIS QUIET PERSEVERANCE AND ABILITY TO LEARN SAW HIM THROUGH A GRUELLING COURSE ROUNDED OFF BY OPERATIONAL TRAINING IN SPITFIRES.

THEIR TRAINING COMPLETED, THE NEWLY FLEDGED FLIERS WERE POSTED TO VARIOUS FIGHTER UNITS. TOM WAS PUZZLED WHEN HE READ THE DESTINATION AGAINST HIS NAME —

TOM HAD PLENTY OF TIME TO FIGURE OUT HIS ASSIGNMENT DURING THE JOURNEY NORTH, BUT EVEN THEN, HE COULDN'T COME UP WITH THE ANSWER.

HERE WE ARE, SIR. H.M.S. FALCON.

SO THAT'S IT — A CARRIER WITH SPITS ON BOARD. STRANGE, THE NAVY'S GOT ITS OWN PILOTS — SHOULDN'T THINK THEY'LL TAKE KINDLY TO THE R.A.F. MUSCLING IN ON THEIR GLORY.

TOM WAS DIRECTED BELOW TO A MESS DECK, WHERE CRAMMED INTO THE CONFINED SPACE WERE TWENTY-FIVE R.A.F. PILOTS. FLIGHT LIEUTENANT BOB CAMPBELL CAME FORWARD TO GREET HIM —

WELCOME ABOARD. MY NAME'S BOB CAMPBELL. BETTER GRAB YOURSELF A BUNK BEFORE SOMEBODY ELSE DOES.

THANKS. I'M TOM SHAW. ANY IDEA WHAT WE'RE DOING ON A CARRIER?

BOB CAMPBELL SHRUGGED HIS SHOULDERS. THERE WAS NO SECURITY LEAK AT ALL TO GIVE THE PILOTS ANY IDEA OF THE DESTINATION.

SEARCH ME, PAL. I'D JUST DONE A TOUR OF OPS ON SPITS WHEN THEY TOLD ME TO GET MY KIT PACKED AND HERE I AM. I DON'T KNOW ANY MORE THAN YOU DO — NOR ANYONE ELSE IN THIS BLACK HOLE OF CALCUTTA.

NO DOUBT WE'LL SOON KNOW ALL ABOUT IT. I COULD DO WITH SOME SLEEP AFTER THE JOURNEY UP HERE.

THE FALCON, WITH A STRONG DESTROYER ESCORT, SLIPPED DOWN THE CLYDE AT DAWN AND HEADED OUT INTO THE BLEAK ATLANTIC TO JOIN A MERCHANT CONVOY OF TWENTY SHIPS.

ATTENTION!... ATTENTION...ALL R.A.F. PERSONNEL! REPORT TO THE FLIGHT BRIEFING ROOM.

AH, NOW FOR IT. THEY SAID THEY'D LET US KNOW OUR DESTINATION AS SOON AS WE WERE OUT OF SIGHT OF LAND.

ALL THE PILOTS REPORTED BELOW —

YOUR DESTINATION IS MALTA. AS SOON AS WE'RE WITHIN FLYING RANGE OF THE ISLAND YOU WILL TAKE OFF FROM THIS DECK. AND BE CAREFUL — JUST REMEMBER HOW BADLY MALTA NEEDS YOU FOR ITS SURVIVAL. THAT IS ALL.

TO MALTA, FIGHTING FOR HER LIFE, STARVING, HER A.A. GUN BARRELS WORN SMOOTH AND HER GALLANT HURRICANES DWINDLING FAST, TWENTY-FIVE FIGHTING SPITFIRES WOULD BE LIKE A BLOOD TRANSFUSION.

THE COMMANDER (FLYING) NEXT READ OFF EACH PILOT'S NAME AND THE NUMBER OF THE AIRCRAFT TO WHICH HE WAS ASSIGNED. WHEN TOM SAW HIS SPITFIRE, THE SHOCK WAS ALMOST A PHYSICAL BLOW.

THE SWORD OF DAKPUR

R.B. 1660, THIS IS THE ONE. GREAT HEAVENS — THAT NAME! AND THE COLOUR...IT'S PAINTED COMPLETELY SILVER!

WHAT'S THE MATTER, CHUM?

TOM KNEW NOTHING OF THE AIRCREW SELECTION OFFICER'S ORDER THAT HE WAS TO FLY DAKPUR'S FIGHTER.

AND I THOUGHT IT WAS JUST A LOAD OF SUPERSTITIOUS HOGSWALLOP! THAT OLD MAN CONTROLS FORCES NEITHER YOU NOR I COULD EVER UNDERSTAND.

WHAT ON EARTH ARE YOU RAVING ABOUT?

BOB CAMPBELL STARED AT TOM. SURELY HE WASN'T GOING BOMB-HAPPY ALREADY?

IT'S A LONG STORY, BOB. LET'S TAKE A STROLL ALONG THE DECK AND I'LL TELL YOU ALL ABOUT IT.

TOM TOLD CAMPBELL EVERY LITTLE DETAIL OF THE AMAZING STORY FROM START TO FINISH.

THAT'S THE WHOLE STORY. U WAN PROPHESIED THAT I'D BECOME A PILOT AND FLY THIS PLANE. I'VE A FEELING THIS NECKLET HAS STRANGE POWERS OVER ME, BUT I FIND IT HARD TO BELIEVE THAT IT COULD ACTUALLY STOP A JERRY ON MY TAIL.

SAME HERE. STILL, YOU KEEP ON WEARING THE FLAMING THING. MAYBE SOME OF ITS LUCK WILL WEAR OFF ON ME.

EIGHT HUNDRED MILES EAST OF GIBRALTAR, THE FALCON, ESCORTED BY TWO DESTROYERS, PRESSED AHEAD AND LEFT THE PLODDING MERCHANT-MEN BEHIND. IT WAS JUST BEFORE SUNRISE WHEN THE TANNOYS CRACKLED, CALLING THE PILOTS TO THEIR PLANES FOR THE ATTEMPT TO REACH MALTA.

RED FLIGHT ONE — READY TO TAKE OFF. COME ON, BLUE FLIGHT ONE, GET THESE SPITS INTO POSITION READY TO FOLLOW. MOVE!

THE DECK OFFICER'S FLAG WHIPPED DOWN THE CHOCKS WERE PULLED CLEAR, AND WITH A BLASTING ROAR FROM HER MERLIN ENGINE THE FIRST SPITFIRE CLAWED HER WAY OFF THE STEEL DECK JUST AS THE SUN ROSE OVER THE SEA'S RIM.

ONE BY ONE THE SPITFIRES TAXIED FOR TAKE-OFF AND CLAWED SKYWARDS. THE FLIGHT DECK WAS CLEARED EXCEPT FOR ONE PLANE — THE LONE SILVER SPITFIRE.

CAN'T YOU FIND THE TROUBLE? COME ON, LET'S HAVE A LOOK AT IT.

SORRY, SIR. WE'LL HAVE TO CHANGE THE GLYCOL PUMP. IT'S HAD IT.

WHILE TOM FRETTED AND FUMED AROUND HIS PLANE, A LIEUTENANT REPORTED THE SITUATION TO THE BRIDGE.

AIRCRAFT FLOWN OFF, SIR, EXCEPT ONE — UNSERVICEABLE.

RIGHT, NUMBER ONE. LOOKS LIKE SHE'LL HAVE TO GO BACK TO U.K. WITH US. MASTER AT ARMS, SIGNAL FLOTILLA TO ALTER COURSE 180 DEGREES.

AYE AYE, SIR.

DESPITE THE HERCULEAN EFFORTS OF THE AERO-ENGINE FITTERS, MALTA WAS ALMOST A HUNDRED MILES OUT OF RANGE WHEN THE SWORD OF DAKPUR WAS FINALLY AIRWORTHY.

SHE'S OK NOW, SIR.

HUH, FAT LOT OF GOOD THAT IS NOW. THANKS, YOU DID ALL YOU COULD.

RADAR TO BRIDGE. UNIDENTIFIED AIRCRAFT APPROACHING. BEARING ZERO NINE EIGHT. HEIGHT — LESS THAN ONE HUNDRED FEET. RANGE — TEN MILES.

THE WARNING MESSAGE BROUGHT QUICK REACTION. ALARM BELLS CLANGED ALL OVER THE CARRIER AND GUN CREWS POUNDED MADLY TO MAN THE SLEEK GUNS.

HERE WE GO AGAIN. ONE OF THESE DAYS WE'LL GET HIT.

SIX BANDITS CLOSING FAST, BEARING ZERO NINE EIGHT. HEIGHT ZERO.

THE CRAFTY DEVILS — TRYING TO SLIP US SOME TORPEDOES.

THE ATTACKING PLANES WERE DORNIER 217s. THEY WERE SNEAKING IN AT WAVE-TOP HEIGHT TO TRY AND TORPEDO THE FALCON.

GOEBBELS SAID THE FALCON WAS SUNK. WE CANNOT LET THEM SAY HE IS A LIAR. SINK HER AT ALL COSTS!

THE CARRIER'S FIGHTERS, FULMARS, CUT TO A BARE MINIMUM TO MAKE ROOM FOR MALTA'S SPITFIRES, WERE TOO SLOW TO HOPE TO CATCH THE SPEEDING DORNIERS, BUT TOM'S SPITFIRE JUST HAPPENED TO HAVE HER ENGINE RUNNING FOR TEST WHEN THE ALARM CAME.

THE CAPTAIN WAS QUICK TO SEIZE THIS OPPORTUNITY TO FOIL THE FAST APPROACHING THREAT.

CAPTAIN TO SPITFIRE PILOT. IF YOUR ENGINE IS SERVICEABLE, TAKE OFF IMMEDIATELY TO INTERCEPT TORPEDO-BOMBERS ATTACKING ON THE STARBOARD BEAM.

YOU WON'T HAVE TO TELL ME TWICE, SKIPPER.

EVERY SECOND WAS VITAL. THERE WAS NO TIME TO PLUG IN HIS RADIO OR CLOSE HIS CANOPY. AS THE SLEEK SILVER SPITFIRE TORE SKYWARDS, TOM'S FLYING HELMET WAS TORN FROM HIS HEAD.

NOW LET'S HAVE YOU, YOU BLACK-CROSSED BUNCH OF SQUAREHEADS!

ALL TOM'S BOTTLED UP FRUSTRATION EXPLODED IN THE DARING FURY OF HIS ATTACK. THE NAZI RAIDERS SCATTERED WILDLY AS HIS GUNS TORE THE LEADING DORNIER TO PIECES. THE SILVER SPITFIRE HAD TASTED ITS FIRST BLOOD.

MEIN GOTT—HE IS A DEVIL!

WITHIN SECONDS TOM STRUCK AGAIN. LIKE A THUNDERCRASH HIS TWIN CANNONS SPOKE —

TWO DOWN, FOUR TO GO.

THE THIRD DORNIER WILTED UNDER A FEARSOME BROADSIDE FROM THE FALCON'S GUNS.

WE TORE 'EM UP PROPER.

SO DID THAT SPIT. GOOD OLD RAF.

CAPTAIN TO RADIO. TELL THE PILOT TO DITCH ALONG- SIDE. WE'LL PICK HIM UP BEFORE HE GETS HIS FEET WET.

SURPRISED AND SHAKEN BY THE VENOMOUS SKILL OF THE SPITFIRE PILOT AND THE TERRIFYING INTENSITY OF THE CARRIER'S FIRE, THE NAZIS' COURAGE BROKE AND THEY FLED FOR SICILY.

IT WAS IMPOSSIBLE TO LAND THE SPITFIRE BACK ON THE FALCON'S DECK SINCE IT HAD NO ARRESTER HOOK TO STOP IT.   THE CAPTAIN'S ORDER WAS THE ONLY ANSWER, BUT TOM HADN'T RECEIVED THE MESSAGE.   THE RADIO PLUG ATTACHED TO HIS FLYING HELMET WAS SINKING SLOWLY TO THE BED OF THE MEDITERRANEAN.

I CAN'T LAND, AND I'LL BE BLOWED IF I'M GOING TO DITCH HER. THEY TOLD US EVERY SPIT IS WORTH ITS WEIGHT IN GOLD IN MALTA, SO IT'S MALTA NEXT STOP.

IT WAS A CRAZY DECISION. TOM KNEW FULL WELL THAT MALTA WAS FAR BEYOND THE SPITFIRE'S RANGE.

THE FOOL WILL NEVER MAKE IT. HE'LL END UP IN THE DRINK, SILVER SPITFIRE AND ALL.

THE CARDS WERE STACKED HEAVILY AGAINST TOM. UNCERTAIN OF THE EXACT POSITION OF THE FALCON, HE ONLY HAD AN APPROXIMATE BEARING TO STEER. IF BY SOME MIRACLE HE EVER SAW LAND AGAIN, IT MIGHT NOT BE MALTA.

MY FUEL MUST BE RUNNING LOW NOW.

SOMEWHERE AROUND PANTELLARIA ISLAND, HE PICKED UP A TWENTY FIVE KNOT TAIL WIND. THE CLOCK REACHED, THEN PASSED THE DEADLINE AND STILL THE ENGINE ROARED STEADILY.

IT'S BEEN ON ZERO FOR THE LAST TWO MINUTES. THIS KITE MUST BE RUNNING ON FRESH AIR.

MALTA RADAR PICKED TOM UP AND HIS AUTOMATIC IDENTIFICATION SIGNAL BOUNCED BACK TO TELL THEM HE WAS 'FRIENDLY'. THEY CALLED HIM IMMEDIATELY.

THIS IS TIMER CALLING. STEER 080. LOSE HEIGHT AT 250 PER MINUTE THEN ORBIT. ENEMY RAID IN PROGRESS. DO NOT ANSWER — REPEAT DO NOT ANSWER. OUT.

BUT TOM RECEIVED NO MESSAGE. HIS HEADSET HAD BEEN LOST ON TAKE-OFF. HE HEADED ON TOWARDS THE VIOLET STREAK AHEAD ON THE HORIZON WHICH WAS MALTA, THE TINY ISLAND THAT THE MIGHT OF GERMAN AND ITALIAN AIR FLEETS COULD NOT SUBDUE. SUDDENLY THE HUNGRY CARBURETTOR GULPED AWAY THE LAST DROPS OF FUEL SLOSHING AROUND IN THE BOTTOM OF THE TANKS.

OH-OH. IT HAD TO COME. SUPPOSE I'D BETTER GET OUT AND PUSH.

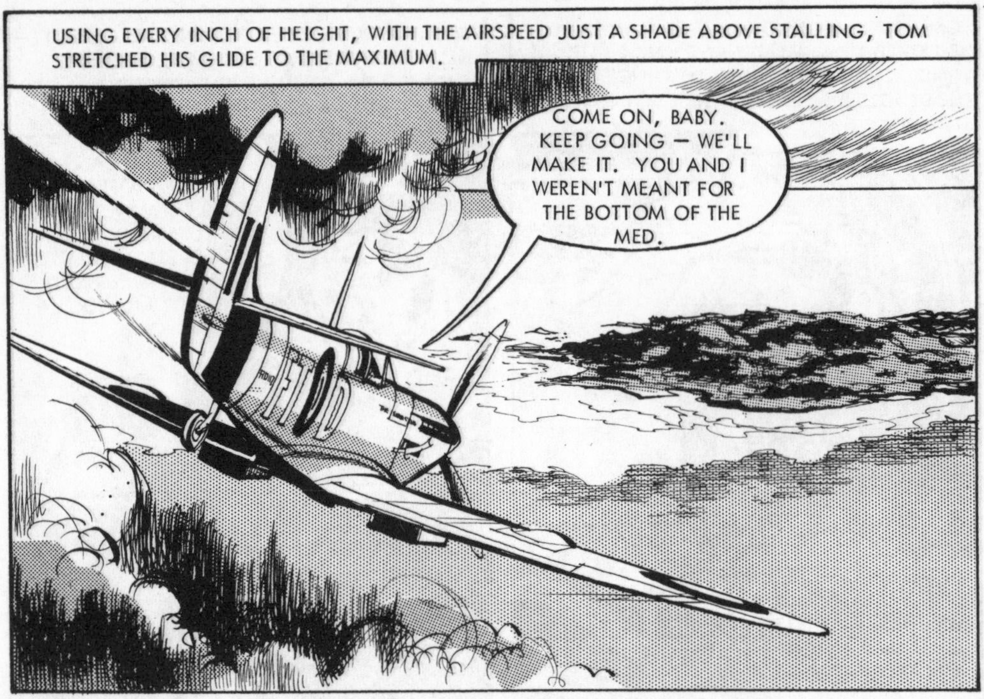
USING EVERY INCH OF HEIGHT, WITH THE AIRSPEED JUST A SHADE ABOVE STALLING, TOM STRETCHED HIS GLIDE TO THE MAXIMUM.
COME ON, BABY. KEEP GOING – WE'LL MAKE IT. YOU AND I WEREN'T MEANT FOR THE BOTTOM OF THE MED.

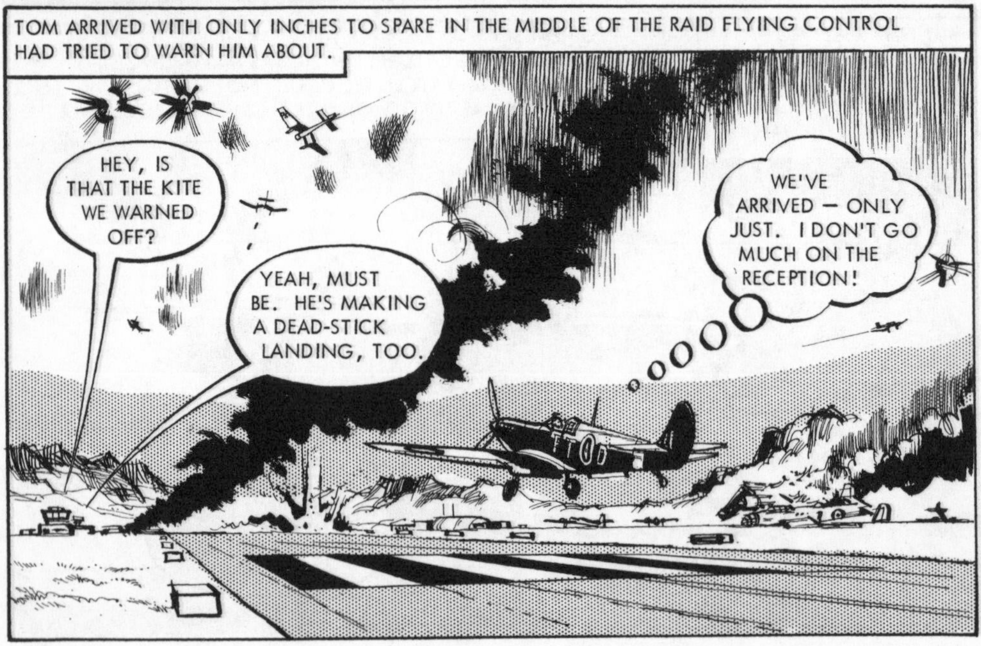
TOM ARRIVED WITH ONLY INCHES TO SPARE IN THE MIDDLE OF THE RAID FLYING CONTROL HAD TRIED TO WARN HIM ABOUT.
HEY, IS THAT THE KITE WE WARNED OFF?
YEAH, MUST BE. HE'S MAKING A DEAD-STICK LANDING, TOO.
WE'VE ARRIVED – ONLY JUST. I DON'T GO MUCH ON THE RECEPTION!

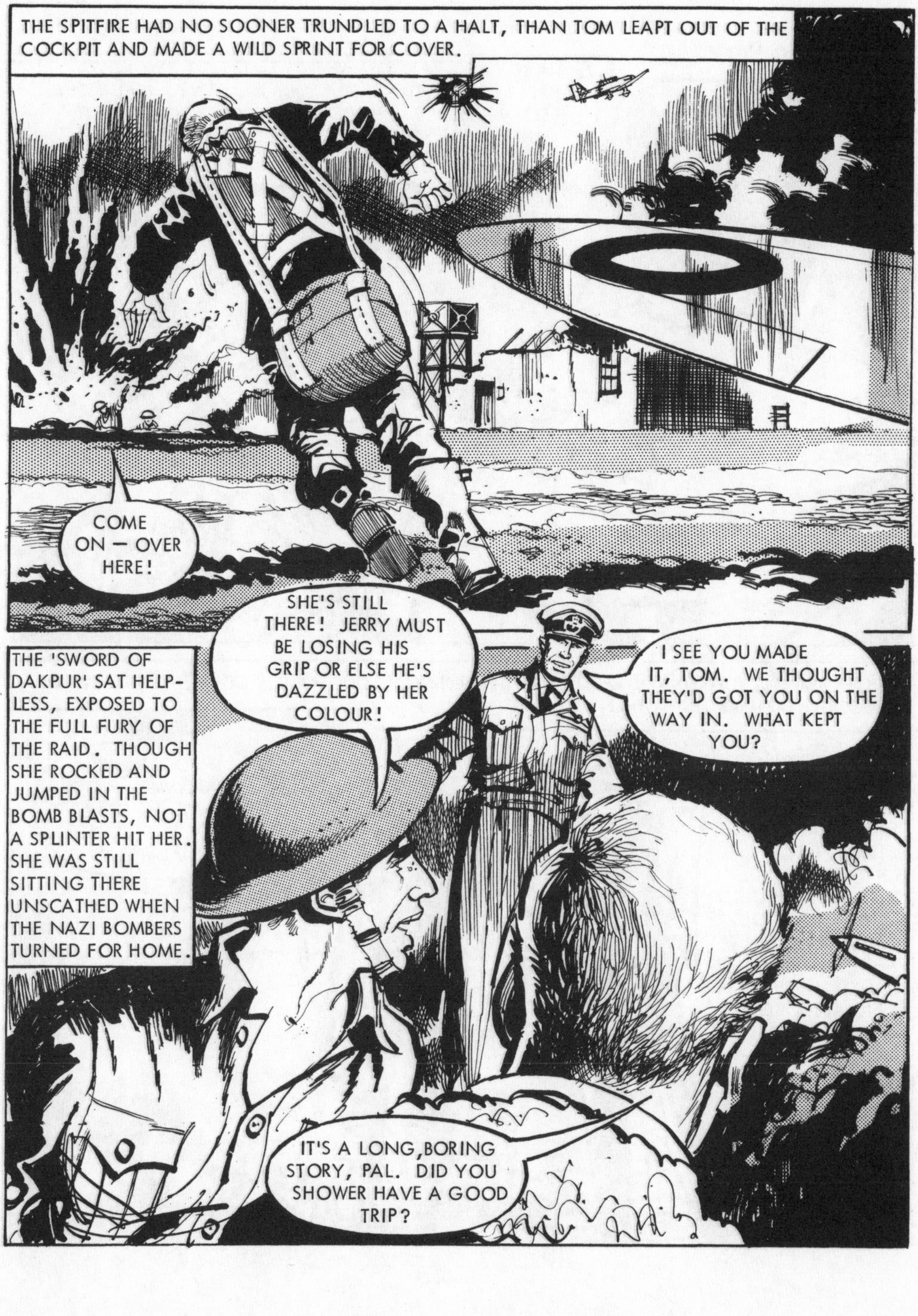
THE SPITFIRE HAD NO SOONER TRUNDLED TO A HALT, THAN TOM LEAPT OUT OF THE COCKPIT AND MADE A WILD SPRINT FOR COVER.
COME ON — OVER HERE!
THE 'SWORD OF DAKPUR' SAT HELPLESS, EXPOSED TO THE FULL FURY OF THE RAID. THOUGH SHE ROCKED AND JUMPED IN THE BOMB BLASTS, NOT A SPLINTER HIT HER. SHE WAS STILL SITTING THERE UNSCATHED WHEN THE NAZI BOMBERS TURNED FOR HOME.
SHE'S STILL THERE! JERRY MUST BE LOSING HIS GRIP OR ELSE HE'S DAZZLED BY HER COLOUR!
I SEE YOU MADE IT, TOM. WE THOUGHT THEY'D GOT YOU ON THE WAY IN. WHAT KEPT YOU?
IT'S A LONG, BORING STORY, PAL. DID YOU SHOWER HAVE A GOOD TRIP?

BOB CAMPBELL'S EYES NARROWED. HE HAD ALREADY TASTED THE BITTERNESS OF WAR IN THE SKIES ABOVE MALTA.

THERE WAS A RAID ON WHEN WE ARRIVED. WE LOST THREE SPITS FIGHTING OUR WAY IN. IT WAS REAL DICEY GETTING DOWN. THEY SAID THIS WAS ONE OF THEIR QUIET DAYS, SO I HOPE I'M NOT AROUND WHEN IT REALLY GETS TOUGH!

BOB CAMPBELL TURNED AND LED TOM UP THE RUNWAY TO A TANGLE OF WRECKAGE, BARELY RECOGNISABLE AS THAT OF AN AIRCRAFT.

THAT WAS THE RESERVE KITE WHICH TOOK YOUR PLACE. JERRY PRANGED IT WITH A FIVE HUNDRED POUNDER JUST AS IT TOUCHED DOWN. POOR OLD SMITH NEVER KNEW WHAT HIT HIM. SOMETHING'S LOOK-ING AFTER YOU ALL RIGHT.

IT LOOKS LIKE IT, ANYWAY. LOOK, I'LL NEED TO GO AND CHECK IN. I'LL SEE YOU LATER.

TOM TURNED AWAY AND MADE FOR THE CREW DUG-OUT.

IF MY ENGINE HADN'T GONE SOUR ON THE FALCON, IF THAT TAIL WIND HADN'T COME UP, IF SOMEBODY HADN'T OVERFILLED BOTH TANKS – IT MUST HAVE BEEN THAT – I'D HAVE BOUGHT IT. AS LONG AS I WEAR THE NECKLET, THEY CAN'T TOUCH ME, IT SEEMS.

INSIDE, TOM SET ABOUT TAKING OFF HIS GEAR –

I SEE THEY'VE GIVEN BOB 'B' FLIGHT AND TUG WILSON'S LEADING 'A'...

BUT TOM DIDN'T EVEN HAVE TIME TO DUMP HIS PARACHUTE WHEN THE STRIDENT CLANG OF THE ALARM-WARNING OF ENEMY RAIDERS   SENT THE PILOTS IN THE DUG-OUT EXPLODING INTO ACTION.

THEY DON'T GET ANY PEACE HERE! STILL, I MANAGED TO BORROW THIS HELMET.

TEN ME109's STREAKED ACROSS THE AIRFIELD, GUNS BLAZING. TOM RACED FOR HIS SPITFIRE. IT HAD ALREADY BEEN REFUELLED AND REARMED AT TOP SPEED.

A BIT TOO CLOSE FOR COMFORT!

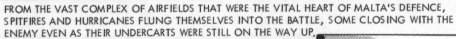

FROM THE VAST COMPLEX OF AIRFIELDS THAT WERE THE VITAL HEART OF MALTA'S DEFENCE, SPITFIRES AND HURRICANES FLUNG THEMSELVES INTO THE BATTLE, SOME CLOSING WITH THE ENEMY EVEN AS THEIR UNDERCARTS WERE STILL ON THE WAY UP.

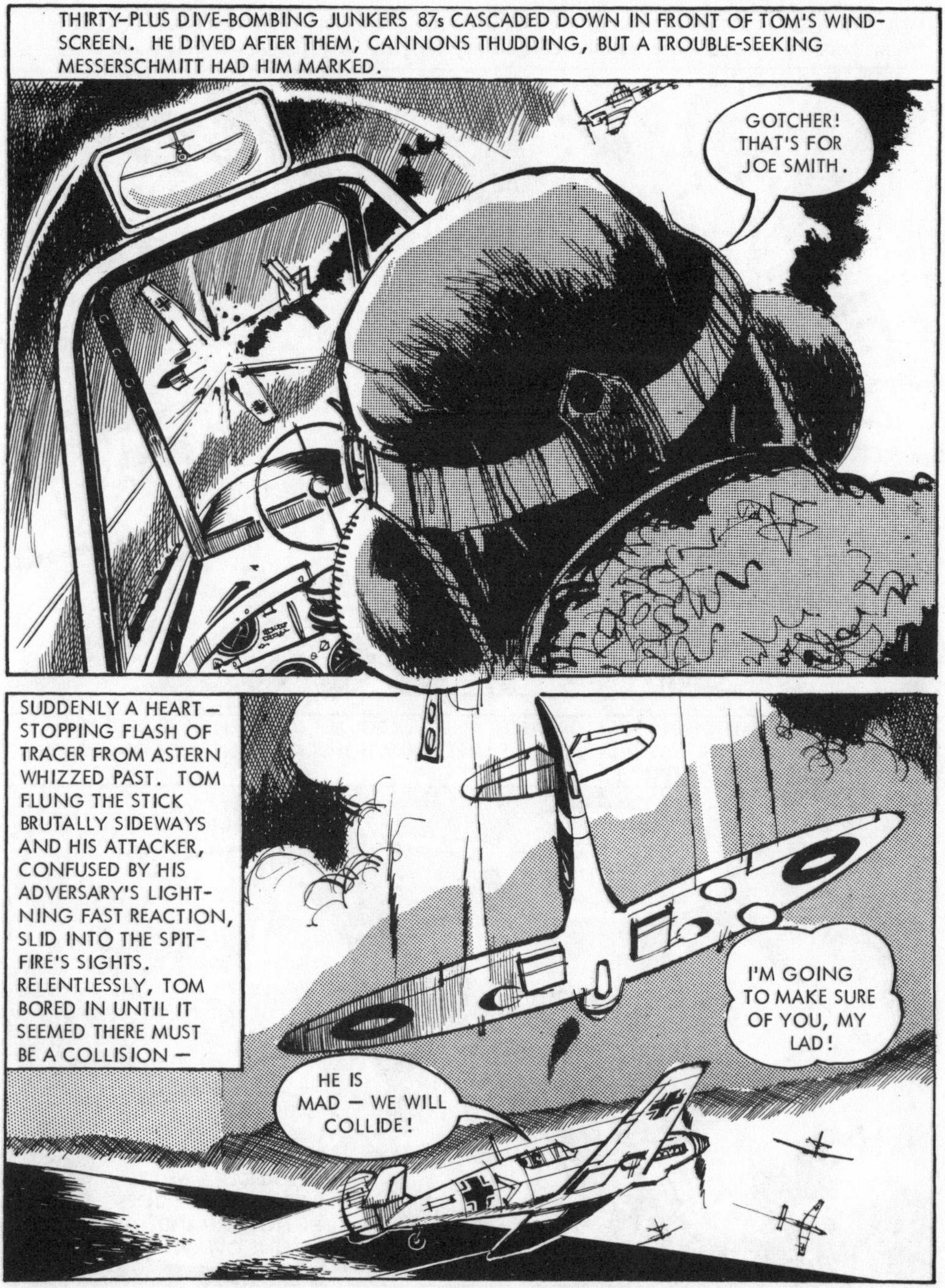
THIRTY-PLUS DIVE-BOMBING JUNKERS 87s CASCADED DOWN IN FRONT OF TOM'S WINDSCREEN. HE DIVED AFTER THEM, CANNONS THUDDING, BUT A TROUBLE-SEEKING MESSERSCHMITT HAD HIM MARKED.
GOTCHER! THAT'S FOR JOE SMITH.
SUDDENLY A HEART-STOPPING FLASH OF TRACER FROM ASTERN WHIZZED PAST. TOM FLUNG THE STICK BRUTALLY SIDEWAYS AND HIS ATTACKER, CONFUSED BY HIS ADVERSARY'S LIGHTNING FAST REACTION, SLID INTO THE SPITFIRE'S SIGHTS. RELENTLESSLY, TOM BORED IN UNTIL IT SEEMED THERE MUST BE A COLLISION —
I'M GOING TO MAKE SURE OF YOU, MY LAD!
HE IS MAD — WE WILL COLLIDE!

AT THE LAST POSSIBLE MOMENT TOM JAMMED HIS THUMB ON THE FIRING BUTTON. THE M.E.109 DISSOLVED INTO TUMBLING FRAGMENTS. THE SPITFIRE BUCKED LIKE A MULE IN THE TEARING BLAST.

WITHOUT ANY HESITATION TOM TORE AFTER ANOTHER BOMBER, BUT WHEN HE PRESSED THE BUTTON ALL HE HEARD WAS THE CLANG OF EMPTY BREECH BLOCKS — AND THE CONDEMNED JUNKERS WAS GIVEN A REPRIEVE.

AW HECK, I'M CLEAN OUT OF AMMO. I'LL HAVE TO TURN BACK.

HIMMEL! I CANNOT SHAKE OFF THIS ACCURSED ENGLANDER. WE ARE DOOMED. WHY DOES HE NOT FIRE AND GET IT OVER?

AS HE BANKED SHARPLY OUT OF THE BATTLE, TOM HEARD THE DESPAIRING CALL OF A MAN STARING DEATH IN THE FACE. IT WAS HIS FLIGHT COMMANDER, TUG WILSON.

DESPERATELY TOM DIVED, HOPING SOMEHOW TO DISTRACT THE SAVAGE ATTACKS OF THE NAZIS BUT IT WAS TOO LATE. LIKE KILLER WOLVES THEY SHEERED OFF IN TRIUMPH FROM THE HOLOCAUST OF FLAME THAT BLOSSOMED UNDER THEIR THUDDING CANNONS.

STILL SHAKEN BY THE SHOCK, TOM MADE A HEAVY LANDING.

WELL DONE, TOM. I SAW YOU DOWN TWO. HEY, WHAT'S UP, ARE YOU HIT?

NO, BOB. IT'S TUG. THEY GANGED UP ON HIM AND TORE HIM TO PIECES. I HEARD HIM YELLING FOR HELP BUT MY AMMO WAS GONE.

THAT NIGHT, AS TOM LAY IN HIS BUNK IN THE DUG-OUT LISTENING TO CRASH OF BOMBS AND THE DRUM-ROLL OF THE GUNS OVER BY VALETTA, BOB CAMPBELL ENTERED.

THE LATEST GEN, TOM. YOU'RE PROMOTED TO LEAD A FLIGHT.

LESS KIDDING, MATE. I'VE JUST ARRIVED.

BECAUSE OF THE CHRONIC SHORTAGE OF MEN AND MACHINES, WHEN A MAN WAS KILLED SOMEONE ELSE HAD TO TAKE HIS PLACE. THEY DIDN'T CALL IT PROMOTION, BUT 'DEAD MEN'S SHOES'. SO TOM, STILL FRESH FROM TRAINING SCHOOL, FOUND HIMSELF A FLIGHT LIEUTENANT.

DON'T GET ON TO ME, MATE. IT'S THE C.O.'S ORDER, AND HE MUST THINK YOU'VE GOT WHAT IT TAKES. ANYWAY, BETWEEN YOU AND ME, I THINK IT'S THAT NECKLET YOU'VE GOT ROUND YOUR NECK.

WHAT'S THAT GOT TO DO WITH IT?

THE TROUBLE WITH BOB CAMPBELL WAS YOU COULD NEVER BE SURE WHEN HE WAS KIDDING OR NOT.

YOU TOLD ME THAT OLD GEEZER IN BURMA SAID YOU'D BE CHIEF OF THE FLYING MACHINES OR SOMETHING. FOR MY MONEY, I'D SAY THAT'D BE A SQUADRON LEADER.

AH, CUT IT OUT, BOB.

BOB LEFT, BUT HIS BANTERING WORDS WENT ROUND AND ROUND IN TOM'S BRAIN. HE KNEW THE ONLY WAY HE'D BECOME C.O. WOULD BE THROUGH THE DEATH OF HIS FRIENDS.

THAT MEANS BOB AND THE OTHER SUPERIOR OFFICERS WILL ALL GET THE CHOP. WHAT A HECK OF A PROSPECT! WHY COULDN'T U WAN HAVE KEPT HIS FLAMING NECKLET TO HIMSELF?

SO THE BATTLE WENT ON. AT TIMES THE NUMBER OF SERVICEABLE FIGHTERS WAS DOWN TO SIX. YET STILL THEY FOUGHT ON, REFUSING TO BE BEATEN.

ANOTHER PLANE TO ADD TO MY SCORE.

THE SWORD OF DAKPUR BECAME THE TERROR OF THE ENEMY. TOM, IT SEEMED, WAS BENT ON SUICIDE. HE FOUGHT LIKE A CORNERED MADMAN.

TOM OFTEN THOUGHT OF THROWING AWAY THE NECKLET, BUT NEVER ACTUALLY DID IT. HE FORGOT ABOUT IT UNTIL ONE DAY THEY WERE DETAILED TO ESCORT IN THE PRECIOUS SURVIVORS OF A BADLY MAULED CONVOY.

AT LAST IT LOOKS LIKE SOME SHIPS WILL MAKE IT. BY THUNDER, I TAKE OFF MY NUMBER ONE HAT TO THESE MATELOTS. IT MUST BE MURDER OUT THERE IN BOMB ALLEY. IT'S STINKING WITH JUNKERS AND DORNIERS.

BE CAREFUL, BOB, FOR PETE'S SAKE. I WISH I WAS COMING, BUT THE ERKS ARE STILL WORKING ON MY MACHINE FROM THE LAST DOGFIGHT.

TOM FELT A VAGUE UNEASINESS — A SENSE OF IMPENDING DISASTER. HE COULDN'T EXPLAIN IT, ONLY WARN BOB OF WHAT HE FELT.

WHAT THE HECK DO YOU TAKE ME FOR? D'YOU THINK I'D CRY OFF BECAUSE IT COULD BE A SHAKY DO? FORGET IT. I CAN LOOK OUT FOR MYSELF.

SEVEN SPITFIRES ROARED SEAWARDS, AND THE HOPES AND FEARS OF ALL ON THE ISLAND WENT WITH THEM. THE NEWS OF THE APPROACHING SHIPS HAD SPREAD LIKE WILDFIRE, LIGHTING UP THE LEAN FACES AND HOLLOW EYES OF SERVICEMEN AND CIVILIANS ALIKE.

GOD GO WITH THEM.

THE AIR RAID SIRENS WERE QUIET. FOR THE FIRST TIME IN MANY WEEKS THE SKIES OVER THE ISLAND WERE CLEAR OF ENEMY AIRCRAFT.

WHAT'S HAPPENED TO JERRY? IS HE HAVING A HOLIDAY OR SUMMAT?

MUST BE ADOLF'S BIRTHDAY. A BIG, DIRTY TORPEDO'S A GOOD PRESENT FOR HIM, I RECKON.

THERE WAS A MORE SINISTER REASON, AS THE SEVEN DISCOVERED AFTER THEY JOINED THE AIR UMBRELLA OVER THE LIMPING, BATTERED SHIPS.

THE AIR WAS FULL OF TUMBLING, DIVING PLANES. A SQUADRON OF CORKSCREW-NOSED MESSERSCHMITTS DIVED TOWARDS THE VALIANT SEVEN. OUTNUMBERED FOUR TO ONE, THEY TURNED TO MEET THE VICIOUS ONSLAUGHT HEAD ON.

AS THE TIME PASSED, TOM SWEATED IT OUT, WAITING ANXIOUSLY FOR ANY NEWS OF THE SAVAGE AIR BATTLE. THEN TWO BATTERED SPITS CAME INTO THE CIRCUIT AND LANDED SHAKILY. THEY WERE PILOTED BY TWO SPROG PILOTS POSTED TO MALTA ONLY A WEEK AGO.

ONLY TWO? WHO ARE THEY?

TARRANT AND MITCHISON. LOOKS LIKE THEY'VE HAD A REAL DOING OVER. THERE'S STILL TIME TO SPARE, THOUGH. THE OTHERS SHOULD BE BACK SHORTLY.

BUT THERE WAS TO BE ONLY ONE MORE SHATTERED AND SMOKING SPITFIRE TO STAGGER DRUNKENLY TOWARDS THE RUNWAY.

IT'S BOB, AND HE'S IN DEAD TROUBLE!

COME ON, YOU BODS — MOVE. IT'S A PILE UP!

THERE WAS A GRINDING SCREECH OF TORTURED METAL AS THE RUINED FIGHTER SMASHED A WINGTIP INTO THE TARMAC AND CARTWHEELED TO FINAL DESTRUCTION.

FRANTICALLY TOM TRIED TO REACH HIS TRAPPED FRIEND, BUT THE HEAT DROVE HIM BACK. THEN HE SAW CAMPBELL STRUGGLING TO FREE HIMSELF AS THE ASBESTOS CLAD FIREMAN DASHED FORWARD TO ASSIST HIM.

MIRACULOUSLY, BOB CAMPBELL SURVIVED WITH ONLY TORN LIGAMENTS IN HIS LEFT LEG. HE WAS SOON HOBBLING ABOUT THE AIRFIELD.

ALL THE OTHERS DEAD, AND IT WAS MY FAULT. IF I'D GOT RID OF THAT NECKLET THEY'D STILL BE ALIVE.

DON'T TALK DAFT. WE TOOK ON THIRTY JERRY CRATES AND KEPT 'EM OCCUPIED WHILE THE OTHER SQUADRONS TORE UP THE BOMBERS.

IF YOU KNEW YOU WERE BEING CONTROLLED BY SOMETHING THAT KILLED OFF ALL YOUR MATES SO YOU COULD GET TO THE TOP, WOULDN'T YOU FEEL SICK? DON'T YOU REALISE, YOU'RE THE NEXT ONE?

LOOK, I'M GROUNDED WITH THIS LEG. YOUR PROMOTION TO SQUADRON LEADER HAS COME THROUGH, SO FORGET ABOUT THE NECKLET OR I'LL BUST YOU ONE.

THE NEWS THAT HE HAD BEEN PROMOTED TO SQUADRON LEADER CAME AS A SHOCK TO TOM. CAMPBELL'S TOUGH ANSWER HAD GIVEN HIM THE JOLT HE NEEDED TO FORGET ABOUT HIS TROUBLES.

HE'S RIGHT, BLAST HIM. IT WAS JERRY BULLETS AND NOTHING ELSE THAT KILLED THE OTHERS. IF I'M TO LEAD THIS SQUAD-RON, BY THUNDER, JERRY'S GOING TO PAY. AS FOR U WAN, HE CAN FIND SOMEBODY ELSE. I'M HAVING NO PART OF HIS CAPER ANY MORE.

BOB CAMPBELL WAITED UNTIL HIS FRIEND WAS OUT OF SIGHT THEN HE HOBBLED OVER TO THE RUBBLE HEAP WHERE THE DISCARDED NECKLET LAY GLEAMING IN THE SUN.

AH, HERE IT IS. CAN'T HAVE TOM LOSING HIS TALISMAN.

PAINFULLY BOB CAMPBELL APPROACHED THE SILVER SPITFIRE AND PULLED HIMSELF UP ON THE WING.

THERE, HE'LL NEVER FIND IT, YET IT WILL ALWAYS FLY WITH HIM.

MAP STOWAGE

NEXT DAY, TOM WAS TOLD FORMALLY OF HIS PROMOTION TO SQUADRON LEADER. AS HE LED HIS FIGHTERS INTO BATTLE FOR THE FIRST TIME, HE SAW BOB WAVE FROM BELOW ON THE RUNWAY.

GOOD LUCK, OLD SON.

TOM NEVER SAW BOB CAMPBELL ALIVE AGAIN. A BURST OF BULLETS FROM A GROUND-STRAFING MESSERSCHMITT KILLED HIM TEN MINUTES LATER.

THE WAR WENT ON AND THE BATTLE OF MALTA WAS WON. NO LONGER DOMINATED BY HIS OBSESSION, TOM LED HIS FLYERS THROUGH THE SICILIAN CAMPAIGN AND INTO THE BITTER SLOGGING MATCH IN ITALY. HIS BITTER FURY STRUCK FEAR INTO ENEMY HEARTS WHENEVER THEY SAW THE SILVER SHAPE OF "THE SWORD OF DAKPUR."

IT IS THE ACCURSED SWORD OF DAKPUR! JETTISON BOMBS. HE LEADS HIS SQUADRON LIKE A MADMAN.

KNOCK 'EM DOWN, FAST!

THE SWORD OF DAKPUR.

BUT LITTLE DID TOM KNOW THAT EVERY TIME HE FLEW INTO ACTION, THE HIDDEN NECKLET WHICH HE THOUGHT TO BE BURIED IN A MALTESE AIRFIELD, WAS WITHIN A HAND'S REACH FROM HIM.

NEW AND MORE DEADLY SPITFIRES JOINED THE GROWING MIGHT OF THE ALLIED AIR FORCES IN ITALY. IT WAS DECIDED THAT TOM'S VETERAN SPITFIRES WERE TO BE TRANSFERRED TO THE FAR EASTERN THEATRE OF WAR.

WELL, SHAW, YOUR ORDERS HAVE COME THROUGH. YOU TAKE OFF AT DAWN FOR CHITTAGONG WHERE YOUR SQUADRON WILL JOIN EASTERN AIR COMMAND. YOUR ROUTE IS OUTLINED HERE.

SIGNALS

I'M ON MY WAY BACK, AS A LEADER, JUST AS U WAN SAID. IT LOOKS LIKE CHUCKING AWAY HIS NECKLET DIDN'T CHANGE THINGS VERY MUCH AT ALL.

WITH LONG RANGE TANKS FITTED, THE SPITFIRES COVERED THE LONG JOURNEY IN EIGHT DAYS, STAYING OVERNIGHT AT STAGING POSTS WHERE FUEL AND FACILITIES WERE AVAILABLE.

THE OLD HURRIES WERE PRETTY HARD PUSHED AGAINST THE ZEROS, BUT WITH THESE WE SHOULD MAKE RINGS ROUND 'EM.

GLAD WE AIN'T GOIN' BY CAMEL TRAIN. THERE'S NEARLY A THOUSAND MILES O' NOTHIN' BEFORE WE HIT BASRA.

THE JAPS WERE ON THE RUN BY THE TIME TOM AND HIS MEN REACHED CHITTAGONG.

THIS PLACE IS AS HOT AS A FURNACE. I COULD DO WITH A LONG, ICE-COLD DRINK.

YOU'VE HAD THAT, SIR. EVEN THE BEER'S AT SEVENTY-FIVE DEGREES.

THE GROUND STAFF FOLLOWED BY AIR TRANSPORT AND WITHIN A COUPLE OF DAYS THE SQUADRON WAS BATTLING AGAINST AN ENEMY EVEN MORE RUTHLESS THAN THE NAZIS. THEY LEARNED THE BITTER CRAFT OF DEALING WITH THE SAVAGE ZEROS THE HARD WAY.

I CAN'T SHAKE HIM OFF! HE'S TOO FAST — AAGH!

DIVE, MAN. DIVE, BEFORE IT'S TOO LATE! BLAST IT, THEY'VE GOT HIM.

THE SWORD OF DAKP

TOM AND HIS PILOTS HAD HAD A HARD TIME IN EUROPE. THEY HAD COME EAST TO FIGHT THE JAPS, THINKING IT WOULD BE AN EASY JOB, DESPITE ALL THEIR C.O.'s WARNINGS TO THE CONTRARY.

PARKER BOUGHT IT TODAY BECAUSE HE TRIED TO MIX IT WITH A ZERO. THESE BABIES CAN OUT-FLY, OUTCLIMB AND OUTMANOEUVRE US, BUT WHERE WE HAVE THEM IS IN A DIVE. I'VE TOLD YOU ALL THIS BEFORE, SURELY NOW IT HAS SUNK IN.

MEANWHILE DESTINY NOW TOOK A STRANGE TURN. THOUSANDS OF MILES AWAY, IN WASHINGTON, U.S.A., AMERICAN INTELLIGENCE, USING A CAPTURED JAPANESE CODE, MONITORED AN ENEMY RADIO MESSAGE.

WELL, HOW NICE FOR YOU, HASHI, OLD PAL. I HOPE YOU HAVE A ROUGH TRIP. HEY, WAIT A MINUTE — THIS COULD BE USEFUL.

RADIO MESSAGE SLIP

7CM 1004.

'78/CM/R4.

1100 HRS. 17 JULY 1943

GEN. HASHIDA.

NIPPONESE COMMANDER N.W. BURMA. WILL LEAVE BANGKOK WITH STAFF IN TWO MITSUBISHI BOMBERS FOR THABAUK AIRSTRIP OBJECT — TOUR OF INSPECTION.

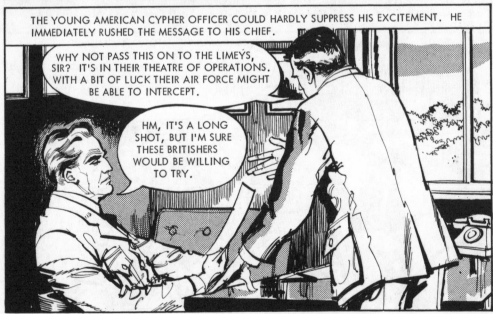

THE YOUNG AMERICAN CYPHER OFFICER COULD HARDLY SUPPRESS HIS EXCITEMENT. HE IMMEDIATELY RUSHED THE MESSAGE TO HIS CHIEF.

WHY NOT PASS THIS ON TO THE LIMEYS, SIR? IT'S IN THEIR THEATRE OF OPERATIONS. WITH A BIT OF LUCK THEIR AIR FORCE MIGHT BE ABLE TO INTERCEPT.

HM, IT'S A LONG SHOT, BUT I'M SURE THESE BRITISHERS WOULD BE WILLING TO TRY.

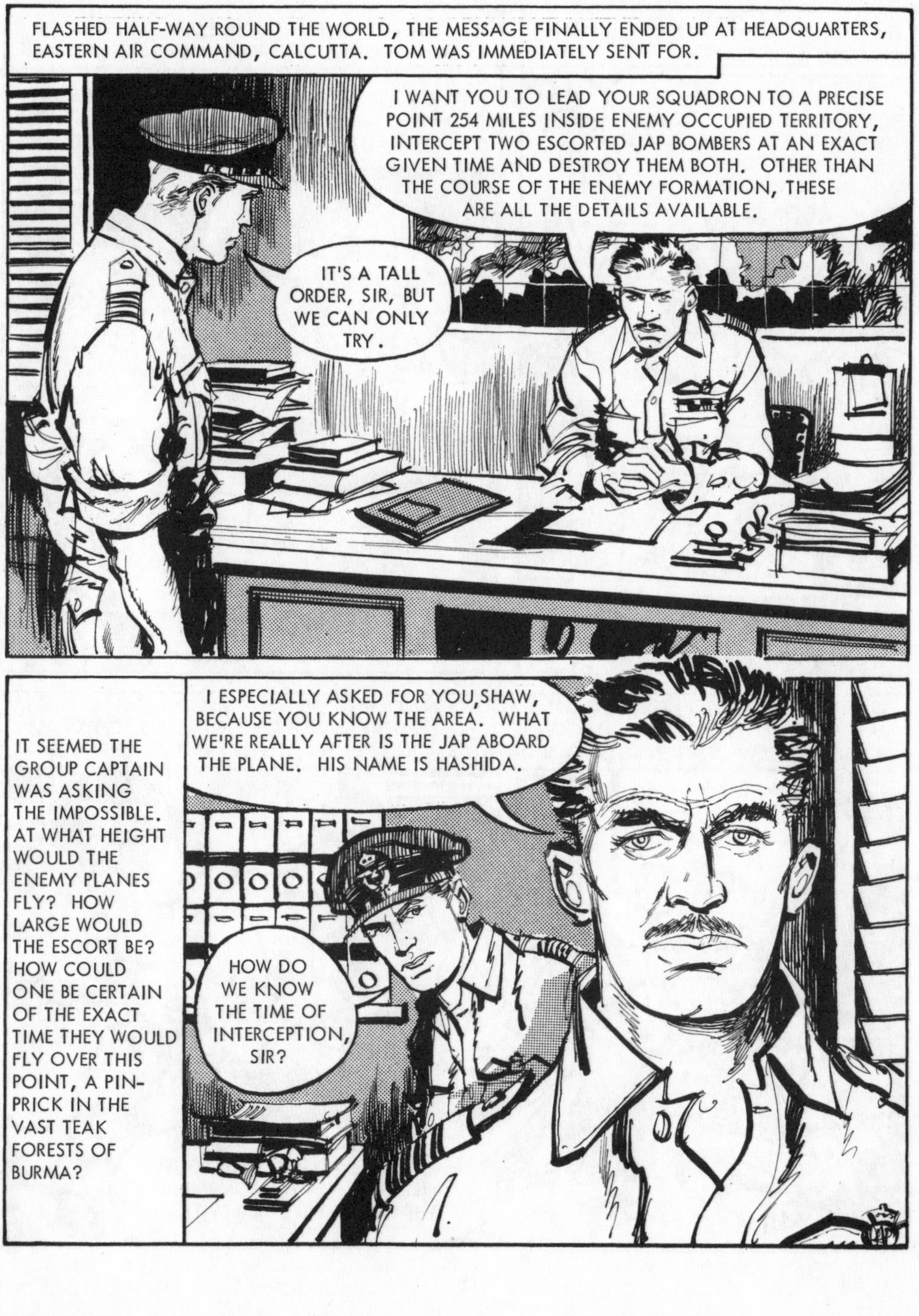
FLASHED HALF-WAY ROUND THE WORLD, THE MESSAGE FINALLY ENDED UP AT HEADQUARTERS, EASTERN AIR COMMAND, CALCUTTA. TOM WAS IMMEDIATELY SENT FOR.
I WANT YOU TO LEAD YOUR SQUADRON TO A PRECISE POINT 254 MILES INSIDE ENEMY OCCUPIED TERRITORY, INTERCEPT TWO ESCORTED JAP BOMBERS AT AN EXACT GIVEN TIME AND DESTROY THEM BOTH. OTHER THAN THE COURSE OF THE ENEMY FORMATION, THESE ARE ALL THE DETAILS AVAILABLE.
IT'S A TALL ORDER, SIR, BUT WE CAN ONLY TRY.
IT SEEMED THE GROUP CAPTAIN WAS ASKING THE IMPOSSIBLE. AT WHAT HEIGHT WOULD THE ENEMY PLANES FLY? HOW LARGE WOULD THE ESCORT BE? HOW COULD ONE BE CERTAIN OF THE EXACT TIME THEY WOULD FLY OVER THIS POINT, A PIN-PRICK IN THE VAST TEAK FORESTS OF BURMA?
I ESPECIALLY ASKED FOR YOU,SHAW, BECAUSE YOU KNOW THE AREA. WHAT WE'RE REALLY AFTER IS THE JAP ABOARD THE PLANE. HIS NAME IS HASHIDA.
HOW DO WE KNOW THE TIME OF INTERCEPTION, SIR?

THE GROUP CAPTAIN MOVED OVER TO A WALL MAP OF BURMA —

THE JAPS HAVE A FETISH FOR PUNCTUALITY, ESPECIALLY HASHIDA, THE MAN WE'RE AFTER. HERE IS YOUR POINT OF INTERCEPTION.

TOM GASPED AS HE READ THE NAME. HE SAW IN A FLASH THAT ALL THAT HAD HAPPENED, AND WAS GOING TO HAPPEN TO HIM, WAS LIKE A GIGANTIC JIG-SAW PUZZLE WHICH WAS NOW COMPLETE. TWO YEARS AGO, SOME MYSTERIOUS POWER HAD GIVEN OLD U WAN THE POWER TO FORESEE THIS.

DAKPUR.

DAKPUR! SO THIS IS THE WAY IT WORKS OUT. I WAS A FOOL FOR BELIEVING I COULD CHANGE THINGS BY CHUCKING AWAY THAT NECKLET.

TOM HURRIED BACK TO HIS SQUADRON. FOURTEEN VOLUNTEERS WERE CALLED FOR AND EVERY MAN JACK STEPPED FORWARD. THOSE NOT CHOSEN WERE OBVIOUSLY GOING TO SCREAM BLUE MURDER, SO TOM ORDERED LOTS TO BE DRAWN AMONG THE SEVENTEEN MOST EXPERIENCED PILOTS.

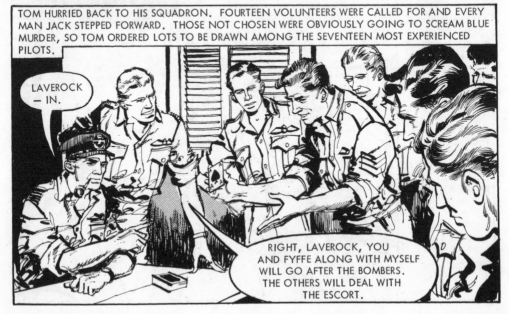

LAVEROCK — IN.

RIGHT, LAVEROCK, YOU AND FYFFE ALONG WITH MYSELF WILL GO AFTER THE BOMBERS. THE OTHERS WILL DEAL WITH THE ESCORT.

NEXT MORNING   FOURTEEN SPITFIRES, LED BY THE DEADLY SILVER SPITFIRE, CLIMBED SHARPLY OVER CHITTAGONG, THEIR SLIPSTREAMS TEARING THE EARLY MORNING MISTS TO SHREDS, THEIR SONG OF POWER ECHOING BACK FROM THE PALACES AND HOVELS OF THE TEEMING CITY.

IF YOU ASK ME, THEY'RE ALL ROUND THE BEND. THEY'LL NEVER PULL IT OFF. BESIDES, THAT AREA'S STINKING WITH ZEROS.

AH, BELT UP. YOU KNOW AS WELL AS I DO, THAT WE'RE JUST ITCHING TO BE GOING OUR- SELVES.

THE DENSE TANGLE OF JUNGLE BENEATH WAS A MONOTONOUS GREEN CARPET WHICH COVERED HILLS AND VALLEYS ALIKE. OCCASIONALLY THERE WAS A JUTTING CRAG OR A CLUSTER OF HUTS. AS THEY APPROACHED THE POINT OF INTER- CEPTION, TOM BEGAN TO IDENTIFY CERTAIN FEATURES HE HAD REMEMBERED FROM HIS EARLIER DAYS.

BUCKSKIN LEADER CALLING. FIFTEEN MINUTES TO OBJECTIVE.

MEANWHILE, IN DAKPUR, THE YOKE OF THE JAPANESE INVADERS HAD GROWN HEAVIER AND HEAVIER AS THE MONTHS PASSED. WITH NO NEWS OF THE WAR EXCEPT THAT WHICH THE JAPS WANTED THEM TO HEAR, MANY OF THE PEOPLE DESPAIRED OF EVER KNOWING FREEDOM AGAIN.

WE MUST NEVER GIVE UP HOPE, MY SON.

HOPE? WE HAVE LOST ALL OUR HOPE, U WAN. DAILY, THE NIPPONESE GRIND US UNDER THEIR BOOTS. IT GOES ON AND ON, AS IF IT WILL NEVER END.

THERE WAS A SUDDEN THUNDEROUS ROAR OVERHEAD. ALL HEADS CRANED UPWARDS AT U WAN'S JOYOUS SHOUT AS THE SPITFIRES, LED BY "THE SWORD OF DAKPUR", FLEW OVERHEAD.

THERE IS YOUR ANSWER — LOOK! THEY HAVE RETURNED.

ENGLISH FLYERS! SHOOT THEM DOWN.

TOM ORGANISED HIS MEN FOR THE ATTACK —

MY SECTION, ORBIT THE VILLAGE. THE REST CLIMB FOR CLOUD COVER AND KEEP YOUR EYES PEELED.

AS HE WAITED FOR WORD FROM THE SEARCHING SPITFIRES ABOVE, TOM GLANCED DOWN AT THE DERELICT AIRSTRIP. IT STILL LOOKED USABLE.

AFTER TWO YEARS OF JAP RULE, IT WOULD CHEER THE VILLAGERS UP NO END TO SEE US NAIL THE BOMBERS.

IT WAS DANNY MARAIS, SHARP EYES TRAINED BY PEERING LONG DISTANCES ACROSS THE SOUTH AFRICAN VELDT, WHO SAW THE APPROACHING JAP FORMATION FIRST.

THERE THEY ARE. TWO BIG FAT BOMBERS AND A SHOWER OF ZEROS — NEARLY TWENTY OF THEM I'D SAY.

IT WAS OBVIOUS THAT THE ESCORT WASN'T EXPECTING TROUBLE. THE RAGGED, SLOPPY FORMATION EVEN FAILED TO NOTICE TOM AND HIS TWO FELLOW SPITFIRES AT FIRST.

LOOK AT THOSE BOMBERS! THEY REMIND ME OF GREAT FAT COMPLACENT COWS. WE'LL STIR 'EM UP. GET STUCK IN.

ACCORDING TO THE PRE-ARRANGED PLAN, TOM'S TWO WING-MEN WENT FOR THE NEAREST FIGHTERS, APPARENTLY BENT ON SUICIDE.

SOME IMPUDENT DOGS OF BRITISHERS MUST HAVE LOST THEIR WAY. DESTROY THEM BOTH.

RIGHT, BOYS, ALL JOIN IN NOW!

THE OTHER SPITFIRES SIZZLED DOWN IN A MURDEROUS ATTACK LIKE A SALVO OF THUNDER-BOLTS. IN SECONDS, A SNARLING, VICIOUS DOGFIGHT WAS BOILING ALL OVER THE SKY.

BUT THE JAP PILOTS WERE CONFUSED AND SHOCKED BY THE SCREAMING PLANES THAT APPEARED FROM NOWHERE TO SLASH THEM WITH FLAMING CANNONS. THE BOMBERS HAD GONE, DIVING TOWARDS THE JUNGLE TO ESCAPE, DOGGEDLY PURSUED BY TOM IN HIS SPITFIRE.

A ZERO CROSSED HIS SIGHTS AND TOM BLASTED IT TO DESTRUCTION IN A FIVE-SECOND BURST OF FURY, BUT THE PILOT HAD BOUGHT A FEW VITAL SECONDS WITH HIS LIFE. THREE MORE ZEROS BURST FROM THE CORDON OF SPITFIRES AND RACED FOR THE LONE SILVER SPITFIRE.

TOM CLOSED IN ON THE FLEEING BOMBERS, WHICH STUCK TOGETHER TO PROTECT EACH OTHER WITH THEIR GUNNERS' CROSSFIRE, CLOSELY FOLLOWED BY THREE ZEROS. IT WAS A RACE TO THE DEATH WITH THE BOMBERS AS THE PRIZE.

TOM FEINTED TO PORT AND LIKE A PACK OF SNARLING WOLVES THE ZEROS FELL FOR IT. AS HE BELTED THE RUDDER SAVAGELY THE OTHER WAY, HE SHOT UNDERNEATH THEIR LASHING TRACER STREAMS AND FOUND HIMSELF IN THE BOMBER'S CROSSFIRE.

THESE ZEROS COULD TURN ON A SIXPENCE. FRENZIEDLY THEY SWUNG BACK TOWARDS TOM, ONLY TO FIND THREE MORE SPITFIRES WERE ON THEM, CUTTING THEM TO FLAMING RIBBONS.

IN A MAD CHASE AT NOUGHT FEET, THE BOMBERS RACED ROUND TREES, OVER ROCKY CRAGS AND TWISTING RIVERS. WITH A COLD, KILLING EYE, TOM LINED UP THE FIRST THAT LOOMED IN HIS SIGHTS AND OPENED FIRE.

THE JAP BLAZED DOWN TO DESTRUCTION. SWIFTLY TOM SWUNG IN PURSUIT OF THE REMAINING BOMBER, GUNNING THE ENGINE OF HIS SILVER SPITFIRE TO THE LIMIT.

HE CAUGHT UP WITH THE SECOND BOMBER AND DREW A MERCILESS BEAD ON IT JUST AS THE VILLAGE OF DAKPUR LOOMED UP AHEAD OUT OF THE JUNGLE.

THE HURTLING WRECKAGE PLUNGED INTO THE JUNGLE CLOSE TO THE AIRSTRIP AND THE ELATED VILLAGERS RUSHED FROM THEIR HUTS, CHEERING THEMSELVES HOARSE. THE BATTLE WAS OVER.

I CERTAINLY SEEM TO HAVE CHEERED THESE VILLAGERS UP ANYWAY.

TOM HAD STRUCK A MIGHTY BLOW AGAINST THE YELLOW INVADERS. WITH THE LOSS OF THE GENERAL AND HIS STAFF, THE JAP RETREAT IN THAT SECTOR BECAME A DEMORALISED ROUT AS HARD-HITTING BRITISH UNITS PRESSED HOME THE ADVANTAGE.

THEY'RE ON THE RUN, LADS. COME ON, KEEP 'EM GOING!

RUN, YOU SLIT-EYED CHARLIES!

AS THE TENTACLES OF THE NIPPONESE OCTOPUS WERE PRISED LOOSE FROM ONE OBJECTIVE AFTER ANOTHER, SQUADRON-LEADER TOM SHAW AND HIS FIGHTING SPITFIRES SCOURGED THE ENEMY UNTIL ONE DAY WHEN A DREADFUL NEW WEAPON BLASTED THE JAPS INTO FINAL SUBMISSION. IT WAS THE ATOM BOMB, DROPPED ON HIROSHIMA.

SHORTLY AFTER THE JAPANESE SURRENDER, TOM FLEW IN WITH HIS SQUADRON TO DAKPUR AIRSTRIP. THE RECEPTION WAS TREMENDOUS AS THE GLEAMING SILVER SPITFIRE TOUCHED DOWN ON THE RUNWAY.

TOM TAXIED HIS SPITFIRE ALL THE WAY TO THE VILLAGE. TO A ROAR OF WELCOME, HE SWUNG IT ROUND ON THE PREPARED CONCRETE BASE IN THE SQUARE AND CUT THE SWITCHES. "THE SWORD OF DAKPUR" HAD FOUND ITS LAST RESTING PLACE, A PERMANENT MEMORIAL TO THE MEN WHO FLEW SPITFIRES.

WELL, THIS IS THE END OF THE ROAD, I RECKON. A NICE GESTURE FROM THE BIG BRASS TO GIVE THE VILLAGERS BACK THIS OLD CRATE.

TOM CLEARED ALL HIS MAPS FROM THE CASE IN HIS COCKPIT, THEN STOPPED SHORT AS HIS EYES CAUGHT THE GLITTER OF A STRANGE, SPINNING NECKLET.

BY ALL THAT'S WONDERFUL, IT'S THE NECKLACE — U WAN'S NECKLACE. NOW HOW ON EARTH DID THAT GET THERE?

THEN TOM REMEMBERED. BOB CAMPBELL HAD BEEN THE ONLY ONE THERE WHEN HE HAD THROWN AWAY THE NECKLET.

POOR OLD BOB — HE KNEW IT WOULDN'T DO HIM ANY GOOD, BUT HE MADE SURE IT ALWAYS FLEW WITH ME.

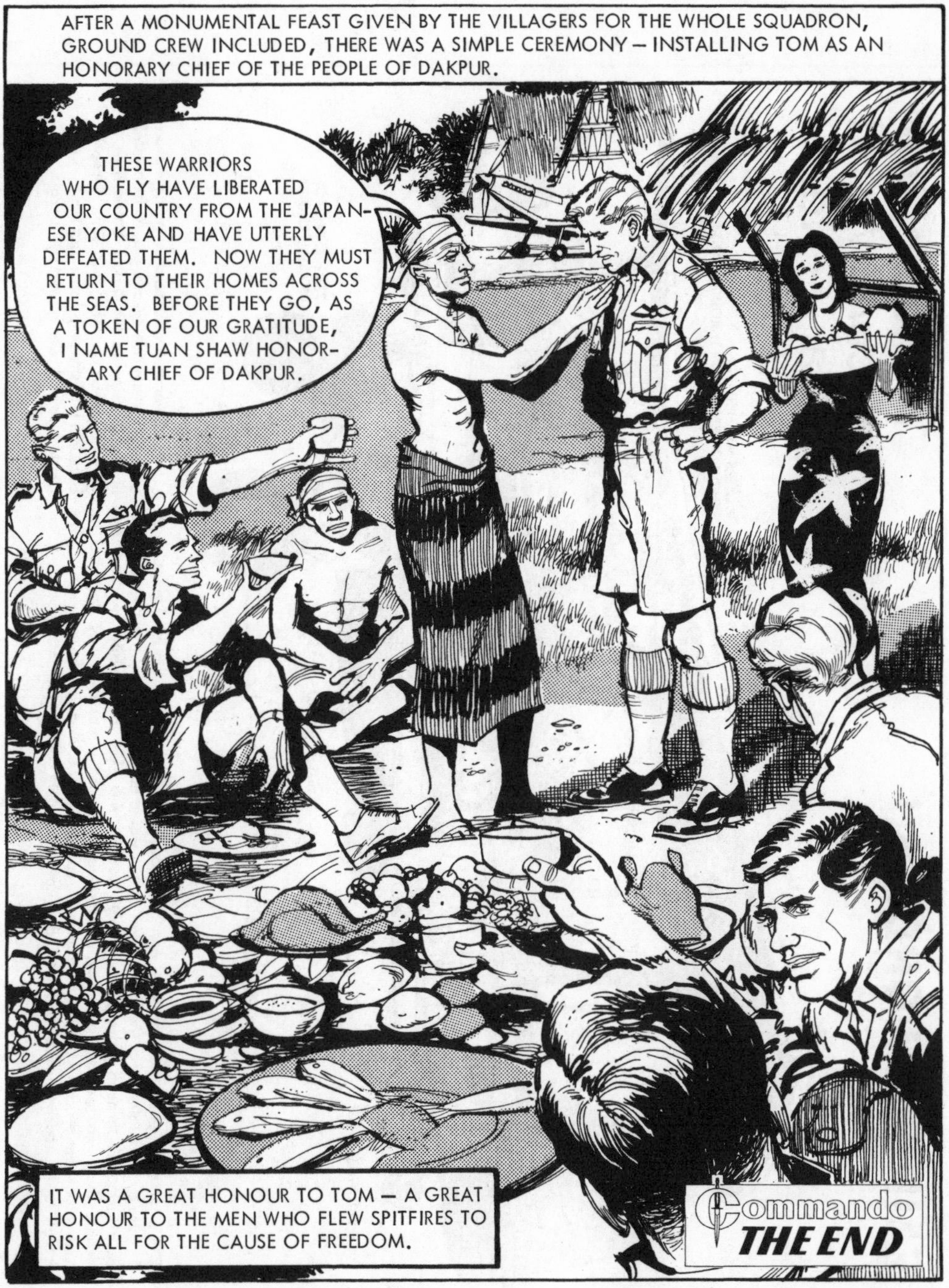
AFTER A MONUMENTAL FEAST GIVEN BY THE VILLAGERS FOR THE WHOLE SQUADRON, GROUND CREW INCLUDED, THERE WAS A SIMPLE CEREMONY – INSTALLING TOM AS AN HONORARY CHIEF OF THE PEOPLE OF DAKPUR.
THESE WARRIORS WHO FLY HAVE LIBERATED OUR COUNTRY FROM THE JAPANESE YOKE AND HAVE UTTERLY DEFEATED THEM. NOW THEY MUST RETURN TO THEIR HOMES ACROSS THE SEAS. BEFORE THEY GO, AS A TOKEN OF OUR GRATITUDE, I NAME TUAN SHAW HONORARY CHIEF OF DAKPUR.
IT WAS A GREAT HONOUR TO TOM – A GREAT HONOUR TO THE MEN WHO FLEW SPITFIRES TO RISK ALL FOR THE CAUSE OF FREEDOM.
Commando
THE END

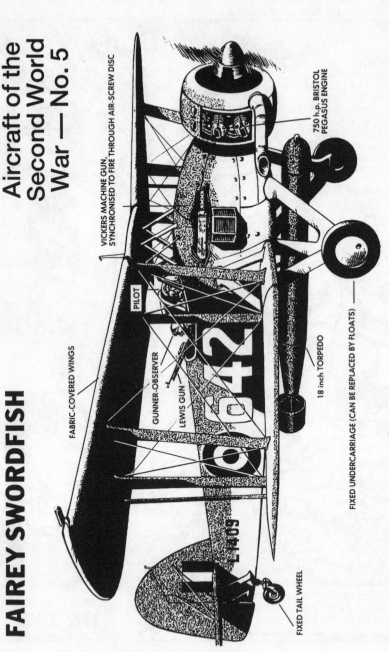

Aircraft of the
Second World
War — No. 5

FAIREY SWORDFISH

VICKERS MACHINE GUN,
SYNCHRONISED TO FIRE THROUGH AIR-SCREW DISC

750 h.p. BRISTOL
PEGASUS ENGINE

FABRIC-COVERED WINGS

PILOT

GUNNER-OBSERVER

LEWIS GUN

18 inch TORPEDO

FIXED UNDERCARRIAGE (CAN BE REPLACED BY FLOATS)

FIXED TAIL WHEEL

THIS amazing plane was already out of date by the beginning of the '39.'45 war, yet it lasted all through those years simply because there was nothing else that could touch it for sheer efficiency. It was a beautiful aircraft to fly, nearly impossible to stall, and it could put up with the kinds of pilot-error that would have caused any other type to fall out of the sky. It actually outlived the Albacore, the plane that was designed to replace it. The men of the Fleet Air Arm affectionately called it the "Stringbag".

The Swordfish secured a permanent place in history when twenty-one planes from HMS Illustrious crippled the Italian battle-fleet at Taranto. This was the first time torpedo-bombers had struck in force and the first time battleships had been routed by aircraft.

SAILOR with WINGS

AS THE PILOTS OF THE ROYAL AIR FORCE BATTLED WITH THE LUFTWAFFE ABOVE BRITAIN, A NEW BREED OF EQUALLY TOUGH, RESOURCEFUL PILOTS TOOK TO THE AIR. THESE WERE THE MEN OF THE FLEET AIR ARM — SAILORS WITH WINGS.

FIERY TEMPERED LIEUTENANT COMMANDER JIM TREGARRON WAS ONE SUCH PILOT.   RECENTLY PROMOTED TO TAKE CHARGE OF THE SQUADRON, HE WAS LEADING HIS MEN ON A STRIKE INTO THE ADRIATIC IN AN ATTEMPT TO CRIPPLE THE ITALIAN FLEET WHICH WAS MENACING VITAL SUPPLY CONVOYS.

THIS JOB'S GOT ME WORRIED — ANTIQUATED KITES, AND PILOTS FRESH FROM FLYING SCHOOL. WE HARDLY STAND A CHANCE.

JIM, SON OF A CORNISH FISHERMAN, HAD PULLED HIS WAY UP THROUGH THE RANKS BY SHEER GUTS AND ABILITY.

KEEP YOUR EYES PEELED, CARSON. WE CAN'T AFFORD TO MESS UP THIS JOB.

DICK CARSON, JIM'S NAVIGATOR, HAD JUST FAILED HIS PILOT'S COURSE AND WAS STILL FEELING BITTER.

AYE AYE, SKIPPER.

THEY SAY HE'S GOT THE BLOOD OF CORNISH PIRATES IN HIS VEINS. I WOULDN'T BE SURPRISED.

IT WAS THE KEEN EYES OF JIM HIMSELF WHICH FIRST SPOTTED THE SHIPS BELOW A FEW MINUTES LATER.

THAT LOOKS LIKE OUR TARGET. THEY'RE ON COURSE FOR CALENTIA TOO.— THE PORT THEY WERE MEANT TO BE HEADING FOR. KEEP FORMATION WHILE I INVESTIGATE.

THE RECEPTION GIVEN BY THE SHIPS BELOW LEFT JIM IN NO DOUBT THAT THIS WAS HIS OBJECTIVE.

THEY'RE EYTIES, OK — TWO CRUISERS AND A BATTLESHIP.

PULLING CLEAR OF THE FLAK, JIM BARKED AN ORDER.

IT'S THEM ALL RIGHT. "A" FLIGHT TAKE THE CRUISERS, "B" FLIGHT FOLLOW ME IN ON THE BATTLESHIP.

EXPERTLY JIM LEVELLED HIS SWORDFISH OUT AND RAN TOWARDS THE BATTLESHIP, REGARDLESS OF THE FLAK.

IT'S UP TO YOU NOW, CARSON. TAKE YOUR TIME AND DON'T RELEASE TOO SOON.

YES, SIR.

DICK CARSON FELT AS NERVOUS AS A KITTEN. IT WAS HIS FIRST SORTIE OF THE WAR.

ANOTHER FEW SECONDS...

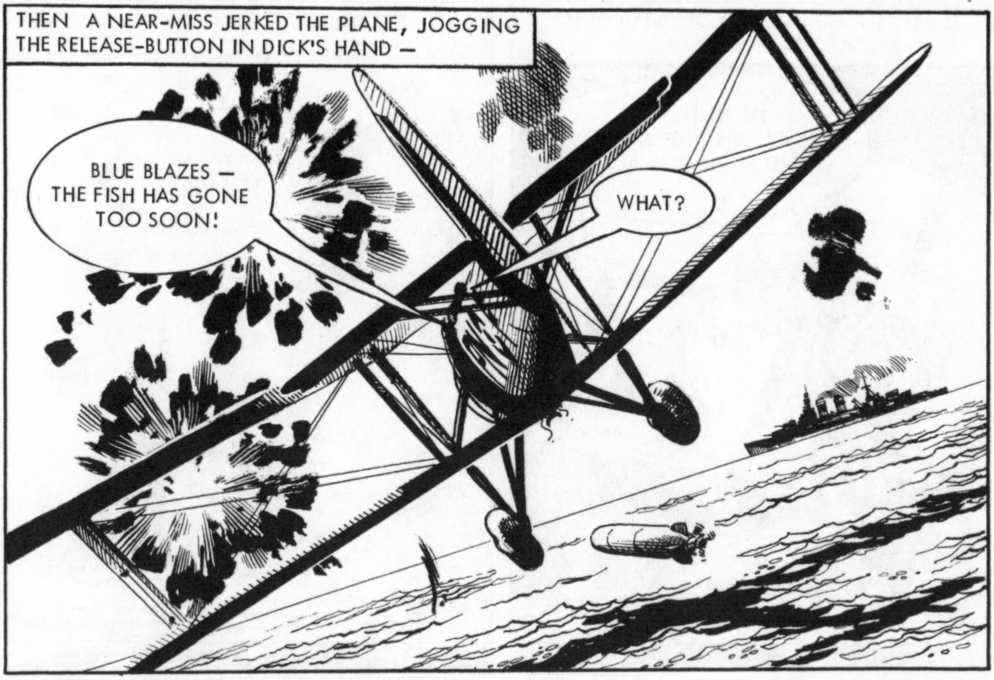
THEN A NEAR-MISS JERKED THE PLANE, JOGGING THE RELEASE-BUTTON IN DICK'S HAND –
BLUE BLAZES – THE FISH HAS GONE TOO SOON!
WHAT?

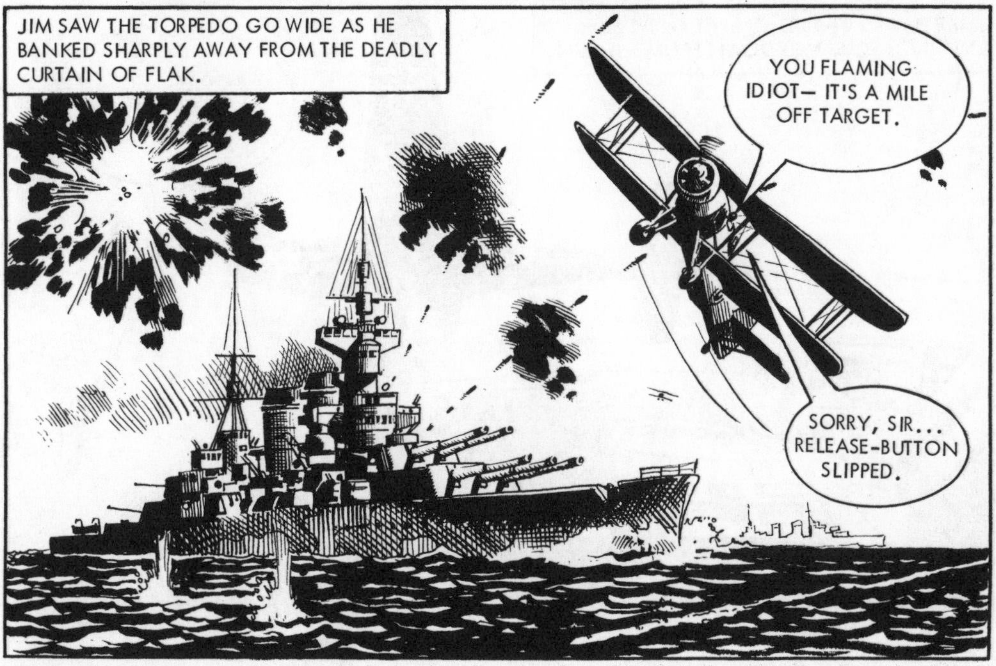
JIM SAW THE TORPEDO GO WIDE AS HE BANKED SHARPLY AWAY FROM THE DEADLY CURTAIN OF FLAK.
YOU FLAMING IDIOT– IT'S A MILE OFF TARGET.
SORRY, SIR... RELEASE-BUTTON SLIPPED.

DICK LISTENED IN BLACK DEPRESSION TO JIM'S ANGRY TIRADE.

YOU BUNGLED IT. YOU COULDN'T HIT BEACHEY HEAD AT THIRTY YARDS...

I'VE HAD IT AS AN OBSERVER NOW.

BUT DICK'S RAGE WAS BROKEN OFF SHARPLY —

FIGHTERS ABOVE, SKIPPER.

LIKE HAWKS DIVING ON FAT GEESE THE ME. 109's SCREAMED DOWN FROM THE SUN.

TAKE EVASIVE ACTION INDEPENDENTLY.

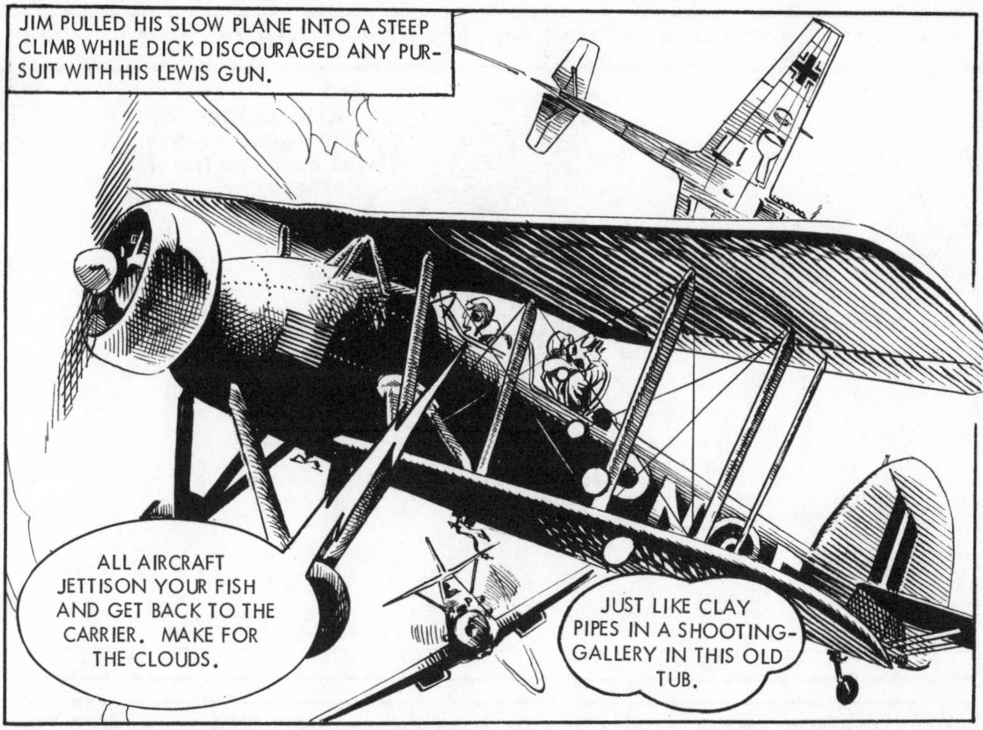
JIM PULLED HIS SLOW PLANE INTO A STEEP CLIMB WHILE DICK DISCOURAGED ANY PURSUIT WITH HIS LEWIS GUN.
ALL AIRCRAFT JETTISON YOUR FISH AND GET BACK TO THE CARRIER. MAKE FOR THE CLOUDS.
JUST LIKE CLAY PIPES IN A SHOOTING-GALLERY IN THIS OLD TUB.

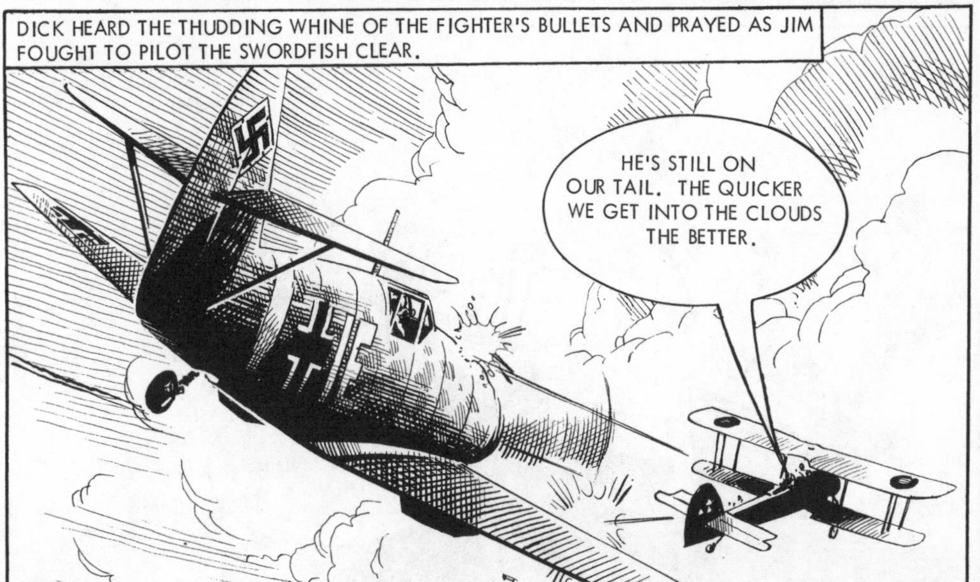
DICK HEARD THE THUDDING WHINE OF THE FIGHTER'S BULLETS AND PRAYED AS JIM FOUGHT TO PILOT THE SWORDFISH CLEAR.
HE'S STILL ON OUR TAIL. THE QUICKER WE GET INTO THE CLOUDS THE BETTER.

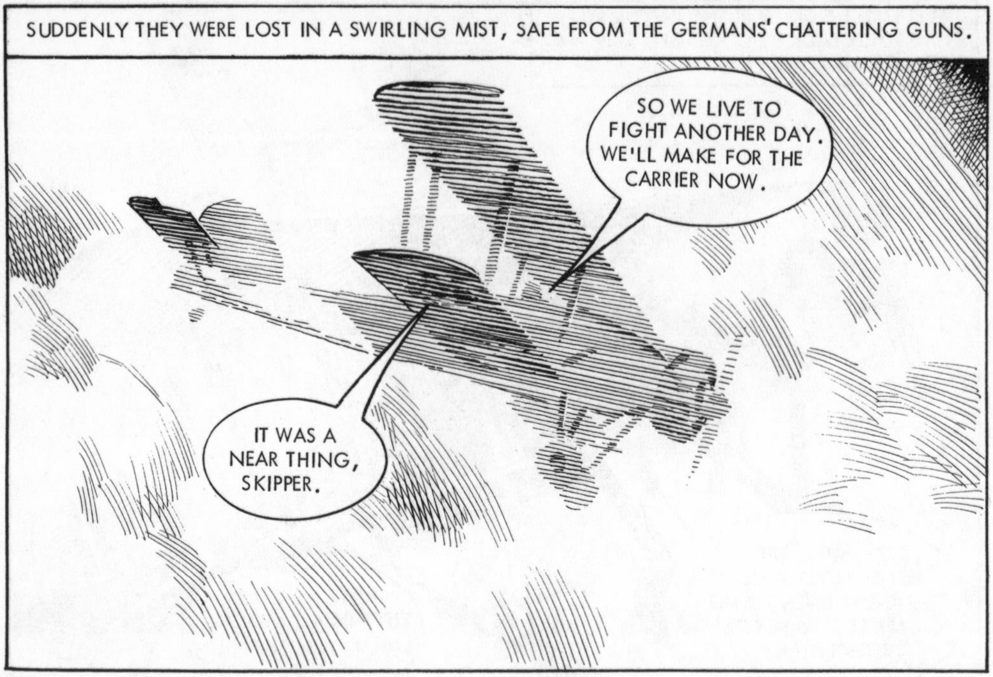
SUDDENLY THEY WERE LOST IN A SWIRLING MIST, SAFE FROM THE GERMANS' CHATTERING GUNS.
SO WE LIVE TO FIGHT ANOTHER DAY. WE'LL MAKE FOR THE CARRIER NOW.
IT WAS A NEAR THING, SKIPPER.

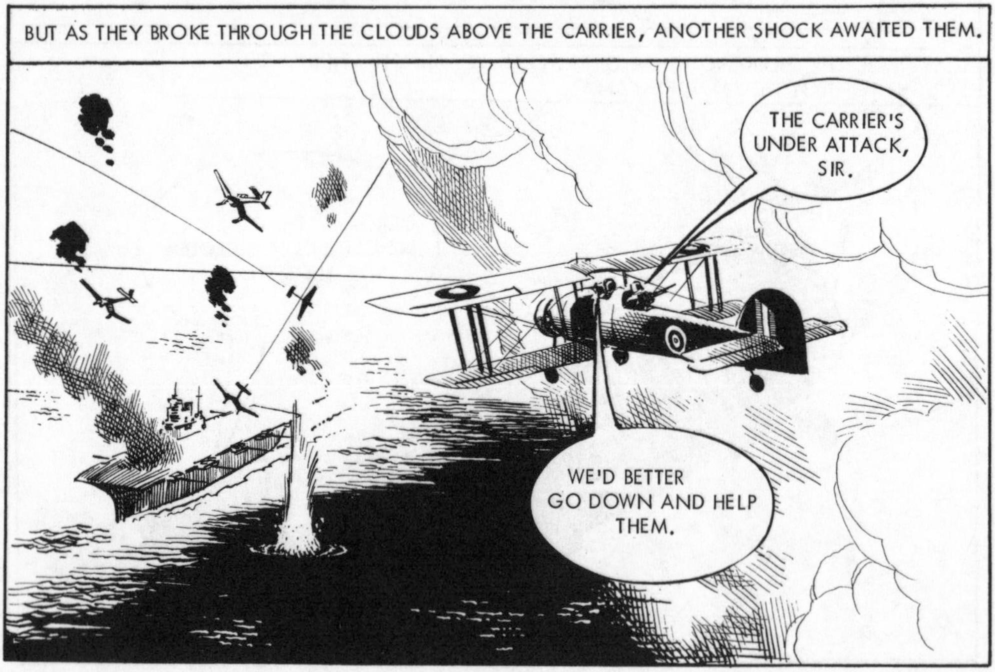
BUT AS THEY BROKE THROUGH THE CLOUDS ABOVE THE CARRIER, ANOTHER SHOCK AWAITED THEM.
THE CARRIER'S UNDER ATTACK, SIR.
WE'D BETTER GO DOWN AND HELP THEM.

IN COLD ANGER JIM PUT HIS PLANE IN A DIVE AFTER ONE OF THE STUKAS, JUST AS THE REMAINING THREE SWORDFISH OF HIS FLIGHT APPEARED.

THE CLUMSY SWORDFISH SWOOPED UNDER THE EVIL-LOOKING GERMAN PLANE AS IT LIFTED FROM ITS BOMBING-DIVE.

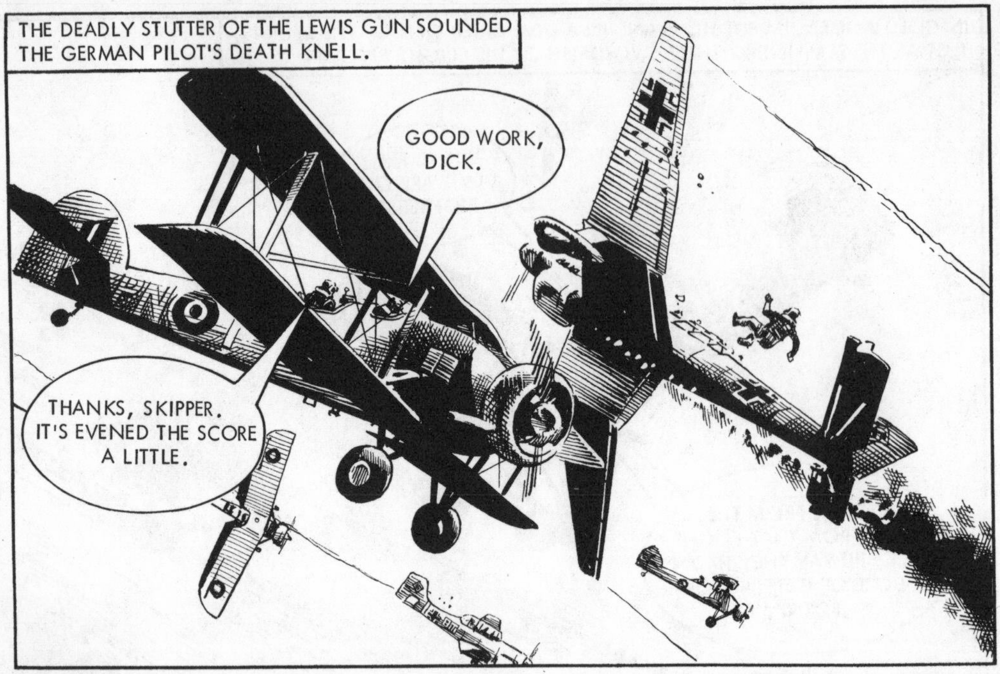
THE DEADLY STUTTER OF THE LEWIS GUN SOUNDED THE GERMAN PILOT'S DEATH KNELL.
GOOD WORK, DICK.
THANKS, SKIPPER. IT'S EVENED THE SCORE A LITTLE.

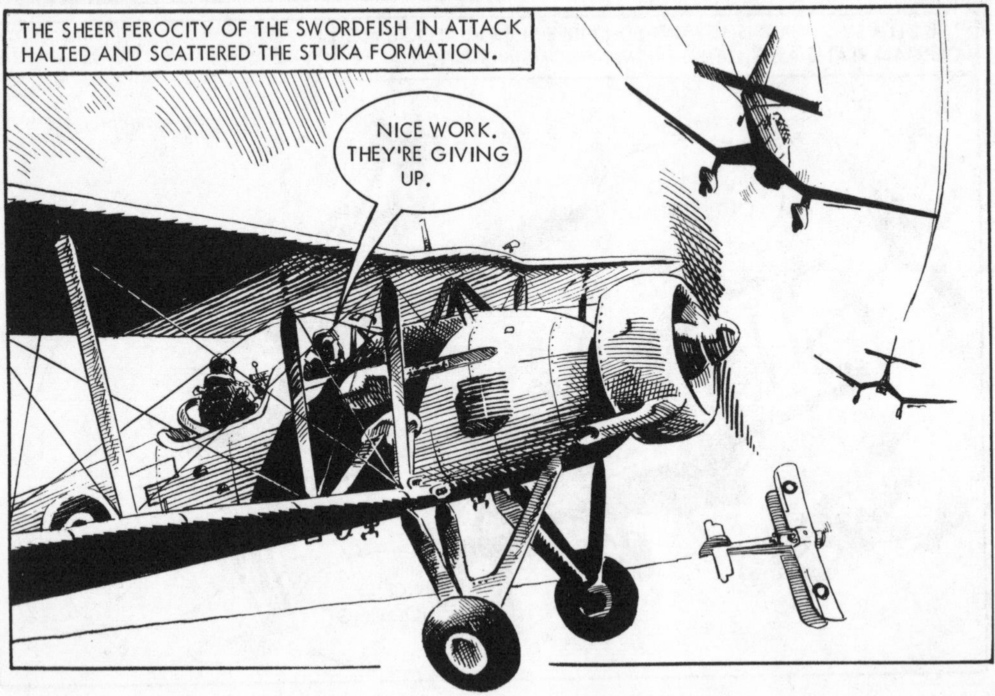
THE SHEER FEROCITY OF THE SWORDFISH IN ATTACK HALTED AND SCATTERED THE STUKA FORMATION.
NICE WORK. THEY'RE GIVING UP.

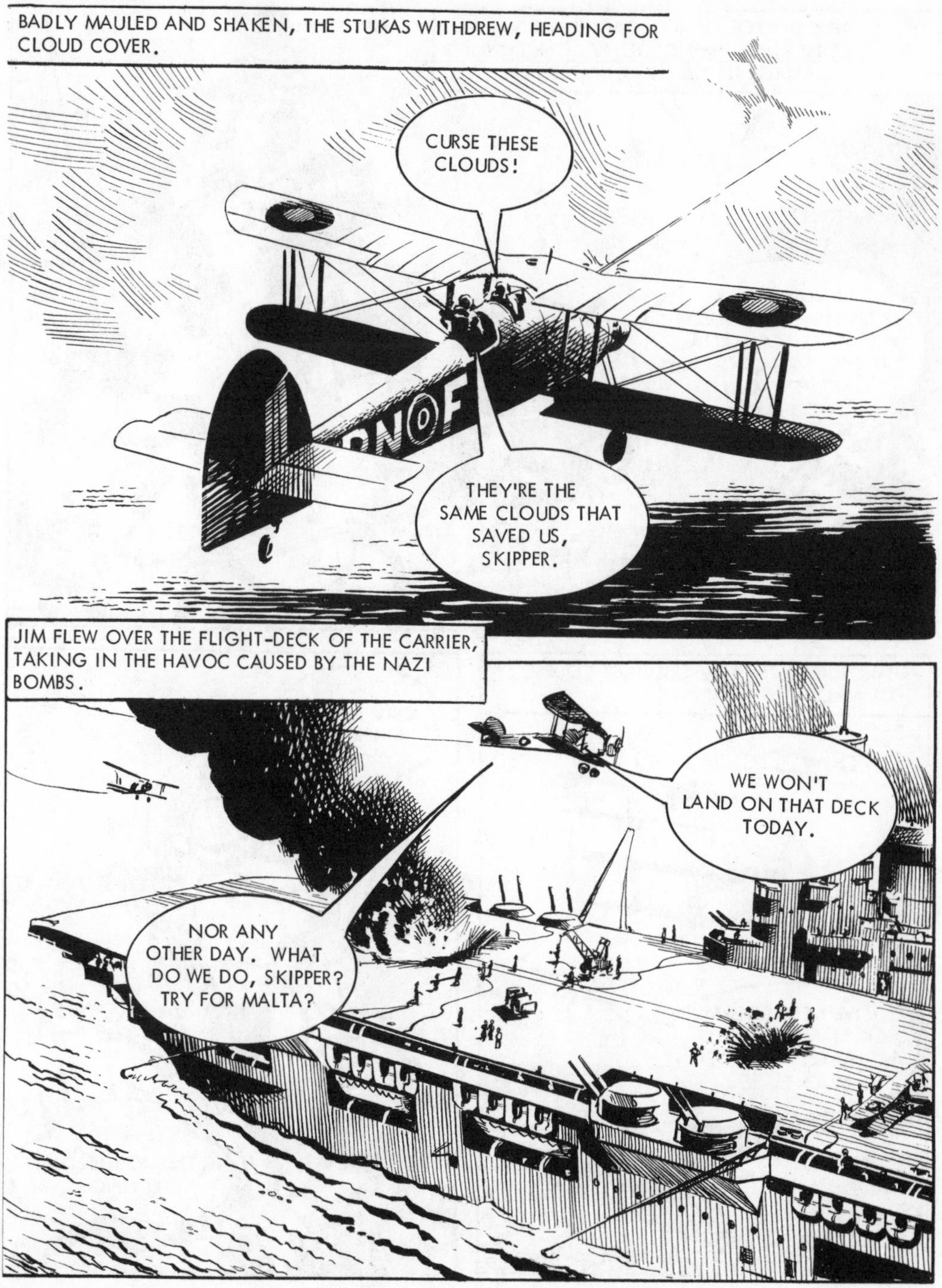
BADLY MAULED AND SHAKEN, THE STUKAS WITHDREW, HEADING FOR CLOUD COVER.
CURSE THESE CLOUDS!
THEY'RE THE SAME CLOUDS THAT SAVED US, SKIPPER.
JIM FLEW OVER THE FLIGHT-DECK OF THE CARRIER, TAKING IN THE HAVOC CAUSED BY THE NAZI BOMBS.
WE WON'T LAND ON THAT DECK TODAY.
NOR ANY OTHER DAY. WHAT DO WE DO, SKIPPER? TRY FOR MALTA?

THE FLIGHT CONTROL OFFICER ON THE AIRCRAFT CARRIER CONFIRMED JIM'S GLOOMY CONCLUSIONS ONCE THE DAMAGE HAD BEEN ESTIMATED.

NO LANDINGS POSSIBLE. SQUADRON WILL MAKE FOR MALTA. REPEAT, SQUADRON WILL MAKE FOR MALTA. GOOD LUCK.

JIM ORDERED THE PLANES TO SET COURSE FOR MALTA.

GIVE ME A COURSE, DICK. MAKE SURE IT'S ACCURATE. WE HAVEN'T MUCH FUEL.

COMING UP, SKIPPER.

I HOPE I'M BETTER AT THIS THAN FLYING.

SOON AFTERWARDS A BLINDING RAIN SQUALL HIT THE SQUADRON, OBSCURING ONE PLANE FROM THE OTHER.

BLINDING RAIN AND MIST — THAT'S ALL WE NEED.

NEVER EXPECTED TO FIND A LONDON PEA-SOUPER OUT HERE.

SUDDENLY THE SQUALL ABATED AS QUICKLY AS IT HAD STARTED.

WHERE IN TARNATION ARE THE OTHERS? CHECK OUR BEARING, CARSON.

RIGHT AWAY, SKIPPER.

DICK HAD HARDLY STARTED PORING OVER HIS MAPS WHEN JIM'S VOICE BURST EXPLOSIVELY IN HIS EAR.

MY COMPASS! IT'S GOT A HOLE IN THE SIDE — A JERRY BULLET MUST HAVE GOT IT. WE COULD BE ANYWHERE IN THE MED!

JIM FOUGHT DOWN HIS PANIC AS HE REALISED HE HAD BEEN FLYING ON A FAULTY COMPASS ALL THIS TIME.

WHAT A MESS! TRY TO GET A FIX FROM THE SUN, WILL YOU?

YES, SIR. I'LL SEE WHAT I CAN DO.

BUT IT WAS WITH A SINKING FEELING THAT DICK BUSIED HIMSELF WITH HIS INSTRUMENTS. HE KNEW HE SHOULD HAVE DONE THIS BEFORE NOW.

AS THEY TALKED, HOWEVER, THE ENGINE SUDDENLY BEGAN TO COUGH AND SPLUTTER.

ENGINE'S PACKING UP. WE CAN'T BE OUT OF FUEL YET.

DICK LEANED OVER THE SIDE TO STUDY THE LAYOUT BELOW THEM, AND —

BLAST! THE FUEL LINE HAS BEEN HOLED, SKIPPER, AND THE FUEL IS LEAKING AWAY.

WE'LL JUST HAVE TO DITCH THEN.

SUDDENLY, HOWEVER, THE LINE OF BLEAK CLIFFS BROKE INTO A FLAT EXPANSE OF SAND.

A BEACH! GLORY BE, A BEACH!

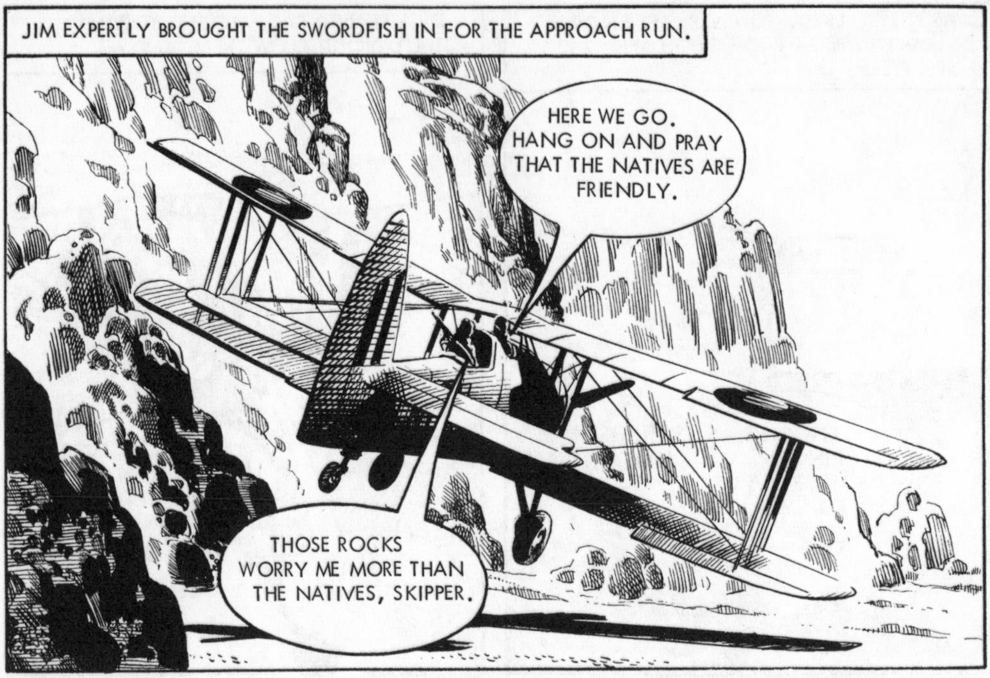
JIM EXPERTLY BROUGHT THE SWORDFISH IN FOR THE APPROACH RUN.
HERE WE GO. HANG ON AND PRAY THAT THE NATIVES ARE FRIENDLY.
THOSE ROCKS WORRY ME MORE THAN THE NATIVES, SKIPPER.

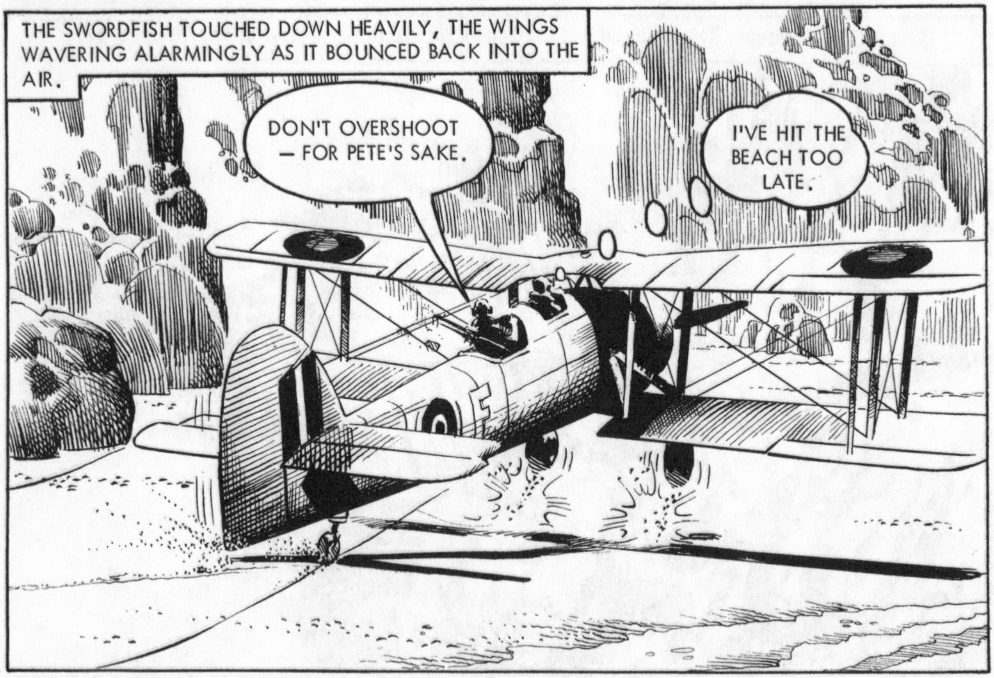
THE SWORDFISH TOUCHED DOWN HEAVILY, THE WINGS WAVERING ALARMINGLY AS IT BOUNCED BACK INTO THE AIR.
DON'T OVERSHOOT – FOR PETE'S SAKE.
I'VE HIT THE BEACH TOO LATE.

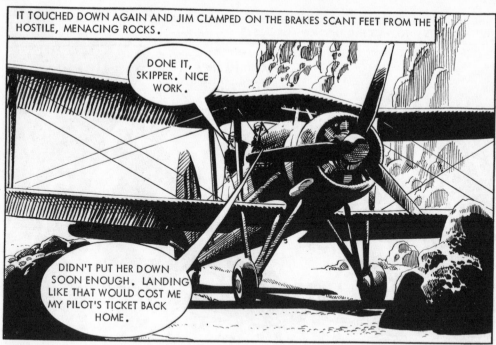

IT TOUCHED DOWN AGAIN AND JIM CLAMPED ON THE BRAKES SCANT FEET FROM THE HOSTILE, MENACING ROCKS.

DONE IT, SKIPPER. NICE WORK.

DIDN'T PUT HER DOWN SOON ENOUGH. LANDING LIKE THAT WOULD COST ME MY PILOT'S TICKET BACK HOME.

EXAMINING THE FUEL TANKS, JIM LOOKED AT THE SMASHED FEED-PIPE FROM THEM.

WE CAN THANK WHATEVER LUCKY STARS WE HAVE WE DIDN'T CATCH FIRE.

WONDER IF ANYONE SAW US LAND? LOOKS PRETTY WILD COUNTRY. AND WHERE THE DEVIL ARE WE, ANYWAY?

THE COUNTRY WAS INDEED WILD, BUT NOT QUITE SO WILD-LOOKING AS THE BUNCH OF CUT-THROATS WHO WATCHED THE NEW ARRIVALS.

JIM AND DICK SAW THEM AS THEY SUDDENLY RUSHED ACROSS THE BEACH, SHOUTING AND BRANDISHING THEIR WEAPONS.

THE TWO FLEET AIR ARM MEN BREATHED A SIGH OF RELIEF WHEN THEY DISCOVERED THE IDENTITY OF THE ROUGH-LOOKING BUNCH.

PLEASE, I AM NIKKI GORGOS, PARTISAN LEADER. THESE ARE MY MEN.

WELL, ARE WE GLAD TO SEE YOU, BOY. AND WHERE ARE WE, EXACTLY?

JIM WAS AMAZED AT THE REPLY.

YOU ARE FIVE KILOMETRES FROM KATINA IN GREECE — NEAR ALBANIAN BORDER.

GREECE! WELL I'LL BE...

RECOVERING HIMSELF, JIM SHOWED NIKKI THE TROUBLE. TO HIS SURPRISE NIKKI GRINNED.

MY MAN STEPHANOS FIX. HE BEST MECHANIC IN GREEK ARMY BEFORE WAR.

FINE, BUT WE'VE STILL GOT A FUEL PROBLEM.

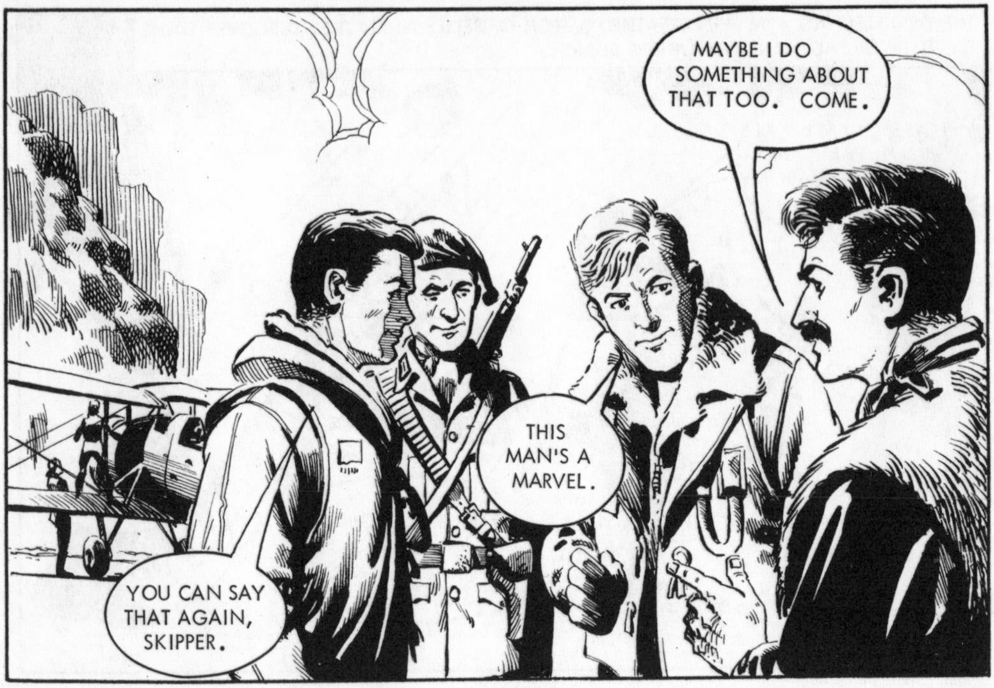
MAYBE I DO SOMETHING ABOUT THAT TOO. COME.
THIS MAN'S A MARVEL.
YOU CAN SAY THAT AGAIN, SKIPPER.

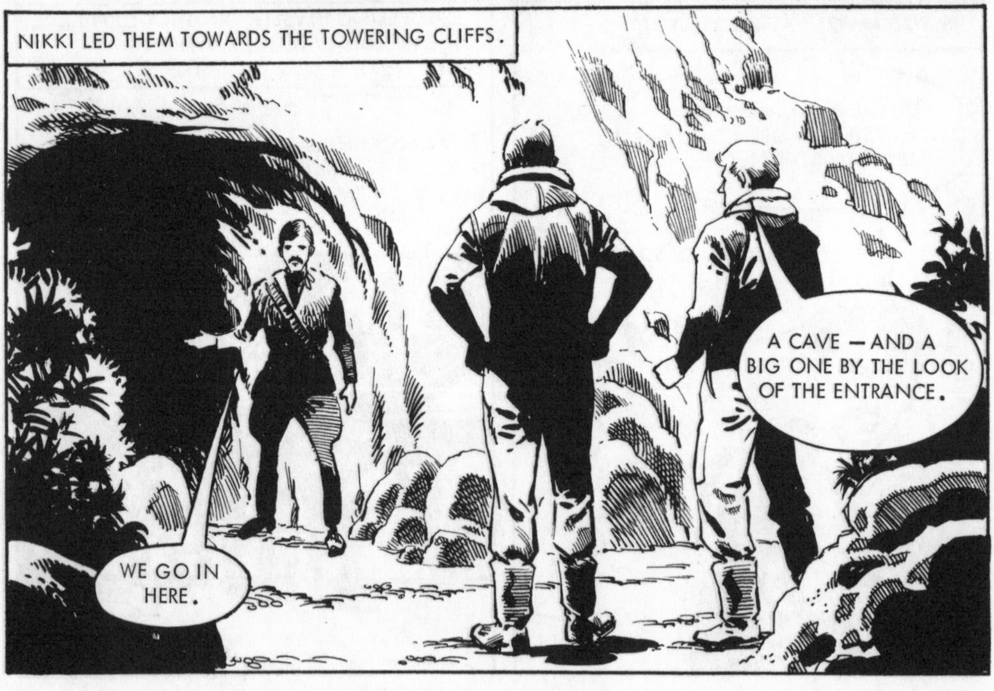
NIKKI LED THEM TOWARDS THE TOWERING CLIFFS.
A CAVE — AND A BIG ONE BY THE LOOK OF THE ENTRANCE.
WE GO IN HERE.

ONCE INSIDE THE LARGE, SPACIOUS CAVE, JIM LET OUT A WHISTLE OF AMAZEMENT.

YE GODS — DRUM UPON DRUM OF PETROL — R.A.F. PETROL.

YOU ARE LUCKY. THIS BEACH WAS CONVERTED INTO AN AIR-STRIP BY R.A.F. DURING FIGHTING IN GREECE. I HID THEIR STORES FROM THE GERMANS IN THIS CAVE. THERE IS A NATURAL ESCAPE AT THE BACK OF THE CAVE TOO.

DARKNESS WAS FALLING AS THEY CAME OUT OF THE CAVE.

YOUR PLANE WILL BE MENDED AND RE-FUELLED. NOW YOU EAT.

DICK AND JIM FOLLOWED THE GIANT GREEK TO ANOTHER CAVE.

I WAS A BOY IN THESE PARTS AND KNEW EVERY CAVE. VERY USEFUL WHEN GERMANS CAME.

CERTAINLY A SAFE SPOT.

THIS OTHER CAVE WAS USED BY THE GUERILLAS AS THEIR H.Q. NIKKI TOLD HIS TWO GUESTS ALL ABOUT HIMSELF.

I WAS A FISHERMAN BEFORE WAR START. MY FAMILY AND WIFE TAKEN TO GERMANY BECAUSE WE SHELTER ALLIED SOLDIERS.

YOU'VE HAD IT ROUGH. NO WONDER YOU HATE JERRIES.

ITALIANS TOO. I WISH WITH ALL MY HEART TO SINK THEIR SHIPS AS THEY PASS HERE EVERY DAY FOR CALENTIA.

CALENTIA? IS IT NEAR, THEN?

FOR ANSWER NIKKI PRODUCED A GREEK ARMY MAP.

IT IS ABOUT ONE HUNDRED AND FIFTY KILOMETRES.

THAT'S ONLY ABOUT ONE HUNDRED MILES. I WONDER...

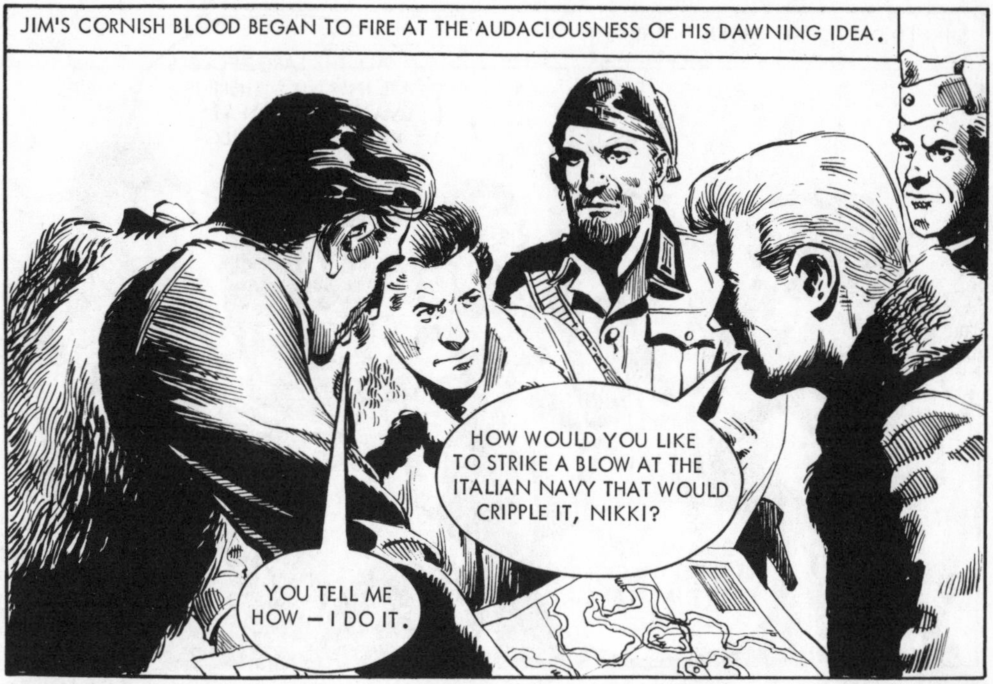
JIM'S CORNISH BLOOD BEGAN TO FIRE AT THE AUDACIOUSNESS OF HIS DAWNING IDEA.
HOW WOULD YOU LIKE TO STRIKE A BLOW AT THE ITALIAN NAVY THAT WOULD CRIPPLE IT, NIKKI?
YOU TELL ME HOW — I DO IT.

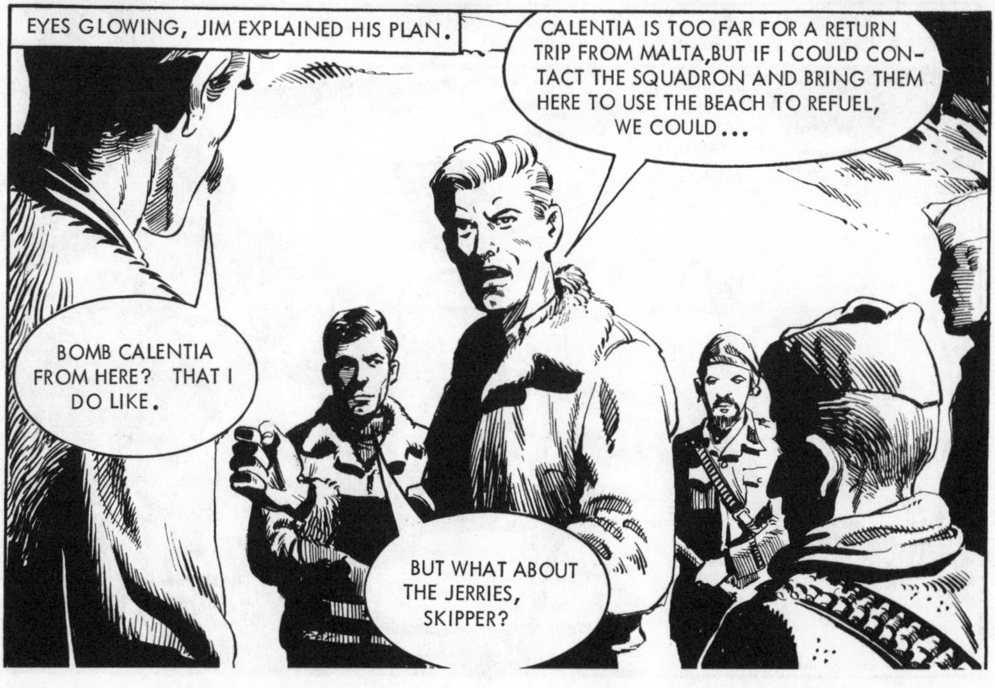
EYES GLOWING, JIM EXPLAINED HIS PLAN.
CALENTIA IS TOO FAR FOR A RETURN TRIP FROM MALTA,BUT IF I COULD CONTACT THE SQUADRON AND BRING THEM HERE TO USE THE BEACH TO REFUEL, WE COULD...
BOMB CALENTIA FROM HERE? THAT I DO LIKE.
BUT WHAT ABOUT THE JERRIES, SKIPPER?

NIKKI DIDN'T SHARE DICK'S DOUBTS.

ALL THE LARGE FORCES ARE INLAND. THERE IS A SMALL GARRISON AT KATINA — TEN KILOMETRES AWAY.

GREAT STUFF. LET'S GET CRACKING WITH THAT PLANE.

BUT AS NIKKI LED THEM BACK TO THE BEACH, A GNARLED FIGURE WATCHED FROM THE CLIFFS ABOVE. IT WAS ANDREOS, THE GOAT HERD.

STRANGERS — I MUST FIND OUT MORE.

CLOSELY FOLLOWED BY THE SNOOPING OLD MAN, THE THREE COMRADES MADE THEIR WAY DOWN TO THE BEACH, WHERE STEPHANOS HAD WORKED HARD PATCHING THE LEAKING FUEL-PIPE.

I THINK SHE HOLD SOME TIME FOR YOU NOW.

GREAT. LET'S GET THE KITE REFUELLED.

MALTA, HERE WE COME.

JIM HAD A SHOCK IN STORE FOR DICK, HOWEVER.

NOT FOR YOU, I'M AFRAID, DICK. YOU STAY HERE AND ORGANISE THE PETROL.

SURELY NOT, SKIPPER?

IT'S THE QUICKEST WAY. YOU CAN HAVE EVERYTHING READY FOR ME COMING BACK.

OK, SKIPPER.

ANDREOS HAD BEEN WATCHING ALL THIS. HE DIDN'T KNOW WHAT WAS GOING ON, BUT HE KNEW AN AEROPLANE WHEN HE SAW ONE.

A BRITISH AEROPLANE. THE GERMAN OFFICER AT KATINA WOULD PAY GOOD MONEY TO KNOW OF THIS.

JUST AT THE MOMENT NIKKI, JIM AND DICK TURNED FROM THE SWORDFISH, ANDREOS CHOSE TO DASH FROM COVER —

STOP OR I SHOOT!

WHEN HE SAW WHO IT WAS, NIKKI'S MANNER CHANGED TO PITYING CONTEMPT.

DO NOT SHOOT. I WAS LOOKING FOR A GOAT THAT STRAYED, MASTER.

IT IS ONLY MAD ANDREOS. ALL RIGHT, OLD MAN — BE ON YOUR WAY AND FORGET WHAT YOU SAW.

IS IT SAFE TO LET HIM GO?

HAVE NO FEAR. HE IS AS SIMPLE AS A CHILD.

BUT AT THE TOP OF THE CLIFF —

I MUST TELL THE GERMANS RIGHT AWAY. THEY SHALL PAY WELL. I WILL HAVE MONEY.

THE REFUELLING WAS COMPLETED IN RECORD TIME BY NIKKI'S MEN.

I'LL BRING THE PLANES IN JUST BEFORE DARK TO AVOID DETECTION.

WE'LL BE WATCHING, SKIPPER. GOOD LUCK.

DESPITE THE SHADOWY MOONLIGHT, JIM TOOK OFF PERFECTLY FROM THE EXCELLENT HOME-MADE RUNWAY.

I'M KEEPING MY FINGERS CROSSED, SKIPPER.

ANDREOS REACHED KATINA IN A FEW HOURS. HE BRAVED THE COLD CONTEMPT OF THE GERMAN GUARDS, DEMANDING TO SEE THE KOMMANDANT, MAJOR HEINRICH BAUER.

WELL, WHAT DO YOU WANT, PEASANT?

I SAW A BRITISH AEROPLANE DOWN BY THE COAST, HERR MAJOR. THE PARTISANS ARE HELPING IT TO ESCAPE.

ANDREOS TOLD BAUER ALL HE HAD LEARNED ABOUT THE PETROL AND THE GUERRILLAS' ACTIVITIES.

YOU HAVE DONE VALUABLE SERVICE TO THE THIRD REICH, OLD MAN. YOU WILL BE REWARDED.

THANK YOU, SIR. BUT HURRY, OR THEY WILL ESCAPE.

MAJOR BAUER LOST NO TIME TURNING OUT HIS MEN. ANDREOS WENT WITH THEM TO SHOW THE WAY.

A SHORT, HAIR-RAISING DRIVE THROUGH THE MOUNTAINS BROUGHT THE NAZIS CLOSE TO THE GUERRILLAS' HIDEOUT.

NIKKI WAS INSIDE THE CAVE ORGANISING THE REMOVAL OF THE PETROL TO THE BEACH WHEN THE TRAP WAS SPRUNG.

DICK HAD BEEN ALONE ON THE BEACH INSPECTING THE RUNWAY, AND THE FIRST HE KNEW OF THE AMBUSH WAS STEPHANOS PULLING HIM INTO THE COVER OF THE ROCKS BY THE CAVE, WHERE THE OTHER PARTISANS WHO HAD AVOIDED CAPTURE WERE HIDING.

AS THE PARTISANS WERE MARCHED AWAY, DICK'S QUESTION WAS ANSWERED BY THE APPEARANCE OF ANDREOS.

ANDREOS. WE SHOULD HAVE SHOT THAT VILLAIN WHEN WE FIRST SAW HIM!

YOU WILL BE PAID WHEN WE REACH KATINA.

QUIETLY, UNDER STEPHANOS' EXPERT LEADERSHIP THEY FOLLOWED THE GERMANS AND PRISONERS.

WE MUST STOP THESE TRUCKS.

BUT HOW?

STEPHANOS BECKONED THEM TO FOLLOW AS HE BEGAN A SPINE-CHILLING DASH ACROSS MOUNTAIN PRECIPICES.

WE GO STRAIGHT BUT THE ROAD WINDS. IF WE HURRY WE CAN GET AHEAD OF THEM.

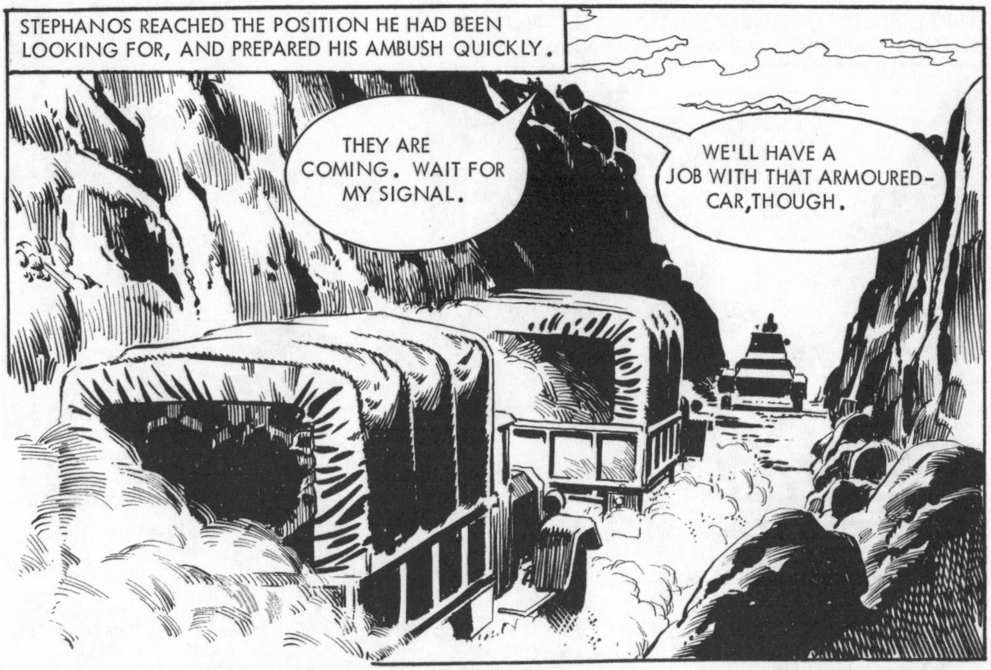
STEPHANOS REACHED THE POSITION HE HAD BEEN LOOKING FOR, AND PREPARED HIS AMBUSH QUICKLY.
THEY ARE COMING. WAIT FOR MY SIGNAL.
WE'LL HAVE A JOB WITH THAT ARMOURED-CAR,THOUGH.

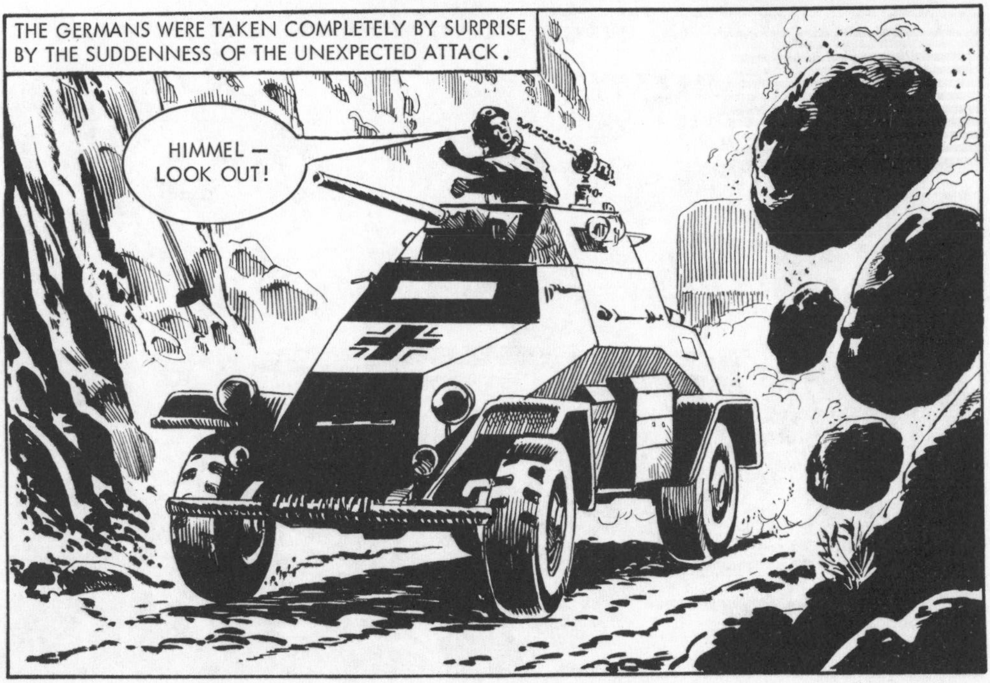
THE GERMANS WERE TAKEN COMPLETELY BY SURPRISE BY THE SUDDENNESS OF THE UNEXPECTED ATTACK.
HIMMEL — LOOK OUT!

THE BOULDERS EFFECTIVELY HALTED THE CONVOY. THE BATTLE BEGAN WITH STEPHANOS HURLING A MOLOTOV COCKTAIL AT THE ARMOURED CAR.

A HUGE SHEET OF FLAME ENVELOPED THE ARMOURED CAR AS THE MOLOTOV COCKTAIL BURST ACCURATELY INSIDE IT.

NIKKI LOST NO TIME IN TAKING ADVANTAGE OF THE DIVERSION.

STEPHANOS HAS NOT FAILED US.

LED BY STEPHANOS, THE PARTISANS FELL UPON THE DOOMED GERMANS. DICK WAS WELL TO THE FRONT OF THE RAMPAGING GREEKS.

KILL EVERY ONE OF THE DOGS!

MY STARS, THIS IS A RIGHT BARNEY.

THE BATTLE WAS BLOODY, BUT SHORT. SOON NIKKI WAS CLAPPING STEPHANOS HEARTILY ON THE BACK.

STEPHANOS, MY OLD FRIEND — I KNEW YOU WOULD COME.

YES, BUT NONE OF THIS WOULD HAVE HAPPENED IF IT WASN'T FOR THE TREACHERY OF ANDREOS THE GOAT HERD.

BUT BEFORE THEY COULD GET ANY FURTHER, A SCUFFLING ON THE ROAD MADE NIKKI LOOK UP.

ANDREOS — THERE HE GOES!

ANDREOS MADE A MAD DASH FOR THE COVER OF BUSHES ABOVE HIM. BUT HE NEVER REACHED THEM.

YOU SHALL BETRAY YOUR COUNTRY NO MORE, TRAITOR.

WITH THE TRAITOR DEALT WITH IN THIS WAY, IT WAS NOW TIME FOR THE PARTISANS TO FADE FROM THE SCENE.

WELL DONE, STEPHANOS. BUT WE'D BETTER GET A MOVE ON WITH OUR PLANS TO REFUEL THE PLANES WHEN THEY APPEAR. THE JERRIES MAY COME AGAIN.

I DON'T THINK ANY OF THEM LIVED TO TELL THE TALE. OUR HIDE-OUT IS PROBABLY STILL OUR SECRET.

BUT NIKKI WAS WRONG. MAJOR BAUER HAD ONLY BEEN CREASED BY THE BULLET WHICH DROPPED HIM.

MUST GET AWAY TO REPORT THIS. HIMMEL, MY HEAD HURTS.

BAUER LEAPT FORWARD TOWARDS THE REMAINING GERMAN TRUCK.

AAAGH!

NOW FOR THE TRUCK!

BAUER WAS IN THE TRUCK AND MOVING BEFORE NIKKI REALISED WHAT HAD HAPPENED.

GET HIM — HE MUST NOT ESCAPE!

THE GERMAN'S LUCK HELD, AND HE DISAPPEARED IN A FLURRY OF ANGRY BULLETS.

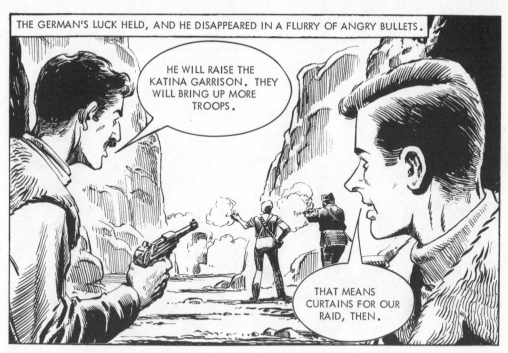

HE WILL RAISE THE KATINA GARRISON. THEY WILL BRING UP MORE TROOPS.

THAT MEANS CURTAINS FOR OUR RAID, THEN.

BUT NIKKI WASN'T GIVING IN YET.

THIS PASS IS THE ONLY WAY TO THE BEACH. WE CAN HOLD IT FOR AS LONG AS YOU NEED.

NICE WORK, NIKKI. YOU HOLD OUT HERE AND I'LL SEE TO THE FUEL.

SO, AS DICK LEFT WITH A FEW PARTISANS, THE OTHERS STAYED WITH NIKKI TO GUARD THE PASS.

THEY ARE TAKING THEIR TIME TO COME. NO DOUBT THEY WILL COME IN FORCE.

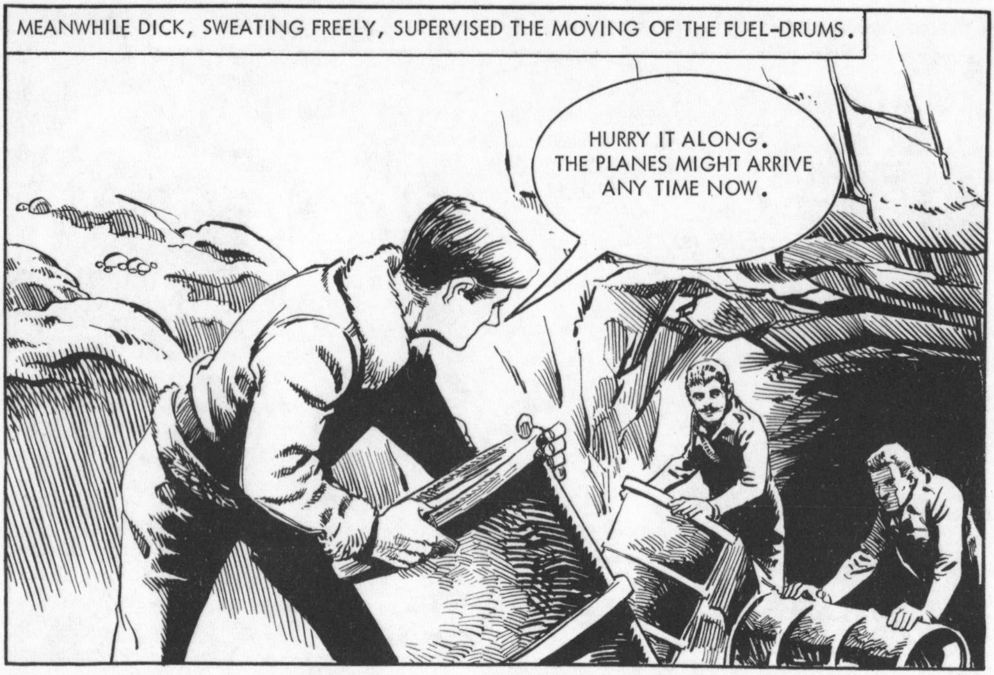
MEANWHILE DICK, SWEATING FREELY, SUPERVISED THE MOVING OF THE FUEL-DRUMS.
HURRY IT ALONG. THE PLANES MIGHT ARRIVE ANY TIME NOW.

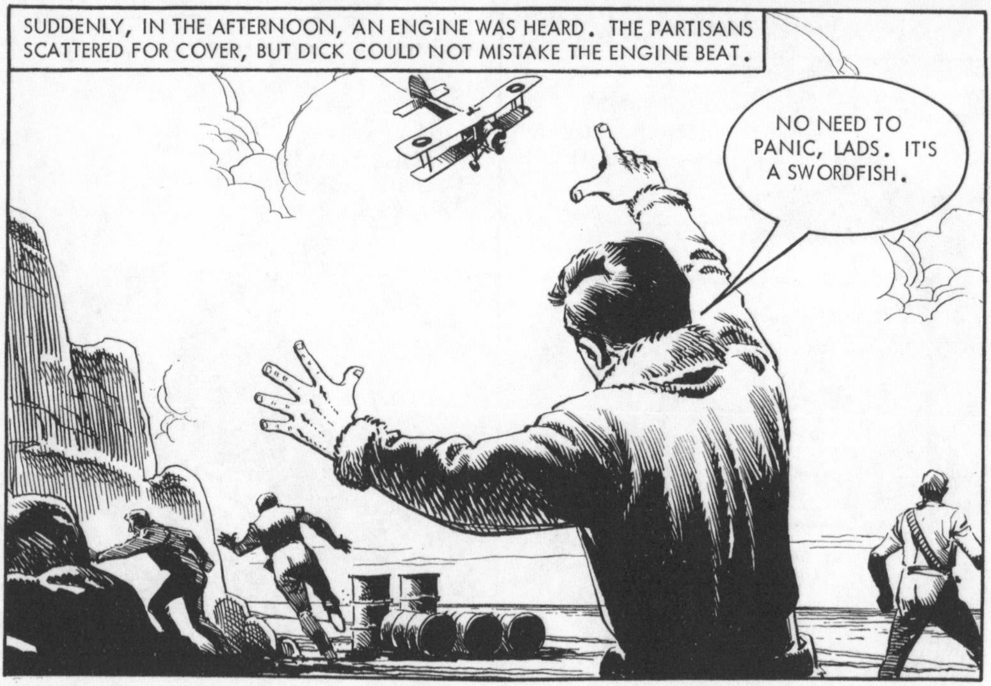
SUDDENLY, IN THE AFTERNOON, AN ENGINE WAS HEARD. THE PARTISANS SCATTERED FOR COVER, BUT DICK COULD NOT MISTAKE THE ENGINE BEAT.
NO NEED TO PANIC, LADS. IT'S A SWORDFISH.

THE SWORDFISH MADE A PERFECT LANDING. IT WAS A SMILING JIM WHO SAW DICK COME TO WELCOME HIM.

THE REST OF THE BOYS MADE IT TO MALTA. FIVE PLANES WILL ARRIVE AT DUSK. WE'LL REFUEL AND TAKE OFF IN MOONLIGHT.

FINE, BUT WE'VE HAD A VISIT FROM JERRY — AND WE'RE EXPECTING ANOTHER.

MEANWHILE, NIKKI HAD SPOTTED TROUBLE ON THE HORIZON.

THEY ARE COMING, STEPHANOS. PASS THE WORD BACK TO THE BEACH.

AT ONCE. THE GERMAN PIGS SEEM TO BE IN FULL STRENGTH, TOO.

A RUNNER INFORMED DICK AND JIM. THEY IMMEDIATELY MADE FOR THE PASS.

IT'LL BE BAD IF THEY CATCH THE WHOLE SQUADRON ON THE GROUND.

BETTER TALK TO NIKKI. HE THINKS HE CAN HOLD 'EM.

THEY SOON REACHED NIKKI.

THE GERMANS COME AGAIN — MANY OF THEM.

JIM PEERED THROUGH NIKKI'S BINOCULARS, GOGGLING AT THE SIGHT WHICH MET HIS EYES.

ARMOURED CARS, ANTI-TANK GUNS, THE LOT. WE'RE REALLY IN FOR A POUNDING.

BUT JIM HADN'T COME THIS FAR TO LET THE GERMANS BEAT HIM NOW.

WE'LL BE NEEDED TO FIGHT, HERE, SKIPPER.

KEEP 'EM OCCUPIED, NIKKI. I THINK WE CAN HELP, DICK. LET'S GO.

JIM INTENDED TO FIGHT — BUT IN HIS OWN WAY. HE RACED BACK TO THE BEACH AND BEGAN TO ORGANISE THE REMOVAL OF THE TORPEDO FROM UNDERNEATH THE SWORDFISH.

HURRY IT ALONG. I WANT THAT KITE IN THE AIR IN THE NEXT TWO MINUTES.

IN RECORD TIME THE PLANE WAS READY AND JOCKEYED AIRBORNE BY JIM.

JUST PRAY THAT WE'RE NOT TOO LATE, DICK.

MEANWHILE, NIKKI HAD NOT BEEN WAITING INNOCENTLY FOR THE GERMANS AT THE PASS. HE HAD LAID ON A SURPRISE FOR THEM.

JUST A LITTLE NEARER — I WILL GIVE THE WORD.

AT NIKKI'S SHOUTED COMMAND, STEPHANOS DEPRESSED THE PLUNGER. THE WHOLE ROAD AROUND THE TWO LEADING ARMOURED CARS SEEMED TO ERUPT IN FLAMES AND SMOKE.

THE GERMANS, FURIOUS AT THIS LATEST OUTRAGE, UNHITCHED THE TWO ANTI-TANK GUNS AND OPENED HEAVY FIRE ON THE GUERRILLAS' POSITION.

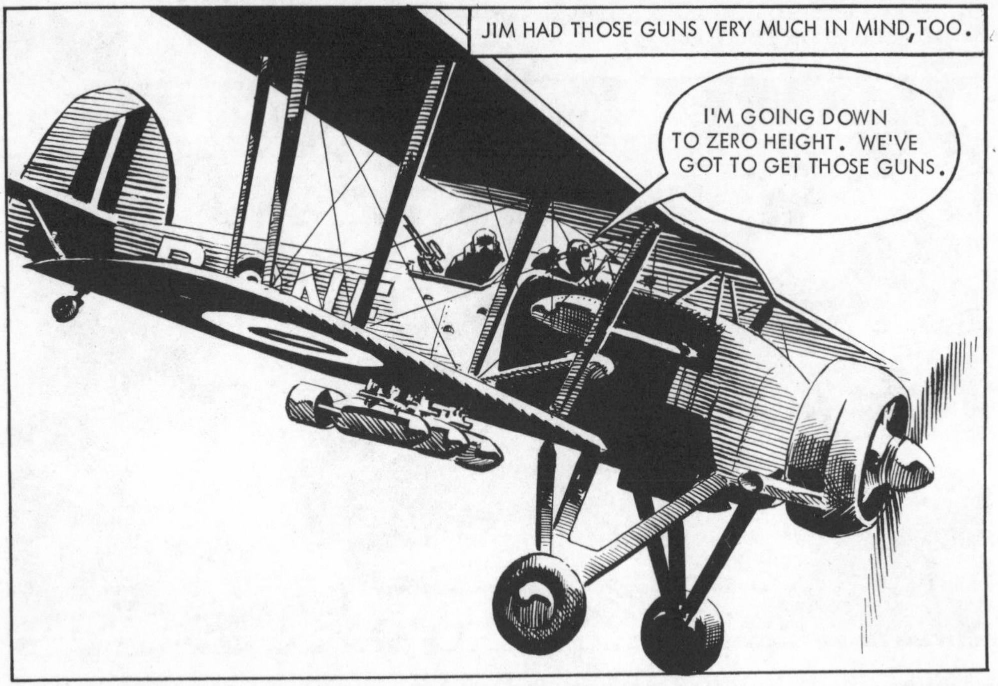
JIM HAD THOSE GUNS VERY MUCH IN MIND, TOO.
I'M GOING DOWN TO ZERO HEIGHT. WE'VE GOT TO GET THOSE GUNS.

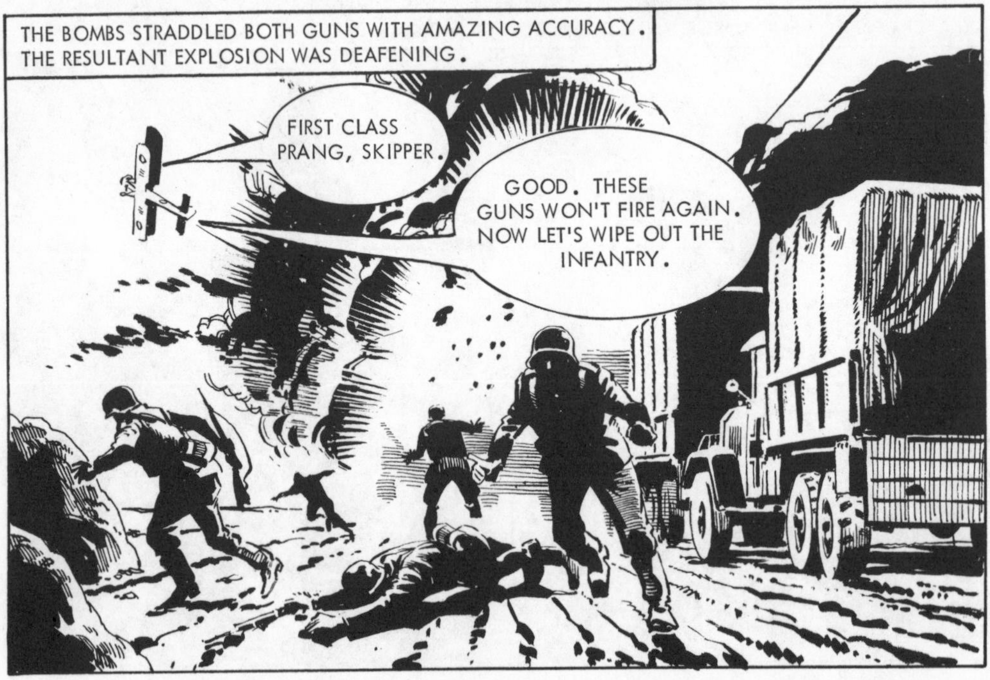
THE BOMBS STRADDLED BOTH GUNS WITH AMAZING ACCURACY. THE RESULTANT EXPLOSION WAS DEAFENING.
FIRST CLASS PRANG, SKIPPER.
GOOD. THESE GUNS WON'T FIRE AGAIN. NOW LET'S WIPE OUT THE INFANTRY.

JIM PILOTED THE PLANE TOWARDS THE OUTCROP OF ROCK HE HAD NOTICED ABOVE THE MAIN GERMAN FORCE.

WE NEED TWO BOMBS JUST BELOW THAT OUTCROP — FAIR AND SQUARE.

WILCO, SKIPPER.

THE TWO BOMBS STRUCK BELOW THE OUTCROP, THE EXPLOSIONS DISLODGING A GREAT WALL OF ROCK.

RUN, YOU NAZIS — RUN!

IT'S GOING TO WIPE THE WHOLE LOT OUT, SKIPPER.

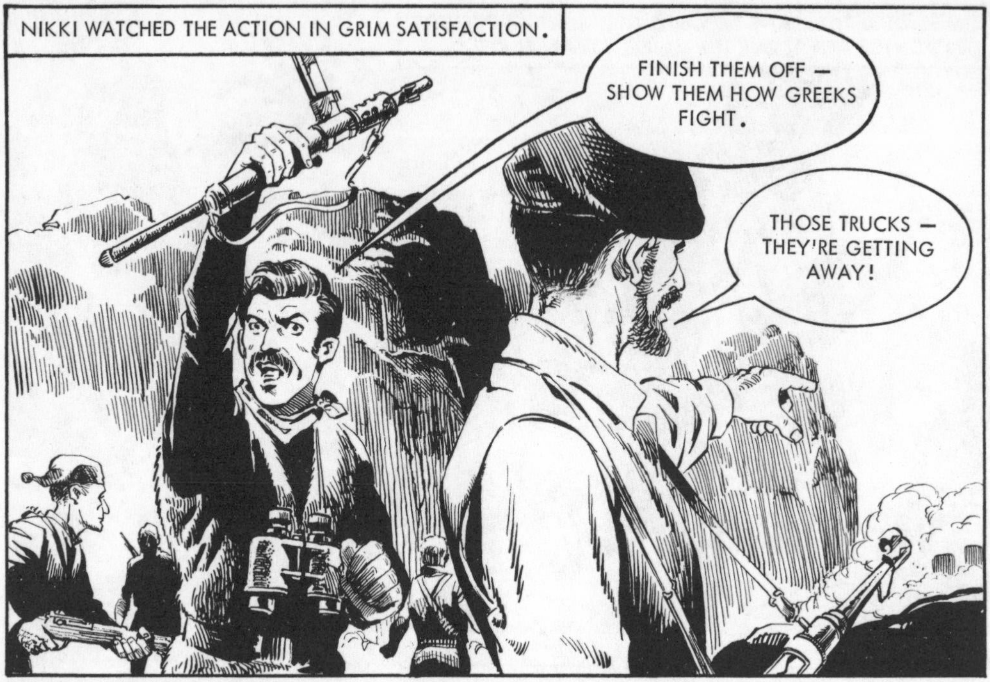
NIKKI WATCHED THE ACTION IN GRIM SATISFACTION.
FINISH THEM OFF — SHOW THEM HOW GREEKS FIGHT.
THOSE TRUCKS — THEY'RE GETTING AWAY!

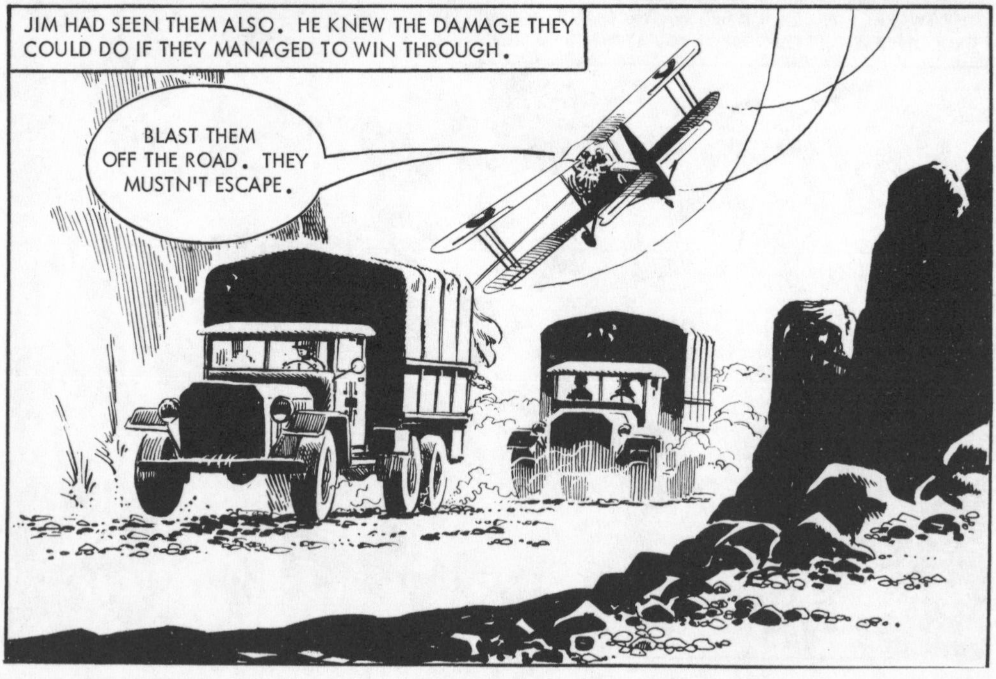
JIM HAD SEEN THEM ALSO. HE KNEW THE DAMAGE THEY COULD DO IF THEY MANAGED TO WIN THROUGH.
BLAST THEM OFF THE ROAD. THEY MUSTN'T ESCAPE.

DICK EMPTIED HIS DRUM OF AMMUNITION INTO THE TRUCKS, THE RESULT BEING DISASTROUS AND SPECTACULAR.

NICE WORK, DICK.

THE BATTLE WAS NOW OVER. NIKKI WAS AT THE BEACH TO CONGRATULATE JIM AS SOON AS HE LANDED.

YOU CAME JUST IN TIME, MY FRIEND.

COULDN'T HAVE BEEN EASIER.

BUT THEN NIKKI'S FACE CLOUDED OVER.

THEY'LL BE BACK. THE GERMANS DON'T GIVE IN EASILY.

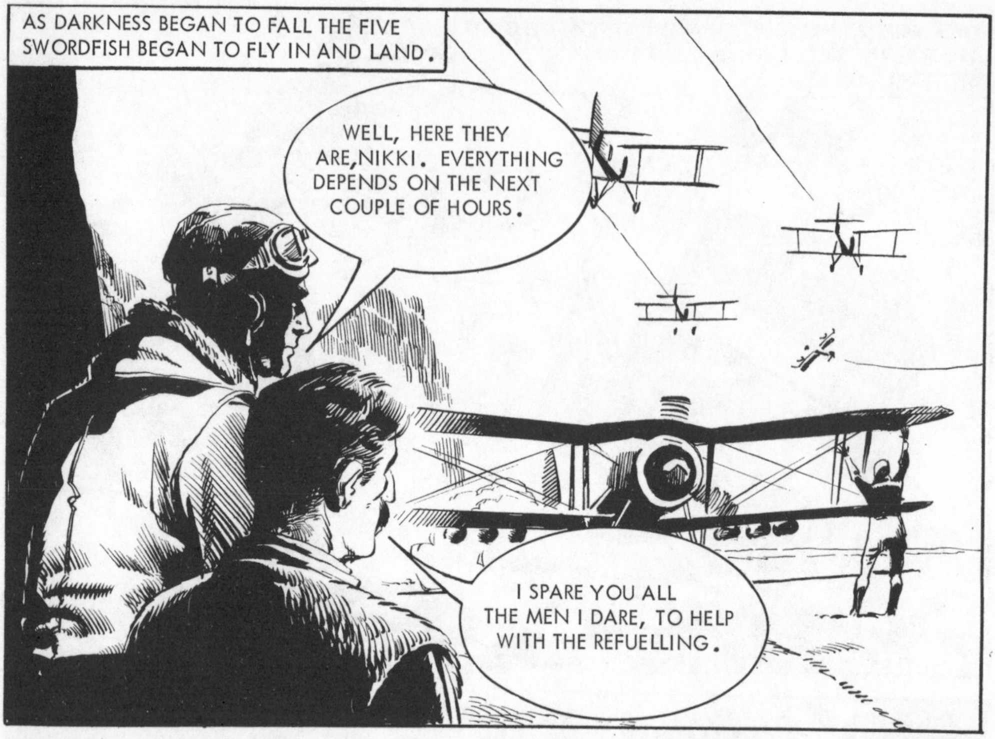
AS DARKNESS BEGAN TO FALL THE FIVE SWORDFISH BEGAN TO FLY IN AND LAND.
WELL, HERE THEY ARE, NIKKI. EVERYTHING DEPENDS ON THE NEXT COUPLE OF HOURS.
I SPARE YOU ALL THE MEN I DARE, TO HELP WITH THE REFUELLING.

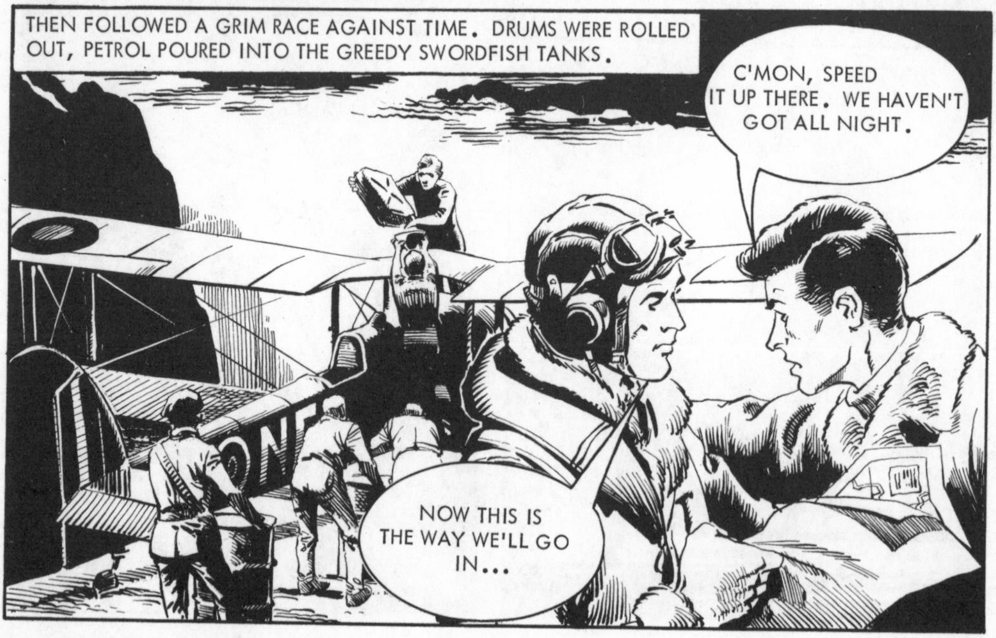
THEN FOLLOWED A GRIM RACE AGAINST TIME. DRUMS WERE ROLLED OUT, PETROL POURED INTO THE GREEDY SWORDFISH TANKS.
C'MON, SPEED IT UP THERE. WE HAVEN'T GOT ALL NIGHT.
NOW THIS IS THE WAY WE'LL GO IN...

MEANWHILE, HOWEVER, THE GERMANS HAD RETURNED AND WERE STORMING THE PARTISANS' POSITION WITH SUICIDAL ANGER.

IS NO GOOD. WE WILL HAVE TO RETREAT.

AS THE GUNFIRE ECHOED NEARER AND NEARER, THE MEN ON THE BEACH SLAVED TO GET THE FIRST OF THE PLANES AIRBORNE. NIKKI CAME WITH BAD NEWS.

THEY HAVE BROKEN THROUGH.

THEY'LL CATCH THE KITES ON THE GROUND!

WE'VE STILL SOME FUEL LEFT IN THE CAVE. I'VE AN IDEA, SKIPPER.

DICK EXPLAINED HIS PLAN TO NIKKI WHO GRINNED HUGELY.

STAY WITH US MY FRIEND. YOU ARE A BORN GUERRILLA FIGHTER!

WHILST NIKKI WENT TO DIRECT OPERATIONS ON THE CLIFF, DICK DASHED TO THE FUEL CAVE.

ROUGH AND READY — BUT THIS FUSE WILL DO THE TRICK.

AS NIKKI RETREATED, HE LED THE GERMANS TOWARDS THE FUEL CAVE AS HE HAD AGREED WITH DICK.

ONCE IN THE CAVE, ESCAPE UP THROUGH THE CHIMNEY TO THE CLIFF. UNDERSTAND?

IT IS MAD, BUT WE DO AS YOU SAY.

AS SOON AS THEY WERE IN THE CAVE, DICK LIT THE FUSE HE HAD ATTACHED TO THE PETROL DRUM WHILST NIKKI COVERED HIM.

HURRY — I CANNOT HOLD THEM LONG.

JUST BE A SEC...

THEY ESCAPED THROUGH THE CHIMNEY TO THE TOP OF THE CLIFF. IT HAD BEEN PREPARED FOR SUCH AN EMERGENCY, BUT STILL NIKKI STUCK —

HAVE YOU OUT IN A JIFFY, MATE.

LEAVE ME. IT IS NOT WORTH... LOOK OUT!

AS DICK TURNED, THE GERMAN'S GUN SPAT, AND A NUMBING PAIN GRIPPED HIS LEFT SHOULDER. HE REELED BACK.

AAAGH!

MY FRIEND!

GLOATING, THE GERMAN MOVED FORWARD TO FINISH NIKKI WITH A BAYONET THRUST...

NOW YOU DIE, PEASANT.

PIG! IF I COULD GET MY GUN...

DICK REVIVED JUST AS THE BAYONET WAS RAISED.   HE MOVED WITH
LIGHTNING SPEED.

AAAGH!

OH NO YOU
DON'T, JERRY!

DESPITE HIS WOUNDED ARM, DICK
STRUGGLED DESPERATELY TO PULL
NIKKI CLEAR BEFORE THE FUSE HE HAD
SET EXPLODED.

JUST IN TIME,
I THINK.

I THINK I AM
THE CORK IN THE
BOTTLE.

THE GERMANS HAD FALLEN HOOK, LINE AND SINKER FOR THE TRAP. THEY HAD RUSHED INTO THE DESERTED CAVE, ONLY TO BE HURLED OUT BY A CONCUSSIVE WAVE OF FLAMING PETROL.

THEY DASHED BACK TO THE BEACH TO FIND JIM REVVING UP THE SWORDFISH. IT WAS THE ONLY ONE STILL ON THE GROUND.

AS THE SWORDFISH SURGED FORWARD, GERMANS BROKE ACROSS THE BEACH FIRING AT THEM.

CLEAR THE WAY, JERRY. WE'RE IN A HURRY.

AAAGH!

THE PLANE LIFTED INTO THE NIGHT SKY, AND NIKKI LED HIS MEN QUICKLY AWAY.

NOW WE HIDE IN THE MOUNTAINS. LET THE GERMANS LOOK FOR GHOSTS.

IT HAS BEEN GOOD WORK THIS NIGHT.

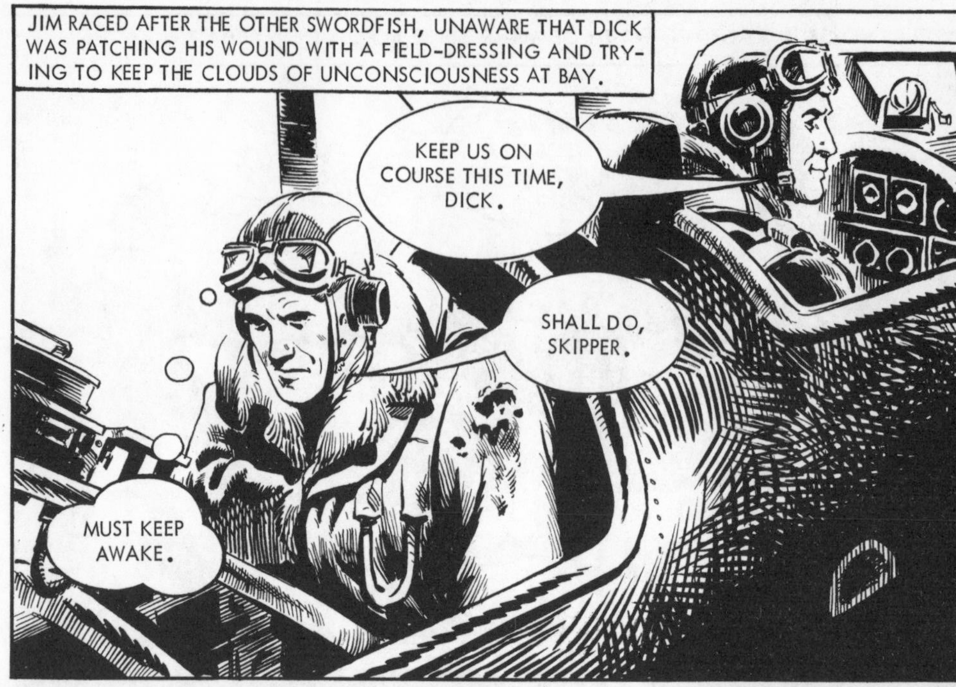
JIM RACED AFTER THE OTHER SWORDFISH, UNAWARE THAT DICK WAS PATCHING HIS WOUND WITH A FIELD-DRESSING AND TRYING TO KEEP THE CLOUDS OF UNCONSCIOUSNESS AT BAY.
KEEP US ON COURSE THIS TIME, DICK.
SHALL DO, SKIPPER.
MUST KEEP AWAKE.

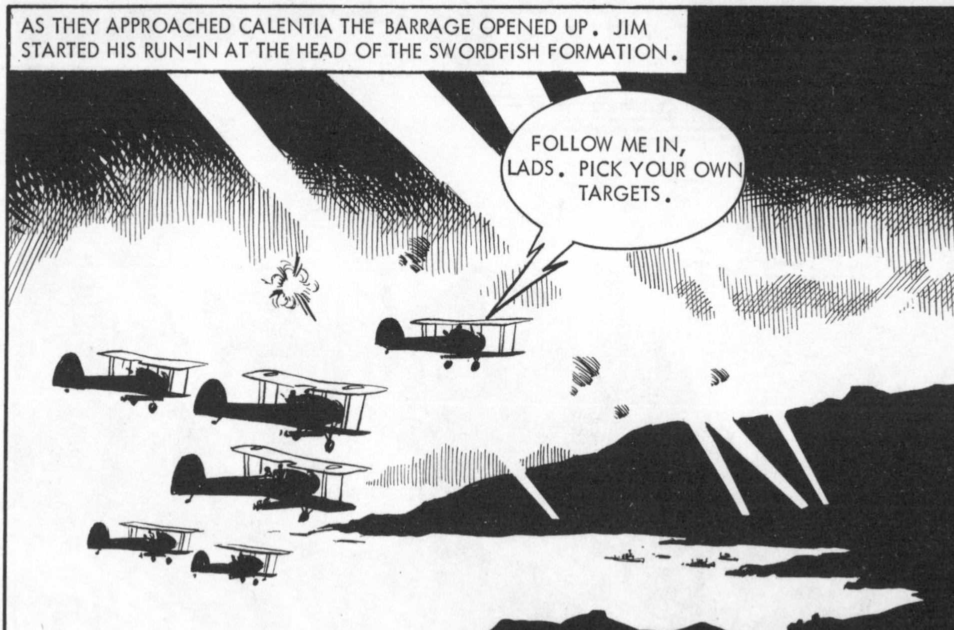
AS THEY APPROACHED CALENTIA THE BARRAGE OPENED UP. JIM STARTED HIS RUN-IN AT THE HEAD OF THE SWORDFISH FORMATION.
FOLLOW ME IN, LADS. PICK YOUR OWN TARGETS.

IT DIDN'T TAKE THE KEEN-EYED JIM LONG TO PICK HIS TARGET.

JIM DROPPED HER DOWN TO ZERO HEIGHT, AND HELD HER STEADY DESPITE THE HEAVY ANTI-AIRCRAFT BARRAGE.

THERE WAS NO DOUBT ABOUT DICK'S AIM, BUT EVEN HE WASN'T EXPECTING THE EXPLOSION WHICH FOLLOWED AS THE MAGAZINE WENT UP.

THE SURPRISE WAS AS COMPLETE AS THE DEVASTATION. TORPEDO AFTER TORPEDO THUMPED HOME WITH SHATTERING RESULTS.

WE'RE REALLY HITTING THEM HARD.

THE WHOLE PLACE IS ON FIRE!

AS THE OTHER SWORDFISH BOMBED THE SHIPS, JIM, HAVING ALREADY DROPPED HIS ON THE GERMANS, SHOT UP THE QUAYSIDE.

THEY WON'T FORGET THIS IN A HURRY!

EVENTUALLY THEY TURNED FOR MALTA, LEAVING CARNAGE AND DESTRUCTION BEHIND. DICK, HOWEVER, HAD LOST INTEREST IN THE PROCEEDINGS.

NICE WORK, DICK — GREAT STARS, HE'S BEEN HIT.

DICK'S NEXT RECOLLECTION WAS OF WAKING UP IN A CLEAN HOSPITAL BED — IN BROAD DAYLIGHT.

WHAT THE DICKENS...WHERE AM I?

IT'S ALL RIGHT, LIEUTENANT. YOU'VE LOST A LOT OF BLOOD, BUT YOU'LL BE OK NOW.

A SHORT WHILE LATER DICK HAD A VISITOR.

DICK, YOU OLD SEA-COOK. WHY DIDN'T YOU SAY YOU'D BEEN WOUNDED?

IT DIDN'T SEEM TO MATTER, SKIPPER.

JIM HAD FAR TOO IMPORTANT NEWS TO LET DICK'S MODESTY BOTHER HIM.

I'VE BEEN PULLING A FEW STRINGS, DICK. YOU'RE GOING BACK TO FLYING-SCHOOL — ON A PILOT'S COURSE!

SKIPPER, THAT'S JUST GREAT!

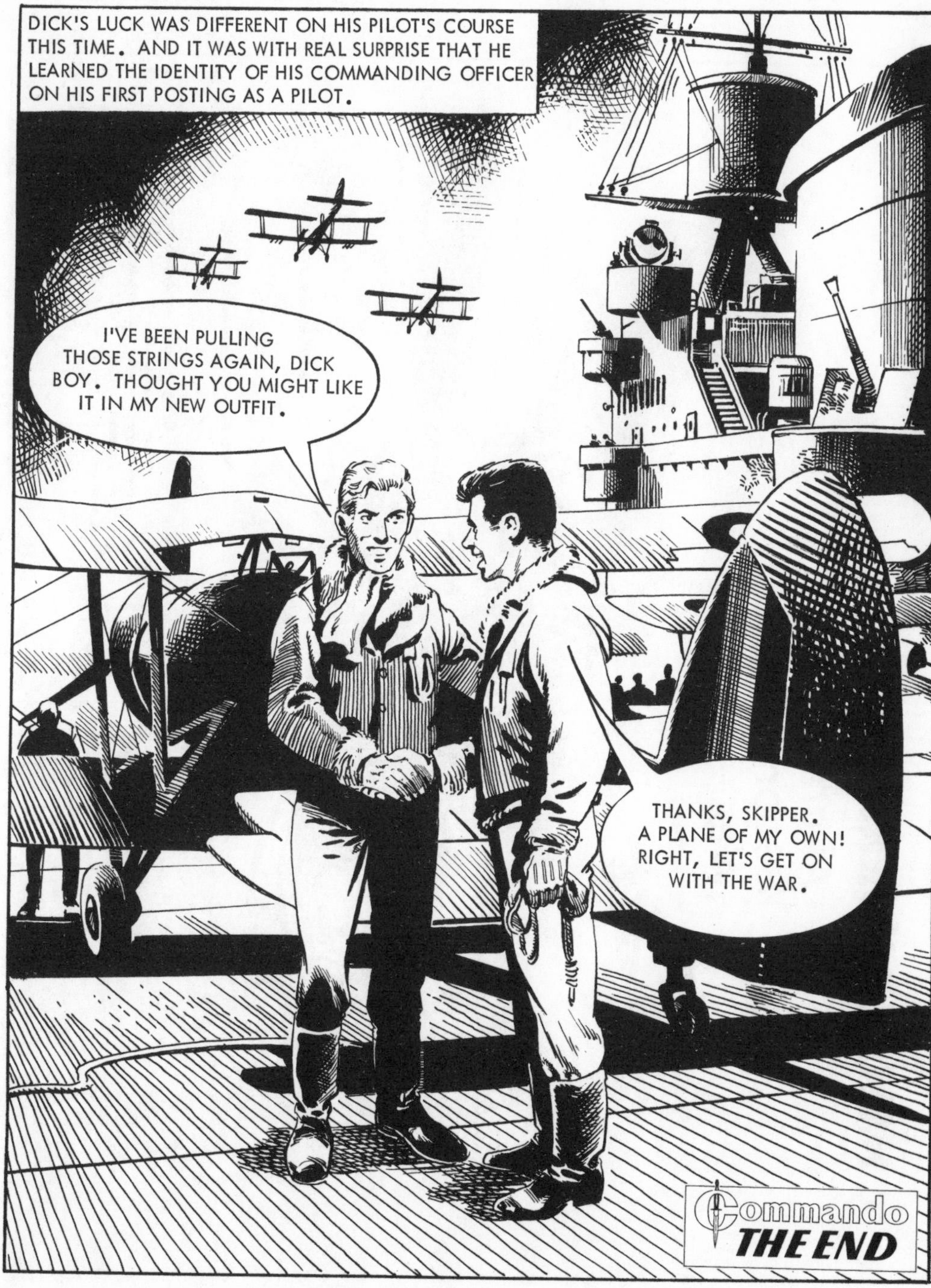
DICK'S LUCK WAS DIFFERENT ON HIS PILOT'S COURSE THIS TIME. AND IT WAS WITH REAL SURPRISE THAT HE LEARNED THE IDENTITY OF HIS COMMANDING OFFICER ON HIS FIRST POSTING AS A PILOT.
I'VE BEEN PULLING THOSE STRINGS AGAIN, DICK BOY. THOUGHT YOU MIGHT LIKE IT IN MY NEW OUTFIT.
THANKS, SKIPPER. A PLANE OF MY OWN! RIGHT, LET'S GET ON WITH THE WAR.
Commando
THE END

HAWKER HURRICANE

Aircraft of the Second World War — No. 10

ROLLS ROYCE MERLIN XX
LIQUID-COOLED ENGINE (1,260hp).

GUN SIGHT

REAR-VIEW MIRROR

RADIO

FLARE CHUTE

LANDING LIGHT

250 lb BOMB BELOW EACH WING

TWO 20mm CANNON IN EACH WING

FUEL TANK IN WING
(One each side)

RETRACTABLE UNDERCARRIAGE

AIR INTAKE

THE famous "Hurri" was the first monoplane fighter used by the R.A.F. and the first British military aircraft capable of more than 300mph. Together with the Spitfire it won the Battle Of Britain, then went on from there to serve in theatres of war all over the world. Many different versions were built. The Fleet Air Arm used it, one type had 40mm cannon below the wings for tank-busting, and it was also carried on a special catapult on merchant ships to protect convoys.
Total production of Hurricanes was 14,533.

HIGH ABOVE THE BATTLE-SCORCHED SANDS OF NORTH AFRICA, R.A.F. HURRICANES OF THE DESERT AIR FORCE FOUGHT IT OUT WITH GERMAN MESSERSCHMITT 109's FOR MASTERY OF THE SKY.

WHILE, ON THE GROUND, FIELD MARSHALL ERWIN ROMMEL FLUNG THE FULL MIGHT OF HIS PANZER DIVISIONS AT THE BRITISH EIGHTH ARMY IN A LIGHTNING BLITZ. IT WAS APRIL, 1941...

IN THE COCKPIT OF HIS HURRICANE MARKED WITH THE EMBLEM OF LONDON'S BOW BELLS, PILOT "GINGER" STUBBS, COCKNEY FIGHTER ACE, CONCENTRATED ON HITTING THE ENEMY.

ALL RIGHT, COME AND PERISHING WELL GET IT. I'VE GOT A BONE TO PICK WITH YOU NAZI SCUM!

SINCE HE'D LEARNT OF HIS PARENTS' DEATH IN A GERMAN BOMBING RAID ON LONDON, GINGER HAD GONE FIGHTING MAD, SCORNING ALL LEAVE.

NOW... TAKE IT AND LIKE IT!

HE LINED UP AN ME. 109 IN HIS GUNSIGHT. HIS THUMB JABBED SAVAGELY AT THE FIRING BUTTON — AND EIGHT BROWNING MACHINE GUNS HAMMERED LEAD INTO THE GERMAN PLANE.

MEIN GOTT ...AARGH!

GOT YOU, YOU RAT!

GINGER'S FRECKLED FACE WORE A MASK OF TRIUMPH, THEN HIS NUMBER TWO SHOUTED A WARNING OVER THE RADIO.

ONE MORE FOR MUM AND DAD... NOW FOR THE NEXT.

GET WEAVING, GINGER — TWO OF 'EM BOUNCING YOU!

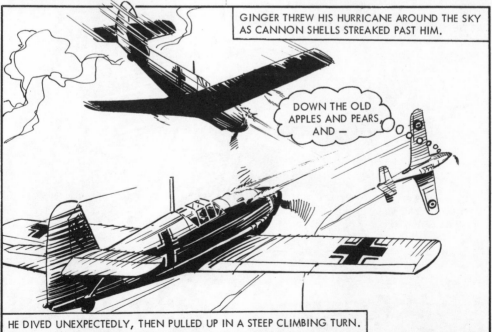

GINGER THREW HIS HURRICANE AROUND THE SKY AS CANNON SHELLS STREAKED PAST HIM.

DOWN THE OLD APPLES AND PEARS, AND —

HE DIVED UNEXPECTEDLY, THEN PULLED UP IN A STEEP CLIMBING TURN.

ZOOMING UP UNDER THE SURPRISED GERMANS, GINGER RIPPED A LONG BURST INTO THE BELLY OF THE NEAREST MESSERSCHMITT. IT SPUN AWAY, OUT OF CONTROL.

DIDN'T EXPECT THAT, DID YOU, MATE? YOU'RE SO FLAMING SLOW YOU COULDN'T EVEN CATCH A COLD!

HE REEFED AROUND HURRIEDLY AND FLEW HEAD-ON AT THE SECOND GERMAN ATTACKING HIM.

LET'S SEE WHO'LL BREAK FIRST, FRITZ!

HIMMEL! THE DUMMKOPF WILL CRASH US BOTH!

THE GERMAN PILOT'S NERVE CRACKED FIRST, AND GINGER RAKED HIM WITH GUNFIRE FROM NOSE TO TAIL AS HE BROKE AWAY.

AND THAT MAKES NUMBER THREE! NOT BAD FOR A DUMB LITTLE COCKNEY LAD!

THE FEW SURVIVING MESSERSCHMITTS FLED BEFORE THE GUNS OF THE VICTORIOUS R.A.F.

ALL THE WAY BACK TO EL ADEM AIRFIELD, SOUTH OF TOBRUK, THE FLIGHT OF HURRICANES SAW BRITISH AND AUSTRALIAN SOLDIERS STRAGGLING WEARILY BACK, IN RETREAT.

WHAT THE BLAZES HAS GONE WRONG NOW?

IT LOOKS TO ME LIKE THE BROWN JOBS HAVE TAKEN A REAL PASTING THIS TIME!

AS THEY CAME IN TO LAND, GINGER WAS SHOCKED TO SEE THE AIRFIELD LOOKING ABANDONED.

BLIMEY, THE PLACE IS DESERTED!

THE SQUADRON C.O. HURRIED UP. HE SEEMED TO HAVE AGED SINCE GINGER HAD SEEN HIM LAST...

WHAT'S THE FLAP ALL ABOUT, SIR?

ROMMEL'S BROKEN THROUGH IN FORCE! HE'S ALMOST ON TOP OF US, AND WE'RE PULLING BACK TO MERSA MATRUH. TAKE OFF AS SOON AS YOU'RE REFUELLED.

GINGER'S LIPS TIGHTENED. A LIGHT OF DEFIANCE FLARED IN HIS EYES.

PULL BACK, IS IT? NOT ME — NOT MRS STUBBS' LITTLE BOY!

I HEAR THE ARMY ARE GOING TO TRY AND HOLD TOBRUK, BUT THAT'S NOTHING TO DO WITH US, SERGEANT.

ISN'T IT, NOW? SOUNDS LIKE MY CHANCE TO TAKE ANOTHER CRACK AT THE NAZIS.

THE C.O. DASHED AWAY. THE FIRST HURRICANE TO BE REFUELLED GOT AIR-BORNE. GINGER STROLLED OVER TO THE PILOT OF THE SECOND FIGHTER...

WHAT'S KEEPING YOU, GINGER? YOU HEARD THE C.O. LET'S BLOW.

YOU SCARPER OFF, MATE. I'LL BE SEEING YOU LATER... MAYBE.

WHEN GINGER TOOK OFF AGAIN, ALONE, HE DID NOT FLY EAST FOR MERSA MATRUH.   HE HEADED NORTH, TO TOBRUK.

REGULAR FORTRESS DOWN THERE... NOW THEY'RE GETTING A ONE-MAN AIR FORCE, WHETHER THEY LIKE IT OR NOT!

HE TOUCHED DOWN ON THE MAIN ROAD INSIDE THE DEFENCE RINGS.   A TRUCK HASTILY PULLED OFF THE ROAD TO GIVE HIM ROOM.

NOTHING TO IT... IT'S AS GOOD AS ANY RUNWAY.

THE STUPID COOT! WHAT SORT OF CAPER DOES HE THINK HE'S ON?

TWO AUSTRALIANS HELPED GINGER TO PUSH HIS PLANE OFF THE ROADWAY. ONE, A HARD-BITTEN VETERAN SERGEANT OF INFANTRY, JEERED...

LOST YER WAY, POMMY? THIS AIN'T NO RUDDY AIR-STRIP, YOU'RE HOLDING UP MILITARY TRAFFIC.

JUST THOUGHT THERE MIGHT BE THE CHANCE OF A FIGHT HERE!

SERGEANT "COBBER" KANE JERKED A DIRTY THUMB AT THE INSIGNIA PAINTED ON GINGER'S AIRCRAFT.

AND WHAT MIGHT THIS BE, SPORT?

SOME PEOPLE ARE DOWNRIGHT IGNORANT! THEM'S THE BOW BELLS, DIGGER ...AND YOU'RE LOOKING AT A REAL LONDON COCKNEY.

THE AUSSIES HAD BEEN DRIVEN HARD, OUT-GUNNED AND DIVE-BOMBED. SHORT OF SLEEP, THEIR TEMPERS WERE ON EDGE. COBBER SUDDENLY FLARED UP.

AND WHERE WERE YOU BRYLCREEM BOYS HIDING WHEN THE JERRIES ATTACKED, EH? JUST TELL ME THAT.

US? WE WERE BASHING ROMMEL'S SUPPLY LINES, ON ORDERS — WHERE WERE YOU?

PRIVATE "WOODY" WOODS, A ROUGH-NECK FROM SYDNEY'S WATERFRONT, BITTERLY RESENTED GINGER'S BLUNT WORDS...

YOU LOT SHOULD HAVE DUG YOUR TOES IN...NOT RUN LIKE RABBITS!

WHY, YOU CRAWLING DINGO, I'LL DO YOU OVER FOR THAT CRACK!

THE AUSSIE LET LOOSE A PUNCH, BUT GINGER DUCKED AND SLAMMED A PILE-DRIVING LEFT TO HIS JAW.

OUCH!

COME ON, DIGGER, I AIN'T EVEN WARMED UP YET!

BELT HIM, WOODY!

ONLY THE UNEXPECTED ARRIVAL OF AN R.A.F. GROUP-CAPTAIN STOPPED A FULL-SCALE PUNCH-UP.

NOW THEN, SERGEANT, WHAT'S GOING ON HERE?

JUST SHOWING ONE OF THE OUTBACK BOYS HOW TO USE HIS MITTS, SIR!

GROUP-CAPTAIN BROWNE, A DESK-PILOT FROM H.Q., FROWNED WHEN HE HEARD GINGER'S STORY AND HIS REQUEST TO BE ALLOWED TO STAY.

YOU SHOULDN'T BE HERE AT ALL, SERGEANT. YOU MUST REJOIN YOUR SQUADRON IMMEDIATELY. EVERY AIRCRAFT WILL BE NEEDED NOW.

SORRY, SIR, I'M CLEAN OUT OF FUEL!

GINGER WAS DETERMINED TO STAY AND FIGHT BACK FROM TOBRUK.

AS BROWNE BEGAN TO SPEAK AGAIN, THERE CAME A SUDDEN DRAMATIC INTERRUPTION...

FORTUNATELY, WE HAVE A SMALL PETROL SUPPLY HERE —

JACK IT IN, YOU JOKERS — THE STUKAS ARE BACK WITH US!

I THOUGHT YOU SAID YOU HAD NO FUEL, SERGEANT?

BET YOU A QUID HE FINDS ENOUGH TO GET OUT OF HERE FAST — TOO RIGHT HE WILL!

GINGER SPRINTED FOR HIS HURRICANE AND VAULTED INTO THE COCKPIT AS GERMAN DIVE-BOMBERS CAME SCREAMING DOWN.

GINGER GUNNED HIS MERLIN ENGINE TO LIFE AND ROARED UPWARDS.

JUST WAIT TILL I GET AT YOU, YOU NAZI VERMIN!

THE BANSHEE WAIL OF JUNKERS JUMO ENGINES SET THE AIR REVERBERATING AS BLACK VULTURE-LIKE STUKAS PLUMMETED DOWNWARD...

THE GUNS OF TOBRUK VOMITED FLAME AND FLYING STEEL...RECKLESSLY, GINGER FOLLOWED THE STUKAS DOWN INTO THE CURTAIN OF SHRAPNEL AND HIGH EXPLOSIVE.

THE FIRST STICK OF BOMBS HIT AN OIL TANKER. INSTANTLY IT BLOSSOMED INTO A FLAMING PYRE.

GINGER TURNED ON A DIME AND WENT HEADLONG AFTER A SECOND STUKA...

HE CLOSED THE GAP, GUNS HAMMERING. THE STUKA, MORTALLY HIT, PLUNGED DOWN WITH ITS BOMBS STILL UNRELEASED.

ACH! MY CONTROLS ARE SHOT AWAY.

GOT HIM! NAILED THE PERISHER!

DOWN BELOW, AUSSIE GUNNERS OF THE 3rd LIGHT A.A. REGIMENT CHEERED LUSTILY AS THE STUKA EXPLODED.

GOOD ON YER, MATE, GIVE 'EM BLAZES!

BLAST 'EM OUT OF THE SKY, YOU BEAUT!

SURPRISED BY THE LONE FIGHTER OF TOBRUK, THE OTHER STUKAS TURNED TAIL — BUT NOT BEFORE GINGER GOT IN A LAST RAKING BURST AT ONE.

LAST ONE — FOR LUCK.

BUT GINGER HAD TO LET THE LAST STUKA ESCAPE. HE KNEW HE HAD NO PETROL TO SPARE FOR A LONG CHASE.

ALL RIGHT, THERE'LL BE ANOTHER TIME.

AS GINGER CAME IN TO LAND, LIEUTENANT COLONEL DEVLIN, AUSTRALIAN INFANTRY, FROWNED THOUGHTFULLY.

WE CAN CERTAINLY USE THAT BOY HERE. I WONDER, NOW...

IT MAKES ME SICK THAT EVEN ONE OF THE RATS GOT AWAY, SIR!

NOT YOUR FAULT, MY BOY. YOU PUT UP A FINE SHOW, AND I'LL BE GLAD TO SEE YOU STAY IN TOBRUK...UNOFFICIALLY!

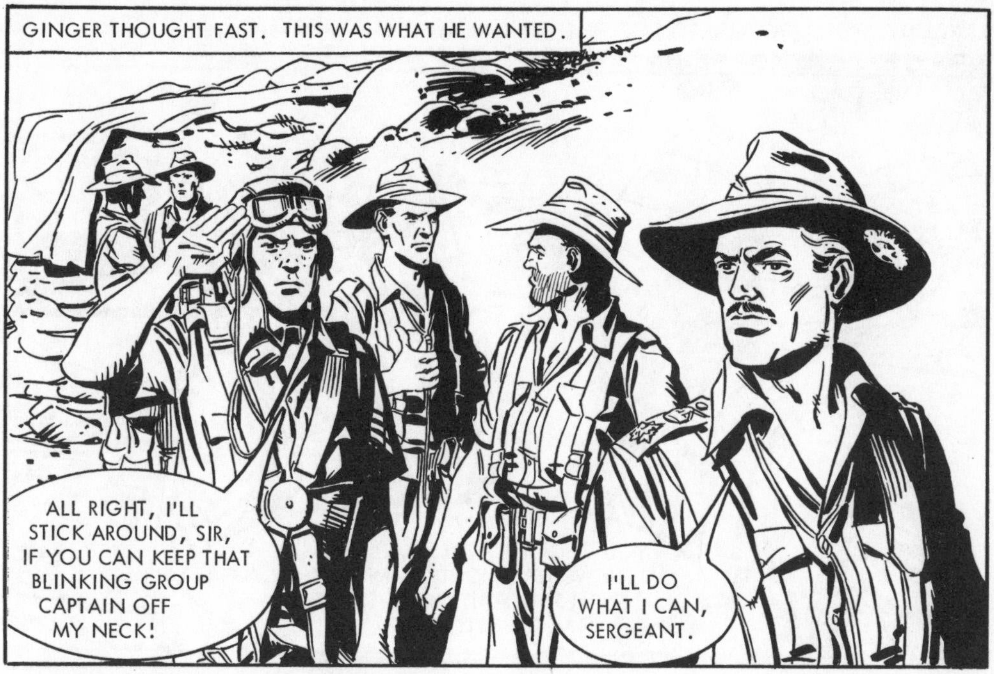
GINGER THOUGHT FAST. THIS WAS WHAT HE WANTED.
ALL RIGHT, I'LL STICK AROUND, SIR, IF YOU CAN KEEP THAT BLINKING GROUP CAPTAIN OFF MY NECK!
I'LL DO WHAT I CAN, SERGEANT.

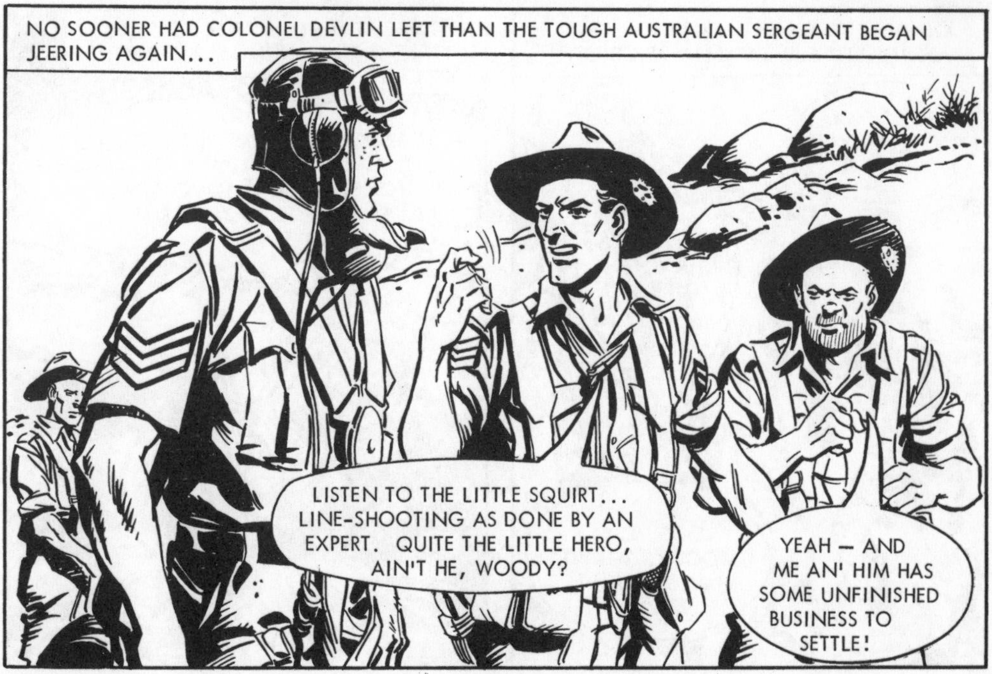
NO SOONER HAD COLONEL DEVLIN LEFT THAN THE TOUGH AUSTRALIAN SERGEANT BEGAN JEERING AGAIN...
LISTEN TO THE LITTLE SQUIRT... LINE-SHOOTING AS DONE BY AN EXPERT. QUITE THE LITTLE HERO, AIN'T HE, WOODY?
YEAH — AND ME AN' HIM HAS SOME UNFINISHED BUSINESS TO SETTLE!

"WOODY" WOODS WANTED TO TAKE UP THE FIGHT WHERE THEY HAD LEFT OFF.

YOU'VE GOT A HOPE, MATE, PICKING ON THE WELTER WEIGHT CHAMP OF THE R.A.F.! AND I'M STILL WAITING TO SEE YOU TACKLE A JERRY.

GINGER TURNED HIS BACK ON THE TWO ASTONISHED AUSSIES AND WALKED OFF.

WHAT D'YOU RECKON TO 'IM NOW, COBBER?

BEATS ME, WOODY. WHO'D HAVE THOUGHT IT?

THAT NIGHT, AS HE SETTLED TO SLEEP UNDER THE STARS, GINGER'S THOUGHTS WERE GRIM.

TOBRUK WILL SUIT ME FINE. IT'S A BOTTLENECK, ROMMEL MUST ATTACK HERE OR STOP DEAD. AND TOMORROW, I'LL KILL SOME MORE NAZIS FOR MUM AND DAD.

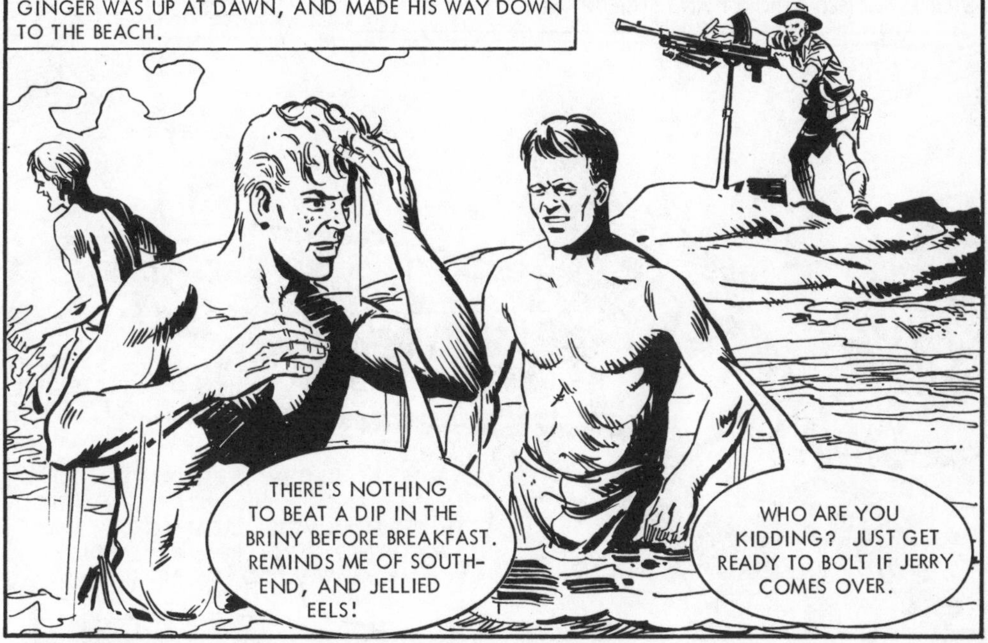
GINGER WAS UP AT DAWN, AND MADE HIS WAY DOWN TO THE BEACH.
THERE'S NOTHING TO BEAT A DIP IN THE BRINY BEFORE BREAKFAST. REMINDS ME OF SOUTH-END, AND JELLIED EELS!
WHO ARE YOU KIDDING? JUST GET READY TO BOLT IF JERRY COMES OVER.

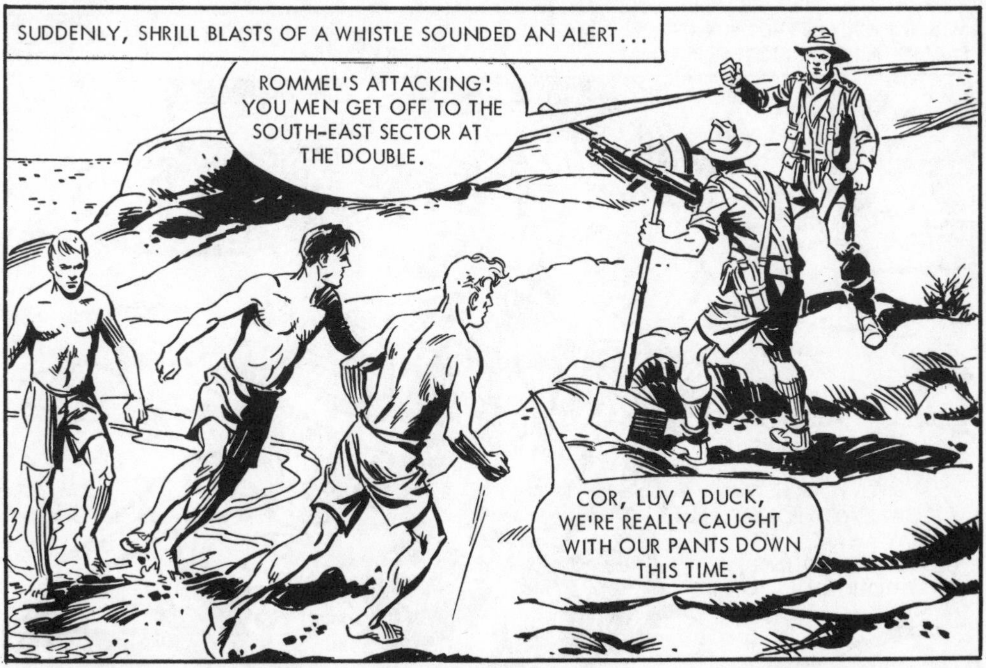
SUDDENLY, SHRILL BLASTS OF A WHISTLE SOUNDED AN ALERT...
ROMMEL'S ATTACKING! YOU MEN GET OFF TO THE SOUTH-EAST SECTOR AT THE DOUBLE.
COR, LUV A DUCK, WE'RE REALLY CAUGHT WITH OUR PANTS DOWN THIS TIME.

GINGER DRESSED QUICKLY AND SPRINTED FOR HIS HURRICANE.

HECK, I SHOULD HAVE REFUELLED LAST NIGHT...AND I DON'T EVEN KNOW WHERE THE PETROL DUMP IS. CLEAN FORGOT I'M MY OWN GROUND CREW NOW! HOLY SMOKE, WHAT DO I DO NEXT?

MEANWHILE, ON THE PERIMETER, BRITISH AND AUSTRALIAN TROOPS BELLIED DOWN IN THE FACE OF A HEAVY MORTAR BARRAGE.

KEEP YOUR HEADS DOWN, YOU JOKERS! BUT STAY AWAKE — JERRY'LL COME SHOOTING THROUGH AS SOON AS THIS LOT STOPS!

TOBRUK, ISOLATED AND SURROUNDED, WAS A BELEAGUERED FORTRESS. AND AGAINST IT, THROUGH THE DUST AND SMOKE, POURED THE MIGHT OF ROMMEL'S ARMY.

HERE THEY COME, SPORTS! RAPID FIRE — POUR IT INTO 'EM!

A HALF-TRACK, NO LESS! THEY MUST HAVE HEARD US AUSSIES WERE HERE.

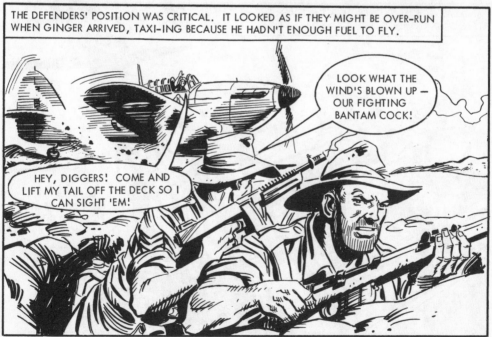

THE DEFENDERS' POSITION WAS CRITICAL. IT LOOKED AS IF THEY MIGHT BE OVER-RUN WHEN GINGER ARRIVED, TAXI-ING BECAUSE HE HADN'T ENOUGH FUEL TO FLY.

LOOK WHAT THE WIND'S BLOWN UP — OUR FIGHTING BANTAM COCK!

HEY, DIGGERS! COME AND LIFT MY TAIL OFF THE DECK SO I CAN SIGHT 'EM!

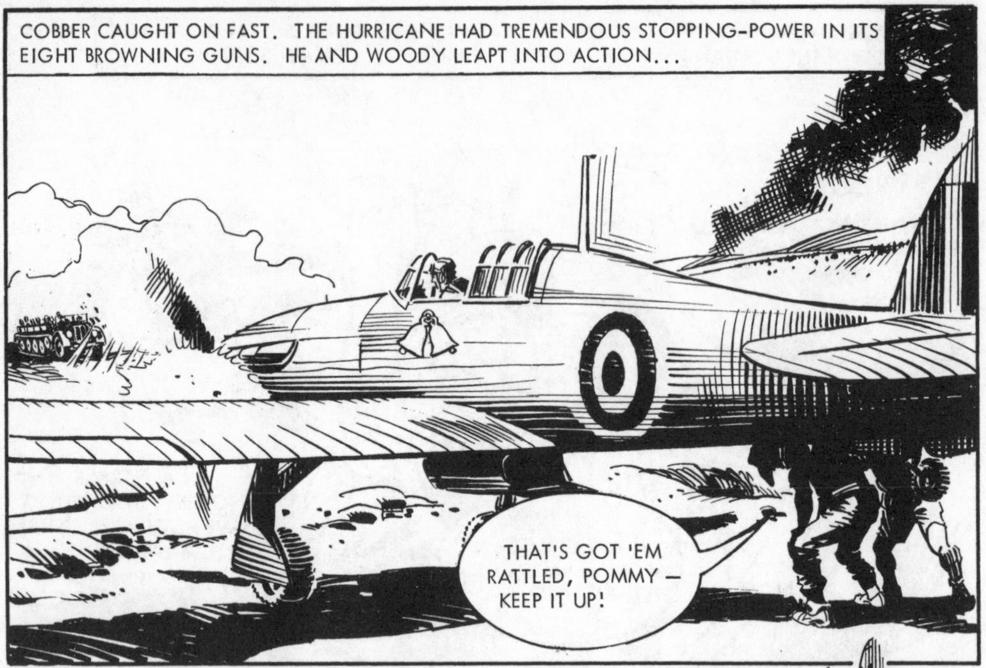
COBBER CAUGHT ON FAST. THE HURRICANE HAD TREMENDOUS STOPPING-POWER IN ITS EIGHT BROWNING GUNS. HE AND WOODY LEAPT INTO ACTION...
THAT'S GOT 'EM RATTLED, POMMY – KEEP IT UP!

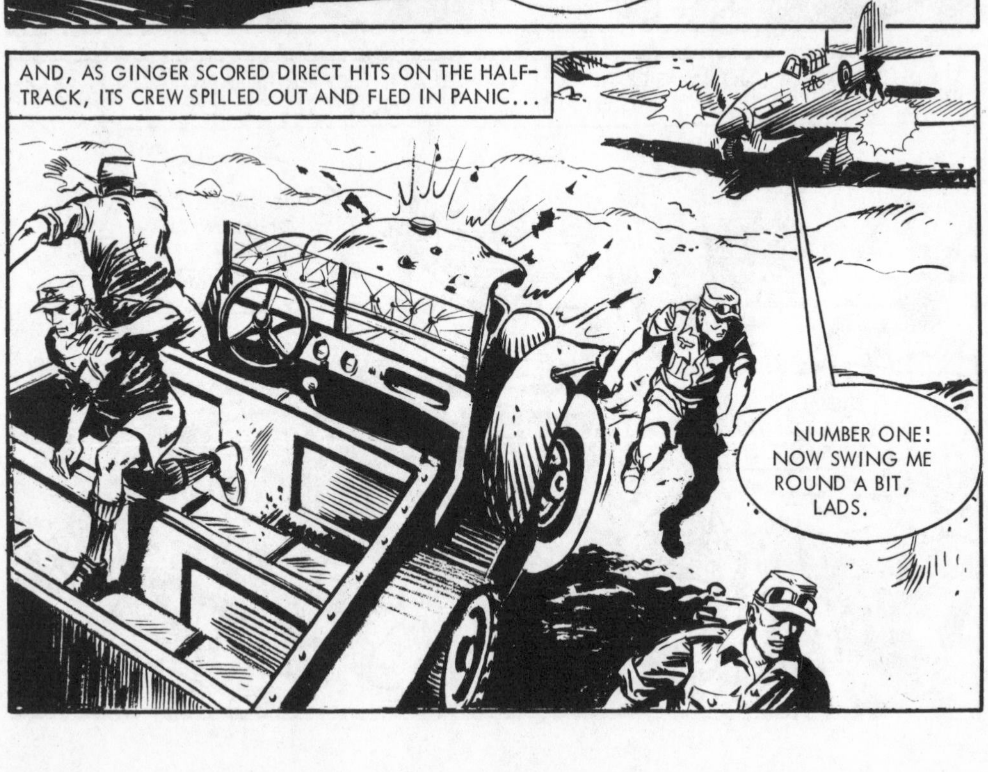
AND, AS GINGER SCORED DIRECT HITS ON THE HALF-TRACK, ITS CREW SPILLED OUT AND FLED IN PANIC...
NUMBER ONE! NOW SWING ME ROUND A BIT, LADS.

FOLLOWING HARD AFTER THE HALF-TRACK CAME GERMAN INFANTRY. GINGER POURED A MURDEROUS FIRE INTO THEIR RANKS.

AARGH!

GOOD-OH! YOU'RE MOWING 'EM DOWN LIKE SKITTLES AT A FAIR-GROUND!

THEN AN UNLUCKY SHOT WINGED GINGER'S SHOULDER. HE GRITTED HIS TEETH AND KEPT FIRING.

I'VE COPPED ONE! CAN'T PACK UP YET...

CAUGHT UNAWARES BY GINGER'S BATTERY OF BROWNINGS, THE ENEMY WERE THROWN INTO CONFUSION, BROKE AND FLED.

THREE CHEERS FOR OUR COCKNEY MATE — HE'S DONE 'EM GOOD AND PROPER.

WOODY! HE'S HIT!

GINGER IGNORED HIS WOUND. HE HAD ONLY ONE IDEA IN HIS HEAD — TO REFUEL AND RE-ARM TO BE READY FOR THE NEXT ATTACK.

I KEEP TELLING YOU, GINGER, YOU NEED TO SEE THE M.O.

KEEP YOUR HAIR ON, TOSH, AND SHOW ME THE PETROL DUMP FIRST. I'M NOT GETTING CAUGHT OUT AGAIN.

BUT COBBER KANE MADE GINGER STOP WHEN THEY REACHED A REGIMENTAL AID POST...

IT'LL BE SORE FOR A DAY OR TWO, SERGEANT. YOU'D BETTER REST UP.

THAT'S ALL YOU KNOW, CHUM!

WATCH IT — HERE COMES THE WINGLESS WONDER!

GROUP-CAPTAIN BROWNE CAME SCURRYING UP, HIS BROAD FACE CREASED IN A FROWN AS HE SAW GINGER AGAIN.

YOU RISKED YOUR AIRCRAFT NEEDLESSLY, SERGEANT. I'M ORDER-ING YOU TO FLY TO REJOIN YOUR SQUADRON IMMEDIATELY.

I'M SORRY, SIR, BUT I'VE JUST BEEN GROUNDED BY THE M.O.

BROWNE FUMED AND FRETTED, BUT THE AUSSIE M.O. FIRMLY BACKED GINGER UP.

I'M AFRAID IT'S TRUE, SIR. YOUR PILOT'S OUT OF ACTION FOR THE PRESENT.

CONFOUND IT! THEN I SUPPOSE HE'LL HAVE TO REMAIN HERE.

OVER HERE, YOU LOT. THE AIR FORCE NEEDS A HAND TO REFUEL.

SO GINGER TAXIED HIS PLANE TO THE PETROL DUMP, AND WILLING HANDS HELPED HIM SERVICE IT.

IT SURE IS LUCKY I WORKED AS A MOTOR MECHANIC BEFORE THIS BUST-UP.

THAT'S YER AMMO BELTS FIXED, MATE. NOW I'M OFF BACK TO THE PERIMETER. BE SEEING YOU.

AFTER COBBER HAD GONE, AND HIS PLANE WAS READY FOR ACTION, GINGER ATE WITH THE AUSSIES. WITHOUT WARNING, THE ENEMY BARRAGE STARTED UP AGAIN.

WHAT, AGAIN? WHY DON'T JERRY PACK IT IN AND GIVE US A REST?

RIGHT IN THE MIDDLE OF OUR ROSIE LEE. WELL, ME AND MY PLANE ARE ALL SET THIS TIME.

DISREGARDING HIS PAINFUL SHOULDER, GINGER TOOK TO THE AIR AND HEADED FOR THE "RED" OUTER DEFENCE LINE RINGING TOBRUK.

DO 'EM OVER, SPORT!

YOU BET YOUR SWEET LIFE I WILL, DIGGER!

THE GERMANS HAD LAUNCHED A SURPRISE ATTACK, EVEN HEAVIER THAN BEFORE. PANZERS AND INFANTRY SWARMED ACROSS THE DESERT BEYOND THE WIRE.

GINGER PUSHED HIS MACHINE AT THE GROUND IN A POWER-DIVE, BROWNINGS CLATTERING. HIS BULLETS CUT A WIDE SWATHE THROUGH THE ATTACKERS.

DOWN BELOW, IN THE RAGING HOLOCAUST OF BATTLE, A BRITISH TWO-POUNDER ANTI-TANK GUN RANGED ON A GERMAN PANZER...

AAAAGH!

...AND ERUPTED FLAME AND THUNDER, TURNING THE MONSTER INTO A METAL COFFIN FOR ITS CREW.

SERGEANT COBBER KANE AND HIS MATE, WOODY, WERE PINNED DOWN, CURSING THE ACCURACY OF THE ENEMY MACHINE GUNNERS.

THE HECK WITH THIS CAPER! A BLOKE CAN'T EVEN POKE HIS HEAD UP TO GET A CRACK AT THE VILLAINS.

THEN KEEP YER NUT DOWN. AT LEAST OUR BOY'S UP THERE, DOING HIS STUFF!

COBBER BIT THE PIN FROM A GRENADE—

GET READY TO CHALK ONE UP TO ME, WOODY, BOY. WONDER WHAT THEY'LL TRY NEXT...

— LOBBED IT UP AND OVER — AND ONE SPANDAU ABRUPTLY CEASED FIRE.

FLYING ABOVE THE BATTLEGROUND, GINGER'S ATTENTION WAS CAUGHT BY THREE GERMAN SOLDIERS, TWO WITH CYLINDERS ON THEIR BACKS. IN A MOMENT OF HORROR, HE REALISED WHAT WAS PLANNED.

FLAME-THROWERS! THE RATS ARE GOING TO BURN THE AUSSIES OUT!

SAVAGELY GINGER HURLED HIS PLANE DOWN, THUMB ON THE FIRING BUTTON. BUT ALREADY A TONGUE OF RED FIRE LICKED OUT FROM THE FLAME-THROWER AND BUILT UP INTO A SOLID WALL OF FLAME.

A TORNADO OF LEAD FROM GINGER'S GUNS SCYTHED INTO THE FLAME-THROWERS AND HURLED THEM TO THE GROUND.

HIS AMMUNITION EXPENDED, GINGER STUBBS RETURNED TO TOBRUK.

...WHERE HE FOUND GROUP-CAPTAIN BROWNE WAITING TO SPRING A SURPRISE ON HIM.

SO THE M.O. SAYS YOU CAN'T FLY, SERGEANT? WELL, YOUR SQUADRON C.O. HAS BEEN IN RADIO CONTACT — AND YOU'RE TO FLY OUT AT ONCE!

COR LUMME, THAT'S REALLY TORN IT!

HEY, COLONEL DEVLIN, SIR! THEY'RE TRYING TO GET RID OF ME, AGAIN!

COLONEL DEVLIN AND CAPTAIN COWAN HURRIED ACROSS. THE AUSSIES WERE RELUCTANT TO LOSE THEIR COCKNEY ACE.

THAT SHOULDER OF YOURS LOOKS PRETTY BAD, SERGEANT. I POSITIVELY FORBID YOU TO FLY!

UNLESS — ER, WE NEED YOU, OF COURSE!

NEXT DAY BROUGHT A NEW TRIAL FOR THE RATS OF TOBRUK. ROMMEL BROUGHT UP HUGE SIX-INCH SIEGE GUNS TO BOMBARD THE FORTRESS.

BLIMEY, WHAT NOW?

SITED ON THE HIGH ESCARPMENT OVERLOOKING THE TOWN AND HARBOUR, THE ENORMOUS GUNS CONTINUED TO LOB THEIR SHELLS ON TO A SITTING TARGET.

FOR PETE'S SAKE, GET UP THERE AND DO SOMETHING TO SPIKE THOSE GUNS!

RIGHT-O, SIR JUST YOU LEAVE 'EM TO ME!

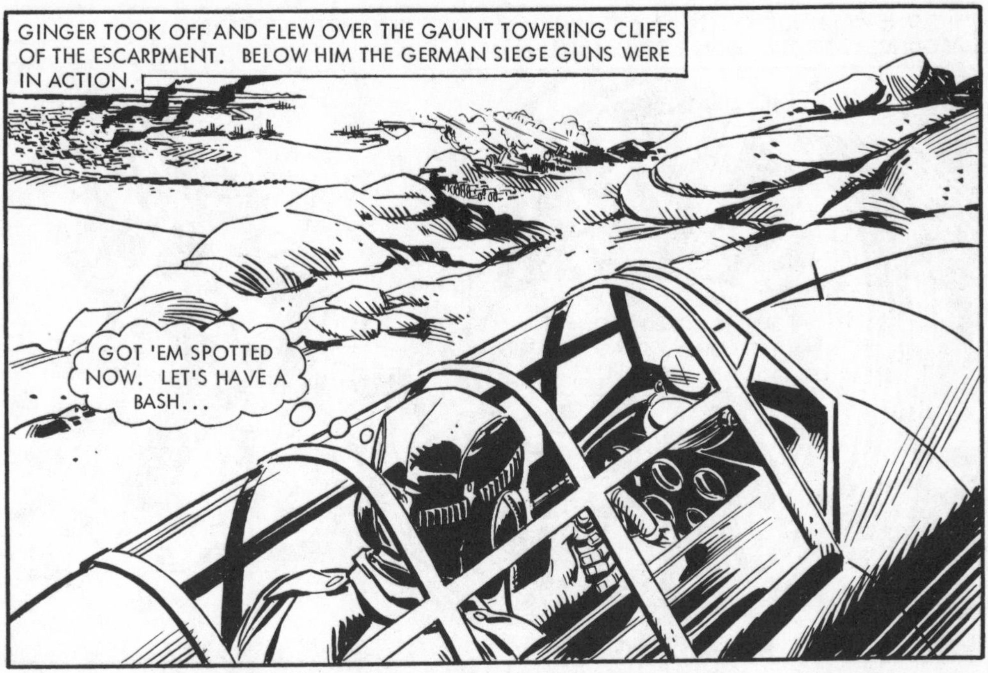
GINGER TOOK OFF AND FLEW OVER THE GAUNT TOWERING CLIFFS OF THE ESCARPMENT. BELOW HIM THE GERMAN SIEGE GUNS WERE IN ACTION.
GOT 'EM SPOTTED NOW. LET'S HAVE A BASH...

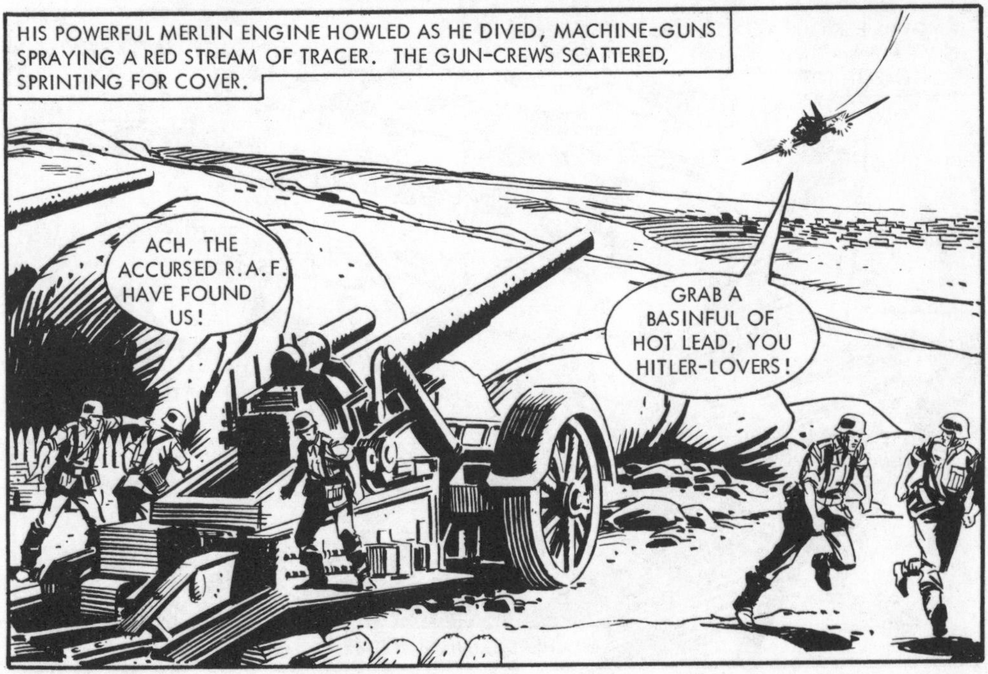
HIS POWERFUL MERLIN ENGINE HOWLED AS HE DIVED, MACHINE-GUNS SPRAYING A RED STREAM OF TRACER. THE GUN-CREWS SCATTERED, SPRINTING FOR COVER.
ACH, THE ACCURSED R.A.F. HAVE FOUND US!
GRAB A BASINFUL OF HOT LEAD, YOU HITLER-LOVERS!

BUT ONE WAS UNLUCKY...GINGER'S BULLETS SLAMMED INTO HIM AND SPUN HIM AROUND. AND THE YOUNG GERMAN LEUTNANT IN COMMAND PANICKED...

HIMMEL! WE SHALL ALL BE KILLED HERE — IT IS TOO OPEN. DRAG THE GUNS BACK. SCHNELL!

GINGER'S FURIOUS ATTACK FORCED THE GERMANS TO WITHDRAW THEIR HEAVY ARTILLERY FROM THE ESCARPMENT.

AND THAT'S BLOOMIN' WELL SETTLED YOUR HASH. HELLO, WHAT'S THIS?

UP AHEAD, GINGER SPOTTED A LONE GERMAN AIRCRAFT...

HE IDENTIFIED THE SMALL HIGH-WING GERMAN MONOPLANE, USED USUALLY AS A TARGET-SPOTTER FOR ARTILLERY, AS A FIESELER STORCH, RUNNING FOR HOME.

A SITTING DUCK IF I EVER SAW ONE. I'LL JUST KNOCK HIM OFF BEFORE I SET DOWN FOR A CUP OF ROSIE!

GINGER RAPIDLY OVERHAULED THE SLOW-MOVING STORCH — AND GOT A SHOCK WHEN A 7.9 MILLIMETRE MACHINE-GUN THREW LEAD AT HIM.

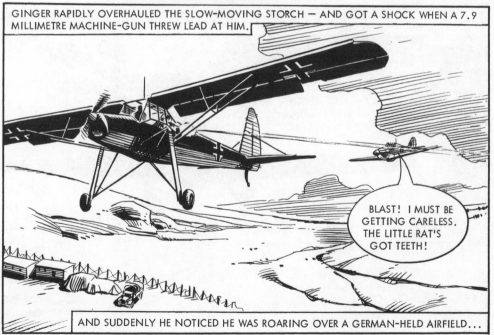

BLAST! I MUST BE GETTING CARELESS. THE LITTLE RAT'S GOT TEETH!

AND SUDDENLY HE NOTICED HE WAS ROARING OVER A GERMAN-HELD AIRFIELD...

HE DID NOT HAVE TIME TO WORRY ABOUT THE STORCH. ENEMY ANTI-AIRCRAFT GUNNERS FLUNG UP A BARRAGE OF CONCENTRATED FIRE, AND SHRAPNEL RIDDLED THE HURRICANE.

HIS ENGINE KNOCKED OUT AND THE CONTROLS DAMAGED, GINGER SOMEHOW GOT CLEAR, SINKING LOWER AND LOWER TOWARDS THE VAST EMPTY WASTE OF SAND STRETCHING TO THE HORIZON.

THEN HE HIT THE GROUND.

GINGER SCRAMBLED OUT OF THE COCKPIT, BRUISED AND SHAKEN. HIS FAITHFUL HURRICANE WAS A WRECK, AND HE FINISHED IT OFF WITH A LIGHTED MATCH.

AND IF I GET BACK, GROUPIE WILL SHIP ME STRAIGHT OUT THIS TIME ALL RIGHT ...A PILOT WITH NO KITE IS A DEAD LOSS.

HE LEFT THE BURNING WRECK IN A STUMBLING RUN.

WHAT I NEED NOW IS COVER — IN CASE THE JERRIES COME LOOKING FOR ME.

HARDLY HAD HE THROWN HIMSELF DOWN IN THE DEEP SHADOW OF SOME DUNES, WHEN —

— THE FIESELER STORCH ARRIVED AND CIRCLED LAZILY OVERHEAD.

THE ENGLANDER IS DEAD, FRANZ.

JAWOHL, NO ONE COULD SURVIVE SUCH A CRASH.

GINGER HID OUT TILL DARK, THEN SET OFF ON FOOT...NOT TOWARDS TOBRUK, BUT BACK TO THE ENEMY AIRFIELD.

THERE'S ONLY ONE PLACE ROUND HERE I CAN GET ANOTHER PLANE — THAT IS, IF THE JERRIES DON'T OBJECT!

HE WALKED FOR HOURS, TILL HIS LEGS ACHED AND HIS FEET BLISTERED. BUT AT LAST —

MESSERSCHMITT 109's — NOW THAT'S WHAT I CALL A SIGHT FOR SORE EYES!

IT WAS DAWN BY THE TIME HE HAD WORKED HIS WAY PAST THE SENTRIES AND INTO RUSHING DISTANCE OF THE PLANES...

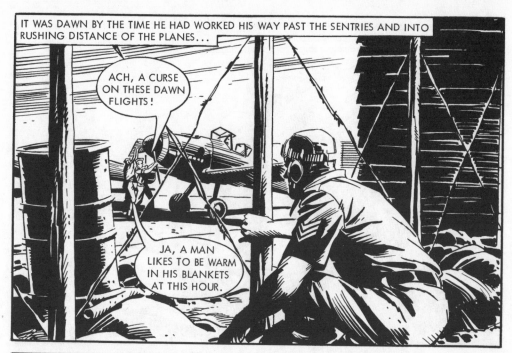

GINGER ROSE AND TOOK A DEEP BREATH. HE RUSHED THE TWO GERMAN MECHANICS SERVICING THE MESSERSCHMITT FIGHTER...

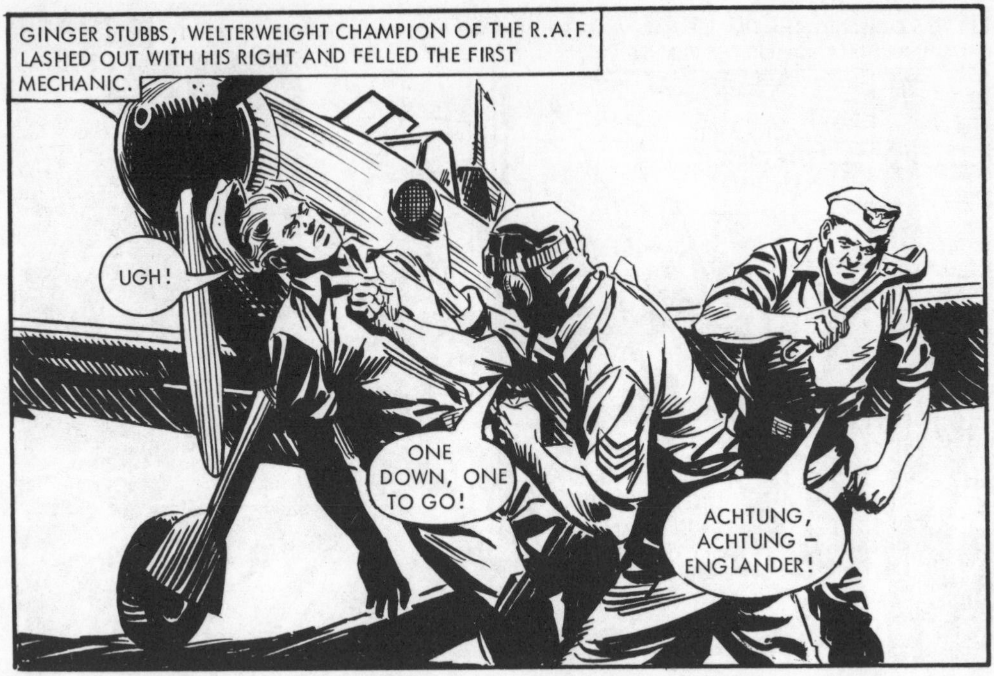
GINGER STUBBS, WELTERWEIGHT CHAMPION OF THE R.A.F. LASHED OUT WITH HIS RIGHT AND FELLED THE FIRST MECHANIC.
UGH!
ONE DOWN, ONE TO GO!
ACHTUNG, ACHTUNG – ENGLANDER!

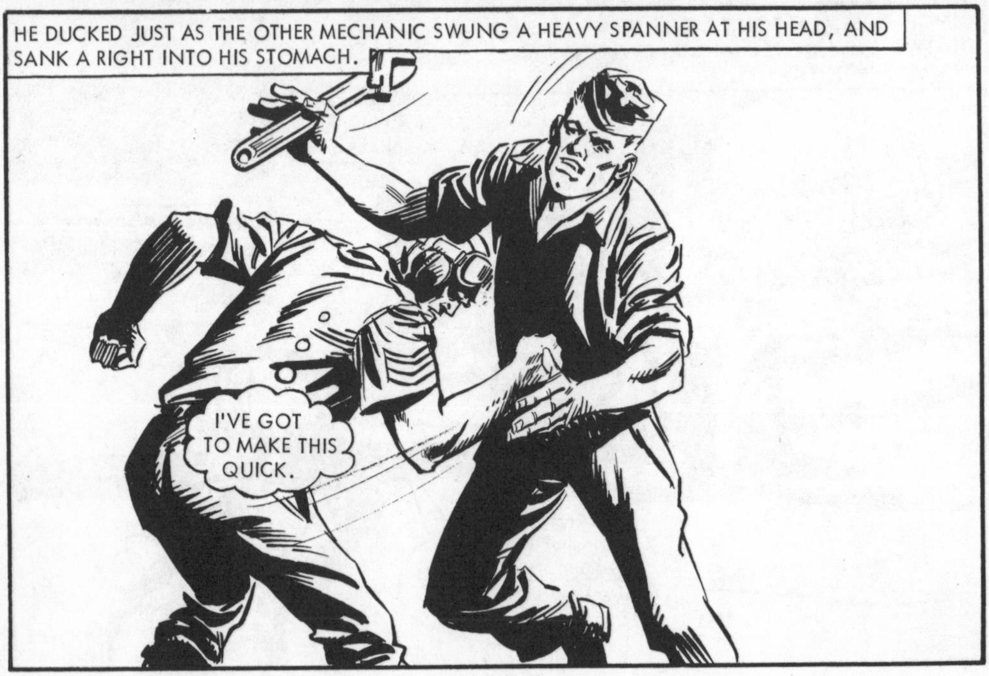
HE DUCKED JUST AS THE OTHER MECHANIC SWUNG A HEAVY SPANNER AT HIS HEAD, AND SANK A RIGHT INTO HIS STOMACH.
I'VE GOT TO MAKE THIS QUICK.

GINGER KNOCKED OUT THE SECOND MECHANIC AS THE MESSERSCHMITT PILOT SPRINTED ACROSS THE AIRFIELD TOWARDS HIM.

AND THAT'S FLAMING WELL SETTLED YOU, MATE! NOW FOR A QUICK GETAWAY.

BUT AS HE CLIMBED INTO THE COCKPIT, THE GERMAN PILOT GRABBED AT HIS LEG. GINGER KICKED OUT SAVAGELY...

BLOW ME DOWN — ANOTHER ONE OF 'EM! GERROFF!

ACH... SCHWEINHUND!

HE SETTLED TO THE CONTROLS AND GOT THE PLANE ROLLING. A WILD SHOUT CAME...

HALT! HALT OR I FIRE!

NOT ON YOUR NELLY, MATE! SHOOT AND BE HANGED!

IN A STORM OF BULLETS, GINGER GUNNED THE ENGINE AND GOT AIRBORNE.

THE ENGLANDER IS ESCAPING! FEUER — FEUER! SHOOT STRAIGHT, YOU FOOLS!

GINGER ESCAPED UNSCATHED...TO FACE ANOTHER PROBLEM.

I'M SHORT OF FLYING TIME ON MESSERSCHMITTS. THIS IS TOO MUCH LIKE BEING CHUCKED IN THE BATHS AND TOLD TO SWIM!

BUT GINGER WAS A NATURAL BORN FLIER, AND QUICKLY GOT THE FEEL OF THE GERMAN FIGHTER.

I'M GETTING THE HANG OF IT NOW. IF I HURRY I'LL JUST BE IN TIME FOR BREAKFAST, I HOPE.

HE FLEW STEADILY NORTH TOWARDS THE COAST, AND TOBRUK.

AND SOON —

IT LOOKS ALMOST LIKE HOME TO A POOR WANDERING COCKNEY BOY.

BUT THE TOBRUK GUNNERS SAW ONLY AN ENEMY AIRCRAFT BEARING BLACK CROSSES, AND OPENED UP WITH A BARRAGE OF HIGH EXPLOSIVE.

CRIKEY! THEY DON'T KNOW IT'S ME IN THIS PERISHING KITE WITH SWASTIKAS PLASTERED ALL OVER IT. THIS IS GOING TO BE A BIT DODGY!

GINGER FLEW THROUGH A CURTAIN OF FLYING STEEL AS SHELLS EXPLODED PERILOUSLY CLOSE TO HIM...

THESE BOYS ARE TOO GOOD! WELL, HERE GOES...

HE RAMMED THE CONTROL STICK FORWARD AND DIVED.

GINGER SET DOWN INSIDE TOBRUK, BREATHLESS AND SHAKEN, BUT UNHURT...AND SAW GRIM-FACED AUSSIES RACING TOWARDS HIM, GUNS COCKED.

C'MON OUT OF THERE, YOU NAZI DINGO — AND WITH YER HANDS HIGH!

AW, LET 'IM HAVE IT, ANYWAY, COBBER!

GINGER CLIMBED OUT QUICKLY, EXPECTING A BULLET FROM A TRIGGER-HAPPY AUSSIE. BUT LUCKILY COBBER AND WOODY WERE TO THE FORE AS USUAL, AND THEIR EXPRESSIONS ALTERED COMICALLY AS THEY RECOGNISED HIM.

TAKE IT EASY, COBBER! REAL FRIENDLY, YOU LOT ARE — I DON'T THINK!

GINGER! WHAT THE HECK ARE YOU DOING IN THAT THING? WE'D GIVEN YOU UP FOR LOST.

THEN THE DESERT RATS GAVE A TREMENDOUS WELCOME TO THEIR POMMY PILOT.

IT'S GOOD TO HAVE YER BACK, SPORT!

I COULDN'T 'ARF DO WITH A CUP OF CHAR, YOU BLOKES.

LOOK OUT, GINGER, HERE COMES THAT STUPID COOT BROWNE AGAIN.

GROUP-CAPTAIN BROWNE, ALONE, DID NOT SEEM PLEASED TO SEE GINGER. ANGRILY, HE SNAPPED OUT HIS WORDS.

WHAT'S THIS, SERGEANT? LOST YOUR HURRICANE, HAVE YOU? AN EXPENSIVE AIRCRAFT WE CAN ILL AFFORD TO SPARE.

BUT I DID A SWOP FOR A 109, SIR!

IT'S MERSA MATRUH FOR YOU NOW, SERGEANT — BY SUBMARINE! YOUR DUTY LIES WITH YOUR SQUADRON. EVERYTHING'S ARRANGED. YOU WILL REPORT TO ME AT 18.00 HOURS!

ALL RIGHT, SIR, IF YOU SAY SO.

COBBER KANE AND WOODY WOODS COULD HARDLY BELIEVE THEIR EARS.

YOU'RE NOT RATTING ON US, GINGER? TAKING ORDERS FROM THAT DEAD-BEAT!

COME OFF IT! I WAS ONLY KID-DING HIM ALONG TO KEEP HIM QUIET FOR A BIT. NOW, I WANT SOME PAINT AND A BRUSH.

QUICKLY GINGER GOT BUSY CONVERTING THE NAZI FIGHTER TO BRITISH IDENTIFICATION, ADDING HIS OWN BOW BELLS EMBLEM.

NOW I'M READY FOR ACTION — LET THEM NAZIS COME!

FIRST, WE'VE GOT TO HIDE YOU FROM THAT FLIPPING GROUP-CAPTAIN!

THE AUSSIES WERE EQUALLY DETERMINED TO KEEP THEIR COCKNEY FIGHTER PILOT IN TOBRUK, HELPING WITH AN AUSSIE SHIRT AND HAT.

RECKON HE WON'T KNOW YER FROM ONE OF US NOW!

EIGHTEEN HUNDRED HOURS CAME AND WENT ...AND BROWNE CAME HUNTING FOR HIS MISSING PILOT.

WHERE IS SERGEANT STUBBS? HAVE ANY OF YOU SEEN HIM? THE SUBMARINE IS WAITING...

NEVER LAID EYES ON HIM, SIR.

THEN THE GROUP-CAPTAIN POINTED STRAIGHT AT GINGER...

YOU, SOLDIER, HAVE YOU SEEN HIM ANY-WHERE? ANSWER ME, MAN!

NO USE ASKING HIM, SIR. HE'S FROM THE OUT-BACK — "OLD SILENT", WE CALLS 'IM! BIT PUNCH-DRUNK, I RECKON.

GROUP-CAPTAIN BROWNE FAILED TO RECOGNISE GINGER...AND, FUMING, STALKED OFF TO SEARCH ELSEWHERE FOR HIM.

SO THE SUBMARINE SAILED WITHOUT THE COCKNEY ACE. BUT GINGER SAW NO ACTION FOR A TIME, WHILE A FIERCE SANDSTORM RAGED OVER TOBRUK.

DAYS PASSED BEFORE THE STORM DIED AWAY. THEN —

JUST BEFORE DAWN, DEVLIN ROUSED GINGER FROM HIS SLEEP...

SERGEANT, WAKE UP, YOU'RE NEEDED! JERRY'S TRYING TO LAND A RAIDING FORCE FROM THE SEA.

ALL RIGHT, KEEP YOUR HAIR ON. I WAS HAVING A LOVELY DREAM.

GINGER FLUNG ON HIS CLOTHES AND RACED FOR HIS CAPTURED MESSERSCHMITT. HE ROARED INTO THE AIR...

WHAT THE DICKENS HAS HAPPENED TO OUR NAVY, THEN? WELL, I'LL SOON PUT THE KIBOSH ON THIS LARK!

ON THE BEACHES, THE AUSSIES FOUGHT WITH COLD STEEL TO FLING THE INVADERS BACK INTO THE SEA. MACHINE-GUNS STUTTERED AND GRENADES CRACKED AS THE BATTLE RAGED.

THE ENEMY SEA-BORNE FORCE HAD ACHIEVED COMPLETE TACTICAL SURPRISE. AND E-BOATS AND LANDING CRAFT POURED IN REINFORCEMENTS.

LUMME, JERRY MEANS BUSINESS THIS TIME! MAYBE THEY THINK THEY'RE BULLET-PROOF OR SOMETHING.

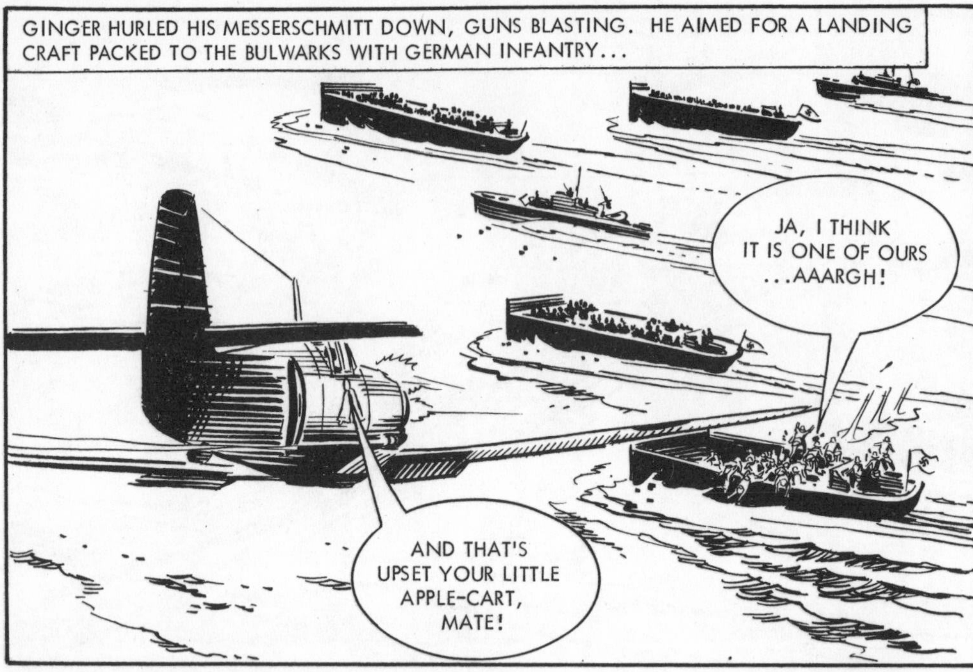
GINGER HURLED HIS MESSERSCHMITT DOWN, GUNS BLASTING. HE AIMED FOR A LANDING CRAFT PACKED TO THE BULWARKS WITH GERMAN INFANTRY...
JA, I THINK IT IS ONE OF OURS ...AAARGH!
AND THAT'S UPSET YOUR LITTLE APPLE-CART, MATE!

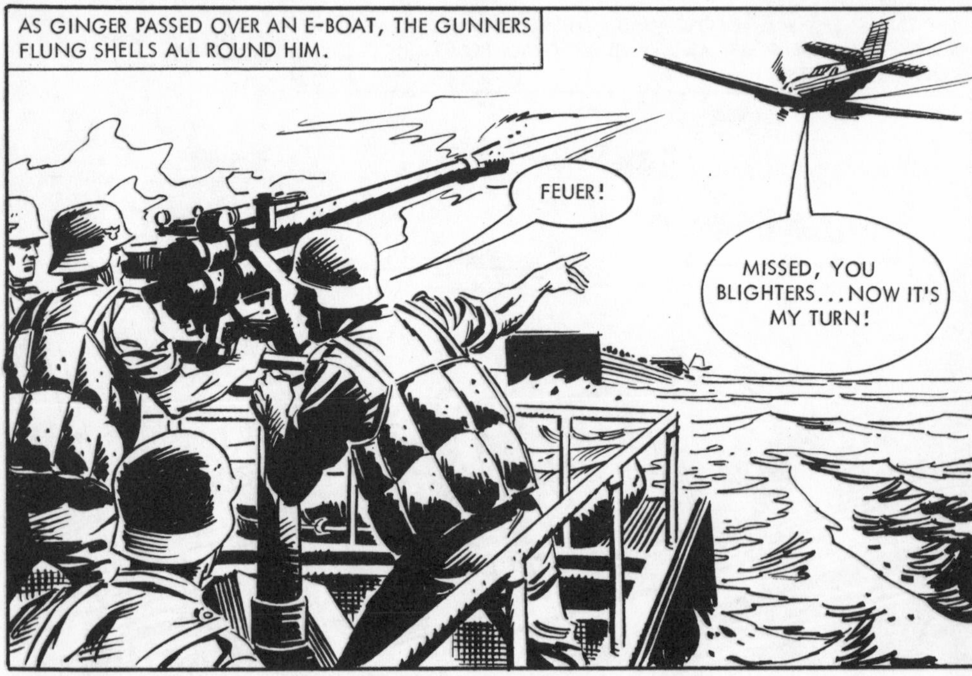
AS GINGER PASSED OVER AN E-BOAT, THE GUNNERS FLUNG SHELLS ALL ROUND HIM.
FEUER!
MISSED, YOU BLIGHTERS...NOW IT'S MY TURN!

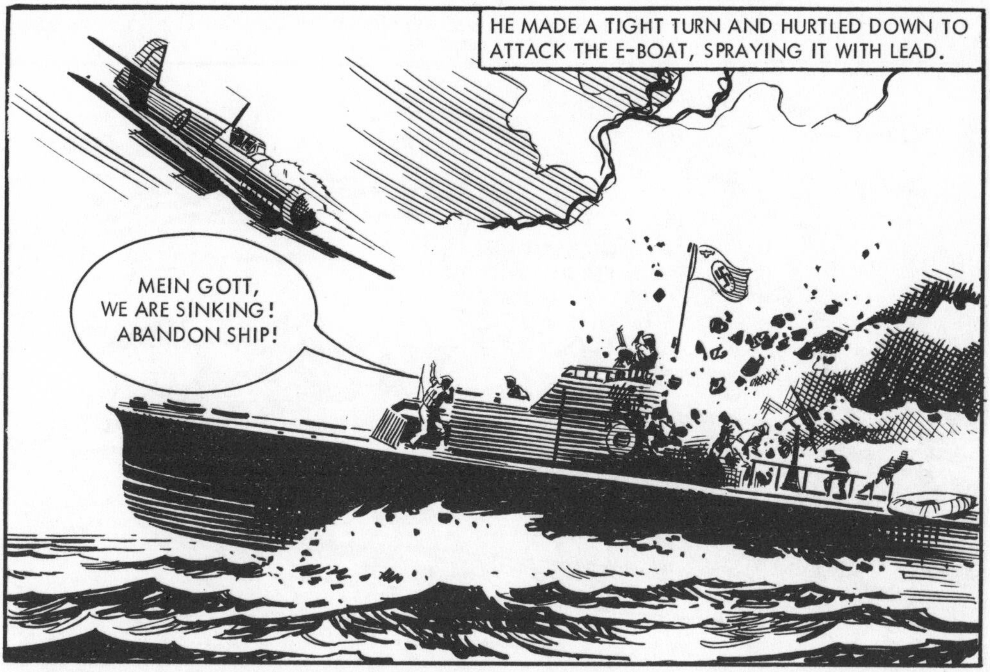
HE MADE A TIGHT TURN AND HURTLED DOWN TO ATTACK THE E-BOAT, SPRAYING IT WITH LEAD.
MEIN GOTT, WE ARE SINKING! ABANDON SHIP!

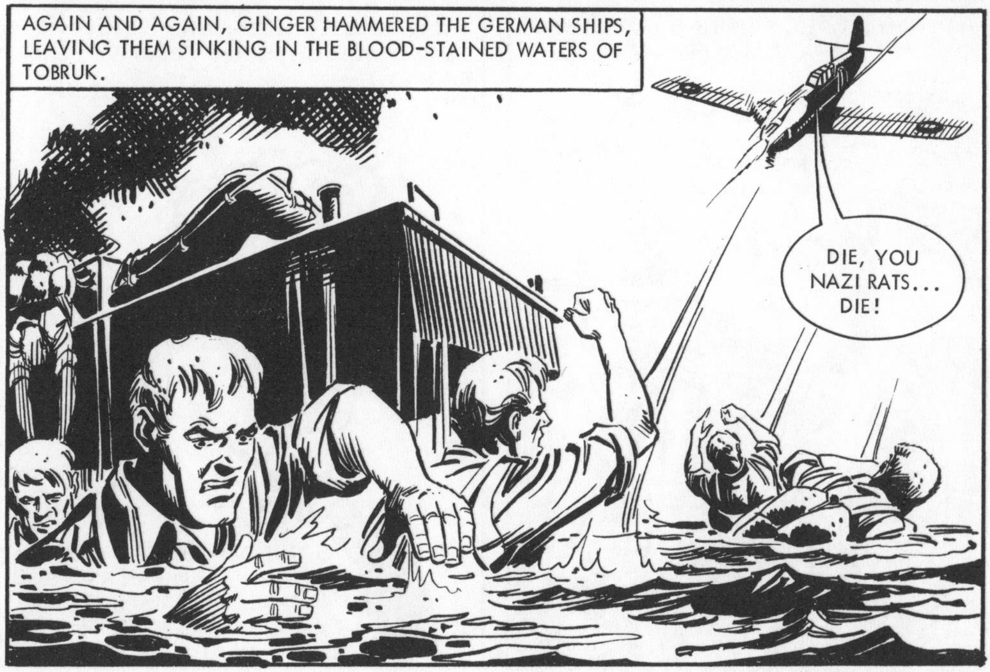
AGAIN AND AGAIN, GINGER HAMMERED THE GERMAN SHIPS, LEAVING THEM SINKING IN THE BLOOD-STAINED WATERS OF TOBRUK.
DIE, YOU NAZI RATS... DIE!

THEN TWO DESTROYERS OF THE BRITISH NAVY ARRIVED TO FINISH THE SLAUGHTER GINGER HAD STARTED.

AND ABOUT TIME, TOO! I'M JUST ABOUT OUT OF AMMO AND FUEL.

SO HE TURNED AND FLEW BACK TO TOBRUK.

WHEN HE LANDED, A SMILING LT. COLONEL DEVLIN CONGRATULATED HIM ON HIS ACTION...

A VERY GOOD SHOW, SERGEANT! I'M PUTTING YOU UP FOR A MEDAL FOR THIS ACTION!

BUT IF THE COLONEL EXPECTED GINGER TO BE DELIGHTED, HE WAS IN FOR A SHOCK...

THANKS, SIR, BUT I DON'T GO MUCH ON GONGS. THEY WON'T BRING ME MUM AND DAD BACK. ALL I WANT IS THE CHANCE TO KILL MORE OF THOSE MURDERING NAZIS!

A FEW DAYS LATER, LT. COLONEL DEVLIN HAD UNEXPECTED NEWS OVER THE RADIO FROM THE BRITISH O.C. IN MERSA MATRUH.

I WONDER...? IT SOUNDS ALMOST TOO GOOD TO BE TRUE.

CAPTAIN, GET ME THAT R.A.F. SERGEANT-PILOT. I'VE GOT JUST THE JOB FOR HIM!

RIGHT, SIR.

AND WHEN GINGER ARRIVED IN THE UNDERGROUND OPS ROOM —

THE BIG NEWS IS, SERGEANT, THAT A RELIEF FORCE IS ON THE WAY. WE'VE WAITED SO LONG IT'S HARD TO BELIEVE, SO I WANT YOU TO CHECK ON IT BEFORE I TELL THE WHOLE GARRISON.

CRIKEY, THAT'D REALLY BE SOMETHING. I'LL JUST NIP UP TOP AND TAKE A DEKKO.

SO GINGER STUBBS TOOK OFF INTO THE BLUE, AND THE RATS OF TOBRUK WAITED HOPEFULLY, NOT REALLY BELIEVING IN THE RELIEF FORCE.

RELIEF, WOODY? I RECKON IT'S JUST ANOTHER RUMOUR, MATE. WE'RE STUCK HERE FOR THE DURATION.

YEAH, YOU SAID IT, COBBER. IF WE EVER GET OUT OF THESE PERISHING CAVES, I'LL GET ME HAIR PERMED!

GINGER FLEW EAST INTO THE SUN, CLIMBING ALL THE TIME ...FINALLY HE GLIMPSED A DUST CLOUD ON THE HORIZON.

BLIMEY! SO IT WAS THE STRAIGHT GEN — WE'RE ON THE MOVE AT LAST. JERRY ISN'T GOING TO LIKE THIS ONE LITTLE BIT, BUT MY DESERT RATS WILL LAP IT UP!

THEN, WHEN GERMAN HEINKEL 111s ROARED OUT OF THE WEST TO BOMB THE ADVANCING
BRITISH, GINGER SWOOPED ON THEM LIKE A HAWK.

HE HAD THE ELEMENT OF SURPRISE IN HIS FAVOUR, AND SPLIT THE GERMAN FORMATION
AT HIS FIRST PASS. SOON HURRICANES OF THE DESERT AIR FORCE RACED UP TO JOIN
THE MELEE.

AS THE HURRICANES POUNCED ON THE TWIN-ENGINED BOMBERS, TRACER SLASHED FANTASTIC PATTERNS ACROSS THE SKY... BUT IT WAS GINGER WHO MADE THE FIRST KILL.

GOT HIM! I GOT THE SO-AND-SO DEAD TO RIGHTS!

AGAIN GINGER WHIRLED INTO POSITION. HIS THUMB STABBED THE FIRING BUTTON...

NUMBER TWO COMING UP. COP THIS LOT, YOU MUG!

HIS BULLETS PUNCHED INTO THE PETROL TANKS OF THE BOMB-LADEN HEINKEL. THERE CAME A SUDDEN BLINDING FLASH, AND METAL FRAGMENTS HURTLED THROUGH THE AIR.

OUT OF AMMUNITION, GINGER BROKE AWAY...

RETURNING TO TOBRUK WITH THE NEWS THAT RELIEF WAS DEFINITELY ON THE WAY, HE SPIED MOVEMENT IN THE DESERT BELOW —

HELLO, WHAT'S THAT DOWN THERE? LOOKS LIKE A JERRY STAFF CAR.

GINGER SWOOPED LOW OVER THE SMALL VEHICLE ZIG-ZAGGING ACROSS THE SAND.

NO AMMO, BUT I CAN STILL BEAT THEM UP AND GIVE 'EM A FRIGHT!

IT IS A MESSERSCHMITT, HERR GENERAL — BUT IT HAS BRITISH MARKINGS!

AS HE BUZZED THE ENEMY STAFF CAR, HE HAD A CLEAR VIEW OF THE MAN SITTING IN THE BACK — AND WAS SHAKEN TO THE CORE.

BLIMEY! IT CAN'T BE...

THE COCKNEY ACE HAD CAUGHT A VERY BIG BUG INDEED — THE BIGGEST — FIELD MARSHAL ROMMEL, THE DESERT FOX HIMSELF.

STOP! WE MUST LEAVE THE CAR, LEUTNANT, AND SEEK COVER.

CURSING THE FACT THAT HE HAD NO AMMUNITION LEFT, GINGER DIVED AT THE DESERT FOX.

RUN, ROMMEL, RUN!

AND SO SERGEANT GINGER STUBBS FROM LONDON TOWN HARASSED AND DISORGANISED THE GERMAN HIGH COMMAND AT A MOST CRITICAL TIME.

ACH — HIS GUNS ARE USELESS. WE ARE WASTING VALUABLE TIME. TO THE CAR, LEUTNANT.

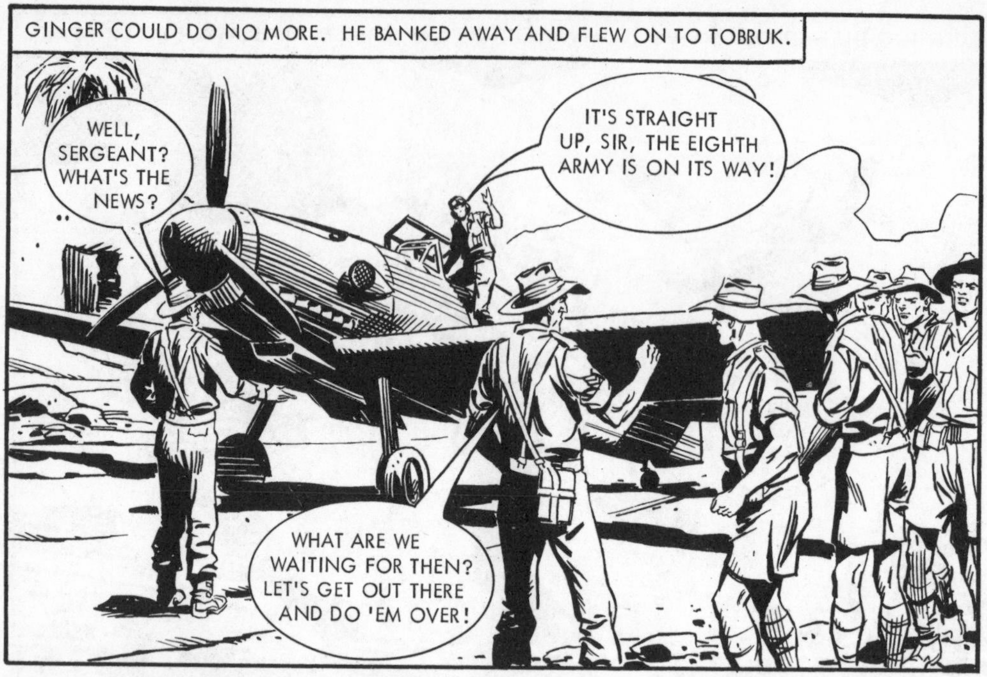
GINGER COULD DO NO MORE. HE BANKED AWAY AND FLEW ON TO TOBRUK.
WELL, SERGEANT? WHAT'S THE NEWS?
IT'S STRAIGHT UP, SIR, THE EIGHTH ARMY IS ON ITS WAY!
WHAT ARE WE WAITING FOR THEN? LET'S GET OUT THERE AND DO 'EM OVER!

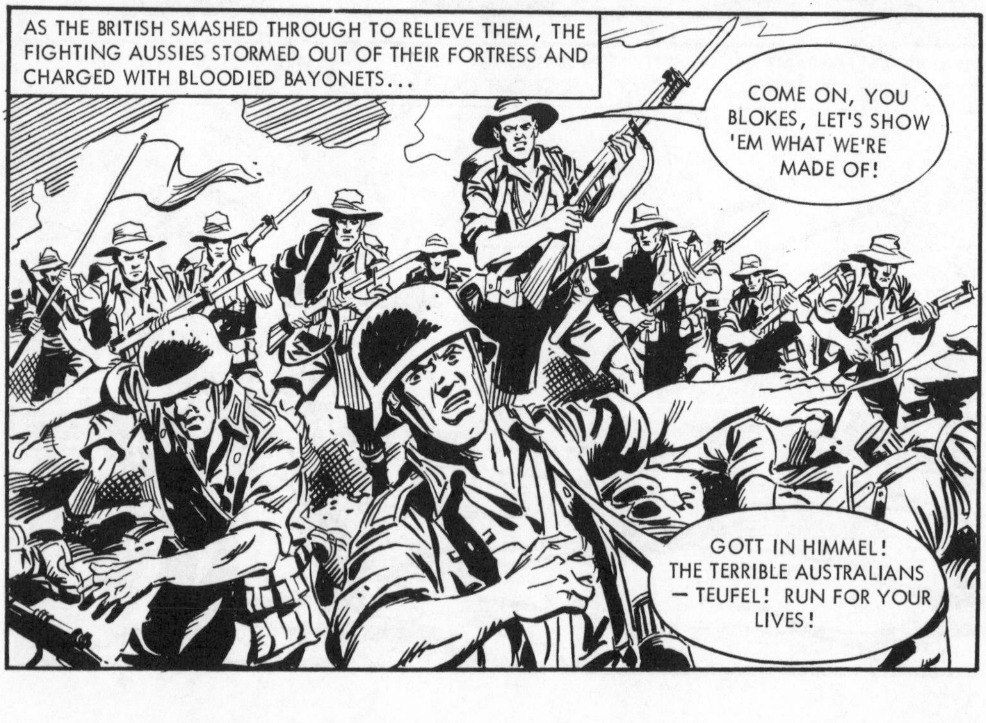
AS THE BRITISH SMASHED THROUGH TO RELIEVE THEM, THE FIGHTING AUSSIES STORMED OUT OF THEIR FORTRESS AND CHARGED WITH BLOODIED BAYONETS...
COME ON, YOU BLOKES, LET'S SHOW 'EM WHAT WE'RE MADE OF!
GOTT IN HIMMEL! THE TERRIBLE AUSTRALIANS — TEUFEL! RUN FOR YOUR LIVES!

AS THE AUSSIES DROVE THE NAZIS BACK, GINGER FLEW PROUDLY AT THEIR HEAD...AND THEY CHEERED THE TOBRUK PILOT WHO, SINGLE-HANDED, HAD FOUGHT THEIR SKY BATTLES FOR THEM.

GIVE 'IM A CHEER, LADS!

YEAH, A REAL AUSSIE CHEER FOR A LITTLE FIGHTING COCKNEY!

WITH TOBRUK BEHIND HIM, GINGER REJOINED HIS SQUADRON. BUT HE NEVER FORGOT THE GREAT FIGHTING QUALITIES AND COMRADESHIP OF HIS MATES FROM DOWN UNDER.

Commando
THE END

Commando FLY PAST

No. 20 — BRISTOL BEAUFIGHTER V1F

Shown in the markings of 29 Squadron, R.A.F. at West Malling, in May, 1943.

SEA BLITZ

DAY AFTER DAY THROUGHOUT THE BATTLE OF BRITAIN, NEWS OF THE GLORIOUS DEEDS OF THE R.A.F. FIGHTER PILOTS WAS FLASHED ROUND THE WORLD, CAPTURING THE IMAGINATION OF ALL WHO BELIEVED IN FREEDOM. AS A RESULT, MANY THOUSANDS VOLUNTEERED TO JOIN THE FLYING SERVICES TO CHANGE "THE FEW" INTO "THE MANY".

ONE OF THEM WAS JIM LAWRENCE WHO LIVED IN A SMALL TOWN IN SOUTH ISLAND, NEW ZEALAND. ONE DAY, HE CAUGHT THE BUS TO DUNEDIN WHERE HE MADE A BEELINE FOR THE ROYAL NEW ZEALAND AIR FORCE RECRUITING CENTRE —

BUT A BITTER DISAPPOINTMENT AWAITED HIM.

YOU'VE PASSED YOUR MEDICAL OK, SO GO HOME NOW AND WE'LL NOTIFY YOU IN ABOUT SIX MONTHS TIME WHERE TO REPORT...

SIX MONTHS! I EXPECTED TO BE IN ACTION BY THEN.

I'M SORRY, LAWRENCE, BUT WE'RE SWAMPED WITH VOLUNTEERS. DON'T WORRY, SIX MONTHS WILL SOON PASS.

SO JIM LAWRENCE, LAURIE TO HIS FRIENDS, WENT BACK TO HIS JOB AS A GARAGE MECHANIC. ONE DAY, HIS WORKMATE CALLED TO HIM.

HEY LAURIE, LISTEN — IT'S A LETTER FROM MY COUSIN IN SCOTLAND. "THERE'S CANADIANS, AUSSIES, NEW ZEALANDERS AND MANY OTHERS IN THE R.A.F. IT'S LIKE A LEAGUE OF NATIONS." WHY DON'T YOU DO IT THAT WAY — GO TO THE OLD COUNTRY AND JOIN THE R.A.F.?

LAURIE WASTED NO TIME IN PUTTING THIS IDEA INTO ACTION. HE BLEW ALL HIS SAVINGS ON A STEAMSHIP TICKET ACROSS THE PACIFIC TO SAN FRANCISCO.

FROM THERE, HE HITCH-HIKED TO THE ATLANTIC COAST.

HE MADE HIS WAY TO A BIG AIRFIELD ON THE EAST COAST WHICH WAS CRAMMED WITH LEASE-LEND AIRCRAFT ON THEIR WAY TO BRITAIN.

THANKS TO THE FRIENDLY CO-OPERATION OF THE AMERICAN FERRY CREWS IT SEEMED THAT THE LAST STAGE OF HIS JOURNEY WAS GOING TO BE EASY.

THE BIG BOMBER TOOK OFF AND HEADED EASTWARDS, PART OF THE VAST SHUTTLE SERVICE OF AIRCRAFT AND WAR SUPPLIES THAT WENT ON DAY AND NIGHT.

TAKE A LOOK DOWN BELOW, KIWI. SEE ALL THOSE SHIPS? THEY'RE CRAMMED TO THE HATCHES WITH WAR SUPPLIES FOR THE LIMEYS.

IT'S QUITE A SIGHT.

UNEXPECTED COLD FRONTS HAD MOVED DOWN FROM THE BITTER WASTES OF GREENLAND RIGHT ACROSS THEIR PATH. TWO HUNDRED MILES WEST OF SCOTLAND, THE LIBERATOR PLUNGED INTO DRIVING RAIN AND THICK CLOUD.

HUH! THE WEATHER BOYS SAID WE'D HAVE VISIBILITY UNLIMITED THE WHOLE WAY.

COULD BE JUST A BELT OF RAIN. MAYBE WE'LL CLEAR IT SHORTLY.

DIVERTED FROM THEIR DESTINATION, THEY HEADED TOWARDS A CLEAR AIRFIELD NEAR THE MORAY FIRTH. BUT DIRECTLY IN THEIR PATH WAITED DISASTER. HIDDEN BY THE DRIVING CLOUDS, A RIDGE OF MOUNTAINS LOOMED UP.

AAH! NO!

THE NEXT INSTANT, THEIR WORLD DISOLVED IN A SHATTERING CRASH AS THE LIBERATOR PLOUGHED INTO A MOUNTAIN ON A HEBRIDEAN ISLAND.

AAGH!

ONE MAN MIRACULOUSLY SURVIVED THE IMPACT — LAURIE. HE NEVER KNEW HOW HE ESCAPED UNSCATHED, AS HE CAME TO IN A NIGHTMARE OF FLAMING WRECKAGE AND SUFFOCATING SMOKE.

WHERE AM I? WHAT HAPPENED?

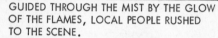

GUIDED THROUGH THE MIST BY THE GLOW OF THE FLAMES, LOCAL PEOPLE RUSHED TO THE SCENE.

OVER HERE! HERE'S ONE OF THEM!

LAURIE WAS TAKEN TO HOSPITAL WHERE A FEW MINOR ABRASIONS AND CUTS WERE CLEANED UP, THEN HE WAS GIVEN A THOROUGH EXAMINATION.

YOU'RE OK, BUT YOU'D BETTER HAVE A LONG REST BEFORE YOU JOIN UP. DELAYED SHOCK, YOU KNOW.

AS LAURIE HAD HOPED, GETTING INTO THE R.A.F. WAS NO PROBLEM. HE GOT THROUGH INITIAL TRAINING, THEN FLYING SCHOOL BEFORE GOING TO ADVANCED TRAINING SCHOOL.

OK, LAWRENCE, NOW YOU'RE IN CONTROL. YOU'RE DOING FINE. WE'LL MAKE A FLIER OF YOU YET.

I CAN'T WAIT TO DO MY FIRST SOLO, SIR!

FLIGHT LIEUTENANT STARKEY, LAURIE'S INSTRUCTOR, TOLD HIM TO HEAD FOR A NEARBY CLOUD BANK.

AS THE CLAMMY MIST ENVELOPED THEM, LAURIE'S MIND FLASHED BACK TO THE AWFUL MOMENTS BEFORE THE LIBERATOR SMASHED INTO THE MOUNTAINSIDE. HE IMAGINED HE WAS RELIVING THE WHOLE MIND-SEARING EXPERIENCE.

HIS FEAR GREW AS VISIBILITY DETERIORATED. PANIC-STRICKEN, HE GLARED AHEAD, HIS EYES STRIVING TO SEE THE HILLSIDE HE WAS CONVINCED LAY DIRECTLY IN HIS PATH. HE GRIPPED THE CONTROL COLUMN AND PULLED IT BACK.

I TOLD YOU TO WATCH YOUR INSTRUMENTS! YOU'RE CLIMBING – LAWRENCE! LET THE CONTROLS GO, YOU'LL STALL.

I'VE GOT TO CLIMB OUT OF THE MIST BEFORE WE HIT...

SOMETHING DRASTIC HAD TO BE DONE, AND QUICKLY. STARKEY POKED LAURIE VIOLENTLY IN THE BACK WITH A LONG METAL TUBE.

WHAT ARE YOU RAVING ABOUT? LET GO THE STICK!

OUCH!

THE SHARP PAIN MADE LAURIE SLACKEN HIS VICE-LIKE GRIP. STARKEY SLAMMED THE STICK FORWARD JUST IN TIME TO AVOID A DISASTROUS STALL.

NOW, KEEP AWAY FROM THE CONTROLS. I'LL LAND HER.

YES, SIR.

DESPITE WHAT HAD HAPPENED, STARKEY KNEW HIS PUPIL HAD THE MAKINGS OF A GOOD PILOT. A SEVERE TICKING-OFF SEEMED THE OBVIOUS REMEDY.

WHAT THE BLAZES WERE YOU PLAYING AT UP THERE? THAT WAS DANGEROUS FLYING.

I'M SORRY, SIR. I JUST SEEMED TO PANIC WHEN WE WENT INTO THAT CLOUD. I COULDN'T SEE ANYTHING AHEAD. IT WON'T HAPPEN AGAIN, SIR.

SOMEONE ELSE HAD NOTICED THE ARGUMENT — PILOT OFFICER NIGEL VARNEY, A NASTY CHARACTER ALTOGETHER. HE STROLLED TOWARDS THE SCENE.

IT HAD BETTER NOT, LADDIE. ANY MORE OF THAT AND YOU'LL BE GROUNDED FOR GOOD. A PILOT WHO PANICS IS A MENACE TO HIMSELF AND OTHERS WHO FLY WITH HIM.

HELLO, THE NEW ZEALANDER'S GETTING A BIG STRIP TORN OFF. MUST HEAR THE GORY DETAILS.

VARNEY, NOT THE MOST POPULAR PUPIL, HAD DECIDED VIEWS ON THOSE HE CALLED "COLONIALS". IN GENERAL, HE DIDN'T LIKE THEM. LAURIE IN PARTICULAR HE HAD SEEMED TO DISLIKE ON SIGHT. THAT NIGHT IN THE MESS —

I THOUGHT THESE COLONIALS WERE ALL WILD MEN, BUT IT APPEARS I WAS MISTAKEN. I JUST HEARD TODAY ABOUT A CERTAIN NEW ZEALANDER WHO TURNED BRIGHT YELLOW WHEN HIS INSTRUCTOR TOOK HIM CLOUD FLYING.

STOW IT, VARNEY. LAWRENCE IS BEHIND YOU.

DELIBERATELY, VARNEY RAISED HIS VOICE.

SO WHAT? IT'S THE TRUTH. LAWRENCE PANICKED WHEN HE COULDN'T SEE WHERE HE WAS GOING. IMAGINE THE CREW OF A LANCASTER PUTTING THEIR LIVES INTO THE HANDS OF A PILOT LIKE THAT.

IF HE DOESN'T BELT UP —

EASY THERE, LAURIE.

ANGERED BY LAURIE'S APPARENT LACK OF REACTION, VARNEY BECAME RECKLESS.

WHY DIDN'T YOU STAY IN YOUR OWN COUNTRY, WHERE THINGS ARE A LOT LESS DANGEROUS?

THAT DOES IT!

LIKE A WHIPLASH, LAURIE STRUCK.

YOU'VE SAID TOO MUCH, BIG MOUTH!

OOF!

IT WAS OBVIOUS WHERE THE SYMPATHIES OF THE OTHERS LAY. ALL WERE DELIGHTED TO SEE VARNEY BEING SORTED OUT. AS A RESULT, NO ONE SAW STARKEY WALK INTO THE ROOM.

GO ON, LAURIE. FIX HIM!

STOP THAT FIGHT RIGHT NOW!

FOR PETE'S SAKE, STOP THEM OR THERE'LL BE TROUBLE.

STARKEY MARCHED THEM THERE AND THEN IN FRONT OF THEIR C.O., SQUADRON LEADER ROBERTS. ROBERTS HAD DECIDED VIEWS ON FIGHTING.

YOU SHOULD BE COURT-MARTIALLED FOR THIS, BUT I DON'T WANT TO LOSE TWO PILOTS, SO I'LL GIVE YOU MY OWN PUNISHMENT — AN HOUR'S DRILL WITH RIFLE AND FULL EQUIPMENT DAILY FOR A FORTNIGHT.

LAURIE TOOK HIS PUNISHMENT IN HIS STRIDE, BUT VARNEY TOOK IT BITTERLY HARD.

THIS IS A DISGRACE. ME ON RIFLE DRILL!

SHUT UP. IT'S NOT SO BAD.

JUST KEEP OUT OF MY WAY, YOU COLONIAL CLOWN.

SUITS ME, MATE!

STOP THAT NATTERING!

ABOUT A WEEK LATER AS LAURIE FLEW TOWARDS THE FIRING RANGES FOR TARGET PRACTICE WITH A CAMERA GUN, HE SPOTTED A MASTER FLYING LOW – DANGEROUSLY LOW.

ON HIS RETURN, LAURIE FOUND A STATE OF ALARM AT THE AIRFIELD.

LAURIE WAS NOT SURPRISED THAT VARNEY HAD COME UNSTUCK AFTER THE DISPLAY HE HAD SEEN EARLIER.

NOT LONG AFTERWARDS VARNEY ARRIVED BACK, UNHURT EXCEPT FOR A FEW MINOR CUTS.

YOU OK, VARNEY?

THERE WILL BE AN ENQUIRY INTO YOUR CRASH. I EXPECT YOU WILL BE CALLED IN A COUPLE OF DAYS.

YES, SIR, BUT I'M AFRAID THE MASTER ISN'T. IT'S BURNT OUT.

ACCORDING TO THE REGULATIONS, AN ENQUIRY HAD TO BE MADE INTO THE CIRCUMSTANCES OF THE CRASH. AS MIGHT BE EXPECTED, VARNEY HAD THOUGHT UP SOME GLIB ANSWERS.

I WAS FLYING AT THE PROPER HEIGHT, SIR. ONE THOUSAND FEET, WHEN THE ENGINE SUDDENLY CUT.

I SEE. CAN YOU GIVE ANY REASON WHY THIS HAPPENED?

AGAIN VARNEY'S ANSWER CAME OUT PAT.

YES, SIR. MY FLIGHT MECHANIC'S A SLOPPY TYPE. IF I HAD MY WAY, I'D DISCIPLINE HIM FOR NEGLIGENCE. IT WAS HIS FAULT.

ALL RIGHT, YOU'VE MADE YOUR POINT. WE CAN'T PROVE THIS, AS THE AIRCRAFT WAS DESTROYED, BUT DUE NOTICE WILL BE TAKEN OF WHAT YOU SAY.

AS A RESULT OF VARNEY'S COMPLAINT, HIS FLIGHT MECHANIC WAS DISCIPLINED. CONTEMPT FANNED LAURIE'S ANGER WHEN HE HEARD THE NEWS.

THAT'S THE LOUSIEST THING I EVER HEARD OF, VARNEY. THE CRASH WAS NOBODY'S FAULT BUT YOUR OWN.

WHAT DO YOU KNOW ABOUT IT? THAT FLIGHT MECHANIC WOULD HAVE BEEN COURT-MARTIALLED IF I'D HAD MY WAY. I COULD HAVE BEEN KILLED.

ALTHOUGH LAURIE COULDN'T PROVE THAT WHAT HE HAD SEEN WAS TRUE, VARNEY REALISED THAT IF THE TRUTH CAME OUT, IT COULD HARM HIS CAREER – FOR HE HAD AMBITIONS TO GET TO THE TOP, AND HE DIDN'T CARE HOW HE GOT THERE.

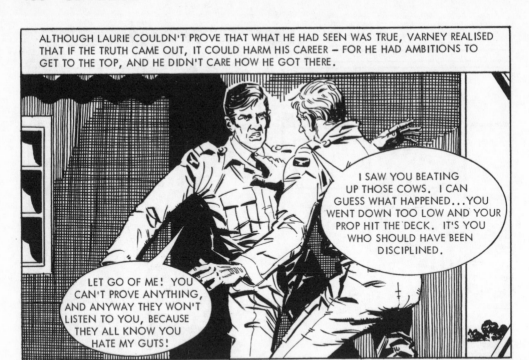

I SAW YOU BEATING UP THOSE COWS. I CAN GUESS WHAT HAPPENED...YOU WENT DOWN TOO LOW AND YOUR PROP HIT THE DECK. IT'S YOU WHO SHOULD HAVE BEEN DISCIPLINED.

LET GO OF ME! YOU CAN'T PROVE ANYTHING, AND ANYWAY THEY WON'T LISTEN TO YOU, BECAUSE THEY ALL KNOW YOU HATE MY GUTS!

A FEW DAYS LATER, THE CLASS BEGAN CROSS-COUNTRY PRACTICE FLIGHTS, FLYING IN PAIRS IN ANSONS, ONE ACTING AS PILOT AND THE OTHER AS NAVIGATOR.

NOW REMEMBER THIS – IF THE WEATHER SHOULD DETERIORATE, MAKE FOR ONE OF THE AIRFIELDS WHICH YOU HAVE LISTED. THE PILOT ALLOTTED TO EACH AIRCRAFT IS LISTED ON THE FLIGHT BOARD.

BUT THE FLIGHT BOARD HELD A SHOCK FOR LAURIE. HIS PILOT WAS NONE OTHER THAN VARNEY.

I'M NAVIGATING FOR YOU!

ANY OBJECTIONS, LAWRENCE? BELIEVE ME, YOU'RE THE LAST MAN I'D PICK.

THEY TOOK OFF INTO A CLEAR SKY, BOTH OF THEM KEEPING THINGS ON AN IMPERSONAL LEVEL.

NAVIGATOR TO PILOT. SET COURSE ONE EIGHT EIGHT DEGREES.

FOR OVER AN HOUR THE ANSON DRONED STEADILY ON. THEY WERE ON THE LAST LEG OF THEIR COURSE WHEN THEY RAN INTO THICK CLOUD.

CHECK COURSE AND ESTIMATED TIME OF ARRIVAL AGAIN, NAVIGATOR. THE WEATHER'S CLOSING DOWN.

THE ANSON BURIED ITSELF DEEP IN THE GREY NOTHINGNESS OF CLOSE-PACKED CLOUD BANKS. DESPERATELY, LAURIE TRIED TO GULP BACK THE FEAR THAT ROSE IN HIS THROAT, CHOKING HIM. HE TURNED TO VARNEY.

BETTER TURN FOR PEMBROKE. IT'S THE NEAREST AIRFIELD. HERE'S THE COURSE.

PEMBROKE? WHY SHOULD WE GO TO PEMBROKE?

CONTEMPTUOUSLY VARNEY CRUMPLED THE MESSAGE SLIP AND THREW IT ASIDE.

WHAT'S THE MATTER? YOU'RE SHAKING LIKE A LEAF. I WAS RIGHT, YOU ARE A FAIR WEATHER FLIER.

YOU KNOW THE ORDERS ABOUT THE BAD WEATHER. YOU'VE GOT TO TURN BACK.

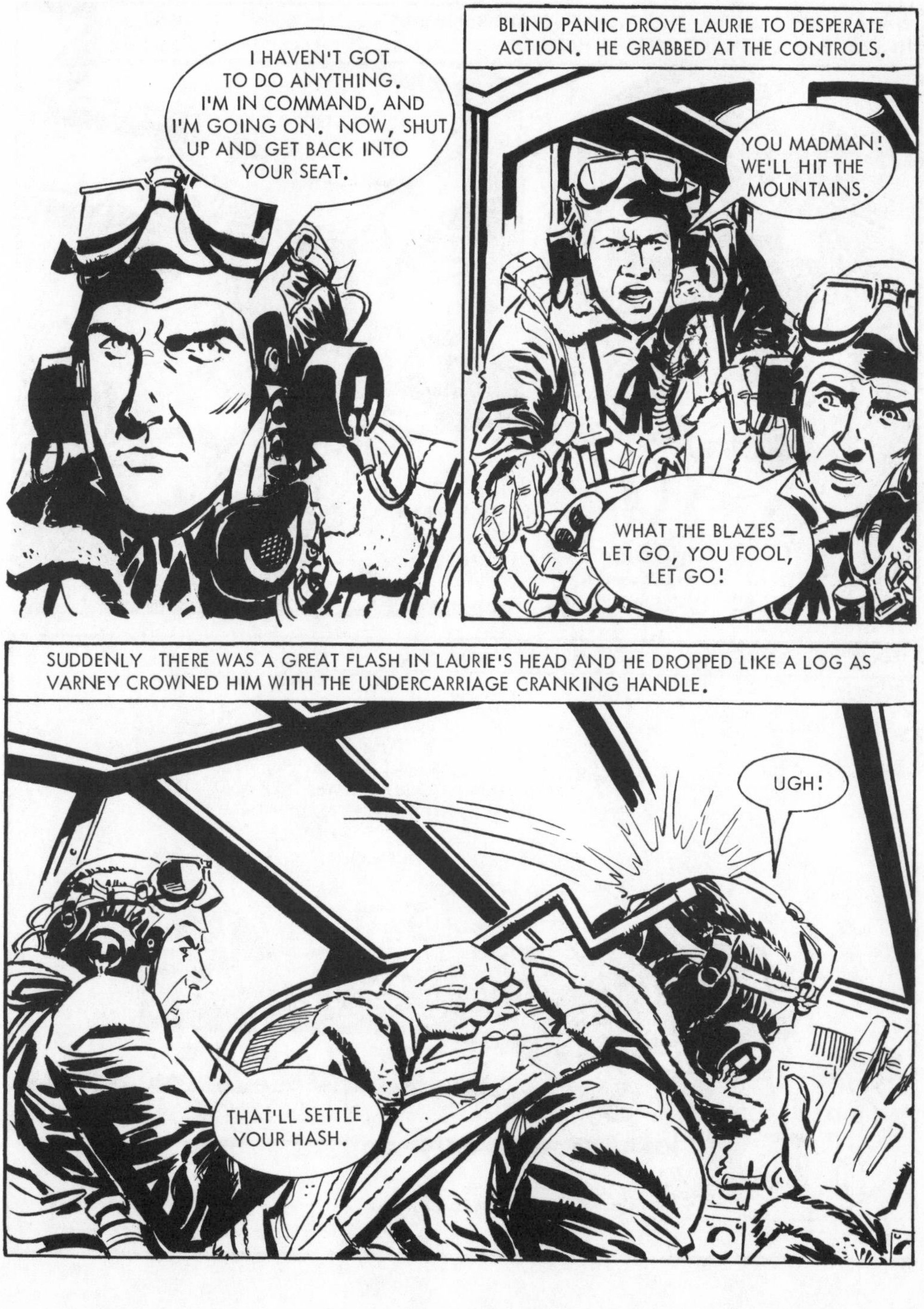
I HAVEN'T GOT TO DO ANYTHING. I'M IN COMMAND, AND I'M GOING ON. NOW, SHUT UP AND GET BACK INTO YOUR SEAT.
BLIND PANIC DROVE LAURIE TO DESPERATE ACTION. HE GRABBED AT THE CONTROLS.
YOU MADMAN! WE'LL HIT THE MOUNTAINS.
WHAT THE BLAZES — LET GO, YOU FOOL, LET GO!
SUDDENLY THERE WAS A GREAT FLASH IN LAURIE'S HEAD AND HE DROPPED LIKE A LOG AS VARNEY CROWNED HIM WITH THE UNDERCARRIAGE CRANKING HANDLE.
UGH!
THAT'LL SETTLE YOUR HASH.

WHEN LAURIE CAME TO, THEY WERE OVER THEIR HOME BASE. BLACK DESPAIR ENGULFED HIM AS HE REALISED JUST WHAT HE HAD DONE.

AH, SO YOU'VE SURFACED!

I'M FINISHED. THEY'LL THROW THE BOOK AT ME FOR THAT. I'LL NEVER BE A PILOT NOW...

VARNEY'S REPLY JOLTED THE FUZZINESS FROM LAURIE'S BRAIN.

DRY YOUR EYES! AS FAR AS I'M CONCERNED, WE RAN INTO BUMPY WEATHER AND YOU HIT YOUR HEAD ON THE ROOF. LAID YOURSELF OUT COLD.

WHAT? I DON'T GET IT. WHY SHOULD YOU DO THIS FOR ME, VARNEY?

ANY ILLUSIONS ABOUT A CHANGE OF HEART ON VARNEY'S PART WERE COMPLETELY DISPELLED AS THEY LEFT THE PLANE.

DON'T GET ME WRONG, LAWRENCE, I'VE GOT NO TIME FOR YOU. WE'RE QUITS NOW. WHAT YOU SAID ABOUT MY LOW FLYING COULD GET ME INTO BIG TROUBLE. WHAT YOU DID TODAY COULD FINISH YOU. IF YOU KEEP QUIET ABOUT ME, I'LL KEEP QUIET ABOUT YOU.

LAURIE DIDN'T KNOW WHETHER TO THANK VARNEY OR TO CURSE HIM. THE THOUGHT OF THIS DEVIL'S BARGAIN SEARED HIM WITH SHAME.

I DON'T KNOW WHAT TO SAY...

ONE THING MORE. KEEP OUT OF MY WAY, AND I'LL KEEP OUT OF YOURS.

THAT WASN'T LAURIE'S ONLY WORRY. SOONER OR LATER, HE WOULD HAVE TO FLY AGAIN IN BAD WEATHER, BUT FATE DECREED THAT HE WOULDN'T HAVE TO FACE THE CONDITIONS HE DREADED FOR SOME TIME YET.

AT LAST CAME THE DAY EAGERLY AWAITED BY LAURIE AND HIS FELLOW FLIERS — THE END OF THE FLYING COURSE. THE NEXT STEP WAS TRAINING IN BATTLE PRACTICE. THEY WERE TO BE SENT TO VARIOUS OPERATIONAL TRAINING UNITS AT HOME AND ABROAD.

GOOD SHOW, LAURIE. YOU'VE GOT YOUR COMMISSION, TOO.

THANK HEAVENS VARNEY'S GOING ELSE-WHERE. WHEN I'VE GOT HIM OFF MY BACK, I CAN START WITH A CLEAN SLATE.

THEY SENT LAURIE TO A LONG RANGE STRIKE FIGHTER TRAINING UNIT FLYING BEAUFIGHTERS.

WHAT A KITE! THIS IS MORE LIKE IT.

THE BEAUFIGHTER WAS A FAST BUT HEAVY MACHINE WHICH PACKED A REAL PUNCH IN THE SHAPE OF FOUR HISPANO CANNON IN ITS NOSE AND SIX MACHINE GUNS IN ITS WINGS.

THE TUITION THAT TURNED A NEW FLEDGLING INTO A FULLY OPERATIONAL STRIKE FIGHTER PILOT WAS INTENSIVE AND UNREMITTING. AND STILL THE SKIES STAYED HOT AND CLOUDLESS, MUCH TO LAURIE'S RELIEF.

AT THE END OF IT ALL, THEY SENT HIM TO A COASTAL COMMAND STATION ON A WINSWEPT AIRFIELD IN CORNWALL. THE C.O. OF THE SQUADRON, SQUADRON LEADER RADLETT, INTRODUCED HIM TO HIS NAVIGATOR, SERGEANT SCOTT.

THE WEEK FOLLOWING LAURIE'S ARRIVAL, THE SQUADRON OPERATIONS WERE CONFINED TO COASTAL CONVOY ESCORTS. AFTER THE FIRST FEW FLIGHTS, LAURIE HAD DECIDED THAT HE AND SCOTTY WOULD MAKE A GOOD TEAM.

A BIT TEDIOUS, MAYBE — ACTING AS NURSEMAID TO THOSE BABIES DOWN THERE. LET'S HOPE SOME REAL ACTION COMES SOON.

THE TEST WAS TO COME TWO DAYS LATER AS A SUNDERLAND FROM ANOTHER SQUADRON SPOTTED THE DARK SHAPE OF A U-BOAT'S CONNING TOWER.

OBJECT IN WATER, NINE O'CLOCK.

IT'S A SUB, SKIPPER!

ACTION STATIONS! RADIO, SEND A SIGHTING REPORT, QUICK. BOMB AIMER, STAND BY — WE'RE GOING IN!

JUST AS THE SUNDERLAND SIGHTED ITS TARGET, THE U-BOAT CRASH-DIVED.

DIVE! DIVE!

THE SUNDERLAND'S ENTIRE LOAD OF DEPTH BOMBS LASHED THE WATER INTO FIRE-STREAKED SPRAY AS THEY EXPLODED IN A PATTERN OF DESTRUCTION ROUND THE SUBMERGING U-BOAT.

ALL BOMBS ON TARGET, SKIPPER!

SPLIT BY THE PUNISHING FORCE OF THE POWERFUL EXPLOSIONS, THE U-BOAT UP-ENDED ITS BOWS OUT OF THE WATER BEFORE VANISHING FOR EVER.

WE GOT IT!

NO DOUBT AT ALL, LADDIE. OUR FIRST KILL.

THE WORDS WERE BARELY OUT OF HIS MOUTH, WHEN TWO VENGEFUL Ju88 LONG RANGE FIGHTERS CAME AT THE GREAT AIRCRAFT LIKE TERRIERS ATTACKING A BULL.

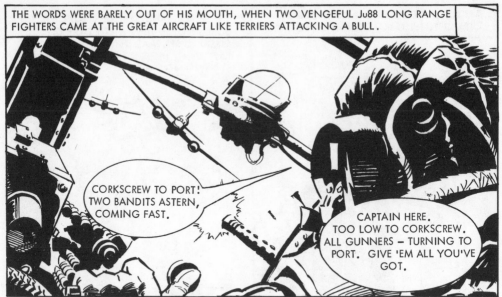

NOT FOR NOTHING DID THEY CALL THE SUNDERLAND THE "FLYING PORCUPINE". A SHATTERING BROADSIDE TORE THE FIRST NAZI AIRCRAFT TO PIECES IN SECONDS.

THE SURVIVING NAZI PILOT WAS A CLEVER FOX. HE DIVED TO SEA LEVEL, ENGINES ROARING AT FULL THROTTLE, THEN SHOT UPWARDS LIKE A ROCKET, ALL GUNS BLAZING. BUT THE SUNDERLAND PILOT WAS NO FOOL EITHER.

OH NO YOU DON'T, FRITZ!

HE'S COMING UP FROM BELOW. STAND BY FOR A TURN!

THE SUNDERLAND CAPTAIN STOOD THE GREAT FLYING BOAT ON ONE WING TIP TO BRING HIS GUNS TO BEAR ON THE JUNKERS. THE GERMAN'S LAST ACT BEFORE HE HIT THE WATER WAS TO PULVERISE BOTH THE SUNDERLAND'S PORT SIDE ENGINES INTO SCRAP.

WE'RE HIT BAD! CRASH STATIONS!

FUEL FROM THE MANGLED PETROL PIPES HAD SPILLED OVER THE HOT ENGINES AND TURNED THE WHOLE PORT WING INTO A FLAMING TORCH. THE SUNDERLAND'S CAPTAIN THREW THE PLANE TOWARDS THE SEA.

EVERYBODY OUT, QUICK. SHE'S GOING TO BLOW UP ANY SECOND!

THEY WERE BARELY CLEAR WHEN THE FLYING BOAT BLEW UP. BUT ANOTHER SUNDERLAND PATROLLING NEARBY HAD COME TO HELP.

IN YOU COME.

BUT A HIDDEN MENACE AWAITED THE RESCUERS. A PIECE OF FLOATING WRECKAGE LAY DIRECTLY IN THEIR LANDING PATH. THERE WAS A RENDING CRASH AS IT STOVE IN THE PLANE'S BOW.

IN THE SECOND SUNDERLAND, NOW CRIPPLED BY THE COLLISION, THE SITUATION WAS DEADLY DANGEROUS, FOR MORE GERMAN FIGHTERS COULD BE EXPECTED AT ANY MOMENT. QUICKLY THE SHOT-DOWN CREW WERE PULLED ABOARD.

WE STOVE IN OUR BOWS ON SOME FLOATING WRECKAGE. WE'LL HAVE TO FIX A PATCH ON HER BEFORE WE CAN GET OFF AGAIN. JUST HOPE NO MORE JERRIES SHOW UP IN THE MEANTIME.

WE'D BETTER KEEP OUR FINGERS CROSSED.

WITH THE REST OF THE MEN DOWN BY THE TAIL TO HOIST THE BOWS CLEAR OF THE WATER, TWO OF THE CREW WORKED AT TOP SPEED TO REPAIR THE DAMAGE.

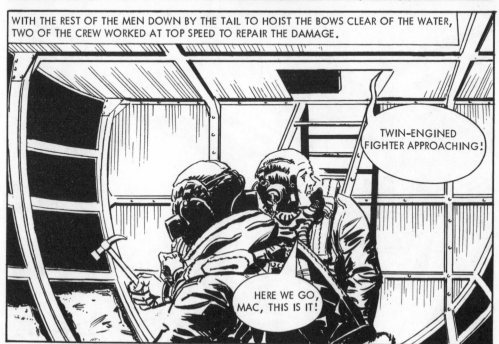

TWIN-ENGINED FIGHTER APPROACHING!

HERE WE GO, MAC, THIS IS IT!

THE NEWCOMER WAS FRIENDLY — A BEAUFIGHTER OF LAURIE'S SQUADRON.

THE SQUADRON'S AIRFIELD WAS LASHED WITH RAIN AND THE SCUDDING CLOUDS WERE DOWN TO THE TREE TOPS. THE SQUADRON HAD FLOWN TO ANOTHER AIRFIELD IN KENT TO REFUEL BEFORE TAKING PART IN A SHIPPING STRIKE. LAURIE AND SCOTTY HAD STAYED BEHIND AS SPARE CREW. LAURIE FELT HIS OLD FEAR COME TO LIFE AS THE ADJUTANT GAVE DETAILS OF THE JOB THEY HAD TO DO.

GET AIRBORNE IMMEDIATELY. IF JERRY FIGHTERS GET THERE BEFORE YOU DO, THOSE BLOKES IN THAT SUNDERLAND HAVE HAD IT.

LAURIE KNEW IT HAD TO HAPPEN SOONER OR LATER. NOW IT WAS HERE, THE SITUATION HE DREADED — FLYING BLIND.

CONTACT!

CONTACT!

THE GROUND CREWS RACED TO THE PLANE TO START IT UP READY FOR TAKE-OFF.

LAURIE AND SCOTTY HURRIED TO THE CREW ROOM TO GET THEIR FLYING KIT. SUDDENLY, LAURIE SLUMPED INTO A CHAIR.

WHAT'S THE MATTER, ARE YOU ILL?

I CAN'T DO IT, I JUST CAN'T.

HE BLURTED OUT THE WHOLE STORY OF THE TERROR THAT DOGGED HIM.

...EVER SINCE I LEFT FLYING SCHOOL, I HOPED I HAD MASTERED THIS FEAR, BUT NOW IT HAS BEGUN ALL OVER AGAIN.

HIS SHOULDERS DROOPED IN THE SHEER MISERY OF SHAME AND DEFEAT.

IT'S THE END OF THE ROAD FOR ME AS A PILOT.

BUT, SKIPPER, YOU CAN'T DO THIS, NOT NOW. COME ON, THE BEAU'S WAITING.

DESPERATE MEASURES WERE NEEDED, AND SCOTTY TOOK THEM. HE SHOUTED INTO LAURIE'S FACE.

YOU'RE MORE CONCERNED ABOUT YOUR OWN SKIN THAN THOSE MEN OUT THERE. IF YOU DON'T GET A GRIP OF YOURSELF AND TAKE OFF NOW, TWO SUNDERLAND CREWS HAVE HAD IT.

SCOTTY'S STINGING WORDS SEARCHED OUT THE REMNANTS OF LAURIE'S SELF RESPECT AND FANNED THEM INTO LIFE...

I'VE FLOWN WITH ALL SORTS, BUT NEVER WITH A WINDY WILLIE. THESE BLOKES OUT THERE ARE FINISHED IF WE DON'T GET OUT AFTER THEM, SO COME ON.

SCOTTY'S ANGER HAD ITS EFFECT. RELUCTANTLY LAURIE GOT TO HIS FEET AND FOLLOWED HIM TO THE WAITING PLANE.

LAURIE TOOK OFF INTO THE LASHING RAIN. SCOTTY'S REASSURING VOICE CAME OVER THE INTERCOM.

SO FAR SO GOOD. YOUR COURSE IS TWO ZERO TWO DEGREES.

FIERCELY LAURIE FOUGHT THE DREAD THAT CHOKED HIM. SCOTTY'S STINGING WORDS RANG IN HIS EARS, FORCING HIM ON.

HE WATCHED HIS INSTRUMENTS WITH A FIERCE CONCENTRATION. FOR ONE PANIC-RIDDEN MOMENT HE WAS SURE HE WAS DIVING, UNTIL HE REMEMBERED HIS INSTRUCTOR'S WORDS — "ALL MEN ARE LIARS, BUT YOUR INSTRUMENTS TELL THE TRUTH".

KEEP GOING, KEEP GOING. YOU'RE OVER THE SEA. I'M NOT SURE — MAYBE WE'RE OFF COURSE.

AFTER AN HOUR, LAURIE SUDDENLY REALISED THAT HIS PREOCCUPATION WITH HIS INSTRUMENT PANEL HAD DRIVEN AWAY HIS CRIPPLING FEAR. JUST THEN, SCOTTY'S VOICE CAME OVER THE INTERCOM. LAURIE LOOKED ROUND.

I'VE GOT A FIX. WE'RE TWELVE MILES SOUTH-WEST OF USHANT.

LAURIE FELT A SURGE OF ELATION AS THE BEAU BROKE INTO A CLEAR SKY. NEXT INSTANT HE GLIMPSED THE SUNDERLAND FAR BELOW – BUT HIS JUBILATION WAS SHORT-LIVED, FOR TWO BLACK SHAPES WERE SPEEDING TOWARDS THE CRIPPLED FLYING-BOAT.

INTENT ON DESTROYING THE HELPLESS SUNDERLAND, THE JUNKERS CREWS PAID SCANT ATTENTION TO THE SKIES ABOVE THEM. TOO LATE THEY REALISED THEIR MISTAKE AS LAURIE HURTLED OUT OF THE SKY ABOVE THEM.

THE FIRST Ju88 SMASHED INTO THE WATER AND WITH A QUICK FLICK OF THE CONTROLS, LAURIE BROUGHT HIS GUNS TO BEAR ON THE OTHER. A TWO SECOND BURST AND IT WAS ALL OVER.

NO MORE ENEMY FIGHTERS SHOWED UP. LAURIE CONTINUED TO CIRCLE THE FLYING BOAT AS THE CREW STRUGGLED TO REPAIR THE GASHED HULL.

AS THE GREAT FLYING BOAT ROSE LIKE A HUGE SEABIRD, LAURIE REALISED THAT BUT FOR HIMSELF AND SCOTTY IT WOULD HAVE BEEN A BULLET-RIDDLED WRECK.

LANDFALL, SKIPPER. I'M SORRY I SPOKE TO YOU THE WAY I DID BEFORE WE TOOK OFF.

I'M NOT SORRY. I CAN'T THANK YOU ENOUGH — IT SAVED TWENTY MEN'S LIVES, AND YOU MADE ME FACE UP TO MY FEAR AND BREAK IT.

FOR THAT DAY'S WORK, LAURIE AND SCOTTY WERE AWARDED THE D.F.C. AND D.F.M. IN THE MONTHS THAT FOLLOWED, LAURIE GAINED IN EXPERIENCE AND IN FLYING HOURS. NEVER AGAIN DID BAD WEATHER BOTHER HIM.

GET A LOAD OF THIS, JERRY!

IN SPITE OF THE OCCASIONAL EXCITEMENT OF AN UNEXPECTED BATTLE, MOST OF THE LONG RANGE FIGHTER WORK WAS BORING ROUTINE. AFTER A TIME THE SQUADRON MOVED TO NORFOLK, WHERE OPERATIONS OFF NORTH GERMANY AND DENMARK USUALLY BROUGHT ACTION OF SOME SORT. INEVITABLY THE LOSSES WERE HIGH.

THREE DAYS AFTER THE LOSS OF SQUADRON-LEADER RADLETT, HIS REPLACEMENT ARRIVED. LAURIE GOT A SHOCK WHEN HE SAW WHO IT WAS.

TO HAVE VARNEY ON THE SAME UNIT WAS THE LAST THING LAURIE WOULD HAVE WISHED. TO HAVE HIM AS HIS C.O. WAS A DISASTER.

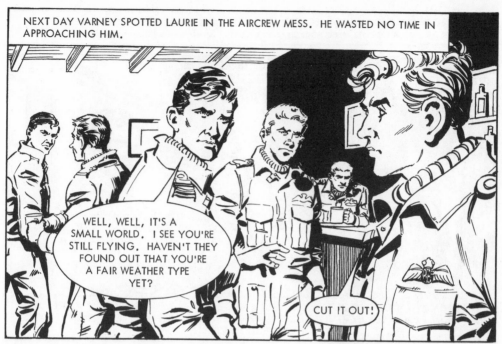

NEXT DAY VARNEY SPOTTED LAURIE IN THE AIRCREW MESS. HE WASTED NO TIME IN APPROACHING HIM.

WELL, WELL, IT'S A SMALL WORLD. I SEE YOU'RE STILL FLYING. HAVEN'T THEY FOUND OUT THAT YOU'RE A FAIR WEATHER TYPE YET?

CUT IT OUT!

ANTAGONISM FLARED BETWEEN THE TWO MEN.

GET THIS, VARNEY, I FLY IN ANY WEATHER. IF YOU THINK OTHERWISE YOU CAN CHECK UP MY LOG BOOK.

YOU'LL HAVE TO PROVE IT PERSONALLY BEFORE I'LL BELIEVE IT. ANOTHER THING, YOU'LL ADDRESS ME WITH RESPECT. I'M YOUR COMMANDING OFFICER.

THEY BOTH REALISED SIMULTANEOUSLY THAT THEY WERE CAUSING A SCENE. ABRUPTLY VARNEY TURNED ON HIS HEEL AND STAMPED OUT, LEAVING LAURIE GRINDING HIS TEETH WITH RAGE.

HOW DID THAT JUMPED-UP CREEP COME TO BE A SQUADRON LEADER? HE MUST HAVE PULLED A HECK OF A LOT OF STRINGS, I RECKON. BLAST HIS ROTTEN HIDE!

IF VARNEY WAS WRONG ABOUT LAURIE, LAURIE WAS EQUALLY WRONG ABOUT VARNEY. HE HAD COME FROM A BEAUFORT TORPEDO SQUADRON WHICH HAD TAKEN SOME HARD KNOCKS. THE LOSS OF OFFICERS SENIOR TO HIMSELF HAD SPEEDED UP PROMOTION.

AS FOR THE INCIDENT AT THE TRAINING SCHOOL WHEN HE MADE HIS MECHANIC CARRY THE CAN FOR HIS MISDEMEANOR, VARNEY NOW DEEPLY REGRETTED HIS ACTION. HE WAS STILL RUTHLESS...BUT ONLY IN FIGHTING THE WAR. HE DIDN'T WASTE ANY TIME IN LETTING HIS NEW COMMAND KNOW IT.

I'VE COME FROM A SQUADRON WHICH HAS A RECORD SECOND TO NONE. IT'S LAST OPERATION BEFORE I LEFT WAS A CLASSIC. WE ATTACKED THROUGH FLAK, FIGHTERS AND DIRTY WEATHER TO SINK AN ENTIRE CONVOY.

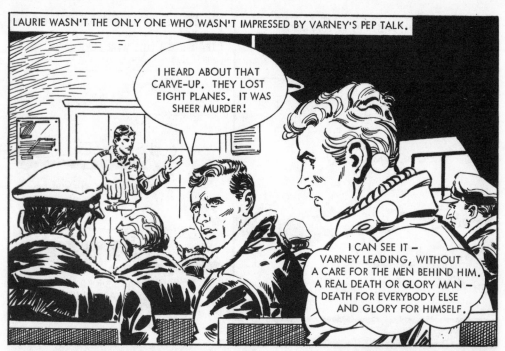

LAURIE WASN'T THE ONLY ONE WHO WASN'T IMPRESSED BY VARNEY'S PEP TALK.

I HEARD ABOUT THAT CARVE-UP. THEY LOST EIGHT PLANES. IT WAS SHEER MURDER!

I CAN SEE IT — VARNEY LEADING, WITHOUT A CARE FOR THE MEN BEHIND HIM. A REAL DEATH OR GLORY MAN — DEATH FOR EVERYBODY ELSE AND GLORY FOR HIMSELF.

VARNEY STUCK HIS CHIN OUT ARROGANTLY AND CONTINUED.

UNDER MY LEADERSHIP, THIS SQUADRON IS GOING TO DO EVEN BETTER THAN THAT, OR I'LL WANT TO KNOW WHY. THAT'S A PROMISE.

BLITHERING IDIOT! HEAVEN HELP US WITH THAT MANIAC IN COMMAND.

THE SQUADRON'S FIRST OPERATION UNDER VARNEY'S COMMAND WAS A STRIKE AGAINST A FLAK-SHIP WITH AN ESCORT OF E-BOATS THAT HAD BEEN SIGHTED OFF THE DUTCH COAST.

PILOT OFFICER PICKFORD AND SERGEANT TRIPP, FRESH FROM AN OPERATIONAL TRAINING UNIT, WERE FLYING THEIR FIRST OPERATION.

SECONDS LATER THE TARGET CAME INTO VIEW. THE BEAUFIGHTERS CIRCLED OUT OF RANGE UNTIL VARNEY GAVE THE ORDER TO ATTACK. THEN THEY TURNED INWARDS SIMULTANEOUSLY, ENGINES THUNDERING AT FULL THROTTLE.

TWISTING AND TURNING TO DODGE THE DEATH-DEALING FLAK, EACH BEAUFIGHTER ATTACKED INDEPENDENTLY. THE MULTI-DIRECTIONAL ATTACK COMPLETELY BEWILDERED THE DEFENCES.

THESE ACCURSED BRITISH ARE EVERYWHERE! WE CANNOT STOP THEM ALL!

THE GERMAN FLAK-SHIP WAS A FORMIDABLE FOE. IT BRISTLED WITH LIGHT AND HEAVY GUNS. THE E-BOATS TOO, SPRAYED THE SKY WITH SHELLS. FACED BY THE THUNDEROUS BARRAGE, THE INEXPERIENCED PICKFORD FALTERED UNCERTAINLY.

THAT FLAK! IT'S — IT'S FANTASTIC! I DIDN'T KNOW IT WOULD BE LIKE THIS —

AS LAURIE DIVED HIS BEAUFIGHTER ON A STRAFING RUN OVER AN E-BOAT HE AND SCOTTY HEARD VARNEY'S AGGRESSIVE TONES OVER THE RADIO.

THEY WERE TOO BUSY ENGAGED IN SLAMMING THEIR ROCKETS IN THE SIDE OF AN E-BOAT TO SEE WHAT PICKFORD AND TRIPP WERE DOING.

BUT EVEN AS SCOTTY SPOKE, THE E-BOAT DISAPPEARED. LAURIE BANKED SHARPLY TO AVOID THE SHATTERING EXPLOSION AS THE FLAK-SHIP EXPLODED UNDER MANY HITS.

THERE GOES THE FLAK-SHIP!

RADIO'S GONE DEAD — BUT WE'RE HEADING FOR HOME. THERE'S NOTHING TO KEEP US. EVERYTHING HAS BEEN SUNK!

DEBRIEFING WAS A TIME FOR RECKONING THE RESULTS — AND THE COST.

WE LOST FOUR. I SAW THEM GOING DOWN, ONE AFTER ANOTHER.

NO DOUBT ABOUT IT, WE'VE TAKEN A HARD KNOCK. THERE'S A CREW MISSING, TOO. WHO ARE THEY, "BRAINS"?

PICKFORD AND TRIPP.

THE HUBBUB OF CONVERSATION SUDDENLY STILLED. THEY TENSED AS THEY HEARD THE UNMISTAKABLE BEAT OF A BEAUFIGHTER'S ENGINES RUNNING ROUGH — VERY ROUGH.

SOMEHOW THE SHATTERED WRECK STAGGERED ROUND THE AIRFIELD. VARNEY GRABBED THE MICROPHONE.

PICKFORD! TRY TO GAIN HEIGHT AND BAIL OUT. CAN YOU HEAR ME?

YES, SIR, I CAN HEAR YOU. I...I THINK TRIPP'S DEAD BUT I'M NOT SURE. I CAN'T BAIL OUT NOT KNOWING IF HE'S ALIVE OR DEAD.

ALL WHO HEARD YOUNG PICKFORD'S VOICE THROUGH THE CONTROL TOWER SPEAKER WERE CONSCIOUS OF THE CRUEL DILEMMA THAT FACED HIM.

TRIPP CAN'T BE ALIVE. BAIL OUT, PICKFORD.

NO...I'M COMING IN.

THE BEAUFIGHTER STAGGERED OVER THE RUNWAY. SUDDENLY BOTH ENGINES CUT DEAD AND THE HEAVY FIGHTER DROPPED LIKE A STONE.

OH, NO! HE'S HAD IT!

IN LESS THAN A SECOND, THE WRECKAGE WAS ABLAZE FROM END TO END. THE BLACK SMOKE MARKED THE FUNERAL PYRE OF TWO GALLANT YOUNG FLIERS.

THERE'S NOTHING ANYBODY CAN DO NOW.

THEY WERE ONLY KIDS...YOU DIDN'T HAVE TO SEND THEM AGAINST THAT FLAK-SHIP.

THIS IS WAR, LAWRENCE, AND IN CASE YOU HADN'T NOTICED, A LOT OF KIDS ARE GETTING KILLED. DO YOU THINK THAT'S THE WAY I WANT IT?

LAURIE FORGOT RESTRAINT AND DISCRETION. AS HE SAW IT, VARNEY WAS DIRECTLY RESPONSIBLE FOR WHAT HAD JUST HAPPENED.

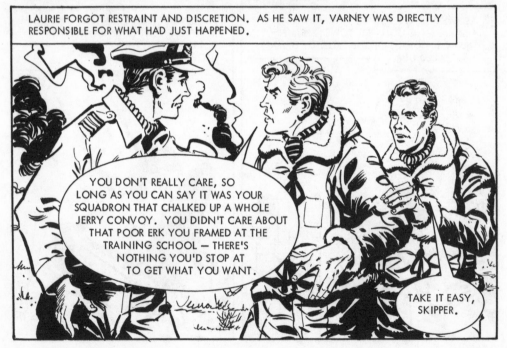

YOU DON'T REALLY CARE, SO LONG AS YOU CAN SAY IT WAS YOUR SQUADRON THAT CHALKED UP A WHOLE JERRY CONVOY. YOU DIDN'T CARE ABOUT THAT POOR ERK YOU FRAMED AT THE TRAINING SCHOOL — THERE'S NOTHING YOU'D STOP AT TO GET WHAT YOU WANT.

TAKE IT EASY, SKIPPER.

FOR A SECOND-RATE PILOT, YOU'VE GOT A LOT TO SAY FOR YOURSELF. NEXT TIME YOU STEP OUT OF LINE, I'LL GROUND YOU. SO WATCH IT.

AS LAURIE TRIED DESPERATELY TO CALM HIS RAGE, VARNEY SWUNG ON HIS HEEL AND LEFT.

FOR TWO PINS, I'D BELT HIM HERE AND NOW!

DON'T DO THAT, SKIPPER. I DON'T WANT TO LOSE MY PILOT.

AT THIS MOMENT, OFF THE NORWEGIAN COAST, ONE OF NAZI GERMANY'S GREATEST GAMBLES SEEMED ALL SET TO PAY OFF. THREE MONTHS PREVIOUSLY, A BIG CARGO LINER, THE "KONIGSHAFEN", HAD LEFT TOKYO, CRAMMED WITH VITAL WAR MATERIALS. SO FAR SHE HAD ELUDED THE ALLIED BLOCKADE, BUT NOW AS SHE REACHED THE MOST HAZARDOUS PART OF THE JOURNEY, THICK FOG CLOSED DOWN.

WE WILL HAVE TO MAINTAIN OUR SPEED DESPITE THE FOG. WE ARE STILL IN RANGE OF THE BRITISH AIR FORCE.

BUT THE SHIP WAS NOT UNOBSERVED. OFF THE BLEAK NORWEGIAN COAST, SOME FISHERMEN SAW HER LOOMING THROUGH THE FOG.

KONIGSHAFEN! THE RESISTANCE MUST KNOW OF THIS. WHAT A TARGET FOR A BRITISH SUBMARINE!

THE NORWEGIANS WERE PATRIOTS. THEY PASSED THE INFORMATION TO THE RESISTANCE, WHO RADIOED IT TO BRITAIN. COASTAL COMMAND SWUNG INTO ACTION.

THAT IS THE POSITION WHERE SHE WAS SIGHTED, BUT IT IS CERTAIN SHE IS STEERING AN ERRATIC COURSE. THIS SHIP MUST BE FOUND AND SUNK AT ALL COSTS.

AS SOON AS THE ORDERS WERE RECEIVED, VARNEY DECIDED THAT IT MUST BE HIS SQUADRON THAT WOULD SINK THE KONIGSHAFEN.

YOU WILL FLY NIGHT AND DAY, IN FAIR WEATHER AND FOUL. YOU WILL FLY UNTIL YOU DROP. THE KONIGSHAFEN IS GOING TO BE SUNK BY THIS SQUADRON.

VARNEY WAS AS GOOD AS HIS WORD. HE DROVE HIS MEN AS HARD AS HE HAD PROMISED, TILL THEY WERE NEARLY OUT ON THEIR FEET. LAURIE AND SCOTTY WERE NO EXCEPTION.

TIGHTEN YOUR HARNESS, SCOTTY. APPROACHING TO LAND. I FEEL ABSOLUTELY WHACKED!

I DON'T FEEL TOO CHIRPY MYSELF, SKIPPER. TWO SEVEN-HOUR PATROLS EVERY DAY ISN'T EXACTLY A HOLIDAY. THE C.O. BADGERING US ALL THE TIME DOESN'T MAKE IT ANY EASIER, EITHER.

AS LAURIE CAME IN TO LAND AN ALARM HOOTER SOUNDED. STARTLED, HE LOOKED DOWN AND SAW TWO RED LIGHTS GLOWING ON HIS INSTRUMENT PANEL.

HE SLAMMED BOTH THROTTLES WIDE OPEN, BUT IT WAS TOO LATE. HIS PROPELLERS CHEWED INTO THE RUNWAY, TEARING OUT LUMPS OF CONCRETE. WITH THE TORTURED SCREECHING OF MANGLED METAL, THE BEAUFIGHTER BELLY-LANDED IN A CLOUD OF DUST AND SPARKS.

FIRST ON THE SCENE WAS VARNEY. HE TURNED ANGRILY ON LAURIE. TEMPERS WERE SHORT, AND THE ANTAGONISM BETWEEN THE TWO MEN FLARED.

SHEER NEGLIGENCE, I CALL IT. HOW THE BLAZES DO YOU EXPECT ME TO KEEP THE SQUADRON AT MAXIMUM EFFORT IF YOU DO THIS KIND OF THING?

LISTEN — I'VE FLOWN FOURTEEN HOURS TODAY....WHAT DO YOU EXPECT, PUSHING US LIKE THIS? WE AREN'T THE ONLY SQUADRON LOOKING FOR THE KONIGSHAFEN, BUT THE OTHERS AREN'T UNDER THE KIND OF PRESSURE WE ARE.

NEXT MORNING THE MET. OFFICER GAVE VARNEY THE WEATHER REPORT.

IT'S HOPELESS, SIR. THE FOG'S CLOSED RIGHT DOWN. THEY'LL NEVER SEE A THING.

THERE WILL BE NO LET-UP. EVERY AIRCRAFT WILL BE IN THE AIR. WE'VE GOT TO FIND THAT SHIP TODAY.

VARNEY HAD A SHOCK FOR LAURIE, TOO, WHEN THEY MET IN THE CREW ROOM.

YOU'LL BE FLYING AS MY NUMBER TWO TODAY, LAWRENCE.

LAURIE'S HACKLES ROSE WHEN HE REALISED WHAT VARNEY MEANT.

YOU'VE STILL GOT TO KEEP AN EYE ON ME — YOU DON'T TRUST ME, DO YOU?

SINCE YOU ASK ME, I DON'T! YOU'VE GOT A THING ABOUT THICK WEATHER. YOU'LL BE MORE OCCUPIED TRYING TO CALM YOUR FEARS THAN WATCHING FOR THAT SHIP.

GIVE ME STRENGTH! WHAT MORE CAN I DO TO CONVINCE YOU? BAD WEATHER DOESN'T WORRY ME ANY MORE!

THE SQUADRON'S BEAUFIGHTERS TOOK OFF IN PAIRS AND DISAPPEARED INTO THE FOG BANKS WHICH BLANKETED THE SEA, EACH PAIR ON A PRECISELY PLOTTED COURSE. VARNEY AND LAURIE WERE FIRST TO GO.

FOR TWO TEDIOUS HOURS, THEY SEARCHED THE FOG-BOUND OCEAN UNTIL THEIR EYES ACHED. SUDDENLY VARNEY AND LAURIE CAME TO A GREAT GAP IN THE FOG. THEY CLIMBED HIGHER – AND THERE, GLEAMING IN THE WATERY SUNLIGHT, WAS THE KONIGSHAFEN. LAURIE DIVED TO THE ATTACK AT ONCE.

THE KONISGHAFEN WAS NO HELPLESS MERCHANT SHIP. AS LAURIE DIVED TO THE ATTACK, HE WAS MET WITH A SOLID CURTAIN OF FLAK.

SOME CARGO LINER! HECK, IT PACKS A WALLOP BIG ENOUGH FOR A BATTLESHIP!

THERE WAS NO DOUBT ABOUT IT. EVERY GUNNER ON BOARD THE KONIGSHAFEN WAS DETERMINED TO BLAST THE LONE BEAUFIGHTER FROM THE SKY. THEY WERE SO NEAR HOME NOW AFTER THOSE LONG WEARY WEEKS AT SEA, SURELY ONE SINGLE AIRCRAFT COULDN'T STOP THEM NOW.

WHERE'S VARNEY? HE SHOULD BE ATTACKING FROM THE OTHER SIDE TO SPLIT THE DEFENCES. CAN YOU SEE HIM, SCOTTY?

HE TURNED AWAY WHEN THE FLAK OPENED UP. HE'S CIRCLING OUT OF RANGE.

HIS AIM SPOILED BY THE FURY OF THE FLAK, LAURIE TURNED AWAY.

THE YELLOW RAT! COME IN, BLACKJACK ONE. WHAT'S THE BIG IDEA, LEAVING ME TO FACE THAT FLAK ON MY OWN? HEY, VARNEY. WHY DON'T YOU ANSWER?

TO LAURIE'S DISGUST, THERE WAS NO REPLY FROM VARNEY. SCOTTY HAD BAD NEWS TOO.

THE FOG'S DISPERSING, SKIPPER. WE CAN EXPECT MESSERSCHMITTS TO SHOW UP AT ANY MOMENT.

WE'D BETTER NAIL HER NOW. HERE WE GO!

TWISTING AND JINKING LIKE A MAD THING, THE BEAUFIGHTER PENETRATED THE FLAK CURTAIN. AS THE DEADLY ROCKETS LEFT THEIR RAILS, A SHELL SMASHED THE STARBOARD ENGINE.

ROCKETS GONE! WOW! WE'RE HIT!

THE CLUSTER OF ROCKETS SMASHED INTO THE KONIGSHAFEN'S SIDE AND BLEW HER BOILERS APART. THE EXPLOSIVE FORCE OF RELEASED HIGH PRESSURE STEAM TORE THE HULL ASUNDER.

WE GOT HER, SKIPPPER. RIGHT IN THE BOILER ROOM. SHE'S HAD IT!

SO HAVE WE, MATE. STAND BY TO DITCH!

WITH THE FLAMES FROM THE RUINED ENGINE SPREADING FAST, LAURIE WASTED NO TIME IN PUTTING THE DOOMED PLANE DOWN IN THE SEA.

GET THE DINGHY OUT, FAST!

VARNEY CIRCLED OVER THE SCENE. FLYING OFFICER PRATT, HIS OBSERVER, SAW THAT THE TWO MEN IN THE WATER WERE IN DEADLY DANGER.

THEY'RE IN TROUBLE, SIR. IT LOOKS AS IF THEIR DINGHY'S BEEN RIPPED BY FLAK.

IF WE DON'T DO SOMETHING QUICKLY, THEY'RE DEAD MEN.

LAURIE AND SCOTTY SAW VARNEY'S AIRCRAFT COMING IN LOW TOWARDS THEM. THEN AS IT CAME CLOSER, THEY SAW THE FLAPS WERE DOWN AND ITS ENGINES STOPPED. WITH A GREAT SPLASH IT WENT IN.

WHAT THE HECK'S HE DOING THAT FOR? HE WASN'T HIT, WAS HE?

AT LEAST WE WON'T DROWN. HE'S GOT A DINGHY WITH NO HOLES IN IT — I HOPE!

QUICKLY, VARNEY AND PRATT LAUNCHED THEIR DINGHY, PADDLED ACROSS TO THE OTHER TWO AND DRAGGED THEM ABOARD. IT WAS A TIGHT SQUEEZE, FOR THE LITTLE RUBBER BOAT WAS MEANT FOR ONLY TWO.

I DON'T GET YOU, VARNEY. YOU CAN'T STOMACH A BIT OF FLAK SO YOU HOLD BACK AND LET ME FACE THE MUSIC... THEN YOU GO AND DO A FOOLHARDY THING LIKE THAT.

YOU UNGRATEFUL PUP! TO START WITH, YOU DISOBEYED MY ORDERS OVER THE RADIO. I TOLD YOU NOT TO ATTACK UNTIL I RADIOED A SIGHTING REPORT TO BASE, SO THEY'D KNOW WHERE THE SHIP WAS.

NEXT INSTANT, VARNEY AND LAURIE WERE AT IT HAMMER AND TONGS.

COME OFF IT. I DIDN'T HEAR ANY ORDER.

WELL, YOUR RADIO, OR MINE, MUST HAVE BEEN DUD — OR YOU CHOSE NOT TO HEAR MY ORDERS.

THE CONTINUED TO ARGUE BITTERLY, INDULGING THEIR DISLIKE FOR EACH OTHER TO THE FULL. THE OTHER TWO OCCUPANTS OF THE DINGHY HAD NO CHOICE BUT TO LISTEN WITH GROWING IMPATIENCE, UNTIL, AT LAST, THEY HAD HAD ENOUGH.

THAT'S YOUR STORY AND YOU'RE STICKING TO IT....

LOOK, PRATT AND I ARE GETTING A BIT FED UP WITH ALL THIS WRANGLING. THERE'S NO POINT IN IT.

SCOTTY'S RIGHT. WE'RE SUPPOSED TO BE FIGHTING GERMANS, NOT EACH OTHER. WHAT'S THE USE OF ALL THAT ARGUMENT? WE'RE ALL IN THE SAME BOAT.

THIS PROTEST BORE FRUIT.

I SUPPOSE YOU'RE RIGHT, PRATT.

SO HE IS. IN THE SAME BOAT, HE SAYS. THAT'S RATHER COMICAL.

SUDDENLY THEY STARTED TO LAUGH UPROARIOUSLY AT PRATT'S UNINTENDED JOKE. BUT JOE PRATT DIDN'T THINK IT SO FUNNY...

WHAT ARE YOU ALL LAUGHING AT? WE MIGHT GET PICKED UP BY JERRY, OR WE MIGHT NOT GET PICKED UP AT ALL. I MUST SAY THE PROSPECT ISN'T VERY AMUSING.

BUT LADY LUCK SMILED ON THEM THAT DAY. THEY WERE PICKED UP WITHIN AN HOUR.

HERE WE GO! RESCUED FOR WHAT? TO ROT IN A PRISON CAMP FOR THE REST OF THE WAR.

IT'S OK, THEY'RE NORWEGIAN.

WITH THE HELP OF THE NORWEGIAN RESISTANCE, THEY GOT BACK TO THE U.K. SAFELY. AFTER ALL CONGRATULATIONS WERE OVER, VARNEY AND LAURIE SAW EACH OTHER DIFFERENTLY.

I'VE BEEN COMPLETELY WRONG ABOUT YOU, LAWRENCE. THE WAY YOU FACED THAT FLAK SHOWED ME YOU'VE REALLY GOT WHAT IT TAKES.

I MISJUDGED YOU TOO, SIR. YOU RISKED YOUR NECK TO SAVE OUR LIVES OUT THERE.

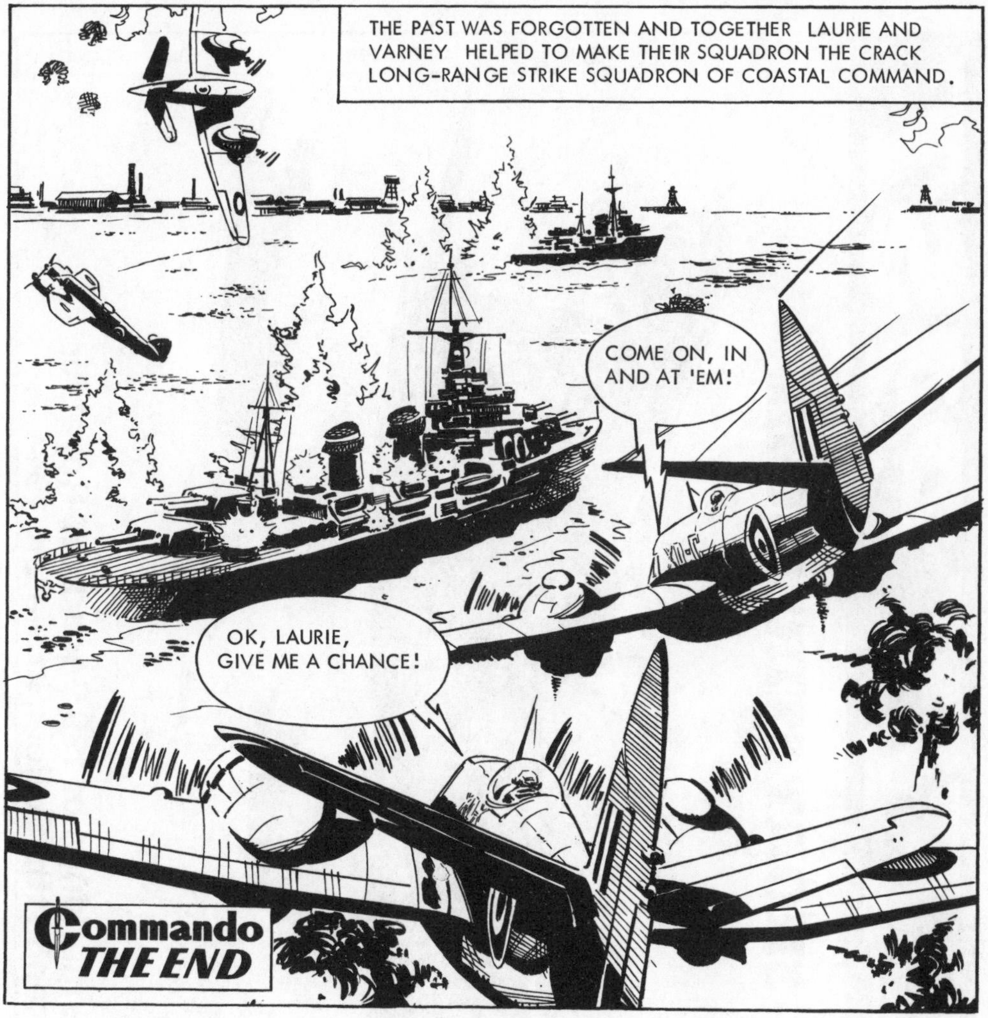
THE PAST WAS FORGOTTEN AND TOGETHER LAURIE AND VARNEY HELPED TO MAKE THEIR SQUADRON THE CRACK LONG-RANGE STRIKE SQUADRON OF COASTAL COMMAND.
COME ON, IN AND AT 'EM!
OK, LAURIE, GIVE ME A CHANCE!
Commando
THE END

Commando **FLY PAST**

No. 37 — SHORT STIRLING III

Shown in the markings of 199 Squadron, Royal Air Force, at Lakenheath, Suffolk, in March, 1944.

A STIRLING CALLED SATAN

PILOTS GET PRETTY FOND OF THEIR AIR-CRAFT, AND FLYING OFFICER SAM GILBERT WAS NO EXCEPTION. BUT THERE CAME A TIME WHEN SAM SUSPECTED THAT HIS BELOVED STIRLING BOMBER WAS A "ROGUE", CURSED WITH MISFORTUNE FROM THE DAY SHE LEFT THE ASSEMBLY-LINE.

AND NONE OF HIS CREW WOULD HAVE DISAGREED — IN FACT THEY GAVE HER THE GRIM NICKNAME OF... SATAN!

HIS TROUBLES REALLY BEGAN MUCH EARLIER, WHILE HE WAS FLYING WHITLEYS. HE LOOKED ROUND TO FIND HIS NAVIGATOR, SERGEANT "TODDY" McKENZIE, DEEPLY ENGROSSED IN HIS WORK.

THE PORT ENGINE'S PLAYING UP AGAIN. WHEN DO WE REACH THE COAST?

FIVE MINUTES, SKIPPER. I'LL PLAN A COURSE TO THE NEAREST AIRFIELD.

THE RADIO OPERATOR, STAN BLYTHE, CROSSED HIS FINGERS AND SMILED GRIMLY AT HIS GREAT PAL, GUNNER REX PARKER.

PHIL NEWTON, THE TAIL GUNNER, SIGHED WITH RELIEF AS THEY CROSSED THE COAST. BUT THEN THE AILING ENGINE SPLUTTERED AND PACKED UP COMPLETELY.

WE'RE IN LUCK, I CAN SEE A RUNWAY. WE'LL GO STRAIGHT IN TO LAND.

FLASHING HIS LIGHTS TO INDICATE AN EMERGENCY, SAM TOUCHED DOWN SMOOTHLY ON THE UNFAMILIAR AIRFIELD.

A PLACE CALLED WINKLETON — IT'S A NON-OPERATIONAL AIRFIELD, SO WE'RE LUCKY EVERYONE WASN'T IN BED.

JUST IN TIME, THE OTHER ENGINE WAS STARTING TO OVERHEAT. WHERE ARE WE, TODDY?

AS THEY PREPARED TO LEAVE THE AIR-FIELD, TODDY NOTICED AN UNFAMILIAR AIRCRAFT.

HEY, LOOK — WHAT'S THAT MONSTER KITE?

SEARCH ME. MUST BE ON THE SECRET LIST. WONDER IF THEY'D SWOP IT FOR OUR BUS?

FLIGHT-LIEUTENANT BOB RAMSAY, AN OLD FRIEND, WAS STATIONED AT WINKLETON, AND THEY MET AT BREAKFAST.

WHAT'S THAT LOVELY FOUR-ENGINED JOB BY THE HANGARS, BOB?

A STIRLING, AND IT'LL SOON BE OPERATIONAL. I'LL SHOW YOU ROUND...

BOB, WHO WORKED FOR THE TEST AND DEVELOPMENT UNIT, WAS VERY PROUD OF THE NEW BOMBER.

FOUR MASSIVE ENGINES, AN EIGHT-TON PAYLOAD, AND SHE HANDLES LIKE A FIGHTER! FANCY A CIRCUIT OR TWO?

JUST TRY TO STOP ME, CHUM! I'D SOONER FLY THAN JUST LOOK AT HER.

A SHORT FLIGHT CONFIRMED SAM'S FIRST IMPRESSIONS.

SHE'S A DREAM, BOB! I'D LIKE TO GET MY HANDS ON ONE OF MY OWN.

THEY'RE PICKING CREWS FOR THE SQUADRONS SOON, AND YOU SHOULD STAND A GOOD CHANCE WITH ALL YOUR OPERATIONAL EXPERIENCE.

LATER THAT DAY, WITH THE WHITLEY REPAIRED, THEY LEFT FOR HOME — BUT SAM'S MIND WASN'T ON HIS JOB.

TAKE A GOOD LOOK, YOU BLOKES! WE'LL BE FLYING ONE SOON.

FOR SEVERAL WEEKS SAM PESTERED THE AUTHORITIES, UNTIL EVENTUALLY HIS PERSISTENCE GOT RESULTS.

JUST WAIT TILL I TELL MY CREW — THERE'LL BE A CELEBRATION TONIGHT, SIR.

YOU'VE THE LUCK OF THE DEVIL, SAM. YOUR APPLICATION'S BEEN ACCEPTED.

BUT THE CREW DIDN'T SEEM TO SHARE HIS ENTHUSIASM — ESPECIALLY TODDY McKENZIE AND PHIL NEWTON THE TAIL GUNNER.

WE'RE ASKING FOR TROUBLE, CHANGING SQUADRONS IN THE MIDDLE OF A TOUR.

TODDY'S RIGHT, SKIPPER. WE'RE USED TO WHITLEYS, AND WE'LL BE NEW BOYS AGAIN ON STIRLINGS.

FOR A MOMENT SAM FEARED IT WOULD MEAN BREAKING UP THE CREW — BUT THEIR LOYALTY PREVAILED.

YOU DON'T HAVE TO CHANGE, THE C.O. WOULD KEEP YOU HERE ON WHITLEYS.

YOU'D NEVER FIND ANY TARGETS WITHOUT US, SKIPPER. I RECKON WE'D BETTER TAG ALONG TO KEEP YOU OUT OF TROUBLE.

A SECOND PILOT, MIKE GRAHAM, MADE UP THEIR NEW CREW WITH GUNNER DAVE STEWART.

SO THEY BEGAN THEIR CONVERSION TRAINING, AND SOON THEY HAD MASTERED THE STIRLING AND LOOKED FORWARD EAGERLY TO ACTION AGAIN.

OUR LAST TRIP, LADS. TOMORROW WE GO TO AN OPERATIONAL SQUADRON.

IT FELT GOOD TO BE IN A SQUADRON AGAIN — BUT TODDY HAD PICKED UP SOME DISQUIETING RUMOURS.

WE'RE ON OPS TOMORROW MORNING. BRIEFING'S AT FIVE, SO WE'D BETTER GET AN EARLY NIGHT.

LET'S HOPE IT ISN'T TOO ROUGH. HAVE YOU TALKED TO THE SENIOR AIR CREWS ABOUT THE OTHER DAYLIGHT RAIDS?

TODDY FROWNED AS SAM ANSWERED HIS QUESTIONS.

THEY'VE HAD A FEW TOUGH ONES, BUT THAT'S ONLY TO BE EXPECTED. THINGS ARE BOUND TO IMPROVE.

WHO ARE YOU KIDDING, SAM? THE STIRLING JUST ISN'T A DAY BOMBER — IT'S TOO SLOW AND CLUMSY.

MIKE, THE SECOND PILOT, HAD ALSO BEEN TALKING WITH SOME OF THE EXPERIENCED CREWS.

IT'S THE JERRY FIGHTERS WE'VE GOT TO WATCH OUT FOR. THEY'LL BE AFTER US ALL THE WAY.

THE OLD HANDS HAVE JUST BEEN TRYING TO WORRY YOU, MIKE. YOU DON'T WANT TO BELIEVE ALL THEIR YARNS.

BUT AS THE STIRLING FORCE AND ITS FIGHTER ESCORT RENDEZVOUSED OVER THE FRENCH COAST.

BANDITS APPROACHING FROM THE NORTH. GET READY TO SEE THEM OFF!

THE SPITFIRES WHEELED IN TIGHT FORMATION AND DIVED TO MEET THE GERMAN THREAT.

AAGH!

FIRST BLOOD TO US, BLUE FORCE!

BUT A SECOND ENEMY FORMATION WAS LYING IN WAIT FOR THE BOMBERS.

GO FOR THE BOMBERS, THEY'RE ON THEIR OWN NOW.

SAM BLINKED AS A MESSERSCHMITT HURTLED OVERHEAD LIKE A THUNDERBOLT.

THEY MUST HAVE DODGED OUR ESCORT.

HE'S GETTING AWFULLY CLOSE. IT'S AS IF OUR KITE IS ATTRACTING THE FIGHTERS.

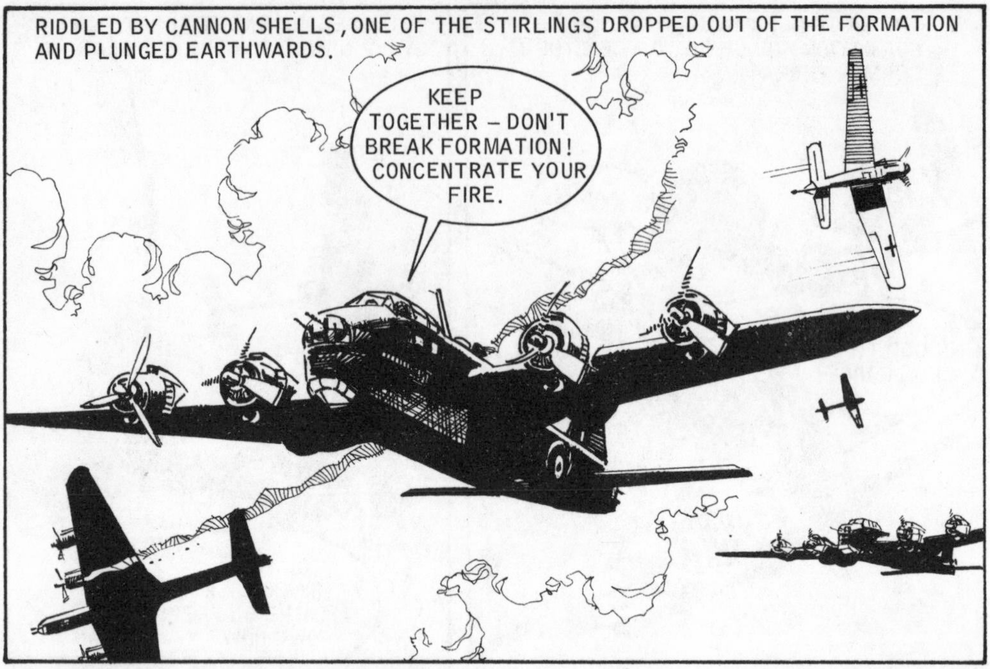
RIDDLED BY CANNON SHELLS, ONE OF THE STIRLINGS DROPPED OUT OF THE FORMATION AND PLUNGED EARTHWARDS.
KEEP TOGETHER – DON'T BREAK FORMATION! CONCENTRATE YOUR FIRE.

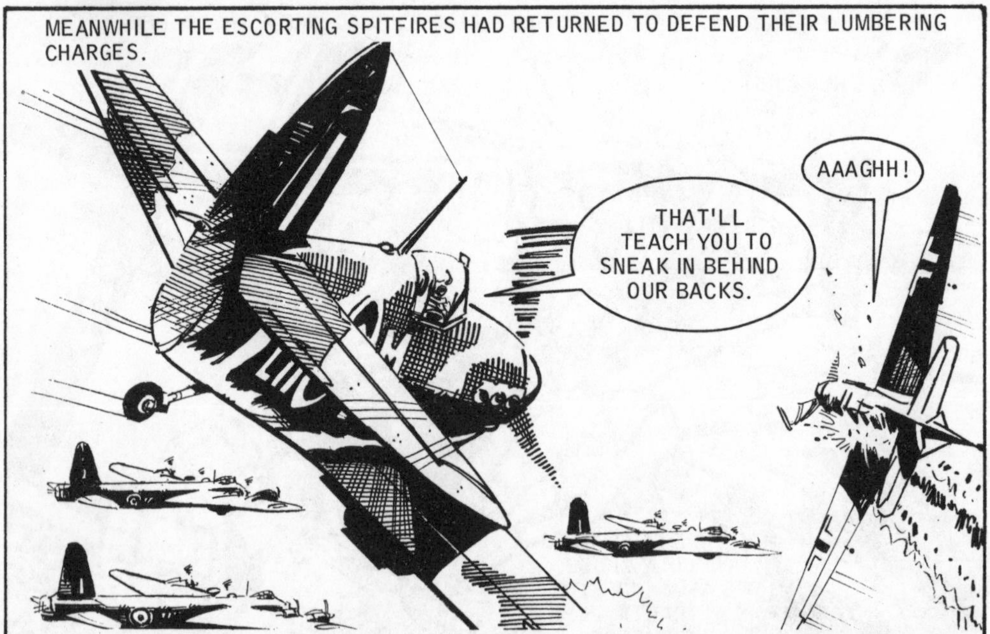
MEANWHILE THE ESCORTING SPITFIRES HAD RETURNED TO DEFEND THEIR LUMBERING CHARGES.
THAT'LL TEACH YOU TO SNEAK IN BEHIND OUR BACKS.
AAAGHH!
EVEN WITH THE SPITFIRES BACK, THE STIRLINGS' TROUBLES WEREN'T OVER...

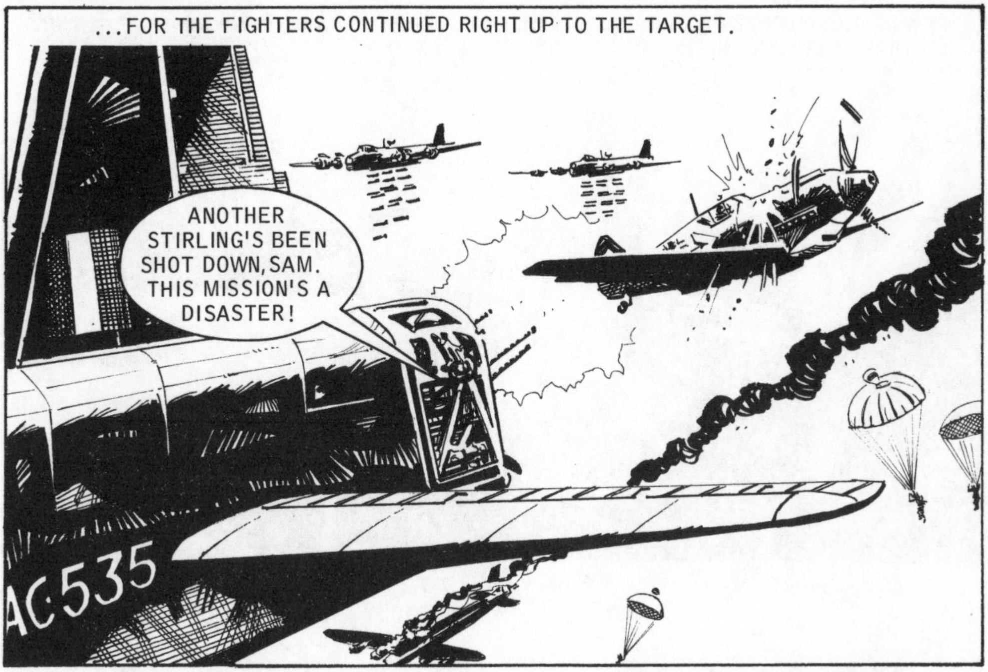
...FOR THE FIGHTERS CONTINUED RIGHT UP TO THE TARGET.
ANOTHER STIRLING'S BEEN SHOT DOWN, SAM. THIS MISSION'S A DISASTER!
AC535

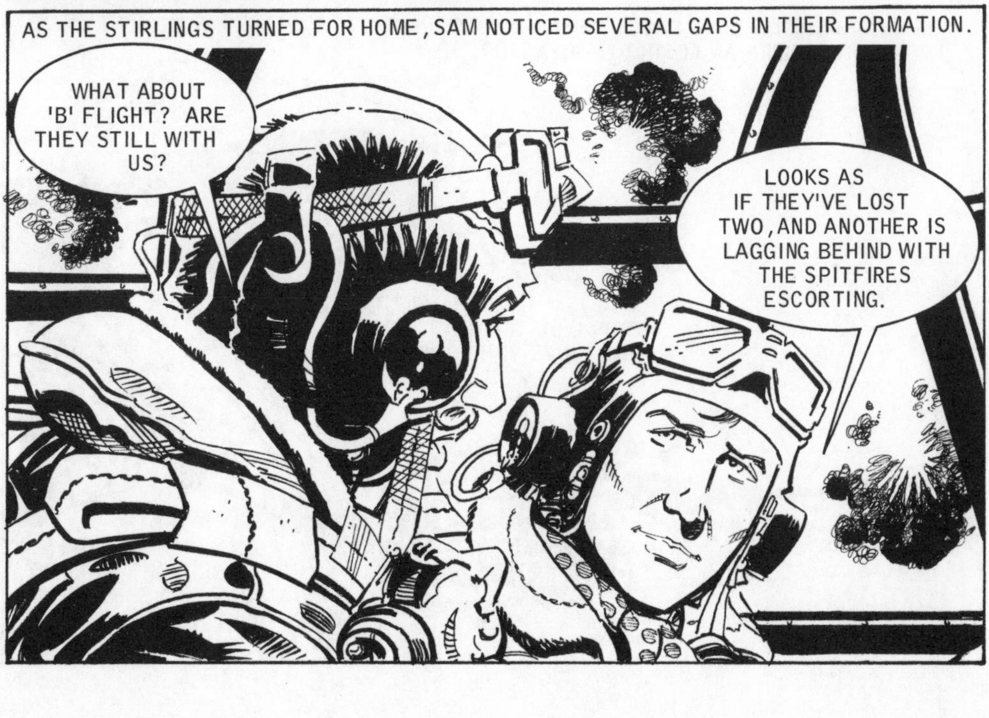
AS THE STIRLINGS TURNED FOR HOME, SAM NOTICED SEVERAL GAPS IN THEIR FORMATION.
WHAT ABOUT 'B' FLIGHT? ARE THEY STILL WITH US?
LOOKS AS IF THEY'VE LOST TWO, AND ANOTHER IS LAGGING BEHIND WITH THE SPITFIRES ESCORTING.

FEW OF THE BOMBERS HAD ESCAPED DAMAGE, AND SAM AGAIN FOUND HIMSELF FLYING ON THREE ENGINES.

HEY, MY COFFEE FLASK'S BEEN SMASHED.

ALL THIS TROUBLE AND TODDY STILL GRUMBLES.

THERE WERE SOME LONG FACES WHEN THEY RETURNED TO BASE, FOR EVERYONE KNEW THE RAID HAD BEEN AN ABSOLUTE DISASTER.

WELL, SAM, I WAS RIGHT. THIS KITE IS A JINX. MAYBE YOU'LL LISTEN NEXT TIME I GIVE YOU SOME ADVICE.

IT'S THE LUCKY OLD STIRLING THAT BROUGHT US HOME, TODDY. FIVE-THREE-FIVE DIDN'T LET US DOWN.

BUT TODDY WASN'T CONVINCED.

THERE'S NOTHING LUCKY ABOUT FIVE-THREE-FIVE, SAM. TRY ADDING THOSE FIGURES TOGETHER. SHE'S A JINX ALL RIGHT.

HEY, YOU'RE RIGHT! I'D NEVER NOTICED THAT — THEY TOTAL THIRTEEN.

LIKE SAILORS, MANY AIRCREW WERE SUPERSTITIOUS — AND SAM SENSED THAT HIS CREW FELT UNEASY.

WELL, LUCKY OR NOT, WE SHAN'T BE FLYING AGAIN UNTIL THEY'VE REPAIRED THE DAMAGE.

MAYBE BY THEN THE TOP BRASS WILL HAVE REALISED THAT STIRLINGS ARE JUST FIGHTER-BAIT IN DAYLIGHT.

ALTHOUGH NOBODY CONSULTED TODDY, AIR MINISTRY PLANNERS HAD REACHED THE SAME CONCLUSION.

SO FROM NOW ON, GENTLEMEN, WE'LL BE REVERTING TO NIGHT BOMBING. THERE'LL BE NO MORE DAYLIGHT RAIDS.

WHOOPEE! NO MORE PLAYING AT CLAY PIGEONS! PERHAPS WE'LL HAVE BETTER LUCK.

SO SAM AND HIS CREW FOUND THEMSELVES ONCE MORE SETTING OUT FOR GERMANY — THIS TIME BY NIGHT.

IT'S A NICE CLEAR NIGHT. NAVIGATION SHOULDN'T BE ANY PROBLEM.

NO, BUT AT THE HEIGHT WE'RE FLYING WE'LL COP ALL THE FLAK.

IT WAS TRUE THE STIRLINGS FLEW LOWER THAN THE REST OF THE BOMBER FORCE, FOR THEIR CEILING WAS LIMITED BY THE HEAVY LOAD THEY CARRIED.

BOMBS GONE, SKIPPER. LET'S GET HOME.

BUT ON THE CREDIT SIDE, THEIR FOUR ENGINES GAVE A GREATER SAFETY MARGIN IF THEY WERE DAMAGED.

YET DESPITE THEIR FEARS, NOTHING HAPPENED THAT NIGHT.

A NICE QUIET RUN, JUST LIKE OLD TIMES. NONE OF THE FLAK CAME NEAR US.

MAYBE OUR KITE ISN'T JINXED AFTER ALL, SKIPPER. BUT YOU'LL NEVER CONVINCE TODDY OF THAT!

SAM LAUGHED. FIVE-THREE-FIVE A JINX? SURELY THIS WOULD CONVINCE EVEN TODDY.

THE UNEVENTFUL TRIP DID CREW MORALE A LOT OF GOOD — AND THAT WAS WHAT THE PLANNERS INTENDED.

THIS IS A VITAL JOB SO IT'S GOT TO BE MAXIMUM EFFORT. WE'RE PUTTING EVERY KITE INTO THE AIR THAT CAN FLY.

THAT'LL MEAN TROUBLE FOR ANYONE WHO DOESN'T FIND THE TARGET. I'D BETTER WATCH MY NAVIGATION.

SOME AIRCRAFT NEVER EVEN GOT AWAY FROM THEIR DISPERSAL AREAS...

CRIKEY, THE C.O. WILL GO NUTS! THAT'S THE THIRD ONE THIS WEEK TO BREAK AN UNDER-CARRIAGE.

HEY, LOOK, ONE OF THE KITES HAS DONE THE SPLITS.

BECAUSE OF A PECULIARITY OF THE UNDERCARRIAGE DESIGN IT WAS EASY TO SHEAR THE SECURING BOLTS IF THE PILOT TURNED TOO SHARPLY — THIS RESULTED IN AN EXPENSIVE REPAIR JOB AND A FURIOUS SQUADRON COMMANDER.

GOOD JOB THAT WASN'T US, SAM, THOSE BLOKES WILL BE ON THE CARPET.

BUT AS THEY CLAMBERED INTO THEIR BOMBER AND STARTED THEIR ENGINES...

CHECK THE FLAPS AGAIN, MIKE. THEY DON'T SEEM TO BE WORKING.

THEY'RE NOT! MUST BE A FAULT SOMEWHERE BECAUSE THE UNDER-CARRIAGE CIRCUIT IS OUT OF ORDER, TOO.

SAM SWITCHED OFF, KNOWING THAT IT WAS HOPELESS TO CONTINUE.

IT'S THESE ELECTRIC MOTORS. DAMP WEATHER AFFECTS THE INSULATION.

AND NOW WE'LL BE ON THE CARPET AS WELL. STILL, THE C.O. CAN'T REALLY SAY IT'S OUR FAULT.

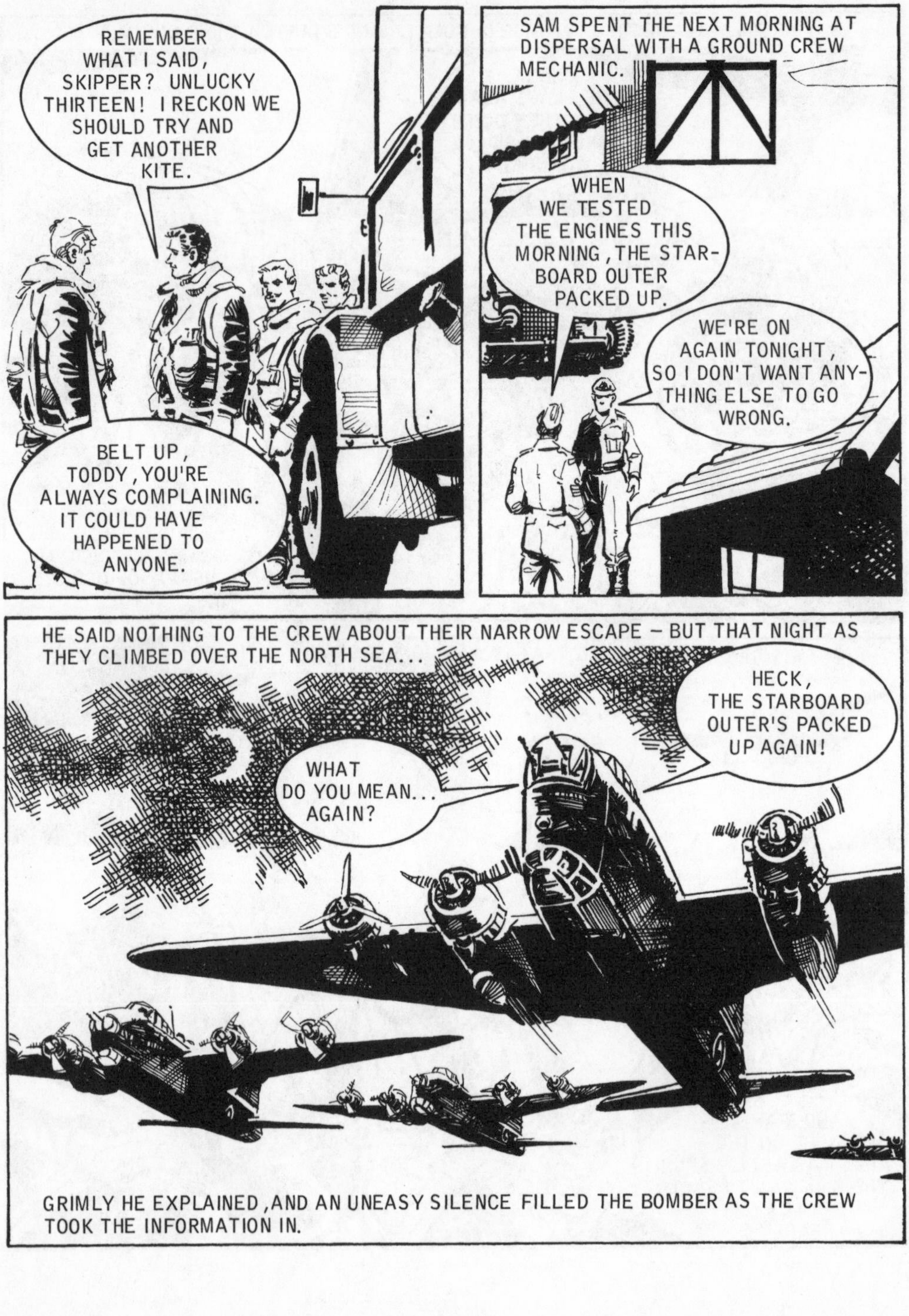
REMEMBER WHAT I SAID, SKIPPER? UNLUCKY THIRTEEN! I RECKON WE SHOULD TRY AND GET ANOTHER KITE.
BELT UP, TODDY, YOU'RE ALWAYS COMPLAINING. IT COULD HAVE HAPPENED TO ANYONE.
SAM SPENT THE NEXT MORNING AT DISPERSAL WITH A GROUND CREW MECHANIC.
WHEN WE TESTED THE ENGINES THIS MORNING, THE STAR-BOARD OUTER PACKED UP.
WE'RE ON AGAIN TONIGHT, SO I DON'T WANT ANY-THING ELSE TO GO WRONG.
HE SAID NOTHING TO THE CREW ABOUT THEIR NARROW ESCAPE – BUT THAT NIGHT AS THEY CLIMBED OVER THE NORTH SEA...
WHAT DO YOU MEAN... AGAIN?
HECK, THE STARBOARD OUTER'S PACKED UP AGAIN!
GRIMLY HE EXPLAINED, AND AN UNEASY SILENCE FILLED THE BOMBER AS THE CREW TOOK THE INFORMATION IN.

SAM NOW FACED A CRITICAL DECISION — TO CONTINUE ON THREE ENGINES, OR TO RETURN TO BASE AND ADMIT ANOTHER FAILURE.

WE CAN MAINTAIN HEIGHT ON THREE ENGINES ALTHOUGH WE'LL BE BELOW THE MAIN STREAM. I'M NOT TURNING BACK.

YOU'RE THE BOSS, BUT I RECKON WE'LL GET SPECIAL ATTENTION FROM THE FLAK.

AND IT CERTAINLY SEEMED AS IF EVERY GUN IN GERMANY WAS FIRING AT THEM AS THEY NEARED THE TARGET.

HEY, SOMEONE TELL THE JERRIES WE'RE NOT THE ONLY KITE AIRBORNE TO-NIGHT!

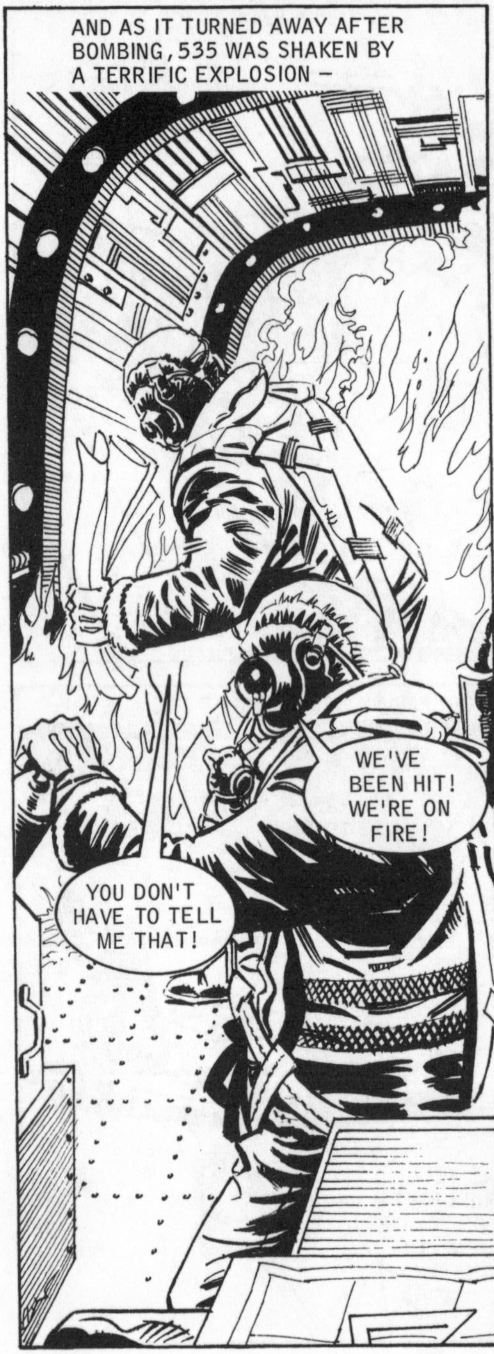
AND AS IT TURNED AWAY AFTER BOMBING, 535 WAS SHAKEN BY A TERRIFIC EXPLOSION –
WE'VE BEEN HIT! WE'RE ON FIRE!
YOU DON'T HAVE TO TELL ME THAT!

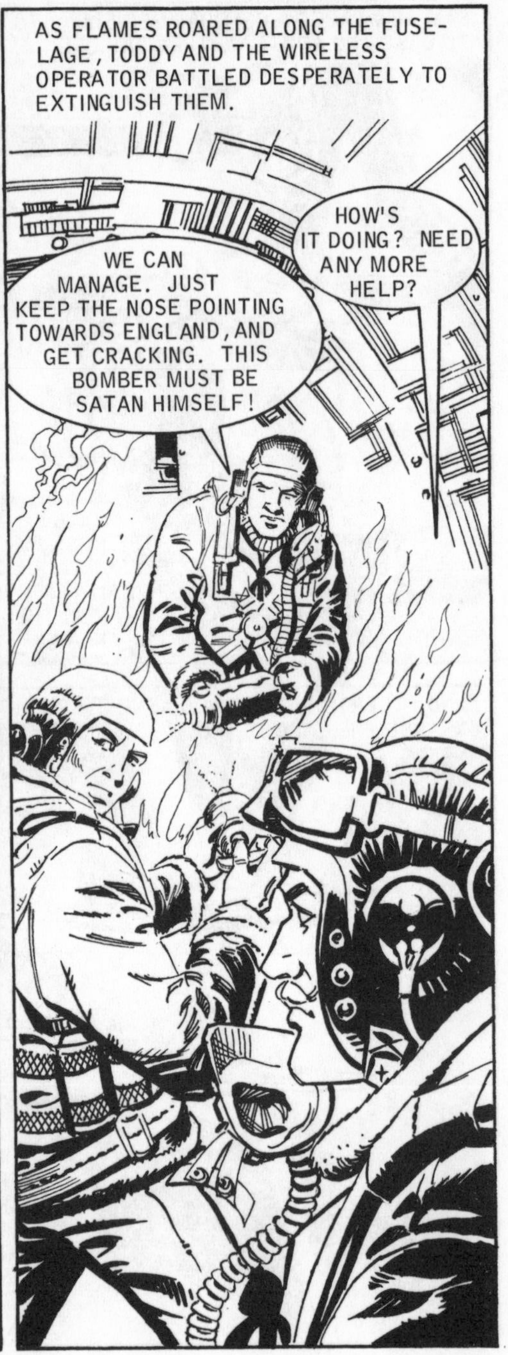
AS FLAMES ROARED ALONG THE FUSELAGE, TODDY AND THE WIRELESS OPERATOR BATTLED DESPERATELY TO EXTINGUISH THEM.
HOW'S IT DOING? NEED ANY MORE HELP?
WE CAN MANAGE. JUST KEEP THE NOSE POINTING TOWARDS ENGLAND, AND GET CRACKING. THIS BOMBER MUST BE SATAN HIMSELF!

THEY GOT THE FIRE OUT EVENTUALLY, BUT TODDY REGARDED IT AS FURTHER PROOF OF 535's JINX.

ALL STIRLINGS ARE BAD, BUT THIS KITE HAS A HOODOO. SAM NEEDS HIS HEAD TESTING FOR LEAVING WHITLEYS.

WE CERTAINLY DON'T HAVE MUCH LUCK, BUT I SUPPOSE IT COULD HAVE BEEN WORSE.

THEY WERE LATE ARRIVING BACK AT BASE, AND MOST PEOPLE HAD GIVEN THEM UP FOR LOST.

A COUPLE OF THE OTHERS ARE MISSING, SAM — UNLESS THEY'VE LANDED SOME-WHERE ELSE.

I DON'T KNOW WHAT HAPPENED TO THEM, BECAUSE WE GOT MOST OF THE FLAK. MAYBE THEY RAN INTO BAD WEATHER.

BUT IT HAD NOT BEEN BAD WEATHER THAT HAD ACCOUNTED FOR THE MISSING AIRCRAFT.

FIGHTERS, SWARMS OF THEM! THEY WERE NIBBLING AT US ALL THE WAY TO THE TARGET.

IT WAS THEIR NIGHT, ALL RIGHT. I SAW THREE WIMPEYS AND TWO STIRLINGS GO DOWN.

YOU HEARD THAT? IF WE'D BEEN WITH THE MAIN FORCE, WE MIGHT HAVE BEEN CHOPPED BY NIGHT FIGHTERS.

INSTEAD WE WERE NEARLY CHOPPED DOWN BY FLAK! SO WHAT DOES THAT PROVE?

TODDY REMAINED UNCONVINCED — BUT SOME OF THE OTHERS WONDERED IF 535 WASN'T LUCKY AFTER ALL.

THE REPAIRS ARE DONE, SO WE'LL BE ON OPS TONIGHT. STILL, I STILL RECKON SAM OUGHT TO GET ANOTHER KITE.

CHANGE THE KITE AND CHANGE OUR LUCK — BUT IT MIGHT CHANGE FOR THE WORSE! OUR KITE ISN'T REALLY THAT BAD, YOU KNOW.

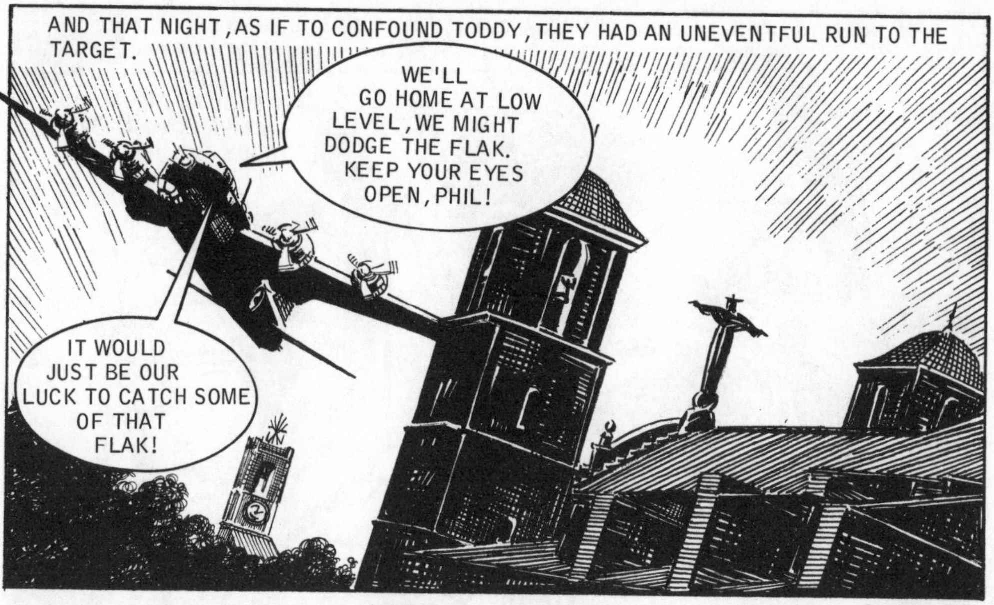
AND THAT NIGHT, AS IF TO CONFOUND TODDY, THEY HAD AN UNEVENTFUL RUN TO THE TARGET.
WE'LL GO HOME AT LOW LEVEL, WE MIGHT DODGE THE FLAK. KEEP YOUR EYES OPEN, PHIL!
IT WOULD JUST BE OUR LUCK TO CATCH SOME OF THAT FLAK!

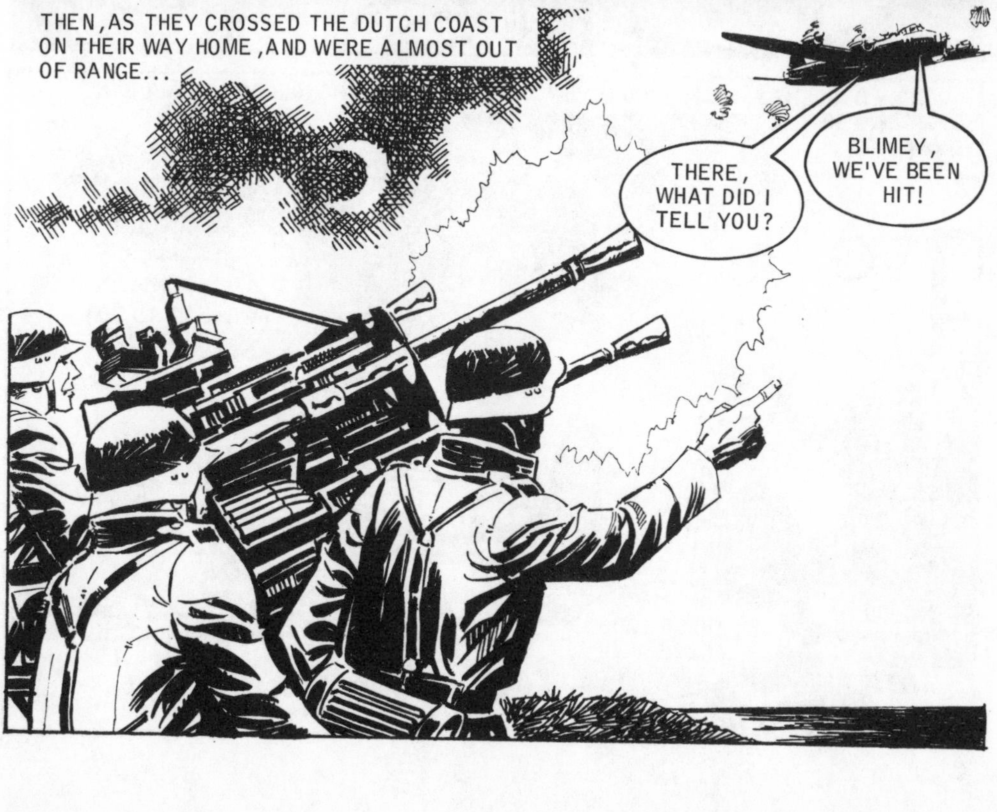
THEN, AS THEY CROSSED THE DUTCH COAST ON THEIR WAY HOME, AND WERE ALMOST OUT OF RANGE...
BLIMEY, WE'VE BEEN HIT!
THERE, WHAT DID I TELL YOU?

SAM TRIED THE CONTROLS GRIMLY TO SEE WHAT DAMAGE HAD BEEN DONE.

WE'LL NEED AN AIRFIELD WITH A LONG RUNWAY, TODDY. WE HAVEN'T ANY BRAKES OR FLAPS WORKING.

THERE'S A NEW EMERGENCY STRIP NEAR MARR-BRIDGE, IN SUFFOLK. I'LL GIVE YOU A COURSE FOR IT.

THEY BROUGHT THE STIRLING IN GENTLY, HOPING THE UNDERCARRIAGE WOULDN'T COLLAPSE.

NOW ALL WE HAVE TO DO IS STOP.

BLIMEY, THESE LADS ARE REALLY SPEEDING.

THEY USED EVERY YARD OF THE EXTRA-LONG RUNWAY, AND FINALLY CAME TO A HALT AT THE FAR END.

NOW WHAT DO YOU THINK OF YOUR JINX KITE? EVERY TIME WE FLY SOMETHING GOES WRONG.

WE GOT BACK, DIDN'T WE? COME ON, LET'S FIND SOMEWHERE TO SLEEP FOR THE REST OF THE NIGHT.

BEFORE TURNING IN, SAM PHONED THEIR BASE TO ARRANGE FOR TRANSPORT THE NEXT DAY.

THEY'RE HAVING AN AIR RAID — SEEMS THEY'VE BEEN HIT BAD!

WHAT DO YOU SAY TO THAT THEN, TODDY? WE'RE LUCKY AGAIN.

WHEN THEY RETURNED TO THEIR OWN AIRFIELD THEY REALISED WHAT A NARROW ESCAPE THEY HAD HAD.

ONE OF THE BOMBS WAS RIGHT BESIDE OUR QUARTERS. IF WE'D BEEN HERE WE MIGHT HAVE COPPED IT!

I'M BEGINNING TO THINK FIVE-THREE-FIVE KNOWS A THING OR TWO. SHE GETS US INTO TROUBLE, BUT SHE GETS US OUT OF A LOT MORE!

AND WHEN 535 HAD BEEN REPAIRED, EVEN TODDY ADMITTED RELUCTANTLY THAT HE COULD HAVE BEEN WRONG.

ALL RIGHT, SHE'S BEAUTIFUL AND LUCKY — BUT THE NEXT TIME ANYTHING GOES WRONG I'LL GET MYSELF TO A NEW CREW!

NOT SO LOUD, TODDY, SHE MIGHT HEAR YOU. AND SHE'S VERY SENSITIVE ABOUT BEING INSULTED!

BUT THE BRIEF TRUCE WAS SOON OVER, FOR THINGS BEGAN TO GO WRONG SOON AFTER TAKE-OFF.

WE'LL BE LATE OVER THE TARGET IF SAM DOESN'T GET A MOVE ON.

WE'RE LOSING POWER ON THE PORT OUTER. WE'LL HAVE TO GO IN LOW AGAIN.

ONCE AGAIN THEY GOT MORE THAN THEIR FAIR SHARE OF FLAK AS THEY APPROACHED THE TARGET.

AT LEAST THIS SHOULD KEEP NIGHT-FIGHTERS AWAY. THEY WOULDN'T WANT TO FLY THROUGH THIS FLAK!

BUT AS THEY RELEASED THEIR BOMBS AND TURNED FOR HOME, THE FLAK STOPPED OMINOUSLY.

THAT MEANS FIGHTERS ANY MINUTE NOW.

YOU'RE RIGHT, PHIL. KEEP YOUR EYES PEELED!

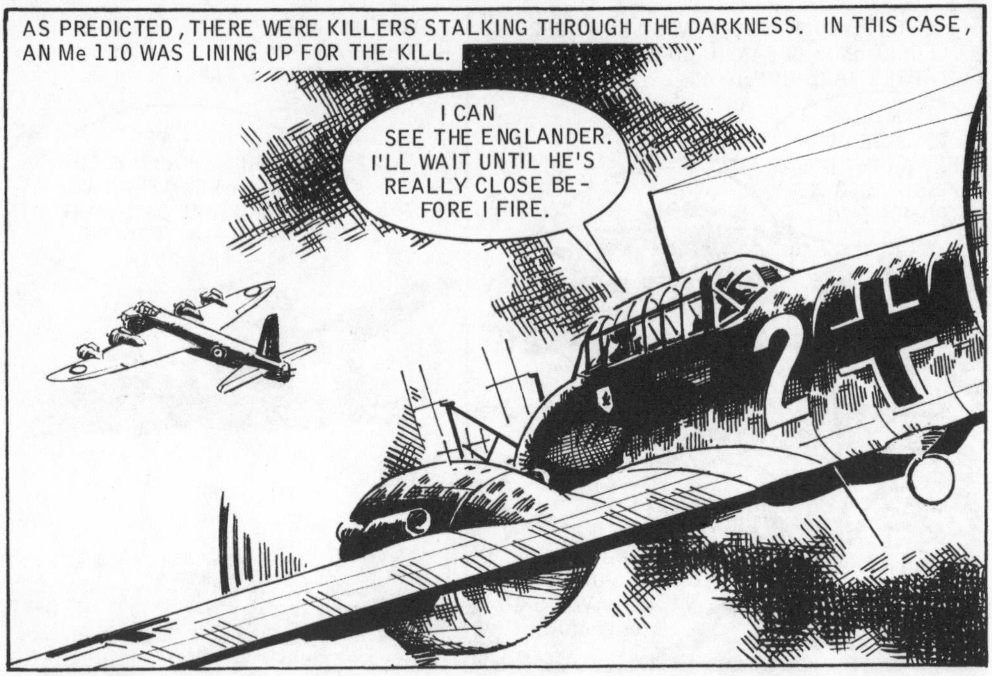
AS PREDICTED, THERE WERE KILLERS STALKING THROUGH THE DARKNESS. IN THIS CASE, AN Me 110 WAS LINING UP FOR THE KILL.
I CAN SEE THE ENGLANDER. I'LL WAIT UNTIL HE'S REALLY CLOSE BE- FORE I FIRE.

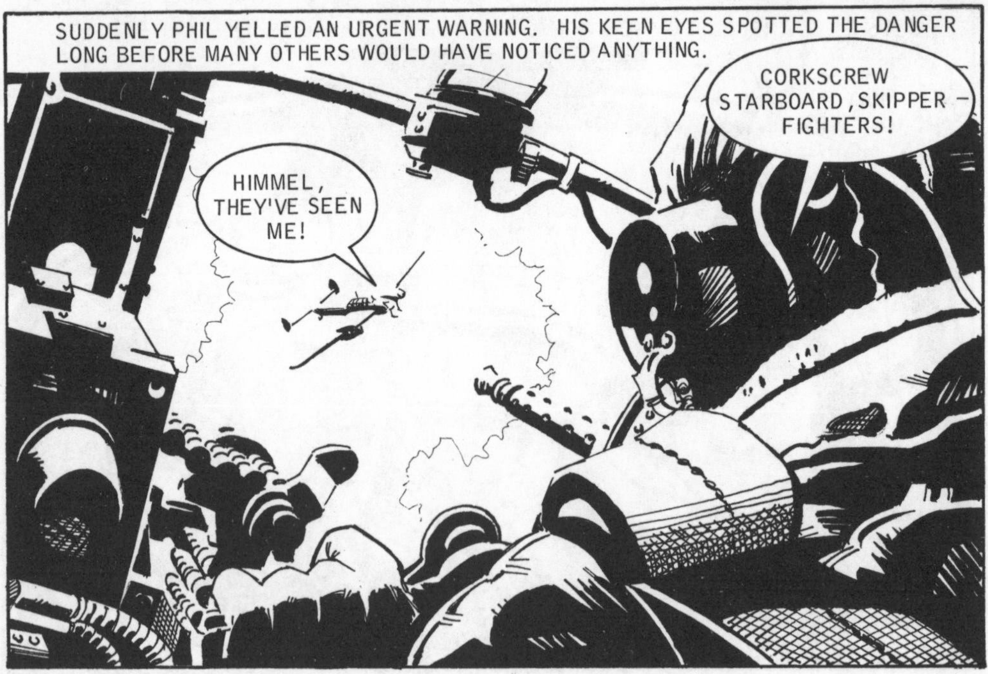
SUDDENLY PHIL YELLED AN URGENT WARNING. HIS KEEN EYES SPOTTED THE DANGER LONG BEFORE MANY OTHERS WOULD HAVE NOTICED ANYTHING.
HIMMEL, THEY'VE SEEN ME!
CORKSCREW STARBOARD, SKIPPER – FIGHTERS!

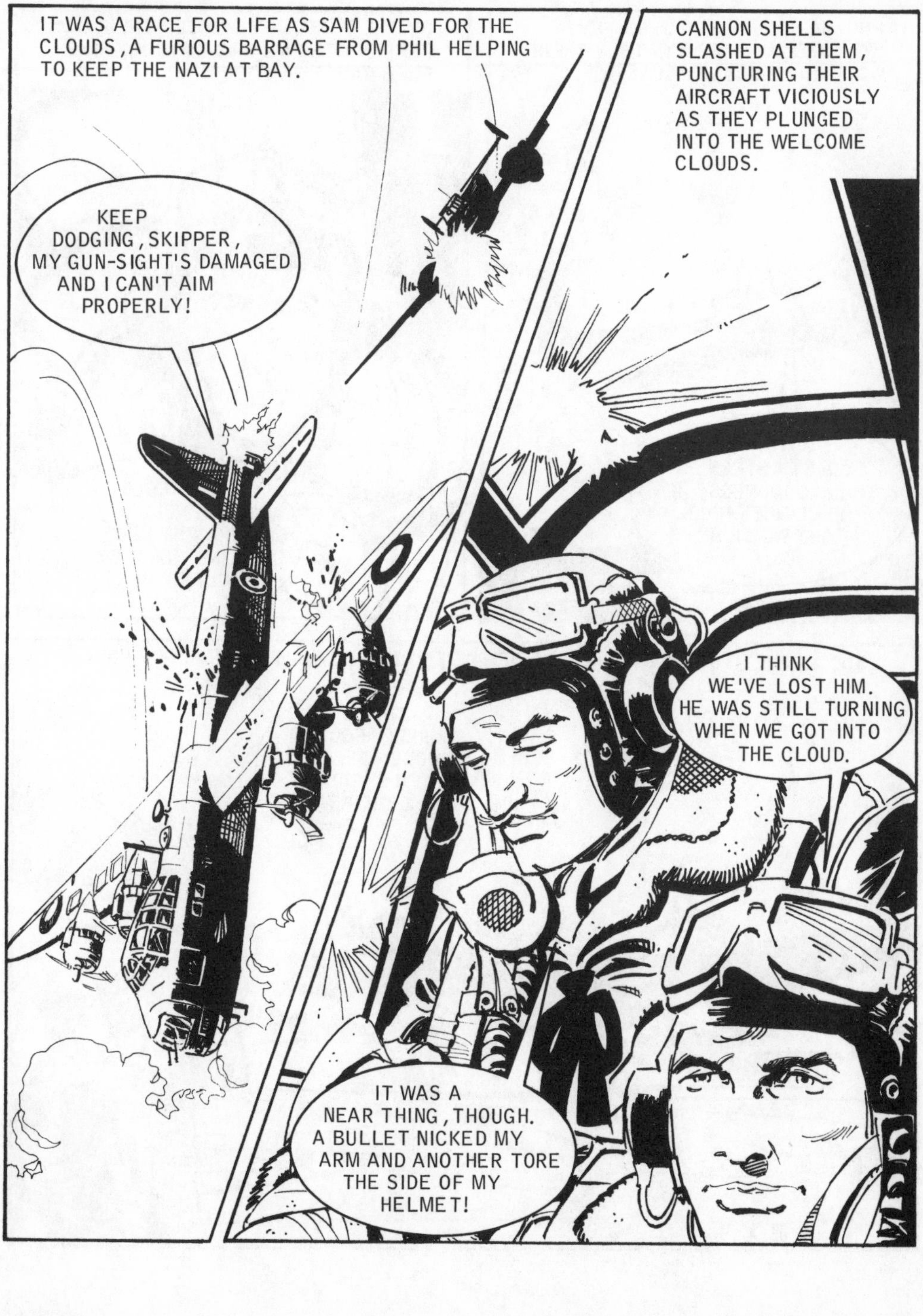
IT WAS A RACE FOR LIFE AS SAM DIVED FOR THE CLOUDS, A FURIOUS BARRAGE FROM PHIL HELPING TO KEEP THE NAZI AT BAY.
KEEP DODGING, SKIPPER, MY GUN-SIGHT'S DAMAGED AND I CAN'T AIM PROPERLY!
CANNON SHELLS SLASHED AT THEM, PUNCTURING THEIR AIRCRAFT VICIOUSLY AS THEY PLUNGED INTO THE WELCOME CLOUDS.
I THINK WE'VE LOST HIM. HE WAS STILL TURNING WHEN WE GOT INTO THE CLOUD.
IT WAS A NEAR THING, THOUGH. A BULLET NICKED MY ARM AND ANOTHER TORE THE SIDE OF MY HELMET!

PHIL HAD ALSO BEEN SLIGHTLY WOUNDED, BUT FORTUNATELY THERE WERE NO SERIOUS CASUALTIES.

DUTCH COAST ASTERN, THANK GOODNESS. IF THE ENGINES HOLD OUT WE'LL BE OK.

BY THE TIME THEY SIGHTED THEIR OWN FLARE-PATH SAM WAS WATCHING THE FUEL GAUGES ANXIOUSLY.

JUST ABOUT ENOUGH FUEL IF WE GO STRAIGHT IN WITHOUT CIRCLING. BETTER CROSS YOUR FINGERS ANYWAY!

AND AS THEY TOUCHED DOWN, TWO OF THE ENGINES CUT OUT FOR LACK OF FUEL.

THERE'S JUST ABOUT ENOUGH LEFT TO FILL YOUR LIGHTER!

AS THEY CLIMBED OUT AND STRETCHED WITH RELIEF, TODDY DELIVERED HIS ULTIMATUM.

I RECKON WE'VE HAD OUR LAST WARNING, SKIPPER. EITHER WE CHANGE KITES, OR I'M CHANGING CREWS.

YOU'RE NOT SERIOUS, TODDY? WE'VE BEEN TOGETHER SINCE THE WAR STARTED!

TODDY WAS DEAD SERIOUS — AND FOR ONCE ALL THE OTHERS AGREED WITH HIM.

TODDY'S RIGHT, SKIPPER. WE'VE PUSHED OUR LUCK FAR ENOUGH. YOU COULD EASILY GET ANOTHER KITE IF YOU ASKED.

OK, OK, IF THAT'S THE WAY YOU ALL FEEL. I DON'T WANT TO FIND ANOTHER CREW AT THIS STAGE.

CHANGING AIRCRAFT WAS NO PROBLEM, FOR 535 WAS IN NEED OF EXTENSIVE REPAIRS.

I FEEL LIKE A TRAITOR, DESERTING POOR OLD FIVE-THREE-FIVE. IT'S A GOOD JOB WE'VE ALMOST FINISHED OUR TOUR.

THE LAST FEW RAIDS WILL BE A PLEASURE, SKIPPER. SOMEONE ELSE CAN HAVE OUR JINX!

WHEN 535 WAS REPAIRED SHE WENT TO A NEW CREW, AND IT LOOKED AS IF SAM'S PROBLEMS WERE OVER.

WE'VE NEVER HAD IT SO QUIET. IT'S ALMOST AS IF THE JERRIES HAVE DECIDED TO LEAVE US ALONE.

AND ON THE LAST RAID OF THEIR TOUR THEY WEREN'T EVEN FIRED AT.

WELL, SAM, THAT'S THE LOT! NOW FOR SOME LEAVE AND SIX MONTHS ON INSTRUCTION DUTIES.

YOU'VE GOT A HOPE. I'VE ALREADY BEEN IN TOUCH WITH BOB RAMSAY AT WINKLETON TO SEE IF HE HAS ANY JOBS GOING.

TEST FLYING? WELL, IT'LL BE A CHANGE FROM STIRLINGS.

I THOUGHT YOU'D BE PLEASED. YOU'D BE BORED STIFF AS AN INSTRUCTOR.

AS THEY LEFT TO BEGIN THEIR LEAVE THEY CAUGHT SIGHT OF AN OLD FRIEND.

LOOK, FIVE-THREE-FIVE WON'T START! NOW THEY KNOW WHAT WE HAD TO PUT UP WITH.

MAYBE SHE'S SORRY TO SEE US LEAVE. I STILL FEEL GUILTY ABOUT DESERTING HER.

AFTER THEIR LEAVE SAM AND HIS CREW REPORTED TO WINKLETON, WHERE BOB RAMSAY WAS STILL WORKING FOR THE TEST AND DEVELOPMENT UNIT. FOR BOB HAD SUCCEEDED IN FINDING THEM A PLACE IN THE ESTABLISHMENT, IN A SECTION CONDUCTING TRIALS ON BOMBER COMMAND EQUIPMENT.

THIS IS IT THEN, LADS, YOUR NEW HOME.

TODDY'S EYES GLEAMED AS HE SAW A HALIFAX — THEN HIS EXPRESSION ALTERED.

MAYBE IT BELONGS TO A VISITOR. WE'LL SOON FIND OUT.

OH, NO — A STIRLING! I THOUGHT WE'D SEEN THE LAST OF THEM.

BOB CONFIRMED THAT THE STIRLING BELONGED TO THE UNIT — AND THAT WAS NOT ALL.

IT'S A HANDY AIRCRAFT WITH LOTS OF ROOM FOR EQUIPMENT. AND AS YOU'VE FLOWN THEM ON OPS YOU CAN TAKE CHARGE OF THE ONE WE'VE GOT. I'LL GIVE YOU THE DETAILS LATER.

I KNEW IT. I HAD A FEELING IN MY BONES THAT THINGS WERE GOING TOO WELL TO LAST!

THEY WERE SOON HARD AT WORK, FOR THERE WAS PLENTY TO BE DONE. TWO 20mm CANNONS WERE TO BE FITTED IN THE TAIL TURRET.

IT'LL BE INTERESTING TO SEE HOW THE ADDED WEIGHT OF THE CANNONS ALTERS THE HANDLING QUALITIES, PHIL.

BETTER TAKE IT EASY AT FIRST, SKIPPER. I DON'T WANT THE TAIL TO FALL OFF WITH ME IN THE TURRET!

NEW GUNS, NEW TURRETS, NEW BOMBS – THEY TESTED THEM ALL.

BOMBS GONE, SKIPPER! IT'S A PIECE OF CAKE WITH THIS NEW RADAR BOMB-SIGHT.

AND TO EVERYONE'S SURPRISE, INCLUDING SAM, THE STIRLING BEHAVED PERFECTLY.

I COULD HAVE BEEN WRONG ABOUT STIRLINGS, SAM. IT WAS JUST FIVE-THREE-FIVE THAT WAS A HOODOO.

YOU WERE EVEN WRONG ABOUT FIVE-THREE-FIVE, BUT I DON'T SUPPOSE THERE'S ANY WAY OF CONVINCING YOU NOW.

THEN ONE MORNING SAM FOUND BOB EXPERIMENTING WITH A CURIOUS DEVICE.

WHAT THE HECK IS THAT? A PETROL SUBSTITUTE?

NO, ROCKET ASSISTANCE. IT'S A NEW SCHEME TO SHORTEN THE TAKE-OFF RUN FOR A HEAVILY LOADED BOMBER.

THE LORRY SKIDDED TO A HALT AS THE ROCKETS BURNED OUT.

WORKS LIKE A CHARM, SIR! A TOUCH OF THE BUTTON AND WE WERE BREAKING THE WORLD SPEED RECORD FOR LORRIES.

THAT'S FINE. WE'LL MODIFY THE GEAR FOR YOUR STIRLING, SAM, AND SEE WHAT SORT OF RESULTS WE GET.

BUT THE FULLY-LOADED STIRLING WAS NOT SO EASY TO PUSH AS A SMALL LORRY.

IT NEEDS MORE THRUST, SIR. I'LL HAVE THE NEW PACKS FITTED — THEY'RE MUCH MORE POWERFUL THAN THE ORIGINAL MODELS.

BUT SAM AND HIS CREW WATCHED DUBIOUSLY AS THE NEW EQUIPMENT WAS FITTED.

WHY DON'T WE TRY IT IN STAGES, BOB? WE DON'T WANT TOO MUCH POWER TO START WITH.

THERE'S NO TIME, SAM, WE'RE BEING PUSHED BY THE BOFFINS. THE AIR MINISTRY WANTS RESULTS — FAST!

AND SO, A LITTLE LATER, SAM CHECKED THAT ALL WAS WELL BEFORE REACHING FOR THE FIRING BUTTONS.

RIGHT, LET'S GO. AS SOON AS WE'RE ROLLING STRAIGHT, I'LL FIRE THE CHARGES.

I'M GLAD WE'RE LOADED WITH SAND-BAGS AND NOT BOMBS. I DON'T TRUST THESE NEW-FANGLED GADGETS.

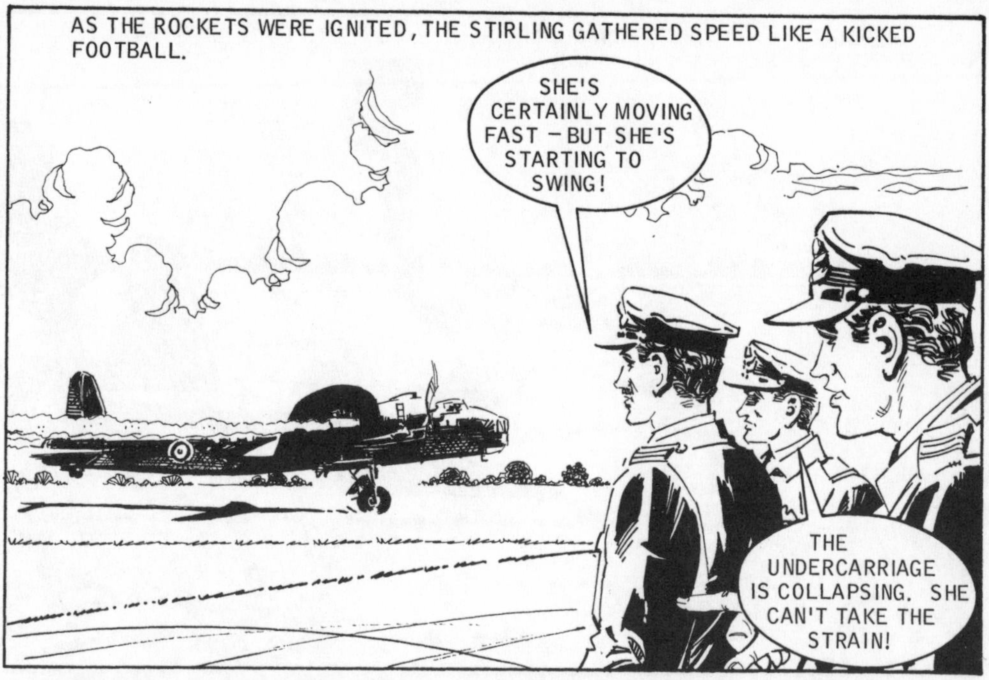
AS THE ROCKETS WERE IGNITED, THE STIRLING GATHERED SPEED LIKE A KICKED FOOTBALL.
SHE'S CERTAINLY MOVING FAST – BUT SHE'S STARTING TO SWING!
THE UNDERCARRIAGE IS COLLAPSING. SHE CAN'T TAKE THE STRAIN!

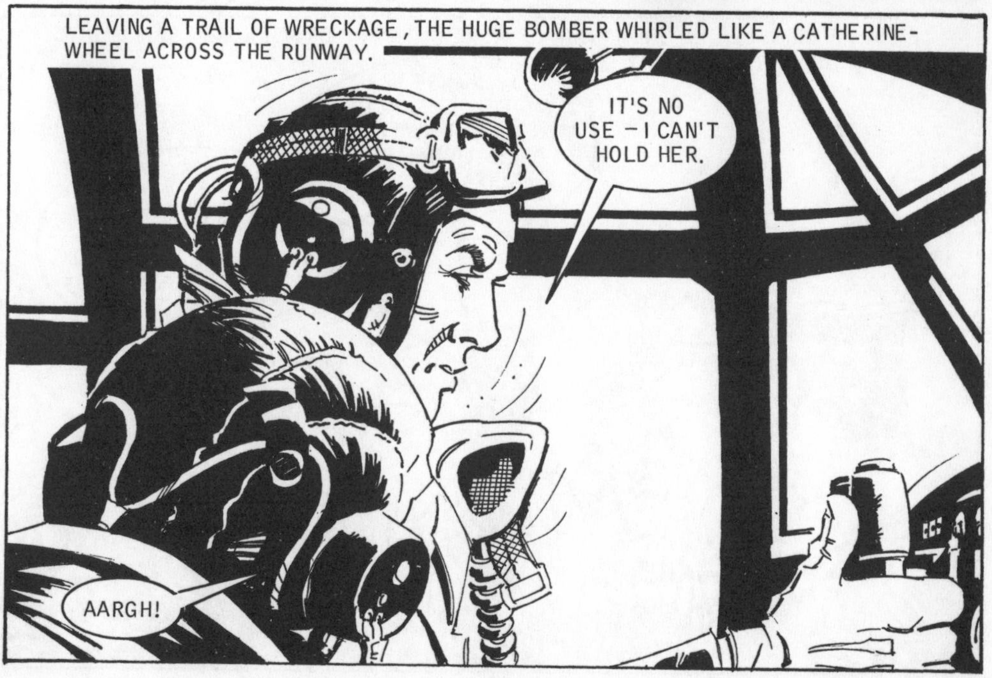
LEAVING A TRAIL OF WRECKAGE, THE HUGE BOMBER WHIRLED LIKE A CATHERINE-WHEEL ACROSS THE RUNWAY.
IT'S NO USE – I CAN'T HOLD HER.
AARGH!

SHEDDING HALF A WING, THE AIRCRAFT HURTLED ON UNTIL IT LANDED IN A DITCH.

NOW I KNOW WHAT A SHELL FEELS LIKE WHEN IT'S BEEN FIRED!

TALK ABOUT SUICIDE KITES!

BY SOME MIRACLE THE ONLY INJURIES WERE CUTS AND BRUISES, BUT SAM HAD TO SOOTHE HIS RUFFLED CREW.

I PROMISE YOU, FELLERS, I'LL APPLY RIGHT AWAY FOR AN OPERATIONAL POSTING ON HALIFAXES. NO MORE STIRLINGS.

THAT'S WHAT YOU SAID WHEN WE LEFT THE SQUADRON — AND LOOK WHAT HAPPENED!

HE APPLIED FOR THE POSTING. BUT IN THE MEANTIME THE ORDINARY WORK OF THE UNIT HAD TO CONTINUE.

ANOTHER STIRLING, BOB? I'LL HAVE A MUTINY ON MY HANDS WHEN I TELL MY CREW — AND THEY'LL PROBABLY LYNCH YOU!

NO MORE ROCKETS, SAM, AND THAT'S A PROMISE. BUT I WANT YOU TO CONTINUE WORKING WITH THE RADAR BOMB SIGHT. WE'LL FIT IT TO THE NEW KITE RIGHT AWAY.

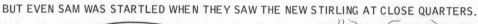

BUT EVEN SAM WAS STARTLED WHEN THEY SAW THE NEW STIRLING AT CLOSE QUARTERS.

THERE'S SOMETHING FAMILIAR ABOUT THAT KITE. THOSE PATCHES ON THE FUSELAGE...

IT'S FIVE-THREE-FIVE! OH, NO, THIS IS LIKE A BAD DREAM. THAT THING IS HAUNTING ME!

BUT IT SEEMED THAT 535 HAD LEFT HER JINX BEHIND, FOR THE TEST PROGRAMME WENT WITHOUT A HITCH.

I CAN HARDLY BELIEVE IT'S THE SAME KITE. WE'VE HAD NOTHING GO WRONG SINCE SHE ARRIVED.

I TOLD YOU SHE WAS ALL RIGHT. OK, LET'S START THE BOMBING RUN, THE RANGE IS CLEAR.

AND THE RADAR BOMB-SIGHT WORKED WITH PIN-POINT PRECISION UNDER ALL CONDITIONS.

SIGNAL FROM THE RANGE, TODDY. THE LAST THREE RUNS WERE DIRECT HITS.

I'M EVEN SURPRISING MYSELF, SKIPPER. THIS SIGHT WILL SHAKE THE JERRIES WHEN IT GOES INTO SERVICE.

AND AFTER SEVERAL WEEKS OF INTENSIVE TESTING, THE NEW SIGHT WAS CLEARED FOR SQUADRON USE.

THAT'LL PLEASE THE LADS. THEY WERE BEGINNING TO THINK WE'D BE HERE FOR THE REST OF THE WAR!

A HALIFAX SQUADRON IS BEING FORMED FOR SPECIAL DUTIES, AND THEY'LL GET THE FIRST DELIVERIES. THE A.O.C. HAS AGREED TO LET YOU JOIN THEM.

MEANWHILE, FAR AWAY ACROSS EUROPE, A PHOTO-RECCE SPITFIRE WAS CIRCLING HIGH ABOVE A PORT IN SOUTHERN ITALY WITH ITS CAMERAS RECORDING EVERYTHING OF INTEREST.

I'D BETTER MAKE ONE MORE RUN — THERE'S SOME INTERESTING SHIPPING DOWN THERE...

THE PHOTOGRAPHS CAUSED GREAT EXCITEMENT AT THE WAR OFFICE.

IT'S THE ADMIRAL EISEN — A JERRY POCKET-BATTLESHIP! SHE MUST HAVE SLIPPED IN FOR REPAIRS.

OUR CRUISERS HIT HER DURING THAT SCRAP LAST WEEK. WE MUST FINISH HER OFF BEFORE SHE CAN GET AWAY AGAIN.

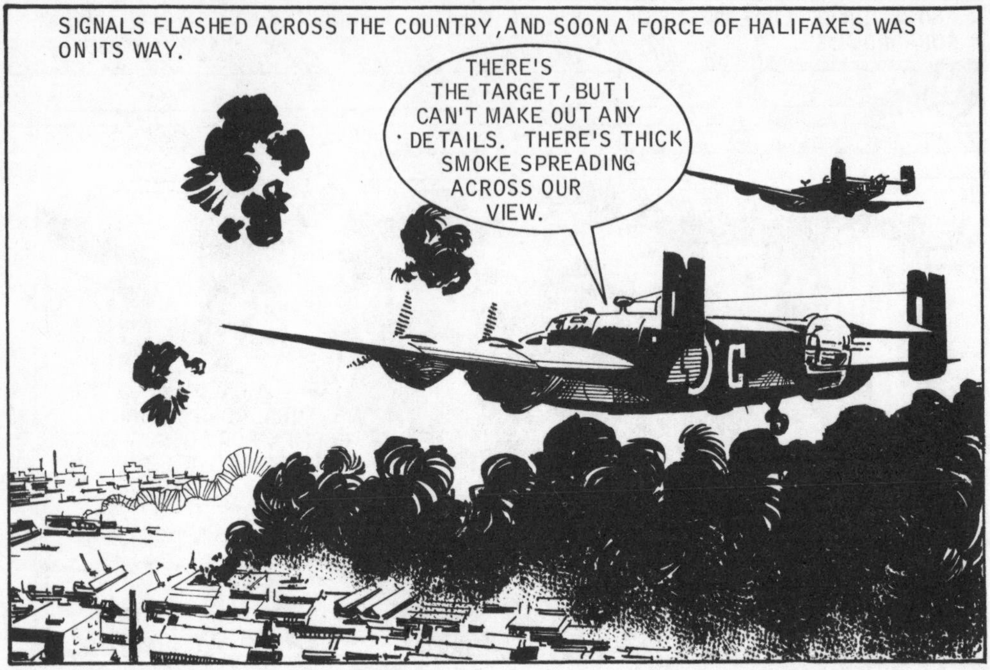
SIGNALS FLASHED ACROSS THE COUNTRY, AND SOON A FORCE OF HALIFAXES WAS ON ITS WAY.
THERE'S THE TARGET, BUT I CAN'T MAKE OUT ANY DETAILS. THERE'S THICK SMOKE SPREADING ACROSS OUR VIEW.
C

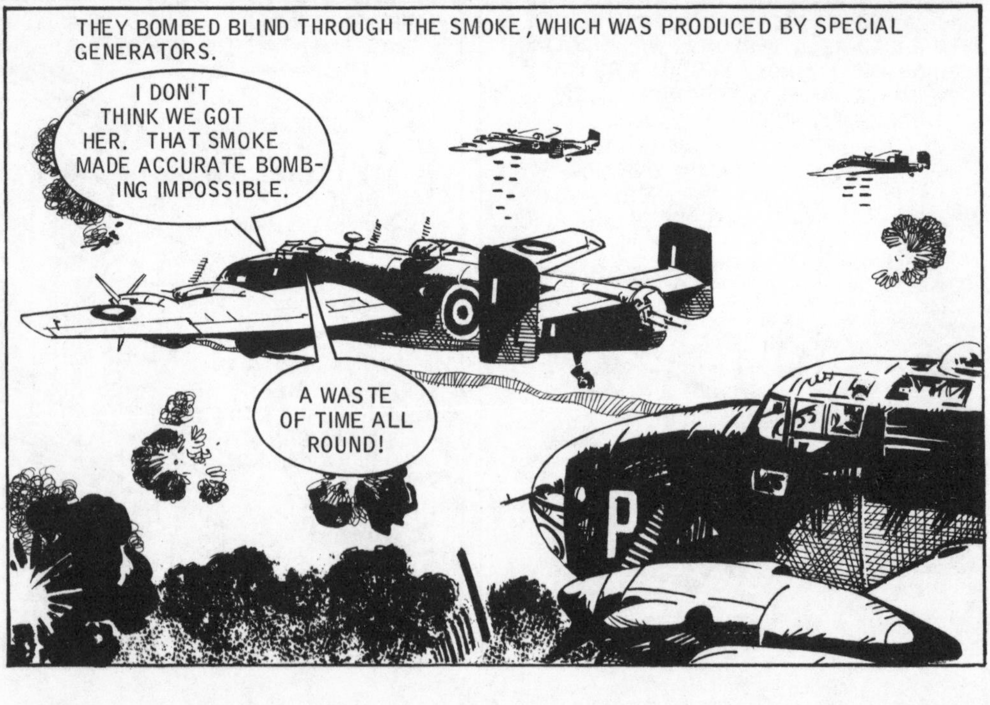
THEY BOMBED BLIND THROUGH THE SMOKE, WHICH WAS PRODUCED BY SPECIAL GENERATORS.
I DON'T THINK WE GOT HER. THAT SMOKE MADE ACCURATE BOMBING IMPOSSIBLE.
A WASTE OF TIME ALL ROUND!
P

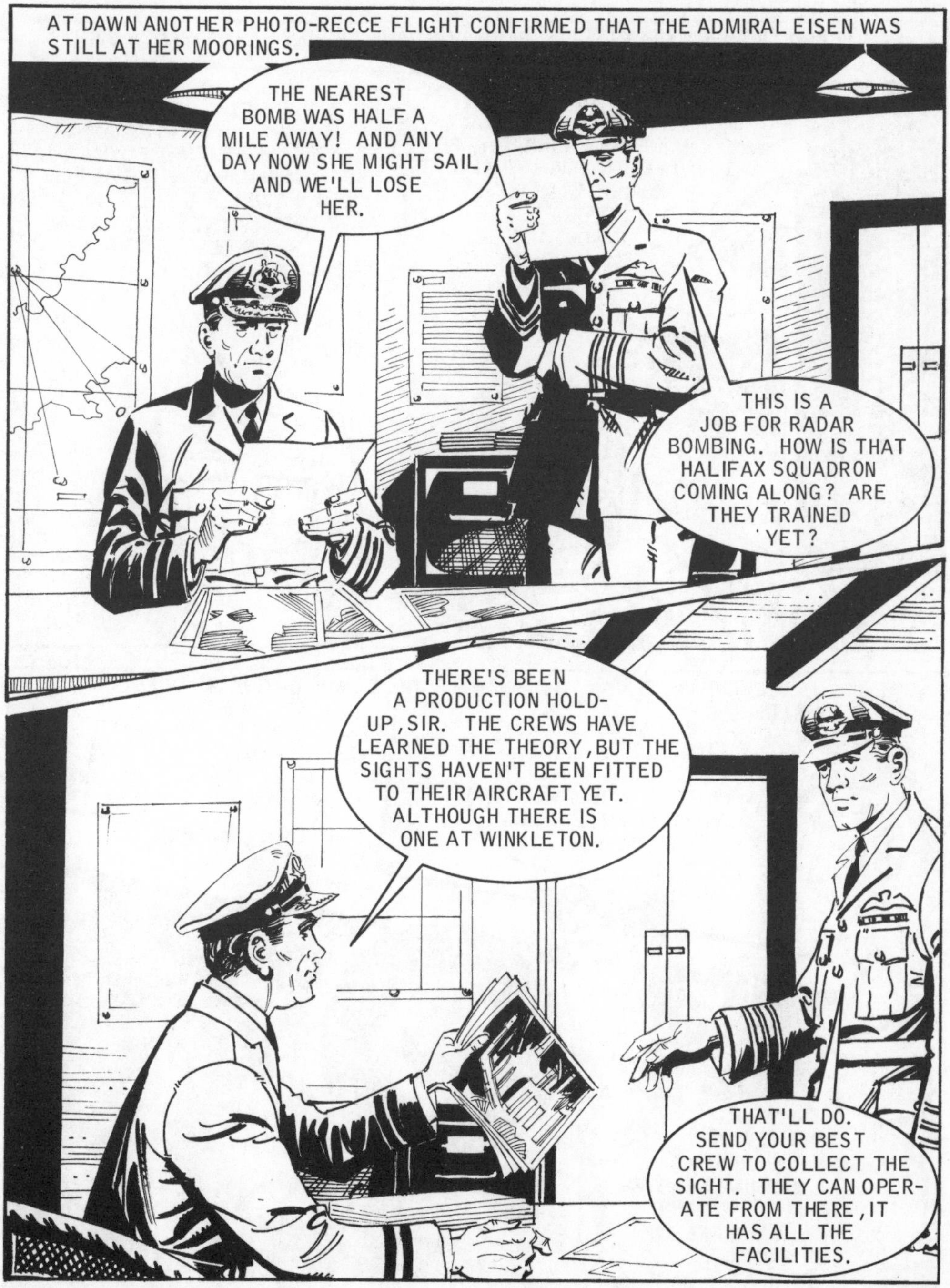
AT DAWN ANOTHER PHOTO-RECCE FLIGHT CONFIRMED THAT THE ADMIRAL EISEN WAS STILL AT HER MOORINGS.
THE NEAREST BOMB WAS HALF A MILE AWAY! AND ANY DAY NOW SHE MIGHT SAIL, AND WE'LL LOSE HER.
THIS IS A JOB FOR RADAR BOMBING. HOW IS THAT HALIFAX SQUADRON COMING ALONG? ARE THEY TRAINED YET?
THERE'S BEEN A PRODUCTION HOLD-UP, SIR. THE CREWS HAVE LEARNED THE THEORY, BUT THE SIGHTS HAVEN'T BEEN FITTED TO THEIR AIRCRAFT YET. ALTHOUGH THERE IS ONE AT WINKLETON.
THAT'LL DO. SEND YOUR BEST CREW TO COLLECT THE SIGHT. THEY CAN OPERATE FROM THERE, IT HAS ALL THE FACILITIES.

SAM HEARD THE NEWS GLUMLY, FOR HE WOULD HAVE LIKED TO TRY THE NEW SIGHT IN ACTION.

IT'S SOME SORT OF SPECIAL TARGET, AND AS THE HALIFAXES ARRIVE WE'RE TO FIT THE SIGHT AND LOAD THEM UP WITH BOMBS. MUST BE PRETTY IMPORTANT.

IT'S A PITY WE WEREN'T FLYING A HALIFAX — THEY MIGHT HAVE LET US FLY THE OP OURSELVES. NOW SOMEONE ELSE GETS ALL THE FUN!

BUT AS THE TECHNICIANS BEGAN TO DISMANTLE THE COMPLICATED RADAR EQUIPMENT ON THE STIRLING...

BAD NEWS, SAM. THE HALIFAX HAS PRANGED ON ITS WAY HERE. NOBODY BADLY HURT, BUT THE KITE'S A WRITE-OFF.

THEN THIS IS OUR CHANCE, BOB. ASK GROUP IF THEY'LL LET US USE FIVE-THREE-FIVE. IT'LL BE QUICKER THAN FLYING UP ANOTHER HALIFAX.

IT WAS AN IRREGULAR REQUEST — BUT THE CIRCUMSTANCES WERE UNUSUAL AND THERE WAS LITTLE TIME TO SPARE.

THE STIRLING CREW ARE VERY EXPERIENCED, SIR. AND THEY'VE HAD LOTS OF PRACTICE WITH THE NEW SIGHT.

ALL RIGHT, WE'LL RISK IT. SEND SOMEONE OVER TO BRIEF THEM, AND ALTER THE TIMING OF THE DIVERSIONARY RAID. IT'S PROBABLY OUR ONLY HOPE, ANYWAY.

AND SO SAM AND HIS CREW FACED THE PROSPECT OF FLYING 535 ON OPERATIONS ONCE AGAIN.

I DON'T KNOW THE TARGET YET, BUT BRIEFING'S IN TEN MINUTES. AND IT'S VOLUNTEERS ONLY!

TAKING OUR JINX KITE ON A SUICIDE RAID? NOW I KNOW I SHOULD HAVE JOINED THE NAVY!

BUT THEIR SPIRITS ROSE WHEN THEY HEARD WHAT THEIR MISSION WAS.

THERE'LL BE A DIVERSIONARY RAID LAID ON TO DRAW THE FLAK AND FIGHTERS AWAY FROM YOU, BUT THE REST IS UP TO YOU. YOU WON'T HAVE ENOUGH FUEL TO MAKE THE RETURN JOURNEY SO YOU'LL HAVE TO CONTINUE ON TO EGYPT.

YOU HEAR THAT, SAM? A POCKET BATTLESHIP — AND SHE'S ALL OURS! WHOOPEE!

FORTUNATELY WINKLETON WAS ABLE TO SUPPLY ALL 535's OPERATIONAL NEEDS.

PITY WE DIDN'T KEEP THOSE BIG CANNONS, SKIPPER. IT LOOKS AS IF WE MIGHT NEED THEM.

WE CAN'T AFFORD THE EXTRA WEIGHT, PHIL. DON'T FORGET WE'VE GOT TO CROSS THE ALPS.

AND AS NIGHT FELL, THEY LUMBERED OFF THE RUNWAY AND CLIMBED SLOWLY OVER THE SEA.

LOOK OUT, MUSSOLINI, HERE WE COME!

BURDENED BY HER HEAVY LOAD OF FUEL AND BOMBS, 535 WAS RELUCTANT TO CLIMB.

AT THIS RATE WE'LL GO THROUGH THE ALPS INSTEAD OF OVER THEM.

WE'LL HAVE USED A LOT OF FUEL BEFORE WE REACH THEM, SO THAT'LL HELP.

AND THE ATTENTION OF THE GERMAN GUNNERS WAS NO HELP ON THEIR JOURNEY OVER FRANCE.

IT'S A GOOD JOB OUR ROUTE AVOIDS THE WORST FLAK CONCENTRATIONS. LET'S HOPE THERE AREN'T ANY FIGHTERS ABOUT...

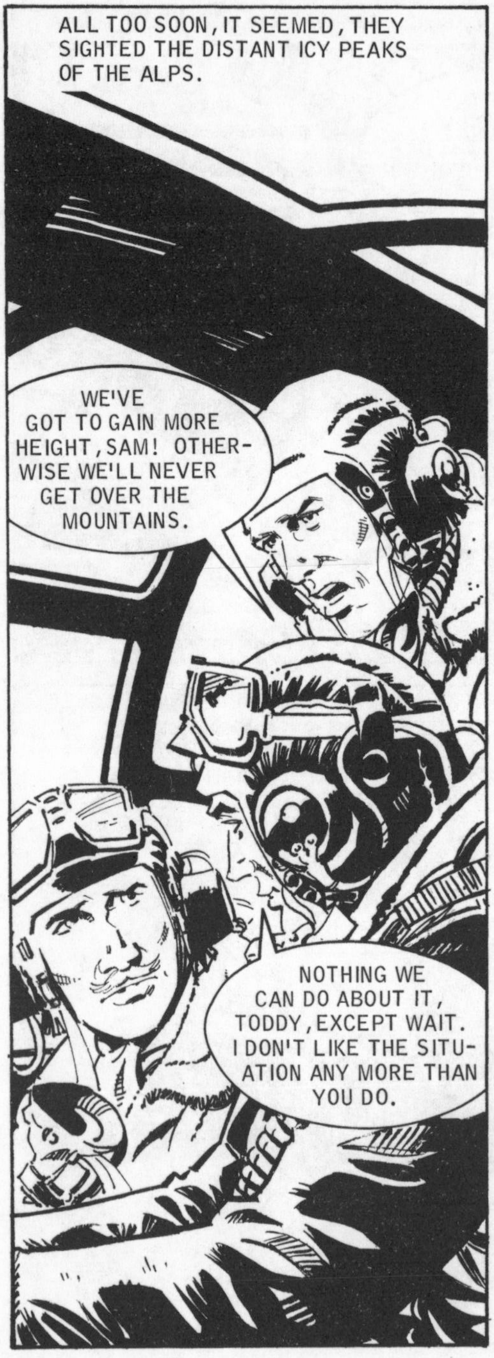
ALL TOO SOON, IT SEEMED, THEY SIGHTED THE DISTANT ICY PEAKS OF THE ALPS.
WE'VE GOT TO GAIN MORE HEIGHT, SAM! OTHERWISE WE'LL NEVER GET OVER THE MOUNTAINS.
NOTHING WE CAN DO ABOUT IT, TODDY, EXCEPT WAIT. I DON'T LIKE THE SITUATION ANY MORE THAN YOU DO.

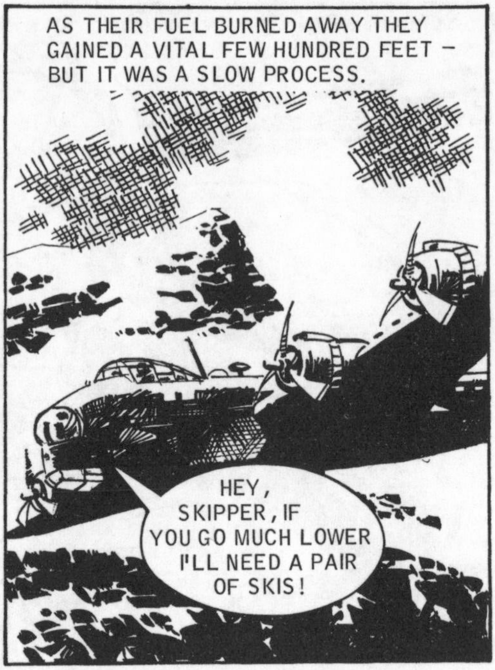
AS THEIR FUEL BURNED AWAY THEY GAINED A VITAL FEW HUNDRED FEET – BUT IT WAS A SLOW PROCESS.
HEY, SKIPPER, IF YOU GO MUCH LOWER I'LL NEED A PAIR OF SKIS!

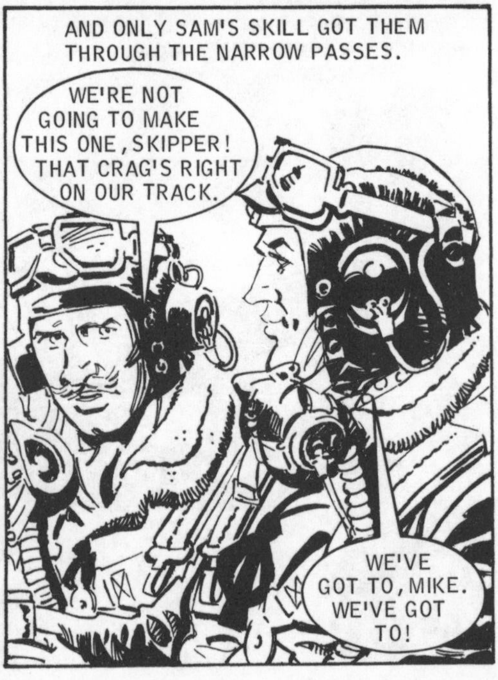
AND ONLY SAM'S SKILL GOT THEM THROUGH THE NARROW PASSES.
WE'RE NOT GOING TO MAKE THIS ONE, SKIPPER! THAT CRAG'S RIGHT ON OUR TRACK.
WE'VE GOT TO, MIKE. WE'VE GOT TO!

THE MOUNTAIN FACE SLIPPED BY PERILOUSLY NEAR THEIR WINGS — THEN SUDDENLY
THERE WERE NO MORE MOUNTAINS AHEAD.

THAT'S IT — WE'RE OVER THE TOP! IT'S DOWNHILL ALL THE WAY FROM NOW ON!

THEY CONTINUED ON THEIR WAY.   THEN FROM FIFTY MILES AWAY THEY COULD SEE THE
FLARES DROPPED BY THE DIVERSIONARY FORCE.

WE'RE LATE, SAM, THE RAID HAS ALREADY STARTED. THEY'LL BE ON THEIR WAY HOME BY THE TIME WE ARRIVE.

THE FLAK REACHED OUT FOR THEM AS THEY NEARED THE TARGET, FOR THE REST OF THE BOMBERS HAD DEPARTED.

TODDY SAYS WE'VE BEEN HIT, SKIPPER. THE HEATING SYSTEM'S PUNCTURED.

WE'LL BE WARM ENOUGH WITHOUT IT. I'VE NEVER SEEN FLAK THIS THICK — EVEN OVER GERMANY!

AS THEY RAN UP TO THE TARGET TODDY CONCENTRATED AS NEVER BEFORE.

LEFT A BIT, SKIPPER, I'VE GOT THE HARBOUR ON THE SCREEN. STEADY AT THAT... STEADY...

NOTHING WAS VISIBLE BELOW, EXCEPT FLAK SPARKLING THROUGH THE DENSE SMOKE-SCREEN.

LUCKY WE'RE USING RADAR, SKIPPER. I CAN'T SEE A THING DOWN THERE.

I JUST HOPE TODDY CAN. I WOULDN'T WANT TO DO THIS TRIP TWICE.

THEN, AS THE NARROW OUTLINE OF THE ADMIRAL EISEN SLID ACROSS THE RADAR SCREEN...

WE'VE BEEN HIT!

ALTHOUGH THE FLAK CAUSED RELATIVELY MINOR DAMAGE TO THE PLANE, DAVE WAS BADLY INJURED BY STRAY SHRAPNEL.

SAM BANKED GRIMLY AND BEGAN A SECOND APPROACH UNDER TODDY'S DIRECTIONS.

I'VE HAD TO FEATHER THE PORT OUTER. WE CAN'T MAINTAIN HEIGHT MUCH LONGER.

ON THE SECOND RUN TODDY PRESSED THE RELEASE BUTTON AND THE BOMBS TUMBLED AWAY.

BOMBS GONE, SKIPPER!

LET'S HOPE IT'S NOT ALL BEEN IN VAIN.

THEY WAITED TENSELY — THEN A BALL OF FIRE ROSE THROUGH THE SMOKE SCREEN.

HIMMEL, THEY'VE HIT THE ADMIRAL EISEN!

THE SHIP WAS DOOMED. BURNING FUEL AND EXPLODING AMMO SOON ENGULFED THE DREADED RAIDER.

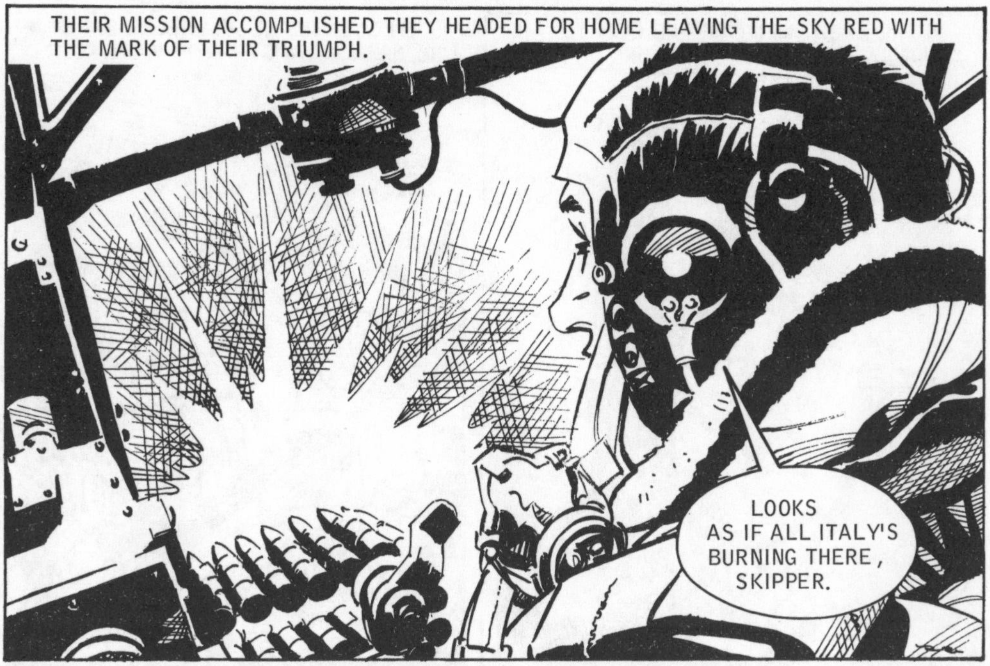
THEIR MISSION ACCOMPLISHED THEY HEADED FOR HOME LEAVING THE SKY RED WITH THE MARK OF THEIR TRIUMPH.
LOOKS AS IF ALL ITALY'S BURNING THERE, SKIPPER.

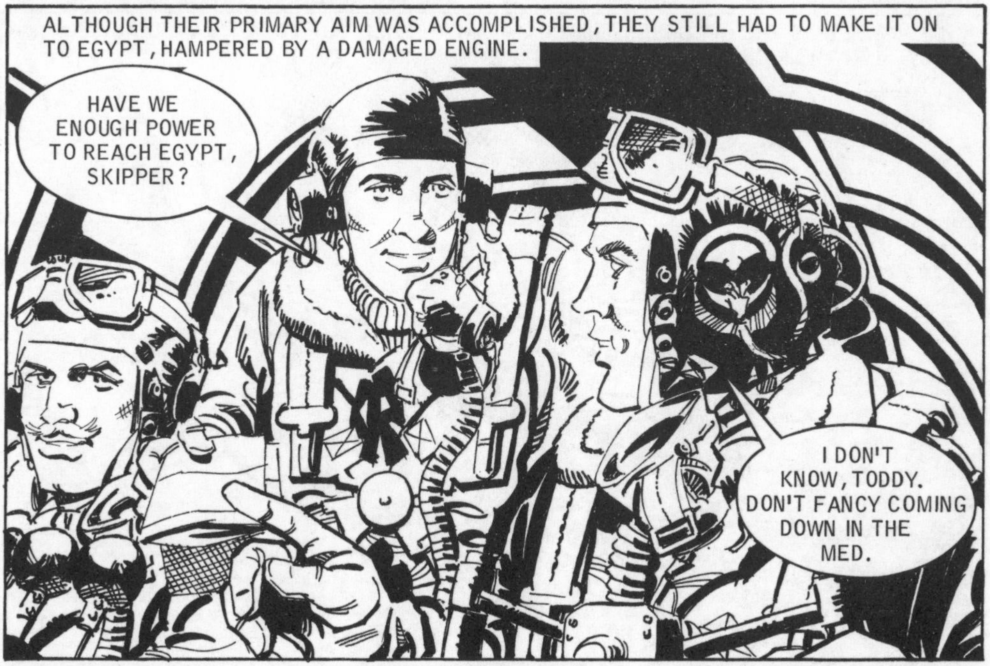
ALTHOUGH THEIR PRIMARY AIM WAS ACCOMPLISHED, THEY STILL HAD TO MAKE IT ON TO EGYPT, HAMPERED BY A DAMAGED ENGINE.
HAVE WE ENOUGH POWER TO REACH EGYPT, SKIPPER?
I DON'T KNOW, TODDY. DON'T FANCY COMING DOWN IN THE MED.

IN THE EXCITEMENT OF THE EVENTS SAM HAD FORGOTTEN THAT ONE OF HIS GUNNERS HAD BEEN INJURED.

HOLD HER ON THIS COURSE, MIKE, I'LL GO BACK AND SEE HOW DAVE IS.

ALTHOUGH HIS LEG HAD BEEN BADLY INJURED, DAVE'S SPIRITS WERE HIGH.

I'LL BE OK, SKIPPER, I'VE COME THROUGH TOUGHER SCRAPES THAN THIS ONE.

MEANWHILE AS THEY CROSSED THE COAST AND HEADED OUT TO SEA SAM REALISED HOW SLIM THEIR CHANCES WERE.

IT'LL BE A NEAR THING. BUT WE SHOULD JUST ABOUT MAKE THE AFRICAN COAST.

WE CAN'T AFFORD ANY ERRORS, SO WE'D BETTER DUMP EVERYTHING WE DON'T NEED.

SPARE AMMUNITION, GUNS, AND EVERYTHING ELSE BULKY WENT OVER THE SIDE AS THEY STAGGERED ON.

BETTER HANG ON TO OUR PARACHUTES. WE MIGHT NEED THEM YET!

WHAT A PESSIMIST!

THEN TODDY MADE A STARTLING DISCOVERY. THERE WAS STILL A BOMB ON BOARD.

I CAN'T RELEASE IT, THE GEAR'S JAMMED. CAN'T WE SHAKE IT LOOSE BY BUCKING AROUND?

WE CAN'T SPARE THE FUEL, TODDY. WE'VE BARELY ENOUGH AS IT IS.

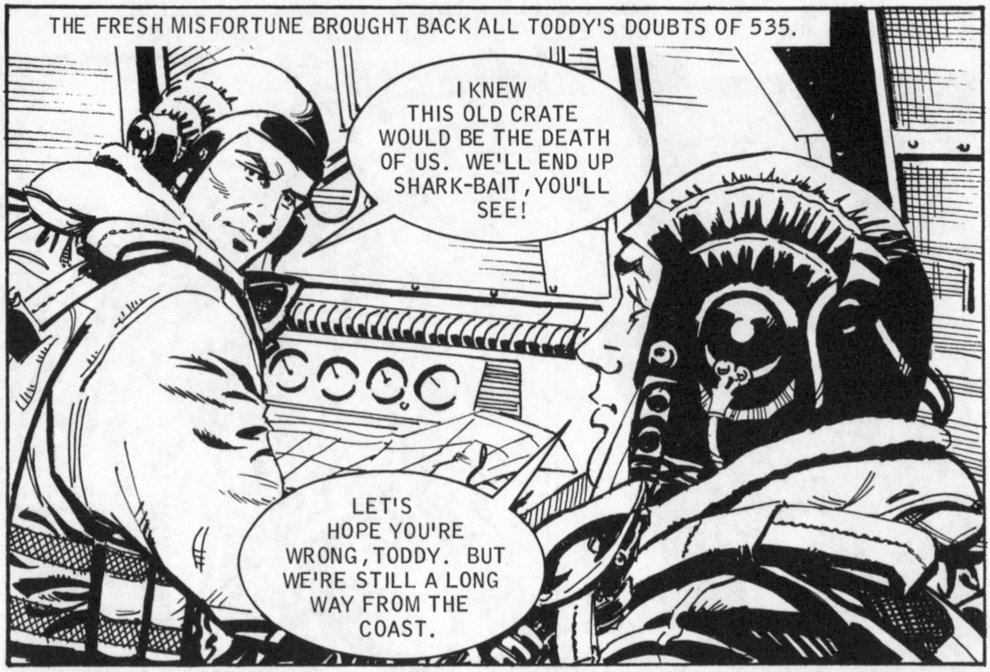
THE FRESH MISFORTUNE BROUGHT BACK ALL TODDY'S DOUBTS OF 535.
I KNEW THIS OLD CRATE WOULD BE THE DEATH OF US. WE'LL END UP SHARK-BAIT, YOU'LL SEE!
LET'S HOPE YOU'RE WRONG, TODDY. BUT WE'RE STILL A LONG WAY FROM THE COAST.

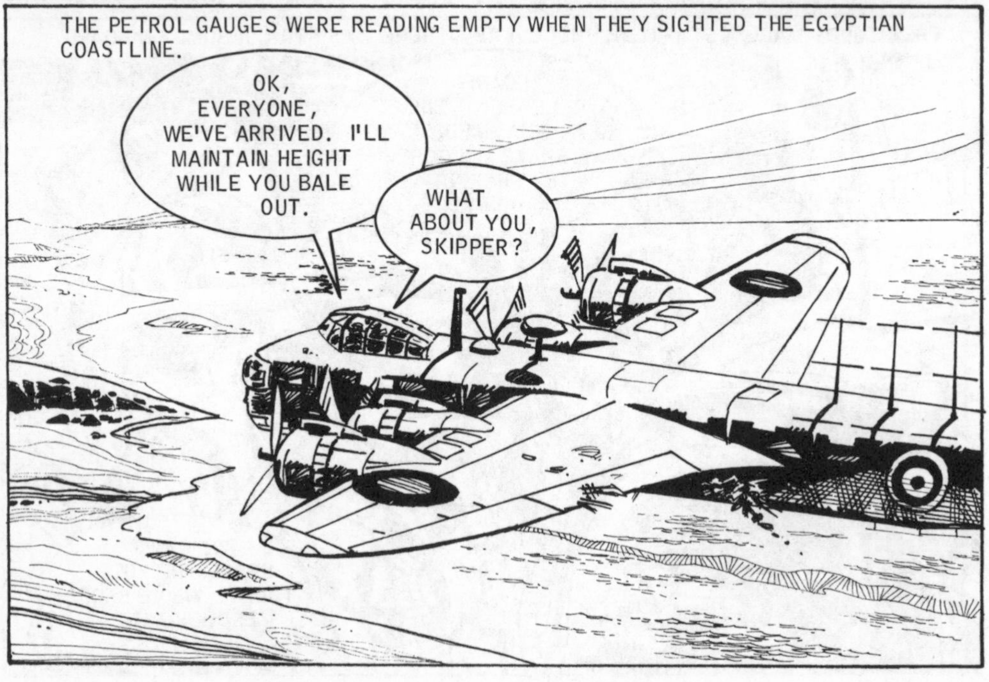
THE PETROL GAUGES WERE READING EMPTY WHEN THEY SIGHTED THE EGYPTIAN COASTLINE.
OK, EVERYONE, WE'VE ARRIVED. I'LL MAINTAIN HEIGHT WHILE YOU BALE OUT.
WHAT ABOUT YOU, SKIPPER?

SAM KNEW THAT THE DAMAGED CONTROLS WOULD FLICK THE STIRLING INTO A ROLL AS SOON AS HE LEFT THEM.

THERE WAS A FURIOUS SNORT FROM TODDY, WHO HAD OVERHEARD THEIR CONVERSATION.

HE TRIED TO MAKE IT AN ORDER, BUT SECRETLY HE WAS PROUD OF THEIR LOYALTY.

EVERYONE AT CRASH POSITIONS? ALL RIGHT... BRACE!

I'VE GOT TO GET DOWN IN ONE PIECE — THE BLOKES ARE RELYING ON ME. COME ON, OLD GIRL, DON'T LET ME DOWN.

THE CREW SAT OR LAY IN THEIR BRACE POSITIONS AS SAM, UNABLE TO LOWER THE UNDERCARRIAGE, TOUCHED DOWN FOR A BELLY-LANDING ON THE SAND.

THIS IS IT!

AS THEY SKIDDED TO A HALT, THE CREW TUMBLED OUT AND RAN.

RUN FOR YOUR LIVES, THE JOLT MIGHT HAVE UPSET THAT BOMB!

THEY HAD BARELY PUT A SAFE DISTANCE BETWEEN THEMSELVES AND THE BOMB WHEN...

THERE SHE GOES!

THAT MUST BE ABOUT THE UNLUCKIEST KITE IN THE R.A.F.

TODDY SCOWLED AS HE GOT TO HIS FEET AND BRUSHED THE SAND FROM HIS CLOTHING

SHE WAS A JINX RIGHT TO THE END. THAT BOMB COULD HAVE BLOWN US ALL APART!

BUT IT DIDN'T. BESIDES, I GAVE YOU A CHANCE TO BALE OUT.

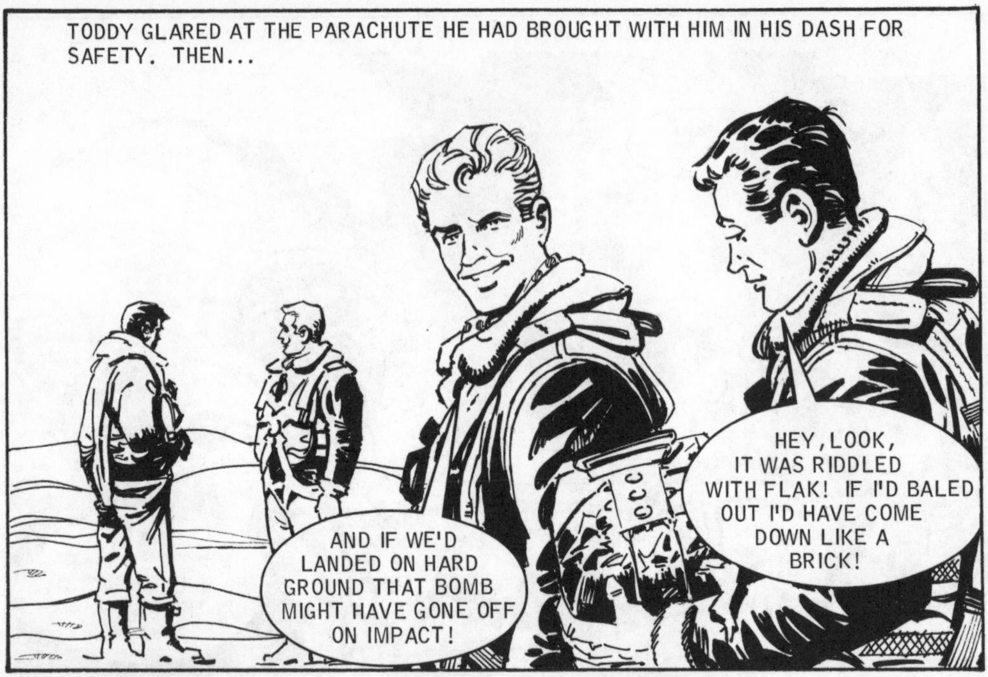
TODDY GLARED AT THE PARACHUTE HE HAD BROUGHT WITH HIM IN HIS DASH FOR SAFETY. THEN...
HEY, LOOK, IT WAS RIDDLED WITH FLAK! IF I'D BALED OUT I'D HAVE COME DOWN LIKE A BRICK!
AND IF WE'D LANDED ON HARD GROUND THAT BOMB MIGHT HAVE GONE OFF ON IMPACT!

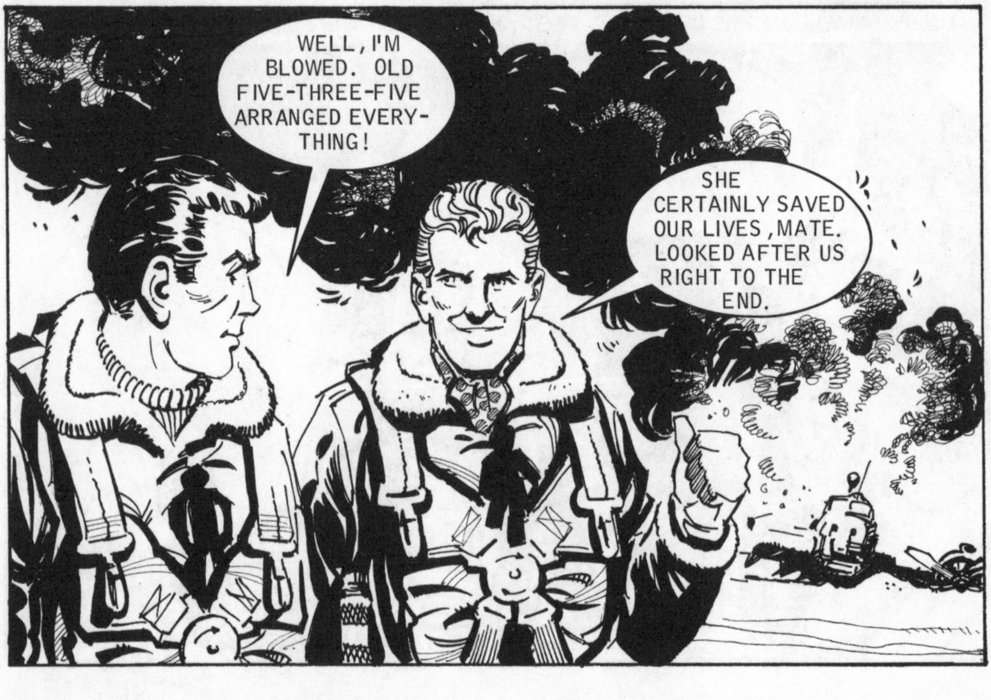
WELL, I'M BLOWED. OLD FIVE-THREE-FIVE ARRANGED EVERY-THING!
SHE CERTAINLY SAVED OUR LIVES, MATE. LOOKED AFTER US RIGHT TO THE END.

FOR ONCE TODDY HAD NO COMMENT TO MAKE. BUT ON THEIR RETURN TO ENGLAND, WHEN AS A REWARD FOR THEIR SUCCESSFUL ATTACK ON THE ADMIRAL EISEN THEY WERE GIVEN A POSTING TO A HALIFAX SQUADRON, HE WAS THE ONE WHO SUGGESTED THE EMBLEM THAT ADORNED THE NOSE OF THEIR NEW AIRCRAFT.

No. 17 — KITTYHAWK 1

Shown in the markings of 112 Squadron, R.A.F., at Sidi Heneish, North Africa, in June, 1942.

LOW-LEVEL LANC

SERGEANT PETER LAWLER, D.C.M., THE SOMME.

SERGEANT MAJOR JOHN LAWLER, V.C., BOER WAR.

TIM LAWLER WAS A BORN AUSSIE — AND PROUD OF IT. BUT HE HAD BEEN REARED ON TALES OF HOW HIS FIGHTING ANCESTORS HAD WON FAME AND HONOUR IN THE BRITISH ARMY. WHEN THE WAR AGAINST NAZI TYRANNY CAME ALONG, TIM JOINED THE R.A.F. AS A PILOT FOR ONE REASON — BECAUSE IT LOOKED THE QUICKEST WAY TO GLORY. AND THE WAY HE FLUNG HIS LANCASTER ABOUT THE SKY HE WAS GOING TO GET JUST THAT — OR DIE IN THE ATTEMPT.

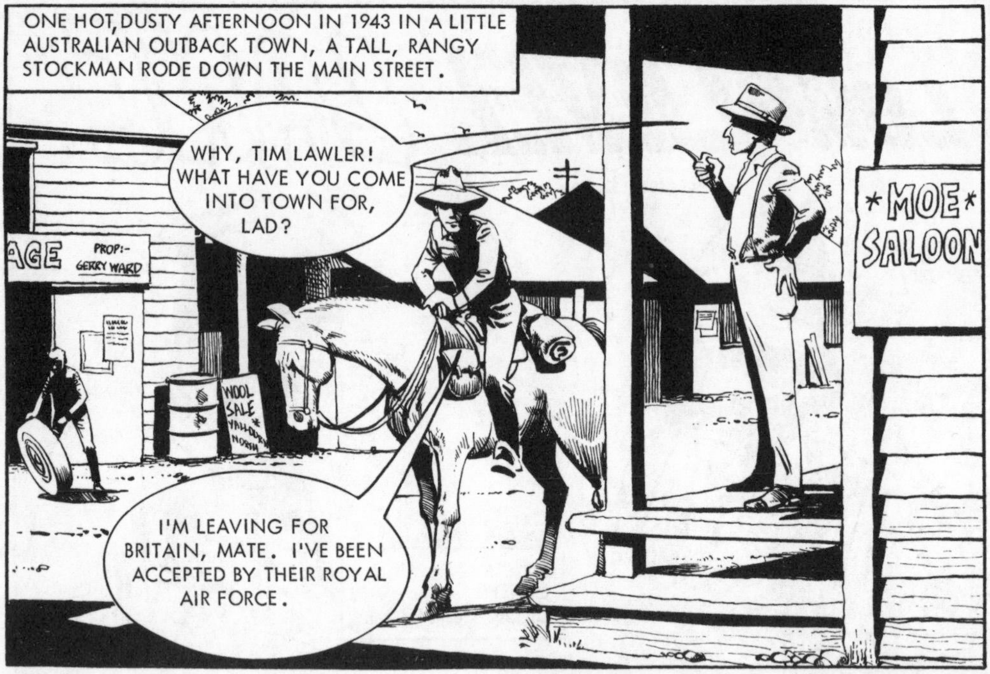
ONE HOT, DUSTY AFTERNOON IN 1943 IN A LITTLE AUSTRALIAN OUTBACK TOWN, A TALL, RANGY STOCKMAN RODE DOWN THE MAIN STREET.
WHY, TIM LAWLER! WHAT HAVE YOU COME INTO TOWN FOR, LAD?
I'M LEAVING FOR BRITAIN, MATE. I'VE BEEN ACCEPTED BY THEIR ROYAL AIR FORCE.
AGE PROP:- GERRY WARD
WOOL SALE
MOE SALOON

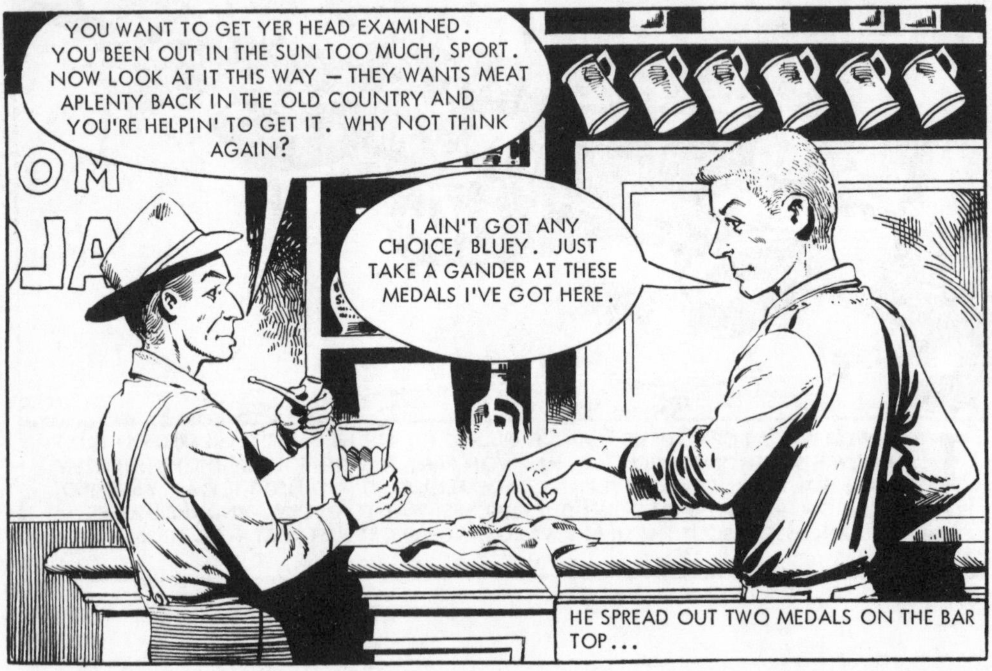
YOU WANT TO GET YER HEAD EXAMINED. YOU BEEN OUT IN THE SUN TOO MUCH, SPORT. NOW LOOK AT IT THIS WAY – THEY WANTS MEAT APLENTY BACK IN THE OLD COUNTRY AND YOU'RE HELPIN' TO GET IT. WHY NOT THINK AGAIN?
I AIN'T GOT ANY CHOICE, BLUEY. JUST TAKE A GANDER AT THESE MEDALS I'VE GOT HERE.
HE SPREAD OUT TWO MEDALS ON THE BAR TOP...

THE DISTINGUISHED CONDUCT MEDAL WAS MY DAD'S. HE GOT IT IN FRANCE AT THE SOMME DURING WORLD WAR ONE. AND THIS OTHER ONE IS THE HIGHEST AWARD YOU CAN GET — THE VICTORIA CROSS. MY GRANDFATHER WON THAT IN THE BOER WAR.

FOR VALOUR

FOR DISTINGUISHED CONDUCT IN THE FIELD

DOWNING HIS BEER, TIM CAREFULLY WRAPPED UP THE MEDALS AGAIN AND PUT THEM BACK INTO HIS POCKET.

I CAN'T BE ODD MAN OUT, CAN I? I'VE GOT TO GET ME SOMETHING TO ADD TO THE COLLECTION, AND I'LL BE AIMING HIGH, I CAN TELL YOU.

WELL, CHEERIO, COBBER. BRING US BACK A SWASTIKA OR A SAMURAI SWORD OR SOMETHIN'.

TIM WAS SOON IN BRITAIN AND UNDERGOING THE HIGH-PRESSURE ROYAL AIR FORCE TRAINING WHICH CHURNED OUT BOMBER PILOTS IN THEIR HUNDREDS. HE DID NOTHING OUTSTANDING, ATTAINING AVERAGE RATINGS ALL THE WAY.

PILOT OFFICER LAWLER. GOOD LUCK!

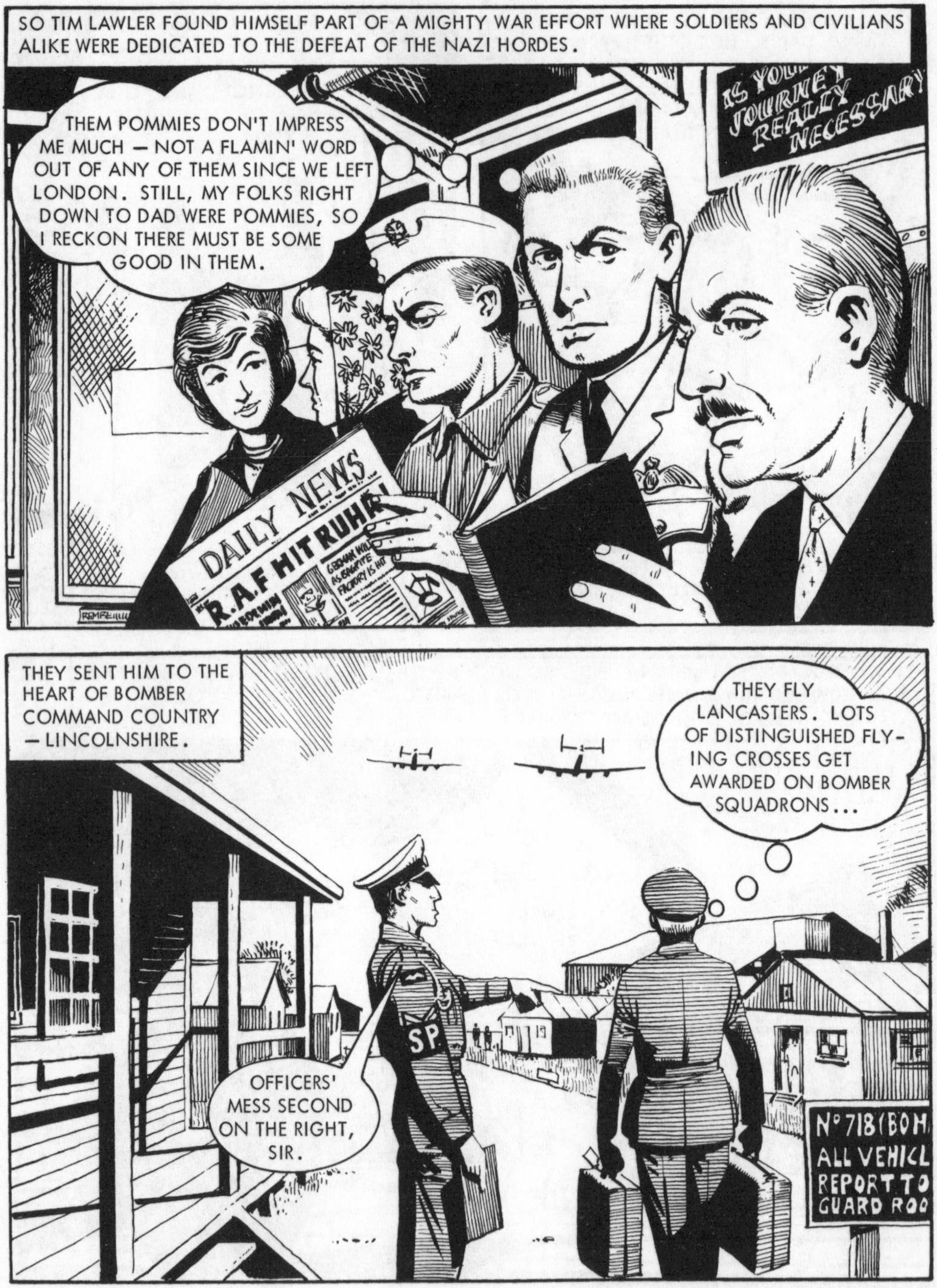
SO TIM LAWLER FOUND HIMSELF PART OF A MIGHTY WAR EFFORT WHERE SOLDIERS AND CIVILIANS ALIKE WERE DEDICATED TO THE DEFEAT OF THE NAZI HORDES.
JOURNEY REALLY NECESSARY
THEM POMMIES DON'T IMPRESS ME MUCH — NOT A FLAMIN' WORD OUT OF ANY OF THEM SINCE WE LEFT LONDON. STILL, MY FOLKS RIGHT DOWN TO DAD WERE POMMIES, SO I RECKON THERE MUST BE SOME GOOD IN THEM.
DAILY NEWS
R.A.F HIT RUHR
THEY SENT HIM TO THE HEART OF BOMBER COMMAND COUNTRY — LINCOLNSHIRE.
THEY FLY LANCASTERS. LOTS OF DISTINGUISHED FLY-ING CROSSES GET AWARDED ON BOMBER SQUADRONS...
SP
OFFICERS' MESS SECOND ON THE RIGHT, SIR.
REPORT TO

FINDING NO ONE IN THE MESS, HE EVENTUALLY CAME TO THE LOUNGE. HIS JOURNEY FROM LONDON HAD BEEN LONG AND TIRING AND THE ARM-CHAIRS LOOKED COMFORTABLE.

NOBODY ABOUT. I'LL JUST REST MY WEARY FEET TILL SOMEBODY SHOWS UP. I COULD DO WITH A REST.

HE PEELED OFF HIS TUNIC, THREW IT OVER THE BACK OF AN ARMCHAIR, THEN FLOPPED DOWN. ABOUT FIVE MINUTES LATER...

YOU THERE. WHAT D'YOU THINK THIS IS, A BALLY HOTEL? ON YOUR FEET, MAN. MOVE!

THE WING COMMANDER WAS SMOOTH AND SNOOTY, HIS VOICE CLIPPED AND ARROGANT — ALL QUALITIES WHICH MANY AUSTRALIANS DESPISE. TIM FELT HIS TEMPER RISING.

YOU ARE SCRUFFY AND SLOPPY. GET OUT AND TIDY YOURSELF AND DO NOT PRESENT YOURSELF IN THE OFFICERS' MESS IN THIS CONDITION AGAIN.

WHAT THE BLAZES — ?

WITH TIM'S TUNIC FLUNG CARELESSLY OVER THE CHAIR, HIS INSIGNIA OF RANK WAS NOT SEEN. HE SAW A WAY TO TAKE THE MAN DOWN A PEG.

WHEN YOU SPEAK TO A GROUP CAPTAIN, STAND TO ATTENTION! I'M IN TRANSIT, ON MY WAY TO YORKSHIRE AND I DO NOT TAKE KINDLY TO BEING SO ADDRESSED. WHAT IS YOUR NAME?

DARCY, S-SIR! I — I'M SORRY. I THOUGHT —

THOUGHT? ARE YOU CAPABLE OF IT? I DOUBT IT. NOW WILL YOU KINDLY GET OUT OF HERE?

WING COMMANDER DARCY SHOT OFF LIKE A FRIGHTENED RABBIT.

MAYBE THAT WAS A CRAZY THING TO DO, BUT IT WAS WORTH IT TO SEE THE LOOK ON HIS DIAL!

NEXT MORNING, THE ADJUTANT INTRODUCED TIM TO HIS CREW.

MEET YOUR CREW, LAWLER. MEN, THIS IS PILOT OFFICER LAWLER, YOUR NEW SKIPPER.

A PRETTY POOR LOOKING LOT, I'M THINKIN'.

SERGEANT COLLINS, THE NAVIGATOR, SEEMED TO BE THEIR SPOKESMAN. HIS VOICE WAS TENSE AND EDGY.

THE BLOKE WHOSE PLACE I'M TAKING, WHAT HAPPENED TO HIM?

HE BOUGHT IT — HANDED IN HIS CHIPS — GOT KILLED. BUT WE'RE STILL ALIVE AND WE MEAN TO STAY THAT WAY. I HOPE YOU GET THE MESSAGE — SIR.

TIM'S ANSWER WAS SHORT AND TO THE POINT.

LISTEN, YOU SHOWER, WE'RE HERE TO DO A JOB, AND IT'LL BE DONE MY WAY.

UNDER THE GUIDANCE OF HIS FLIGHT COMMANDER, HE TOOK A LADEN LANCASTER INTO THE AIR FOR THE FIRST TIME FOR LOCAL FLYING PRACTICE.

WE TOOK OFF THAT TIME, LAWLER, BUT ONLY BECAUSE I WAS HERE TO LIFT THE FLAP LEVER WHICH YOU DIDN'T CONSIDER NECESSARY. IF YOU DON'T WATCH IT YOU WON'T LAST LONG.

SORRY, COBBER. I'VE NEVER FLOWN TOTING A BOMB CARGO BEFORE.

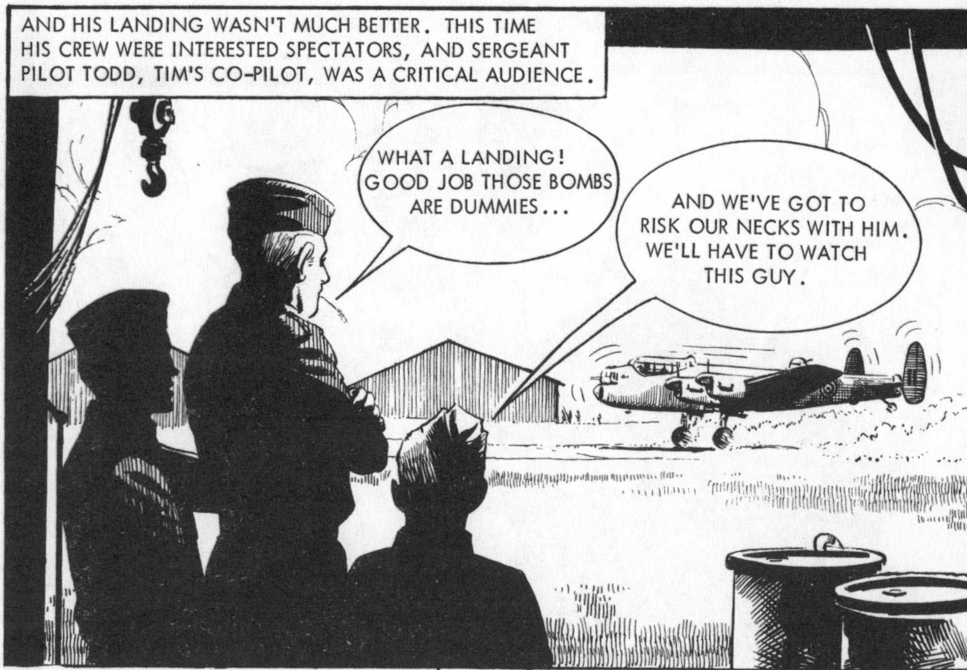
AND HIS LANDING WASN'T MUCH BETTER. THIS TIME HIS CREW WERE INTERESTED SPECTATORS, AND SERGEANT PILOT TODD, TIM'S CO-PILOT, WAS A CRITICAL AUDIENCE.
WHAT A LANDING! GOOD JOB THOSE BOMBS ARE DUMMIES...
AND WE'VE GOT TO RISK OUR NECKS WITH HIM. WE'LL HAVE TO WATCH THIS GUY.

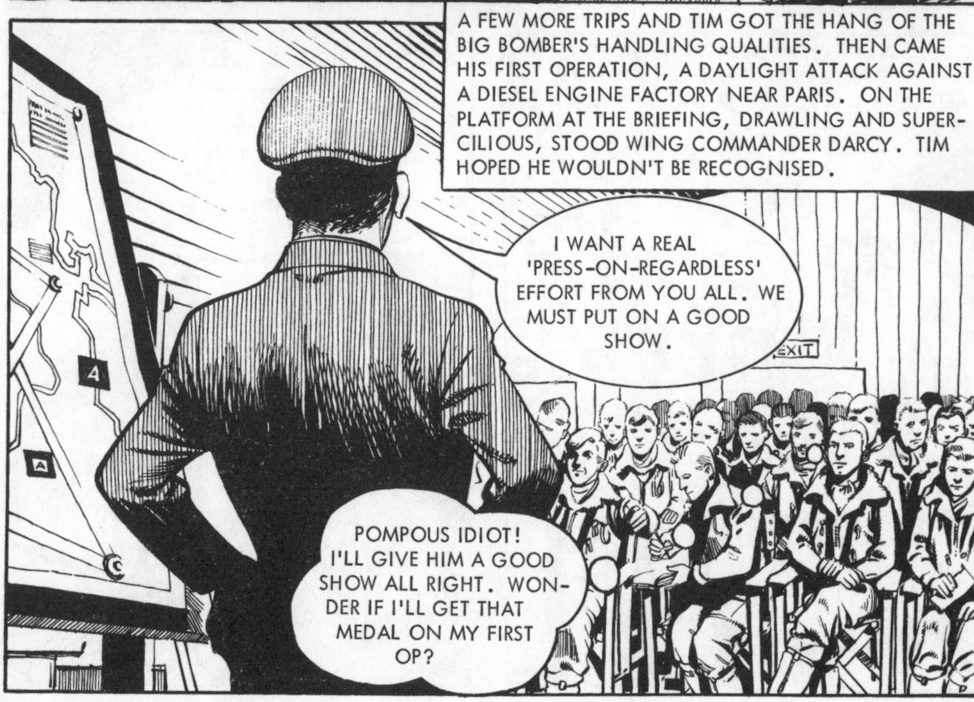
A FEW MORE TRIPS AND TIM GOT THE HANG OF THE BIG BOMBER'S HANDLING QUALITIES. THEN CAME HIS FIRST OPERATION, A DAYLIGHT ATTACK AGAINST A DIESEL ENGINE FACTORY NEAR PARIS. ON THE PLATFORM AT THE BRIEFING, DRAWLING AND SUPERCILIOUS, STOOD WING COMMANDER DARCY. TIM HOPED HE WOULDN'T BE RECOGNISED.
I WANT A REAL 'PRESS-ON-REGARDLESS' EFFORT FROM YOU ALL. WE MUST PUT ON A GOOD SHOW.
EXIT
POMPOUS IDIOT! I'LL GIVE HIM A GOOD SHOW ALL RIGHT. WONDER IF I'LL GET THAT MEDAL ON MY FIRST OP?

THEN DARCY HESITATED, AND STUTTERED. TIM FOUND HIMSELF LOOKING STRAIGHT INTO HIS EYES.

CONTROLLING HIMSELF WITH A MIGHTY EFFORT, DARCY CONTINUED HIS BRIEFING. AFTER IT WAS OVER, THERE WAS A MESSAGE FOR TIM...

DARCY'S VOICE WAS ICY.

IT WASN'T SO MUCH THE DRESSING DOWN THAT ANGERED TIM — HE WAS EXPECTING THAT. IT WAS THE HAUGHTY TONES OF WING COMMANDER DARCY.

THIS ISN'T AN "AUSSIE SQUADRON". MARK THIS WELL — I'LL BE WATCHING YOU LIKE A HAWK. JUST GIVE ME THE EVIDENCE AND I'LL JUMP ON YOU HARD. UNDERSTOOD?

AW, HORSEFEATHERS! SOME OF YOU POMMIES CAN'T EVEN TAKE A JOKE.

N	WARD. G.	✓
L	BEAR. M	✓
B	TAYLOR. B.	✓
S	GREENBAUM.	✓
T	ROBERTS. J.	X
U	BILLIMOREE.	
Y	PETTS. S.	
C	PERRY.	
M.	KEMB	

LUCKILY, ZERO-HOUR FOR THE OPERATION WAS IMMINENT AND TIM'S HOT TEMPER COOLED AS HE WAITED HIS TURN FOR TAKE-OFF. SOON TIM'S PLANE, X FOR X-RAY, ROARED INTO THE AIR.

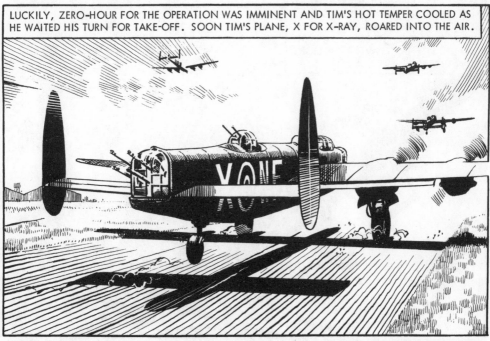

THE WARM AFTERNOON AIR THRUMMED AND SHOOK AS THE GATHERING WAVES OF BOMBERS JOINED 718 SQUADRON IN A MIGHTY WHEELING ORBIT OVER THE PEACEFUL COUNTRY-SIDE.

NAVIGATOR TO PILOT. SET COURSE ONE-EIGHT-NINE DE-GREES THIRTY SECONDS FROM NOW...NOW!

ROGER, TURNING ON ONE-EIGHT-NINE DEGREES.

AS THE MASS FORMATION CROSSED THE ENGLISH COAST, IT DROPPED TO FIFTY FEET TO FOX THE ENEMY RADAR, THEN WHEN IT REACHED THE FRENCH COAST, CLIMBED STEEPLY TO AVOID THE LIGHT FLAK THAT HOSE-PIPED UP TO IT.

HIGH ABOVE, SPITFIRES FOUGHT SAVAGELY AGAINST HORDES OF FOCKE-WULF 190s. AHEAD, HURRI-BOMBERS BLASTED ENEMY AIRFIELDS. THERE WOULD BE NO GERMAN FIGHTERS TO KEEP THE BOMBERS FROM THEIR DEADLY WORK.

ARROW LEADER TO SQUADRON. WATCH THAT RUNWAY — ANYBODY TRIES TO TAKE OFF, BLAST HIM. KEEP 'EM GROUNDED.

FROM THE LEADING LANCASTER, A DOUBLE GREEN FLARE ROSE, THE SIGNAL THAT THE ESTIMATED TIME OF ARRIVAL ON TARGET WAS EXACTLY ONE MINUTE. TIM'S MOMENT OF GLORY HAD COME...

RIGHT, BOMB-AIMER, I'M GOING IN AT TWO HUNDRED FEET. SET YOUR BOMBSIGHT ACCORD-INGLY.

LAWLER, YOU'RE MAD. WE'RE A SITTING DUCK DOWN THERE.

YOU NUT! YOU CAN'T DO THIS — YOU'LL KILL US ALL!

TIM LET RIP AN ANGRY RETORT.

SHUT UP, THE LOT OF YOU. YOU'RE YAPPING AWAY LIKE A MOTHERS' MEETING. NOW GET THIS. I'M SKIPPER AND I GIVE THE ORDERS. WE'RE GOING IN TO PUT OUR LOAD SLAP IN THAT MACHINE SHOP. BUT FIRST, I'VE GOT TO FIND IT.

AS THEY ROARED OVER THE INDUSTRIAL SUBURBS OF THE GREAT CITY, SEARCHING FOR THE VITAL HEART OF THE DIESEL FACTORY, THE FLAK BUILT UP TO FANTASTIC INTENSITY.

TIM KNEW THAT THE CHANCES OF BOMBING ACCURACY WERE LESS LIKELY WITH A JITTERY CREW ABOARD. THERE WAS ONLY ONE THING TO DO.

YOU WINDY LOT! BOMB-AIMER, SWITCH YOUR BOMB RELEASE OFF — I'LL DO THE JOB MYSELF. I'M SICK OF YOUR MOANING SO I'M DISCONNECTING MY INTERCOM.

FOR FULLY FOUR MINUTES, THE BOMBER WEAVED BACK AND FORTH THROUGH THE HOLOCAUST. TO THE TREMBLING NAVIGATOR, IT SEEMED LIKE FOUR HOURS. THEN HE FELT THE NOSE DROPPING SHARPLY.

WE'VE HAD IT. WE'RE HIT!

BUT IT WAS ONLY A DIVE. TIM HAD LOCATED HIS TARGET AND WAS SCREAMING IN TO DROP HIS BOMBS.

A VISITING CARD, RIGHT IN JERRY'S FRONT DOOR!

CORBIEL ET CIE

THE ENTIRE BUILDING ERUPTED IN FLAME AND FLYING METAL. THE RACING LANCASTER LURCHED VIOLENTLY IN THE TEARING BLAST.

IT HAD BEEN RECKLESS, STUPID FLYING...BUT IT HAD SERVED ITS PURPOSE.

AS TIM OPENED UP THE THROTTLES WIDE TO CATCH UP THE MAIN BOMBER FORCE ALREADY ON ITS WAY HOME, HE FELT JUBILANT ABOUT HIS SUCCESS.

SERGEANT TODD DIDN'T REALLY CARE MUCH WHERE OMDURMAN WAS. ALL THAT INTERESTED HIM WAS THAT THEY HAD SURVIVED WITH WHOLE SKINS.

I SUPPOSE IT'S SOME DUST-HEAP IN THE AUSTRALIAN DESERT.

YOU IGNORAMUS! THE BATTLE OF OMDURMAN IN THE SUDAN, IN EIGHTEEN NINETY-EIGHT. SERGEANT HENRY LAWLER, MY GRANDFATHER, LED FIFTY MEN AGAINST TWO THOUS-AND HOWLING DERVISHES AND STOLE THEIR FLAG. GOT A MEDAL FOR THAT, HE DID.

EVERY GENERATION OF LAWLERS SINCE THE CRIMEA HAS GOT MEDALS IN SOME BATTLE OR OTHER. I'VE GOT 'EM ALL BACK IN MY BILLET. THEY'VE BEEN HANDED DOWN TO ME. SO, I AIN'T GOING TO BE ODD MAN OUT. MAYBE THEY'LL GIVE ME A D.F.C. FOR TODAY'S DO, BUT IT WON'T BE THANKS TO YOU.

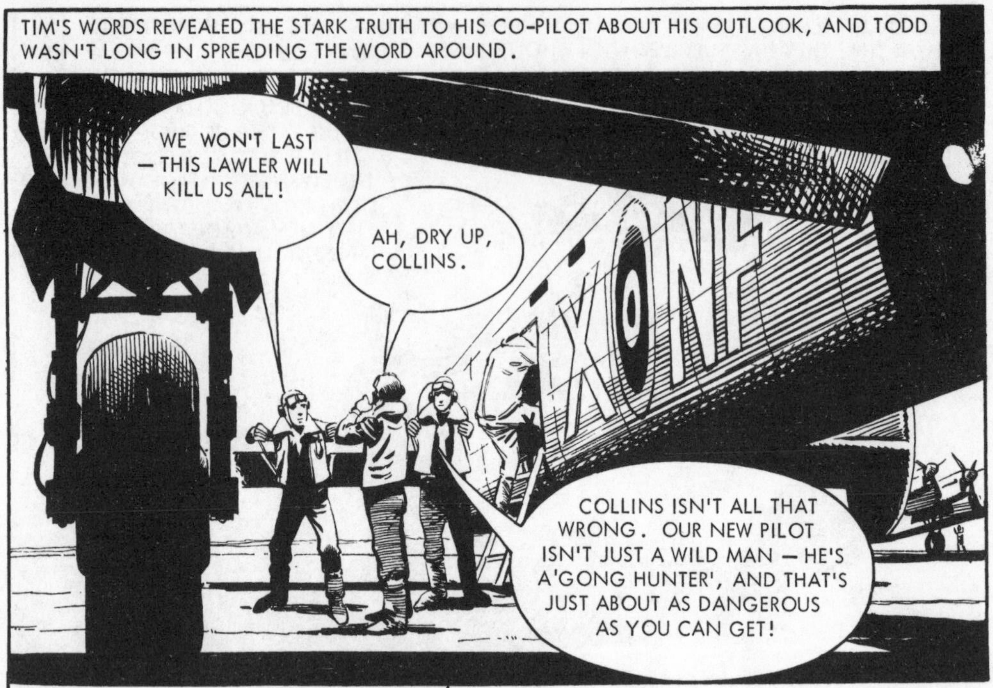
TIM'S WORDS REVEALED THE STARK TRUTH TO HIS CO-PILOT ABOUT HIS OUTLOOK, AND TODD WASN'T LONG IN SPREADING THE WORD AROUND.
WE WON'T LAST — THIS LAWLER WILL KILL US ALL!
AH, DRY UP, COLLINS.
COLLINS ISN'T ALL THAT WRONG. OUR NEW PILOT ISN'T JUST A WILD MAN — HE'S A 'GONG HUNTER', AND THAT'S JUST ABOUT AS DANGEROUS AS YOU CAN GET!

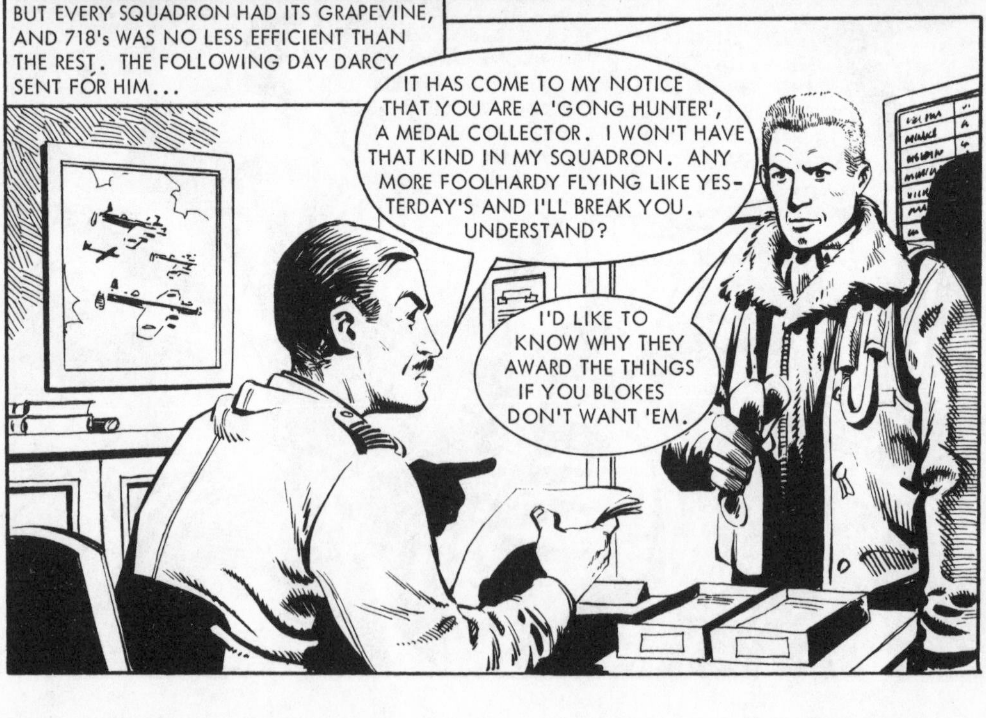
BUT EVERY SQUADRON HAD ITS GRAPEVINE, AND 718's WAS NO LESS EFFICIENT THAN THE REST. THE FOLLOWING DAY DARCY SENT FOR HIM...
IT HAS COME TO MY NOTICE THAT YOU ARE A 'GONG HUNTER', A MEDAL COLLECTOR. I WON'T HAVE THAT KIND IN MY SQUADRON. ANY MORE FOOLHARDY FLYING LIKE YES-TERDAY'S AND I'LL BREAK YOU. UNDERSTAND?
I'D LIKE TO KNOW WHY THEY AWARD THE THINGS IF YOU BLOKES DON'T WANT 'EM.

DARCY EXPLODED.

YESTERDAY, WHEN YOU WENT IN LOW, YOU KNOCKED THE WHOLE STRIKE PLAN FOR SIX. NOBODY COULD DROP THEIR BOMBS WHILE YOU WERE CROSSING OVER THAT FACTORY, AND YOU CROSSED IT ABOUT SIX TIMES!

TIM LEFT, BOILING WITH ANGRY FRUSTRATION.

I WISH I'D NEVER JOINED THIS FLYING LOONEY-BIN — STRAIGHT I DO. THEY DON'T EVEN GIVE YOU CREDIT FOR DOING A GOOD JOB.

HE HAD NOT YET LEARNT THE ONE ESSENTIAL QUALITY OF A BOMBER PILOT — TO FIT IN WITH A TEAM.

EVEN TIM'S OWN CREW HAD BEEN SCARED TO DEATH BY HIS FLYING. THEY MEANT TO DO SOMETHING ABOUT IT...

I SAY, LET'S PUT IN AN APPLICATION FOR TRANSFER NOW.

IT'S NO GOOD, TODD. THEY DON'T TAKE YOU OFF OPERATIONS BECAUSE YOU DON'T LIKE YOUR PILOT. NO, WE'LL HAVE TO SEE IF THERE'S A WAY TO GET RID OF THIS MANIAC. I MIGHT BE ABLE TO THINK OF SOMETHING SOON.

THEY HOPED THAT, UNTIL THEY COULD GET RID OF TIM, THEY WOULDN'T GET TOO MANY STICKY OPERATIONS. BUT THEIR HOPES WERE DASHED TWO DAYS LATER.

TIM WAS EXUBERANT — BUT HE WAS THE ONLY ONE ABOARD WHO FELT THAT WAY. THE OTHERS KEPT THINKING OF THE EIGHT TONS OF HIGH-EXPLOSIVE AND INCENDIARY BOMBS STOWED AWAY IN THE VAST BOMB-BAY.

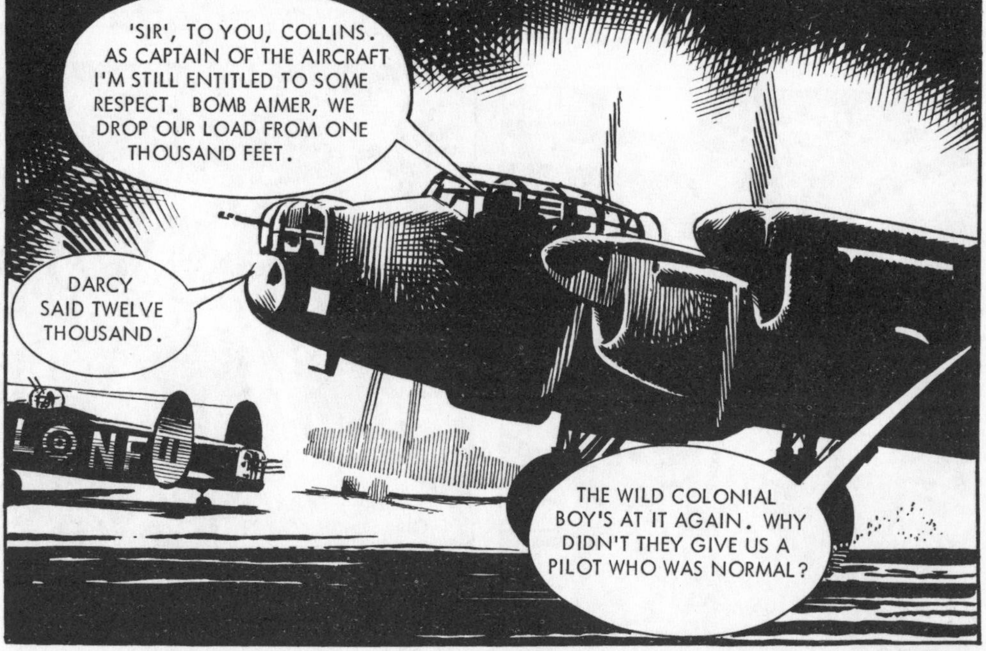
'SIR', TO YOU, COLLINS. AS CAPTAIN OF THE AIRCRAFT I'M STILL ENTITLED TO SOME RESPECT. BOMB AIMER, WE DROP OUR LOAD FROM ONE THOUSAND FEET.
DARCY SAID TWELVE THOUSAND.
THE WILD COLONIAL BOY'S AT IT AGAIN. WHY DIDN'T THEY GIVE US A PILOT WHO WAS NORMAL?
LONF

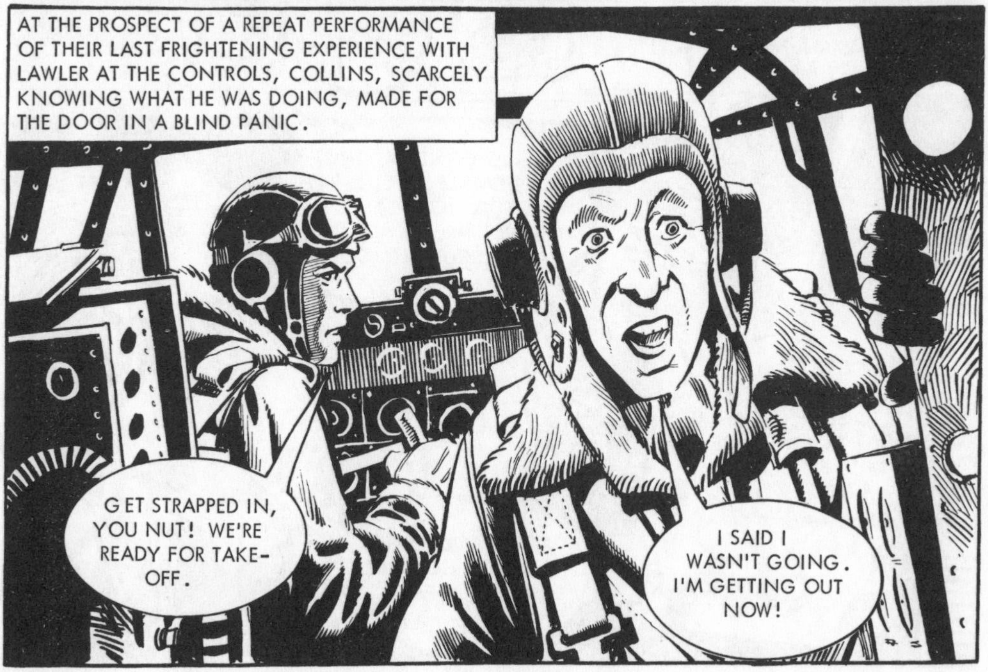
AT THE PROSPECT OF A REPEAT PERFORMANCE OF THEIR LAST FRIGHTENING EXPERIENCE WITH LAWLER AT THE CONTROLS, COLLINS, SCARCELY KNOWING WHAT HE WAS DOING, MADE FOR THE DOOR IN A BLIND PANIC.
GET STRAPPED IN, YOU NUT! WE'RE READY FOR TAKE-OFF.
I SAID I WASN'T GOING. I'M GETTING OUT NOW!

LIKE A STREAK OF LIGHTNING, TIM LAWLER WHIPPED HIS STRAPS OFF AND THREW HIMSELF AFTER THE FLEEING COLLINS. HE SPUN HIM ROUND VIOLENTLY.

THE PANIC-STRICKEN MAN HAD TO BE SILENCED QUICKLY. TIM LET LOOSE A PILE DRIVING RIGHT TO HIS JAW.

COME BACK HERE, YOU!

THERE'S ONLY ONE PLACE YOU'RE GOING AND THAT'S HAMBURG.

MEANWHILE, IN THE CONTROL TOWER, WING COMMANDER DARCY WAS TEARING HIS HAIR.

HELLO CONTROL, THIS IS L-LEATHER. TELL X-RAY TO GET A MOVE ON — MY ENGINE S ARE SO HOT I'LL HAVE TO CUT THEM SOON.

YE GODS! LAWLER AGAIN! THE FOOL'S GONE TO SLEEP OUT THERE. I'LL HAVE HIM WHEN HE GETS BACK FROM THIS SORTIE.

CONTROL TOWER TO X-RAY, CONTROL TOWER TO X-RAY...

WHILE THE TWO MEN STRUGGLED INSIDE THE LANCASTER, DARCY LEAPT INTO ACTION.

IF X-RAY DOESN'T GET OFF THE GROUND SOON OUR PLUGS ARE GOING TO BE OILED UP!

FOR PETE'S SAKE, SHIFT HIM SOMEHOW.

BUT ALREADY TIM HAD RESUMED HIS SEAT AND THE NAVIGATOR HAD SLUMPED TO THE DURAL FLOOR, UNCONSCIOUS.

ANY MORE OF YOU WANT A MOUTHFUL OF FIST? BECAUSE YOU'LL GET IT IF THERE'S ANY MORE TROUBLE. SOMEBODY STRAP COLLINS IN, WE'RE ON OUR WAY!

WHEN COLLINS OPENED HIS EYES, X-RAY WAS JUST CLEARING THE SUFFOLK COASTLINE.

WHEN THE CLOUDS HAVE CLEARED FROM THAT TINY BRAIN OF YOURS, COLLINS, I WANT THE FIRST COURSE BEARING. WE'VE LOST THE MAIN BOMBER FORCE, THANKS TO YOUR LITTLE STUPIDITY BEFORE TAKE-OFF.

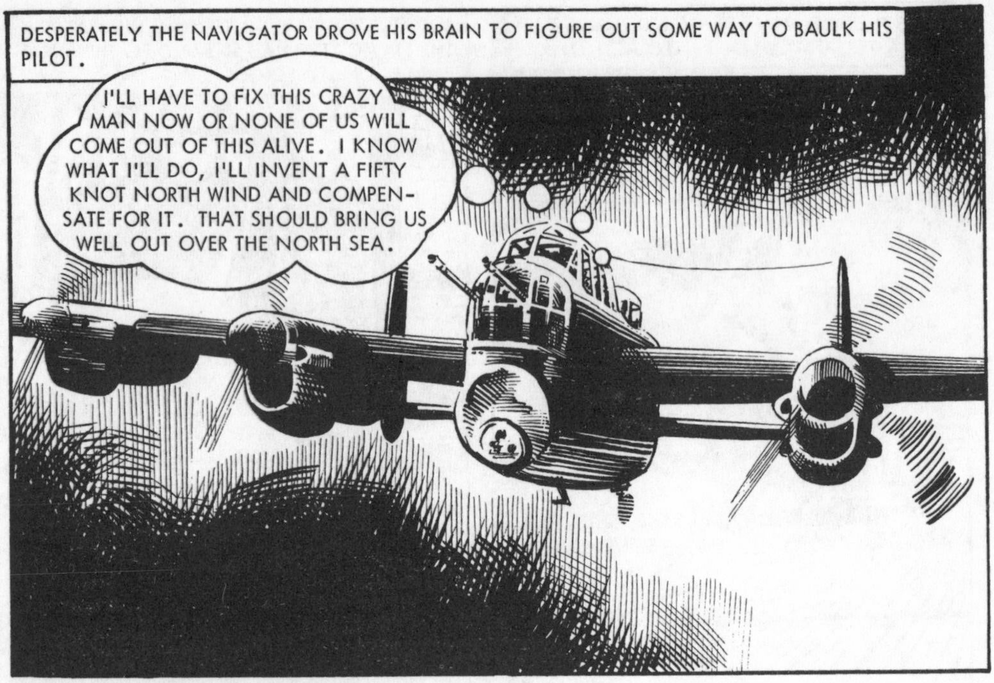
DESPERATELY THE NAVIGATOR DROVE HIS BRAIN TO FIGURE OUT SOME WAY TO BAULK HIS PILOT.
I'LL HAVE TO FIX THIS CRAZY MAN NOW OR NONE OF US WILL COME OUT OF THIS ALIVE. I KNOW WHAT I'LL DO, I'LL INVENT A FIFTY KNOT NORTH WIND AND COMPEN-SATE FOR IT. THAT SHOULD BRING US WELL OUT OVER THE NORTH SEA.

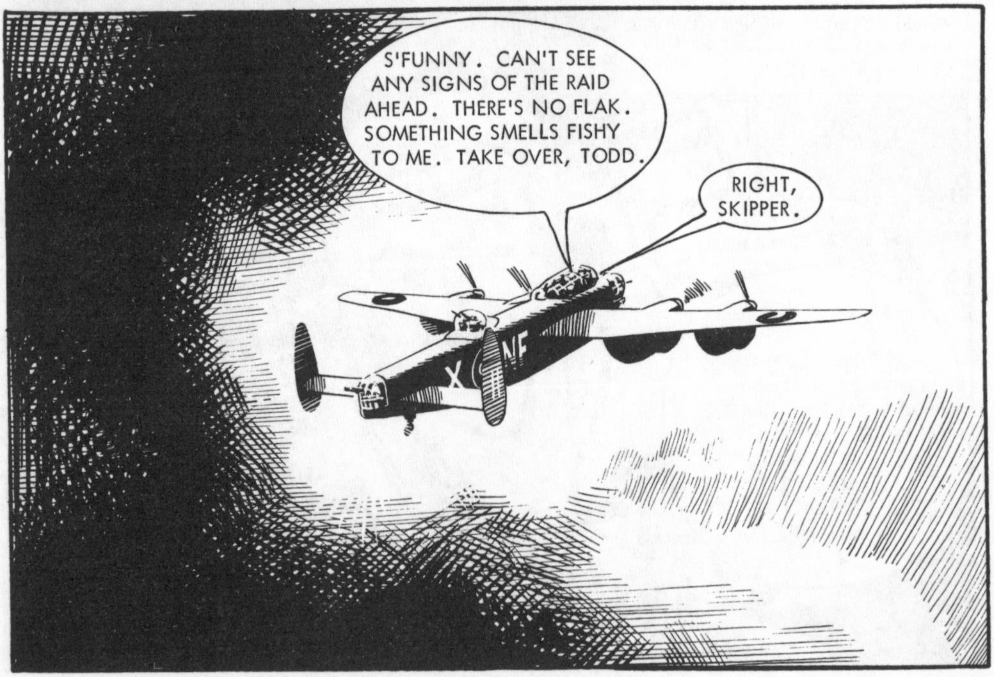
S'FUNNY. CAN'T SEE ANY SIGNS OF THE RAID AHEAD. THERE'S NO FLAK. SOMETHING SMELLS FISHY TO ME. TAKE OVER, TODD.
RIGHT, SKIPPER.
X NF

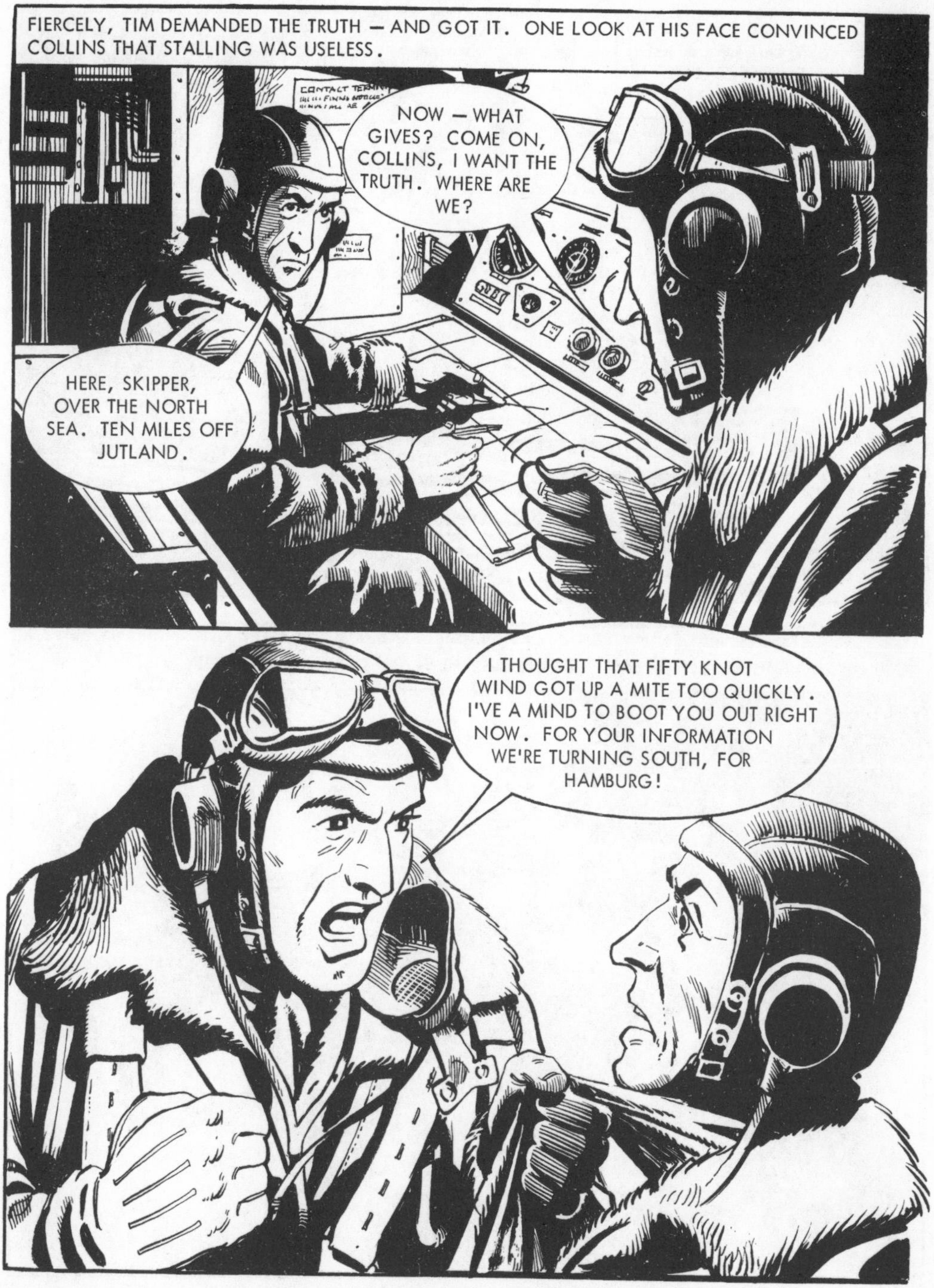
FIERCELY, TIM DEMANDED THE TRUTH — AND GOT IT. ONE LOOK AT HIS FACE CONVINCED COLLINS THAT STALLING WAS USELESS.
NOW — WHAT GIVES? COME ON, COLLINS, I WANT THE TRUTH. WHERE ARE WE?
HERE, SKIPPER, OVER THE NORTH SEA. TEN MILES OFF JUTLAND.
I THOUGHT THAT FIFTY KNOT WIND GOT UP A MITE TOO QUICKLY. I'VE A MIND TO BOOT YOU OUT RIGHT NOW. FOR YOUR INFORMATION WE'RE TURNING SOUTH, FOR HAMBURG!

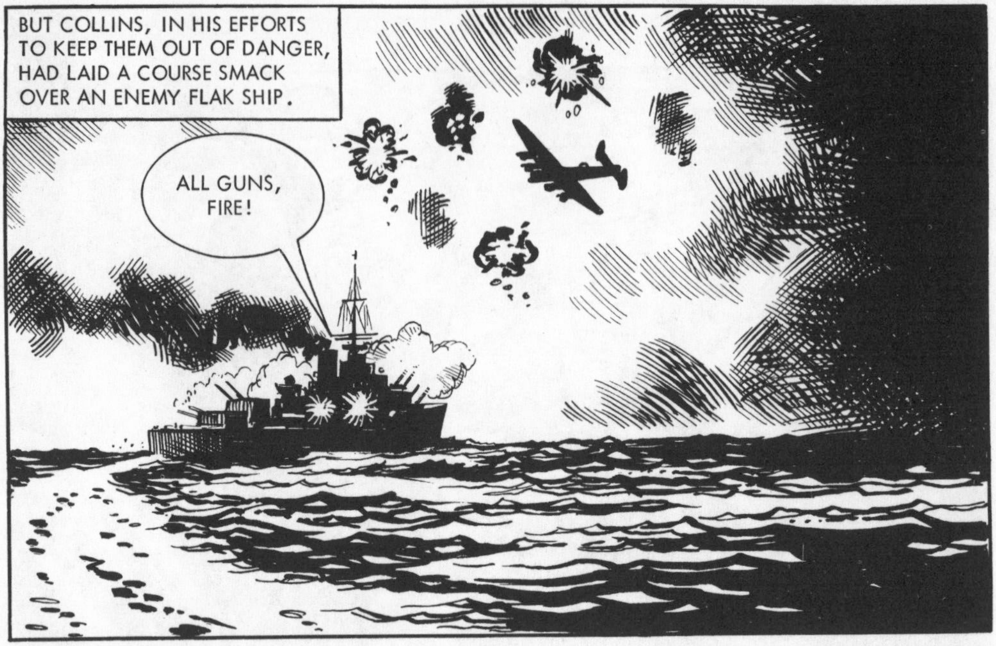
BUT COLLINS, IN HIS EFFORTS TO KEEP THEM OUT OF DANGER, HAD LAID A COURSE SMACK OVER AN ENEMY FLAK SHIP.
ALL GUNS, FIRE!

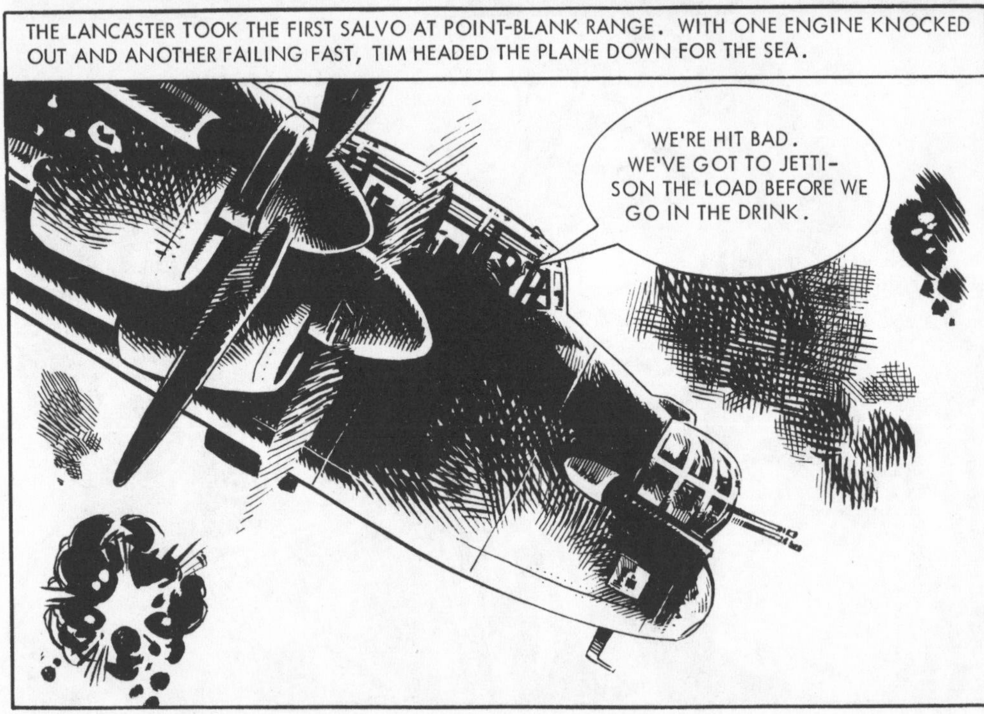
THE LANCASTER TOOK THE FIRST SALVO AT POINT-BLANK RANGE. WITH ONE ENGINE KNOCKED OUT AND ANOTHER FAILING FAST, TIM HEADED THE PLANE DOWN FOR THE SEA.
WE'RE HIT BAD. WE'VE GOT TO JETTI-SON THE LOAD BEFORE WE GO IN THE DRINK.

WITH THE DRAG OF THE PROPELLERS REDUCED BY FEATHERING THE BLADES AND THE DUMPING OF THE BOMB LOAD, THEY REMAINED AIRBORNE — JUST.

WITH A BIT OF LUCK, WE'LL MAKE IT. ANYBODY HURT?

COLLINS — HE'S HIT. I THINK HE'S DEAD!

WHAT HAD KILLED COLLINS WAS A TINY SHELL SPLINTER, PLUMB IN THE CENTRE OF HIS FOREHEAD.

IT'S CRAZY. HE'D MOST LIKELY HAVE MADE IT IF HE HADN'T COOKED OUR COURSE AND WE'D GONE TO HAMBURG. MY REPORT CAN'T HURT HIM NOW — BUT THAT MAKES NO DIFFERENCE, I'LL HAVE TO TELL THE TRUTH.

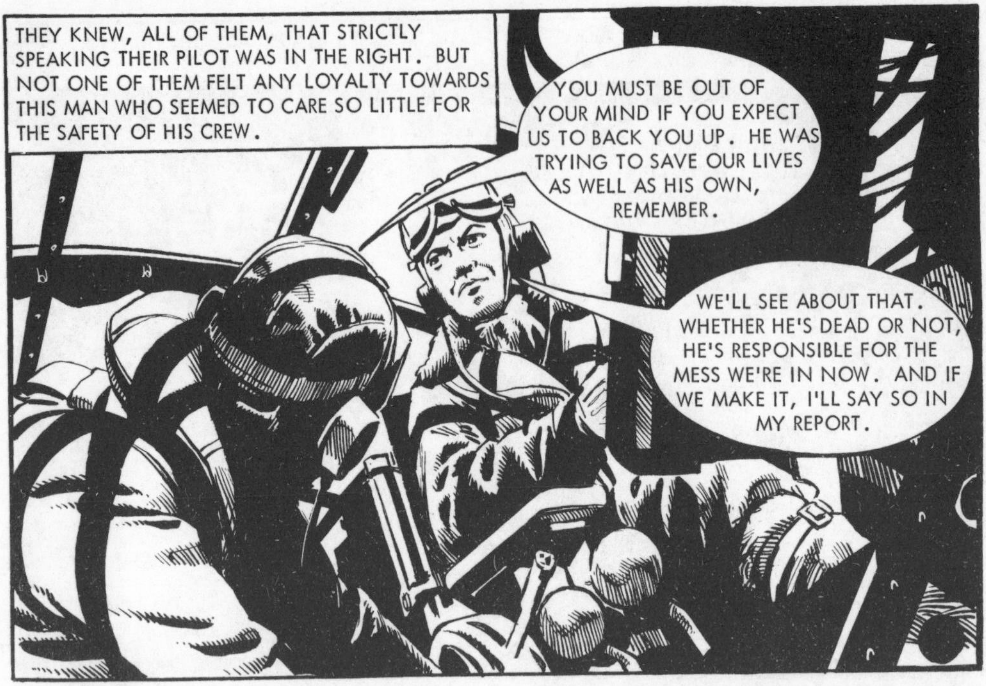
THEY KNEW, ALL OF THEM, THAT STRICTLY SPEAKING THEIR PILOT WAS IN THE RIGHT. BUT NOT ONE OF THEM FELT ANY LOYALTY TOWARDS THIS MAN WHO SEEMED TO CARE SO LITTLE FOR THE SAFETY OF HIS CREW.
YOU MUST BE OUT OF YOUR MIND IF YOU EXPECT US TO BACK YOU UP. HE WAS TRYING TO SAVE OUR LIVES AS WELL AS HIS OWN, REMEMBER.
WE'LL SEE ABOUT THAT. WHETHER HE'S DEAD OR NOT, HE'S RESPONSIBLE FOR THE MESS WE'RE IN NOW. AND IF WE MAKE IT, I'LL SAY SO IN MY REPORT.

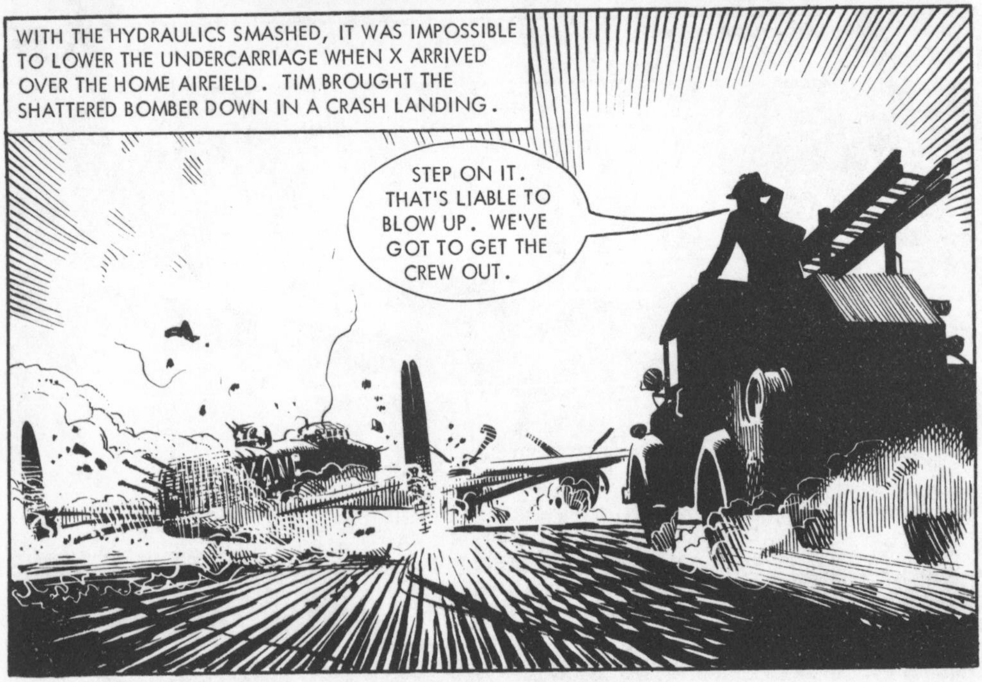
WITH THE HYDRAULICS SMASHED, IT WAS IMPOSSIBLE TO LOWER THE UNDERCARRIAGE WHEN X ARRIVED OVER THE HOME AIRFIELD. TIM BROUGHT THE SHATTERED BOMBER DOWN IN A CRASH LANDING.
STEP ON IT. THAT'S LIABLE TO BLOW UP. WE'VE GOT TO GET THE CREW OUT.

AT DEBRIEFING, THE CREW TOLD THEIR STORY, LEAVING OUT THE VITAL BITS THAT INCRIMINATED THE DEAD NAVIGATOR. THIS GAVE THE IMPRESSION THAT RESPONSIBILITY FOR THE NON-ARRIVAL OF X-RAY OVER THE TARGET LAY SQUARELY ON THE AUSTRALIAN'S SHOULDERS, AND DARCY POUNCED ON IT.

SO, YOU STEERED TEN DEGREES OFF COURSE AND HAD TO JETTISON YOUR BOMBS SIXTY MILES NORTH OF HAMBURG. JUST PICTURE WHAT WOULD HAVE HAPPENED IF ALL THE FOUR HUNDRED AND FIFTY LANCASTERS HAD DUMPED THEIR LOADS IN THE NORTH SEA.

I TELL YOU MY NAVIGATOR GAVE ME THE WRONG COURSE.

TIM LAWLER DROPPED HIS HANDS HELPLESSLY BY HIS SIDES. WITH A HOSTILE CREW AND A VINDICTIVE COMMANDING OFFICER, HE KNEW HE COULD NOT WIN.

TO BLAME A DEAD MAN FOR INCOMPET-ENCE IS CONTEMPTIBLE, LAWLER.

ALL RIGHT, DARCY. CUT THE CACKLE AND GET IT OVER WITH.

ALL RIGHT, LAWLER, HERE IT IS. YOU WILL BE OFF THE STATION IN TWO DAYS' TIME. IN MY OPINION YOUR ATTITUDE MAKES YOU TOTALLY UNFIT FOR FLYING BOMBERS. WE'LL SEE WHAT COASTAL COMMAND OPERATIONS OVER THE NORTH SEA CAN DO FOR YOU. OH, AND DON'T TRY ANY GONG-COLLECTING THERE, THEY'VE GOT NO TIME FOR IT.

STUNNED, TIM RETURNED TO HIS QUARTERS TO PACK. WHAT CHANCE DID HE HAVE OF MAKING A NAME FOR HIMSELF ON THE DREARY ROUTINE PATROLS OF COASTAL COMMAND? HE SMOULDERED WITH RESENTMENT.

HE HAD TO ATTEND A TORPEDO BOMBER CONVERSION COURSE, WHICH WAS EVEN FURTHER REMOVED FROM FIGHTING THE ENEMY — AND WINNING MEDALS.

IT IS IMPORTANT TO STUDY THE CHARACTERISTICS OF ENEMY MERCHANT SHIPS. FOR INSTANCE, THE FAST CARGO CARRIERS OF THE NEPTUNE CLASS HAVE A DISTINCTIVE SQUARE-CUT STERN.

WHAT A WASTE OF TIME. ALL THE GERMAN MERCHANT FLEET'S BOTTLED UP TIGHT BY THE BLOCKADE.

LECTURE FOLLOWED LECTURE. ONLY WHEN TIM SAW THE BEAUFORT TORPEDO BOMBERS WHICH HE WAS TO TRAIN ON DID HIS INTEREST QUICKEN.

MAYBE, IF I'M LUCKY, ONE DAY I MIGHT SEE SOMETHING FLYING THE SWASTIKA FLAG I CAN AIM THESE TIN FISH AT.

RIGHT NOW YOU'VE GOT THE CHANCE TO PRAC-TISE FOR THAT DAY. GET ABOARD, LAWLER. WE'LL SEE WHAT YOU CAN DO.

TRAINEES PRACTISED ON A TARGET SHIP, WITH DUMMY TORPEDOES SET TO RUN JUST UNDER ITS HULL.

WHAT HEIGHT SHALL I DROP IT FROM?

HAVEN'T YOU LISTENED TO WHAT WE'VE BEEN DRUMMING INTO YOU? THIRTY FEET — NO MORE, NO LESS. GOT IT?

THEY FLEW OVER THE NEARBY COASTLINE, AND WHEN TIM SAW THE TARGET HE DROPPED THE RACING BEAUFORT ALMOST TO WAVE-TOP HEIGHT.

TIM PRESSED THE TORPEDO RELEASE BEFORE HE LEVELLED OUT, CAUSING THE TORPEDO TO HIT THE WATER TAIL FIRST. THERE IT BEHAVED EXACTLY LIKE A PORPOISE.

THEY RETURNED TO THE AIRFIELD, TOOK ON ANOTHER TORPEDO AND TOOK OFF AGAIN FOR A FURTHER TRY. AS THE BEAUFORT RACED TOWARDS THE TARGET TIM CHECKED AND RE-CHECKED HEIGHT, TRIM, FLYING ANGLE AND SPEED.

THAT'S BETTER. IT'S A GOOD RUN THIS TIME.

THE TARGET VESSEL FILLED THE TORPEDO SIGHT ON THE BEAUFORT'S WIND-SCREEN AND STILL TIM HELD THE PLANE DOWN.

BLIMEY! THIS GEEZER'S GOING TO HIT US!

PULL UP, LAWLER. PULL UP!

WHEN IT SEEMED NOTHING COULD SAVE THE HURTLING BEAUFORT FROM DESTRUCTION, TIM HAULED BACK ON THE STICK AND THEY CLEARED THE MASTHEAD WITH ONLY INCHES TO SPARE. THE TORPEDO JOLTED AGAINST THE SIDE OF THE TARGET SHIP, THEN SANK SLOWLY TO THE BOTTOM.

I MADE CERTAIN OF IT THAT TIME, SIR.

YOU BLITHERING IDIOT. YOU DARN NEARLY KILLED US BOTH! RETURN TO BASE IMMEDIATELY.

THE INSTRUCTOR BOTTLED UP HIS ANGER UNTIL THE BEAUFORT LANDED. AT TIM'S COMMENTS, HE EXPLODED —

IF THAT SHIP HAD BEEN AN ENEMY DES- TROYER, IT WOULD HAVE BEEN SUNK. I CAN'T UNDERSTAND WHAT YOU'RE BEEFING ABOUT — YOU DON'T WIN MEDALS BY BEING CAUTIOUS.

MEDALS? FOR HEAVEN'S SAKE, MAN, IF THAT HAD BEEN AN ENEMY SHIP THE ONLY CROSS YOU'D HAVE WOULD BE THE ONE ON YOUR GRAVE — IF THEY COULD FIND ENOUGH PIECES OF YOU TO BURY. AS FOR SINKING A SHIP, YOU'RE 'WAY OFF THE BEAM. THE TORPEDO HAS TO RUN FOR TWO HUNDRED YARDS BEFORE IT'S LIVE.

HOWEVER, THE INSTRUCTORS WERE PATIENT MEN, AND THEY SUCCEEDED IN MAKING A FAIR TORPEDO PILOT OUT OF TIM LAWLER. BUT ALL AGREED HIS FUTURE PROSPECTS WERE GLOOMY.

THERE'S ONE MAN I RECKON WILL BE LUCKY IF HE LASTS FOR THREE TORPEDO STRIKES. THAT AUSSIE, LAWLER.

HE'S GOT A TWIST THAT ONE. I CAN'T QUITE GET HIS ANGLE. HE'S AFTER THE GLORY ALL RIGHT, BUT THE SAFETY OF HIS CREW, EVEN THE SUCCESS OF THE OPERATION, ARE UN-IMPORTANT TO HIM. IT'S ALL DOWN IN HIS RECORDS.

TIM WAS SENT TO A BLEAK, ISOLATED AIRFIELD IN THE NORTH OF SCOTLAND.

BRR! THAT WIND WOULD TAKE THE SKIN OFF YOUR NOSE. AND TO THINK IT'S ABOUT A HUN-DRED DEGREES IN THE SHADE IN MELBOURNE.

BUT THEN HE FORGOT THE COLD AS HE REALISED WHAT HE WAS LOOKING AT. IT PACKED A KNOCK-OUT PUNCH IN THE SHAPE OF FOUR MASSIVE CANNONS BENEATH ITS BELLY AND SIX MACHINE GUNS IN ITS WINGS. AND SLUNG BELOW, A 2000lb AIR TORPEDO. IT WAS A TORPEDO-CARRYING BEAUFIGHTER KNOWN AS THE TORBEAU, THE MOST FORMIDABLE STRIKE AIRCRAFT OF THE WAR...

PHEW! WILL YOU JUST LOOK AT THAT!

YES, SIR. SHE'S A BEAUTY ALL RIGHT. MY NAME'S CLIFFORD CONWAY, BY THE WAY. I JUST GOT HERE THIS MORNING. THEY TELL ME YOU'RE MY PILOT.

TIM TORE HIS AWED GAZE FROM THE PLANE AND HIS EYES FLICKED OVER CONWAY'S UNIFORM. THE FLYING BADGE HAD LONG SINCE LOST ITS NEW GLEAM, WHICH TOLD THAT THIS MAN HAD FLOWN MANY HOURS — BUT HE ALSO NOTED THAT THERE WERE NO MEDAL RIBBONS.

GLAD TO KNOW YOU, CONWAY. I RECKON WE SHOULD GET ON PRETTY WELL AS A CREW.

HAVE YOU BEEN ON OPS BEFORE, SIR?

TOO RIGHT I HAVE. LANCASTERS. I HAD A LOUSY CREW SO I CAN'T SAY I WAS SORRY TO LEAVE 'EM. ONE THING I INSIST ON — THE DRIVER'S THE MAN IN CHARGE. THEY DIDN'T APPROVE.

I GET THE MESSAGE. I WON'T LET YOU DOWN.

MEANWHILE THE COMMANDING OFFICER, SQUADRON LEADER OLIVER, WAS DISCUSSING THE NEW ARRIVALS WITH FLIGHT LIEUTENANT DERRY, HIS ADJUTANT.

I HESITATE ENTRUSTING A GOOD MAN LIKE CONWAY TO THIS LAWLER. HIS FLYING RECORD'S A SHOCKER, BUT WE'RE DESPERATELY SHORT OF PILOTS.

MAYBE CONWAY COULD STRAIGHTEN HIM OUT A BIT.

THE DANGEROUS TRADE OF TORPEDO BOMBING CALLED FOR STEADINESS AND FLYING DISCIPLINE OF A HIGH ORDER — A PILOT WHO LACKED THESE WAS A DANGER TO HIMSELF AND THE MAN WHO FLEW WITH HIM. TIM LAWLER'S CONFIDENTIAL RECORDS MADE IT CLEAR TO OLIVER THAT SENDING THIS MAN ON A TORPEDO STRIKE WOULD BE LIKE CONDEMNING HIM TO DEATH.

THEY CAN DO BLOCKADE PATROLS FOR A WEEK OR TWO — LAWLER CAN'T VERY WELL GET INTO TROUBLE ON THAT STINT. MAYBE CONWAY WILL HAVE SOME STEADYING INFLUENCE ON HIM, AND IF HE BECOMES A NICE DOCILE LITTLE LAD I'LL LET HIM GO ON TORPEDO STRIKES.

AND SO, AFTER A QUICK CONVERSION COURSE, TIM STARTED HIS NEW JOB. THE BRITISH NAVY AND R.A.F. COASTAL COMMAND THROUGHOUT THE WAR BLOCKADED THE ATLANTIC AND THE NORTH SEA SO EFFECTIVELY THAT SEABORNE SUPPLIES WERE COMPLETELY DENIED TO THE ENEMY. ONE PART OF THE VAST OPERATION WAS CONTINUOUS PATROLLING OF THE NORTH SEA BY THE TORBEAUS OF COASTAL COMMAND.

NOT A SIGHTING FOR DAYS. WE'RE THE ONLY ONES WHO ARE STUPID ENOUGH TO COME OUT IN THIS LOT.

THESE WERE ARDUOUS DUTIES BECAUSE THE CREWS HAD TO FLY THROUGH THE WORST WEATHER CONDITIONS, AND MONOTONOUS BECAUSE TENS OF THOUSANDS OF MILES WERE FLOWN WITHOUT ANYTHING BEING SEEN.

IN THE FOLLOWING WEEKS, THE DULL MONOTONY OF THESE PATROLS HAD THEIR IRRITABLE EFFECT ON A MAN OF TIM LAWLER'S OUTLOOK. HE BECAME MOROSE AND SNAPPY FROM SHEER BOREDOM.

WELL WELL, THERE'S THE NORWEGIAN COAST AGAIN. NOW ISN'T THAT EXCITING? JUST WHERE IT WAS YESTERDAY, AND THE DAY BEFORE THAT, AND THE DAY BEFORE THAT...

OCCASIONALLY THEY DID CONVOY ESCORT WORK, BUT EVEN THEN THEY SAW NO ACTION.

AT LEAST WE AREN'T CARRYING OUR TORPEDO AROUND ON THIS JOB.

SO WHAT? WE NEVER GET THE CHANCE TO DROP ONE ANY-WAY.

ONE MORNING THERE WAS TENSE EXCITEMENT IN THE AIR. A SUNDERLAND HAD SIGHTED A GERMAN CONVOY OF TEN SHIPS HEADING NORTH THROUGH THE SKAGERRAK. THE TORBEAU CREWS WERE BRIEFED TO MAKE A STRIKE — ALL EXCEPT TIM AND CLIFF.

LOOK AT THAT — WE'RE STUCK WITH THE PATROL AGAIN. I RECKON WE'RE LONG OVERDUE FOR A TURN AT STRIKE OPERATION. IF THINGS GO ON LIKE THIS, I'LL BE THE FIRST LAWLER IN NEARLY A HUNDRED YEARS WHO DIDN'T BRING BACK A MEDAL.

CONVOY STRIKE
TAKE OFF 11·00 HRS
R AREA. PATROL :-
LAWLER & CONWAY
A PATROL :-
PSON & WARD.
PATROL :-
MANN & PET
ALL REPORTS
ELLIGENCE OF

CLIFF SAID NOTHING AS THE PLANE BORED INTO THE MIST BANKS THAT BLEW IN OVER THE BLEAK COASTLINE. HE KNEW THAT ANY COMMENT WOULD PROBABLY RESULT IN SOME TESTY REPLY.

I CAN'T BLAME HIM. FOR SOME REASON WE DO SEEM TO BE GETTING LEFT OUT OF THINGS.

BUT THIS TIME THEY SAW SOMETHING. IT WAS HALF WAY ACROSS THE NORTH SEA...

SHIPS, DEAD AHEAD. I CAN'T IDENTIFY.

WE'LL JUST HAVE A LOOK.

IT WAS A FLOTILLA OF THREE BRITISH DESTROYERS ON A SPECIAL ANTI-SUBMARINE PATROL.

IT'S ONE OF OURS, NUMBER ONE. TELL GUNS TO SHOOT UP THE DAY'S COLOURS.

AYE, AYE, SIR.

USUALLY, FLARES WERE FIRED, A DIFFERENT COLOUR FOR EACH DAY IN ORDER THAT FLYERS WOULD BE ABLE TO IDENTIFY FRIENDLY SHIPS. BECAUSE OF THE MIST, THE FLOTILLA COMMANDER HAD DECIDED TO USE EXTRA-BRIGHT STAR SHELLS INSTEAD.

THERE WAS NO ANXIETY ABOARD THE DESTROYER, NOR ANY REASON FOR IT. THESE PATROLLING FLIERS WERE EXPERT AT SHIP RECOGNITION AND ALL SERVICE UNITS IN THE AREA WERE INFORMED AT MIDNIGHT OF THE COLOURS FOR THE FOLLOWING DAY.

BUT ON THIS OCCASION, BAD VISIBILITY OBSCURED THE BURSTING SHELL FROM THE TORBEAU'S CREW, BUT NOT THE FLASH OF THE GUN THAT FIRED IT.

THEY'RE FIRING AT US. THAT SETTLES IT, THEY'RE GERMAN. MOST LIKELY HEADING SOUTH TO TAKE OVER ESCORT OF THAT CONVOY THAT WAS SIGHTED. BY THUNDER — ACTION AT LAST!

WAIT, SKIPPER. MAKE CERTAIN FIRST.

A HAIL OF CANNON SHELLS SLASHED TOWARDS THE MIST-ENSHROUDED FLOTILLA LEADER.

IF I WASTE TIME FLYING AROUND UNTIL YOU MAKE UP YOUR MIND, WE'LL LOSE 'EM IN THE MIST. I'M GOING AFTER THAT FLOTILLA LEADER NOW AND PUT THE TORPEDO WHERE IT HURTS MOST. SHOULD BE GOOD FOR A D.F.C. AT LEAST.

THE DESTROYERS TOOK EVASIVE ACTION, ALDIS LAMPS FLASHED AND CREWS CURSED AS THE RACING TORBEAU LEVELLED OFF.

THE FOOL'S SOFTENING US UP FOR A TORPEDO ATTACK. STAND BY, GUNNERS — DON'T FIRE UNLESS I GIVE THE ORDER. 'B' TURRET GUN RELOAD WITH STAR-SHELL. SHOOT IT CLOSE TO HIM — IF IT HITS HIM IT'S HIS OWN STUPID FAULT.

AYE AYE, SIR!

FINGERS HOVERED ON FIRING BUTTONS AND THE TENSION MOUNTED. ANY SECOND NOW...

SO HELP ME, I'LL BLAST YOU OUT OF THE SKY AS SOON AS THE SKIPPER GIVES THE WORD, FLY-BOY!

TIM'S FINGER TIGHTENED ON THE TORPEDO RELEASE BUTTON...

ANOTHER FOUR SECONDS...

I DON'T LIKE THIS. NO OPPOSITION!

WITH TWO SECONDS TO GO, A BRILLIANT GREEN AND RED EXPLOSION BLINDED THEM BOTH AND THE BLAST ROCKED THE AIRCRAFT VIOLENTLY, AS THE STAR-SHELL EXPLODED JUST FIVE YARDS AHEAD AND TO ONE SIDE.

BREAK OFF, FOR HEAVEN'S SAKE, MAN. IT'S THE COLOURS OF THE DAY. THEY'RE OURS!

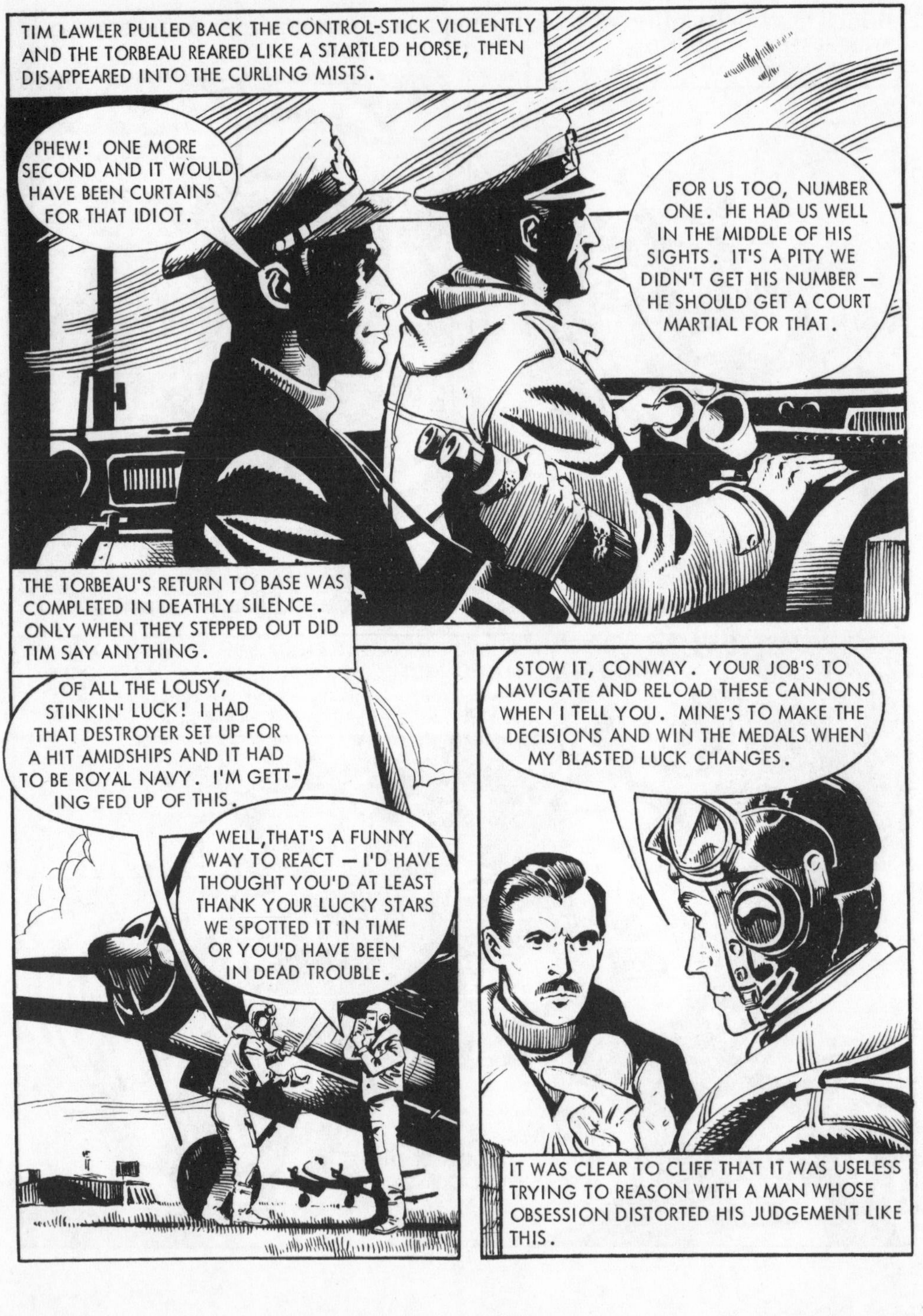
TIM LAWLER PULLED BACK THE CONTROL-STICK VIOLENTLY AND THE TORBEAU REARED LIKE A STARTLED HORSE, THEN DISAPPEARED INTO THE CURLING MISTS.
PHEW! ONE MORE SECOND AND IT WOULD HAVE BEEN CURTAINS FOR THAT IDIOT.
FOR US TOO, NUMBER ONE. HE HAD US WELL IN THE MIDDLE OF HIS SIGHTS. IT'S A PITY WE DIDN'T GET HIS NUMBER — HE SHOULD GET A COURT MARTIAL FOR THAT.
THE TORBEAU'S RETURN TO BASE WAS COMPLETED IN DEATHLY SILENCE. ONLY WHEN THEY STEPPED OUT DID TIM SAY ANYTHING.
OF ALL THE LOUSY, STINKIN' LUCK! I HAD THAT DESTROYER SET UP FOR A HIT AMIDSHIPS AND IT HAD TO BE ROYAL NAVY. I'M GETT-ING FED UP OF THIS.
WELL,THAT'S A FUNNY WAY TO REACT — I'D HAVE THOUGHT YOU'D AT LEAST THANK YOUR LUCKY STARS WE SPOTTED IT IN TIME OR YOU'D HAVE BEEN IN DEAD TROUBLE.
STOW IT, CONWAY. YOUR JOB'S TO NAVIGATE AND RELOAD THESE CANNONS WHEN I TELL YOU. MINE'S TO MAKE THE DECISIONS AND WIN THE MEDALS WHEN MY BLASTED LUCK CHANGES.
IT WAS CLEAR TO CLIFF THAT IT WAS USELESS TRYING TO REASON WITH A MAN WHOSE OBSESSION DISTORTED HIS JUDGEMENT LIKE THIS.

A COUPLE OF NIGHTS LATER, TIM, OFF DUTY, WALKED THE BLACKED-OUT STREETS OF THE NEARBY TOWN, WHICH WAS ALSO A NAVAL PORT, FED UP WITH THE SQUADRON AND THE LUCK THAT DOGGED HIM.

I'LL GET A CUP OF COFFEE AND THEN GET BACK TO CAMP.

AS HE WAITED IN THE QUEUE, HE COULDN'T AVOID OVERHEARING THE REMARKS OF A GROUP OF SAILORS IN FRONT OF HIM.

...SOME IDIOT PILOT CAME AT US WITHOUT WARNING, AND OPENED FIRE. I DIDN'T LIKE THE LOOK OF HIS TORPEDO EITHER.

STUPID NIT. SOME OF THOSE FLY-BOYS WANT THEIR EYES TESTED.

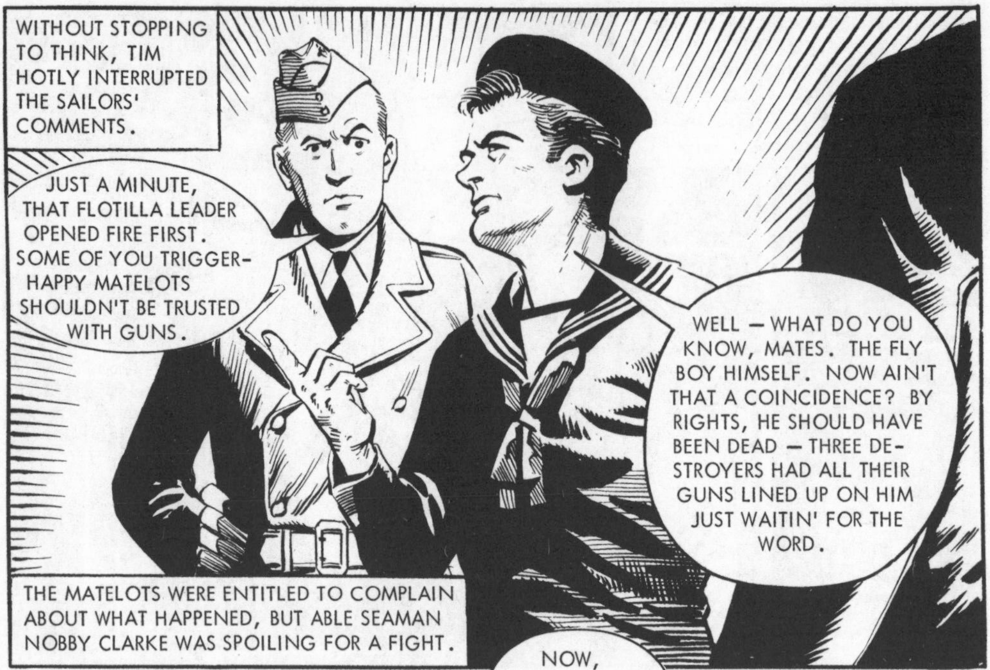
WITHOUT STOPPING TO THINK, TIM HOTLY INTERRUPTED THE SAILORS' COMMENTS.
JUST A MINUTE, THAT FLOTILLA LEADER OPENED FIRE FIRST. SOME OF YOU TRIGGER-HAPPY MATELOTS SHOULDN'T BE TRUSTED WITH GUNS.
WELL – WHAT DO YOU KNOW, MATES. THE FLY BOY HIMSELF. NOW AIN'T THAT A COINCIDENCE? BY RIGHTS, HE SHOULD HAVE BEEN DEAD – THREE DE-STROYERS HAD ALL THEIR GUNS LINED UP ON HIM JUST WAITIN' FOR THE WORD.
THE MATELOTS WERE ENTITLED TO COMPLAIN ABOUT WHAT HAPPENED, BUT ABLE SEAMAN NOBBY CLARKE WAS SPOILING FOR A FIGHT.

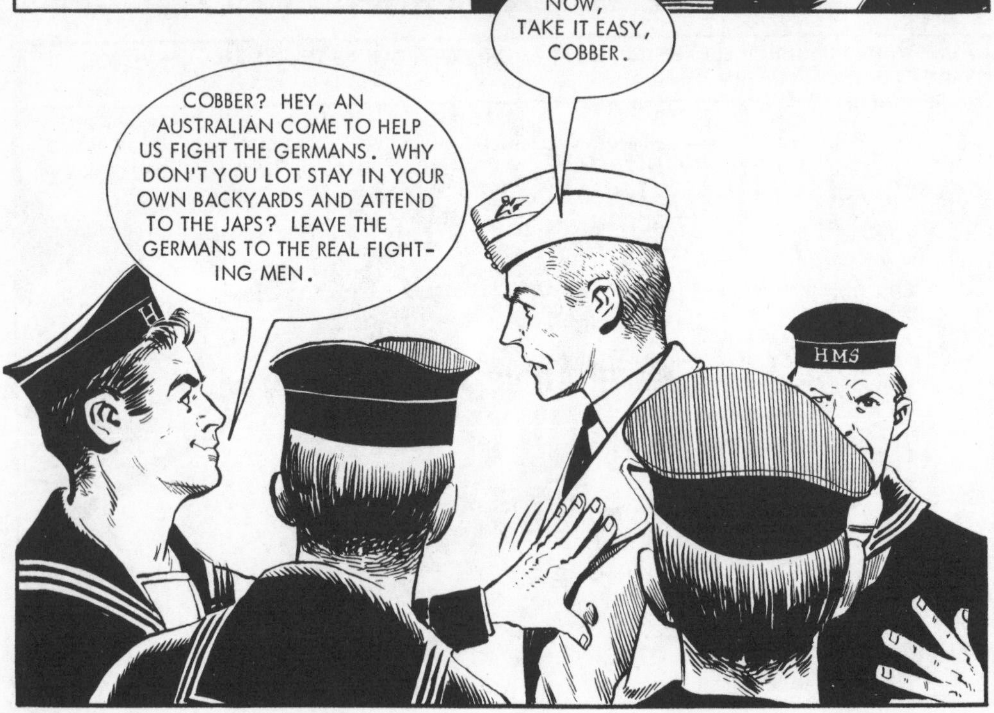
NOW, TAKE IT EASY, COBBER.
COBBER? HEY, AN AUSTRALIAN COME TO HELP US FIGHT THE GERMANS. WHY DON'T YOU LOT STAY IN YOUR OWN BACKYARDS AND ATTEND TO THE JAPS? LEAVE THE GERMANS TO THE REAL FIGHT-ING MEN.
HMS

AS THE MATELOT CONTINUED TO PUSH HIM ABOUT, TIM'S TEMPER FLARED.

DON'T PUSH ME AROUND, COBBER, OR —

OR WHAT, FLY-BOY?

WITH A CRACK THAT COULD BE HEARD OVER THE WHOLE CANTEEN TIM FLOORED THE SAILOR WITH A SLASHING RIGHT CROSS.

OR THIS!

UGH!

HEY, YOU DON'T GET AWAY WITH THAT, CHUM!

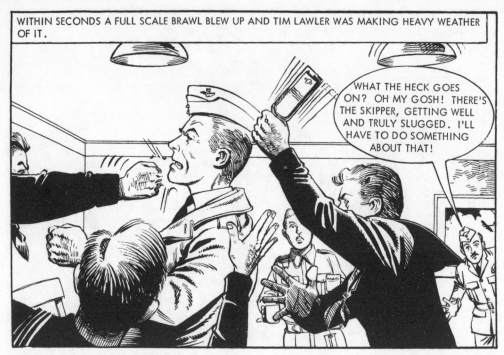

WITHIN SECONDS A FULL SCALE BRAWL BLEW UP AND TIM LAWLER WAS MAKING HEAVY WEATHER OF IT.

WHAT THE HECK GOES ON? OH MY GOSH! THERE'S THE SKIPPER, GETTING WELL AND TRULY SLUGGED. I'LL HAVE TO DO SOMETHING ABOUT THAT!

CLIFF WADED IN LIKE A TORNADO.

BREAK IT UP THERE!

LOOK OUT! SHORE PATROL!

CLIFF HAD TO GET HIS PILOT AWAY BEFORE THE SERVICE POLICE GOT TO HIM. IF HE WAS CAUGHT IT WOULD MEAN A COURT MARTIAL.

WE'VE GOT TO GET OUT OF HERE FAST. R.A.F. OFFICERS DON'T BRAWL WITH MATELOTS. IF YOU'RE CAUGHT, YOU'RE IN BIG TROUBLE! COME ON — THIS WAY.

FIRE EXIT

LUCK WAS ON THEIR SIDE. THEY GOT CLEAR AWAY AND KEPT ON GOING, HEADING FOR THE AIRFIELD WHICH WAS ON THE OUTSKIRTS OF THE TOWN.

I CAN'T THANK YOU ENOUGH FOR WHAT YOU DID. YOU'RE A REAL COBBER AND A DARN GOOD OBSERVER AT THAT — ONLY I WAS TOO DIM TO REALISE IT.

OH, WRAP IT UP, SIR.

CLIFF CONWAY'S CONCERN FOR HIS SKIPPER MADE TIM FEEL ASHAMED OF THE CHURLISH WAY HE'D TREATED HIM.

AND YOU CAN DROP THE 'SIR'. THINGS ARE GOING TO BE DIFFERENT FROM NOW ON, CLIFF. WE'RE A TEAM.

MEANWHILE, SOMEWHERE BETWEEN THE SHETLANDS AND NORWAY, A LARGE, FAST MERCHANT SHIP, THE LUBECK, RACED SOUTHWARDS. SHE HAD COME A LONG WAY — FROM JAPAN, DODGING ALLIED NAVAL PATROLS AND KEEPING WELL OFF THE SHIPPING ROUTES. SHE WAS CRAMMED TO THE HATCHES WITH VALUABLE MINERALS VITAL TO GERMANY'S WAR MACHINE.

CLEVERLY CAMOUFLAGED WITH WOODEN BOARDING AND FLYING THE STARS AND STRIPES, THE LUBECK WAS AN EXACT COPY OF AN AMERICAN CARGO LINER. HIDDEN AWAY BEHIND THE DISGUISE WERE POWERFUL BATTERIES OF FLAK GUNS OF ALL CALIBRES — JUST IN CASE.

NOW, ON THE MOST HAZARDOUS PART OF THE JOURNEY, THE LAST FEW HUNDRED MILES, A BLANKET OF SLEET AND DRIVING MIST HAD CLOSED DOWN. IT LOOKED AS IF SHE WAS GOING TO MAKE IT.

NOT LONG NOW, HERR KAPITÄN. AND THE WEATHER IS ON OUR SIDE. WHAT A RE-CEPTION THERE WILL BE WHEN WE ENTER THE INNER HARBOUR AT KIEL! THE FUEHRER WILL BE THERE.

JA, HORSTMANN. WE HAVE ENOUGH TUNG-STEN, MERCURY ORE, COPPER, AND MOLYBDENUM IN OUR HOLDS TO KEEP THE WAR MACHINE WELL SUPPLIED.

BACK AT THE R.A.F. BASE, TIM AND CLIFF WERE MAKING READY TO TAKE OFF ON ANOTHER ROUTINE PATROL WHEN...

JUST A MOMENT, CONWAY. A WORD WITH YOU.

I TOLD YOU BEFORE, CONWAY, YOU MUST WEAR THAT MEDAL RIBBON — YOU'VE NO OPTION. REGULATIONS SAY SO. NOW, WHEN YOU RETURN YOU WILL GET IT SEWN INTO PLACE. IS THAT CLEAR?

IT WAS THE WORD 'MEDAL' THAT MADE TIM PRICK UP HIS EARS.

WHAT WAS THAT ABOUT A MEDAL RIBBON? HAVE YOU GOT A MEDAL?

WELL, ACTUALLY, I HAVE. I'VE GOT YOUR COURSE WORKED OUT — WANT IT NOW?

TIM KNEW HIS OBSERVER WAS RELUCTANT TO TALK, BUT HE KEPT PRESSING HIM.

COME ON, CLIFF, SPILL IT. WHAT'S THE MEDAL?

IT'S — IT'S THE VICTORIA CROSS, ACTUALLY. IT WAS THE BIGGEST SURPRISE OF MY LIFE WHEN THEY GAVE ME IT. I WAS ON A STRIKE AGAINST DESTROYERS OFF THE DUTCH COAST. WE TOOK A BEATING AND WENT ON FIRE. I PUT IT OUT — THAT'S ALL. NOW HERE'S YOUR COURSE, SKIPPER.

AS THE GREAT ENGINES THUNDERED ON EACH SIDE OF HIM, TIM LAWLER TOOK A LONG, COOL LOOK AT HIMSELF...

THEY DON'T GIVE V.C.'S JUST FOR PUTTING FIRES OUT. MY STARS! THE TOP AWARD FOR COURAGE AND HE WANTS TO KEEP IT DARK! MAKES ME FEEL ASHAMED WHEN I THINK OF THE WAY I WENT ON ABOUT GETTING A MEDAL. NO WONDER NO-BODY COULD STAND ME, BINDING ABOUT IT ALL THE TIME.

TIM DECIDED IT WAS TIME HE CHANGED — HIGH TIME!

THAT'S WHY I ALMOST TORPEDOED THAT DESTROYER. ALL I WAS THINKING ABOUT WAS GETTING A GONG. IDENTIFICATION OF THE TARGET I NEVER EVEN CONSIDERED. RIGHT, TIM LAWLER, YOU'RE IN THE R.A.F. TO DO A JOB — GET ON WITH IT!

THEY CARRIED OUT THE USUAL SEARCH PROCEEDURE, THEN IT WAS TIME TO RETURN TO BASE. IT LOOKED LIKE ONE MORE UNEVENTFUL PATROL.

TURNING POINT NOW, SKIPPER. COURSE TO BASE IS TWO-SEVEN-THREE DEGREES.

OK, CLIFF. NOTHING ON THE SLATE AGAIN TODAY.

SUDDENLY, THROUGH THE MIST, TIM CAUGHT SIGHT OF THE DARK SHAPE OF THE LUBECK.

LOOK, CLIFF. A SHIP, DEAD AHEAD. A BIG ONE.

EVERYTHING APPEARED TO BE IN ORDER.

SHE'S FLYING THE STARS AND STRIPES. JUDGING BY HER SILHOUETTE I'D SAY SHE'S ONE OF THESE BIG CARGO LINERS USED BY THE AMERICAN EXPORT LINES. CARRYING SOME TROOPS TOO, SHE IS. THEY'RE SO FAST THEY SEND THEM ACROSS WITHOUT AN ESCORT.

SHE'S FLASHING A MESSAGE. "HIYA LIMEY! SOME MORE G.I.s COMING TO WIN THE WAR FOR YOU!"

WITH TYPICAL TEUTONIC EFFICIENCY, THE GERMANS HAD CAMOUFLAGED THE SHIP DOWN TO THE SMALLEST DETAIL.

AN EXCELLENT IDEA OF YOURS, HORSTMANN, TO HAVE THE CREW LINING THE RAILS WEARING AMERICAN STEEL HELMETS!

CHEEKY DEVILS! WE'LL GIVE 'EM A LOW PASS THEN HEAD FOR HOME. THE FUEL'S GETTING LOW.

THE TORBEAU RACED ACROSS THE WATER AT AN ALTITUDE OF TWENTY FEET.

AT LEAST THEY'VE BROKEN THE MONOTONY FOR US.

THEY TURNED FOR HOME. BUT THEN A VAGUE SUS-PICION BEGAN TO NIGGLE AWAY AT THE BACK OF TIM'S MIND.

IT ISN'T USUAL FOR A YANK FREIGHTER TO BE SAILING DOWN THE MIDDLE OF THE NORTH SEA. THEY DIDN'T WARN US TO LOOK OUT FOR HER. I WONDER...? I'M GOING BACK FOR ANOTHER LOOK.

OK, SKIPPER. BUT YOU SAID THE FUEL WAS A BIT LOW, REMEMBER.

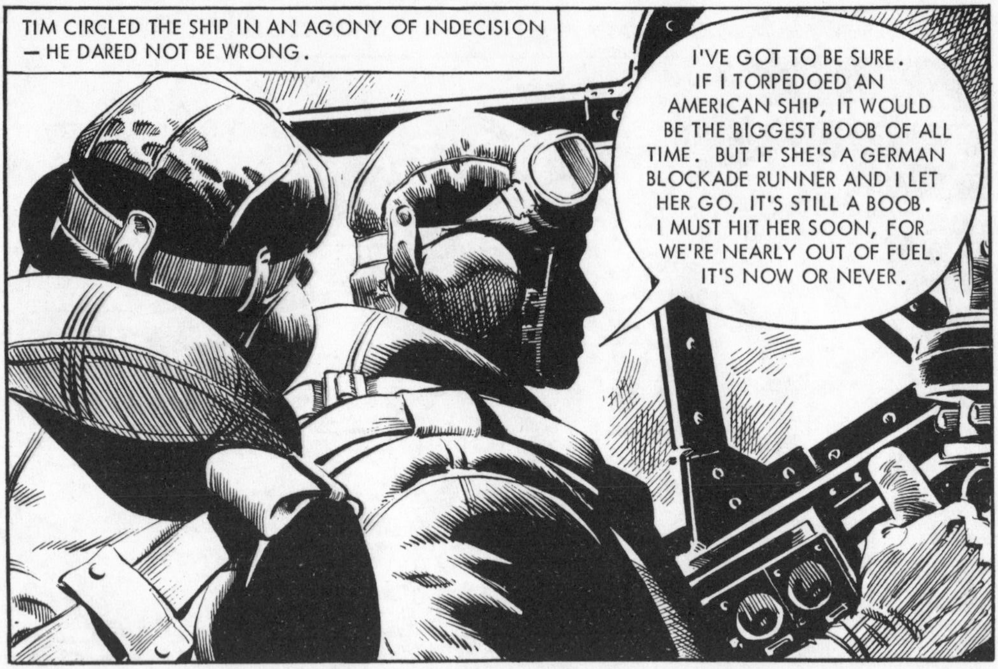
TIM CIRCLED THE SHIP IN AN AGONY OF INDECISION – HE DARED NOT BE WRONG.
I'VE GOT TO BE SURE. IF I TORPEDOED AN AMERICAN SHIP, IT WOULD BE THE BIGGEST BOOB OF ALL TIME. BUT IF SHE'S A GERMAN BLOCKADE RUNNER AND I LET HER GO, IT'S STILL A BOOB. I MUST HIT HER SOON, FOR WE'RE NEARLY OUT OF FUEL. IT'S NOW OR NEVER.

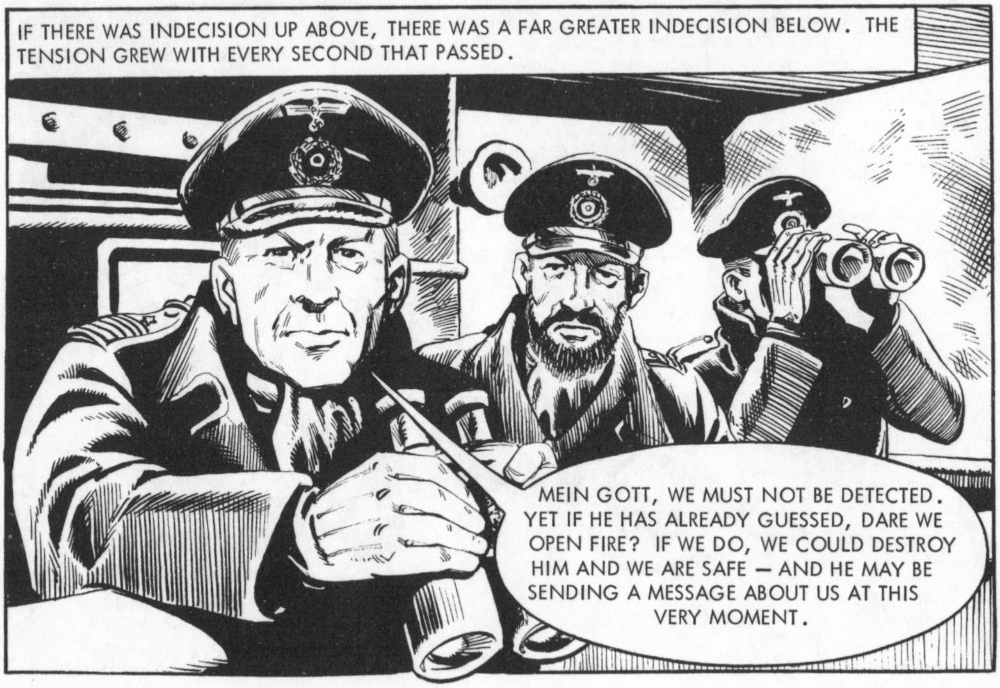
IF THERE WAS INDECISION UP ABOVE, THERE WAS A FAR GREATER INDECISION BELOW. THE TENSION GREW WITH EVERY SECOND THAT PASSED.
MEIN GOTT, WE MUST NOT BE DETECTED. YET IF HE HAS ALREADY GUESSED, DARE WE OPEN FIRE? IF WE DO, WE COULD DESTROY HIM AND WE ARE SAFE – AND HE MAY BE SENDING A MESSAGE ABOUT US AT THIS VERY MOMENT.

THEN THE DECISION WAS TAKEN OUT OF THE CAPTAIN'S HANDS. A GUNNER, NERVOUS AFTER WEEKS OF DANGER, LOST HIS HEAD. ONE OF THE FLAK BATTERIES SHED ITS CAMOUFLAGE AND POURED A DEVASTATING BLAST OF FIRE AT THE TORBEAU.

WE CANNOT MISS — FEUER!

THE SPEEDING TORBEAU STAGGERED AS A HAIL OF FLYING METAL TRANSFIXED IT. TIM FELT A SEARING PAIN IN HIS SHOULDER, AND THEN A WAVE OF DIZZINESS.

AAAH!

A SUDDEN WEAKNESS CLOUDED HIS MIND AS HE FELT BLOOD RUNNING DOWN HIS CHEST BUT THROUGH THE WEAKNESS CAME ONE CLEAR THOUGHT. SINK THIS SHIP, AT ALL COSTS!

SKIPPER, YOU'RE HIT!

I'M ALL — ALL RIGHT. JUST A SPLINTER IN THE SHOULDER. GOT TO GET THAT SHIP OR — OR SHE'LL ESCAPE IN THE MIST. I'M GOING T-TO ATTACK!

TIM BANKED AND CAME IN AT THE SHIP, HIS CANNONS AND MACHINE-GUNS LOOSING OFF A SOLID HAIL OF FIRE.

AAAAH!

THEN HE WAS OVER THE SHIP AND AWAY. SHAKING HIS HEAD TO CLEAR THE GROGGINESS, HE SWUNG ROUND AGAIN TO TURN AND COME BACK ON HIS TORPEDO-RUN.

THE PLANE SHUDDERED TO THE IMPACT OF MURDEROUS FIRE FROM THE LUBECK. WITH IMPLACABLE COURAGE TIM FOUGHT OFF THE WAVES OF PAIN TO HOLD THE TORBEAU FLAT AND LEVEL IN A PERFECT RUN-IN TO THE TARGET. AND THEN —

FRANTICALLY THE CAPTAIN TRIED TO DODGE, BUT DOOM WAS APPROACHING FAST AND SURE, AND THERE WAS NOTHING HE COULD DO ABOUT IT.

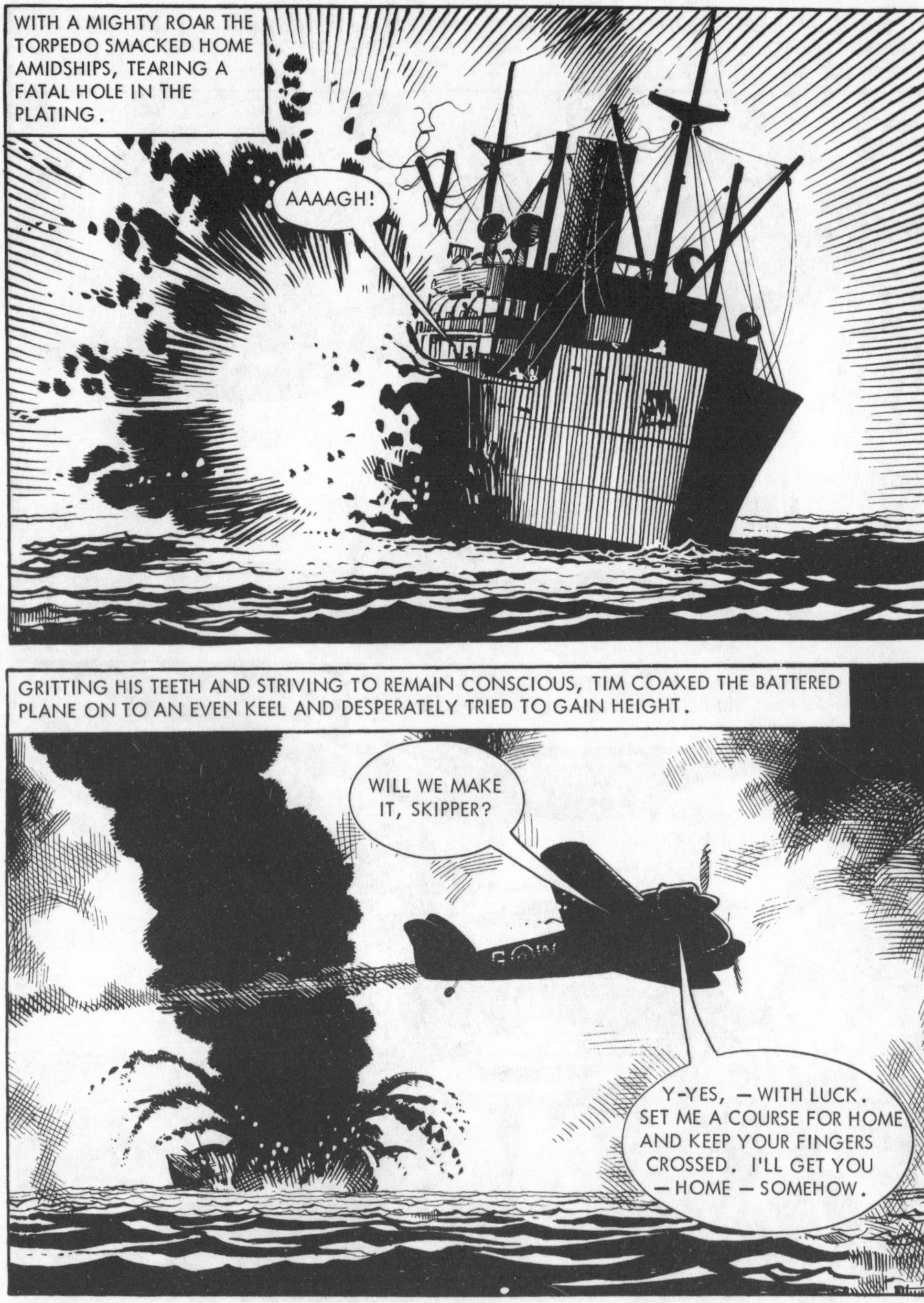
WITH A MIGHTY ROAR THE TORPEDO SMACKED HOME AMIDSHIPS, TEARING A FATAL HOLE IN THE PLATING.
AAAAGH!
GRITTING HIS TEETH AND STRIVING TO REMAIN CONSCIOUS, TIM COAXED THE BATTERED PLANE ON TO AN EVEN KEEL AND DESPERATELY TRIED TO GAIN HEIGHT.
WILL WE MAKE IT, SKIPPER?
Y-YES, — WITH LUCK. SET ME A COURSE FOR HOME AND KEEP YOUR FINGERS CROSSED. I'LL GET YOU — HOME — SOMEHOW.

WITH THE LAST FEW PINTS OF FUEL IN THE TANKS THE TORBEAU STAGGERED OVER THE AIRFIELD BOUNDARY. WITH A JAMMED UNDERCARRIAGE, TIM GATHERED UP HIS LAST RESERVES OF STRENGTH FOR A CRASH LANDING.

EVEN BEFORE THE WRECK STOPPED MOVING, TIM LAWLER SLUMPED UNCONSCIOUS OVER THE CONTROLS.

HOW — HOW IS HE?

HE'S IN A BAD WAY — LOST A LOT OF BLOOD. DUNNO HOW HE BROUGHT THE PLANE DOWN IN THIS STATE.

CLIFF'S ARM WAS BROKEN IN THE LANDING, BUT OTHERWISE HE WAS UNHURT. HE BLURTED OUT THE WHOLE STORY OF THE ATTACK TO SQUADRON LEADER OLIVER.

HE WENT INTO THE ATTACK AFTER HE HAD BEEN HIT. HE WAS AS STEADY AS A ROCK. I'VE NEVER SEEN ANYTHING LIKE IT...

OK, YOUNG FELLER. NOW GET INTO THAT AMBULANCE, RIGHT NOW!

IT TOOK MORE THAN GERMAN SHRAPNEL TO KILL A TOUGH AUSSIE. SOON TIM LAWLER WAS WELL ENOUGH TO RECEIVE VISITORS, AND HIS FIRST TWO HAD SOME NEWS FOR HIM...

YOUR CAMERA GUN CONFIRMED CONWAY'S STORY, SO NOW I CAN TELL YOU TO HURRY UP AND GET ON YOUR FEET AGAIN. YOU'VE GOT A DATE — AT BUCKINGHAM PALACE!

YOU'VE DONE IT AT LAST, TIM! ANOTHER GONG FOR THE LAWLER COLLECTION. THIS TIME IT'S THE DISTINGUISHED FLYING CROSS.

BUT STRANGELY ENOUGH THE NEWS AROUSED NO ELATION IN TIM. ALL HE FELT WAS A STRANGE SENSE OF GRATITUDE.

YOU DON'T KNOW HOW MUCH YOU'VE TAUGHT ME, CLIFF. FROM NOW ON, I'M GOING TO STOP GONG-HUNTING. THE MEN WHO ARE GOING TO WIN THIS WAR ARE THE ONES WHO CONCENTRATE ON DOING THE JOB IN HAND, WITH NO HEROICS OR STUPID RISKS.

SO TIM LAWLER HAD WON HIS MEDAL, BUT HE HAD ALSO LEARNT TO WEAR IT WITH MODESTY AND HUMILITY. BACK IN THE AIR AGAIN, HE AND CLIFF MADE THE BEST BEAUFIGHTER TEAM IN THE BUSINESS, COMBINING TRUE BRAVERY AND SPIRIT WITH COOL PRECISION — THE WAY WARS ARE REALLY WON...

THINK OUR TORPEDO WILL FIND A HOME TODAY, CLIFF?

WITH YOU FLYING, MATE, HOW CAN WE MISS!

Commando
THE END

AVRO LANCASTER HEAVY BOMBER

Aircraft of the Second World War — No. 16

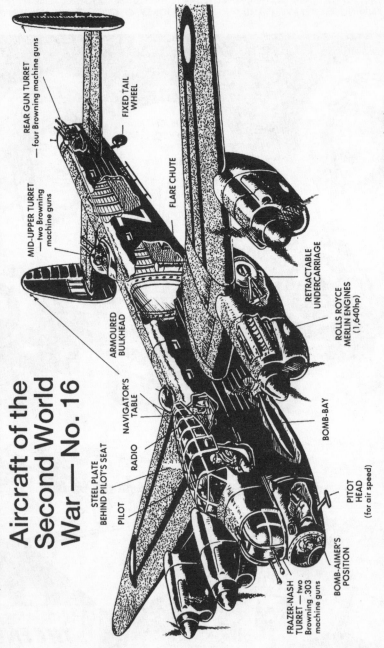

REAR GUN TURRET
— four Browning machine guns

FIXED TAIL WHEEL

MID-UPPER TURRET
— two Browning machine guns

FLARE CHUTE

ARMOURED BULKHEAD

RETRACTABLE UNDERCARRIAGE

ROLLS ROYCE MERLIN ENGINES (1,640hp)

STEEL PLATE BEHIND PILOT'S SEAT

PILOT

RADIO

NAVIGATOR'S TABLE

BOMB-BAY

PITOT HEAD (for air speed)

FRAZER-NASH TURRET — two Browning .303 machine guns

BOMB-AIMER'S POSITION

DESCRIBED as the finest bomber of the war, the Lanc's main feature was its ability to take ever-increasing bomb loads. Designed originally to carry 4000 lb its pay-load was doubled and then trebled to 12,000 lb! Special modifications later enabled Lancasters to carry the fantastic Grand Slam bomb weighing 22,000 lb!

Probably their most famous exploit was the Dam Busters raid, a strike which made these planes and their crews a living legend.

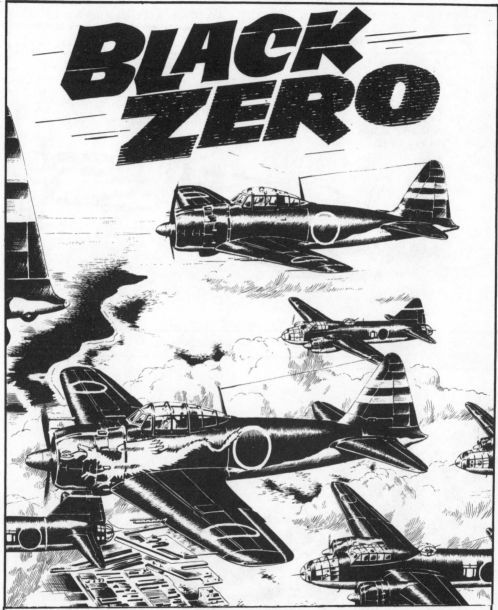

BLACK ZERO

ALL BLACK WITH A GOLDEN DRAGON PAINTED ON THE SIDE — THAT WAS THE BLACK ZERO, PERSONAL AIRCRAFT OF CAPTAIN JIRAI SAITO OF THE JAPANESE ARMY AIR FORCE. RUTHLESS AND AMBITIOUS, SAITO HAD LED HIS HAND-PICKED SQUADRON OF ACE PILOTS TO EARLY VICTORIES UNTIL THEY RULED THE SKIES OF THE PACIFIC — OR SO THEY THOUGHT.

ALLIED FIGHTER AIRCRAFT WERE FEW, AND MOSTLY AMERICAN-PILOTED CURTISS P-40 s. ALTHOUGH VETERANS AT FIGHTING THE JAP PILOTS, THE AMERICANS WERE HANDICAPPED, FOR THE STURDY P-40 WAS NO MATCH FOR THE FAST AND AGILE ZERO.

THIS IS LIKE CHASING A SPORTS CAR IN A TRUCK. THESE DARN ZEROS CAN TURN ON A DIME.

THE ZERO SOON PROVED ITSELF KING OF THE PACIFIC SKIES AS IT FLEW RINGS ROUND THE HEAVIER P-40.

BANZAI!

AAARGH!

BUT THE SUPERB JAP FIGHTER HAD ITS WEAK SPOTS. ONE OF THESE WAS ITS HABIT OF FLARING UP LIKE A TORCH WHEN IT WAS HIT.

TOO BAD YOU DON'T HAVE SELF-SEALING FUEL TANKS, TOJO!

THE LIGHTWEIGHT ZERO ALSO LACKED ARMOUR-PLATING FOR THE PILOT.

THE AMERICAN PILOTS LEARNED TO COMBAT THE ZEROS THROUGH TRIAL AND ERROR — BUT THE LESSONS PROVED COSTLY IN LIVES.

THE POOR, CRAZY KID. I TOLD HIM YOU CAN'T OUT-TURN A ZERO.

THE AMERICANS DEVISED SPECIAL ATTACK METHODS FOR DEALING WITH THE SLIPPERY JAPS. TOP-SCORING AMERICAN ACE WAS CAPTAIN JOHNNY PAYNE.

KNOWN AS "JOHNNY ZERO" BECAUSE OF HIS MANY VICTORIES OVER THE SPEEDY JAP FIGHTERS, JOHNNY HAD ORDERED SHARK'S-TEETH INSIGNIA TO BE PAINTED ON HIS AIRCRAFT.

HE WAS A COLD AND MERCILESS AIR FIGHTER.

HE HOWLED DOWN AT THE ESCAPING JAP.

CAPTAIN JIRAI SAITO, IN HIS ALL-BLACK ZERO EMBLAZONED WITH A DRAGON, WAS JOHNNY'S SWORN ENEMY. THEY HAD DUELLED MANY TIMES.

NEARLY GOT HIM THAT TIME.

THE SHARK PILOT'S SKILL IS ALMOST THE EQUAL OF MINE. HE HUNTS ME WITH A FEROCITY OF A SAMURAI.

SHORT OF FUEL, JOHNNY BROKE OFF THE FIGHT AND RETURNED TO HIS BASE NEAR DARWIN IN NORTH AUSTRALIA.

HOW MANY DID YOU GET TODAY, JOHNNY?

TWO. PAINT 'EM ON THE FUSELAGE, BUTCH.

BUTCH GIBSON HAD BEEN JOHNNY'S MECHANIC FOR YEARS.

THEN JOHNNY REPORTED TO THE STATION COMMANDER, COLONEL O'DONNEL.

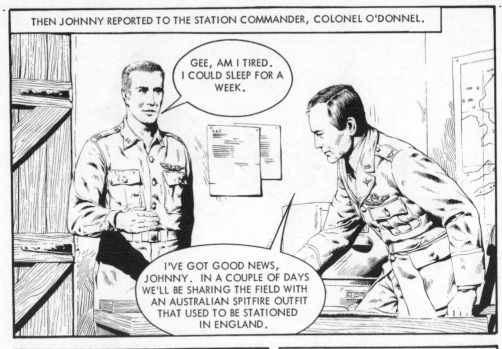

GEE, AM I TIRED. I COULD SLEEP FOR A WEEK.

I'VE GOT GOOD NEWS, JOHNNY. IN A COUPLE OF DAYS WE'LL BE SHARING THE FIELD WITH AN AUSTRALIAN SPITFIRE OUTFIT THAT USED TO BE STATIONED IN ENGLAND.

IT'S ABOUT TIME WE HAD SOME HELP. HOW BIG IS THIS OUTFIT?

ONLY A SQUADRON, BUT THEY HAD A FINE REPUTATION IN THE BATTLE OF BRITAIN.

JOHNNY'S EYES BLAZED ANGRILY.

ONLY A SQUADRON! THE JAPS WILL WIPE OUT THESE GUYS IN A WEEK. WE NEED PLANES, NOT REPUTATIONS. THE BATTLE OF BRITAIN DOESN'T MEAN A THING OUT HERE.

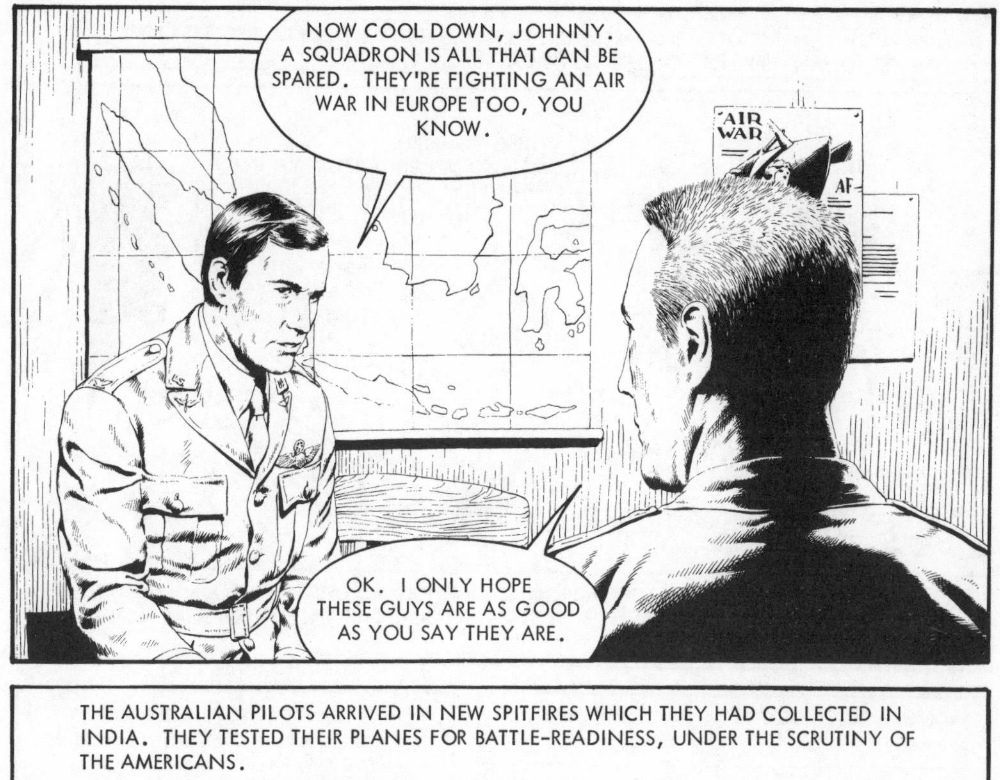
NOW COOL DOWN, JOHNNY. A SQUADRON IS ALL THAT CAN BE SPARED. THEY'RE FIGHTING AN AIR WAR IN EUROPE TOO, YOU KNOW.
AIR WAR
OK. I ONLY HOPE THESE GUYS ARE AS GOOD AS YOU SAY THEY ARE.

THE AUSTRALIAN PILOTS ARRIVED IN NEW SPITFIRES WHICH THEY HAD COLLECTED IN INDIA. THEY TESTED THEIR PLANES FOR BATTLE-READINESS, UNDER THE SCRUTINY OF THE AMERICANS.

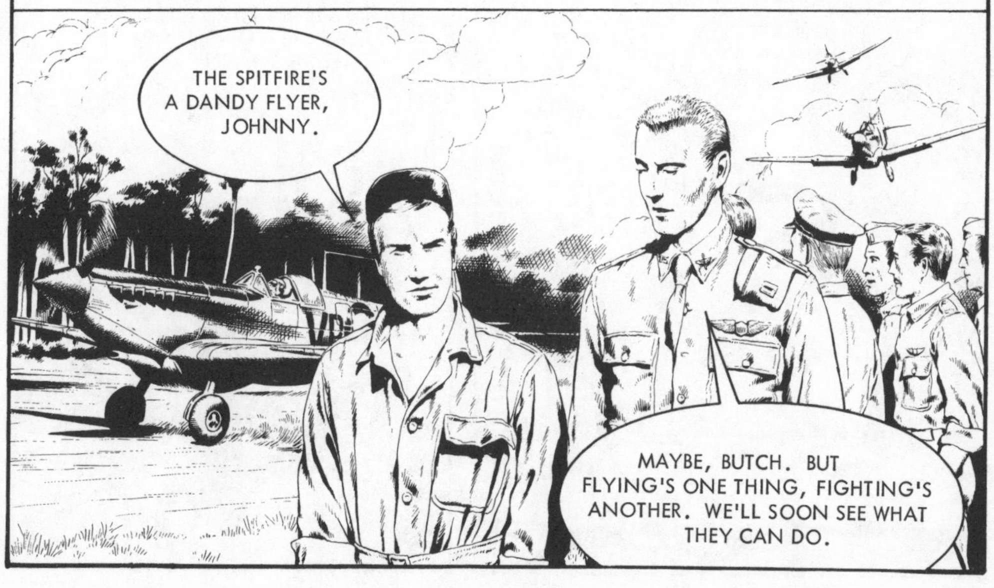
THE SPITFIRE'S A DANDY FLYER, JOHNNY.
MAYBE, BUTCH. BUT FLYING'S ONE THING, FIGHTING'S ANOTHER. WE'LL SOON SEE WHAT THEY CAN DO.

THAT NIGHT, IN THE OFFICERS' MESS, THE TWO SQUADRONS MET FOR THE FIRST TIME. ONE OF JOHNNY'S PILOTS CALLED TO HIM AS HE CAME IN.

HEY, JOHNNY. COME AND MEET THE BOSS OF THE NEW SPITFIRE OUTFIT.

NICK KIRBY, THE AUSTRALIAN SQUADRON LEADER, HAD ALREADY GOT TO KNOW BUDDY ROGERS, ONE OF JOHNNY PAYNE'S PILOTS. HE LOOKED UP WITH INTEREST AS BUDDY CALLED TO THE AMERICAN ACE.

BUDDY ROGERS QUICKLY INTRODUCED THEM. JOHNNY DID NOT APPEAR PLEASED.

GLAD TO KNOW YOU, JOHNNY.

HI.

I'M TOLD YOU GUYS WERE PRETTY GOOD AGAINST THE KRAUTS. WELL, BELIEVE ME, PAL, YOU'RE GONNA FIND THE JAPS TWICE AS SLICK — BUT WE CAN HANDLE 'EM. THEY CALL ME JOHNNY ZERO.

NICK LOOKED QUIETLY AT THE AMERICAN. ONE THING HE COULD NOT STAND WAS A LINE-SHOOTER.

WELL, WE'LL JUST HAVE TO SEE HOW THINGS GO. THE BATTLE OF BRITAIN WASN'T EXACTLY A PICNIC, YOU KNOW.

FORGET ALL THAT BATTLE OF BRITAIN STUFF. OUT HERE THAT DOESN'T MEAN A THING. YOU'RE ALL BEGINNERS AS FAR AS THE JAPS — AND ME — ARE CONCERNED. YOU'RE GOING TO NEED ALL THE ADVICE YOU CAN GET.

OPEN HOSTILITY FLARED BETWEEN THE TWO MEN.

THANK YOU FOR THE CHARMING WELCOME. EVEN THOUGH WE ARE GOING TO USE THE SAME FIELD, I DON'T IMAGINE THERE'LL BE ANY NEED FOR US TO GET IN EACH OTHER'S WAY.

OK, YOU LEARN TO FIGHT THE JAPS THE HARD WAY. BUT DON'T SAY I DIDN'T OFFER TO HELP.

WITH THAT, NICK TURNED ON HIS HEEL AND LEFT. AND WHEN THE REST OF HIS PILOTS REJECTED THE ADVICE AND HELP OF THE AMERICANS, TROUBLE BEGAN TO BREW.

SEEMS TO ME YOU YANKS ARE DEAD SCARED OF THE JAPS!

ARE YOU CALLING US CHICKEN?

HEY, WATCH IT!

SOON THE PLACE WAS IN COMPLETE UPROAR AS THE TWO RIVAL OUTFITS WADED INTO EACH OTHER.

TRY THAT FOR SIZE, BUDDY!

COP THIS, YANK!

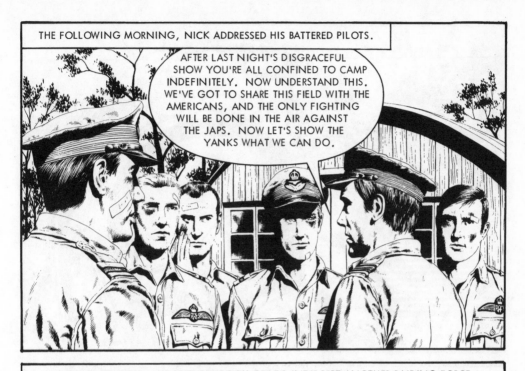

THE FOLLOWING MORNING, NICK ADDRESSED HIS BATTERED PILOTS.

AFTER LAST NIGHT'S DISGRACEFUL SHOW YOU'RE ALL CONFINED TO CAMP INDEFINITELY. NOW UNDERSTAND THIS. WE'VE GOT TO SHARE THIS FIELD WITH THE AMERICANS, AND THE ONLY FIGHTING WILL BE DONE IN THE AIR AGAINST THE JAPS. NOW LET'S SHOW THE YANKS WHAT WE CAN DO.

AT THE NEXT ALERT, THE SPITFIRES TOOK OFF TO INTERCEPT ANOTHER RAIDING FORCE OF JAP BOMBERS ESCORTED BY ZERO FIGHTERS.

TALLY—HO! HIT THE BOMBERS FIRST, THEN TAKE CARE OF THE FIGHTERS.

BUT THE SPEEDY ZEROS SOON SURPRISED THE AUSTRALIANS WITH THEIR INCREDIBLE MANOEUVRABILITY. EVEN NICK WAS AMAZED BY THE AGILITY OF THE ENEMY FIGHTERS.

UNFORTUNATELY FOR NICK AND HIS MEN, THEY HAD RUN INTO THE BLACK DRAGON AND HIS ELITE SQUADRON — A BAD OUTFIT TO TACKLE ON THEIR FIRST OPERATIONAL FLIGHT. AS ALWAYS, SAITO WAS COLD AND RUTHLESS.

I HAVE HEARD MUCH OF THE BRITISH SPITFIRES. THEY ARE FAST — BUT THE PILOTS ARE NEW TO THE WAYS OF THE ZERO. THAT IS GOOD.

NICK SPOTTED THE ALL-BLACK JAP FIGHTER AND WENT AFTER IT.

MUST BE A JAP ACE IN THAT FANCY KITE. LET'S SEE HOW HOT HE REALLY IS.

HE SOON FOUND OUT. AS HE BLASTED DOWN ON THE DRAGON ZERO, IT WHIPPED OUT OF DANGER WITH A QUICK SIDE-TURN.

MISSED HIM BY A MILE. NEVER SEEN A HUN TURN AS FAST AS THAT.

WHILE NICK DUELLED WITH SAITO, THE OTHER SPITFIRES TOOK A SAVAGE MAULING FROM THE JAP FIGHTERS.

THE ZEROS SHOT DOWN THREE SPITFIRES.

SUDDENLY THE FIGHT ENDED, AS THE JAPS TURNED TAIL AND FLEW OFF. NICK HEAVED A SIGH OF RELIEF.

OK, BOYS, RETURN TO BASE. A TOUGH FIGHT, BUT AT LEAST WE STOPPED THEM BOMBING DARWIN TODAY.

NICK WAS FAR FROM PLEASED WITH THE SQUADRON'S FIRST SHOWING, AND HE WAS NOT ALONE. HIS GROUP CAPTAIN, ERIC BLOOM, SENT FOR HIM.

A BAD SHOW, KIRBY. I EXPECTED MORE FROM YOU. YOU LOST THREE SPITFIRES FOR ONLY TWO JAPS. TWO PILOTS ARE SAFE, BUT OUR RESERVE MACHINES WILL SOON BE USED UP AT THIS RATE.

I'M SORRY, SIR, BUT THE ZEROS ARE NEW TO US. IF YOU JUST GIVE US A LITTLE TIME, WE'LL CUT THEM TO PIECES.

THE GROUP CAPTAIN STARED COLDLY AT HIM.

THAT'S JUST IT. WE HAVE NEITHER TIME NOR AIRCRAFT TO SPARE. I'M HAVING A VETERAN AMERICAN PILOT TAKE TEMPORARY COMMAND OF YOUR SQUADRON. HE WILL INSTRUCT YOUR MEN ON HOW TO TACKLE THE ZERO.

NICK FELT LIKE A SCHOOLBOY WHO HAD FLUNKED HIS EXAMS.

BUT, SIR, WE DON'T NEED TO BE TAUGHT HOW TO FIGHT!

NOT AGAINST JERRIES, BUT JAPS ARE ANOTHER MATTER. THAT'S ALL, KIRBY.

AND NICK'S HUMILIATION WAS COMPLETE WHEN THE AMERICAN PILOT TURNED OUT TO BE JOHNNY PAYNE.

WELL, WHAT D'YOU KNOW? SO YOU GUYS NEED ME AFTER ALL.

LOOK, PAYNE, WE'VE GOT TO SUFFER YOU ON ORDERS. JUST GET ON WITH YOUR JOB AND WE'LL LISTEN.

NEXT DAY JOHNNY LECTURED THE AUSTRALIANS ON THE TRIED AND TESTED METHODS OF FIGHTING THE ZERO.

TRY AND FIGHT ON THE DIVE AND CLIMB. AND ABOVE ALL AVOID HORIZONTAL TURNS. A ZERO WILL OUT-TURN YOU EVERY TIME. ONE OTHER POINT. LEAVE THE BLACK DRAGON TO ME. HE'S MY SPECIAL PROPERTY.

JOHNNY PUT DOWN THE POINTER AND FACED HIS PUPILS.

THEORY IS ONE THING, FIGHTING'S ANOTHER. I SHALL LEAD THE SQUADRON INTO ACTION UNTIL I THINK YOU ARE READY TO TACKLE THE JAPS ON YOUR OWN. THAT'S ALL.

AS SOON AS THE LECTURE WAS OVER, NICK CONFRONTED THE AMERICAN.

NOW LOOK HERE, PAYNE, WE DON'T NEED YOU. WE CAN FIGHT OUR OWN BATTLES.

LET'S GET THIS CLEAR, KIRBY. I'M IN COMMAND OF THIS OUTFIT NOW. SO JUST YOU DO AS YOU'RE TOLD, OK?

FOR AN INSTANT THE NORMALLY COOL NICK NEARLY LOST HIS TEMPER.

WHY, YOU BIG-MOUTHED...

SAVE IT FOR THE JAPS, PAL. NOTHING WOULD GIVE ME GREATER PLEASURE THAN TO BUST YOU ON THE JAW. BUT IT WILL KEEP.

AT THE NEXT ALERT THE SHARK-FACED P-40 LED THE SPITFIRES INTO THE HOSTILE SKIES, AND A STREAM OF INSTRUCTIONS CRACKLED OVER THE RADIO.

THE SPITFIRES GAINED HEIGHT AND DIVED OUT OF THE SUN AT THE JAP FORMATION THAT HAD JUST APPEARED. THE P-40 SCREAMED THROUGH THE RING OF ESCORTING FIGHTERS AND BLASTED A BOMBER TO PIECES.

NICK WAS NEXT TO SCORE A KILL. HIS CANNON AND MACHINE-GUNS ROARED, AND ANOTHER BOMBER DISAPPEARED AS ITS BOMB-LOAD EXPLODED.

MUSTN'T LET BIGHEAD PAYNE DO ALL THE WORK.

AFTER CLOBBERING THE BOMBERS, THE SPITFIRES TURNED TO DEFEND THEMSELVES AGAINST THE ZEROS WHICH NOW STREAKED IN TO WREAK THEIR VENGEANCE.

YOU DIE, BRITISH PIG!

NICK SINGLED OUT A ZERO AND OPENED FIRE. BUT THE WILY JAP MADE A LIGHTNING TURN, AND NICK'S BULLETS SLASHED EMPTY AIR.

MISSED HIM!
HE'S SIDESLIPPED, BUT HE
WON'T GET AWAY.

AND FORGETTING JOHNNY'S ADVICE, NICK SWEPT ROUND IN A TIGHT TURN. BUT THE ZERO TURNED FASTER AND BULLETS THUDDED INTO NICK'S SPITFIRE.

PHEW — THAT'S
TOO CLOSE FOR
COMFORT.

SUDDENLY, AS THE ZERO DIVED AWAY, NICK FLIPPED UP HIS SPITFIRE AND LET FLY. SECONDS LATER, THE ZERO WAS A FLAMING WRECK.

RIGHT IN
THE FUEL TANK!

BUT MEANWHILE THE OTHER SPITFIRE PILOTS, IGNORING PAYNE'S HARD-LEARNED LESSONS, WERE FIGHTING IN THEIR OLD STYLE — BUT WITHOUT THE SUCCESS THEY HAD AGAINST THE GERMANS. PAYNE WAS HOPPING MAD.

THE CRAZY FOOLS! NOW THEY'RE GOING TO DIE, BECAUSE THEY WON'T LISTEN!

NEXT INSTANT THE AMERICAN SPOTTED YET ANOTHER SPITFIRE IN DEEP TROUBLE.

THAT STUPID GUY'S GONNA JOIN HIS BUDDY UNLESS I SAVE HIM.

THROWING THE HEAVY P-40 INTO A HOWLING DIVE, JOHNNY HURTLED DOWN ON THE JAP WITH GUNS BLAZING.

A MOMENT LATER, THE ANGRY AMERICAN WAS FLASHING ACROSS THE WAR-TORN SKY TO RESCUE ANOTHER SPITFIRE.

NICK HAD SEEN JOHNNY RESCUE THE TWO AUSTRALIANS — AND A SMALL SPARK OF RESPECT WAS KINDLED FOR THE DARE-DEVIL AMERICAN.

HE MAY BE A BIG-MOUTH — BUT HE DOES BACK IT UP WITH ACTION. NO WONDER THEY CALL HIM JOHNNY ZERO.

BUT MOMENTS LATER NICK SAW SOMETHING WHICH KILLED HIS NEWBORN REGARD FOR THE AMERICAN.

THAT JAP IS DONE FOR — HE'S TRYING TO DITCH — YET PAYNE'S STILL GOING AFTER HIM LIKE A BULLDOG THAT CAN'T LET GO.

SAY YOUR PRAYERS, TOJO!

NICK WATCHED WITH GROWING CONTEMPT AS JOHNNY PURSUED THE CRIPPLED ZERO AND FINALLY BLASTED IT TO UTTER DESTRUCTION.

THAT'S COLD-BLOODED MURDER! THERE WAS NO NEED FOR THAT.

BACK AT THE AIRFIELD AFTER THE FIGHT, JOHNNY PAYNE GAVE THE AUSTRALIANS A TONGUE-LASHING.

YOU GUYS MAKE ME SICK. YOU CAN'T TAKE ADVICE, SO YOU PAY FOR IT WITH YOUR LIVES. THAT WON'T WIN THE WAR. YOU HAD BETTER LEARN TO FIGHT MY WAY — FAST!

THE PILOTS SAT IN COWED SILENCE — ALL EXCEPT NICK, WHO STOOD UP ANGRILY.

WE'LL TAKE YOUR ADVICE, PAYNE, BUT NOT YOUR RUTHLESS METHODS. THERE WAS NO NEED TO GO FOR THAT DAMAGED JAP. HE WAS FINISHED, OUT OF THE FIGHT —

THE AMERICAN EXPLODED WITH FURY.

LOOK, BUD, THIS IS NO GAME OF CRICKET. IT'S KILL OR BE KILLED — AND NO MERCY FOR THE LOSER. THE SOONER YOU LEARN THAT, THE SOONER WE'LL WIN THIS LOUSY WAR!

AFTER JOHNNY PAYNE HAD STORMED OFF, NICK TURNED TO HIS PILOTS.

OK, BOYS. LOOKS LIKE CAPTAIN PAYNE IS RIGHT. THE SOONER WE LEARN TO TACKLE THE JAPS CORRECTLY, THE SOONER WE GET RID OF CAPTAIN PAIN-IN-THE-NECK!

TOO RIGHT, SKIPPER!

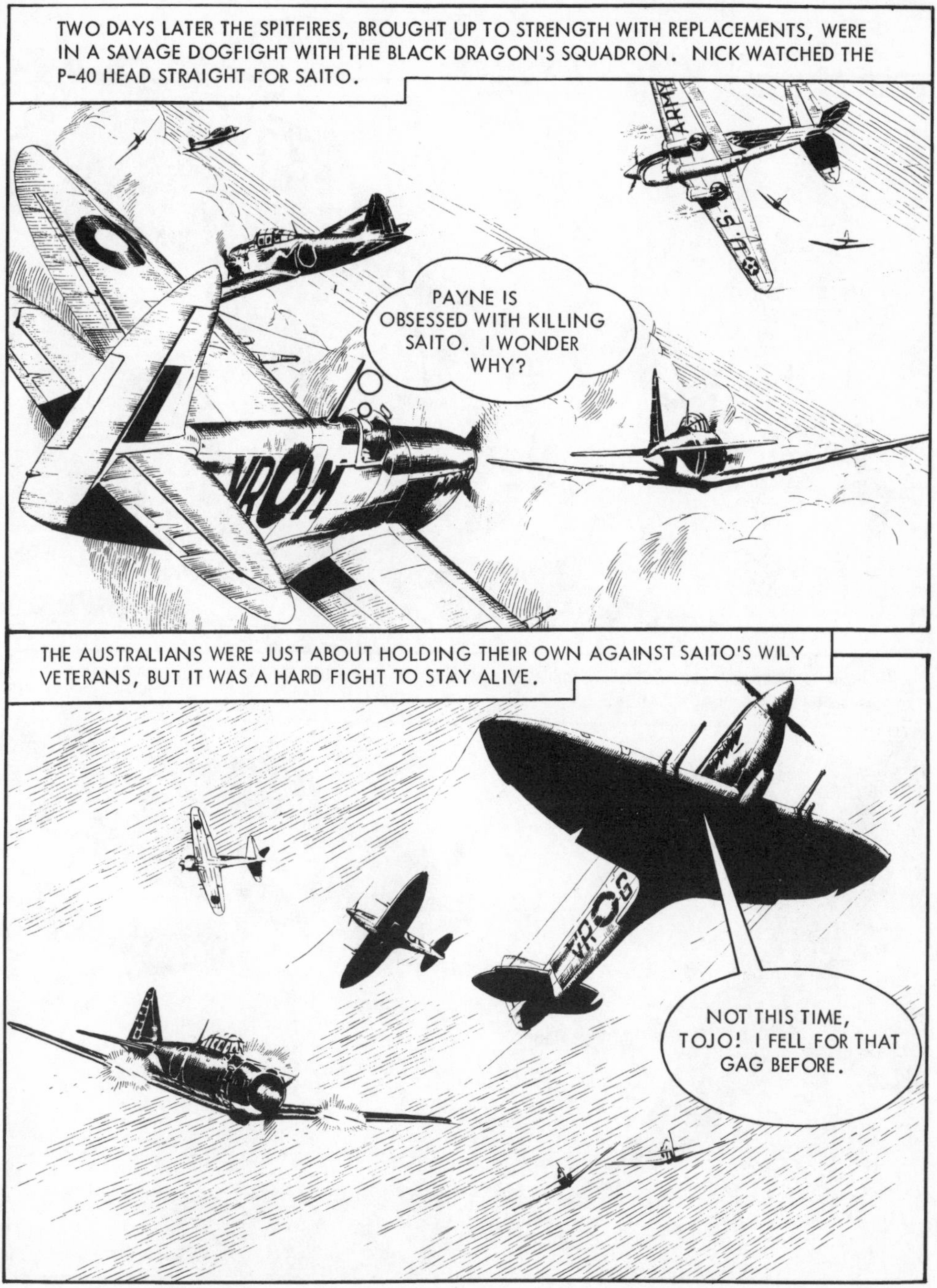
TWO DAYS LATER THE SPITFIRES, BROUGHT UP TO STRENGTH WITH REPLACEMENTS, WERE IN A SAVAGE DOGFIGHT WITH THE BLACK DRAGON'S SQUADRON. NICK WATCHED THE P-40 HEAD STRAIGHT FOR SAITO.
PAYNE IS OBSESSED WITH KILLING SAITO. I WONDER WHY?
THE AUSTRALIANS WERE JUST ABOUT HOLDING THEIR OWN AGAINST SAITO'S WILY VETERANS, BUT IT WAS A HARD FIGHT TO STAY ALIVE.
NOT THIS TIME, TOJO! I FELL FOR THAT GAG BEFORE.

BUT THEN SAITO GOT A BURST IN AT JOHNNY.

BANZAI!

HECK! HE'S GOT ME!

JOHNNY'S PLANE, ITS FUSELAGE RIDDLED, PLUNGED TOWARDS THE SEA IN A DEATH DIVE, TRAILING THICK, BLACK SMOKE.

THE SHARK PILOT IS DOOMED AT LAST. TIME TO RETURN TO BASE.

NICK WATCHED THE P-40 HURTLE TOWARDS THE SEA — BUT THEN, TO HIS ASTONISHMENT, THE DOOMED PLANE ZOOMED UPWARDS IN A MIRACULOUS RECOVERY.

I CAN'T BELIEVE IT! THE FIRE'S OUT, AND HE'S CLIMBING!

MOMENTS LATER, JOHNNY ZERO JOINED THE SURVIVING SPITFIRES AND HIS VOICE CRACKLED OVER THE RADIO.

OK, YOU GUYS, THE JAPS HAVE GONE. LET'S BEAT IT BACK HOME.

WHEN THE SQUADRON LANDED AT THE FIELD, A PUZZLED NICK WATCHED JOHNNY JUMP OUT OF HIS BATTERED PLANE.

PAYNE'S THE LUCKIEST MAN ALIVE. HE'S NOT EVEN SCRATCHED. I WAS SURE HE'D BOUGHT IT.

THOROUGHLY INTRIGUED BY THE AMERICAN'S FANTASTIC SURVIVAL, NICK WALKED OVER TO THE RIDDLED P-40 AFTER JOHNNY HAD LEFT.

HOW ON EARTH DID HE RECOVER SO COMPLETELY FROM THAT DEATH-DIVE? I'LL HAVE A LOOK AT HIS KITE.

WHAT HE SAW PUZZLED HIM EVEN MORE.

THE COCKPIT'S PUNCHED FULL OF HOLES. NOBODY COULD LIVE AFTER THAT. BUT PAYNE HAS.

THE MYSTERY DEEPENED.

AND THE PLANE WAS ON FIRE, WITH SMOKE POURING FROM UNDERNEATH. I'LL TAKE A SQUINT...

BUT BEFORE THE AUSTRALIAN COULD EXAMINE THE UNDERSIDE OF THE P-40, BUTCH GIBSON ARRIVED.

CAN I HELP YOU?

ER...NO – NO, THAT'S ALL RIGHT, BUTCH. JUST SEEING HOW BADLY CAPTAIN PAYNE'S KITE WAS DAMAGED.

NOT WISHING TO REVEAL HIS BURNING INTEREST IN THE MACHINE, NICK WALKED OFF.

BUT, LATER, UNABLE TO CONTAIN HIS CURIOSITY ANY LONGER, HE WENT TO SEE JOHNNY PAYNE.

WELL, WHAT DO YOU WANT — PRAISE FOR TODAY'S COMBAT? SO WE ONLY LOST ONE PLANE. THAT'S ONE TOO MANY.

NO, I DON'T WANT PRAISE — I CAME TO SAY, AMONG OTHER THINGS, THAT I'M GLAD YOU CAME OUT ALIVE.

THE TOUGH AMERICAN WAS A LITTLE TAKEN ABACK BY NICK'S CONCERN FOR HIM.

YEAH, WELL...I'VE BEEN IN TIGHTER SPOTS.

ONE THING PUZZLES ME. HOW DID YOU SURVIVE THOSE HITS ON THE COCKPIT?

JOHNNY ZERO ALLOWED HIMSELF A FROSTY SMILE.

AN INTERESTING QUESTION. OK, I'LL LET YOU INTO A SECRET. PUNCH ME IN THE CHEST. GO ON.

NICK HESITATED, THEN SHRUGGED HIS SHOULDERS AND LET FLY WITH A RIGHT HAND PUNCH TO JOHNNY'S CHEST. NEXT SECOND HE YELLED IN PAIN AS HIS FIST CRUNCHED AGAINST SOMETHING IMMOVABLE.

AAAH!

SOME SURPRISE, HUH?

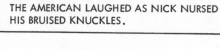

THE AMERICAN LAUGHED AS NICK NURSED HIS BRUISED KNUCKLES.

NOW YOU KNOW! I'M WEARING A BULLET-PROOF VEST, SPECIALLY MADE FOR ME. AND TAKE SOME GOOD ADVICE — GET YOURSELF ONE BEFORE THE JAPS DRILL YOU FULL OF HOLES.

BUT NICK WAS NEITHER AMUSED NOR IMPRESSED.

THANKS, BUT I DON'T THINK I'LL NEED ONE. AFTER A BIT MORE EXPERIENCE I'LL BE ABLE TO HANDLE ANY ZERO.

THE SMILE VANISHED FROM JOHNNY ZERO'S FACE. HE SNAPPED AT NICK.

SUIT YOURSELF, IT'S YOUR FUNERAL. AND THE WAY YOU GUYS ARE FALLING, FUNERAL IS RIGHT.

LET US WORRY ABOUT THAT. INCIDENTALLY, I THOUGHT YOUR KITE WAS FINISHED WHEN SAITO BASHED YOU. HOW DID YOU STOP THE FIRE?

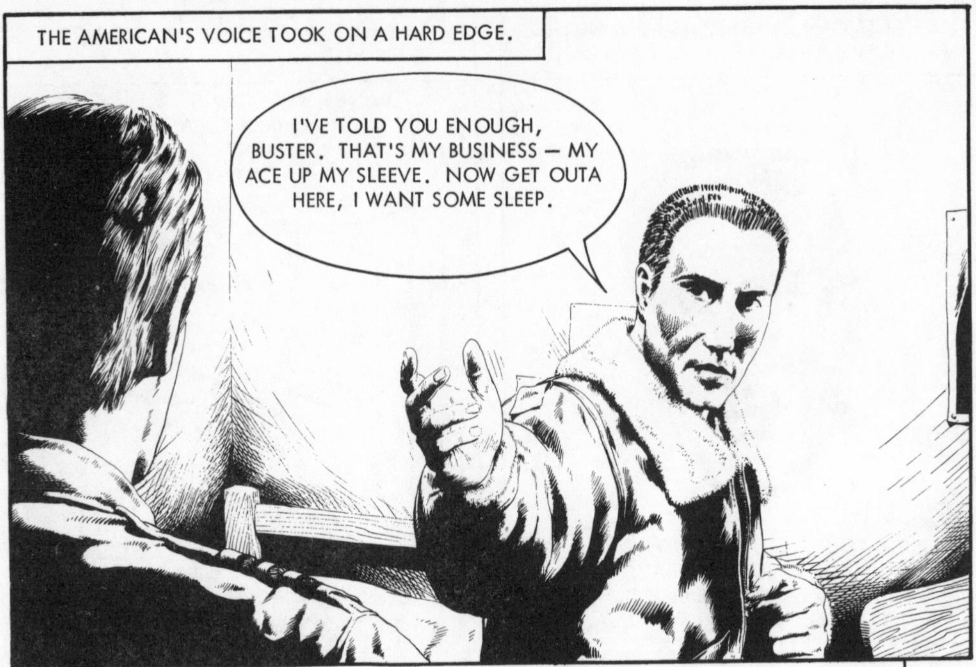
THE AMERICAN'S VOICE TOOK ON A HARD EDGE.
I'VE TOLD YOU ENOUGH, BUSTER. THAT'S MY BUSINESS — MY ACE UP MY SLEEVE. NOW GET OUTA HERE, I WANT SOME SLEEP.

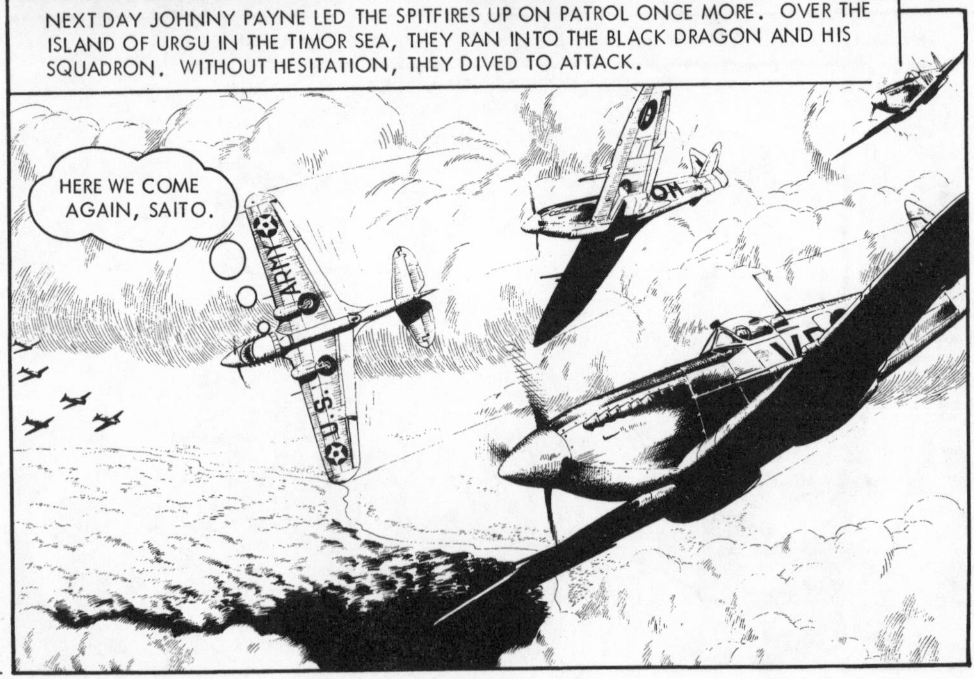
NEXT DAY JOHNNY PAYNE LED THE SPITFIRES UP ON PATROL ONCE MORE. OVER THE ISLAND OF URGU IN THE TIMOR SEA, THEY RAN INTO THE BLACK DRAGON AND HIS SQUADRON. WITHOUT HESITATION, THEY DIVED TO ATTACK.
HERE WE COME AGAIN, SAITO.

THE MORE AGILE ZERO QUICKLY GAINED AN ADVANTAGE. SAITO SNARLED AS HE SAW THE P-40 IN HIS SIGHTS.

SO YOU ESCAPED, DID YOU? ALL RIGHT, THIS TIME YOU DIE.

THE BLACK DRAGON STABBED HIS GUN BUTTON, BUT NOTHING HAPPENED.

BY SHINTO! MY GUNS HAVE JAMMED!

AND ONCE AGAIN JOHNNY ZERO WAS SAVED.

THE AMERICAN SOON REALISED THAT SAITO WAS HAVING TROUBLE WITH HIS GUNS. HE BORE DOWN ON THE TWISTING BLACK ZERO, GRAVITY HELPING HIS HEAVIER PLANE OVERTAKE THE JAP.

I'VE WAITED A LONG TIME FOR THIS MOMENT.

BUT SAITO PROVED A VERY ELUSIVE QUARRY. TIME AND AGAIN JOHNNY PAYNE'S SEARCHING BULLETS LASHED INTO EMPTY AIR.

HE'S AS CUNNING AS A WAGONLOAD OF MONKEYS.

BLACK DRAGON CALLING LIEUTENANT TAKAGI. MY GUNS ARE JAMMED — SHOOT DOWN THE FOOL CHASING ME.

TAKAGI WAS SAITO'S WINGMAN. HE HAD STRICT ORDERS NOT TO INTERFERE IN HIS LEADER'S DUELS WITH THE P-40 UNLESS OTHERWISE ORDERED.

BUT NOW THE ORDER HAD COME. TAKAGI BROKE AWAY EAGERLY FROM THE MAIN FIGHT AND SPED AFTER THE P-40. JOHNNY GROWLED AS HE SAW THE ZERO ROAR IN AT HIM.

WHAT'S THIS, ANOTHER ONE? WHY, YOU BUCK-TOOTHED LITTLE PUNK! I'LL TEACH YOU TO POKE YOUR NOSE IN.

JOHNNY ZERO TURNED TO MEET HIS ATTACKER. HE PRESSED HIS GUN BUTTON — BUT NOTHING HAPPENED.

AW, HECK! I'M OUT OF AMMO. NOW I NEED SOME HELP TOO.

NEXT SECOND, NICK'S EARPHONES CRACKLED URGENTLY.

I'M OUT OF AMMO... GET THIS GUY ON MY TAIL, KIRBY!

BE RIGHT WITH YOU.

IT TOOK NICK SEVERAL SECONDS TO COME TO JOHNNY'S AID — AND IT WAS SEVERAL SECONDS TOO MANY.

AS NICK AND TAKAGI FOUGHT IT OUT HIGH ABOVE, JOHNNY PAYNE BALED OUT. HE WAS WOUNDED IN THE LEG.

THE SPITFIRE WAS JUST AS NIMBLE AS THE ZERO, AND NICK, NOW AN EXPERIENCED JAP FIGHTER, CAUGHT TAKAGI WITH A FULL BURST.

BUT HIS VICTORY WAS SHORT-LIVED. SAITO, HIS GUNS NOW CLEARED, SWOOPED DOWN LIKE AN AVENGING EAGLE AND BLASTED NICK'S SPITFIRE INTO A WRECK.

JOHNNY PAYNE, FLOATING DOWN ON HIS PARACHUTE, LOOKED UP AND SAW NICK BALE OUT. HE SNORTED IN CONTEMPT.

WHAT A SUCKER! SAITO GETS HIM WITH ONE BURST. STILL, I'M GLAD HE'S ALIVE. I'LL GIVE HIM WHAT FOR WHEN I SEE HIM AGAIN.

AND SO NICK, JOHNNY AND TAKAGI FLOATED DOWN TOWARDS THE JUNGLE-COVERED ISLAND OF URGU. NICK LOOKED DOWN THANKFULLY.

IT'S A GOOD THING OUR OWN TROOPS ARE ON THE ISLAND.

THE ALLIED PILOTS KNEW THAT AUSTRALIAN TROOPS HAD LANDED ON URGU A MONTH BEFORE.

JOHNNY PAYNE WAS FIRST TO LAND. HE MADE A CRUDE WOODEN CRUTCH WITH THE HELP OF A HUNTING KNIFE HE ALWAYS CARRIED.

THAT SHOULD DO IT. NOW TO LOOK FOR THE AUSSIE BASE.

JOHNNY BEGAN STUMBLING THROUGH THE JUNGLE, THE PAIN FROM HIS LEG WOUND ADDING FUEL TO HIS ANGER AT BEING SHOT DOWN.

I SHOULD NEVER HAVE JOINED THIS OUTFIT IN THE FIRST PLACE. ALL THESE PUNK PILOTS. LET 'EM GET SHOT TO PIECES, WHO CARES. IT'S MY OWN DARN FAULT GETTING MIXED UP WITH JERKS LIKE THEM.

THERE WAS NO SIGN OF NICK. GRIMLY THE AMERICAN STRUGGLED ON ALONE.

AFTER AN HOUR'S AGONISED HOBBLING, JOHNNY FELL TO THE GROUND, EXHAUSTED. SUDDENLY HE HEARD A RUSTLING IN THE UNDERGROWTH.

SOMEONE'S COMING THIS WAY... PROBABLY NICK KIRBY.

BUT IT WAS NOT NICK WHO BURST INTO THE OPEN — IT WAS LIEUTENANT TAKAGI.

THE JAP!

I NO KILL YOU IN THE AIR, SO I KILL YOU NOW!

THE JAP ADVANCED TOWARDS JOHNNY, HIS FINGER TIGHTENING ON THE TRIGGER OF HIS PISTOL.

DIE, AMERICAN PIG!

MEANWHILE NICK WAS ALSO STRIKING SOUTH. GUNFIRE MADE HIM STOP IN HIS TRACKS.

PISTOL SHOTS... NOT FAR AWAY. WHAT'S GOING ON?

HE SOON FOUND THE SPOT.

ARE YOU ALL RIGHT?

LATE AGAIN, KIRBY!

JOHNNY GESTURED TOWARDS THE JAPANESE PILOT.

THE JAP BUSHWHACKED ME WITH A PISTOL, BUT HE DIDN'T KNOW ABOUT MY BULLET-PROOF VEST. HE LET ME HAVE TWO SLUGS BEFORE I GOT HIM WITH MY KNIFE.

JOHNNY CRAWLED OVER TO THE DEAD TAKAGI, TURNED HIM OVER AND RETRIEVED HIS HUNTING KNIFE.

THAT'S ANOTHER HAPPY JAP GONE TO JOIN HIS ANCESTORS. COME ON, LET'S GO.

NICK TURNED ANGRILY TOWARDS THE AMERICAN.

JUST AS CYNICAL AS EVER, AREN'T YOU?

AND YOU'RE JUST AS LATE AS EVER. SEEMS YOU'RE NEVER AROUND WHEN I'M IN A TOUGH SPOT.

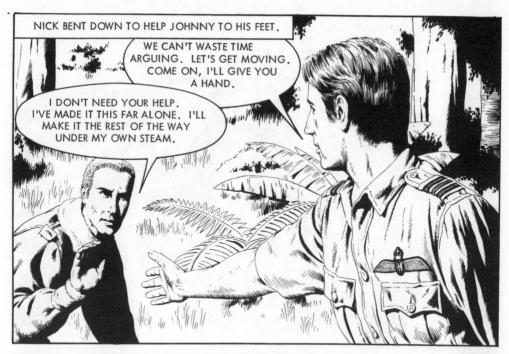

NICK BENT DOWN TO HELP JOHNNY TO HIS FEET.

WE CAN'T WASTE TIME ARGUING. LET'S GET MOVING. COME ON, I'LL GIVE YOU A HAND.

I DON'T NEED YOUR HELP. I'VE MADE IT THIS FAR ALONE. I'LL MAKE IT THE REST OF THE WAY UNDER MY OWN STEAM.

THE PILOTS STRUGGLED ON IN UNFRIENDLY SILENCE. FINALLY THEY RAN INTO AN AUSTRALIAN PATROL.

IT'S ABOUT TIME YOU GUYS SHOWED UP. WHAT KEPT YOU?

YOU'RE LUCKY WE FOUND YOU, YANK.

TAKE NO NOTICE OF HIM, COBBER. HE JUST DOESN'T LIKE US AUSSIES.

AND SO THE TWO FIGHTER ACES, THE ENMITY BETWEEN THEM JUST AS STRONG AS EVER, WERE RETURNED TO THEIR BASE. THE AMERICAN'S LEG WOUND HEALED QUICKLY AND HE WAS GIVEN A SPITFIRE TO REPLACE HIS P-40.

I SEE YOU'VE LOST NO TIME IN PAINTING ON THE SHARK'S TEETH.

THAT'S SO SAITO WILL RECOGNISE ME. AND ANOTHER THING. NOBODY — BUT NOBODY, TOUCHES THIS SPIT EXCEPT BUTCH. THAT'S AN ORDER.

NICK SHRUGGED AND WALKED AWAY.

I WONDER WHY HE'S SO SECRETIVE ABOUT HIS KITES. FIRST THE P-40, NOW THE SPIT. ANYONE WOULD THINK HE HAD A SECRET WEAPON ABOARD.

LATER THAT DAY, INSIDE A LOCKED AND DESERTED HANGAR, BUTCH AND JOHNNY FITTED A DEVICE UNDERNEATH THE NEW SPITFIRE.

THAT'S IT, JOHNNY, ALL FIXED.

GOOD WORK, BUTCH. THIS GIMMICK HAS SAVED MY LIFE BEFORE, AND I RECKON IT'LL DO IT AGAIN TOO.

AT THAT MOMENT, MANY MILES AWAY, A CODED JAP MESSAGE WAS INTERCEPTED ON THE RADIO AT ALLIED H.Q.

GET A LOAD OF THIS!

THE MESSAGE WAS RUSHED TO THE DECODING ROOM, WHERE EXPERTS LOST NO TIME IN TRANSLATING IT.

WHAT A BREAK, THE JAPS ARE STILL USING THE CODE WE BUSTED LAST WEEK. AND BOY, IS THIS HOT STUFF!

LATER, AT A TOP-LEVEL MEETING, THE TEXT OF THE MESSAGE WAS FINALLY DISCLOSED.

WE HAVE INFORMATION THAT ADMIRAL MOTO WILL BE MAKING A FLIGHT TO THE ISLAND OF TUKABOR, THE JAP'S BIGGEST BASE.

THIS IS A SPLENDID OPPORTUNITY TO DISPOSE OF JAPAN'S MOST BRILLIANT NAVAL BRAIN. YOUR PILOTS MUST SHOOT HIM DOWN AT ALL COSTS.

ADMIRAL MOTO HAD BEEN THE CHIEF ARCHITECT OF THE SUCCESSFUL JAPANESE SWEEP THROUGH THE PACIFIC.

THE TASK OF INTERCEPTING ADMIRAL MOTO'S FLIGHT WAS GIVEN TO NICK'S SQUADRON. IN THE BRIEFING ROOM...

THE OPERATION IS A TOUGH ONE. MOTO'S BOMBER WILL BE HEAVILY ESCORTED. YOUR JOB IS TO BREAK THROUGH THE FIGHTERS AND GET MOTO. AND I REPEAT — YOU MUST GET HIM. THAT'S ALL. GOOD LUCK.

GOOD LUCK! HE MEANS GOODBYE!

IT WAS INDEED A TOUGH JOB. JOHNNY ZERO WAS FAR FROM HAPPY. NICK, TOO, HAD MISGIVINGS.

TOUGH, THE MAN SAYS. MORE LIKE SUICIDAL. AND ME LUMBERED WITH A BUNCH OF KNUCKLE-HEADED AUSTRALIANS. I'VE GOT A FEELING THIS WILL BE MY LAST FLIGHT.

THE BRASS-HATS ARE ASKING FOR A MIRACLE. THEY EXPECT US TO CUT THROUGH THE WHOLE ESCORT WITH ONLY TWELVE PLANES.

AS DAWN TINGED THE SKY OVER DARWIN, THE SPITFIRES TOOK OFF ON THEIR FORMIDABLE TASK. JOHNNY ZERO'S VOICE CRACKLED OVER THE INTERCOM.

NOW LISTEN GOOD, YOU GUYS. WE CAN'T AFFORD ANY STUPID MISTAKES THIS TIME...

NICK FELT LIKE INTERRUPTING AS THE AMERICAN ISSUED A STREAM OF LAST MINUTE INSTRUCTIONS, BUT HE KEPT HIS THOUGHTS TO HIMSELF.

THE YANK'S STILL FULL OF CONTEMPT FOR US. BUT THE BOYS ARE READY FOR ANYTHING NOW — ESPECIALLY A FEW ZEROS.

MEANWHILE   THE BOMBER CARRYING ADMIRAL MOTO WAS FLYING SECURELY IN THE MIDDLE OF THE MASSED ZERO ESCORT.

THE JAPANESE WERE TAKING NO CHANCES. MOTO'S PLANE WAS SURROUNDED BY A CLOUD OF FIGHTERS.

THE ADMIRAL WAS DEEP IN THOUGHT. HE WAS ON HIS WAY TO A TOP-LEVEL MEETING IN WHICH HE WOULD REVEAL HIS PLAN FOR THE INVASION OF AUSTRALIA.

THIS WILL BE MY CROWNING ACHIEVEMENT. I HAVE CREATED THE PLAN, AND I ALONE WILL TAKE FULL CREDIT.

THE AMBITIOUS ADMIRAL WAS ALSO HIGHLY SUSPICIOUS. HE TRUSTED NOBODY, NOT EVEN HIS OWN STAFF. ONLY A SINGLE MASTER PLAN EXISTED, AND THAT WAS IN THE BRIEFCASE AT HIS FEET.

AND SO AUSTRALIA'S DESTINY FLEW IN THAT SINGLE JAP BOMBER, GUARDED BY THREE CRACK SQUADRONS OF ZEROS — COMMANDED BY NONE OTHER THAN CAPTAIN SAITO.

IT IS A GREAT HONOUR TO HAVE BEEN CHOSEN TO LEAD THE ADMIRAL'S ESCORT.

BUT SAITO'S VAIN THOUGHTS WERE RUDELY INTERRUPTED AS THE HUNTING SPITFIRES CRASHED DOWN ON THE JAP FORMATION WITH GUNS BLAZING. FOR A FEW VITAL SECONDS THEY HAD THE ADVANTAGE. JOHNNY'S VOICE CRACKLED OVER THE AIR.

REMEMBER, YOU GUYS — STRAIGHT FOR MOTO'S PLANE!

THE SPITFIRES KNIFED THROUGH THE TOP LAYER OF ZEROS, AND JOHNNY HIMSELF WAS THE FIRST TO GET A BEAD ON THE ADMIRAL'S PLANE.

RIGHT, MOTO, YOU'VE HAD IT NOW. I CAN'T MISS AT THIS RANGE.

BUT MISS HE DID. HIS AIM WAS SHATTERED BY A STREAM OF BULLETS FROM THE ALL-BLACK ZERO.

SAITO!

NOW THAT HE HAD SEEN HIS HATED RIVAL, JOHNNY WAS BLIND TO EVERYTHING ELSE. HE TURNED TO ENGAGE THE BLACK DRAGON.

NICK SAW THE AMERICAN'S RASH ACTION AND SHOUTED TO HIM OVER THE RADIO.

PAYNE, YOU CRAZY FOOL, FORGET ABOUT SAITO! WE'RE HERE TO GET MOTO!

BUT JOHNNY IGNORED THE CALL. HE WAS TOTALLY OBSESSED WITH KILLING THE JAP ACE. HE CAUGHT SAITO WITH A WILD BURST, BUT THE DRAGON ZERO WAS FAR FROM FINISHED.

IT'S BEEN A LONG TIME, YOU RAT. BUT NOW I'M IN A PLANE AS GOOD AS YOURS.

SO IT WAS NICK WHO BLASTED THE ADMIRAL'S PLANE INTO FLAMING SCRAP. UNKNOWINGLY THE AUSTRALIAN HAD SAVED HIS COUNTRY FROM INVASION.

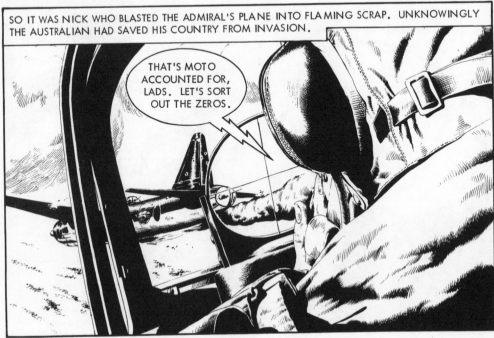

THAT'S MOTO ACCOUNTED FOR, LADS. LET'S SORT OUT THE ZEROS.

NOW FREED FROM THEIR FIRST DUTY, THE EAGER SPITFIRES TORE INTO THE JAP FIGHTERS WITH FURIOUS ZEAL.

SOON THE SKY WAS FILLED WITH FALLING ZEROS. THE AUSTRALIANS MORE THAN MADE UP FOR THEIR PREVIOUS MAULINGS.

BUT IN THE DUEL BETWEEN SAITO AND PAYNE IT WAS THE JAP ACE WHO FINALLY OUTSMARTED THE AMERICAN. WHIPPING ROUND IN A TIGHT TURN, HE HIT THE SPITFIRE WITH A STREAM OF BULLETS.

BANZAI!

THE SHARK-FACED SPITFIRE DIVED AWAY, PLUMING THICK SMOKE, WITH SAITO FOLLOWING, A COLD SMILE ON HIS YELLOW FACE.

AH, SO THE AMERICAN THINKS HE CAN TRICK ME AGAIN WITH THE SMOKE-MAKING DEVICE. THIS TIME I MAKE CERTAIN OF HIM.

JOHNNY'S SECRET DEVICE CONSISTED OF TWO SMOKE CANISTERS WHICH HE COULD ACTIVATE TO MAKE THE ENEMY THINK HE WAS CRASHING.

BUT THIS TIME IT HAD NOT FOOLED THE SHREWD SAITO.

BEFORE JOHNNY REALISED THAT HIS TRICK HAD FAILED, THE JAP ACE PUMPED THE SPITFIRE SO FULL OF BULLETS THAT THE PLANE BEGAN TO BREAK UP IN THE AIR. JOHNNY SLAMMED BACK THE CANOPY TO BALE OUT.

AS JOHNNY DANGLED HELPLESSLY BENEATH HIS PARACHUTE, THE RUTHLESS BLACK DRAGON SWOOPED DOWN UPON HIM AND OPENED FIRE.

SAITO'S BULLETS LASHED INTO THE HELPLESS MAN, AND THE JAP FLEW AWAY IN SAVAGE SATISFACTION.

JOHNNY'S HEAD FELL FORWARD ON HIS CHEST, AND HE DANGLED LIMPLY IN THE HARNESS.

BUT NICK HAD WITNESSED THE FOUL DEED. BOILING WITH RAGE, HE SPED AFTER THE BLACK DRAGON.

MADE CARELESS BY HIS VICTORY OVER THE AMERICAN, SAITO RECEIVED A RUDE AWAKENING AS NICK'S SHELLS SMASHED INTO THE BLACK ZERO.

THE DESTRUCTION OF SAITO'S PLANE KNOCKED THE FIGHT OUT OF THE JAPS. THE FEW SURVIVORS TURNED TAIL AND FLED, LEAVING THE SPITFIRES VICTORS OF THE SKIES. NICK AND HIS MEN HEADED FOR HOME.

WHEN THE SPITFIRES LANDED, NICK WALKED OVER TO BUTCH GIBSON, WHO WAS STILL WATCHING THE SKY FOR THE SHARK-FACED MACHINE TO RETURN.

I'M SORRY, BUTCH, BUT JOHNNY WON'T BE COMING BACK. SAITO KILLED HIM AFTER HE BALED OUT. BUT I GOT THE RAT FOR HIM.

I KNEW IT WOULD END LIKE THIS. EITHER HE WOULD GET SAITO, OR THAT LOUSY JAP WOULD GET HIM.

BUTCH'S ANSWER PROMPTED NICK TO ASK ABOUT JOHNNY'S LONG FEUD WITH THE BLACK DRAGON.

WHY DID JOHNNY HATE SAITO SO MUCH?

BECAUSE HE KILLED JOHNNY'S KID BROTHER, SAME AS HE GOT JOHNNY — HANGING UNDER A PARACHUTE.

NOW THAT NICK UNDERSTOOD THE REASON FOR JOHNNY'S RUTHLESS APPROACH TO AIR FIGHTING, HIS DISLIKE FOR HIM VANISHED. HE TURNED AND WALKED AWAY.

WAR'S A DIRTY BUSINESS. I DON'T BLAME HIM FOR FEELING AS HE DID. I'D FEEL THE SAME WAY. ANYWAY, IT'S ALL OVER FOR HIM NOW.

NICK COULDN'T HAVE BEEN MORE WRONG, FOR SEVERAL DAYS LATER   JOHNNY ZERO SUDDENLY APPEARED.

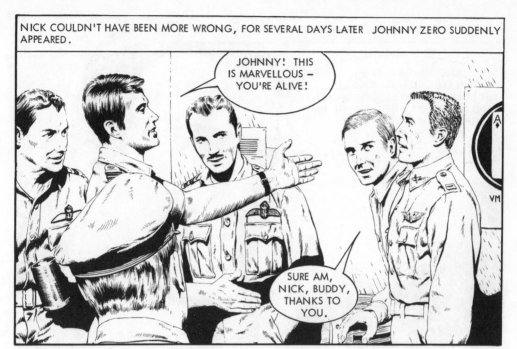

THE TWO MEN SHOOK HANDS WARMLY, REAL FRIENDS AT LAST.

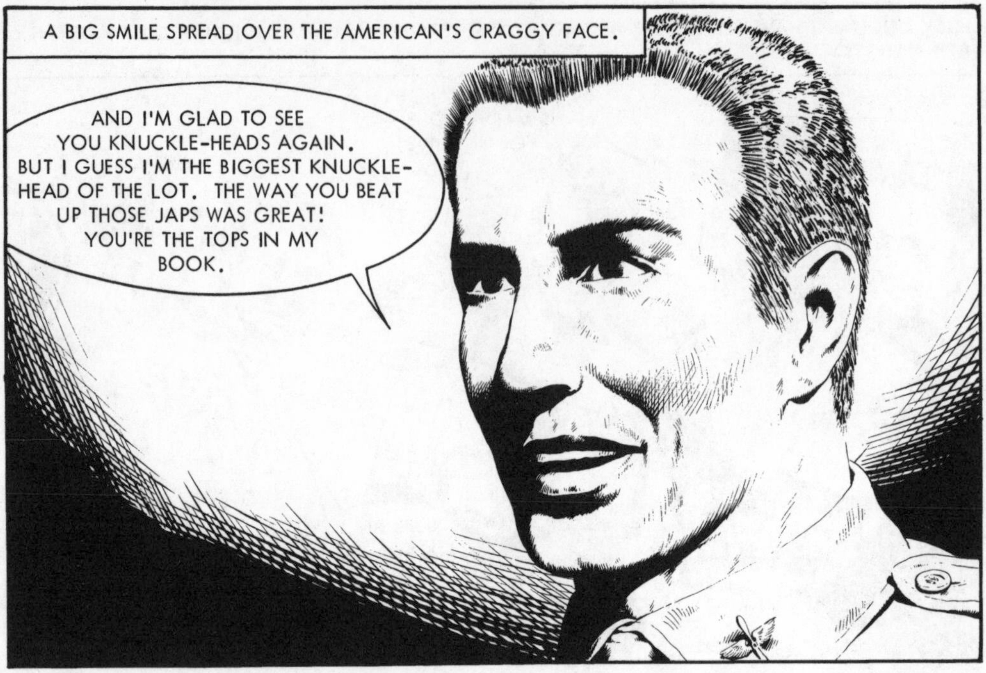
A BIG SMILE SPREAD OVER THE AMERICAN'S CRAGGY FACE.
AND I'M GLAD TO SEE YOU KNUCKLE-HEADS AGAIN. BUT I GUESS I'M THE BIGGEST KNUCKLE-HEAD OF THE LOT. THE WAY YOU BEAT UP THOSE JAPS WAS GREAT! YOU'RE THE TOPS IN MY BOOK.

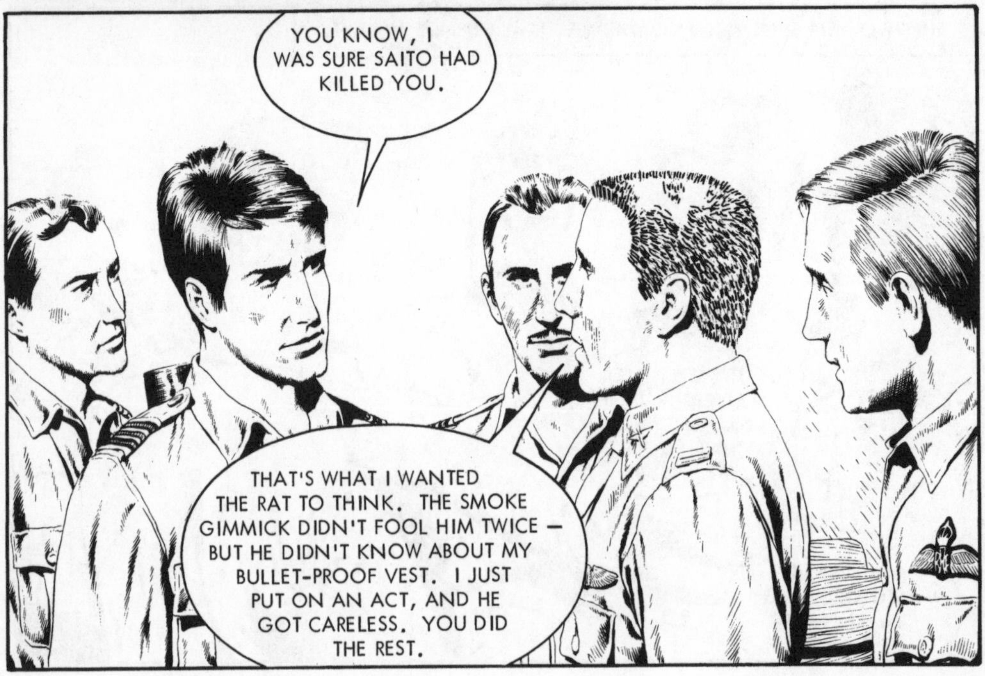
YOU KNOW, I WAS SURE SAITO HAD KILLED YOU.
THAT'S WHAT I WANTED THE RAT TO THINK. THE SMOKE GIMMICK DIDN'T FOOL HIM TWICE — BUT HE DIDN'T KNOW ABOUT MY BULLET-PROOF VEST. I JUST PUT ON AN ACT, AND HE GOT CARELESS. YOU DID THE REST.

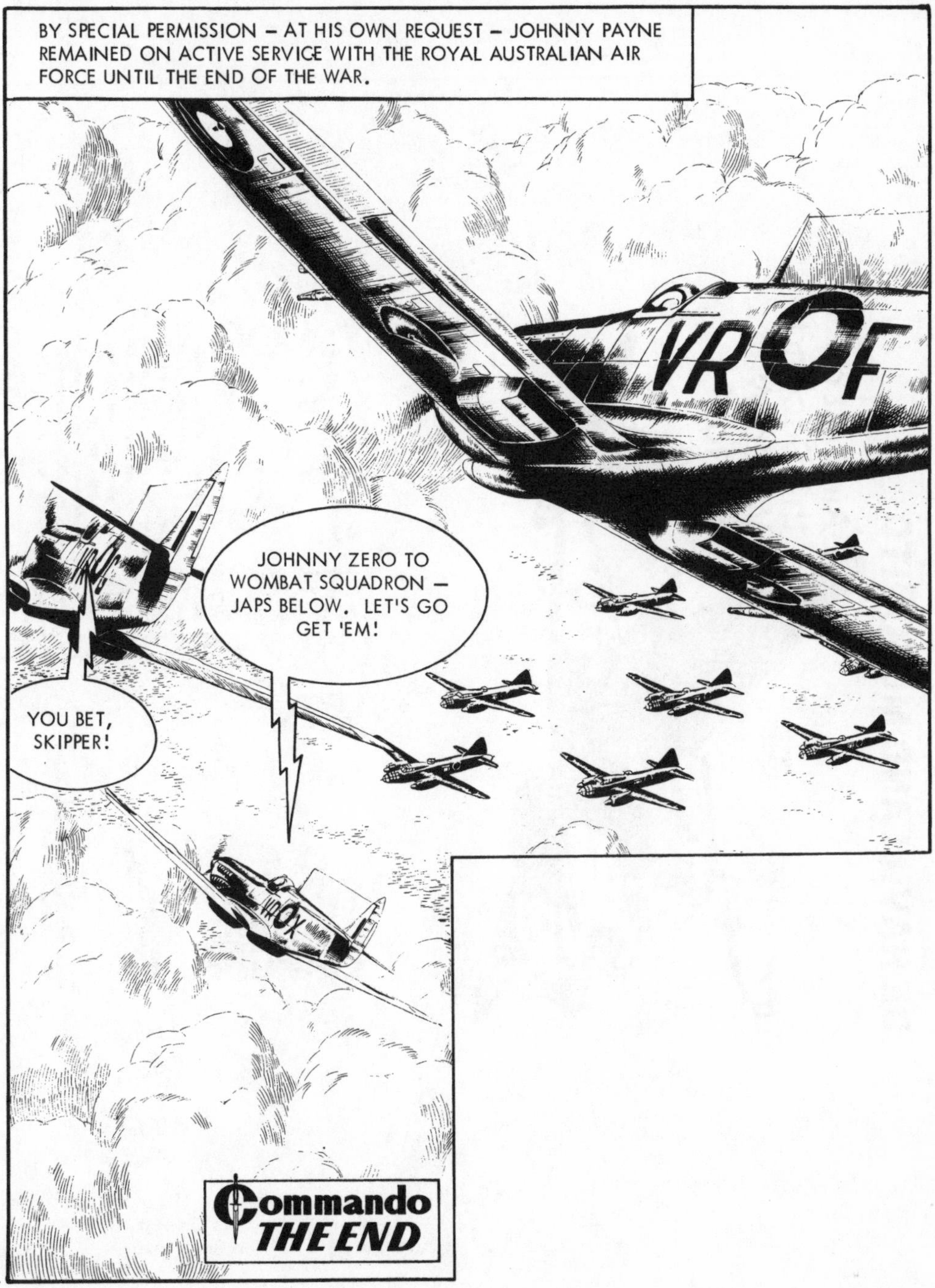
BY SPECIAL PERMISSION – AT HIS OWN REQUEST – JOHNNY PAYNE REMAINED ON ACTIVE SERVICE WITH THE ROYAL AUSTRALIAN AIR FORCE UNTIL THE END OF THE WAR.
JOHNNY ZERO TO WOMBAT SQUADRON – JAPS BELOW. LET'S GO GET 'EM!
YOU BET, SKIPPER!
Commando
THE END

DE HAVILLAND MOSQUITO

Aircraft of the Second World War — No. 14

NOSE OF MK. VI FIGHTER VERSION
FOUR M/GUNS AND FOUR CANNON

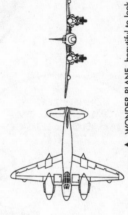

A WONDER-PLANE, beautiful to look at, successful in everything it did, and able to lick the fastest enemy fighters to a frazzle . . . that was the amazing "Mossie", the fighter-bomber that left its opponents wondering what had hit them. Built of steel-strong plywood at a time when supplies of metal were running low, it used its amazing speed to penetrate deep into enemy territory and drop its 4000 lb bomb-load from roof-top level with hair-splitting accuracy.

SPECIFICATION

POWER PLANT —
TWO ROLLS-ROYCE
"MERLIN" TWELVE-
CYLINDER VEE
LIQUID-COOLED
ENGINES POWERING
THREE-BLADED
CONSTANT-SPEED
FULLY-FEATHERING
AIRSCREWS.

DIMENSIONS —
SPAN 54ft 2in (16.5m)
LENGTH — 40ft 4in (12.3m)

BOMB LOAD — Up to 4,000 lb (1814 kg)
SPEED — 408mph (565km/h)

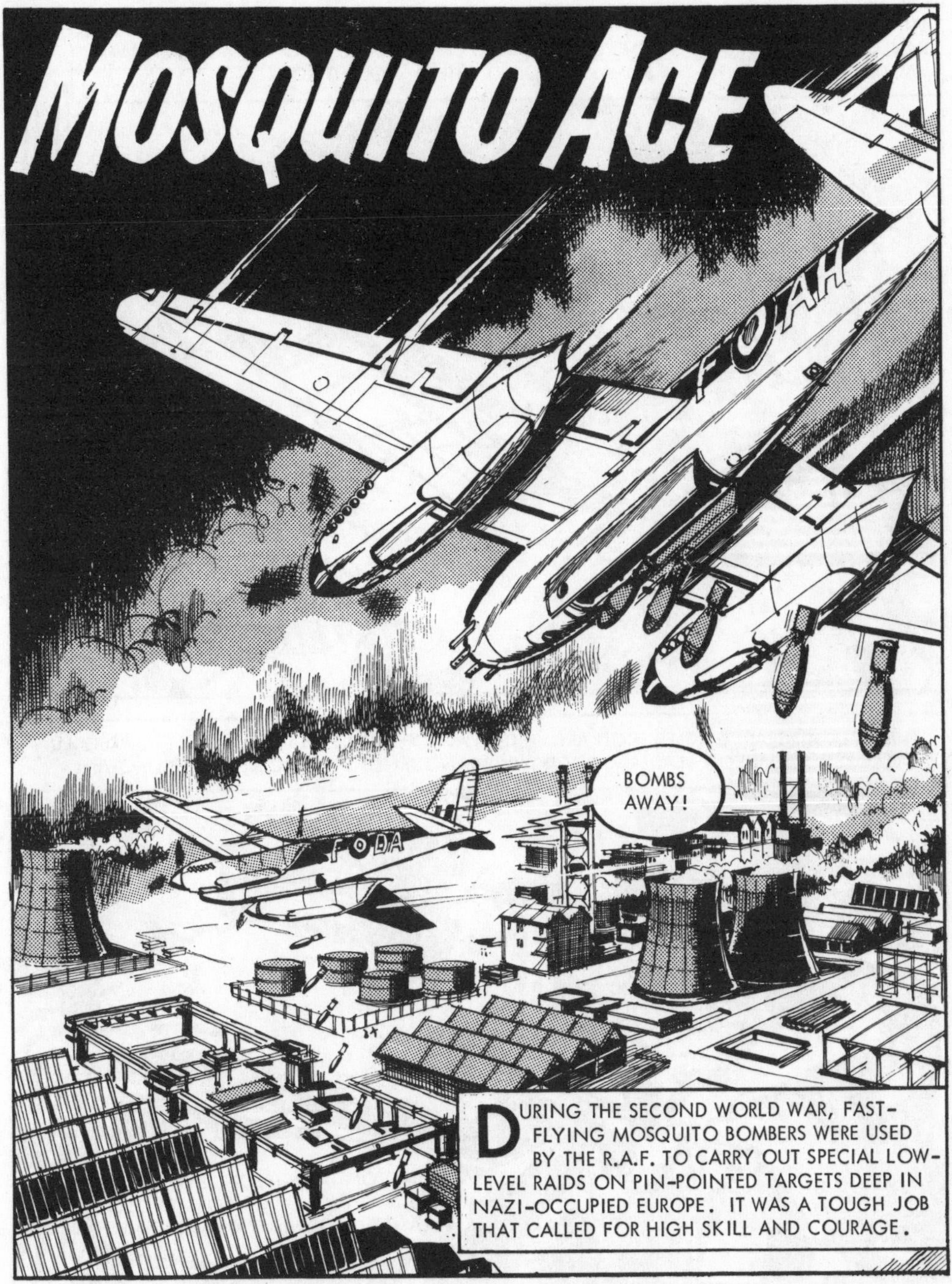
MOSQUITO ACE
F O A H
F O D A
BOMBS AWAY!
DURING THE SECOND WORLD WAR, FAST-FLYING MOSQUITO BOMBERS WERE USED BY THE R.A.F. TO CARRY OUT SPECIAL LOW-LEVEL RAIDS ON PIN-POINTED TARGETS DEEP IN NAZI-OCCUPIED EUROPE. IT WAS A TOUGH JOB THAT CALLED FOR HIGH SKILL AND COURAGE.

IN OCTOBER 1943, MOSQUITOES OF A CRACK NEW ZEALAND SQUADRON DROPPED THEIR PAYLOADS OF DESTRUCTION AND CLIMBED STEEPLY ABOVE THE ROOF OF A GERMAN WAR FACTORY. BELOW THEM THE BOMBS EXPLODED WITH A VIOLENT ROAR.

THE SLEEK AIRCRAFT CIRCLED HIGH ABOVE THE PALL OF SMOKE THAT CLOAKED THE WRECKED FACTORY. SQUADRON-LEADER HARRY 'KIWI' DEAN TURNED TO HIS OBSERVER, BILL OWEN.

WELL, BILL, WHAT'S THE VERDICT?

BANG ON THE BUTTON, SKIPPER. DOES MY HEART GOOD TO GIVE JERRY A BASINFUL OF HIS OWN MEDICINE.

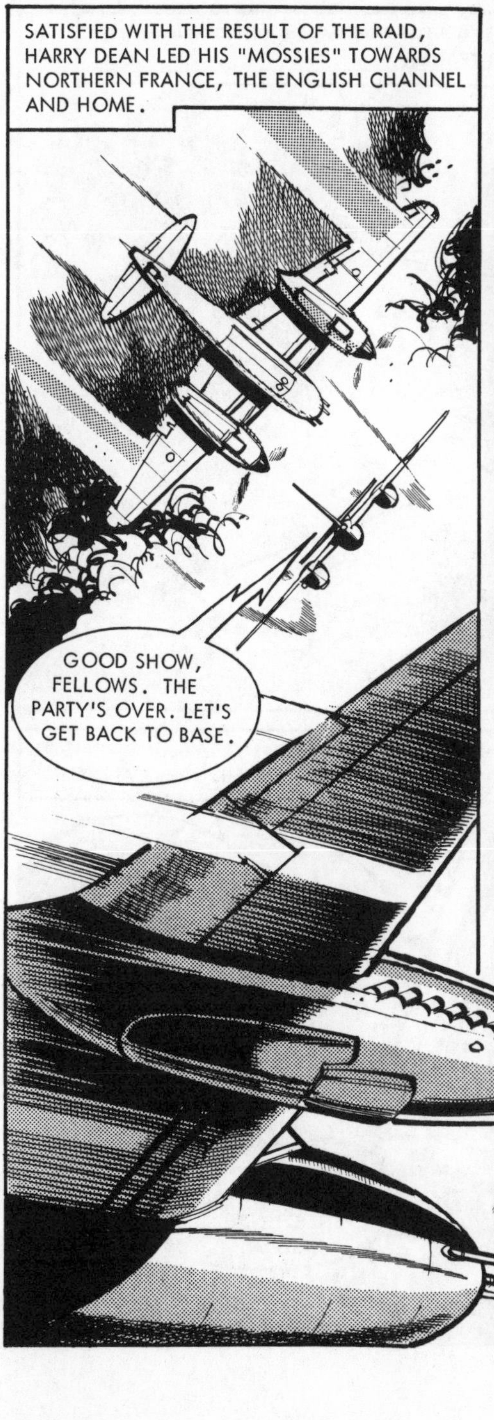
SATISFIED WITH THE RESULT OF THE RAID, HARRY DEAN LED HIS "MOSSIES" TOWARDS NORTHERN FRANCE, THE ENGLISH CHANNEL AND HOME.
GOOD SHOW, FELLOWS. THE PARTY'S OVER. LET'S GET BACK TO BASE.

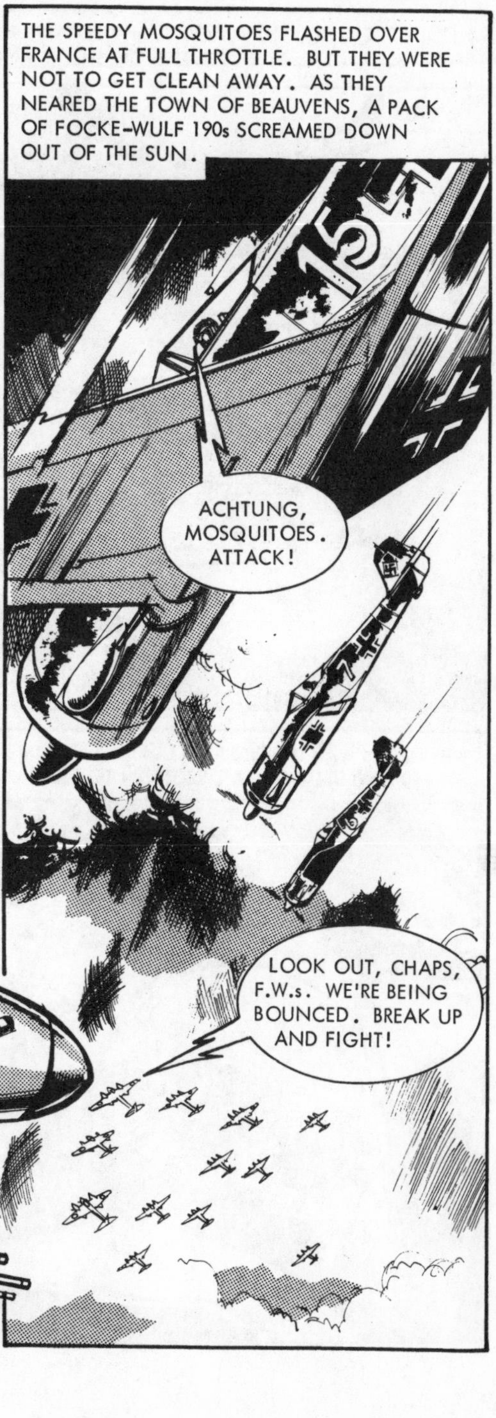
THE SPEEDY MOSQUITOES FLASHED OVER FRANCE AT FULL THROTTLE. BUT THEY WERE NOT TO GET CLEAN AWAY. AS THEY NEARED THE TOWN OF BEAUVENS, A PACK OF FOCKE-WULF 190s SCREAMED DOWN OUT OF THE SUN.
ACHTUNG, MOSQUITOES. ATTACK!
LOOK OUT, CHAPS, F.W.s. WE'RE BEING BOUNCED. BREAK UP AND FIGHT!

WITHIN SECONDS, THE PEACEFUL SKY BECAME FILLED WITH ANGRY, TWISTING WARPLANES SPITTING OUT STREAMS OF CANNON SHELLS AND TRACER.

KIWI DEAN WAS THE FIRST TO CLAIM A VICTIM. HE TACKED ON THE REAR OF A BLUNT-WINGED FW 190 AND BLEW ITS TAIL SECTION TO PIECES WITH A SHORT BURST FROM HIS 20mm CANNON.

GOT HIM!

RIGHT IN THE SWASTIKA. GREAT SHOOTING, SKIPPER.

THE DARE-DEVIL NEW ZEALANDERS THREW THEIR ALL-WOOD AIRCRAFT AROUND THE WIDE BLUE ARENA WITH BREATH-TAKING EASE. SOON, THEIR SHARP SKILL NAILED TWO MORE OF THE ENEMY.

SO LONG, JERRY. THAT'LL TEACH YOU NOT TO TANGLE WITH THE KIWIS.

THE DOGFIGHT WAS WELL IN HAND, BUT KIWI KNEW THAT IF ANY MORE NAZIS ARRIVED, THEY'D HAD IT.

BLUE ONE CALLING...BETTER BREAK OFF THE SCRAP, LADS. FUEL AND AMMO'S RUNNING SHORT. LET'S SHOW THESE BLIGHTERS JUST HOW FAST A MOSSIE CAN MOVE.

BUT AS THE MOSQUITOES BROKE AWAY, TWO FOCKE-WULFS SCREAMED DOWN ON HARRY'S AIRCRAFT.

OY! BILL, WE'VE BEEN PRANGED.

YOU'RE NOT KIDDING. THIS KITE'S LIKE A FLAMING SIEVE!

WHEN THEY SAW THEIR LEADER'S PLANE PLUNGE DOWN PLUMING SMOKE, THE OTHER NEW ZEALANDERS WENT BLAZING MAD.

THEY'VE GOT THE SKIPPER! LET'S RIP THESE HUNS TO PIECES FOR THIS, LADS.

BUT KIWI'S FIRM VOICE SOON PUT A STOP TO THAT.

LISTEN, YOU CLOTS! CLEAR OFF NOW AND GET TO BASE — THAT'S AN ORDER. BILL AND I WILL BE OK, WE'RE GOING TO BALE OUT.

RELUCTANTLY THE PILOTS OBEYED THEIR LEADER. TEDDY WILSON, KIWI'S BEST PAL, TOOK OVER COMMAND...

THE SKIPPER'S RIGHT, YOU BLOKES. NO USE ALL COPPING IT.

SO LONG, KIWI, AND THE BEST OF LUCK!

OK, TEDDY, YOU'RE THE BOSS NOW.

SECONDS LATER, KIWI AND BILL WERE FLOATING GENTLY DOWN.

WELL, I GUESS IT HAD TO COME. TWO YEARS OF OPS WITHOUT BUYING IT ONCE IS PUSHING LUCK AS FAR AS SHE'LL GO.

IF THERE'S ONE THING I HATE, IT'S THE THOUGHT OF ROTTING IN A JERRY P.O.W. CAMP.

AFTER THE TWO NEW ZEALANDERS HAD LANDED THEY WERE QUICKLY SURROUNDED BY GERMAN SOLDIERS. SECONDS LATER, AN ARROGANT OFFICER ARRIVED IN A STAFF CAR.

ALL RIGHT, FELDWEBEL, I'LL TAKE CHARGE OF THE ENEMY FLIEGERS. THEY ARE WANTED FOR IMMEDIATE INTERROGATION AT H.Q. I SHALL ONLY NEED ONE GUARD.

JAWOHL, HERR HAUPTMANN! BAMBERG, YOU WILL ESCORT THE PRISONERS.

MINUTES LATER, KIWI AND BILL WERE SPEEDING ALONG IN THE MERCEDES COVERED BY THE BARRELS OF A LUGER AND A SCHMEISSER SUB-MACHINE GUN.

AFTER A LITTLE TALK AT H.Q. YOU WILL BE TAKEN TO A P.O.W. CAMP. TRY TO ESCAPE AND YOU WILL BE SHOT.

AW, PUT A SOCK IN IT, WILL YOU? YOU'RE GIVING ME GOOSE PIMPLES.

AS THE CAR ROARED ALONG THE TWISTING COUNTRY ROADS, A DESPERATE PLAN CAME INTO BILL'S HEAD.

A LITTLE LATER, AS THE BIG MERCEDES SWUNG ROUND STEEPLY, BILL SPRANG LIKE A TIGER...

AND KIWI GOT RIGHT ON THE BALL.

THE HAUPTMANN'S GUN HAND WAS FORCED DOWN BEFORE HE COULD MOVE.

ACH, PIG!

NO YOU DON'T, SQUAREHEAD!

AS THE HUGE CAR SPED ON, A SAVAGE LIFE OR DEATH STRUGGLE RAGED AMONG THE FOUR. BILL WAS THE FIRST TO WIN HIS BOUT.

OUT YOU GO, FRITZ!

AAAARGH!

A SECOND LATER, KIWI SMASHED THE GERMAN OFFICER UNCONSCIOUS.

ACH — !

GOOD ON YOU, KIWI. NOW FOR THE DRIVER...

BILL RAMMED THE SCHMEISSER HARD INTO THE DRIVER'S NECK.

STOP, YOU, OR YOU'LL HAVE NO HEAD!

BUT THE DRIVER WAS A REAL NAZI FANATIC. WITH COMPLETE DISREGARD FOR HIS OWN LIFE HE SPUN THE WHEEL OF THE CAR AND HURTLED IT OFF THE ROAD TO DESTRUCTION.

LOOK OUT, BILL, WE'RE GOING TO CRASH!

JA, ENGLANDER. WE WILL ALL DIE TOGETHER.

BILL BELTED THE DRIVER, BUT NEXT INSTANT THE SPEEDING MERCEDES SLAMMED INTO THE TREE WITH A SICKENING CRUNCH, BOUNCED AND ROLLED AWAY.

AAAARGH!

ONLY ONE FIGURE STAGGERED OUT OF THE FEARFUL CRASH ALIVE — KIWI DEAN.

POOR OLD BILL. I — I MUST GET AWAY FROM HERE...MAYBE MAKE MY WAY TO THE COAST. IF I'M CAUGHT I'LL BE SHOT FOR SURE.

AFTER SEVERAL MILES OF CROSS-COUNTRY WALKING, THE DAZED AND GRIEVING PILOT SPOTTED A LONELY FARM.

THIS LOOKS LIKE A GOOD PLACE TO REST. I COULD SLEEP FOR A WEEK.

THOROUGHLY EXHAUSTED, THE NEW ZEALANDER SANK DOWN GRATEFULLY IN THE SOFT HAY AND IMMEDIATELY FELL INTO A DEEP SLEEP. LATER, WHEN HE OPENED HIS EYES...

DON'T BE ALARMED, MON AMI, YOU ARE IN GOOD HANDS. I AM A PATRIOT. I WILL BRING YOU FOOD AND THEN CONTACT A RESISTANCE GROUP.

MERCI, M'SIEUR.

LOOKS LIKE I'VE HIT A LUCKY STRIKE.

GASTON, THE FARMER, WAS TRUE TO HIS WORD. A DAY LATER, KIWI FOUND HIMSELF IN THE HOME OF RESISTANCE SECTION LEADER, CRIPPLED PAUL THIERRY, IN THE TOWN OF BEAUVENS.

THIS IS MY YOUNG BROTHER, RAOUL, AND MY MOTHER AND FATHER, SQUADRON-LEADER. YOU WILL BE SAFE HERE WITH US UNTIL WE CAN SMUGGLE YOU BACK TO ENGLAND.

I'M VERY GRATEFUL. BUT IF THE NAZIS DISCOVER THAT YOU ARE HIDING ME THEY WILL SHOOT YOU ALL.

THAT IS A RISK WE ARE GLAD TO TAKE. WE ARE FREE MEN, NOT THE SLAVES OF THOSE GESTAPO DOGS!

BUT KIWI HAD ONLY STAYED WITH THE THIERRY FAMILY A FEW DAYS, WHEN —

THE GESTAPO! WE'VE BEEN BETRAYED. QUICKLY, WE MUST ALL ESCAPE.

NO, PAUL. TAKE M'SIEUR DEAN AWAY WHILE I HOLD THE SWINE UP.

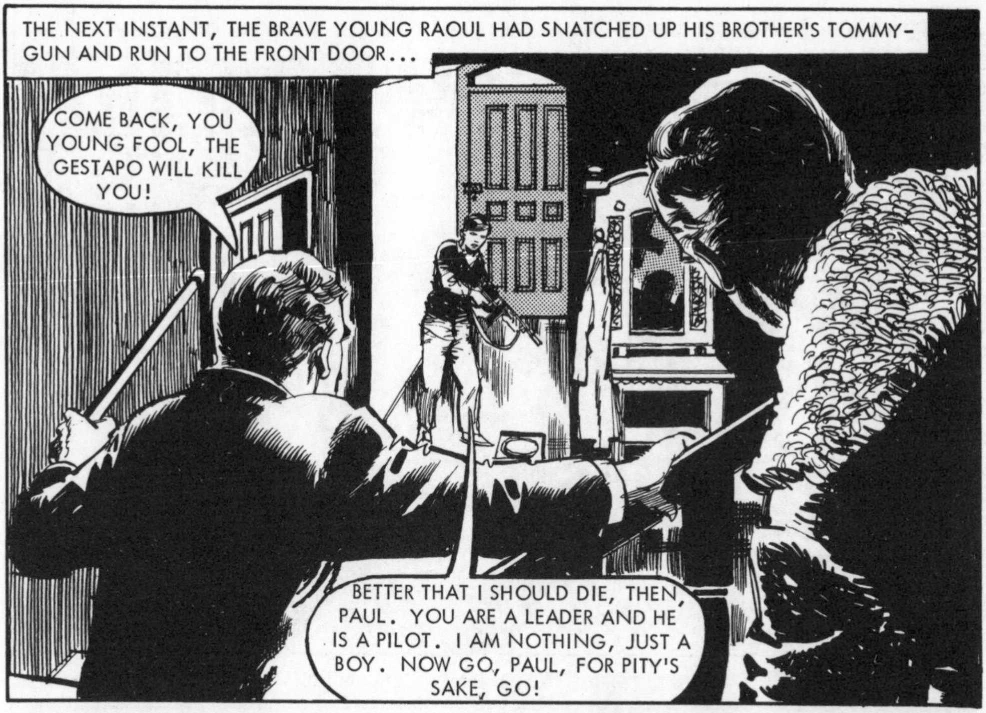
THE NEXT INSTANT, THE BRAVE YOUNG RAOUL HAD SNATCHED UP HIS BROTHER'S TOMMY-GUN AND RUN TO THE FRONT DOOR...
COME BACK, YOU YOUNG FOOL, THE GESTAPO WILL KILL YOU!
BETTER THAT I SHOULD DIE, THEN, PAUL. YOU ARE A LEADER AND HE IS A PILOT. I AM NOTHING, JUST A BOY. NOW GO, PAUL, FOR PITY'S SAKE, GO!

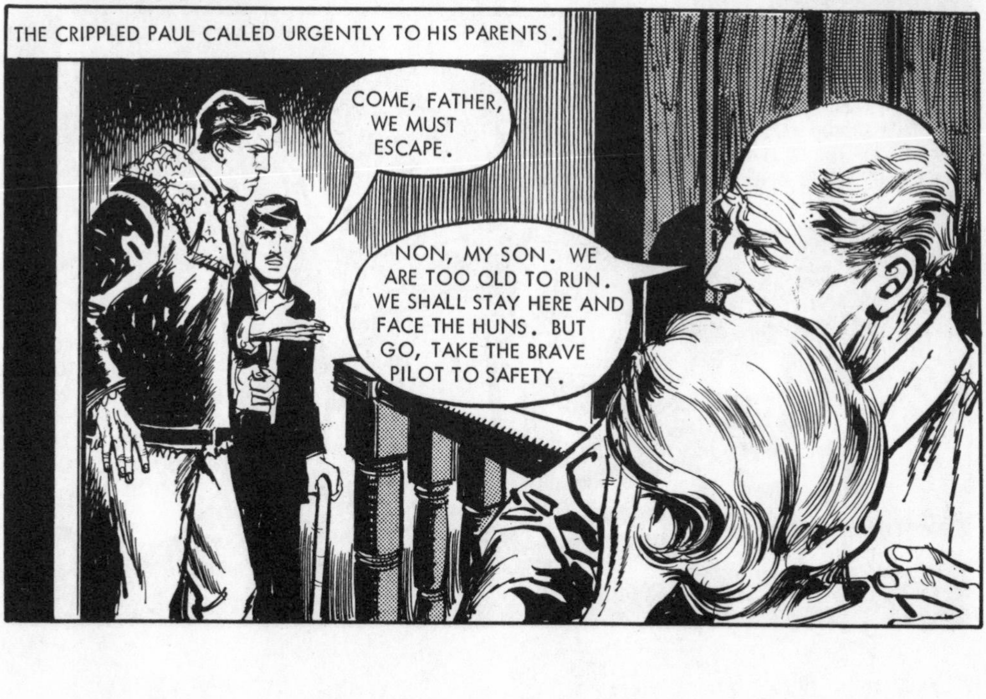
THE CRIPPLED PAUL CALLED URGENTLY TO HIS PARENTS.
COME, FATHER, WE MUST ESCAPE.
NON, MY SON. WE ARE TOO OLD TO RUN. WE SHALL STAY HERE AND FACE THE HUNS. BUT GO, TAKE THE BRAVE PILOT TO SAFETY.

AND SO DID YOUNG RAOUL THIERRY DIE A HERO'S DEATH TO BUY TIME AND FREEDOM FOR HIS BROTHER AND KIWI DEAN.

VIVE LA FRANCE...!

IT WAS A SACRIFICE THAT THE NEW ZEALAND PILOT WAS NEVER TO FORGET.

LATER, AT A SECRET LANDING FIELD NEAR THE FRENCH COAST, KIWI BID FAREWELL TO PAUL THIERRY.

THANKS, PAUL. I — I JUST DON'T FEEL WORTHY OF IT ALL — YOUR BROTHER DEAD, YOUR PARENTS IN THE HANDS OF THE GESTAPO, JUST SO THAT I COULD ESCAPE AND FIGHT AGAIN.

THIS IS WAR, MON AMI. RAOUL WILL NOT HAVE DIED IN VAIN IF YOU RETURN WITH YOUR AIRCRAFT AND STRIKE THE NAZIS HARD AND OFTEN. GOOD LUCK.

ON THE FLIGHT BACK TO BRITAIN, KIWI'S MIND WAS ABLAZE WITH THOUGHTS OF VENGEANCE...

WHICHEVER WAY YOU LOOK AT IT, I'M TOTALLY RESPONSIBLE FOR THE FATE OF THE THIERRY FAMILY. I OWE PAUL A DEBT I CAN NEVER REPAY. BUT I'LL GET MY REVENGE ON THOSE GESTAPO BRUTES AT BEAUVENS SOMEHOW, I SWEAR IT.

THE SQUADRON REJOICED AT THEIR POPULAR LEADER'S SAFE RETURN.

GOOD ON YOU, SKIPPER. I KNEW YOU WERE TOO SLIPPERY FOR THE SQUAREHEADS TO HOLD. HOW DID YOU DO IT?

STOW IT, TEDDY, I DIDN'T DO A THING. OTHERS HELPED ME ESCAPE...AND DIED DOING IT.

YOUNG RAOUL'S DEATH WILL HAUNT ME FOR EVER UNLESS I CAN SQUARE THE ACCOUNT.

IT WASN'T LONG BEFORE KIWI AND HIS SQUADRON WERE ONCE AGAIN OPERATIONAL OVER GERMANY.

TARGET DEAD AHEAD, BOYS. LET'S GIVE IT A REAL BASHING!

THE MOSQUITOES SWEPT IN LOW AT NERVE-RACKING HEIGHTS AND SENT THEIR BOMBS SKIMMING TOWARDS THE NAZI TANK AND MUNITIONS FACTORIES.

BOMBS AWAY! THAT'S GOING TO KNOCK A HOLE IN HITLER'S WAR EFFORT.

AS HARRY BANKED HIS MACHINE ABOVE THE EXPLODING TARGET, HIS OBSERVER SAM HARRIS NOTED THE RESULT OF THE RAID WITH SATISFACTION.

BANG ON, SKIPPER. COULDN'T BE BETTER.

GOOD. NOW LET'S GET OUT OF HERE.

WITH ANOTHER SUCCESSFUL RAID TO THEIR CREDIT THE NEW ZEALANDERS ROARED HOMEWARDS. AS THE SLEEK MOSQUITOES ATE UP THE AIR MILES, AN IDEA SUDDENLY HIT KIWI, AS IF HE FELT HE HADN'T CAUSED ENOUGH TROUBLE TO THE NAZIS FOR ONE DAY.

BLUE ONE CALLING — HOW D'YOU FEEL ABOUT A LITTLE UNOFFICIAL STRAFING JOB, BOYS? I'VE A SCORE TO SETTLE WITH GESTAPO H.Q. IN BEAUVENS. IT'S WAY OFF COURSE, BUT WHAT D'YOU SAY?

TEDDY WILSON ANSWERED HIS CHIEF.

BLUE TWO HERE. COME OFF IT, KIWI, YOU KNOW WE'RE SUPPOSED TO GO STRAIGHT HOME TO MUM AFTER A RAID!

KIWI THOUGHT FOR A MOMENT. ALTHOUGH HE WAS BURNING FOR REVENGE, HE DIDN'T WANT TO INVOLVE HIS MEN IN HIS OWN PERSONAL FEUD.

YEAH, PERHAPS YOU'RE RIGHT, TEDDY. BUT, DARN IT, I MUST HAVE A CRACK AT THOSE GESTAPO RATS. TELL YOU WHAT, YOU TAKE THE BLOKES OFF HOME. I'LL CATCH YOU UP LATER.

BUT THE THOUGHT OF LEAVING KIWI ALONE IN ENEMY SKIES DIDN'T APPEAL TO WILSON AND THE OTHERS. AS KIWI BANKED TO TURN OFF —

AW, TO HECK WITH ORDERS! IF YOU GO, KIWI, WE GO. RIGHT, LADS?

TOO RIGHT, TEDDY. THAT'S WHAT WE'RE IN THIS WAR FOR — TO CLOBBER AS MANY GERMANS AS POSS. LET'S GO, SKIPPER!

WITH PERFECT PRECISION, THE SQUADRON OF MOSQUITOES SWUNG OFF COURSE AND HEADED FOR BEAUVENS. SOON —

THIS IS WHAT I'VE BEEN WAITING FOR, A CRACK AT THOSE BLACK-UNIFORMED SKUNKS WHO GOT RAOUL AND HIS PARENTS.

NEXT INSTANT, THE HATED BUILDING WHICH FLEW THE CROOKED CROSS OF NAZISM FLASHED INTO SIGHT.

THERE IT IS, CHAPS, GESTAPO H.Q. LET'S RIP IT TO PIECES. TALLYHO!

THE DREADED HOUSE OF TERROR SEEMED TO ROCK IN AGONY AS THE HURTLING MOSQUITOES UNLEASHED A BROADSIDE OF 20mm CANNON SHELLS AND MACHINE GUN BULLETS.

THOSE RATS AREN'T USED TO PEOPLE HITTING BACK!

INSIDE THE BUILDING OF FEAR, HIMMLER'S JACK-BOOTED SECRET POLICE WERE RUNNING FOR THEIR LIVES. BUT MANY MET THEIR DOOM UNDER THE STEEL-TIPPED STING OF THE ATTACKING MOSQUITOES.

AAARGH!

RADIO FOR THE — UUURGH!

BACK AND FORTH SWEPT THE MOSQUITOES, HAMMERING THE BUILDING WITH AN AVALANCHE OF DESTRUCTION. KIWI SMILED GRIMLY AS HE SENT HIS PERSONAL TORRENT OF DEATH THROUGH A THIRD FLOOR WINDOW.

I WOULDN'T LIKE TO PAY THEIR BARRACK ROOM DAMAGES, SAM!

AFTER SEVERAL MINUTES OF THE VENGEANCE STRIKE, FLAMES BEGAN TO SWEEP THROUGH THE GESTAPO H.Q. AND THE BLACK UNIFORMED MEN RAN INTO THE STREET...

THE RATS HAVE JUMPED OUT OF THE FRYING PAN INTO THE FIRE! TAKE THAT, ME CROP-'EADED BEAUTIES!

OUT OF AMMO, KIWI BANKED HIS PLANE ABOVE THE BLAZING BUILDING. BUT SUDDENLY, HE WAS SWEPT BY A SENSE OF IMPENDING DANGER...

OK, LADS, LET'S BEAT IT, WE'VE THROWN EVERYTHING EXCEPT OUR BOOTS AT 'EM. JUST PRAY WE DON'T MEET ANY JERRY FIGHTERS ON THE WAY HOME. IF WE DO, WE'LL BE IN DEAD TROUBLE WITH NO AMMO.

AND AS FATE WOULD HAVE IT, THAT WAS EXACTLY WHAT HAPPENED. ALERTED TO THE STRAFING MOSQUITOES, A PACK OF FOCKE-WULF 190s SCREAMED DOWN ON THE LOW-FLYING NEW ZEALANDERS AS THEY TURNED FOR THE COAST.

LOOK OUT, BOYS, BANDITS 9 O'CLOCK HIGH! FULL THROTTLE, EVERYONE. LET'S GIVE 'EM A RUN FOR THEIR MONEY.

WEAVING AND TWISTING IN THE TRACER-TORN SKY, THE DEFENCELESS MOSQUITOES DID THEIR BEST TO AVOID THE BARBED-TEETH OF THE GERMAN HAWKS. SPEED WAS THEIR ONLY HOPE.

ALTHOUGH THE MOSQUITOES HAD THE EDGE IN SPEED OVER THE FW 190s, ONE OR TWO COULDN'T ESCAPE THE RIPPING STREAMS OF NAZI SLUGS.

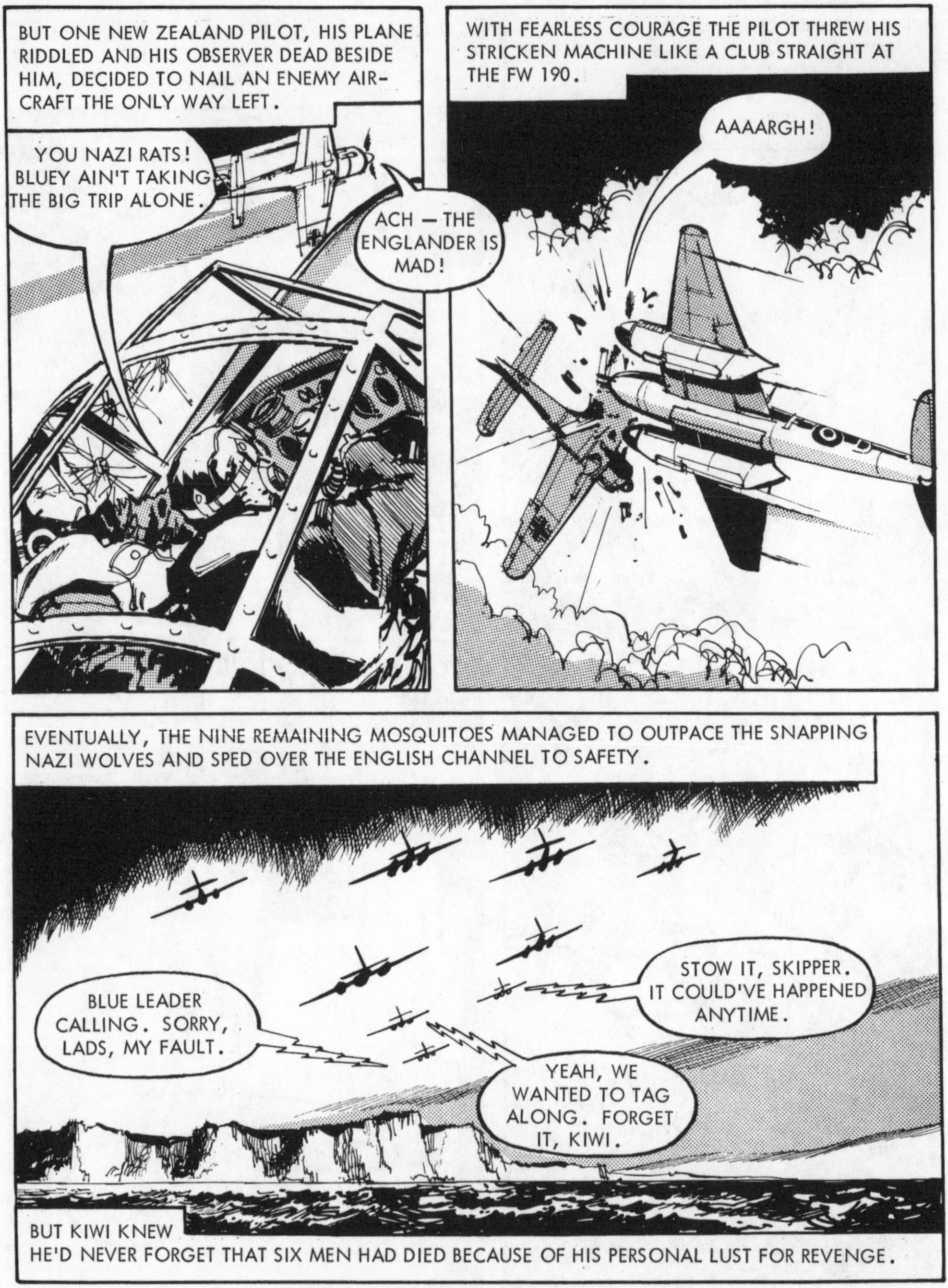
BUT ONE NEW ZEALAND PILOT, HIS PLANE RIDDLED AND HIS OBSERVER DEAD BESIDE HIM, DECIDED TO NAIL AN ENEMY AIRCRAFT THE ONLY WAY LEFT.
YOU NAZI RATS! BLUEY AIN'T TAKING THE BIG TRIP ALONE.
ACH — THE ENGLANDER IS MAD!
WITH FEARLESS COURAGE THE PILOT THREW HIS STRICKEN MACHINE LIKE A CLUB STRAIGHT AT THE FW 190.
AAAARGH!
EVENTUALLY, THE NINE REMAINING MOSQUITOES MANAGED TO OUTPACE THE SNAPPING NAZI WOLVES AND SPED OVER THE ENGLISH CHANNEL TO SAFETY.
BLUE LEADER CALLING. SORRY, LADS, MY FAULT.
STOW IT, SKIPPER. IT COULD'VE HAPPENED ANYTIME.
YEAH, WE WANTED TO TAG ALONG. FORGET IT, KIWI.
BUT KIWI KNEW
HE'D NEVER FORGET THAT SIX MEN HAD DIED BECAUSE OF HIS PERSONAL LUST FOR REVENGE.

LATER, KIWI HAD TO FACE HIS BRITISH STATION COMMANDER.

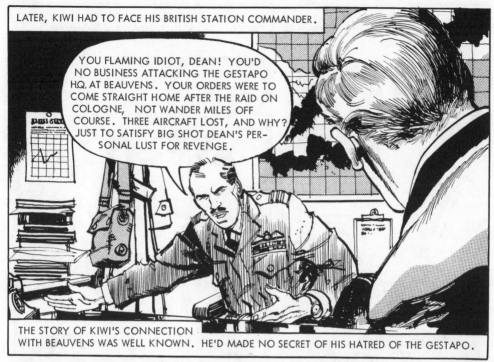

YOU FLAMING IDIOT, DEAN! YOU'D NO BUSINESS ATTACKING THE GESTAPO H.Q. AT BEAUVENS. YOUR ORDERS WERE TO COME STRAIGHT HOME AFTER THE RAID ON COLOGNE, NOT WANDER MILES OFF COURSE. THREE AIRCRAFT LOST, AND WHY? JUST TO SATISFY BIG SHOT DEAN'S PERSONAL LUST FOR REVENGE.

THE STORY OF KIWI'S CONNECTION WITH BEAUVENS WAS WELL KNOWN. HE'D MADE NO SECRET OF HIS HATRED OF THE GESTAPO.

KIWI'S RAGE AND GRIEF SUDDENLY EXPLODED.

YES, REVENGE! BUT THAT'S SOMETHING YOU WOULDN'T UNDERSTAND. YOU SIT HERE WITH YOUR MAPS, COLOURED FLAGS, AND FIGHT THE WAR TO A RULE-BOOK. WELL I'M NOT LIKE THAT. THOSE GESTAPO RATS DESERVED WHAT WE GAVE 'EM.

AS THE TWO MEN GLARED AT EACH OTHER, KIWI SUDDENLY REMEMBERED THE SIX MEN HE HAD LOST.

I — I DIDN'T REALISE WE WERE SO LOW ON AMMO, SIR. IT WON'T HAPPEN AGAIN.

YOU'RE DARNED RIGHT. IT WON'T HAPPEN AGAIN, AND I'LL TELL YOU WHY!

WING-COMMANDER SHAW'S NEXT WORDS STRUCK KIWI WITH THE FORCE OF A SLEDGE-HAMMER.

THERE'LL BE NO MORE OPERATIONAL DUTIES FOR YOU, DEAN. YOU'RE UN-RELIABLE, LET YOUR EMOTIONS RULE YOUR HEAD. I'M SENDING THROUGH A REPORT ON THIS AND ASKING THAT YOU BE TRANSFERRED TO A TRAINING WING.

OH, NO...!

THE SQUADRON-LEADER WALKED OUT OF THE OFFICE IN A DAZE. TEDDY WILSON AND THE BOYS SURROUNDED HIM.

WELL, KIWI, WHAT DID THE OLD MAN SAY?

GAVE YOU A DIRTY BIG ROCKET, EH, SKIPPER?

WING COMMANDER

NOT JUST A ROCKET, BEN, A RUDDY GREAT BLOCK-BUSTER. I'M BEING KICKED OFF THE STATION TO TRAINING DUTIES.

THE PILOTS WERE SHATTERED.

WHY, OF ALL THE ROTTEN DEALS!

NO QUIBBLES, BOYS. I ASKED FOR IT.

BUT SHAW DIDN'T HAVE TO THROW THE BOOK AT YOU. AFTER ALL, WE DID WRECK THE GESTAPO H.Q. I'M GOING TO HAVE A WORD WITH THAT STRAIGHT-LACED PONGO.

TEDDY WILSON STORMED INTO THE WING-COMMANDER'S OFFICE AND PROCEEDED TO GIVE THE ENGLISHMAN A MOUTHFUL OF NEW ZEALAND STRAIGHT TALK.

NOW LOOK HERE, WINGCO, THE BOYS AND I RECKON YOU'RE BEING TOO DARNED ROUGH ON THE SKIPPER. YOU KNOW DARN WELL HARRY'S A FIRST-RATE NUMBER ONE, AND THE BEST LOW-LEVEL FLYING BLOKE IN THE BUSINESS.

THAT'S QUITE ENOUGH, WILSON! ANY MORE OF THIS AND I'LL KICK YOU OFF THE STATION, TOO. THAT'S THE TROUBLE WITH YOU NEW ZEALANDERS — LACK OF DISCIPLINE. AND I'M GOING TO SEE THAT YOU GET SOME FROM NOW ON.

REALISING HE'D GONE TOO FAR, WILSON FOUGHT TO GET SOME RESPECT INTO HIS VOICE.

SORRY, SIR. BUT WE DO FEEL STRONGLY ABOUT THIS. KIWI'S LEARNT HIS LESSON, THE HARD WAY. WON'T YOU PLEASE GIVE HIM ANOTHER CHANCE, SIR?

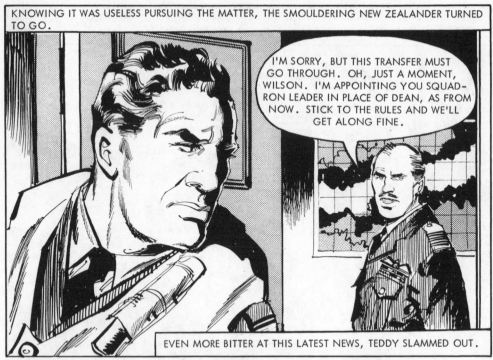

KNOWING IT WAS USELESS PURSUING THE MATTER, THE SMOULDERING NEW ZEALANDER TURNED TO GO.

I'M SORRY, BUT THIS TRANSFER MUST GO THROUGH. OH, JUST A MOMENT, WILSON. I'M APPOINTING YOU SQUADRON LEADER IN PLACE OF DEAN, AS FROM NOW. STICK TO THE RULES AND WE'LL GET ALONG FINE.

EVEN MORE BITTER AT THIS LATEST NEWS, TEDDY SLAMMED OUT.

JUST BEFORE HE LEFT, KIWI AND TEDDY SHOOK HANDS WARMLY.

DON'T WORRY, KIWI, I'LL LOOK AFTER THE BOYS FOR YOU. WHAT A LOUSY BREAK FOR A BLOKE LIKE YOU.

IT COULD'VE BEEN WORSE, TEDDY. I'M LUCKY THAT "RULE-BOOK" SHAW DIDN'T MARCH ME BEFORE A COURT-MARTIAL. JUST BASH THE HUNS FOR ME, OLD SON, THAT'S ALL I ASK.

GOOD LUCK, SKIPPER! THE OLD OUTFIT WON'T BE THE SAME WITHOUT YOU.

BUT HARRY DEAN WAS MORE UPSET ABOUT HIS TRANSFER THAN HE CARED TO SHOW...

NOW I'LL NEVER BE ABLE TO REPAY MY DEBT TO THE THIERRY FAMILY. RAOUL GAVE HIS LIFE SO THAT I COULD ESCAPE AND HAMMER THE NAZIS, NOT TO BE NURSE-MAID TO A LOT OF ROOKIES. BLAST! I'VE MADE SUCH A FLAMING MESS OF THE WHOLE SHOW.

SO ONE OF THE R.A.F.'S FINEST LOW-LEVEL BOMBING PILOTS TOOK UP HIS TRAINING DUTIES. FOR ALL HIS BITTERNESS, KIWI DID HIS NEW JOB WELL. BUT HIS RAGE FOR VENGEANCE STILL BURNED FIERCELY IN HIS HEART.

NOT BAD, FELLOWS, NOW LET'S DO IT AGAIN.

WHAT I WOULDN'T GIVE TO BE BLASTING THE HUNS. THIS IS NO JOB FOR A MAN WITH AN UNFINISHED ACCOUNT ON HIS HANDS. I WONDER WHAT PAUL THIERRY'S DO-ING NOW?

BUT KIWI WOULD'VE HATED TO SEE PAUL AT THAT MOMENT. NOW PROMOTED TO AREA LEADER, HE HAD JUST FALLEN INTO THE HANDS OF THE GESTAPO!

THE GAME'S UP, THIERRY. YOU AND ALL YOUR COMRADES WILL BE TAKEN TO BEAUVENS PRISON, QUESTIONED AND LATER SHOT.

WE HAVE BEEN BETRAYED! HOW ELSE COULD THE NAZI RATS HAVE GOT ON TO US?

THROUGH THE TREACHERY OF THE UNKNOWN INFORMER, THE GESTAPO HAD MANAGED TO ROUND UP NEARLY A HUNDRED RESISTANCE FIGHTERS IN THE BEAUVENS AREA, INCLUDING A GREAT NUMBER OF KEY LEADERS.

GET INSIDE, FRENCH SCHWEIN!

COCHONS!

GUT. PERHAPS WE HAVE AT LAST CRUSHED THE ACCURSED RESISTANCE IN THIS REGION.

THE CAPTURE OF THEIR LEADERS HAD DEALT THE FRENCH UNDERGROUND MOVEMENT A CRIPPLING BLOW. SO VITAL WERE THESE MEN THAT SOMETHING HAD TO BE DONE TO RESCUE THEM. RACING AGAINST TIME THE FEW MAQUIS LEADERS STILL FREE BEGAN TO PLAN...

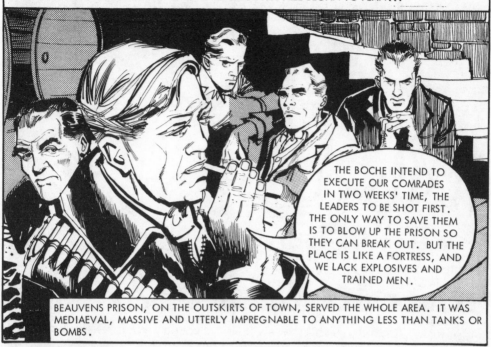

THE BOCHE INTEND TO EXECUTE OUR COMRADES IN TWO WEEKS' TIME, THE LEADERS TO BE SHOT FIRST. THE ONLY WAY TO SAVE THEM IS TO BLOW UP THE PRISON SO THEY CAN BREAK OUT. BUT THE PLACE IS LIKE A FORTRESS, AND WE LACK EXPLOSIVES AND TRAINED MEN.

BEAUVENS PRISON, ON THE OUTSKIRTS OF TOWN, SERVED THE WHOLE AREA. IT WAS MEDIAEVAL, MASSIVE AND UTTERLY IMPREGNABLE TO ANYTHING LESS THAN TANKS OR BOMBS.

THE GROUP FELL SILENT FOR A MOMENT, THEN A GRIM-FACED FRENCHMAN SPOKE.

THEN THERE'S ONLY ONE ANSWER TO OUR PROBLEM... WE MUST ASK THE R.A.F. TO STRIKE FROM THE SKY AND BREACH THE PRISON WALLS WITH BOMBS.

BUT CAN IT BE DONE WITHOUT KILLING THE MEN INSIDE?

SOME WILL DIE, BUT MANY WILL ALSO ESCAPE. IT WILL BE UP TO THE R.A.F. TO DROP THEIR BOMBS WITH PINPOINT ACCURACY. I SEE NO OTHER SOLUTION. BUT BEFORE WE ACT WE MUST GET A MESSAGE THROUGH TO OUR LEADERS, ASK IF THEY ARE WILLING.

JACQUES DESPARD IS STILL A WARDEN THERE, AND LOYAL TO US...

THE NEXT DAY THE FAITHFUL JACQUES ON HIS CLEANING ROUND WHISPERED BRIEFLY INTO EACH PACKED CELL FULL OF MAQUIS.

...AIRCRAFT TO BOMB, BREAK DOWN THE WALLS...FREEDOM...

FREEDOM!

A WHISPERED CONFERENCE WAS HELD BETWEEN THE CELLS. IN PAUL THIERRY'S CELL —

BUT WE MAY ALL BE KILLED!

SO? WHO OF US WOULD NOT RISK DEATH FOR FREE-DOM? I SAY "YES", LET THE R.A.F. SEND THEIR BOMBERS.

AND SOON PAUL HAD FIRED THE MEN WITH HIS OWN SPIRIT OF DEFIANCE.

BUT IN THE CELL AT LEAST ONE PARTISAN, GASTON BRENNER, THE LOCAL INNKEEPER, WASN'T HAPPY WITH THE DECISION AT ALL. HIS PALE, FAT FACE WAS BEADED WITH COLD SWEAT.

BUT THIS IS MADNESS! WE SHALL BE CRUSHED LIKE BEETLES, IS IT NOT? I SAY NON, NON MERCI!

LIKE FAT SLUGS, YOU MEAN, GASTON! BE QUIET, YOU FOOL. IT IS OUR ONLY CHANCE.

AND SO THE DESPERATE DECISION WAS PASSED ON TO OLD JACQUES.

ONLY SEVEN DAYS OF "INTERROGATION" WERE LEFT BEFORE THEIR DAY OF EXECUTION. THE REMAINING RESISTANCE LEADERS RADIOED BRITAIN REQUESTING THAT THE R.A.F. BURST BEAUVENS PRISON WIDE OPEN TO FREE THEIR LEADERS.

THE MESSAGE WAS RECEIVED AND IN BRITAIN THE WHEELS OF WAR BEGAN TO TURN. NEARLY AN ENTIRE QUARTER OF FRANCE'S INTELLIGENCE SET-UP, RESISTANCE LEADERS, ALL STOOD TO BE DESTROYED IF THE MEN IN THAT PRISON TALKED — OR DIED.

GENTLEMEN, WE PLAN TO UNDERTAKE THE LOW-LEVEL PRECISION BOMBING OF BEAUVENS PRISON TO FREE VITAL RESISTANCE MEN. IT MUST BE DONE BY A CRACK SQUADRON. I AWAIT YOUR SUGGESTIONS...

THE CHIEFS OF BOMBER COMMAND SOON PICKED THE UNIT FOR THIS SPECIAL TASK.

THERE'S NO DOUBT IN MY MIND, GENTLEMEN, THAT THERE'S ONE UNIT ONLY THAT COULD HANDLE THIS TICKLISH JOB — THEIR RECORD IS TERRIFIC.

THEY'RE NEW ZEALANDERS, AREN'T THEY?

YES, AND THEY'RE THE TOPS IN PRECISION BOMBING.

THE NEW ZEALANDERS WERE AS KEEN AS MUSTARD WHEN THEY HEARD THE NEWS. THEY HAD GREAT CONFIDENCE IN THEIR OWN ABILITY AND GREAT TRUST IN THEIR NEW LEADER, TEDDY WILSON. BUT TEDDY'S THOUGHTS WERE ELSEWHERE...

SO WE'RE TO BUST OPEN BEAUVENS JAIL. THIS IS JUST THE SORT OF CAPER KIWI WOULD GIVE HIS RIGHT ARM TO BE IN ON. WHAT LOUSY LUCK FOR HIM. STILL, THE SQUADRON WON'T LET HIM DOWN.

THE MEN WERE BRIEFED BY WING-COMMANDER SHAW, WHO LEFT NO DOUBT IN THEIR MINDS THAT THIS WAS TO BE A VERY TOUGH MISSION INDEED.

PRISON FRONT

MAIN GATE

GRASS STRIP ON ROAD

YOU WILL STRIKE THE OUTER WALLS FIRST. IT'S GOING TO MEAN SOME REAL LOW-LEVEL FLYING, RIGHT DOWN ON THE GROUND. THE WALLS ARE JUST OVER TWENTY FEET HIGH, THAT MEAN RUNNING IN AT TEN OR FIFTEEN FEET!

PHEW — THAT MEANS JUST ABOUT SCRAPING THE DECK!

SHAW TURNED FROM THE MAP TO A SCALE-MODEL OF BEAUVENS JAIL.

ZERO HOUR WILL BE IN SIX DAYS' TIME. UNTIL THEN YOU'LL STUDY THIS MODEL AND HUNDREDS OF PHOTOS UNTIL YOU KNOW THE PLACE INSIDE OUT. ALSO, YOU'LL BE DOING A NUMBER OF DUMMY RUNS OVER A MOCK-UP OF THE TARGET. THESE MEN'S LIVES AND A WHOLE INTELLIGENCE SET-UP WITH YEARS OF WORK BEHIND IT DEPEND ON YOU NEXT WEEK. THEY ARE DUE TO BE EXECUTED IN SEVEN DAYS.

BEAUVENS PRISON

IN THE DAYS THAT FOLLOWED THE EAGER NEW ZEALANDERS TRAINED LIKE DEMONS AND NONE MORE SO THAN SQUADRON-LEADER TEDDY WILSON.

THAT WAS PRETTY GOOD, FELLOWS...NOW LET'S DO IT AGAIN AND TRY TO GET DOWN LOWER.

BUT THE NEXT DAY DISASTER STRUCK! WHILE SKIMMING OVER A MOCK-UP OF THE REAL TARGET, TEDDY WILSON MISJUDGED HIS HEIGHT BY A FRACTION.

HOLY SMOKE — I'VE CLIPPED THE ROOF!

TEDDY'S MOSQUITO STAGGERED SICKENINGLY IN MID-AIR, HIT THE GROUND AND SKIDDED CRAZILY FOR A HUNDRED YARDS BEFORE FINALLY SMASHING INTO A LORRY.

QUICK, GET THE CREW OUT BEFORE THAT KITE GOES UP!

A RESCUE SQUAD RUSHED TO THE WRECKED PLANE AND MANAGED TO DRAG OUT THE BADLY-INJURED WILSON AND HIS OBSERVER WITH ONLY SECONDS TO SPARE.

WELL DONE, LADS! JUST MADE IT AND NO MORE.

WING-COMMANDER SHAW WAS FACED WITH A SERIOUS PROBLEM.

WILSON WILL BE OUT OF ACTION FOR MONTHS. I MUST HAVE A NUMBER ONE WHO'S REALLY FIRST-CLASS...I THINK FLIGHT-LIEUTENANT CARTER WILL FILL THE BILL. HE'S THE ONLY ONE LEFT IN THE UNIT WHO'S READY FOR THE JOB.

AND SO BEN CARTER TOOK OVER THE TASK OF LEADING THE SQUADRON THROUGH THE PRELIMINARY DRILL FOR ONE OF THE MOST DARING LOW-LEVEL BOMBING STRIKES IN HISTORY. BUT BAD LUCK SEEMED TO DOG THIS WHOLE OPERATION.

FLAMING CYCLIST! HE MUST BE CRAZY.

BEN SPUN THE STEERING WHEEL IN A DESPERATE EFFORT TO MISS THE PUSH-BIKE.

FOR A SPLIT SECOND THE M.G. GRIPPED THE ROAD, THEN SKIDDED AND HURTLED TOWARDS THE DITCH.

AAARGH!

BEN CARTER STAGGERED OUT WITH A BROKEN ARM.

I'M SORRY, MATE. ARE YOU ALL RIGHT?

I'M STILL ALIVE, IF THAT'S WHAT YOU MEAN, YOU STUPID CLOT!

WHY DID THIS HAVE TO HAPPEN TO ME NOW! WHAT AN ALMIGHTY MESS-UP.

IT SEEMED THAT OPERATION 'JERICHO' WAS DOOMED TO FAILURE FROM THE START. ONCE AGAIN THE SQUADRON WAS WITHOUT A LEADER.

WHEN WING-COMMANDER SHAW HEARD THE NEWS HE WAS PLUNGED INTO DEEP DESPAIR.

FOR HEAVEN'S SAKE, CARTER, HOW THE BLAZES DID YOU MANAGE THIS? THERE'S NOT ANOTHER SOUL IN THE SQUADRON WHO'S READY TO LEAD THIS RAID. IT'S TOO LATE TO BRING IN AN OUTSIDER. THIS JOB HAD SIMPLY GOT TO BE A SUCCESS.

I'M TERRIBLY SORRY, SIR. IT SEEMS EVERYTHING'S GOING WRONG WITH THIS SHOW. I AGREE THAT THERE'S NO ONE ELSE UP TO THE JOB, NOT YET ANYWAY.

THEN WE'VE NO ALTERNATIVE. I'LL HAVE TO TELL H.Q. TO CALL OFF THE RAID.

WITH SINKING HEART BEN TURNED TO GO. BUT THEN HIS EYES FELL ON A GROUP PHOTOGRAPH OF THE SQUADRON ON THE OFFICE WALL, AND ONE FACE IN PARTICULAR...

WAIT A MINUTE, SIR, I'VE GOT AN IDEA. CAN'T YOU BRING BACK KIWI DEAN? HE'S JUST THE BLOKE FOR A DICEY JOB LIKE THIS...

SHAW'S EYES BLAZED WITH SUDDEN ANGER.

THAT'S OUT OF THE QUESTION, CARTER! I DON'T WANT DEAN BACK IN THIS UNIT. HE PROVED HIMSELF UNRELIABLE. IT'S TOO LATE NOW ANYWAY. NO, I WON'T EVEN CONSIDER THE IDEA.

BUT BEN HAD DETECTED A SLIGHT NOTE OF HESITATION IN HIS C.O.'S VOICE.

KIWI'S THE BEST MAN YOU COULD HOPE TO GET FOR THIS MISSION, SIR. HE KNOWS BEAUVENS INSIDE OUT, AND HE CAN SWOT UP ON AN OP FASTER THAN ANY BLOKE I KNOW.

NO! GET OUT, CARTER, BEFORE I THROW YOU OUT!

BUT LATER, ALONE WITH HIS THOUGHTS, SHAW WEIGHED UP THE DILEMMA WHICH FACED HIM.

I CAN EITHER CALL OFF THE SHOW AND CONDEMN DOZENS OF BRAVE FRENCHMEN TO DEATH, OR BRING BACK THAT CLOT DEAN TO TAKE OVER THE SQUADRON. HE'S STILL THE BEST MAN FOR THE JOB, AND HE DOES KNOW THE AREA. IT LOOKS AS IF CARTER IS RIGHT...

AND SO IT WAS THAT DESTINY RETURNED KIWI DEAN TO HIS OLD UNIT. A GRIM-FACED SHAW GAVE HIM A PEP TALK.

DEAN, I'M GIVING YOU ANOTHER CHANCE. BUT REMEMBER THIS — YOU MUST STICK STRICTLY TO OUR PLAN. THE SLIGHTEST DEVIATION COULD MUCK UP THE WHOLE SHOW. EVERY MAN'S BEEN BRIEFED FOR A TEAM JOB WHICH MUST BE PLAYED TO THE RULES.

YES, SIR, I UNDERSTAND.

THIS IS JUST WHAT I'VE BEEN WAITING FOR, ANOTHER CRACK AT THE NAZIS, AND AT BEAUVENS, TOO.

WITH ONLY A FEW DAYS LEFT BEFORE OPERATION 'JERICHO' WOULD BE UNDER WAY, KIWI THREW HIMSELF HEART AND SOUL INTO THE DETAILS OF THE DELICATE MISSION.

NOW REMEMBER, LADS, YOU MUST WATCH YOUR TIMING SO THAT YOU DON'T FLY INTO THE BLAST OF EACH OTHER'S BOMBS — BOMBS WITH FIVE-SECOND FUSES, AS YOU KNOW...

AS KIWI INDICATED THE WIDE, STRAIGHT BOULEVARD WHICH LED UP TO THE PRISON, WINGCO SHAW CAME IN.

THIS LONG, DEAD-STRAIGHT AVENUE WILL GUIDE US BANG ON TARGET. I'LL BE GOING IN FIRST...

JUST A MINUTE, SQUADRON-LEADER. I'VE GOT SOME FURTHER ORDERS FOR YOU.

AND THE ORDERS WERE ENOUGH TO MAKE ANY MAN'S HAIR STAND ON END.

MAIN CELL BLOCK

GUARD HOUSE

MAIN GATE

CENTRAL GRASS RESERVATION

THE INTELLIGENCE BOYS WANT US TO PICK UP A VITAL RESISTANCE AREA LEADER WHO WILL TRY TO ESCAPE WHEN THE WALLS ARE KNOCKED DOWN. HE HAS ORDERS TO BE JUST OUTSIDE THE BROKEN WALL. CAN YOU FLY ALONE, LAND YOUR AIRCRAFT ON THE BOULE-VARD, PICK UP THIS MAN IN THE SQUARE, AND TAKE OFF AGAIN?

SHAW GAVE KIWI A LONG, PENETRATING LOOK.

IT'S A TALL ORDER I KNOW, BUT SO IS THIS ENTIRE OPERATION. I WANT YOU TO ATTEMPT THE PICK-UP BECAUSE I'M CERTAIN YOU CAN BRING IT OFF.

TALL ORDER IS AN UNDER-STATEMENT, SIR. I'D SAY IT'S ALMOST IMPOSSIBLE. BUT I'LL GIVE IT A GO...

CENTRAL GRASS RESERVATION

BY THE WAY, SIR, WHO IS THIS V.I.P.?

MAIN

GUARD HOUSE.

HIS NAME IS PAUL THIERRY. I BELIEVE YOU KNOW HIM.

THE FAMILIAR NAME HIT KIWI LIKE A BOMB.

PAUL THIERRY! SAY NO MORE, WINGCO. THIS RAID AND THE PICK-UP WILL BE A BLINDING SUCCESS, I PROMISE YOU.

WHAT FANTASTIC LUCK. NOW'S MY CHANCE TO REPAY PAUL AND HIS FAMILY FOR ALL THEY DID FOR ME.

BUT ON THE DAY PLANNED FOR OPERATION 'JERICHO', A RAGING BLIZZARD GROUNDED ALL AIRCRAFT IN SOUTHERN ENGLAND. WINGCO SHAW STOOD WITH KIWI WATCHING THE SLANTING WHITE FLAKES WHICH HAD PUT PAID TO THE MISSION.

IT SEEMS THIS JOB HAS BEEN JINXED FROM THE START. TODAY WAS TO HAVE BEEN ZERO HOUR, AND WE ONLY HAVE ABOUT THIRTY-SIX HOURS LEFT.

WE CAN'T TAKE OFF IN THIS, SIR. WE'LL JUST HAVE TO PRAY THAT THE SNOW STOPS BEFORE IT'S TOO LATE.

MEANWHILE, IN BEAUVENS PRISON, PAUL THIERRY AND HIS CONDEMNED COMRADES WAITED HOPEFULLY FOR THE JAIL-BUSTING MOSQUITOES WHICH DIDN'T COME.

THE R.A.F. CANNOT COME IN THIS WEATHER. SOON THEY WILL TAKE US ALL OUT TO BE SHOT, UNLESS SOMEONE CRACKS UP FIRST AND GIVES OUR WHOLE ORGANISATION AWAY. THEN HE WILL BE SAFE WHILE WE AND HUNDREDS OF OTHERS DIE. NOTHING CAN SAVE US NOW... FIRST RAOUL, THEN MY PARENTS, AND NOW ME.

BUT NEXT DAY, ONE DAY BEFORE THE EXECUTIONS WERE DUE TO BEGIN, THE SNOW BLIZZARD CEASED. KIWI SUPERVISED A FRANTIC CLEARING OF THE RUNWAY AND REPORTED TO WINGCO SHAW.

I THINK WE CAN JUST ABOUT TAKE OFF, SIR. IF WE WAIT ANY LONGER IT'LL BE TOO LATE. THE RUNWAY'S ICY, BUT I RECKON WE CAN DO IT. I DON'T KNOW ABOUT COMING BACK.

ORDERS ARE NOT TO TAKE OFF UNTIL THE WEATHER BODS GIVE US THE ALL CLEAR. BUT I AGREE WITH YOU, DEAN. THIS IS ONE TIME WE'RE BOTH GOING TO IGNORE AN ORDER. GET CRACKING, AND GOOD LUCK!

MINUTES LATER, THE SQUADRON OF BOMB-LADEN MOSQUITOES WITH AN ESCORT OF TYPHOON FIGHTERS ROARED OVER THE ICY RUNWAYS AND KNIFED INTO THE COLD GREY SKY.

HERE WE GO, BOYS — NEXT STOP BEAUVENS!

AFTER CROSSING THE FRENCH COAST, KIWI TOOK HIS MOB RIGHT DOWN ON TO THE DECK AND STREAKED OVER THE SNOW-BLANKETED LANDSCAPE TOWARDS THEIR OBJECTIVE.

BLUE LEADER CALLING... MAXIMUM SPEED TO TARGET. LET'S GET THERE BEFORE JERRY RUMBLES SOMETHING'S BREW-ING.

WHILE AT BEAUVENS PRISON, THE NERVES OF A CERTAIN GASTON BRENNER, WHO'D BEEN AGAINST THE MOSQUITO SCHEME FROM THE START, HAD STRETCHED TAUT TO BREAKING POINT AND THEN — SNAPPED!

LET ME OUT! GUARDS, GUARDS! THE R.A.F. PLANES WILL COME NOW THE SNOW HAS STOPPED. YOU PROMISED YOU WOULD FREE ME!

TOO LATE, GASTON REALISED THAT HE'S SEALED HIS FATE, EITHER WAY. OF THE GERMAN GUARDS THERE WAS NO SIGN.

I THINK WE HAVE FOUND OUR TRAITOR, COMRADES. INFORM PAUL...

THE RESISTANCE QUESTIONED HIM, DEBATED, AND DECIDED THE FATE OF GASTON BRENNER IN JUST TWENTY-THREE SECONDS. THERE WAS ONLY ONE ROAD FOR A MAN WHO WAS TOO FOND OF LIVING FAT TO BE LOYAL TO HIS COUNTRYMEN. THEY CLOSED IN ON THE GIBBERING INNKEEPER AS ONE MAN...

AAA—URGH!

SOON KIWI'S SQUADRON SIGHTED BEAUVENS, AND ON THE OUTSKIRTS THE GRIM, FORTRESS-LIKE JAIL.

OK, BOYS, YOU'VE GOT THE STORY. I'M GOING IN FIRST — TALLYHO!

KIWI DIPPED THE NOSE OF HIS PLANE AND FLASHED ALONG THE BROAD BOULEVARD WHICH LED TO THE GAUNT PRISON. AT ONLY TWELVE FEET FROM THE GROUND THE MOSQUITO HURTLED TOWARDS THE WALL THAT LOOMED HIGH ABOVE IT...

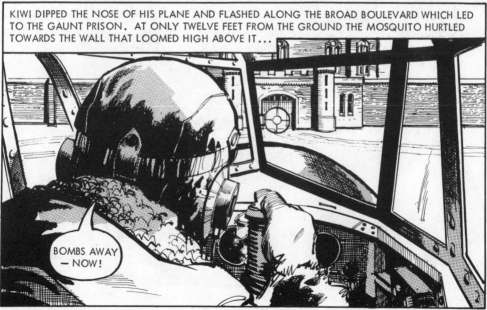

BOMBS AWAY — NOW!

THE TWO BOMBS FELL AWAY FROM THE SPEEDING MOSQUITO, STRUCK THE ICY ROAD AND SHOT TOWARDS THE BASE OF THE PRISON WALL LIKE BULLETS.

BETTER GRAB SOME HEIGHT, QUICK!

WITH ONLY A FOOT TO SPARE, KIWI PULLED BACK THE STICK AND THE MOSSIE SCREAMED UP AND OVER THE TOWERING WALL, JUST CLEARING THE ROOF OF THE MAIN PRISON BUILDING BY INCHES! IT WAS FANTASTIC FLYING.

PHEW! SCRATCHED THE PAINT ON HER BELLY THAT TIME.

INSIDE THE PRISON THE MAQUIS DANCED WITH JOY AS SOON AS THEY HEARD THE SCREAMING WHINE OF THE MOSQUITOES.

AS KIWI CLIMBED AND BANKED, THE TWO BOMBS WHICH HAD BURIED THEMSELVES INTO THE BASE OF THE THICK WALL EXPLODED WITH A MIGHTY ROAR.

BANG ON! NOW IT'S UP TO THE LADS TO DO THE REST. I'LL STOOGE AROUND UNTIL IT'S TIME TO LAND.

WITH CLOCKWORK PRECISION THE MOSQUITOES HURTLED ALONG THE GUIDING LENGTH OF THE BROAD BOULEVARD AND PLACED THEIR BOMBS IN THE PINPOINTED POSITIONS, ONE OF WHICH WAS THE GERMAN GUARDHOUSE.

HERE YOU GO, FRITZ! WITH THE COMPLIMENTS OF THE SQUADRON.

THE TWO DEADLY MISSILES SKIDDED ACROSS THE WIDE PRISON YARD AND CANNONED INTO THE BIG GUARDHOUSE. AT THEIR MID-MORNING BREAK, MOST OF THE GERMANS WERE TOO STUPEFIED TO GET OUT IN TIME.

AAARGH!

WITH THE OUTER WALLS BREACHED ON BOTH SIDES, OTHER MOSQUITOES LAID THEIR DEADLY EGGS HERE AND THERE AGAINST THE WALLS OF THE MAIN PRISON BUILDINGS IN PLACES NOT TOO NEAR THE CELLS, AS PLANNED IN THE DETAILED BRIEFING.

SECONDS LATER, THE THICK WALLS SHATTERED IN A SERIES OF BRIGHT ORANGE FLASHES AND THUNDEROUS EXPLOSIONS. THE ENTIRE NAZI GARRISON WAS IN A PANIC.

BUT THE LOW-FLYING MOSQUITOES DID NOT GET OFF SCOT-FREE. ONE PILOT MISTIMED HIS RUN-IN BY A SECOND AND SPED INTO A BLAST OF EXPLODING BOMBS.

A PILOT'S SLIGHTEST ERROR WAS HIS LAST. THERE WERE NO SECOND CHANCES ON OPERATION 'JERICHO'.

ANOTHER MACHINE FAILED TO CLEAR THE MAIN PRISON ROOFTOP.

BUT THE REMAINING MOSQUITOES COMPLETED THEIR TOUGH MISSION WITH AMAZING SKILL. THE PRISON WAS CAREFULLY REDUCED TO A SHAMBLES WITH HARDLY ANY OF THE MAQUIS BEING SERIOUSLY HURT.

AND THE MINUTE THE BOMBING HAD STOPPED, THE PRISONERS SWARMED THROUGH THE GAPING HOLES TO FREEDOM. AMONG THEM WAS THE LIMPING FIGURE OF PAUL THIERRY.

OUTSIDE THE SHATTERED JAIL, A SPECIAL FORCE OF RESISTANCE FIGHTERS WERE READY TO AID THE ESCAPERS.

MEANWHILE, KIWI WAS BRINGING IN HIS MOSQUITO FOR THE DARING LANDING ON THE BOULEVARD...

HERE WE GO! THE MAQUIS HAVE DONE A GOOD JOB IN KEEPING THE ROAD CLEAR. LIGHT TAIL CROSS-WIND...

KIWI PUT THE MOSSIE DOWN LIKE A FEATHER, A WHEEL EXACTLY ON EITHER SIDE OF THE GRASS STRIP. THEN HE WAS TAXI-ING ALONG THE ICY BOULEVARD TOWARDS THE SQUARE FRONTING THE PRISON, BRAKING LIKE MAD.

HOLY SMOKE! JERRIES! AS IF I HADN'T ENOUGH TROUBLE STANDING ON THE ANCHORS TO GET STOPPED. NOW HERE I AM WITHOUT EVEN A PEASHOOTER AND MY GUNS POINTING INTO MID AIR!

KIWI ACTED LIKE LIGHTNING WITH A TRICK ONLY AN ACE PILOT WOULD HAVE TRIED — OR EVEN THOUGHT OF.

HE JAMMED THE BRAKES ON TIGHT, REVVED UP AND EASED THE CONTROL COLUMN GENTLY FORWARD. AS THE PLANE CAME UP INTO THE FLYING POSITION, ROARING AND BUCKING AGAINST THE BRAKES, HE COULD LINE UP HIS GUNS ON THE GERMAN LORRY.

THAT'LL SETTLE THEIR HASH!

AAAAARGH!

THE BATTERED, DRIVERLESS TRUCK CAREERED CRAZILY ACROSS THE SQUARE AND CRUNCHED INTO THE WALL OF BEAUVENS JAIL.

KIWI HEAVED A SIGH OF RELIEF, LET HIS TAIL DOWN AND BEGAN LOOKING AROUND FOR PAUL.

BUT ALREADY A LIMPING FIGURE WAS HURRYING TOWARDS HIM.

HOP IN AS QUICK AS YOU CAN, PAUL, WE'VE NO TIME TO LOSE.

SQUADRON-LEADER DEAN! THIS IS A PLEAS- ANT SURPRISE. IT'S GOOD TO SEE YOU, MON AMI.

AS SOON AS PAUL CLAMBERED IN, KIWI SWUNG THE MACHINE AROUND.

KEEP YOUR FINGERS CROSSED AND HOPE FOR A CLEAR ROAD, AND A DROP IN THE WIND, PAUL.

HARRY GUNNED THE POWERFUL ENGINES AND THE MOSSIE RACED ALONG THE ICY BOULE- VARD FOR THE TAKE OFF.

FASTER AND FASTER RACED THE MOSQUITO DOWN THE AVENUE — AND NEARER AND NEARER SPED AN OMINOUS DARK SHAPE FROM THE OPPOSITE DIRECTION, BRINGING KIWI'S HEART TO HIS MOUTH.

GREAT SCOTT — A TANK!

AS THE BLACK–CROSSED PANZER LOOMED BIGGER, KIWI UNLEASHED A HURRICANE OF CANNON SHELLS IN SHEER DESPERATION IN AN EFFORT TO HALT THE ONCOMING TANK.

UNSTICK, BABY! GET UP!

SACRE BLEU!

BUT AT THE VERY LAST MOMENT FATE ONCE AGAIN SMILED ON THE BOLD KIWI DEAN...THE ARMOUR-PIERCING CANNON SHELLS STOPPED THE TANK FOR A FEW SECONDS. KIWI JERKED BACK THE STICK OF THE MOSSIE, JUST SCRAPED OVER THE TANK'S TURRET AND CLAWED FOR HEIGHT.

PHEW! CLOSE!

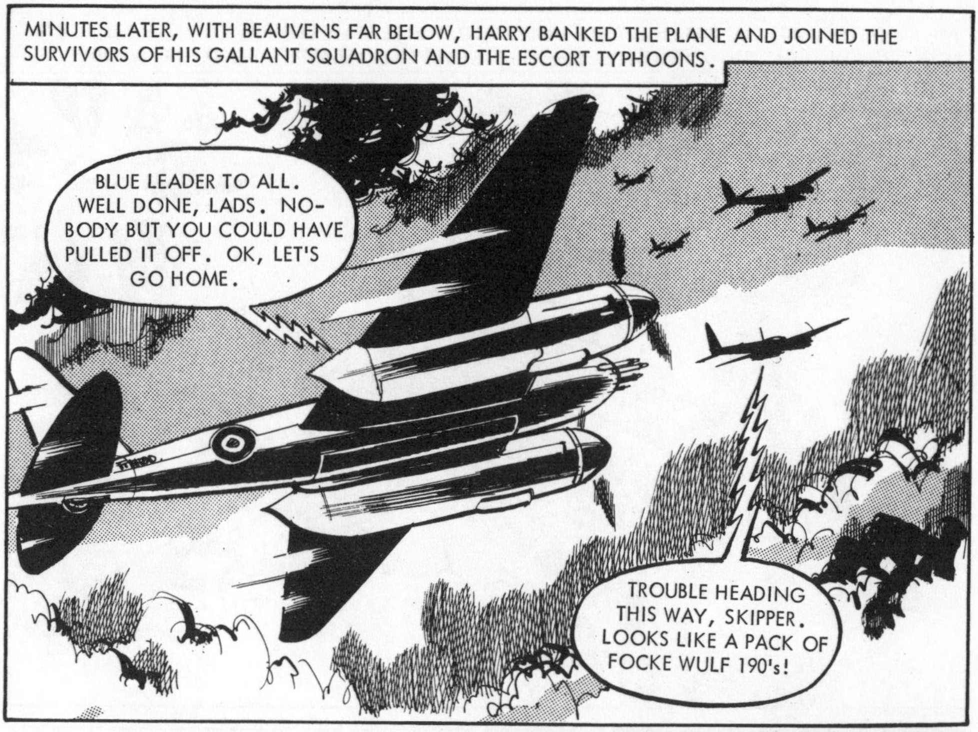
MINUTES LATER, WITH BEAUVENS FAR BELOW, HARRY BANKED THE PLANE AND JOINED THE SURVIVORS OF HIS GALLANT SQUADRON AND THE ESCORT TYPHOONS.
BLUE LEADER TO ALL. WELL DONE, LADS. NOBODY BUT YOU COULD HAVE PULLED IT OFF. OK, LET'S GO HOME.
TROUBLE HEADING THIS WAY, SKIPPER. LOOKS LIKE A PACK OF FOCKE WULF 190's!

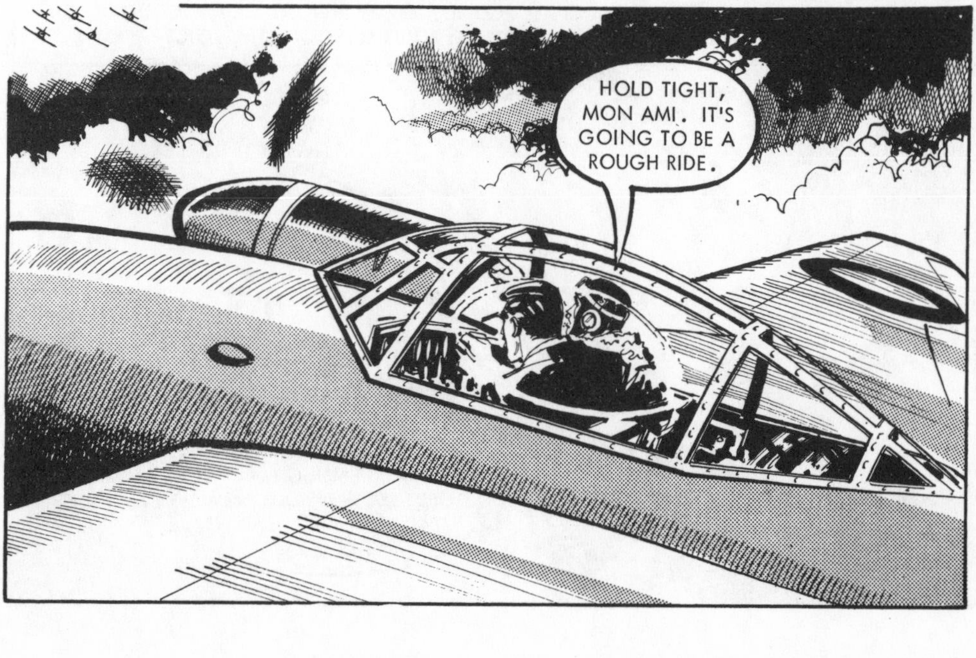
HOLD TIGHT, MON AMI. IT'S GOING TO BE A ROUGH RIDE.

THE NEXT INSTANT, THE BRITISH PLANES KNIFED INTO THE ENEMY FORMATION WITH ALL GUNS BLAZING. KIWI CAUGHT A NAZI FIGHTER IN HIS SIGHTS AND BLASTED IT INTO OBLIVION, MUCH TO PAUL'S DELIGHT.

MA FOI! KIWI DEAN IS INDEED A TIGER. MY YOUNG BROTHER RAOUL DID NOT DIE IN VAIN.

IT PROVED A BAD DAY FOR THE GERMANS ALL ROUND. THE TYPHOONS AND MOSQUITOES CUT THE LUFTWAFFE UNIT TO SHREDS, AS THEY BLASTED THROUGH. SOON, THE VOICE OF KIWI CRACKLED OVER THE RADIO.

BLUE ONE CALLING ...THAT'S ENOUGH, BOYS, DON'T USE ALL YOUR AMMO. BREAK NOW AND HEAD FOR HOME.

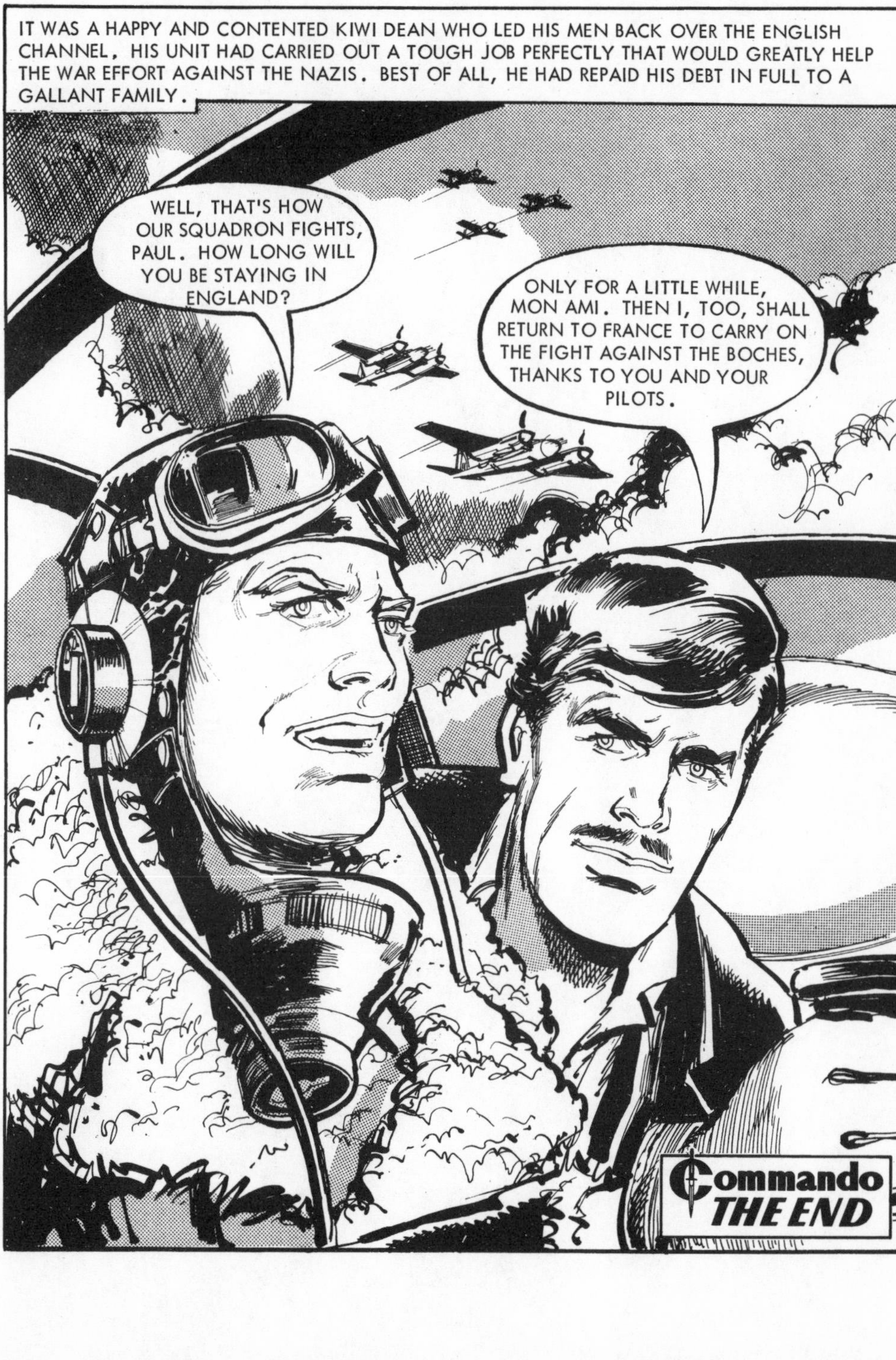
IT WAS A HAPPY AND CONTENTED KIWI DEAN WHO LED HIS MEN BACK OVER THE ENGLISH CHANNEL. HIS UNIT HAD CARRIED OUT A TOUGH JOB PERFECTLY THAT WOULD GREATLY HELP THE WAR EFFORT AGAINST THE NAZIS. BEST OF ALL, HE HAD REPAID HIS DEBT IN FULL TO A GALLANT FAMILY.
WELL, THAT'S HOW OUR SQUADRON FIGHTS, PAUL. HOW LONG WILL YOU BE STAYING IN ENGLAND?
ONLY FOR A LITTLE WHILE, MON AMI. THEN I, TOO, SHALL RETURN TO FRANCE TO CARRY ON THE FIGHT AGAINST THE BOCHES, THANKS TO YOU AND YOUR PILOTS.
Commando
THE END

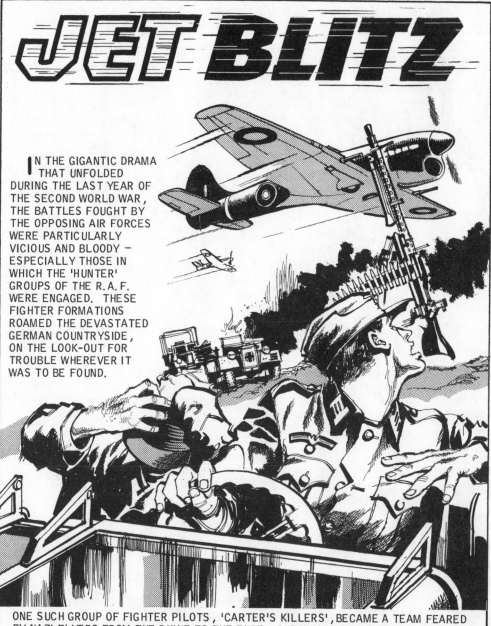

JET BLITZ

IN THE GIGANTIC DRAMA THAT UNFOLDED DURING THE LAST YEAR OF THE SECOND WORLD WAR, THE BATTLES FOUGHT BY THE OPPOSING AIR FORCES WERE PARTICULARLY VICIOUS AND BLOODY — ESPECIALLY THOSE IN WHICH THE 'HUNTER' GROUPS OF THE R.A.F. WERE ENGAGED. THESE FIGHTER FORMATIONS ROAMED THE DEVASTATED GERMAN COUNTRYSIDE, ON THE LOOK-OUT FOR TROUBLE WHEREVER IT WAS TO BE FOUND.

ONE SUCH GROUP OF FIGHTER PILOTS, 'CARTER'S KILLERS', BECAME A TEAM FEARED BY NAZI FLYERS FROM THE RHINE TO THE ELBE. BUT WHAT LAY BEHIND THAT AMAZING TEAMWORK WAS A FANTASTIC STORY...

THE LUFTWAFFE HAD BEEN TAKING A BEATING. STRUGGLING TO STEM THE AVALANCHE OF ALLIED PLANES, ITS FIGHTERS WERE UNABLE TO CONCENTRATE IN SUFFICIENT NUMBERS TO HIT BACK EFFECTIVELY — UNTIL ONE DAY IN OCTOBER 1944 WHEN AN UNUSUAL OPPORTUNITY AROSE.

THESE FOOLS OF ENGLANDERS HAVE BEEN CARELESS. ONE OF OUR AGENTS ON A BRITISH AIRFIELD OVERHEARD FULL DETAILS OF TODAY'S OPER-ATION. HIGH COMMAND HAS MOVED SWIFTLY, AND NOW THIS WHOLE GRUPPE IS WAITING TO MEET AND ANNIHILATE — THEM.

IT WAS AN R.A.F. STRIKE AGAINST ENEMY TRANSPORT MOVING UP REINFORCEMENTS TO THE EINDHOVEN AREA, AND WHAT BEGAN AS A NORMAL OPERATION RAPIDLY BECAME A DESPERATE BATTLE FOR SURVIVAL.

BATTLEAXE THREE TO BATTLEAXE LEADER — FORTY PLUS BANDITS, ELEVEN O'CLOCK HIGH.

ANOTHER FORTY PLUS AT 2 O'CLOCK. COMING DOWN FAST, SKIPPER.

HOLY SMOKE, ANOTHER LOT! THEY'RE LIKE A SWARM OF BEES.

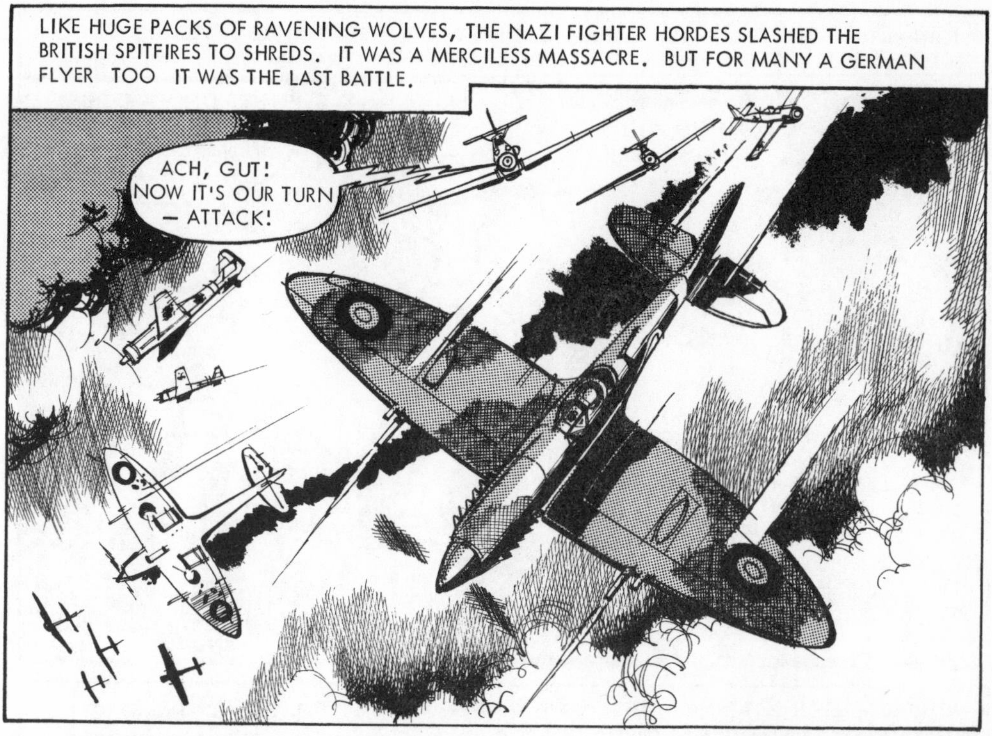
LIKE HUGE PACKS OF RAVENING WOLVES, THE NAZI FIGHTER HORDES SLASHED THE BRITISH SPITFIRES TO SHREDS. IT WAS A MERCILESS MASSACRE. BUT FOR MANY A GERMAN FLYER TOO IT WAS THE LAST BATTLE.
ACH, GUT! NOW IT'S OUR TURN — ATTACK!

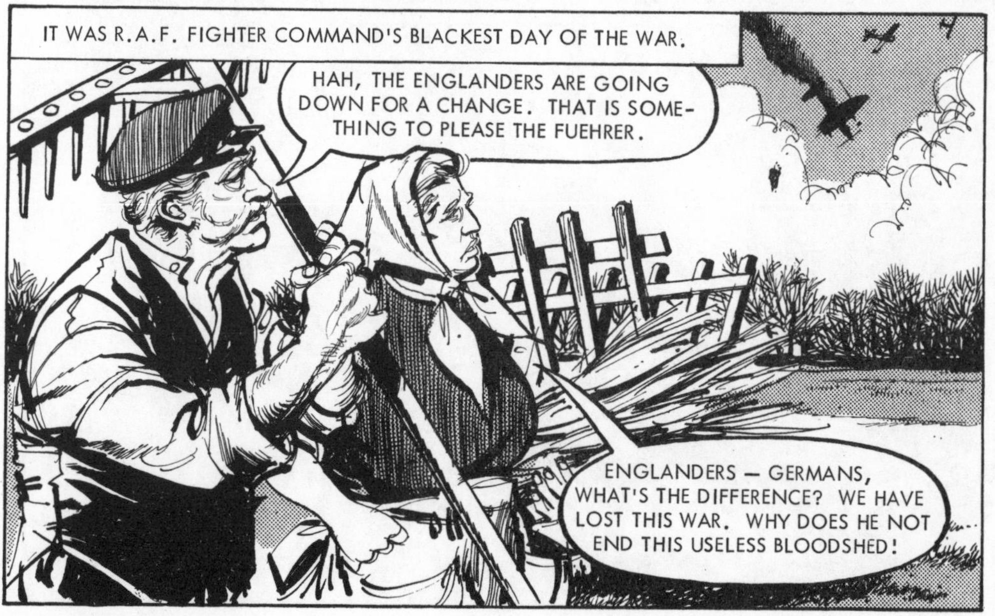
IT WAS R.A.F. FIGHTER COMMAND'S BLACKEST DAY OF THE WAR.
HAH, THE ENGLANDERS ARE GOING DOWN FOR A CHANGE. THAT IS SOMETHING TO PLEASE THE FUEHRER.
ENGLANDERS — GERMANS, WHAT'S THE DIFFERENCE? WE HAVE LOST THIS WAR. WHY DOES HE NOT END THIS USELESS BLOODSHED!

FLIGHT-LIEUTENANT TOM CARTER, 635 SQUADRON'S B FLIGHT COMMANDER, STEERED HIS CRIPPLED, BULLET-RIDDEN FIGHTER BACK TO BASE, AN AIRFIELD NEAR BRUSSELS.

COME ON, YOU LOT — MOVE!

WE COULD HAVE A CUSTOMER.

HE'S ONLY THE THIRD. THE OTHERS SHOULD'VE BEEN BACK HALF AN HOUR AGO.

WITH THE SCREECH OF TORTURED METAL, THE SHATTERED PLANE PLUNGED AND BUCKED TO FINAL DESTRUCTION. THE DAY OF THE DISASTER WAS OVER.

HURRY, MAN! WE'VE GOT TO GET HIM OUT OF THERE BEFORE SHE BLOWS UP.

FLAMES LICKED ANGRILY ROUND THE COCKPIT AS TOM STRUGGLED TO FREE HIMSELF. THEN STRONG HANDS DRAGGED HIM CLEAR.

THANKS, THAT'S BETTER. THAT JEEP, CAN I BORROW IT?

YEAH, IT'S THE ENGINEER OFFICER'S, HE WON'T MIND. BUT — ARE YOU ALL RIGHT? I MEAN, SHOULDN'T YOU LET THE DOC LOOK YOU OVER?

IMPATIENTLY HE BRUSHED ASIDE THE HELPING HANDS.

COME ON, SIR. BACK TO SICK QUARTERS, LET THE MEDICAL OFFICER CHECK YOU OVER.

LET GO OF ME! I'M ALL RIGHT. THERE'S SOMETHING I'VE GOT TO DO — RIGHT NOW.

TOM'S FACE WAS SET AND GRIM. HE CRASHED THE JEEP'S GEARS AND TORE OFF DOWN THE RUNWAY TOWARDS THE AIRFIELD BUILDINGS.

THAT'S QUEER, HE COULDN'T GET TO THAT JEEP FAST ENOUGH. WHERE'S HE OFF TO?

SHOCK, THAT'S WHAT IT IS. MAKES BLOKES DO ODD THINGS SOMETIMES.

UNDER THE SAVAGE IMPACT OF TOM'S FLYING-BOOT, THE CREW ROOM DOOR CRASHED OPEN.

WHAT THE BLAZES! FLIGHT-LIEUTENANT CARTER — SO YOU GOT BACK,TOO.

WELL, WELL! IF IT ISN'T FLYING-OFFICER SMITH AND MILTON. SO THIS IS WHERE YOU'RE SKULKING. I WATCHED YOU SCUTTLE FOR HOME BEFORE THE ENEMY WERE IN RANGE.

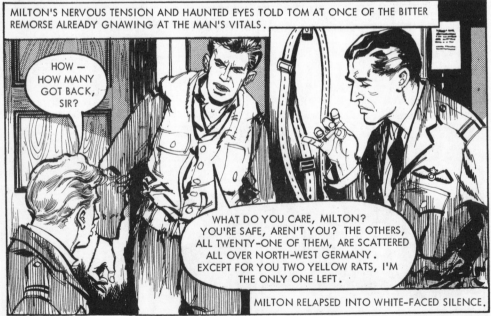

MILTON'S NERVOUS TENSION AND HAUNTED EYES TOLD TOM AT ONCE OF THE BITTER REMORSE ALREADY GNAWING AT THE MAN'S VITALS.

HOW — HOW MANY GOT BACK, SIR?

WHAT DO YOU CARE, MILTON? YOU'RE SAFE, AREN'T YOU? THE OTHERS, ALL TWENTY-ONE OF THEM, ARE SCATTERED ALL OVER NORTH-WEST GERMANY. EXCEPT FOR YOU TWO YELLOW RATS, I'M THE ONLY ONE LEFT.

MILTON RELAPSED INTO WHITE-FACED SILENCE.

BUT SMITH WAS A HORSE OF A DIFFERENT COLOUR, AND TOM FELT HIS SELF-CONTROL WAVERING UNDER THE MAN'S CASUAL INSOLENCE.

WELL, CONGRATULATIONS, SKIPPER, ON YOUR GOOD LUCK. LIKE I ALWAYS SAID, IT AIN'T HEALTHY THIS FLYING. ME — I'M FINISHED WITH IT. YOU CAN HAVE ME BUSTED DOWN TO A.C.2. IF YOU LIKE. I'LL BE QUITE HAPPY WORKING IN THE COOKHOUSE OR AS STATION POSTMAN, MAYBE. IT'S A DARN SIGHT SAFER THAN BEING A FLY BOY.

IN A RED MIST OF RAGE HE SLAMMED SMITH AGAINST THE WALL.

LET GO OF ME BIG BOY, OR I'LL BUST YOU ONE!

YOU RAT, I COULD HAVE YOU COURT-MARTIALLED FOR COWARDICE AND DRUMMED OUT OF THE SERVICE FOR WHAT YOU DID TODAY.

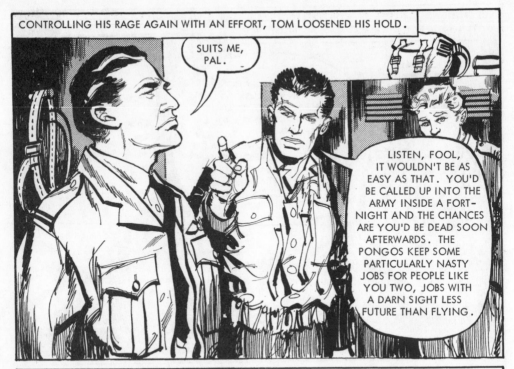

CONTROLLING HIS RAGE AGAIN WITH AN EFFORT, TOM LOOSENED HIS HOLD.

SUITS ME, PAL.

LISTEN, FOOL, IT WOULDN'T BE AS EASY AS THAT. YOU'D BE CALLED UP INTO THE ARMY INSIDE A FORT-NIGHT AND THE CHANCES ARE YOU'D BE DEAD SOON AFTERWARDS. THE PONGOS KEEP SOME PARTICULARLY NASTY JOBS FOR PEOPLE LIKE YOU TWO, JOBS WITH A DARN SIGHT LESS FUTURE THAN FLYING.

MILTON HAD JUST JOINED 635 SQUADRON TWO WEEKS PREVIOUSLY ON COMPLETION OF HIS TRAINING. THIS HAD BEEN HIS FIRST OPERATIONAL FLIGHT.

SIR, DON'T — PLEASE DON'T SAY ANYTHING ABOUT THIS. MY FATHER — HE GOT THE V.C. IN THE LAST WAR. HE WOULD NEVER LIVE IT DOWN IF HE KNEW I'D ACTED THE COWARD. CAN'T YOU GIVE ME ANOTHER CHANCE?

IT'S A BIT LATE IN THE DAY FOR THAT. TWENTY-ONE MEN HAVE BEEN KILLED, AND THEY'VE GOT TO BE AVENGED. THAT SEEMS LIKE A JOB FOR YOU TWO, AND ME. I'LL LEAVE YOU TO THINK THAT OVER BEFORE I REPORT THIS.

AND TOM CARTER SLAMMED OUT.

SMITH WAS WORRIED — HE KNEW BY THE DISLIKE ON CARTER'S FACE THAT PITY OR SPORTSMANSHIP WOULDN'T STOP HIM REPORTING THEM. BUT MILTON WAS IN THE DEPTHS OF SHAME.

I — I JUST COULDN'T FACE THEM, SMITH. ALL THOSE FOCKE-WULFS, LIKE A SWARM OF WASPS. IF ONLY I COULD'VE GOT A GRIP OF MYSELF, STOPPED PANICKING.

YEAH — AND YOU'D HAVE BEEN THE TWENTY-SECOND DEAD PILOT. WHY DON'T YOU GET WISE? BETTER A LIVE COWARD THAN A DEAD HERO, ANY DAY.

WHAT'D CARTER MEAN WHEN HE SAID WE COULD AVENGE THEM? WILL WE BE COURT-MARTIALLED? IF WE ARE, MY FATHER'LL HEAR ABOUT IT. WHAT'LL I DO, SMITH? TELL ME, MAN!

BROODING GUILT WAS ALREADY PLAYING ON MILTON'S NERVES.

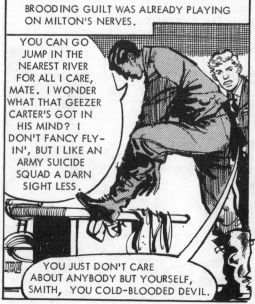

YOU CAN GO JUMP IN THE NEAREST RIVER FOR ALL I CARE, MATE. I WONDER WHAT THAT GEEZER CARTER'S GOT IN HIS MIND? I DON'T FANCY FLY-IN', BUT I LIKE AN ARMY SUICIDE SQUAD A DARN SIGHT LESS.

YOU JUST DON'T CARE ABOUT ANYBODY BUT YOURSELF, SMITH, YOU COLD-BLOODED DEVIL.

SMITH SUDDENLY GOT SICK OF MILTON'S WHINING.

STOP SNIVELLING, YOU LITTLE RAT. HAVEN'T I GOT ENOUGH WORRIES OF MY OWN WITHOUT LISTENING TO YOUR MOANING?

A SQUADRON THAT HAS ONLY TWO AIRCRAFT IS OPERATIONALLY USELESS. THEY SENT OFF THE GROUND STAFF AND THE THREE SURVIVORS TO AN AIRFIELD NEAR THE NORTHUMBERLAND COAST TO REFORM AND RE-EQUIP.

THE AFTERNOON AFTER ARRIVAL, A SINGLE AIRCRAFT LANDED. ITS SIZE AND MIGHTY PROPELLER SPOKE OF TERRIFIC POWER AND RUGGED STRENGTH. THIS WAS THE TEMPEST, THE LATEST AND DEADLIEST FIGHTER OF THEM ALL. THE ENGINEER OFFICER GAVE TOM A RUN-DOWN.

THERE YOU ARE, TOM, THE FIRST OF THE SQUADRON'S NEW PLANES. IT'S A REAL TOUGH EGG, CAN TAKE LOADS OF PUNISHMENT. BUT YOU HAVE TO TREAT THAT ENGINE RIGHT, IT'S LIABLE TO OVERHEAT. WHY DON'T YOU GIVE IT A TRY OUT?

GLAD TO, WHENEVER SHE'S READY.

A TEMPEST TAKE-OFF WAS LIKE A TREMENDOUS PUNCH IN THE BACK — THE ACCELERATION WAS TERRIFIC.

WHAT A BABY — CLIMBS LIKE A BUBBLE IN A BATH!

THE HUGE SABRE ENGINE ROARING THUNDEROUSLY, THE TEMPEST REACHED 30,000 FEET WITH MAGICAL SWIFTNESS. TOM FLIPPED IT ON ITS BACK AND DROPPED THE NOSE —

HERE WE GO, DOWN TO THE DECK...

THE TEMPEST'S GREAT WEIGHT PLUNGED IT EARTHWARDS AT A FANTASTIC SPEED. LEVELLING OUT, TOM TORE RIGHT ACROSS ENGLAND AT TREE-TOP HEIGHT.

FESTERIN' FLIERS! I'LL COMPLAIN TO THE AIR MINISTRY ABOUT THIS JOKER. BE TURNING MY MILK SOUR, HE WILL.

HOLY SMOKE! SIX HUNDRED AND FORTY MILES AN HOUR IN THAT DIVE.

IMPRESSED BY THE TEMPEST'S PERFORMANCE, TOM DECIDED THIS WAS THE IDEAL WEAPON FOR HIS PLAN OF VENGEANCE. HE ORDERED MILTON AND SMITH TO GET THEIR FLYING KIT.

I THOUGHT YOU'D GET US GROUNDED RIGHT AWAY.

I TOLD YOU WE HAD A JOB TO DO, DIDN'T I? THESE ARE WHAT WE'RE GOING TO DO IT IN. NOW TAKE THIS ONE UP TO GET THE FEEL OF IT.

FOR THE REMAINDER OF THAT DAY, MILTON, SMITH AND TOM FLEW THE TEMPEST ON LOCAL TRIPS, LANDINGS AND TAKE-OFFS.

IF HE'S HANDLED CAREFULLY, I RECKON MILTON MIGHT BECOME A GOOD FIGHTER PILOT YET — IF HE'D ONLY RELAX A BIT. BUT SMITH, NOW, I'M NOT SO SURE OF HIM. HE'S A BAD LOT AND I CAN'T SEE HIM CHANGING.

WITHIN A VERY SHORT TIME FLYING REPLACEMENTS ARRIVED, AND MORE TEMPESTS FLEW IN FROM MAINTENANCE UNITS WHERE NEW AIRCRAFT FROM THE FACTORIES WERE FITTED WITH GUNS, OXYGEN AND OTHER OPERATIONAL EQUIPMENT.

URGENT MESSAGE, SIR, JUST CAME IN ON THE TELE-PRINTER.

THANKS.

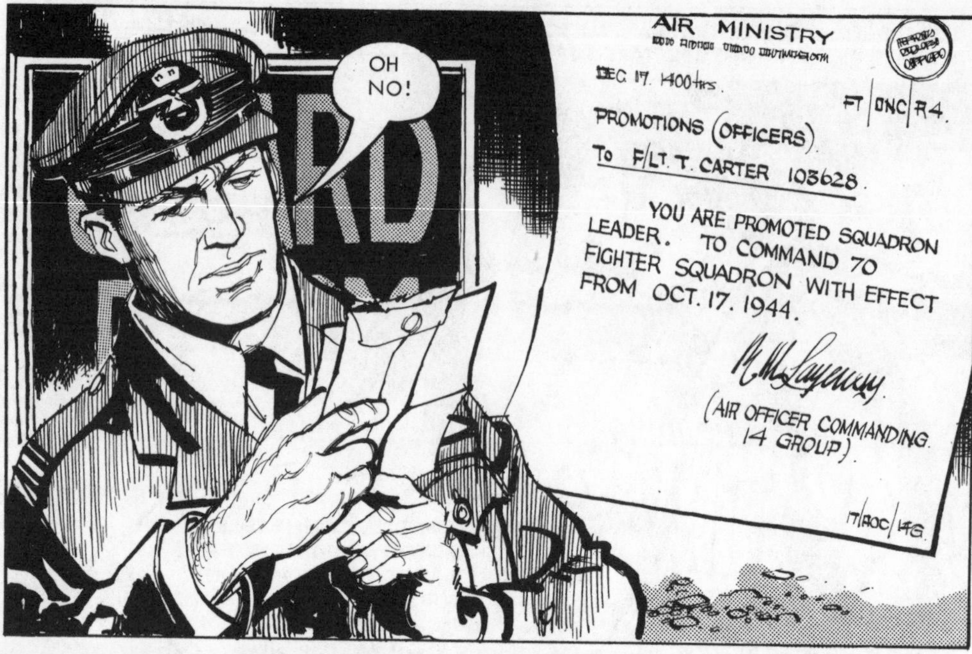
OH NO!
AIR MINISTRY
DEC. 17. 1400hrs.
FT/ONC/R4.
PROMOTIONS (OFFICERS).
To F/LT. T. CARTER 103628.
YOU ARE PROMOTED SQUADRON LEADER. TO COMMAND 70 FIGHTER SQUADRON WITH EFFECT FROM OCT. 17. 1944.
(AIR OFFICER COMMANDING. 14 GROUP).
17/AOC/14G.

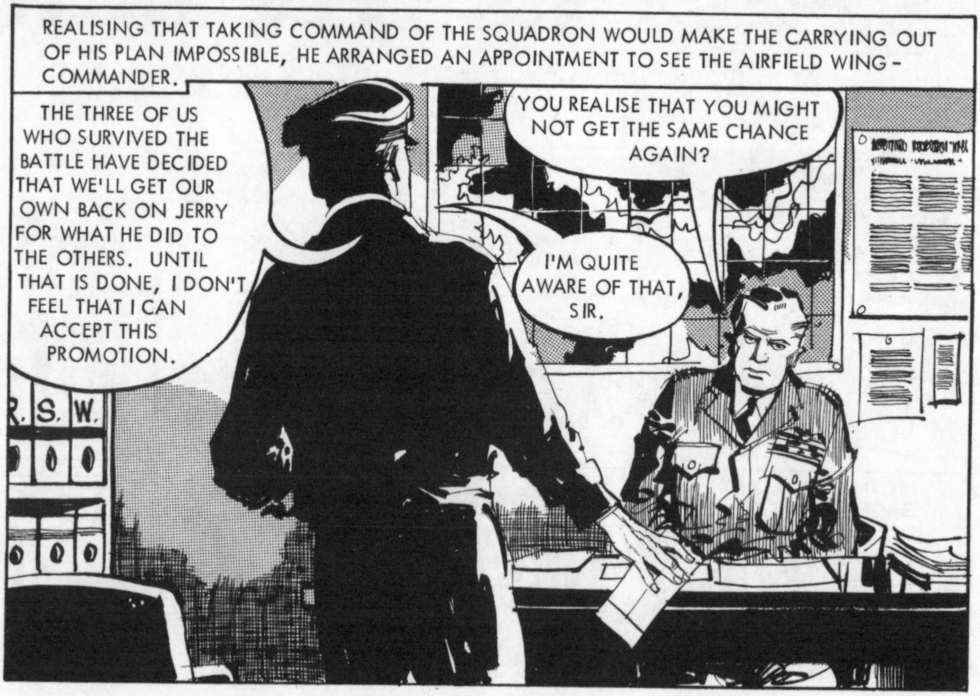
REALISING THAT TAKING COMMAND OF THE SQUADRON WOULD MAKE THE CARRYING OUT OF HIS PLAN IMPOSSIBLE, HE ARRANGED AN APPOINTMENT TO SEE THE AIRFIELD WING-COMMANDER.
THE THREE OF US WHO SURVIVED THE BATTLE HAVE DECIDED THAT WE'LL GET OUR OWN BACK ON JERRY FOR WHAT HE DID TO THE OTHERS. UNTIL THAT IS DONE, I DON'T FEEL THAT I CAN ACCEPT THIS PROMOTION.
YOU REALISE THAT YOU MIGHT NOT GET THE SAME CHANCE AGAIN?
I'M QUITE AWARE OF THAT, SIR.
R.S.W.

BECAUSE OF TOM'S REFUSAL TO TAKE COMMAND, THEY SENT ANOTHER IN HIS PLACE, SQUADRON-LEADER ELLIOT. SOON 70 SQUADRON WAS AT FULL STRENGTH. TOM WASTED NO TIME IN MAKING HIS REQUEST TO THE NEW MAN.

I WANT TO LEAD A FORMATION OF TEMPESTS, SIR, ON ROVING COMMISSIONS WHEN WE'RE BACK IN ACTION IN EUROPE. GIVE ME SMITH AND MILTON, AND I'LL TRAIN THEM INTO A REAL FIGHTING MACHINE. WE THREE HAVE A BIG SCORE TO SETTLE, AND FLYING A 'HUNTER' FLIGHT WOULD BE THE BEST WAY TO DO IT.

BUT WITH THE ALLIED ARMIES HAMMERING AT THE APPROACHES TO THE RHINE, EVERY AVAILABLE FIGHTER AND BOMBER WOULD SOON BE NEEDED TO BLAST THE ENEMY'S RESISTANCE IF THE CROSSING OF THE GREAT RIVER WAS TO SUCCEED. AND ELLIOT KNEW THIS.

GROUP H.Q. WANT 70 SQUADRON OPERATIONALLY TRAINED WITHIN A FORTNIGHT, READY FOR ITS RETURN TO BELGIUM. THERE WON'T BE ANY TIME FOR PRIVATE WARS, CARTER, SO JUST FORGET IT.

BUT, SIR...!

IT APPEARED THAT THE REVENGE SCHEME WAS DOOMED BEFORE IT COULD BEGIN, BUT THERE WAS NO STOPPING A MAN WITH AN OBSESSION LIKE TOM'S.

IF ELLIOT THINKS THAT'S THE END OF IT, HE'S AWAY OFF THE BEAM. THAT PAIR AREN'T GOING TO GET AWAY WITH THIS. I'LL FIGURE OUT SOMETHING...

TOM'S SCHEMING BRAIN SOON CAME UP WITH A PLAN.

I'VE PUT A LETTER IN THE WINGCO'S SAFE GIVING ALL THE EVIDENCE AGAINST YOU TWO. INSTRUCTIONS ON IT SAY IT IS ONLY TO BE OPENED IF ANYTHING HAPPENS TO ME. IT'S UP TO YOU TO SEE IT STAYS IN THERE.

YOU MEAN...

I MEAN THAT WHEN THEY SEND US BACK TO BELGIUM, YOU'RE GOING TO FLY AND FIGHT UNDER MY ORDERS. YOU'LL BE SO BUSY MAKING SURE NOTHING HAPPENS TO ME THAT YOU WON'T HAVE TIME TO WORRY ABOUT YOUR OWN SKINS.

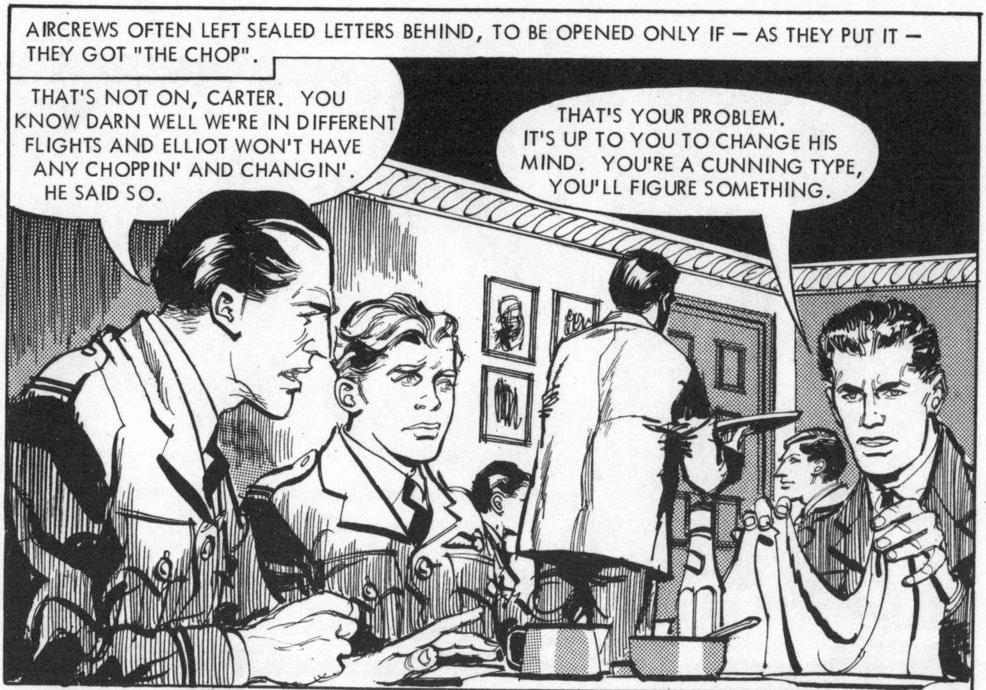
AIRCREWS OFTEN LEFT SEALED LETTERS BEHIND, TO BE OPENED ONLY IF — AS THEY PUT IT — THEY GOT "THE CHOP".
THAT'S NOT ON, CARTER. YOU KNOW DARN WELL WE'RE IN DIFFERENT FLIGHTS AND ELLIOT WON'T HAVE ANY CHOPPIN' AND CHANGIN'. HE SAID SO.
THAT'S YOUR PROBLEM. IT'S UP TO YOU TO CHANGE HIS MIND. YOU'RE A CUNNING TYPE, YOU'LL FIGURE SOMETHING.

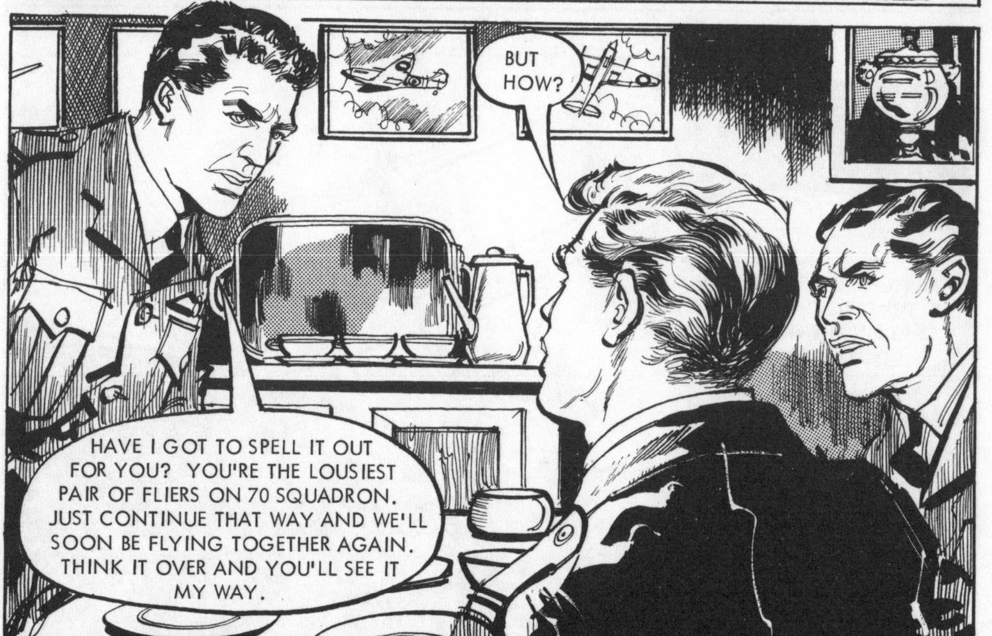
BUT HOW?
HAVE I GOT TO SPELL IT OUT FOR YOU? YOU'RE THE LOUSIEST PAIR OF FLIERS ON 70 SQUADRON. JUST CONTINUE THAT WAY AND WE'LL SOON BE FLYING TOGETHER AGAIN. THINK IT OVER AND YOU'LL SEE IT MY WAY.

70 SQUADRON CHALKED UP A FORMIDABLE TOTAL OF FLYING HOURS AND GUNNERY PRACTICE.

SERGEANT ELLISON. A GOOD ATTACK, PLENTY HITS.

THE ROOKIE FLIERS LEARNED FAST, THEIR EAGERNESS FOR ACTION SPURRING THEM ON. THEN IT WAS SMITH'S TURN —

FLYING-OFFICER SMITH — WRONG APPROACH, WRONG HEIGHT, MILES WIDE OF THE TARGET. THAT CLOT COULDN'T HIT THE ROCK OF GIBRALTAR!

MILTON CAME NEXT, AND HIS EFFORTS WERE JUST AS LAMENTABLE.

FLYING-OFFICER MILTON — TOO STEEP. HE'S EVEN WORSE THAN SMITH. WHAT'S HE TRYING TO DO, DIG A HOLE FOR HIMSELF?

DAILY BECOMING MORE EXASPERATED, THE HARASSED SQUADRON-LEADER ELLIOT TRIED TO PULL SMITH AND MILTON INTO LINE.

YOU'RE A DEAD LOSS, BOTH OF YOU. SMITH, HOW IS IT YOU MANAGE TO GET LOST ON A FLIGHT OF TWENTY MILES? I COULDN'T DO THAT IF I TRIED. AND YOU, MILTON, IF I SEND ANY MORE TEMPESTS IN FOR CHECK-UP AFTER YOUR ROPEY LANDINGS, I'LL HAVE ALL THE AIRFRAME FITTERS ON STRIKE. FOR PETE'S SAKE PULL YOUR SOCKS UP — THERE'S STILL TIME.

	NAVIGATION	GUNNERY	AIRM...
LEWIS	�★★★★	✦✦✦✦✦	✦✦✦
GREENE	✦✦✦✦	✦✦✦	✦✦
EADEN	✦✦✦✦	✦✦✦	✦✦
PIPER	✦✦✦✦✦	✦✦✦✦	✦✦✦
WATSON	✦✦✦✦	✦✦✦✦	✦✦✦
LIMB	✦✦✦✦	✦✦✦	✦✦
PENROSE	✦✦✦✦✦	✦✦✦	✦✦✦
LAING	✦✦✦✦	✦✦✦✦	
SMITH	✦	✦	
MILTON	✦✦	✦	
OUVRY	✦✦✦✦	✦✦✦✦✦	
GLENNY	✦✦✦✦	✦✦✦	✦✦✦

BUT ELLIOT COULD SEE BY THEIR DEADPAN EXPRESSIONS THAT HE WAS WASTING HIS BREATH. THIS PAIR OF DEADBEATS WAS A LIABILITY. IF ONLY HE COULD FIND SOME WAY OF GETTING RID OF THEM...

IT BEATS ME WHY CARTER WANTS THE TWO WORST PILOTS IN THE SQUADRON!

THE NEXT MORNING THE STRIDENT CLAMOUR OF THE ALARM WARNED OF APPROACHING RAIDERS.

COME ON YOU LOT — SCRAMBLE!

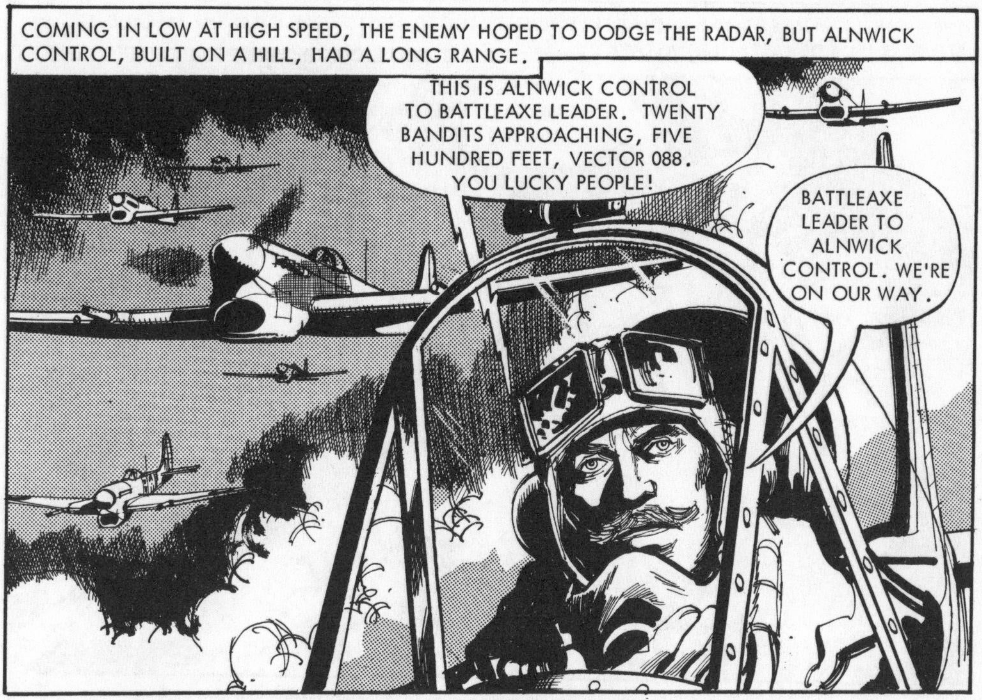
COMING IN LOW AT HIGH SPEED, THE ENEMY HOPED TO DODGE THE RADAR, BUT ALNWICK CONTROL, BUILT ON A HILL, HAD A LONG RANGE.
THIS IS ALNWICK CONTROL TO BATTLEAXE LEADER. TWENTY BANDITS APPROACHING, FIVE HUNDRED FEET, VECTOR 088. YOU LUCKY PEOPLE!
BATTLEAXE LEADER TO ALNWICK CONTROL. WE'RE ON OUR WAY.

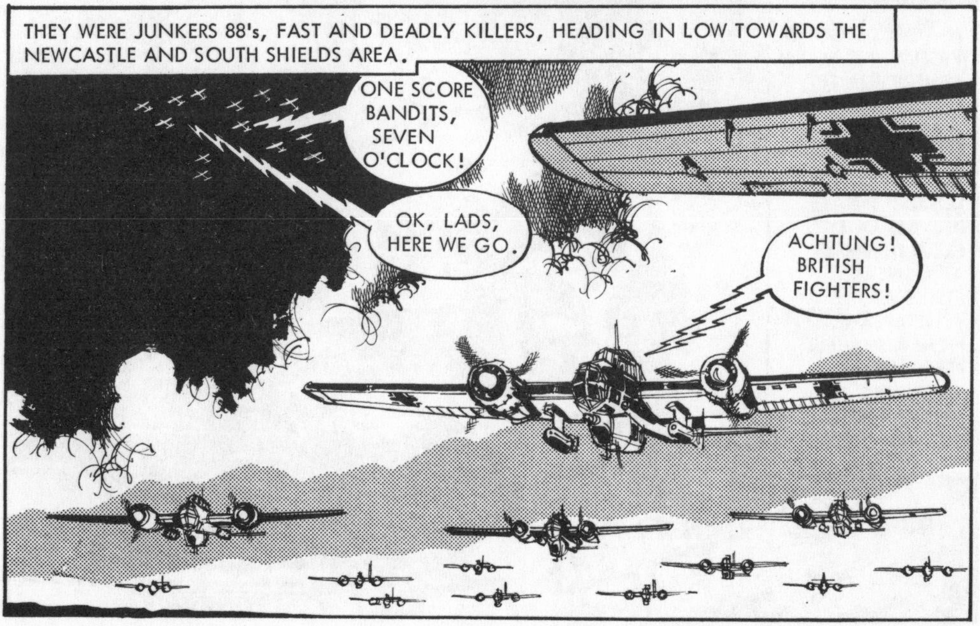
THEY WERE JUNKERS 88's, FAST AND DEADLY KILLERS, HEADING IN LOW TOWARDS THE NEWCASTLE AND SOUTH SHIELDS AREA.
ONE SCORE BANDITS, SEVEN O'CLOCK!
OK, LADS, HERE WE GO.
ACHTUNG! BRITISH FIGHTERS!

THEIR SABRE ENGINES SNARLING AT FULL BOOST, THE TEMPESTS TORE INTO THE MARAUDING BOMBERS IN A DEVASTATING ATTACK.

YAHOO! I GOT ONE!

AS TOM'S SECOND VICTIM AND MANY OTHERS FELL TO FLAMING RUIN, THE SHOCKED NAZI SURVIVORS JETTISONED THEIR LOADS. WHAT HAD SET OUT FROM DENMARK AS A SNEAK STRIKE AT THE TYNE AREA WAS NOW A SHAKEN REMNANT, STREAKING TO A SAFETY WHICH DID NOT EXIST.

THEY'RE CHUCKING THEIR BOMBS AWAY. THEY'VE HAD IT!

KEEP AFTER THEM. NONE OF THEM MUST GET BACK.

ONE AFTER ANOTHER, THE SURVIVING JUNKERS FELL TO THE ROARING CANNONS OF THE TEMPESTS. NOT UNTIL THE LAST ONE HAD PLOUGHED INTO THE GREY WATERS OF THE NORTH SEA DID 70 SQUADRON TURN FOR HOME.

NICE WORK, LADS. LET'S GO HOME. ALL PRESENT AND CORRECT?

NO SIR, TWO MISSING, SMITH AND MILTON.

THE NEWS STRUCK TOM LIKE A BODY BLOW — BUT NOT SO WITH ELLIOT...

SMITH AND MILTON BOUGHT IT. OH NO!

AIR SEA RESCUE WILL BE OUT — LET'S HOPE THEY PICK THEM UP.

I WANTED RID OF THEM ALL RIGHT, BUT NOT THIS WAY.

THE PILOTS CELEBRATED THEIR TOTAL VICTORY WITH A MONUMENTAL BEAT UP OF THE AIR FIELD. ANOTHER SHOCK AWAITED TOM — TWO TEMPESTS ALREADY LANDED THERE BELONGED TO SMITH AND MILTON.

NOBODY COULD HAVE KNOWN OF THEIR PREVIOUS COWARDICE. YET IT SEEMED TO THEM ALL THAT SMITH AND MILTON MUST HAVE DELIBERATELY AVOIDED THIS FIGHT.

THERE AND THEN, ELLIOT ORDERED SMITH'S GUNS TO BE GROUND TESTED.

WHILE MILTON'S TEMPEST WAS AT ONCE TAKEN UP BY ANOTHER PILOT FOR AN AIR TEST.

NO FAULT COULD BE FOUND WITH EITHER PLANE. THE PROOF WAS PLAIN, BUT MILTON STILL PROTESTED INNOCENCE. AND IN HIS CASE, A TEMPORARY ENGINE FAULT HAD EXISTED, BUT IT HAD RIGHTED ITSELF.

YOUR GUNS ARE PERFECT, SMITH. MILTON, YOUR TEMPEST HAS BEEN AIR-TESTED. THERE'S NO EVIDENCE OF OVERHEATING AT ALL. SO YOU WERE BOTH LYING.

BUT, SIR, IT WAS TRUE. THE FIRE WARNING LIGHT WAS SHOWING!

THE THREE FLIGHT COMMANDERS OF THE SQUADRON HAD ASKED FOR AN IMMEDIATE INTERVIEW WITH SQUADRON-LEADER ELLIOT, AND WERE SHOWN IN AT ONCE.

CAN WE SPEAK FREELY, SIR?

GO AHEAD.

THE PILOTS SAY THEY REFUSE TO FLY WITH THESE TWO ANY MORE. THEY'RE A LET-DOWN TO THE WHOLE SQUADRON.

THE VICTORY OVER THE BOMBERS HAD BOOSTED MORALE SKY-HIGH, AND THEIR GROWING SQUADRON PRIDE DEMANDED THAT THE TWO SHIRKERS SHOULD GO.

I'D GET RID OF THAT PRECIOUS PAIR TOMORROW IF I COULD, BUT GROUP H.Q. HAVE VETOED ALL OUR POSTINGS UNTIL FURTHER NOTICE. I'D LIKE TO SEND THEM TO TIMBUCTOO!

BUT SOMETHING WILL HAVE TO BE DONE, SIR. MEN MIGHT GET THE CHOP JUST BECAUSE THEY'RE ABSENT OR SLACKING.

AND NOW TOM SAW HIS CHANCE AT LAST, AND JUMPED AT IT.

EXCUSE ME, SIR. WHY NOT LET ME HAVE THEM AS I SUGGESTED BEFORE. I GUARANTEE TO TURN THEM INTO FIRST-CLASS TEMPEST PILOTS OR KILL THEM BOTH IN THE ATTEMPT.

ELLIOT HESITATED. THE IDEA WAS UNORTHODOX, BUT IT WASN'T EVERY DAY A COUPLE OF NUMB-SKULLS LIKE SMITH AND MILTON KEPT A WHOLE SQUADRON GROUNDED.

WELL...WE'VE GOT THREE RESERVES WHO COULD TAKE YOUR PLACES. YES, CARTER, YOU'RE WELCOME TO THEM. PERSONALLY, I DON'T KNOW WHY YOU'RE SO KEEN, BUT PLEASE — JUST KEEP THEM OUT OF MY HAIR.

THAT NIGHT THERE WAS A WILD MESS PARTY TO CELEBRATE THE SQUADRON'S SUCCESS AGAINST THE JUNKERS. ALL WENT WELL UNTIL SMITH TRIED TO TAKE PART.

GOOD OLD 70, "THE JUNKERS BASHERS"!

HOW ABOUT A SONG, LADS?

SIT DOWN AND SHUT UP, YOU FOOL.

AT THAT, THE PILOTS' DISLIKE AND RESENTMENT FLARED INTO OPEN HOSTILITY.

WE WANT A BIT OF FRESH AIR AROUND HERE. WHY DON'T YOU AND YOUR YELLOW PAL LEAVE? WE DON'T WANT YOU AROUND.

WHY, YOU—!

ALL RIGHT, SMITH. TAKE IT EASY. I'LL SEE YOU BOTH OUT.

OUTSIDE, SMARTING UNDER THE CONTEMPTUOUS WORDS, THE TWO MEN TURNED ON TOM BITTERLY.

BLASTED SHOWER OF IGNORANT SPROGS! WAIT TILL THEY TANGLE WITH THE FOCKE-WULFS, THEN THEY'LL CHANGE THEIR TUNE.

YELLOW, THEY SAID, YELLOW! IT'S ALL YOUR FAULT, CARTER. YOU ORDERED US TO GET INTO TROUBLE. I'LL SHOW YOU AND ALL THOSE FOOLS IN THERE I'M NOT SCARED.

ANGERED BY THEIR STUPIDITY, AND REALISING THAT LEADING THESE OUTCASTS WOULD MAKE HIM AN OUTCAST TOO, TOM LASHED THEM WITH BITTER WORDS.

LISTEN! KNOW WHAT A PARIAH IS? AN OUTCAST. YOU'VE BEEN PARIAHS SINCE YOU RAN AWAY THAT DAY OVER GERMANY. YOU'LL STAY PARIAHS UNTIL YOU PROVE OTHERWISE. NOW GET OUT OF MY SIGHT UNTIL MORNING. WE THREE TAKE OFF EARLY — FOR BELGIUM.

SOON AFTER DAWN NEXT DAY, 70 SQUADRON ROARED ITS WAY BACK TO THE BATTLE-TORN SKIES OF EUROPE TOWARDS EVELLE AIRFIELD, NEAR THE DUTCH BORDER OF BELGIUM.

70 SQUADRON WERE FLYING THEIR FIRST OFFENSIVE PATROL THE DAY AFTER THEIR ARRIVAL AT EVELLE. BUT THE THREE TEMPESTS OF THE 'HUNTER' FLIGHT HEADED NORTHWARDS ON A VERY DIFFERENT KIND OF MISSION, LED BY TOM.

HALF AN HOUR AFTER TAKE OFF, THEY SKIRTED THE TREMENDOUS FLAK BARRAGE THAT ROSE FROM HELIGOLAND, AND HEADED ON TOWARDS SCHLESWIG-HOLSTEIN.

CEASE FIRING! IT IS USELESS TO WASTE AMMUNITION. THE ENGLANDERS ARE OUT OF RANGE.

TOM HAD SELECTED AN EASY TARGET FOR THEIR FIRST OPERATION — A LUFTWAFFE TRAINING AIRFIELD THAT FACED THE SHELTERED WATERS OF THE BALTIC.

TARGET AHEAD. IF EITHER OF YOU RUNS AWAY FROM THIS LOT, I'LL PERSONALLY TAKE HIM APART WHEN WE GET BACK.

ALL THE WAY FROM TAKE OFF, MILTON'S STOMACH HAD BEEN TWISTING IN AN AGONY OF APPREHENSION. WHEN HE SAW THE GERMAN FORMATION AHEAD, A TERRIBLE URGE SEIZED HIM.

TH-THERE THEY ARE. M-MUST GET IT — OVER WITH QUICKLY. I'VE G-GOT TO PROVE I'M NOT SCARED.

THE PUPILS PRACTISING FORMATION FLYING SCATTERED DESPERATELY AS MILTON'S HURTLING TEMPEST SEEMED ABOUT TO CRASH INTO THEM IN WHAT LOOKED LIKE A WILD ATTEMPT AT SUICIDE. TOM, ABOUT TO NAIL HIS VICTIM, SPOTTED THE SUDDEN FLURRY FROM THE CORNER OF HIS EYE.

MEIN GOTT — A MADMAN!

FOR THE LOVE OF MIKE! MILTON, YOU FOOL!

MILTON PRESSED THE FIRING BUTTON A FRACTION OF A SECOND LATER, AND THE HENSCHEL HE WAS ALMOST ON TOP OF BLEW UP IN HIS FACE UNDER THE LASH OF THE TEMPEST'S SHELLS.

MIRACULOUSLY, MILTON'S BATTERED TEMPEST SURVIVED THE RAIN OF WRECKAGE THAT SMASHED INTO WINGS, PROPELLER AND FUSELAGE. ONE OF THE OTHERS FROM THE FORMATION, FORGETTING IN HIS PANIC ALL HE HAD LEARNT ABOUT RECOVERING FROM A SPIN, SMASHED INTO THE GROUND.

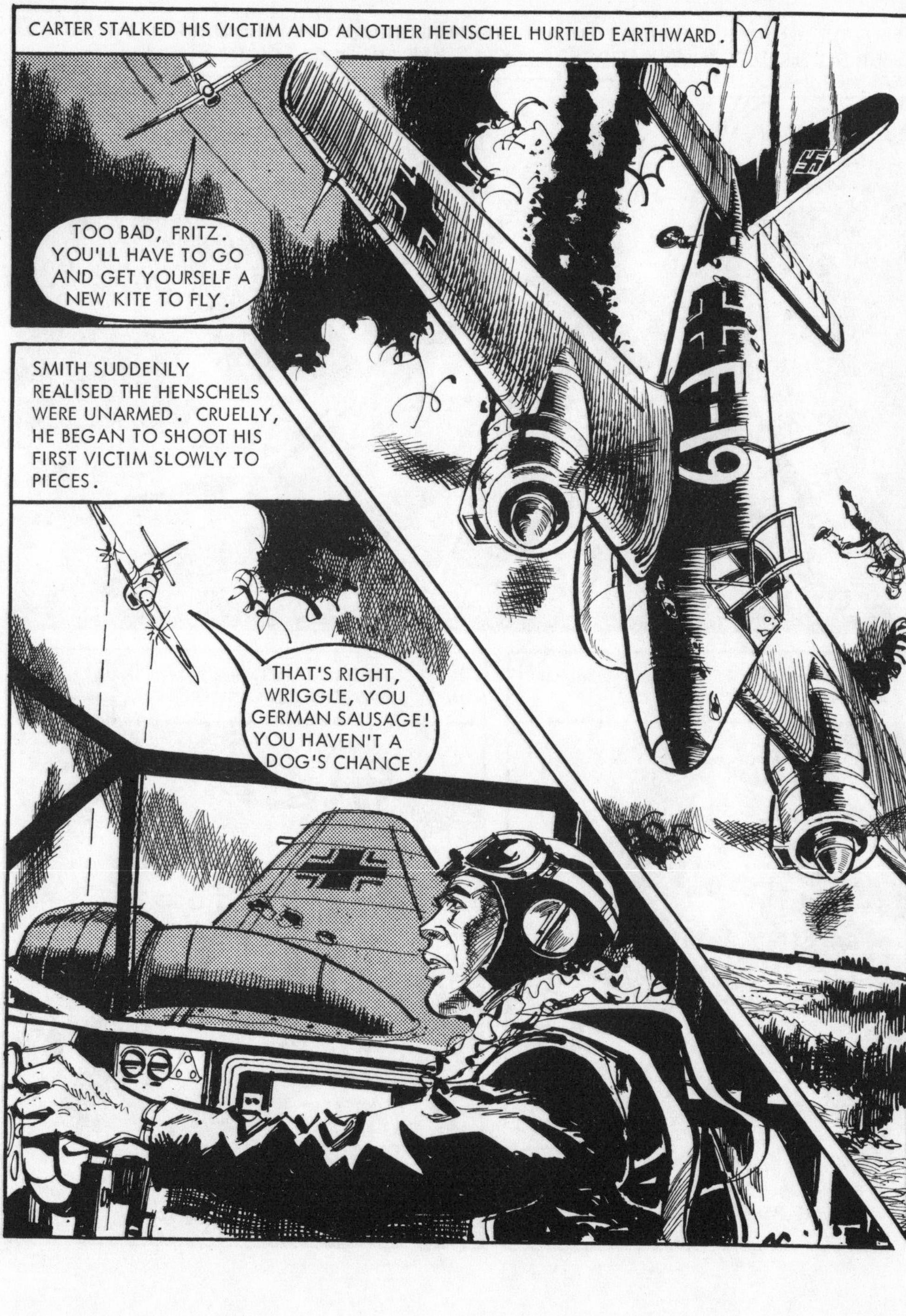
CARTER STALKED HIS VICTIM AND ANOTHER HENSCHEL HURTLED EARTHWARD.
TOO BAD, FRITZ. YOU'LL HAVE TO GO AND GET YOURSELF A NEW KITE TO FLY.
SMITH SUDDENLY REALISED THE HENSCHELS WERE UNARMED. CRUELLY, HE BEGAN TO SHOOT HIS FIRST VICTIM SLOWLY TO PIECES.
THAT'S RIGHT, WRIGGLE, YOU GERMAN SAUSAGE! YOU HAVEN'T A DOG'S CHANCE.

WHEN THE HENSCHEL WAS BARELY STAYING AIRBORNE, RIDDLED AND RUINED, SMITH DELIBERATELY ANNIHILATED THE COCKPIT — AND THE PILOT. CARTER WATCHED IN DISGUST.

YOU SHOULDN'T HAVE JOINED, CHUM.

SMITH! YOU DIDN'T HAVE TO DO THAT. HE'D HAD IT ALREADY.

BUT SMITH ONLY PROCEEDED TO RIP UP ANOTHER FROM NOSE TO TAIL.

WHAT'S CARTER BEEFING ABOUT? WE'RE SUPPOSED TO KILL 'EM. HERE'S ANOTHER HAD HIS CHIPS.

THE FLAK BEGAN TO COME UP IN STREAMS NOW THE SKY WAS CLEARED OF HENSCHELS.

HUNTER FLIGHT BREAK OFF ACTION OVER...

AT THE DE-BRIEFING AFTERWARDS, THE CLENCHED FISTS AND JUMPING MUSCLES IN MILTON'S FACE BETRAYED HIS TENSE NERVOUSNESS.

UNWIND, MILTON, CAN'T YOU? YOU'RE LIKE A TIGHT FIDDLE STRING.

IT — IT WAS THAT HENSCHEL — IT BLEW UP IN MY FACE. I SHOWED THEM THOUGH, DIDN'T I? I'M NOT SCARED. I — I CAN DO IT ALL RIGHT.

ALL RIGHT, LADDIE. YOU'VE PROVED WHAT? LAST TIME YOU GOT SO SCARED YOU RAN AWAY. THIS TIME YOU GOT SO SCARED YOU NEARLY KILLED YOURSELF. AND FOR WHAT? TWO OLD HENSCHELS BEING USED AS TRAINERS. UNARMED, TOO!

UNARMED! I DIDN'T KNOW..

THAT NIGHT SMITH BOASTED OF HIS SUCCESS. THEY LISTENED, SICKENED — BUT HE PRATTLED ON REGARDLESS —

LIKE ONE O' THEM CHINESE TORTURES — "DEATH OF A THOUSAND CUTS"! FIRST I SHOT HIS WINGTIPS OFF, THEN I RIDDLED HIS RUDDER, AND FINALLY I BLASTED HIS WHOLE COCKPIT TO SMITHEREENS.

ALL RIGHT, BRAVE BOY, SPARE US THE GORY DETAILS. SO YOU GOT YOURSELF A POOR LITTLE UNARMED HENSCHEL. SOUNDS LIKE MURDER!

SMITH WAS TOO STUPID TO SEE WHAT THE PILOT REALLY MEANT BY "MURDER". AS THE OTHERS TURNED AWAY IN DISGUST, TOM STRODE OVER —

IT CERTAINLY WAS. THAT FLAK! OH, BUT THAT AIN'T ALL. I GOT ANOTHER. SPLIT HIM UP THE MIDDLE, I DID. OH BOY, YOU SHOULD HAVE SEEN THE BITS FLY OFF.

SHUT UP, YOU RUDDY LINESHOOTER. THE POOR DEVILS DIDN'T EVEN HAVE ANYTHING THEY COULD THROW AT YOU. IT WAS JUST AN EXERCISE IN GUNNERY, ONLY YOU HAD TO GO AND MAKE A MEAL OF IT.

TOM NOW SAW THAT PLANNING REVENGE ON THE ENEMY WAS ONE THING, BUT GETTING IT WITH THE HELP OF THESE TWO DEADBEATS WAS ANOTHER. ALL THAT KEPT THEM IN LINE WAS THE SEALED LETTER.

CAN I DO ANYTHING WITH SMITH? HE'S A NATURAL COWARD, AND TOO THICK-SKINNED TO KNOW IT. AND MILTON'S TURNED NASTY AND DANGEROUS. MY STARS! WHAT HAVE I TAKEN ON?

NEXT DAY THEY STRUCK DEEP INTO GERMANY ITSELF ON A 'HUNTER' OPERATION, LOOKING FOR TROUBLE.

WITHIN FIFTEEN MINUTES, THEY FOUND THEIR FIRST TARGET.

TARGET AT TWO O'CLOCK — LET'S GO!

SMITH'S BLOOD LUST WAS UP. BEFORE HE HAD FIRED A SHOT, HE WAS VISUALISING THE DEATH AND DESTRUCTION THAT WAS TO COME.

HOLD THAT, SQUAREHEADS. JUST LIKE A FIREWORK DISPLAY. WOW! LOOK AT THESE JERRIES BITING THE DUST.

BELT UP, SMITH, AND GET ON WITH THE JOB.

THEN IT WAS MILTON'S TURN. TOM HAD BEEN EXPECTING INTERFERENCE, AND HE WASN'T DISAPPOINTED.

HUNTER LEADER HERE. FOUR FW'S ARE DIVING TO ATTACK. CARRY ON WITH ATTACK, BUT BE READY. WHEN I SHOUT 'BREAK' — CLIMB LIKE THE DEVIL AND THEN EVERY MAN FOR HIMSELF.

FOUR FOCKE-WULF 190's, THIRSTING FOR VENGEANCE, HURTLED DOWN ON THE WATCHFUL TEMPESTS, THINKING TO TAKE THEM UNAWARES.

TEUFEL! LOOK AT THE MESS THEY'VE MADE OF THAT TRAIN. SHOOT THE DOGS DOWN!

AT THE VERY MOMENT WHEN THE GERMAN FIGHTER PILOTS MOVED TO PRESS THEIR FIRING BUTTONS, TOM GAVE THE SIGNAL.

BREAK!

THREE THROTTLES SLAMMED WIDE OPEN. THE SURGING POWER OF THE MIGHTY SABRE ENGINES ROCKETED THEM SKYWARDS AS THEY PULLED THEIR STICKS BACK.

UPS A DAISY!

OVER ON THEIR BACKS THEY WENT, AND DOWN AGAIN BEHIND THE GERMAN FIGHTERS' TAILS.

NOW'S YOUR CHANCE, BOTH OF YOU. WE'VE GOT THEM COLD.

ACH, WHERE ARE THEY?

IT WAS A MASTERLY PIECE OF FIGHTER TACTICS, EXPLOITING THE FLYING QUALITIES OF THE TEMPESTS TO THE FULL.

THAT'S THE IDEA, LADS. WE REALLY SHOOK THEM RIGID.

THE SURVIVOR CLIMBED AWAY TOWARDS THE EAST. LIKE AN AVENGING FURY, MILTON TORE AFTER HIM.

COME BACK, YOU NIT. MILTON, LEAVE IT! HEAD FOR BASE, SMITH. I'M GOING AFTER THAT CRACKPOT. HE'S REALLY GOT THE BIT BETWEEN HIS TEETH THIS TIME.

SOMEWHERE OVER THE WESER RIVER, TWO STRANGE SHAPES STREAKED UPWARDS FROM THE GREEN GERMAN PLAIN.

OH, MY GOSH! THERE ARE TWO JETS AFTER HIM. MILTON, LOOK OUT. DIVE, MAN, DIVE, AND HEAD FOR HOME. THE FOOL'S STILL GOT HIS TRANSMITTER ON, HE CAN'T HEAR ME.

BUT MILTON DID HEAR THE WARNING AND SENT THE TEMPEST PLUMMETING EARTH-WARDS.

ITS GREAT WEIGHT GAVE IT THE EXTRA SPEED TO ESCAPE FROM THE LIGHTNING-FAST JETS, MESSERSCHMITT 262's.

AFTER THE ENGLANDER!

IN A MAD BUT DEADLY HUNT, THE THUNDERING JETS RAPIDLY OVERHAULED THE FLEEING TEMPEST, WITH TOM FRANTICALLY PURSUING ALL THREE.

TOM ALMOST BLACKED OUT UNDER THE TERRIFIC G FORCE AS HE PULLED OUT OF HIS DIVE AT MORE THAN 600 MILES AN HOUR. AS THE MISTS CLEARED FROM HIS BRAIN, HE FELT THE HOT BLAST FROM THE REARMOST JET'S ENGINES.

THREE SHELLS WENT UP THE VENT PIPE AND BLEW THE SPINNING IMPELLER INTO TEARING LETHAL FRAGMENTS WHICH PRACTICALLY CUT THE MESSERSCHMITT'S FUSELAGE IN TWO.

AAAGH!

TOM'S MOMENTUM TOOK HIM WITHIN RANGE OF THE SECOND JET. AS IT OPENED FIRE ON MILTON'S FRANTICALLY DODGING PLANE, HIS SHELLS ABRUPTLY ENDED THE SHORT LIFE OF ANOTHER OF HITLER'S NEW JETS.

OK, THAT'S SETTLED HIS HASH. NOW GET BACK TO BASE, MILTON. I'VE GOT A BONE TO PICK WITH YOU.

ON ARRIVAL AT BASE, TOM WASTED NO TIME IN GIVING MILTON A WELL DESERVED DRESSING DOWN.

IF I HADN'T NAILED THOSE JETS YOU'D HAVE BEEN A DEAD DUCK. I'M WARNING YOU, MILTON, OBEY MY ORDERS IN FUTURE — OR ELSE!

STILL OUTCASTS, THE HUNTERS RANGED FAR AND WIDE OVER ENEMY TERRITORY. AVOIDING DEFENDED AREAS AND LOOKING FOR THE LESS OBVIOUS TARGETS, THEIR TERRIFIC SPEED AND LOW LEVEL TACTICS GOT MAXIMUM RESULTS WITH MINIMUM RISK.

ANOTHER COUPLE OF SQUAREHEADS SCORED OFF THE LIST.

IMPRESSED BY THE HUNTERS' SPECTACULAR RECORD, FIGHTER COMMAND HEADQUARTERS TOOK A HAND.

SQUADRON-LEADER ELLIOT TELLS ME CARTER HAS WORKED WONDERS WITH THEM. HE'S TURNED THEM FROM SQUADRON THROW-OUTS INTO A FIRST CLASS FIGHTING TEAM. BY ATTACKING OFF-BEAT TARGETS THEY ARE GIVING THE ENEMY AN OUTSIZE HEADACHE.

I PROPOSE THAT WE ALLOT THREE SPECIAL MARKS OF TEMPEST TO THEM, WITH EXTRA FUEL CAPACITY AND ARMED WITH ROCKETS.

WITH THE INCREASED RANGE THAT COULD TAKE THEM DEEP INTO HITLER'S EUROPE, CARTER'S KILLERS, AS THEY BECAME KNOWN, WERE DREADED BY NAZIS EVERYWHERE WHO'D THOUGHT THEMSELVES SAFE.

THAT'S ONE BIG FAT GERMAN GENERAL WHO WON'T BE DINING IN PRAGUE TONIGHT!

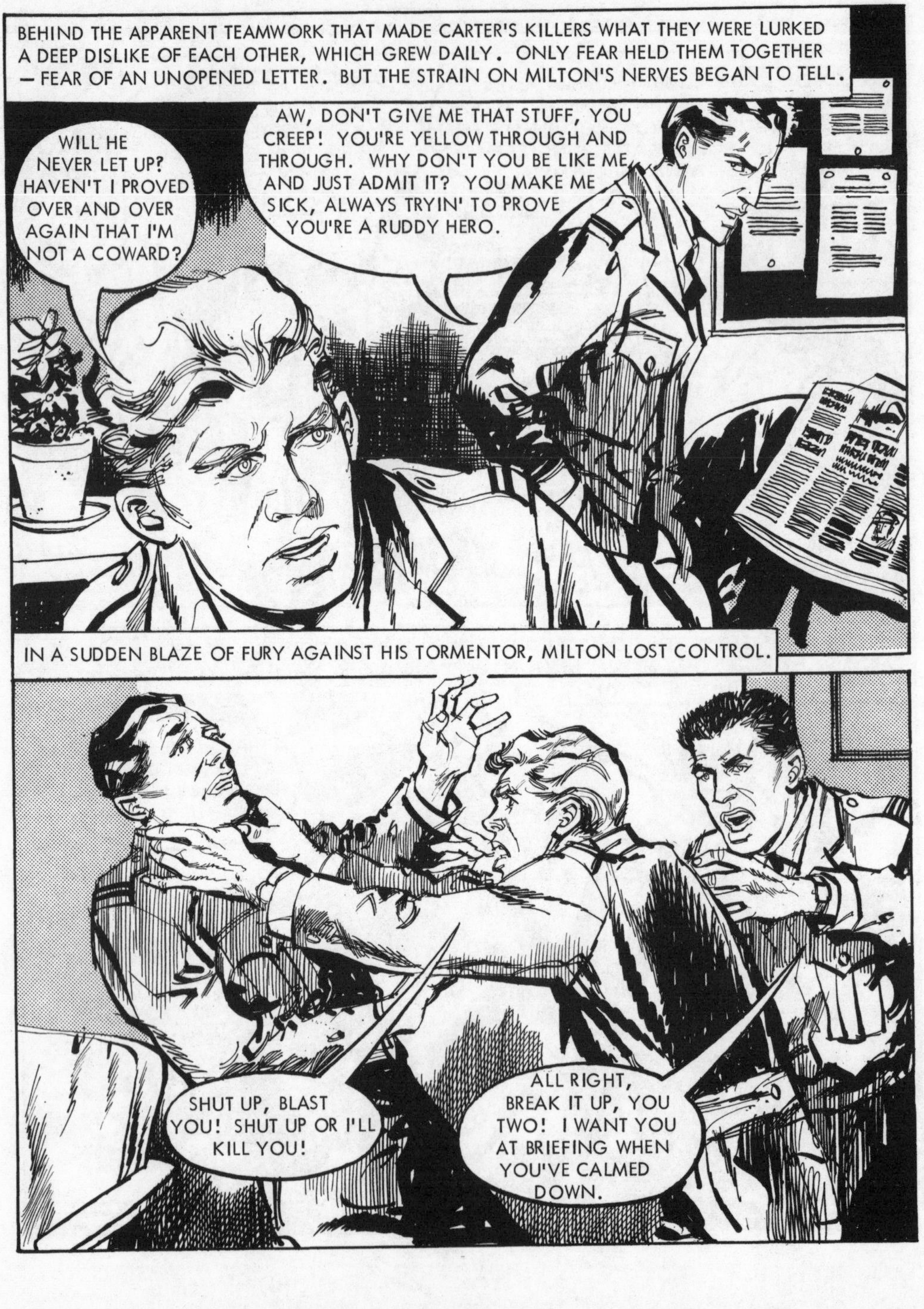
BEHIND THE APPARENT TEAMWORK THAT MADE CARTER'S KILLERS WHAT THEY WERE LURKED A DEEP DISLIKE OF EACH OTHER, WHICH GREW DAILY. ONLY FEAR HELD THEM TOGETHER — FEAR OF AN UNOPENED LETTER. BUT THE STRAIN ON MILTON'S NERVES BEGAN TO TELL.
WILL HE NEVER LET UP? HAVEN'T I PROVED OVER AND OVER AGAIN THAT I'M NOT A COWARD?
AW, DON'T GIVE ME THAT STUFF, YOU CREEP! YOU'RE YELLOW THROUGH AND THROUGH. WHY DON'T YOU BE LIKE ME AND JUST ADMIT IT? YOU MAKE ME SICK, ALWAYS TRYIN' TO PROVE YOU'RE A RUDDY HERO.
IN A SUDDEN BLAZE OF FURY AGAINST HIS TORMENTOR, MILTON LOST CONTROL.
SHUT UP, BLAST YOU! SHUT UP OR I'LL KILL YOU!
ALL RIGHT, BREAK IT UP, YOU TWO! I WANT YOU AT BRIEFING WHEN YOU'VE CALMED DOWN.

TWO DAYS PREVIOUSLY, A SPITFIRE XIV WAS FLYING A ROUTINE MISSION OVER A SHATTERED NAZI AIRFIELD WEST OF HANOVER, CALLED LANGENDORF.

WHAT A BIND! FIVE TIMES IN THREE WEEKS I'VE PHOTOGRAPHED THIS PLACE — IT STILL LOOKS THE SAME RUBBISH HEAP TO ME. HECK — WHAT'S THAT? FLAK! THERE MUST BE SOMETHING AFTER ALL.

FOR THE PAST FEW WEEKS A HEAVY TOLL HAD BEEN TAKEN OF THE SWARMS OF ALLIED BOMBERS THAT POUNDED BY DAYLIGHT THE VAST HEART OF NAZISM — BERLIN. MESSERSCHMITT 262 JETS, ARMED WITH CANNONS AND ROCKETS, APPEARED FROM A CLEAR SKY AND DISAPPEARED AFTERWARDS WITHOUT TRACE. THEN PHOTOGRAPHS FOR THE FIRST TIME SEEMED TO ANSWER THE RIDDLE OF WHERE THEY CAME FROM.

WE'VE GOT IT! THESE FRESH TYRE MARKS, THE DIFFERENT SHAPE OF THESE BOMB CRATERS — JERRY'S REPAIRED THE RUN-WAYS AND PAINTED DUMMY CRATERS ON THEM. IT'S THE JET BASE, WITHOUT A DOUBT, UNDER-GROUND HANGARS AND ALL.

THE AMERICANS ARE PUTTING ON A BIG STRIKE AGAINST BERLIN TOMORROW. THAT AIRFIELD'S GOT TO BE KNOCKED OUT — FAST!

SPEED AND DECISIVENESS WERE VITAL IF THE HIDDEN PERIL WAS TO BE COUNTERED.

NO TIME FOR BOMBING, AND MONTY AND IKE ARE YELLING FOR EVERY FIGHTER THEY CAN GET FOR THE RHINE CROSSING. WE WANT A SMALL FORCE TO PRANG 'EM JUST BEFORE TAKE-OFF. CARTER'S KILLERS ARE THE ONLY ONES FOR THIS JOB.

TOM DIDN'T LIKE THIS. TO SADDLE CARTER'S KILLERS WITH A VITAL OP LIKE THIS WAS COURTING FAILURE. BUT THEY'D NO CHOICE.

FOR A CHANGE, THIS IS NO EASY OP. THERE'LL BE FLAK, BAGS OF IT. BUT IF WE STICK TO OUR TIMING, NONE OF THEIR JETS SHOULD GET OFF THE GROUND. NOW DON'T FORGET, THESE NEW NAPALM BOMBS ARE LIKE THE VERY FLAMES OF HADES. DROP 'EM BELOW 100 FEET AND YOU'LL MOST LIKELY GET THE FULL BENEFIT YOURSELF.

WHILE THE REST OF THE SQUADRON WERE PLAYING THEIR PART IN THE CROSSING OF THE RHINE, THE HUNTERS WERE PRECISELY TIMED TO ATTACK THE JET BASE JUST BEFORE THE JETS WERE DUE TO TAKE OFF AND INTERCEPT THE APPROACHING ARMADA OF U.S. BOMBERS.

SO NOTE THAT, MILTON. KEEP UP UNTIL YOU'VE GOT RID OF YOUR EGGS. SMITH — YOU'LL DEAL WITH THE FLAK, USING YOUR CANNONS.

AW, HECK, I DON'T FANCY FLAK. IF THEY HIT ONE OF THESE NAPALM THINGS, I'LL GO UP LIKE A TORCH.

DON'T WORRY. YOUR LOAD'S GOING TO BE ALL ROCKETS, TO USE ON THE NAZI GUNS.

WITH THEIR MASSIVE LETHAL LOAD, THE TEMPESTS WERE SLOW TO GET AIRBORNE. TOM FELT THE SWEAT START OUT ON HIS BACK AS THE BOUNDARY HEDGE RACED NEARER.

TO MISLEAD THE ENEMY, THE HUNTERS HEADED IN THE DIRECTION OF MAGDEBURG. THEN, WHEN THEY WERE DUE SOUTH OF LANGENDORF, THEY SWUNG SHARPLY INTO A RIGHT-ANGLED TURN.

A VITAL THREE MINUTES — THE U.S. BOMBERS, EIGHT HUNDRED AND FIFTY FORTRESSES AND LIBERATORS, WERE ALREADY SHAKING THE WINDOWS IN DUTCH BORDER TOWNS WITH THEIR THUNDEROUS APPROACH. SO FAR, FIGHTER OPPOSITION HAD BEEN LIGHT. THE FIELD HAD BEEN LEFT CLEAR FOR THE LANGENDORF JETS.

AT LANGENDORF, UNDER WHAT SEEMED FROM THE AIR TO BE TUMBLED WRECKAGE, JET TURBINES BEGAN TO WHINE. FROM THE SIDE OF AN IRREGULARLY SHAPED HILLOCK, CONCEALING AN UNDERGROUND HANGAR, A RAMP WAS UNCOVERED.

ACHTUNG! PILOTS, MAN YOUR AIR-CRAFT.

HURRY UP THERE, THE PILOT IS WAITING.

SURPRISE WAS COMPLETE. THE ROARING TEMPESTS HURTLED OVER THE PERIMETER, CANNONS THUMPING, AT 450 MPH.

HUNTER TWO, MARK YOUR TARGET. HUNTER THREE, GET THOSE GUNS!

SEARCHING FOR A TARGET FOR HIS NAPALM BOMBS, A PAIR OF TAXI-ING JETS LOOMED IN TOM'S SIGHTS. HE JAMMED HIS THUMB ON THE FIRING BUTTON.

NO YOU DON'T. YOU'RE NOT FLYING TODAY — OR ANY OTHER DAY.

SUDDENLY TOM SPOTTED THE UNCOVERED RAMP. HE RACED TOWARDS IT AND SLAMMED DOWN THE RELEASE LEVER.

IMPRESSIVE THOUGH THE RESULTS WERE, HE GROANED WITH DISMAY WHEN HE SAW HE HAD FAILED.

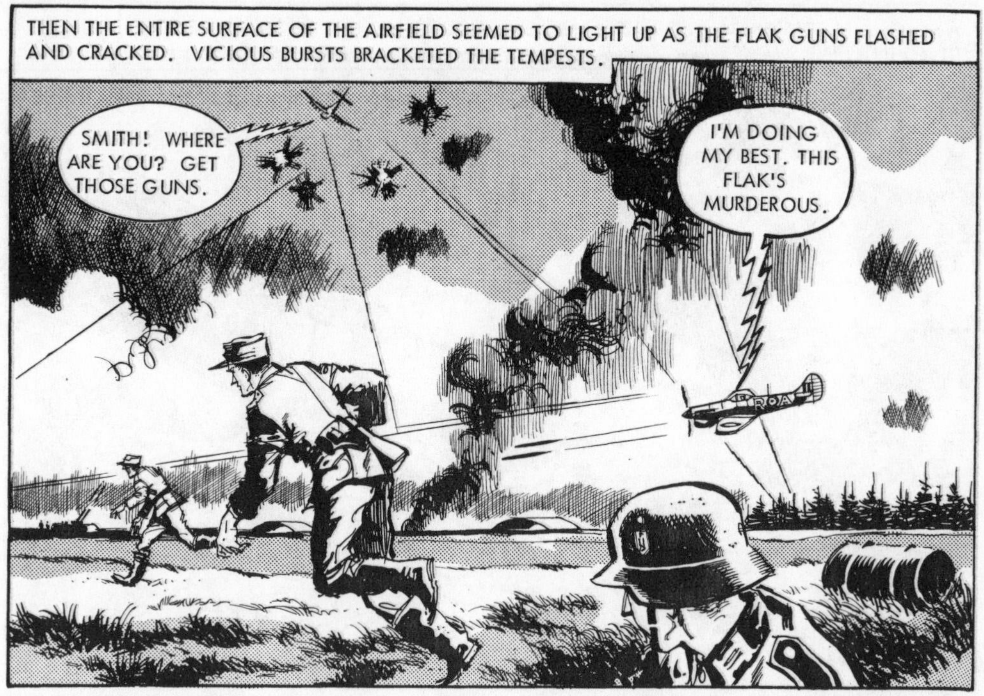
THEN THE ENTIRE SURFACE OF THE AIRFIELD SEEMED TO LIGHT UP AS THE FLAK GUNS FLASHED AND CRACKED. VICIOUS BURSTS BRACKETED THE TEMPESTS.
SMITH! WHERE ARE YOU? GET THOSE GUNS.
I'M DOING MY BEST. THIS FLAK'S MURDEROUS.

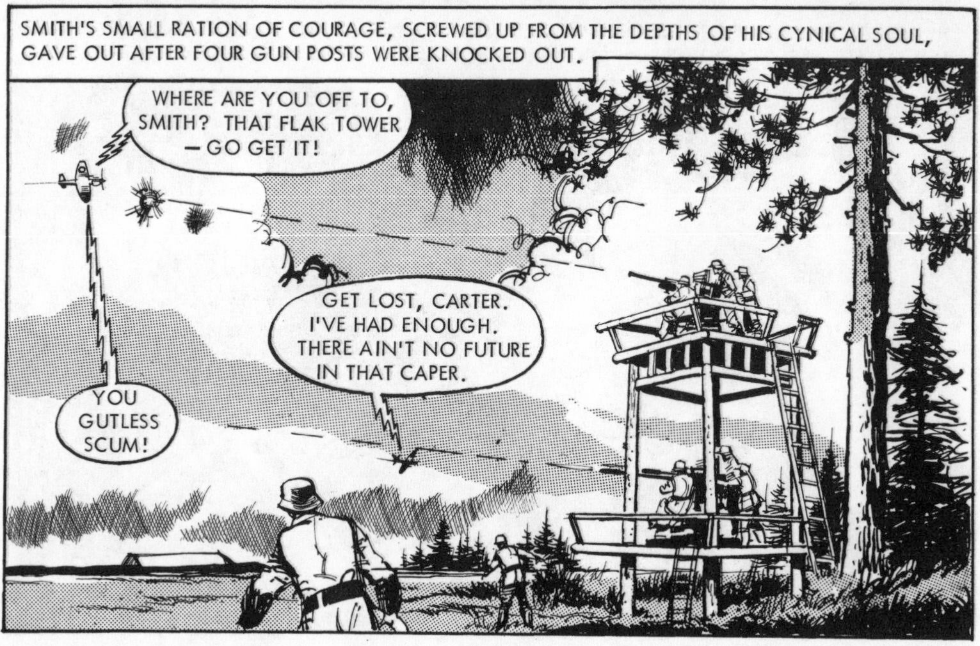
SMITH'S SMALL RATION OF COURAGE, SCREWED UP FROM THE DEPTHS OF HIS CYNICAL SOUL, GAVE OUT AFTER FOUR GUN POSTS WERE KNOCKED OUT.
WHERE ARE YOU OFF TO, SMITH? THAT FLAK TOWER — GO GET IT!
GET LOST, CARTER. I'VE HAD ENOUGH. THERE AIN'T NO FUTURE IN THAT CAPER.
YOU GUTLESS SCUM!

A SINGLE JET DESPERATELY TRIED TO TAKE OFF THROUGH A HAIL OF SHELLS AS TOM DIVED INTO THE SMOKE.

I MIGHT HAVE KNOWN SMITH DIDN'T HAVE WHAT IT TAKES.

OH, NO YOU DON'T, FRITZ.

HE LOOSED TWO ROCKETS. AS THEY BLASTED THE JET'S TAIL UP, ITS FUSELAGE BOUNCED ON THE TARMAC AND DISSOLVED IN A SHOWER OF FRAGMENTS FROM SMASHED WINGS AND TAIL PLANES.

HE FLUNG HIS TEMPEST IN A SWEEPING ARC, HIS WING-TIP ONLY INCHES FROM THE GROUND AND LOOSED ALL HIS REMAINING ROCKETS IN A DEVASTATING SALVO, SQUARE INTO THE RAMP ENTRANCE.

BULLSEYE!

THE ROCKET'S EXPLOSIONS BECAME ONLY A PART OF A VAST SPREADING DETONATION AS JET FUEL, AMMUNITION AND FIGHTER ROCKETS BLEW UP, THE WHOLE HILL CRUMBLING.

WE'LL NEVER KNOW HOW MANY JETS THEY HAD DOWN THERE — AND IT DOESN'T MATTER MUCH NOW.

SQUADRON-LEADER CARTER'S YELL OF TRIUMPH CHANGED TO A GASP OF HORROR AS HE SAW MILTON'S TEMPEST NOW THUNDERING OVER LANGENDORF AIRFIELD ONLY TWENTY FEET ABOVE GROUND.

MILTON — HE'S MAKING A RUN TO DROP HIS NAPALM. HE'S MILES TOO LOW.

CLIMB, BLAST YOU, MILTON — CLIMB!

BUT MILTON DIDN'T HEAR — OR WOULDN'T LISTEN. THE INTOLERABLE MENTAL STRAIN SEEMED TO HAVE SNAPPED HIS OVERSTRETCHED NERVES AT LAST.

A HANGAR FULL OF 'EM. WHAT A FIRE IT'LL BE, A DOZEN JETS — AND ONE TEMPEST!

THE STARK HORROR OF WHAT MILTON THEN DID SHOCKED CARTER TO THE ROOTS OF HIS BEING. HE ZOOMED RIGHT INTO THE HANGAR TO RELEASE HIS DEADLY NAPALM BOMBS.

MILTON! WHY DID YOU DO IT, YOU CRAZY FOOL.

CARTER FOUND HIMSELF UNABLE TO LOOK AT THE HORROR THAT WAS TO COME. NO ONE COULD SURVIVE DROPPING NAPALM BOMBS THAT LOW.

WHEN THEY LOOKED DOWN AGAIN, SECONDS LATER, THE HANGAR DISSOLVED IN A MASS OF BOILING FLAMES, AN ALL-CONSUMING FUNERAL PYRE. GESCHWADER 295 HAD BEEN WIPED OFF THE MAP AS IF IT HAD NEVER EXISTED.

POOR YOUNG MILTON...HE CERTAINLY WENT OUT IN STYLE. AND I THOUGHT HE'D NO GUTS!

SUDDENLY SMITH SAW SOMETHING THAT WAS WILDLY IMPOSSIBLE.

YOU'RE WRONG, BY THUNDER, YOU'RE WRONG! LOOK, CARTER LOOK — HE'S GOT AWAY WITH A FLAMIN' MIRACLE!

EVEN THE FLAK DEFENCES FIRED WILDLY FOR A FEW MINUTES AS THEIR CREWS GAPED, STAGGERED BY THE REMARKABLE ESCAPE OF THE SCORCHED AND STAGGERING TEMPEST WHOSE SPEED HAD TAKEN IT RIGHT THROUGH THAT INFERNO.

NOW I'VE SEEN EVERYTHING. MILTON, YOU'LL NEVER GET A SECOND CHANCE LIKE THAT. YOU'RE LIVING ON BORROWED TIME. MILTON, CAN YOU HEAR ME?

BUT ONE FLAK CREW WAS STILL ON THE BALL. MILTON'S SMOKING FIGHTER STAGGERED AS A LANCE OF 20MM SHELLS IMPALED IT. HIS BORROWED TIME WAS RUNNING OUT FAST.

BLAZES! THE STINKIN' NAZIS HAVE NAILED HIM. BALE OUT MAN, QUICK. YOU CAN MAKE IT.

AS THE HURTLING BODY TRAILED A SUDDEN WHITE FLASH OF SILK THE TENSION BROKE AND SMITH LAUGHED WITH RELIEF.

HE'S GOING TO MAKE IT!

BUT A NEW DANGER NOW FACED MILTON. THE FLAK CREW, ENRAGED BY THE RUINS OF LANGENDORF, WANTED REVENGE.

HAVE ANOTHER LOOK, SMITH. THAT FLAK TOWER'S STILL FIRING — AT MILTON — THANKS TO YOU, YOU YELLOW RAT. IF YOU'D PRANGED IT AS I ORDERED I COULD'VE HAD A CRACK AT PICKING HIM UP. BUT NOW THE POOR DEVIL HASN'T A CHANCE. THEY MEAN TO GET HIM AND I CAN'T DO A THING ABOUT IT. MY AMMO'S DONE.

YOU TALK TOO MUCH, CARTER. GET DOWN THERE AND PICK HIM UP. I'LL FIX THAT TOWER.

BUT HOW — ? YOU HAVEN'T ANY SHELLS LEFT EITHER, HAVE YOU?

BUT SMITH ONLY POINTED THE TEMPEST'S WIDE NOSE AT THE TOWER AND DIVED.

THE AIR AROUND SMITH'S SPEEDING FIGHTER CRACKLED WITH EXPLODING SHELLS, BUT IT HELD ITS UNWAVERING COURSE. THIS TIME, ITS PILOT DID NOT FLINCH.

AFTER SEEING MILTON COME THROUGH THAT FIRE, I'M NOT GOING TO SIT UP HERE WATCHING THEM SHOOT HIM TO BITS. NOW SHUT UP AND GO GET HIM, CARTER. GOOD LUCK.

TOM WATCHED AND HELD HIS BREATH, WAITING FOR SMITH'S CANNONS TO OPEN UP. ONLY IN THE LAST SPLIT SECOND DID HE REALISE THAT SMITH'S GUNS WOULD STAY SILENT FOR ALL ETERNITY.

AT 470 MILES AN HOUR HE WENT SMACK INTO THE FLAK TOWER, A WHIRLWIND OF FLAMES AND FRAGMENTS SCATTERING IN THE SKY.

UNDER THE PROTECTION OF THE BILLOWING SMOKE, TOM EXPERTLY LANDED HIS TEMPEST CLOSE TO MILTON.

ARE YOU ALL RIGHT? COME ON, I HAVEN'T GOT ALL BLOOMING DAY — GET ABOARD. I'LL SIT ON YOUR LAP AND DRIVE.

HAMPERED BY HIS AWKWARD PERCH, TOM MADE A ROPEY TAKE-OFF BUT THEY MADE IT — CLIMBING FREE INTO THE CLEAR SKY, HEADING WESTWARDS.

WHY DID HE DO IT? HE HATED MY GUTS. HE TOLD ME SO.

DON'T ASK ME — BUT I RECKON WHEN IT COMES TO THE PUSH THERE'S ALWAYS SOMETHING INSIDE A MAN THAT MAKES HIM DO THE RIGHT THING, NO MATTER WHO HE IS. NOW SHUT UP AND LET'S CONCENTRATE ON FLYING THIS THING. IT'S AWKWARD ENOUGH WITH YOU TAKING UP ALL THE ROOM.

BACK IN THEIR MESS, FREED NOW FROM THE BURDEN OF HIS CONSCIENCE, THE DEEP LINES OF TENSION THAT WERE ETCHED ON MILTON'S FACE FADED. HE SMILED AGAIN, FOR THE FIRST TIME IN MANY WEEKS.

BETWEEN US, WE'VE GOT ABOUT THIRTY-FIVE ENEMY PLANES. I RECKON THAT WIPES THE SLATE CLEAN. POOR OLD SMITHY TURNED UP TRUMPS IN THE END AND I RECKON YOU'VE TURNED INTO A FIRST CLASS FIGHTER PILOT. MAYBE THEY'VE GOT ROOM FOR US NOW WITH THE REST OF THE SQUADRON.

BUT ABOUT THAT, ER — LETTER...

TOM SMILED AND GOT UP. TOGETHER THEY WALKED ACROSS TO THE FIRE.

I GOT THAT FROM THE SAFE THIS MORNING. THERE'S ONLY ONE PLACE FOR IT NOW...

THEY MADE TOM A SQUADRON-LEADER SHORTLY AFTERWARDS, AND WITH MILTON AS ONE OF HIS FLIGHT COMMANDERS THEY FORMED A RED-HOT TEAM. THE HUNTER FLIGHTS OF 70 SQUADRON ROAMED THE FORWARD BATTLE AREAS, PLAYING A VITAL PART IN THE FINAL CONFLICT THAT SMASHED THE NAZI REIGN OF TERROR OVER EUROPE INTO RUINS FOR GOOD.

Commando
THE END

Commando

FOR ACTION AND ADVENTURE

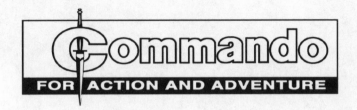

THE COVERS

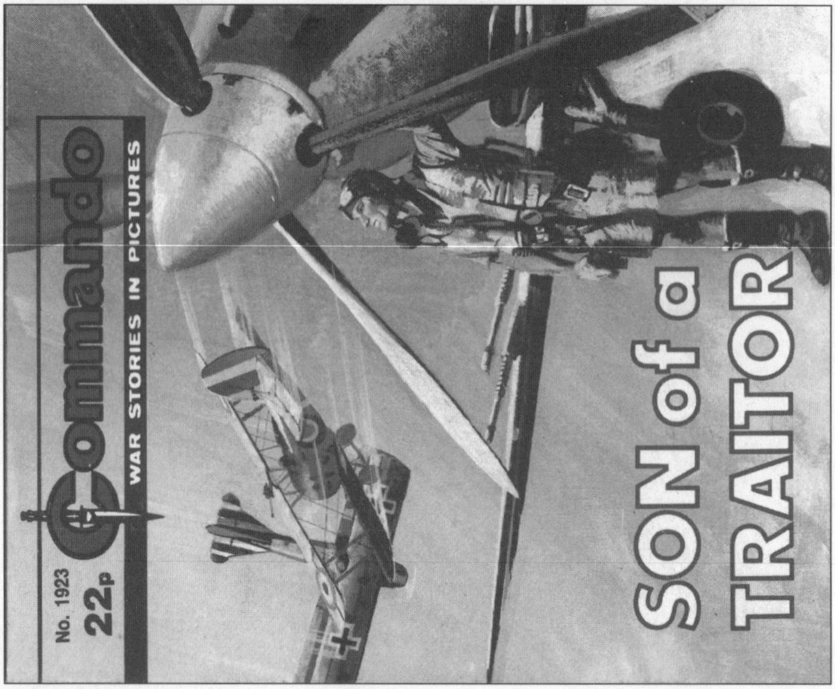
No. 1923
22p
Commando
WAR STORIES IN PICTURES
SON of a
TRAITOR

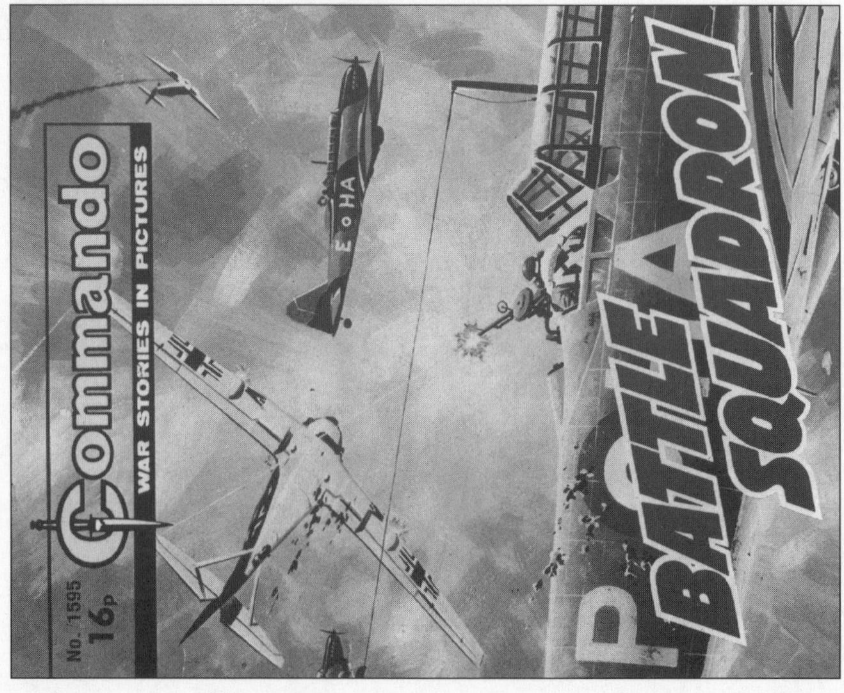
No. 1595
16p
Commando
WAR STORIES IN PICTURES
BATTLE
SQUADRON

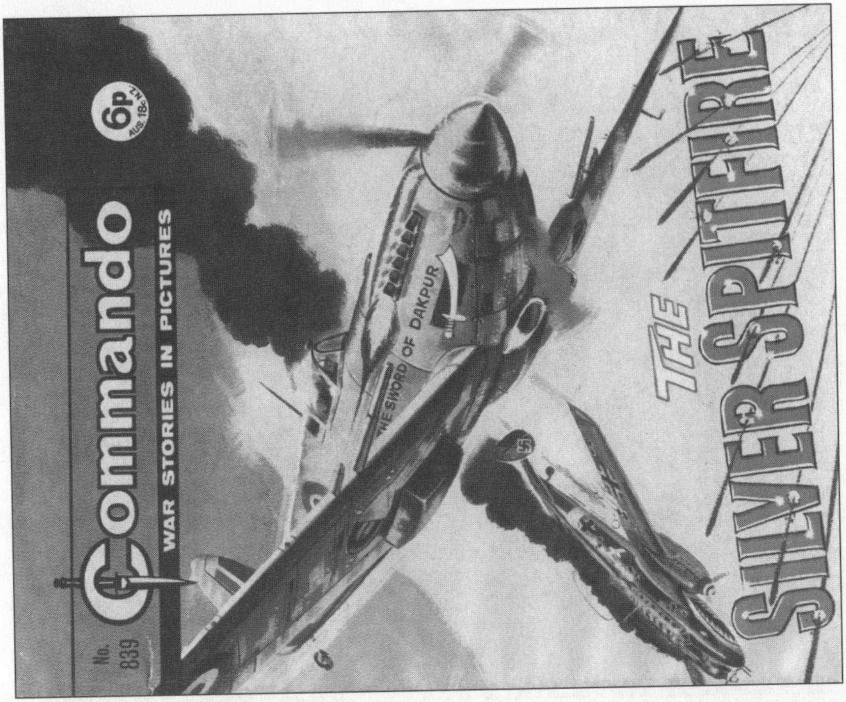
No. 839
Commando
WAR STORIES IN PICTURES
6p
AUS. 18c N.Z.
THE SWORD OF DAKPUR
THE SILVER SPITFIRE

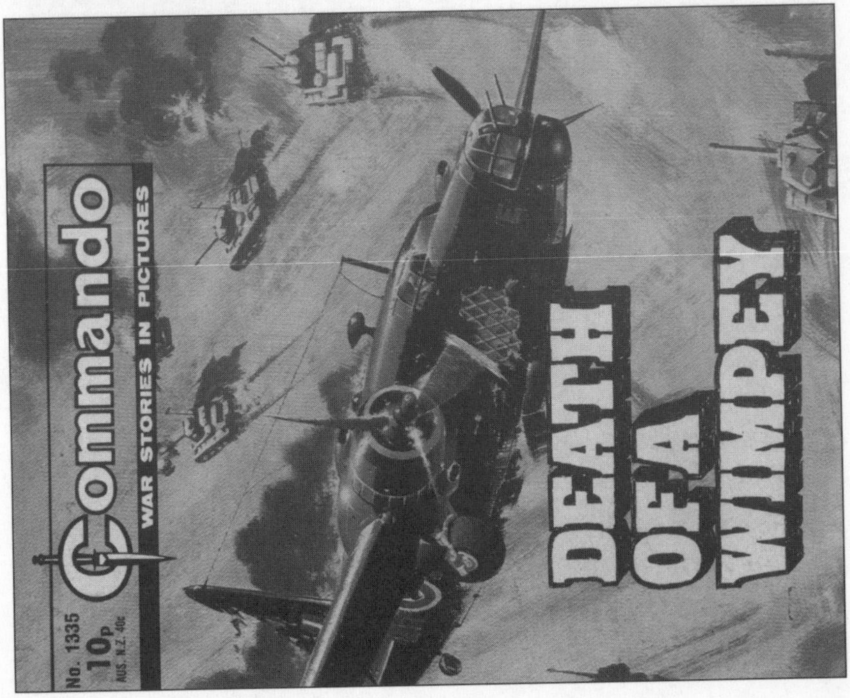
No. 1335
10p
AUS. N.Z. 40c
Commando
WAR STORIES IN PICTURES
DEATH OF A WIMPEY

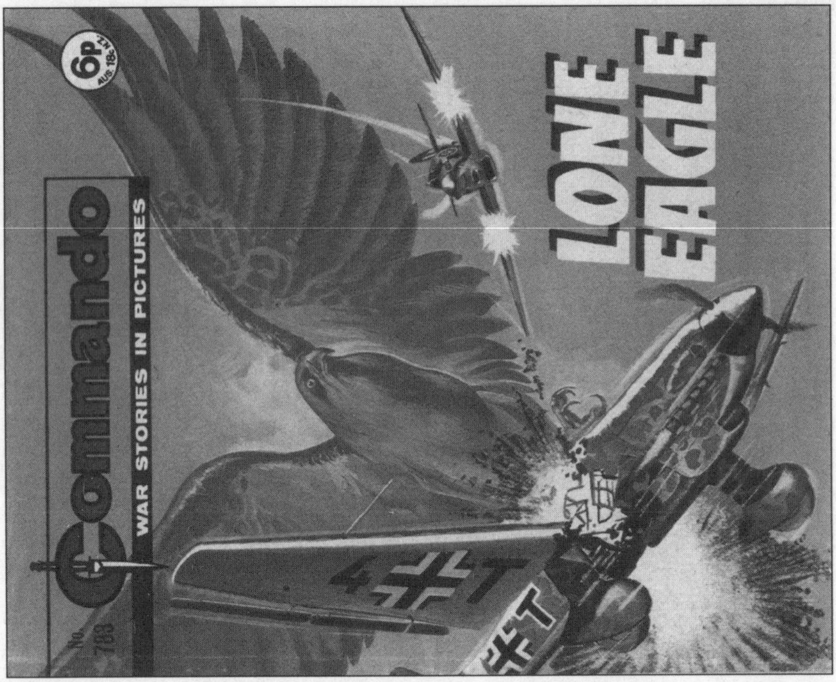
No. 783
Commando
WAR STORIES IN PICTURES
6p
LONE EAGLE

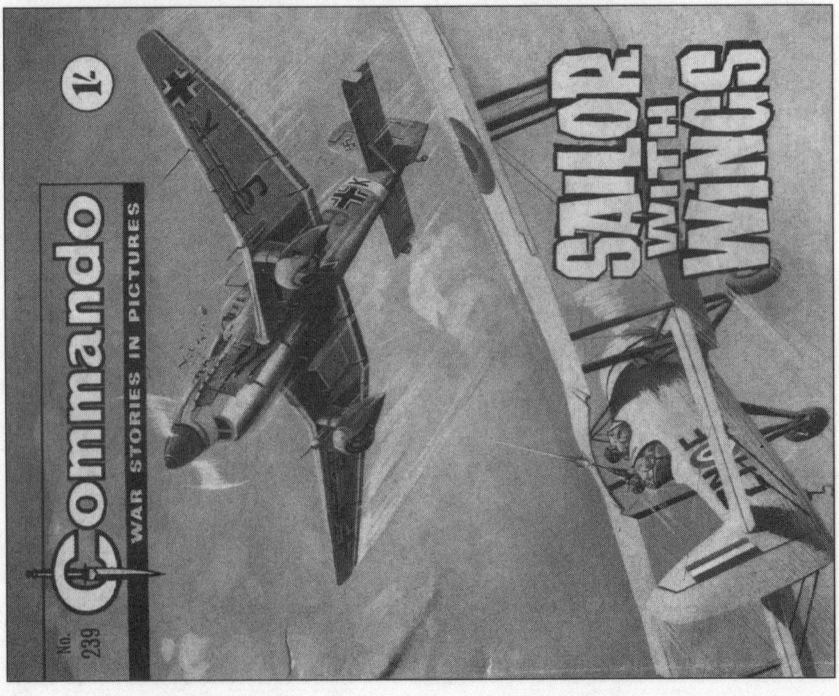
No. 239
Commando
WAR STORIES IN PICTURES
1/-
SAILOR WITH WINGS

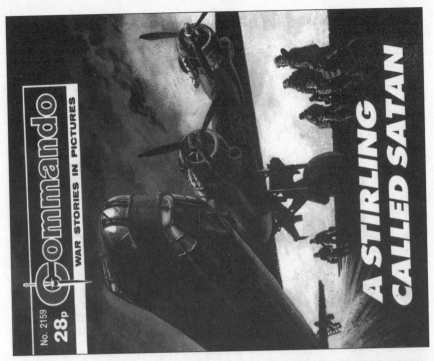

Commando
WAR STORIES IN PICTURES

No. 2159 28p

A STIRLING CALLED SATAN

Commando
WAR STORIES IN PICTURES

1/-

SEA BLITZ

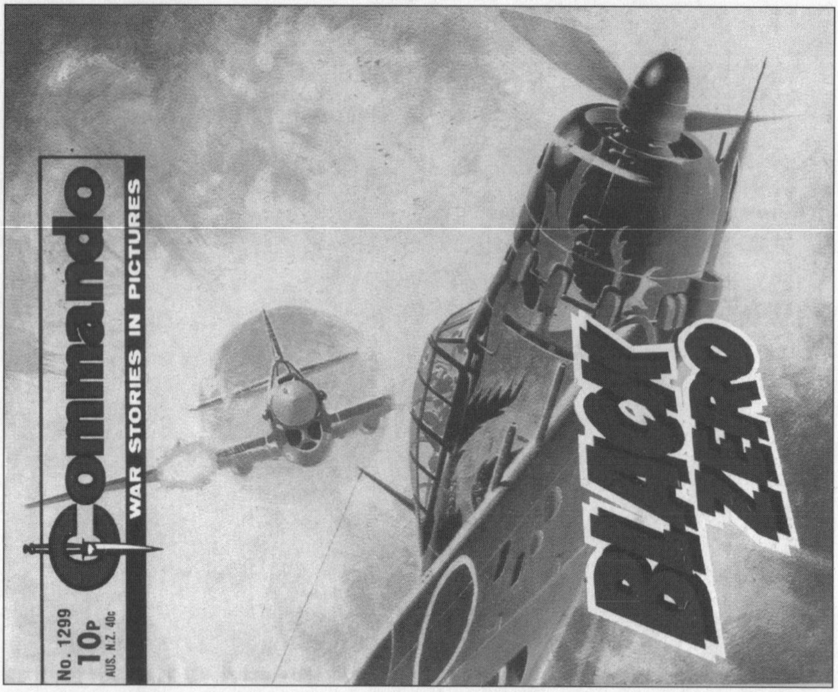
No. 1299
10P
AUS. N.Z. 40c
Commando
WAR STORIES IN PICTURES
BLACK ZERO

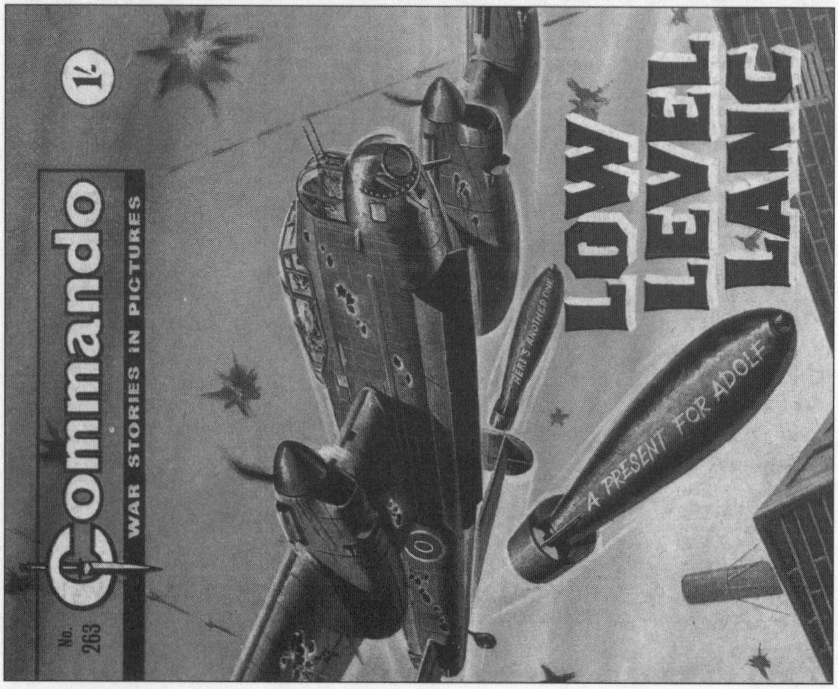
No. 263
Commando
WAR STORIES IN PICTURES
1/-
LOW LEVEL LANC
HERE'S ANOTHER ONE
A PRESENT FOR ADOLF

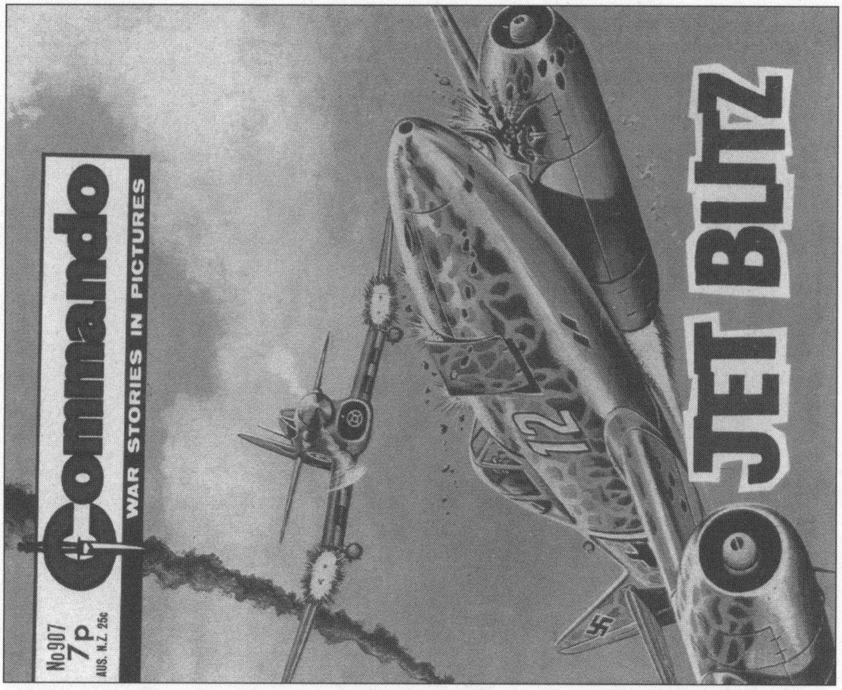
No907
7p
AUS. N.Z. 25c
Commando
WAR STORIES IN PICTURES
JET BLITZ

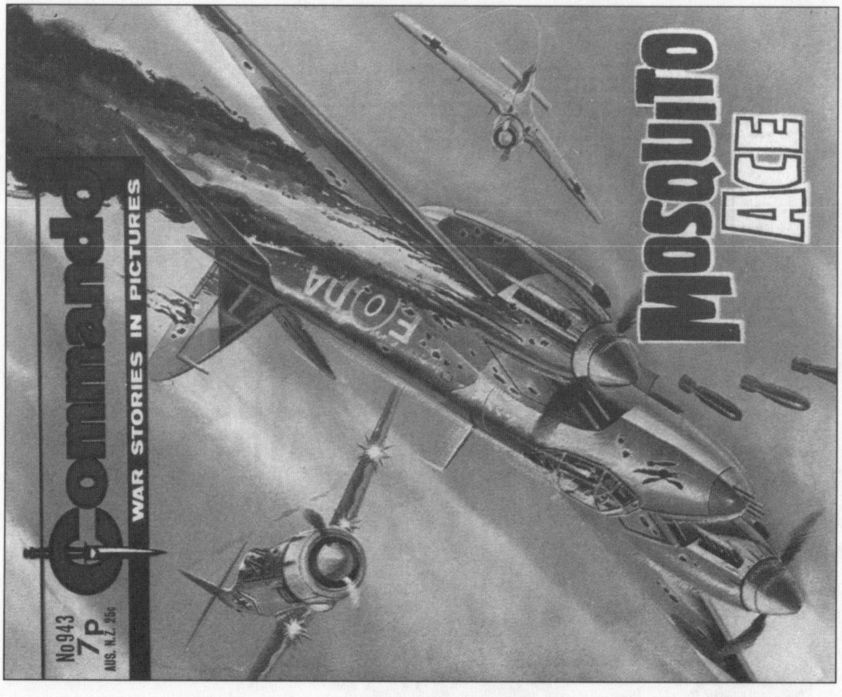
No943
7p
AUS. N.Z. 25c
Commando
WAR STORIES IN PICTURES
MOSQUITO ACE

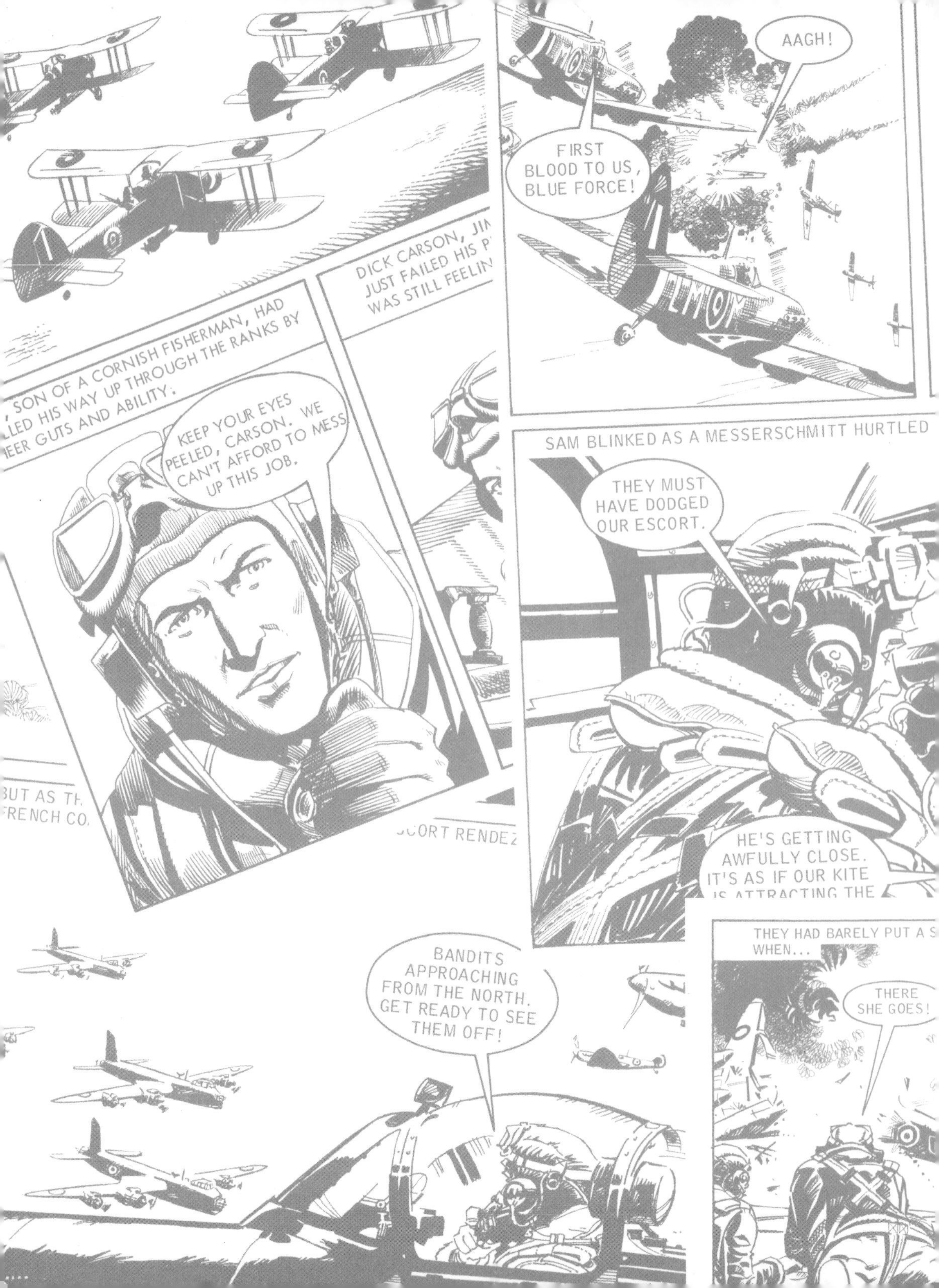
AAGH!
FIRST BLOOD TO US, BLUE FORCE!
DICK CARSON, JI
JUST FAILED HIS P
WAS STILL FEELIN
, SON OF A CORNISH FISHERMAN, HAD
LLED HIS WAY UP THROUGH THE RANKS BY
EER GUTS AND ABILITY.
KEEP YOUR EYES PEELED, CARSON. WE CAN'T AFFORD TO MESS UP THIS JOB.
BUT AS TH
FRENCH CO
SCORT RENDEZ
SAM BLINKED AS A MESSERSCHMITT HURTLED
THEY MUST HAVE DODGED OUR ESCORT.
HE'S GETTING AWFULLY CLOSE. IT'S AS IF OUR KITE
THEY HAD BARELY PUT A S
WHEN...
THERE SHE GOES!
BANDITS APPROACHING FROM THE NORTH. GET READY TO SEE THEM OFF!